AN EXPLORER'S GUIDE

Orlando, Central & North Florida

Kathy Wolf

Orlando, Central & North Florida

Sandra Friend & Kathy Wolf

FIRST EDITION

The Countryman Press ✷ Woodstock, Vermont

First Edition

No entries or reviews in this book have been solicited or paid for.

ISSN 1549-0009
ISBN 0-88150-603-6

Maps by Mapping Specialists Ltd., Madison, WI, © The Countryman Press
Text and cover design by Bodenweber Design
Composition by PerfecType, Nashville, TN
Front cover photograph © David Ball/Index Stock Imagery
Interior photographs by the authors unless otherwise indicated

Published by The Countryman Press,
P.O. Box 748, Woodstock, Vermont 05091

Distributed by W. W. Norton & Company, Inc
500 Fifth Avenue, New York, NY 10110

Printed in the United States of America

10 9 8 7 6 5 4 3 2 1

DEDICATION

To Sunny, for bringing us together

"If there were no mystery left to explore life would get rather dull, wouldn't it?"
—Sidney Buchman

Also by Sandra Friend
50 Hikes in North Florida
50 Hikes in Central Florida
50 Hikes in South Florida
Along the Florida Trail
Florida
The Florida Trail: The Official Hiking Guide
Sinkholes

EXPLORE WITH US!

Welcome to the first edition of *Orlando, Central & North Florida: An Explorer's Guide*, the most comprehensive travel guide you'll find on the Sunshine State. All of the attractions, accommodations, restaurants, and shopping have been included on the basis of merit (primarily close personal inspection by your authors) rather than paid advertising. The following points will help you understand how the guide is organized.

WHAT'S WHERE

The book starts out with a thumbnail sketch of the most important things to know about traveling in Florida, from where the waterfalls are (yes, waterfalls!) to which beaches you should head to first. We've included important contact information for state agencies and advice on what to do when you're on the road.

LODGING

All selections for accommodations in this guide are based on merit; most of them were inspected personally or by a reliable source known to one or both of us. No businesses were charged for inclusion in this guide. Many B&Bs do not accept children under 12 or pets, so if there is not a specific mention in their entry, ask them about their policy before you book a room. Some places have a minimum-stay requirement, especially on weekends.

Rates: Rates quoted are for double occupancy, 1 night, before taxes. When a range of rates is given, it spans the gamut from the lowest of low season (which varies around the state) to the highest of the high season; a single rate means the proprietor offers only one rate. Rates for hotels and motels are subject to further discount with programs like AAA and AARP, and may be negotiable depending on occupancy.

RESTAURANTS

The distinction between *Eating Out* and *Dining Out* is based mainly on price, secondarily on atmosphere. Dining in Florida is more casual than anywhere else in the United States—you'll find folks in T-shirts and shorts walking into the dressiest of steak houses. If a restaurant has a dress code, it's noted.

Smoking is no longer permitted within restaurants in Florida, if the bulk of the business's transactions are in food rather than drink. Many restaurants now provide an outdoor patio for smokers.

KEY TO SYMBOLS

Special Value. The special value symbol appears next to lodgings and restaurants that offer quality not usually enjoyed at the price charged.

Child-friendly. The crayon symbol appears next to places or activities that accept children or appeal to families.

♿ **Handicapped access.** The wheelchair symbol appears next to lodgings, restaurants, and attractions that provide handicapped access, at a minimum with assistance.

🐾 **Pets.** The pet symbol appears next to places that accept pets, from B&Bs to bookstores. All lodgings require that you let them know you're bringing your pet; many will charge an additional fee.

Prices for lodgings and restaurants are subject to change, and shops come and go. Your feedback is essential for subsequent editions of this guide. Feel free to write us at Countryman Press, P.O. Box 748, Woodstock, Vermont 05091, or Explorer's Guide, P.O. Box 424, Micanopy, Florida 32667, or e-mail ExploreFLA@aol.com with your opinions and your own treasured finds.

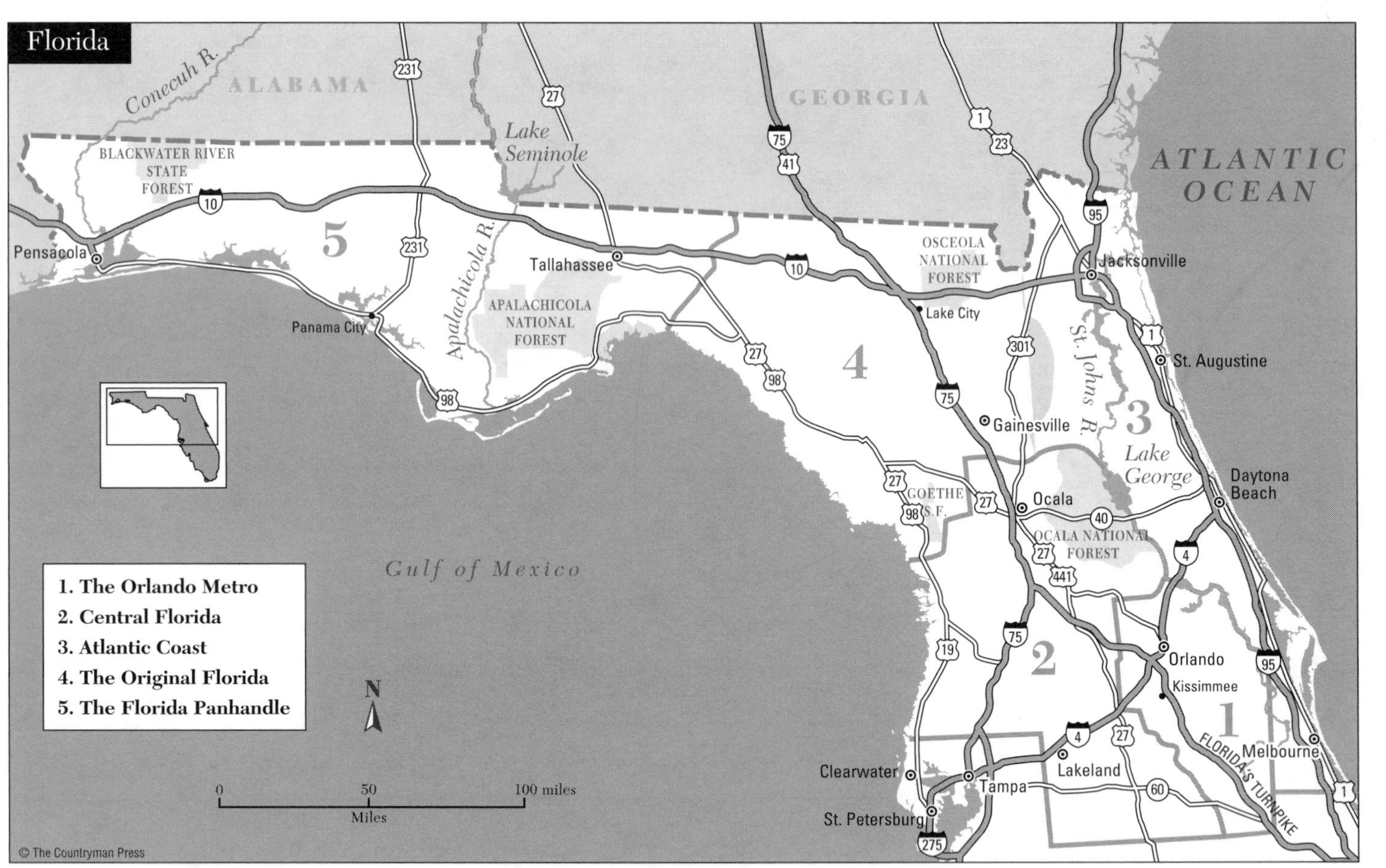

Florida
ALABAMA
GEORGIA
ATLANTIC OCEAN
Gulf of Mexico
Conecuh R.
Lake Seminole
Apalachicola R.
St. Johns R.
Lake George
BLACKWATER RIVER STATE FOREST
APALACHICOLA NATIONAL FOREST
OSCEOLA NATIONAL FOREST
GOETHE S.F.
OCALA NATIONAL FOREST
Pensacola
Panama City
Tallahassee
Lake City
Jacksonville
St. Augustine
Gainesville
Ocala
Daytona Beach
Orlando
Kissimmee
Melbourne
Lakeland
Tampa
Clearwater
St. Petersburg
FLORIDA'S TURNPIKE
1. The Orlando Metro
2. Central Florida
3. Atlantic Coast
4. The Original Florida
5. The Florida Panhandle
N
0
50
100 miles
Miles
© The Countryman Press

CONTENTS

INTRODUCTION

Lunching one afternoon in historic Micanopy with my friend Judy, I struck up a conversation with a British couple at the next table. They were wrapping up a couple of winter weeks roaming Florida, and dreading the weather awaiting them back in Oxford. Unlike the majority of British tourists who settle down into winter vacation homes around Kissimmee, they made a point of learning more about Florida.

"We're exploring," the gentleman said. "If we see a sign that looks interesting, we follow it. If someone recommends a town to us, we look for it." They'd just wrapped up an enjoyable stay in Cedar Key, and stopped in Micanopy—thanks to a billboard out on I-75—en route to Mount Dora. "We've done the theme parks and the beaches. Now we'd like to see the real Florida."

I explained my involvement in this book, and they became animated. "That's exactly what we need! An Explorer's Guide to Florida!"

It was a few months later that I met Kathy Wolf, and the rest is history. Together we've ranged across our home state to discover untold treasures, the story behind the phenomenon that is Florida tourism. I took my first steps on Florida sand at the tender age of 3 (screaming, mind you, "Yow bug!" at the flood of palmetto bugs that poured into the gutter under the streetlights in Silver Springs at night in the 1960s), and moved here with my family in the 1970s before settling here permanently after college. Thanks to my involvement with the Florida Trail Association and the 50 Hikes guides, I've poked around every wild nook and cranny of this state; taking on reviews of travel destinations was a whole different ball game. But I've always loved old-time Florida, savoring places like St. Augustine and Micanopy, Cedar Key and Pensacola, so it was a delight to discover more treasures within a day trip of home—walking the hills of Mount Dora for the first time, marveling at the antiques shops in Sanford, falling in love with the fishing village of Apalachicola, and finding out that Lakeland, once you get past the stuff around its edges, has an incredibly beautiful downtown. And as for Orlando—for all the years I worked and played there, I never saw it through a local's eyes quite the way I did while researching this guide. I knew about the art scene and the theme parks, but had never made the deep connection with its history and architecture before. It just goes to prove that you can be a tourist in your own backyard!

Given the historic importance of tourism to Florida's economy, there is no way to capture the breadth and depth of what this region of the state has to offer in a single book. Rather, Kathy and I delve into what we, as residents, appreciate the most: places of cultural and historic interest, and outdoor recreation. "The Best Of" is a purely subjective judgment on our parts. But I think you'll be pleased with our finds, and you'll use this book as a launch pad for your own exploration of Florida. In some cases our picks lead you into off-the-beaten-path places that are worthy of note in their entirety: the fishing villages of Steinhatchee and St. Marks, for example, or the quiet river towns of White Springs and Apalachicola, or the lakeside towns of Mount Dora and McIntosh. In other cases exploration means getting past the outer rim of strip malls and chain restaurants to discover the beauty in a city's heart—which is the certainly the case for cities like Orlando, Jacksonville, Gainesville, Ocala, and Lakeland.

Having watched the shift in tourism from the hokey roadside attractions of the 1960s to the slick theme parks of today, I take my Florida with a good dose of nostalgia, reflecting on the thousands of years of human settlement and five centuries of European culture that shape our towns and cities, the unique botanical wonders of our state, and its little-known geological oddities. Florida's multicultural melting pot includes Hispanic families whose ancestors settled here in the 1600s, descendants of British gentry with their vast indigo and rice plantations in the 1700s, Minorcans and Greeks who colonized in the early 1800s and established fishing villages still vibrant today,

Broken up into five distinct regions, this book captures the essence of the peaceful Panhandle, the stately historic towns of North Florida, the coastal strands of the Atlantic Ocean, and the rolling hills and lakes of Central Florida. Covering metropolitan Orlando and Jacksonville, it also touches on sophisticated city life.

ACKNOWLEDGMENTS

Many, many people worked shoulder to shoulder with us on pulling together information for this guidebook, setting up our research trips, and just plain being there when we needed someone to call on, so we'd like to acknowledge our many helpers along the way; without your help, we'd never have completed this immense project.

Bonnie Barns, Bonnie Barns Visionary; Steve Beck, St. Mary's Fish Camp; Debra Benjamin, Tallahassee Area Convention & Visitors Bureau; Becca Bides and Dagmar Cardwell, SeaWorld; Amber Bowers, Orlando/Orange County Convention & Visitors Bureau; Tangela Boyd and Susan McLain, Daytona Beach Area CVB; Gary Buchanan and Lisa Boisvert, Walt Disney World; Tracey Butcher, Jackie Hendry, and Margo McKnight, Brevard Zoo; Harvey Campbell, Original Florida Tourist Development Council; Mary Ann Carroll, St. John & Partners Advertising & Public Relations; Leon Corbett and Rachel Bray-Stiles, Visit Florida; Lee Cort, St. Augustine Historic Inns; Mary Craven, Citrus County TDC; Carol DeHaven-McLeod and Fay Downing, Central Florida VCB; Doug and Jill de Leeuw, Azalea House B&B; Susan Flower, Discovery Cove; Dean Fowler and Gentry Baumline, Steinhatchee Landing Resort; Victoria and Robert Freeman, House on Cherry Street B&B; Stacey Garrett, Pensacola CVB; Zoe Golloway, Gadsden Art Center; Anita Gregory, Apalachicola CVB; Carolyn Haney, Amelia Island Tourist; Kathy Harper, Jacksonville & the Beaches CVB, and her dad, Vernon Harper; Kenyatta Harris, Pasco County TDC; Michele Harris, Gatorland and Silver Spurs Rodeo; Amanda Hartley and Laura Richeson, Seminole County CVB; Sheila Hauser, Anchor Vacation Properties, Inc.; Erin Heston, CKPR, on behalf of Lake County; Herbert L. Hiller, on Putnam County and the author of *Guide to the Small and Historic Lodgings of Florida*; Jennifer Hodges, Loews Hotels at Universal Orlando; Jay Humphreys, St. Augustine, Ponte Vedra & the Beaches VCB; Linda Jarosz and Dick Morris, Flagler Chamber of Commerce; Gene Johnson, Madison Chamber of Commerce; Judy Johnson, Cedar Key Chamber of Commerce; Mary C. Kenny, The Kessler Collection; Michel Lester and Leanne Vollmer, The Zimmerman Agency; Megan MacPherson and Ashley Chisolm, E. W. Bullock Associates, Pensacola; Abby Montpelier, Kissimmee–St. Cloud CVB; Dick Morris and Linda Jarosz, Flagler County Chamber of Commerce; Jayna M. Leach, Panama City CVB; Bob and

Chong Murphy, Island Aerial Tours; Rhonda Murphy, Universal Studios Orlando; Deb Nordstrom, Amelia Island Inns; Paula Ramsey Pickett, Visit Gulf; Allison Pope, YPB&R Public Relations; John Pritchard and Kerstin Strom, Alachua County CVB; Susan Rupe and Laurel Parmelee, Hernando County Tourism; Keith Salwoski and Joyce McCormick, Gaylord Palms; Chuck Sims, Jackson County Chamber of Commerce; Phyllis Smith, Greater Dade City Chamber of Commerce; Mark Thomas Sperberg, Tishman Hotel Corporation; Laurilee Thompson, Dixie Crossroads and the Space Coast Birding and Wildlife Festival; Trevor Thompson and the gang at Skyventure, Skycoaster, and G-Force; Dawna Thorstad, Space Coast Nature Tours and Titusville Chamber of Commerce; Cindy Turner and Joy Mills, Bok Sanctuary; Jackie Vasquez, Wonderworks; Carol Lee Wallis, Team Spirit; Renee Wente-Tallevast, St. Johns River Country; Louise at the West Nassau Chamber of Commerce; and numerous attractions and establishments that put us up, fed us, and showed us a really good time. Many thanks.

In addition, Sandra would like to thank friends Gary and Millie Buffington, Carl and Sylvia Dunnam, Joan Jarvis, Linda Patton, and G. K. Sharman for putting me up (or putting up with me) in my travels and introducing me to some of the delights of their regions; Jim Warnke, for sharing his knowledge of Florida's ghost towns; Grace Hagedorn, for her College Park history lesson; Eva Knapp, for filling me in on Pasco and Hernando Counties; and Rob Smith, for sharing the joys of urban Orlando with a historian's eye for accuracy, including his voluminous out-of-print tome known as *Orlando: A Centennial History* by Eve Bacon. If it weren't for my parents, I wouldn't have the intimate knowledge I do of the Walt Disney World Resort; and thanks to friends in the Florida Trail Association and the Florida Outdoor Writers Association who suggested their favorite places to dine and stay.

Kathy would like to thank my daughter, Sherri Lemon, who explored the extreme world with me; my son Jaime Jimino, who explored the tamer countryside and waterways; Sherri's husband, Chris, who kept my car in check; my brother, Kevin Karnes, who kept cellular company with me on many, many long drives home from northeast Florida, and his wife, Susan, who typed up my cryptic notes; Chelsea VerBerkmoes, who spent hours on data entry and proof checking; my day boss, Terry Myers, for accommodating my schedule, and my co-workers there who listened endlessly to my escapes every Monday morning; Phyllis Malinski—who I promise will get to go shopping next time; Steve Beck, who drove me in his stretch limo across state lines in search of an Irish wolfhound, and Jack Manser who lent me his RV; my mentor, Marion Robertson; my muse Mary Ellen Carey; and Ron Mercer—who opened my eyes and taught me to explore.

WHAT'S WHERE IN FLORIDA

ADMISSION FEES If an admission fee is $5 or less, it's simply listed as "fee." Fees greater than $5 are spelled out. Although fees were accurate when this book went to press, keep in mind that yearly increases are likely, especially for the larger attractions and theme parks.

AIRBOAT RIDES Airboats are an exciting way to get out in the backcountry of Florida. These shallow boats can skim over only a few inches of water. Boat sizes range from small four-seaters to massive floating buses holding up to 30 people and dictate the type of experience you can expect. The smaller, intimate boats will be more one-on-one, will get into tighter places, and may be more expensive. Most of the larger boats provide handicapped assistance. All airboats require hearing protection, which is provided by the operators.

AIR SERVICE Major international airports in the region covered by this book include **Greater Orlando International Airport** (407-825-2001; www.state.fl.us/goaa/) and **Jacksonville International Airport** (904-741-4902). Smaller regional airports served by commuter flights are listed in their respective chapters.

AREA CODES

As Florida's population grows, its area codes continue to fragment. You must dial the area code (407) in Orlando in front of *every* local call; the need for the area code varies depending where you are in any particular county, since the phone systems do not correspond to county lines. (850) remains the area code for the entire Florida Panhandle.

ALLIGATORS No longer an endangered species, the American alligator is a ubiquitous resident of Florida's lakes, rivers, streams, and retention ponds. Most alligators will turn tail and hit the water with a splash when they hear you coming—unless they've been fed or otherwise desensitized to human presence. Do not approach a sunning alligator, and never, ever feed an alligator (it's a felony, and downright dangerous to do) in the wild. Nuisance alligators should be reported to the **Florida Fish and**

Sandra Friend

Wildlife Conservation Commission (352-732-1225; www.florida conservation.org).

AMTRAK Two daily Amtrak (1-800-USA-RAIL; www.amtrak.com) trains make their way from New York/ Washington, DC, to Florida: the **Silver Service/Palmetto**, ending in either Tampa or Miami, and the **AutoTrain**, bringing visitors (and their cars) to Sanford. Stops are noted in *Getting There*.

ANTIQUES While **Mount Dora** is the state's top destination for antiques collectors, you'll also find **Micanopy**, **Dade City**, **DeLand**, and **Havana** worth at least a full day for antiques browsing. Since 1985, the free magazine ***Antiques & Art Around Florida*** (352-475-1336; www.aarf .com) has kept up with the trends throughout the Sunshine State; pick up a copy at one of the antiques stores you visit, or browse their web site to do a little pretrip planning. I've found some real bargains in **Bartow**, **Lake Alfred**, **Winter Haven**, and downtown **Lakeland**, while **St. Augustine** boasts a don't-miss antiques row on San Marcos Ave. No matter what you're collecting, it's out there somewhere!

ARCHEOLOGY Florida's archeological treasures date back more than 10,000 years, including temple mound complexes such as those found near Tallahassee at **Leitchworth Mounds** and **Lake Jackson Mounds**, and thousands of middens (prehistoric garbage dumps) of oyster shells found along the state's rivers, streams, and estuaries. Of the middens, the most impressive in size and area are those at **Timucuan Preserve** in Jacksonville, **Mount Royal** in Welaka, and at **Shell Mound** near Cedar Key. More recent archeological finds focus on the many **shipwrecks** found along Florida's coasts and in its rivers, protected by underwater preserves. For information about archeological digs and shipwrecks, contact the **Florida Division of Historical Resources, Bureau of Archeological Research** (dhr.dos.state.fl.us/bar/index.html).

ART GALLERIES Florida is blessed with many creative souls drawing their inspiration from our dramatic landscapes, working in media that range from copper sculpture and driftwood to fine black-and-white photography, giclee, and watercolor. Many artists gravitate into communities, so you'll find clusters of art galleries in places like **Apalachicola**, **Cedar Key**, **Cocoa**, **DeLand**, **St. Augustine**, and **Mount Dora**; of these, I'd happily drop a bundle in Apalachicola for the beautiful Florida paintings and photography I found there.

ARTS COUNCILS Many cities and counties have public art displays (such as "art in the parks" in Orlando, Bartow, Cocoa, and Melbourne, and the swans of Lakeland) thanks to their local arts councils. The **Florida Cultural Affairs Division** (www.florida-arts.org/index.asp) offers resources, grants, and programs to support the arts throughout Florida; its Florida Artists Hall of Fame recognizes great achievements in the arts.

AVIATION While Florida may not be the birthplace of aviation, it is definitely its nursery school and post-doctorate program. Florida's aviation history includes the many World War II training bases and the birth of naval aviation in 1914; the first scheduled commercial airline flight from St. Petersburg to Tampa was also in 1914, and the first nonstop flight across the nation came soon after. The rocket technology of NASA brings modern aviation into the space age. Four aviation museums in this book team up with their Pastport Flight of Four. The $44 admission allows access to **Fantasy of Flight**, **Flying Tigers**, **Florida Air Museum**, and **Valiant Air Command**.

BALLOONING, GLIDING, AND PARASAILING The unique topography of the Florida peninsula makes it ideal for aerial sports, since strong thermals rise down the center of the peninsula. **Orange Blossom Balloons** in Orlando offers a splendid ride over the treetops, where you can watch the sunrise over the Magic Kingdom and downtown Orlando. Near Clermont, the **Seminole Gliderport** gives unique trips in unpowered gliders, where you feel like a bird as you catch a thermal to climb thousands of feet in the air. Parasailing floats you over lakes or ocean from the back platform of a boat. **Boggy Creek Parasail** takes you on a gentle ride over East Lake Tohopekaliga, and there are several companies that will fly you off the windier Atlantic Coast. No longer is hang gliding restricted to mountain zones. The folks at **Wallaby Ranch** near Central Florida will take you high up so you can soar like a bird.

BASEBALL Florida is home to Major League Baseball's annual spring training, and although most teams train in the southern portion of the state, you'll catch players hanging out in Central Florida, including the **Atlanta Braves** at Disney's Wide World of Sports. Polk County is *the* hot spot for spring training, with the **Cleveland Indians, Toronto Blue Jays, Detroit Tigers,** and **Kansas City Royals** playing exhibition games in venues around the county.

BEACHES Where to start? Florida's 2,000-mile coastline means plenty of beaches for every taste, from the busy social scene at **Daytona Beach** to the remote serenity of **Dog Island**. In the Panhandle, resorts and condos cluster around the beaches at **Fort Walton–Destin**, **Pensacola Beach**, and **Panama City Beach**; if you want a quieter experience on the same brilliant sands, seek out **Mexico Beach**, **Cape San Blas**, and **St. George Island**. On the peninsula **Amelia Island** offers beautiful strands with luxurious resorts, and the north end of **New Smyrna Beach** has broad beaches with serious wave action for surf fanatics. **Cocoa Beach** is Surf

Central, where the annual Easter competition packs in the college crowd. Public lands are your best places to enjoy pristine dunes and uncluttered beachfronts—my personal favorites in this region include **St. Joseph Peninsula State Park**, **St. George Island State Park**, **Little Talbot Island State Park**, and **Anastasia State Park**, and I'll never pass up a trip to **Gulf Islands National Seashore**.

BED & BREAKFASTS Given the sheer number of B&Bs throughout Florida, this book doesn't list every B&B in the regions it covers, but it does give you selections from what I feel are the best I've encountered. There is a mix of historical B&Bs, working ranches, rustic lodges, and easygoing family homes. Some of my choices, but not all, are members of associations such as **Superior Small Lodging** (www.superiorsmall lodging.com) or the **Florida Bed & Breakfast Inns** (281-499-1374 or 1-800-524-1880; www.florida-inns .com), both of which conduct independent inspections of properties. All of the B&B owners I stayed with were eager to tell their story; most have a great love for the history of their home and their town. I find B&B travel one of the best ways to connect with the *real* Florida, and strongly encourage you to seek out the experiences listed throughout the book. Some motels will offer breakfast so that they can list their establishment as a B&B. I have tried to note this wherever possible, as Internet sites can be misleading.

BICYCLING Bike Florida (www.bike florida.org) is your gateway to statewide bicycling opportunities. Regional groups have done a great job of establishing and maintaining both on-road bike routes and off-road trails suitable for mountain biking, and information on these routes and trails is listed in the text. Check in with the **Office of Greenways and Trails** (see *Greenways*) for information on rail-trail projects throughout the state.

BIRDING As the home to millions of winter migratory birds, Florida is a prime destination for bird-watching. The **Great Florida Birding Trail** (floridabirdingtrail.com), supported by the Florida Fish and Wildlife Conservation Commission, provides guidance to birders on the best overlooks, hiking trails, and waterfront parks to visit and which species you'll find at each location. Sites listed in the regional Great Florida Birding Trail brochures are designated with brown road signs displaying a stylized swallow-tailed kite. Certain sites are designated "Gateways" to the Great Florida Birding Trail, where you can pick up detailed information and

Kathy Wolf

speak with a naturalist. In the region covered by this guidebook, these sites include **Fort Clinch State Park**, **Merritt Island National Wildlife Refuge**, and **Tenoroc Fish Management Area** for the East Section, and **Paynes Prairie Preserve State Park** for the West Section. The Florida Game and Fresh Water Fish Commission (www.floridaconservation.org; 850-414-7929) also has a bird-watching certificate program called Wings Over Florida.

BOAT AND SAILING EXCURSIONS Exploring our watery state by water is part of the fun of visiting Florida, from the blasting speed of an airboat skipping across the marshes to the gentle toss of a schooner as it sails across Matanzas Bay. Many ecotours rely on quiet electric-motor pontoon boats to guide you down Florida's rivers and up to its first-magnitude springs. I greatly recommend a sail on the **Schooner *Freedom*** in St. Augustine, the **Schooner *Wanderer*** in Port Canaveral, and a cruise on **Silver Springs**'s classic glass-bottomed boats, but you'll find almost any boat tour you take a delight.

BOOKS To understand Florida, you need to read its authors, and none is more important than **Patrick Smith**, whose *A Land Remembered* is a landmark piece of fiction tracing Florida's history from settlement to development. A good capsule history of Florida's nearly 500 years of European settlement is *A Short History of Florida*, the abbreviated version of the original masterwork by **Michael Gannon**. To see through the eyes of settlers who tried to scratch a living from a harsh land, read the award-winning books of **Marjorie Kinnan Rawlings**, including *The Yearling*, *Cross Creek*, and *When the Whipoorwill*. For insights into the history of African American culture in Florida, seek out novelist **Zora Neale Hurston**; her works *Their Eyes Were Watching God* and *Jonah's Gourd Vine* touch the soul. For a taste of frontier Florida, try the Cracker western novels of **Lee Gramling**, which draw deeply from Florida's history.

The nonfiction classic *Palmetto Leaves* from **Harriett Beecher Stowe** captures life during Reconstruction along the St. Johns, and to understand Florida culture, read *Palmetto Country* by **Stetson Kennedy**, a Florida icon who worked to compile Florida's folklore with the 1940s WPA project and went on to fight for civil rights throughout the South. For a glimpse of Florida's frenetic development over the past century, *Some Kind of Paradise: A Chronicle of Man and the Land in Florida*, by **Mark Derr**, offers serious insights. All visitors to Florida who love the outdoors should read *Travels* by **William Bartram**, a botanist who recorded his adventures along the St. Johns River during the 1700s, as well as the *A Thousand-Mile Walk to the Gulf* by **John Muir** and *A Naturalist in Florida: A Celebration of Eden* by **Archie Carr**. *River of Lakes: A Journey on Florida's St. Johns River* by **Bill Belleville** is a wonderful celebration of our state's mightiest river. When you plan your outdoor activities, don't forget that Florida has more than 2,500 miles of hiking trails—and Sandra walked a large percentage of them while compiling *50 Hikes in North Florida*, *50 Hikes in Central Florida*, *Along the Florida Trail*, and *The Florida Trail: The Official Hiking Guide*.

BUS SERVICE **Greyhound** (1-800-229-9424; www.greyhound.com) covers an extensive list of Florida cities; see their web site for details and the full schedule. Stops are noted in the text under *Getting There*.

CAMPGROUNDS Rates are quoted for single-night double-occupancy stays; all campgrounds offer discounts for club membership as well as weekly, monthly, and resident (6 months or more) stays, and often charge more for extra adults. If pets are permitted, keep them leashed. Also see the *Parks* section of each chapter for campgrounds at state and county parks. The Florida State Parks system now uses Reserve America (1-800-326-3521) for all campground reservations; a handful of sites are kept open for drop-ins. Ask at the gate.

CHILDREN, ESPECIALLY FOR The crayon symbol  identifies activities and places of special interest to children and families.

CITRUS STANDS, FARMER'S MARKETS, AND U-PICKS Citrus stands associated with active groves are typically open seasonally Nov–Apr. I've listed permanent stands as well as places you're likely to see roadside fruit and vegetable sales (often out of the backs of trucks and vans) from local growers. All U-pick is seasonal, and Florida's growing seasons run year-round with citrus in winter and spring, strawberries in early spring, blueberries in late spring, and cherries in early summer. If you attempt U-pick citrus, bring heavy gloves and wear jeans: Citrus trees have serious thorns. Also, don't pick citrus without permission: It's such a protected crop in Florida that to pluck an orange from a roadside tree is a felony. For a full listing of farmer's markets around the state, visit the **USDA Florida Marketing Services** (www.ams.usda.gov/farmersmarkets/States/Florida.htm) web site.

CIVIL WAR As the third state to secede from the Union, Florida has a great deal of Civil War history to explore, particularly in the Panhandle and North Florida. Civil War buffs shouldn't miss Olustee Battlefield, site of Florida's largest engagement, and should check out **Florida Civil War Events** (www.extlab1.entnem.ufl.edu/olustee/related/fl-cw.htm) for a calendar of reenactments held throughout the state.

CRABS Florida can lay claim to some of the freshest crabs anywhere in its seafood restaurants, with blue crabs and stone crabs caught along the Gulf Coast; some restaurants, like **Pecks Old Port Cove** in Ozello, raise their own crabs in the Gulf's salty waters. October is Crab Festival time in **St. Marks**, and you'll find them celebrating the seafood harvest down at **Cedar Key** that month, too. Eat your crab legs with melted butter for optimum effect.

Sandra Friend

DIVE RESORTS Dive resorts cater to both open-water and cave divers, with an on-site dive shop. They tend toward utilitarian but worn accommodations—wet gear can trash a room! Lodgings categorized under this header will appeal to divers because of their location, not because of their quality.

DIVING Certification for open-water diving is required for diving in Florida's rivers, lakes, and streams; certification in cave diving is required if you plan to enter the outflow of a spring. Expertise in open-water diving does *not* translate to cave diving, and many experienced open-water divers have died attempting to dive Florida's springs. Play it safe and stick with what you know. A DIVER DOWN flag is required when diving.

THE DIXIE HIGHWAY Conceptualized in the 1910s by Carl Graham Fisher and the Dixie Highway Association as a grand route for auto touring, the Dixie Highway had two legs that ran along the East Coast of the United States into Florida, both ending in Miami. Since it ran along both coasts of Florida, you'll find OLD DIXIE HIGHWAY signs on both US 1 and US 17 on the east coast and along US 19, 27, and 41 on the west coast, and even US 441 in the middle—the highway ran through places as diverse as Jacksonville, Daytona, Melbourne, Tallahassee, Micanopy, Ocala, downtown Orlando, and Fort Meade. The original brick pavement that still exists on the Old Tampa Highway in Loughman was part of the Dixie Highway route.

EMERGENCIES Hospitals with emergency rooms are noted at the beginning of each chapter. Dial **911** to connect to emergency service anywhere in the state. For highway accidents or emergencies, contact the **Florida Highway Patrol** at *FHP on your cell phone or 911.

FACTORY OUTLETS You've seen the signs, but are they really a bargain? Several factory outlets, particularly in the Orlando area, offer brand and designer names for less, but you may also get great deals at smaller shops and even the local mall. I've listed some factory outlets that I found particularly fun to shop at that also had a nice selection of eateries and close access to major highways.

FERRIES Florida has few remaining ferryboats; in the region covered by this book, you'll find FL A1A crossing the St. Johns River on the **Mayport Ferry**, and the **Fort Gates Ferry** crossing from the Ocala National Forest to Welaka.

FISH CAMPS Rustic in nature, fish camps are quiet retreats for anglers and their families to settle down along a lake or river and put in some quality time fishing. Accommodations listed under this category tend to be older cabins, mobile homes, or concrete

Kathy Wolf

block structures, often a little rough around the edges. If the cabins or motel rooms at a fish camp are of superior quality, I list them under those categories.

FISHING The **Florida Fish and Wildlife Conservation Commission** (www.floridaconservation.org) regulates all fishing in Florida, offering both freshwater and saltwater licenses. To obtain a license, visit any sporting goods store or call 1-888-FISH-FLO for an instant license; you can also apply online at www.floridafisheries.com. No fishing license is required if you are on a guided fishing trip, are fishing with a cane pole, are bank fishing along the ocean (varies by county), or are 65 years or older; choose from short-term, annual, 5-year, or lifetime options.

FLAUSA **Visit Florida** (www.flausa.com), the state's official tourism bureau, is a clearinghouse for every tourism question you might have. Their partners cover the full range of destinations, from the sleepy hamlets of the Big Bend to the snazzy new hotels along I-Drive in Orlando. Utilize their web site resources to preplan your trip, from the interactive map that lets you explore destination possibilities in regions, to Sunny, the online vacation planner, which assists you in compiling your itinerary.

FLORIDA TRAIL The **Florida Trail** is a 1,300-mile footpath running from the Big Cypress National Preserve north of Everglades National Park to Fort Pickens at Gulf Islands National Seashore in Pensacola. With its first blaze painted in 1966, it is now one of only eight congressionally designated National Scenic Trails in the United States, and is still under development—but you can follow the orange blazes from one end of the state to the other. The Florida Trail and other trails in state parks and state forests, known as the Florida Trail System, are built and maintained by volunteer members of the nonprofit **Florida Trail Association** (352-378-8823 or 1-877-HIKE-FLA; www.floridatrail.org), 5415 SW 13th St, Gainesville 32608; the association is your primary source for maps and guidebooks for the trail.

FORESTS, NATIONAL There are three national forests in Florida (Apalachicola, Ocala, and Osceola), administered out of the **USDA Forest Service** (850-523-8500; www.southernregion.fs.fed.us/florida) offices in Tallahassee. Established in 1908 by President Theodore Roosevelt, **Ocala National Forest** is the oldest national forest east of the Mississippi River.

FORESTS, STATE The Florida Division of Forestry (www.fl-dof.com) administers **Florida State Forests**, encompassing thousands of acres of public lands throughout North and Central Florida; the **Blackwater River State Forest** and **Withlacoochee State Forest** are the largest in Florida. Each offers an array of outdoor activities from hiking, biking, trail riding, and camping to fishing, hunting, and even motocross and ATV use. Most (but not all) developed state forest trailheads charge a per-person fee of $2–3 for recreational use. For $30, you can purchase an annual day-use pass good for the driver and up to eight passengers: a real bargain for families! If you're a hiker, get involved with the **Trailwalker** program, in which you tally up miles on hiking trails and receive patches and certificates; a similar program is in place for equestrians, called the **Trailtrotter** program. Information on both programs can be found at trailhead kiosks or on the Florida State Forests web site.

GAS STATIONS Gas prices fluctuate wildly around the state—and not in proportion to distance from major highways, as you might think. You'll find your best bargains for filling your tank along US 441 between Tavares and Apopka, along US 27 south of Clermont through Polk County, along US 19 from Crystal River to Port Richey, and in the Oviedo-UCF area of Orlando. The highest prices cluster around Lake Buena Vista and Walt Disney World, and it's always painful to top off the tank in Gainesville. When traveling near the Georgia border it may be worth it to drive across a few miles to tank up.

GENEALOGICAL RESEARCH In addition to the excellent resources found at the **Florida State Archives** in Tallahassee and **Elmer's Genealogical Library** in Madison, check the **State Library of Florida, Florida Collection** (dlis.dos.state.fl.us/stlib/genealres.html) for the Florida GenWeb project, census data, vital records, pioneer families, and links to the state's many historical societies.

GOLFING Golfing is a favorite pastime for many Florida retirees, and there are hundreds of courses across the state, impossible for me to list in any detail; a good resource for research is **Play Florida Golf** (www.playfla.com/pfg/index.cfm), the state's official golf course web site. I've covered courses that are particularly interesting or feature exceptional facilities. Florida is home to both the PGA and LPGA headquarters.

GREENWAYS Florida has one of the nation's most aggressive greenway programs, overseen by the **Office of Greenways and Trails** (850-245-2052 or 1-877-822-5208; www.dep.state.fl.us/gwt/), which administers the state land acquisition program under the Florida Forever Act and works in partnership with the Florida Trail Association, Florida State Parks, water management districts, and regional agencies in identifying crucial habitat corridors for preservation and developing public recreation facilities.

HANDICAPPED ACCESS The wheelchair symbol ♿ identifies lodgings, restaurants, and activities that are, at a minimum, accessible with minor assistance. Many locations and attractions provide or will make modifications for people with disabilities, so call beforehand to see if they can make the necessary accommodations.

HIKING I note the best hiking experiences in each region under the *Hiking* section, and you can find additional walks mentioned under *Green Space*. Your most comprehensive hiking guides for this portion of Florida include Sandra Friend's *50 Hikes in Central Florida* and *50 Hikes in North Florida* (Backcountry Guides), and *The Florida Trail: The Official Guide* by Sandra Friend (Westcliffe Publishing).

HERITAGE SITES If you're in search of history, watch for the brown signs with columns and palm trees that mark official Florida Heritage Sites—everything from historic churches and graveyards to entire historic districts. According to the **Florida Division of Historical Resources** (dhr.dos.state.fl.us/bhp/markers/markers_map.html), to qualify as a Florida Heritage Site a building, structure, or site must be at least 30 years old and have significance in the areas of architecture, archeology, Florida history, or traditional culture, or be associated with a significant event that took place at least 30 years ago.

HISTORIC SITES With nearly five centuries of European settlement in Florida, historic sites are myriad—so this book's coverage of Florida history is limited to sites of particular interest. For the full details on designated historic sites in Florida, visit the state-administered **Florida's History Through Its Places** (dhr.dos.state.fl.us/HistoricPlaces/Atlas.html) web site. Historic sites that belong to the **Florida Trust for Historic Preservation** (850-224-8128; www.floridatrust.org), P.O. Box 11206, Tallahassee 32302, honor the **Florida's Historic Passport** program, in which you can purchase a passport for $35 ($50 family) that offers special access to member sites—some for free, others for discounted admissions.

HOTELS AND MOTELS In general, chain hotels and motels are not listed in this guide because of their ubiquitous nature. I've included a handful that are either the only lodging options in a particular area or happen to be outstanding places to stay.

HUNTING Hunting is regulated by the **Florida Fish and Wildlife Conservation Commission** (www.floridaconservation.org), with general gun season falling between Oct and Feb in various parts of the state. Check the web site for specific hunt dates, the wildlife management areas (WMAs) open to hunting, and hunting license regulations.

INFORMATION Several kiosks and roadside billboards will taunt you to come in for vacation deals. Most are tied to time-shares or are operating in their own interest. True visitors centers will offer information without trying to sell you something. At the beginning of each section under *Guidance* I have listed the visitors bureaus and chambers with no commercial affiliation.

INSECTS Florida's irritating insects are myriad, especially at dawn and dusk during summer months. We love our winters when they get chilly enough to kill the little buggers off. If you don't like DEET and you can't stand citronella, you'll spend 99 percent of your time indoors. Flying annoyances include the mosquito (which comes in hundreds of varieties), gnat, and no-see-um; troublesome crawling bugs are the chigger (also known as redbug), a microscopic

Kathy Wolf

critter that attaches itself to your ankles to feed; the tick, which you'll find in deeply wooded areas; and red ants, invaders that swarm over your feet leaving painful bites if you dare step in their nest. Bottom line—use insect repellent, and carry an antihistamine with you to counter any reactions you have to communing with these native residents.

JELLYFISH At almost any time of the year you will find jellyfish in the ocean and washed up on the shore. Take particular care with the blue man o'war jellyfish; the sting from this marine creature is excruciatingly painful. Do not touch the dead ones on the beach, as their venom is still potent. Contrary to popular belief they won't chase you down, but in case you get stung, consider carrying a small bottle of white vinegar in your beach bag; this seems to help alleviate some of the pain. Then seek medical attention. Just as with bee stings, reactions vary.

THE KINGS HIGHWAY Established between 1763 and 1819 to connect coastal communities south from Brunswick through Cow Ford (Jacksonville) and St. Augustine to New Smyrna, this military trail is now approximated by the route of US 1; you will see KINGS HIGHWAY signs on historic sections of the road that are not part of US 1, most notably between Dupont Center and Ormond Beach.

MARITIME HERITAGE In a state where many still pull their living from the sea, it's only appropriate that we have a **Florida Maritime Heritage Trail** (dhr.dos.state.fl.us/maritime/index.html) that ties together the elements of our maritime heritage: working fishing villages such as Tarpon Springs, Steinhatchee, and Apalachicola; coastal fortresses built to defend Florida from invasion; lighthouses; historic shipwrecks; and our endangered coastal communities such as the coastal pine flatwoods and coastal scrub. Visit the web site for a virtual travel guide to Florida's maritime heritage.

MUSEUMS Explore our centuries of history: The **Florida Association of Museums** (850-222-6028; www.flamuseums.org) provides a portal to more than 340 museums throughout the state, from the frontier **Fort Christmas Museum** in Christmas to the high-tech **Florida Museum of Natural History** in Gainesville. Their web site also provides a calendar of exhibits in museums around the state.

Sandra Friend

OYSTERS Nowhere in the United States can compare to **Apalachicola** and its oysters, pulled fresh from the Gulf estuaries along the Panhandle. A lack of industrial pollution and a small population mean the waters are clean and the oysters prime; eat them locally, where the steamed or fried oysters melt like butter in your mouth, and you'll be hooked for life.

PADDLING Canoeing and kayaking are extraordinarily popular activities in Florida, especially during the summer months. A new phenomenon is the appearance of clear-bottomed Lexan kayaks along many of the rivers in North Florida that boast beautiful crystalline waters and springs—look straight down and enjoy the view! Most state parks have canoe livery concessions, and private outfitters are mentioned throughout the text.

PARKS, STATE The **Florida State Parks** system (850-245-2157; www.floridastateparks.org) is one of the United States's best and most extensive state park systems, encompassing 147 parks at most recent count; it seems that new ones open all the time! All Florida state parks are open 8 AM–sunset daily. If you want to watch the sunrise from a state park beach, you'll have to camp overnight. Camping reservations are centralized through **Reserve America** (1-800-326-3521), 8–8 EST, and can be booked through the Florida State Parks web site. Walk-in visitors are welcome on a first-come, first-served basis. An annual pass is a real deal if you plan to do much traveling in the state: Individual passes are $40 plus tax, and family passes are $80, plus tax, per year. The family pass is good for up to a maximum of eight people in one vehicle. Vacation passes are also available in 7-day increments for $20 plus tax, covering up to eight people in your vehicle. These passes are honored at all state parks except Madison Blue Spring, Homosassa Springs, and the Sunshine Skyway Fishing Pier, where they are good for a 33 percent discount. Pick up a pass at any state park ranger station, or order through the web site.

Navarre Beach Chamber

Sandra Friend

PETS The dog-paw symbol 🐾 identifies lodgings and activities that accept pets. Always inform the front desk that you are traveling with a pet, and expect to pay a surcharge.

POPULATION According to the 2000 federal census, Florida's population is closing in on 16 million people. What's scary to those of us who live here is that there is a net gain of 800 people moving into Florida *every day*—which means an increasingly serious strain on our already fragile water resources.

RAILROADIANA Florida's railroad history dates back to 1836 with the **St. Joe & Lake Wimico Canal & Railroad Company,** followed shortly by the 1837 opening of the mule-driven **Tallahassee & St. Marks Railroad** bringing supplies from the Gulf of Mexico to the state capital. Railroad commerce shaped many Florida towns, especially along David Yulee's **Florida Railroad** (circa 1850) connecting Fernandina and Cedar Key, and the later grandiose efforts of Henry Plant and the **Plant System** (later the **Seaboard Air Line**) on the west coast and Henry Flagler's **Atlantic Coast Line** on the east coast. This category notes sites of interest to railroad history buffs.

RATES The range of rates provided spans the lowest of low season to the highest of high season (which varies from place to place), and does not include taxes or discounts such as AARP, AAA, and camping club discounts.

RIVERS For recreation on the **Suwannee River** and its tributaries, contact the Suwannee River Water Management District (386-362-1001; www.srwmd.state.fl.us), 9225 CR 49, Live Oak 32060, for a map with boat ramps; you can also download their recreational guide from their web site. The St. Johns Water Management District (386-329-4500; www.sjwmd.com), 4049 Reid St, Palatka 32177, can provide similar information on the **St. Johns River** and its tributaries, and has an excellent free guidebook to recreation on their public lands. The North Florida Water Management District oversees major rivers in the Panhandle, such as the **Apalachicola** and **Blackwater**, and the South West Florida Water Management District is the caretaker of the Green Swamp and the tributaries of the **Withlacoochee River**.

SCENIC HIGHWAYS The Florida Department of Transportation has designated nine scenic highways throughout the state. In North and Central Florida, enjoy a drive on the **Scenic & Historic A1A Scenic Highway**, **A1A Ocean Shore Scenic Highway**, and **A1A River & Sea Trail Scenic Highway**, on the First Coast; the **Indian River Lagoon Scenic Highway** on the Space Coast; the **Old Florida Heritage Highway**, which includes 48 miles of back roads around Gainesville; and the **Pensacola Scenic Bluffs Highway**. In addition to these state-level routes, you'll find local designations such as the **Apalachee Savannahs Scenic Byway**, and county-designated **canopy roads** in places like Tallahassee, Alachua County, Marion County, and Volusia County where the dense live oak canopy overhead makes for a beautiful scenic drive.

SEASHORES, NATIONAL Encompassing large portions of Santa Rosa Island and Perdido Key, **Gulf Islands National Seashore** provides vast unbroken stretches of white quartz beaches near Pensacola, perfect for sunning and swimming. Between New Smyrna and Titusville, **Canaveral National Seashore** protects a slender strip of coastal strand just outside the Kennedy Space Center.

SEASONS Florida's temperate winter weather makes it ideal for vacationers, but we do have a very strong tropical delineation of wet and dry seasons, which strengthens the farther south you venture. Daily thundershowers are an absolute in summer from Ocala southward. Winter is generally dry and crisp, with nighttime temperatures falling as low as the 20s in the Panhandle, 30s in North Florida, and 40s in Central Florida.

SHARKS Yes, they are in the water. At any given time there are a dozen or more just offshore, but for the most part they will leave you alone. To avoid being bitten, stay out of the water if there is a strong scent of fish oil in the air, which means that fish are already being eaten and you may be bitten by mistake. You will also want to avoid swimming near piers and jetties, which are active feeding zones.

SHRIMP You'll find different types of shrimp fried, broiled, sautéed, and blackened up and down the coast from Fernandina to Titusville. The most sought after are red, white, pink, rock, "brownies," and "hoppers," all of which are served at Shrimp Central—**Dixie Crossroads**.

THE SUNSHINE STATE The moniker ***Sunshine State*** was an effective 1960s advertising slogan that was also required on motor vehicle tags; it became the state's official nickname in 1970 by a legislative act.

TAXES Florida's base **sales tax** is 6 percent, with counties adding up to another 1.5 percent of discretionary sales tax. In addition, a **tourist development tax** of up to 10 percent may be levied on hotel accommodations in some cities and counties, including Orange County (Orlando metro).

THEME PARKS You could say Florida is the birthplace of the theme park, starting with glass-bottomed boats drawing tourists to **Silver Springs** in 1878 and tourists gawking at alligators in the **St. Augustine Alligator Farm** in 1893. But the real heyday came with Dick Pope's water ski and botanical garden wonder called **Cypress Gardens**, circa 1932, soon followed by **Weeki Wachee Springs**, the "Spring of Living Mermaids," in 1947. The 1960s saw an explosion in roadside attractions and zoos like **Gatorland**, and fancier parks like **Rainbow Springs** and **Homosassa Springs** showing off Florida's natural wonders. But when Walt Disney started buying up Osceola County in the 1950s, Florida changed forever. After **Walt Disney World** opened in 1971, most of the old roadside attractions that made Florida so much fun in the 1960s folded. If you want to see all the attractions today, you'll need at least 2 full months for the Orlando area alone.

TRAIL RIDING Bringing your own horses? You'll find working ranches and B&Bs with boarding stables listed in this guide, and believe it or not, some hotels will put up your horse—the **Ocala Hilton** (352-854-1400 or 1-877-602-4023; www.ocalahilton.com) currently offers free boarding for your horse with your stay. Remember, under state law, riders utilizing trails on state land must have proof with them of a negative Coggins test for their horses. If you're interested in riding, hook up with one of the many stables listed in the text. Under state law, equine operators are not responsible for your injuries if you decide to go on a trail ride.

WATERFALLS Yes, Florida has natural waterfalls! You'll find them flowing into deep sinkholes (such as the ones at **Falling Waters State Park** and **Devils Millhopper Geologic State Park**) or dropping over limestone ledges along creeks and rivers (**Steinhatchee Falls**, **Falling Creek**, **Disappearing Creek**, and others). Florida's highest concentration of waterfalls is along the Suwannee River and its tributaries; the farthest south you'll find a natural waterfall with at least a couple-of-foot drop is in Polk County.

Kathy Wolf

WEATHER Florida's weather is perhaps our greatest attraction. Balmy winters are the norm, with daytime temperatures in the 70s and evenings in the 50s common for Central Florida; in North Florida and the Panhandle, temperatures can drop into the 50s for daytime and 30s at night. When it snows (which is rare), it doesn't stick for long. Our summers are predictably hot and wet, with thunderstorms guaranteed on a daily basis and temperatures soaring up to the 90s in Central Florida, the 80s in North Florida and the Panhandle. Florida thunderstorms come up fast and carry with them some of the world's most violent and dangerous lightning. It's best to get indoors and out of or off the water should you see one coming. Hurricane season runs June–Nov, and when the big winds from Africa start moving across the Atlantic, it pays to pay attention—follow public announcements on what to do in the event of a tropical storm or hurricane.

WHERE TO EAT I've limited choices to local favorites and outstanding creative fare, avoiding the chains seen everywhere across America. However, several Florida-based chains deserve a mention; you'll enjoy their cuisine when you find them. **Harry's**, a Cajun restaurant found in many cities, delights with tasty seafood and steaks. **Shells**, a family seafood restaurant, serves ample portions for reasonable prices; **R. J. Gators** appeals to the sports-bar crowd. **Too Jays**, a New York–style deli, shines with big breakfasts, stellar sandwiches, and their yummy Mounds Cake. **Woodies** has consistently excellent barbecue at reasonable prices. The **Holiday House** buffets are especially popular with seniors, and you'll find the **Ice Cream Churn**, with 28 flavors of homemade ice cream, tucked away inside convenience stores throughout the state.

WHITEWATER RAFTING Believe it or not, you *can* go whitewater rafting in Florida! When water levels are right, the **Big Shoals of the Suwannee River** provide more than a mile of Class III whitewater fun. Rafters use the canoe portage route to run the rapids over and over, and then float downstream to their pickup point in White Springs.

WINERIES Florida's wineries run the gamut from small family operations to large production facilities, and some partner together to provide a storefront in a high-traffic region while the growing, fermenting, and bottling is done in an area more favorable for agriculture. Native muscadine grapes are the cornerstones of the state's wines. For an overview of Florida wineries, contact the **Florida Grape Growers Association** (941-678-0523; www.fgga.org), 343 W Central Ave, #1, Lake Wales 33853.

The Orlando Metro

CITY NEIGHBORHOODS

ORLANDO NORTH

ORLANDO SOUTH

THEME PARKS

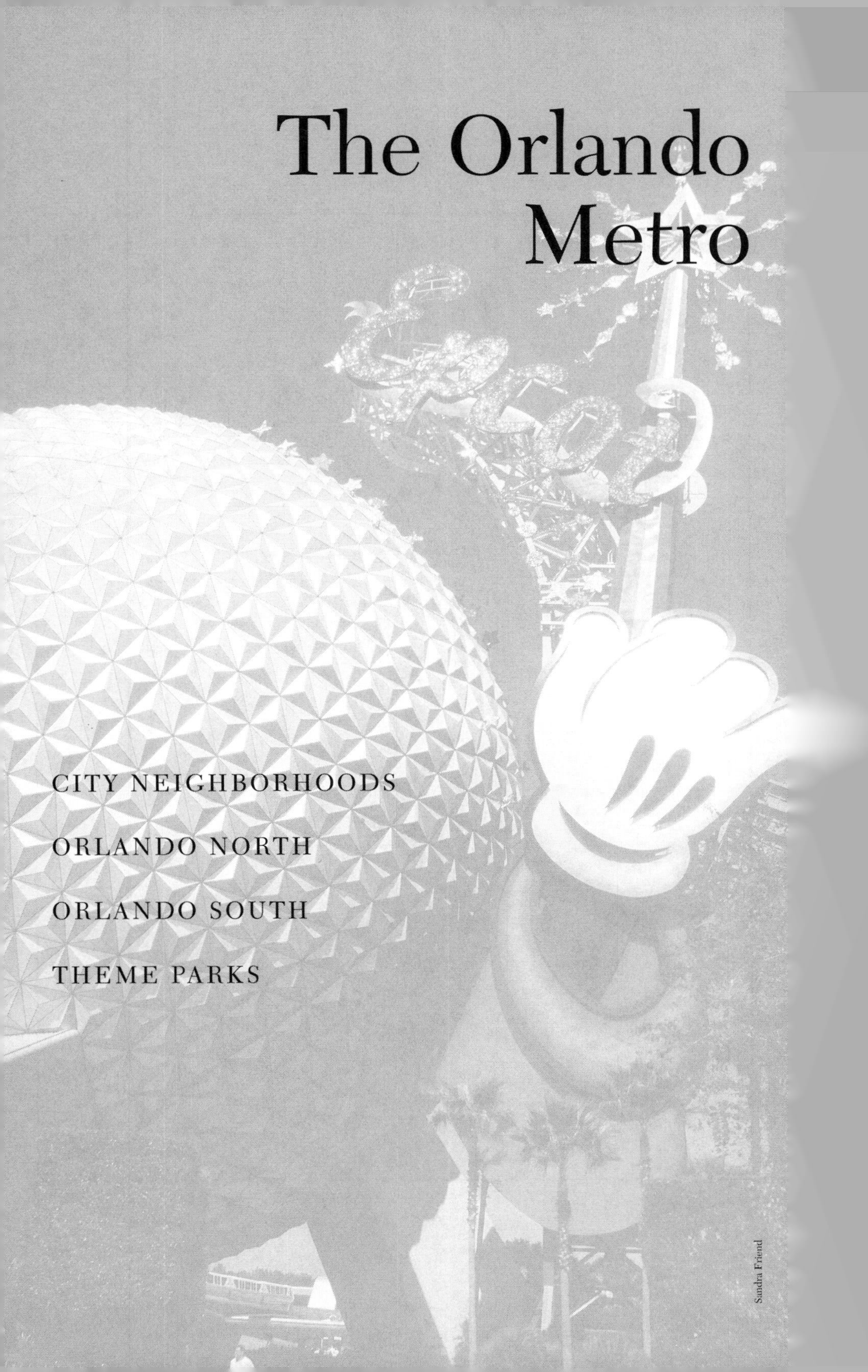

Sandra Friend

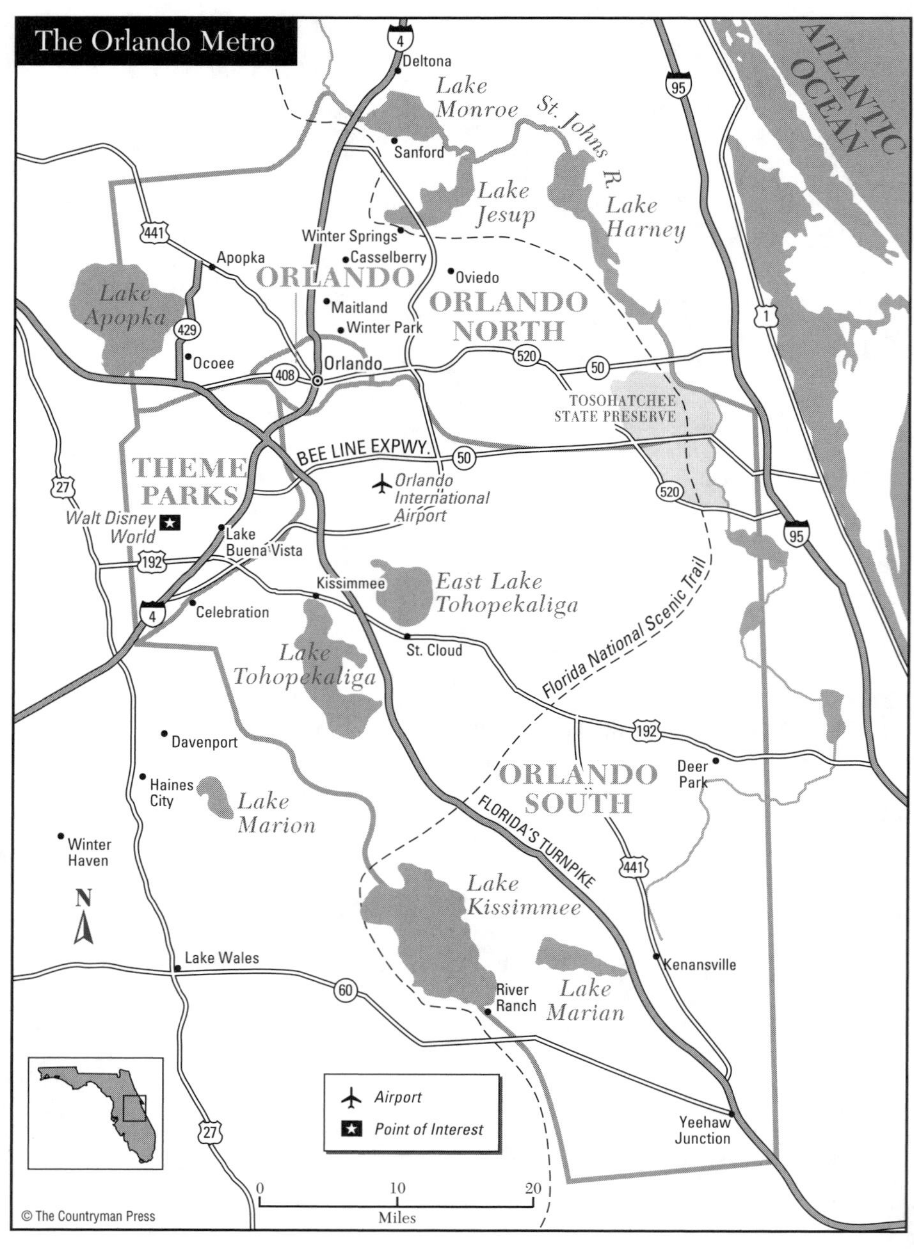
The Orlando Metro
ATLANTIC OCEAN
Deltona
Lake Monroe
St. Johns R.
Sanford
Lake Jesup
Lake Harney
Winter Springs
Casselberry
Apopka
ORLANDO
Oviedo
Lake Apopka
ORLANDO NORTH
Maitland
Winter Park
Ocoee
Orlando
TOSOHATCHEE STATE PRESERVE
BEE LINE EXPWY.
THEME PARKS
Orlando International Airport
Walt Disney World
Lake Buena Vista
East Lake Tohopekaliga
Kissimmee
Celebration
St. Cloud
Florida National Scenic Trail
Lake Tohopekaliga
Davenport
Deer Park
Haines City
ORLANDO SOUTH
Lake Marion
FLORIDA'S TURNPIKE
Winter Haven
N
Lake Kissimmee
Lake Wales
Kenansville
River Ranch
Lake Marian
Airport
Point of Interest
Yeehaw Junction
0
10
20
Miles
© The Countryman Press

THE ORLANDO METRO

Rich in history, the Orlando metro is the vibrant heart of Central Florida, centered on a frontier town that grew up to shape the space age. It all began during the Second Seminole War in the 1830s, when a string of fortresses were built by the U.S. Army to push the Seminoles southward: Fort Christmas and Fort Mellon (on the St. Johns River, in what is now Sanford) were the first. Built in 1838 along the military trail to Fort Mellon, Fort Gatlin formed the core of a new settlement in Central Florida. To accelerate the removal of the Seminoles from Florida, the U.S. Armed Occupation Act offered settlers on the Florida frontier up to 160 free acres as long as they would build a home and maintain a farm for at least 5 years. Aaron Jernigan moved to Fort Gatlin in 1843 with 700 head of cattle, becoming Mosquito County's first resident; the settlement around his spread was called Jernigan. After Florida achieved statehood in 1845, Mosquito County was renamed Orange County (the better to attract settlers), and Jernigan served as the county's first representative in the state legislature. The fledging settlement along Lake Eola bore his name. By 1856 the county required a permanent seat, and the name decided upon was *Orlando*. One account claims frontier Judge James G. Speer named the town for his appreciation of Shakespeare's *As You Like It*. Another credits Orlando Rees, an army officer who died on the shores of Lake Eola during a Seminole attack in 1835; "Orlando's Grave" became a stopping point along the military trail.

DISNEY MONORAIL AT EPCOT

Sandra Friend

Spreading out from its city core in Orange County, the Orlando metro encompasses Seminole and northern Osceola Counties, with commuters coming in to work from adjoining Lake, Volusia, and Polk Counties. More than a million people live in this bustling region, where the population exploded during the 1940s—more than 100,000 servicemen were stationed in Orlando at various bases, receiving military training during World War II. After the war, the space race began, and the defense and aerospace industries started to grow, with what is now Lockheed Martin becoming an anchor employer in the northern suburbs.

In the late 1950s animator Walt Disney came to town, quietly buying up land. As early as 1967, accounts in local publications touted the coming wonder that was Walt Disney World, and the opening of the Magic Kingdom in 1971 triggered an explosive spurt of growth on the southern edge of the metro area—hotels, restaurants, and more theme parks. The Orlando metro area now hosts the largest number of tourists in the world, with more than 43 million visitors arriving annually to the undisputed center of Florida tourism.

CITY NEIGHBORHOODS

With nearly 200,000 residents within its city limits, Orlando is a vibrant modern city with deep roots in Florida's long and storied history. As part of a string of defenses for the U.S. Army, Fort Gatlin was built in 1838 near the Council Oak, a meeting place for the Seminoles. Soon after, Aaron Jernigan moved to what was then Mosquito County to set up a homestead and start cattle ranching near the fort; he served as a volunteer in the army as the settlement grew. By 1854 there was a sawmill and trading post along **Lake Eola**, and a steady stream of settlers picked out spreads around the region's many lakes: the Hugheys on Lake Lucerne, the Patricks and Barbers on **Lake Conway**, and the Speers on Lake Ivanhoe. It was a rough-and-tumble frontier town, the "Wild West" of Florida—cattle rustling from the free-range herds was common, and the herds were indeed the cash cow of the region, as the Spanish would pay in gold for Florida beef to be shipped to Cuba; drovers stopped at **Fern Creek** on their way south to water the herds. Florida's top cattle baron, Jacob "King of the Crackers" Summerlin, settled his family in Orlando in 1873 to take advantage of its central location along his cattle-droving route from St. Augustine to Punta Rassa; he built a large home on Main St and purchased the 200 acres surrounding Lake Eola. In a power struggle with General Henry Sanford over the location of the county seat, Summerlin offered to front $10,000 to build a proper county courthouse if the county seat would remain at Orlando; the courthouse became reality, as did the incorporation of the village of Orlando, a mile square surrounding the courthouse.

The 1880s ushered in the region's railroad era, when the newly incorporated Florida Southern Railroad brought in tourists and settlers entranced by the descriptions of the area written by promoter W. W. Harney. The influx of visitors created a need for hotels and services. Many newcomers planted their land as citrus groves. The old frontier ways yielded to a more genteel class of people attracted by the growing citrus industry; the cows were officially herded out of downtown (by law) in 1882, and sidewalks went in. Jacob Summerlin donated the land that became Lake Eola Park. By 1885 more than 600,000 crates of oranges were shipped north from the region, which saw a wave of British immigrants who invested in Florida land from afar, based on descriptions of the "outdoors life" that residents enjoyed. Mule-drawn streetcars provided transportation

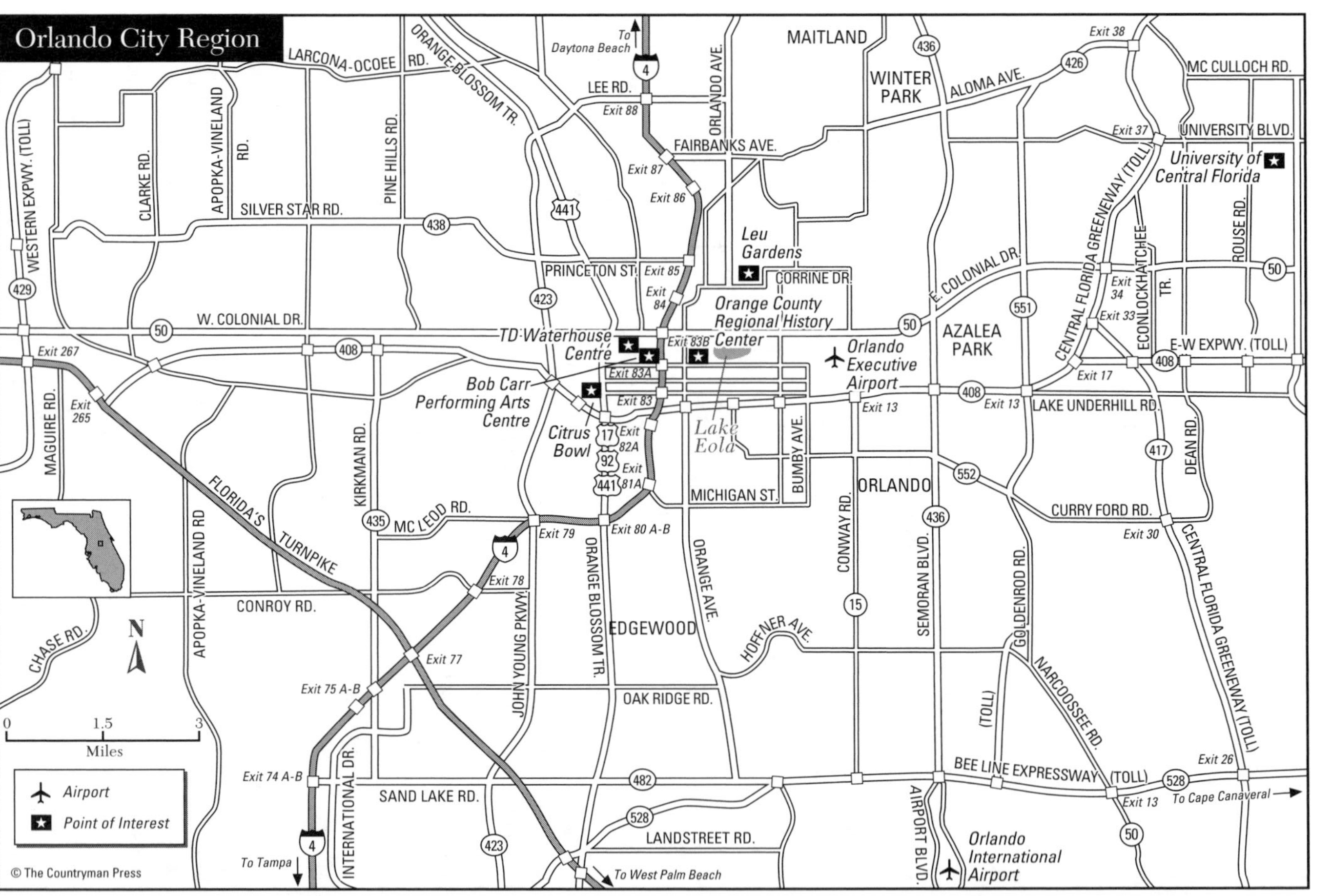

Orlando City Region
MAITLAND
WINTER PARK
AZALEA PARK
ORLANDO
EDGEWOOD
University of Central Florida
Leu Gardens
Orange County Regional History Center
TD Waterhouse Centre
Bob Carr Performing Arts Centre
Citrus Bowl
Lake Eola
Orlando Executive Airport
Orlando International Airport
LARCONA-OCOEE RD.
ORANGE BLOSSOM TR.
LEE RD.
ORLANDO AVE.
FAIRBANKS AVE.
ALOMA AVE.
MC CULLOCH RD.
UNIVERSITY BLVD.
WESTERN EXPWY. (TOLL)
CLARKE RD.
APOPKA-VINELAND RD.
PINE HILLS RD.
SILVER STAR RD.
PRINCETON ST.
CORRINE DR.
E. COLONIAL DR.
W. COLONIAL DR.
CENTRAL FLORIDA GREENEWAY (TOLL)
ECONLOCKHATCHEE TR.
ROUSE RD.
E-W EXPWY. (TOLL)
LAKE UNDERHILL RD.
DEAN RD.
MAGUIRE RD.
KIRKMAN RD.
MC LEOD RD.
BUMBY AVE.
MICHIGAN ST.
CURRY FORD RD.
CONWAY RD.
SEMORAN BLVD.
GOLDENROD RD.
FLORIDA'S TURNPIKE
CONROY RD.
CHASE RD.
JOHN YOUNG PKWY.
ORANGE AVE.
HOFFNER AVE.
NARCOOSSEE RD.
OAK RIDGE RD.
BEE LINE EXPRESSWAY (TOLL)
INTERNATIONAL DR.
SAND LAKE RD.
LANDSTREET RD.
AIRPORT BLVD.
(TOLL)
To Daytona Beach
To Tampa
To West Palm Beach
To Cape Canaveral
Exit 38
Exit 37
Exit 34
Exit 33
Exit 17
Exit 13
Exit 30
Exit 26
Exit 88
Exit 87
Exit 86
Exit 85
Exit 84
Exit 83B
Exit 83A
Exit 83
Exit 82A
Exit 81A
Exit 80 A-B
Exit 79
Exit 78
Exit 77
Exit 75 A-B
Exit 74 A-B
Exit 267
Exit 265
4
17
92
441
50
408
417
423
426
429
435
436
438
482
528
551
552
15
N
0
1.5
3
Miles
Airport
Point of Interest
© The Countryman Press

downtown. In the first 6 years that the railroad connected Orlando to the outside world, the population increased 20-fold, and the city was dubbed "The Phenomenal City," its rows of shops and businesses generating business "equal to a city three times its size." A passenger coach was sent to the 1893 Columbian Exposition, filled with Florida's fabulous citrus and tropical fruit products, exhibiting the best of Florida to the citizens of Chicago. And the people continued to come.

The big freeze of 1895 dealt a harsh blow to the region's burgeoning citrus industry. As the century turned, interests were diversified to lumbering and turpentine; banking and real estate speculation began to boom. Ravaged by fires, the old wooden buildings of the city were replaced with edifices of brick and stone. As subdivisions began to radiate away from downtown, new communities like **Colonialtown** appeared. At his factory at Orange Ave and Princeton Dr, Dr. Phillip Phillips developed a rotary juice press and a method of pasteurizing orange juice that introduced consumers to a safer, better-tasting product, leading to expanded exports for the citrus industry. After the post–World War I economic downturn, the subsequent 1920s Florida land boom brought new growth to the region. But World War II accelerated the city's population growth to epic proportions. In 1940 an Army Air Corps training field opened, and military personnel and their families moved in. The year 1941 ushered in the Pine Castle Air Force Base, which served as Strategic Air Command for B-52 bombers. More than 100,000 servicemen were stationed in Orlando. The boom continued after World War II, with industries tied to military weaponry and the defense contractor The Martin Company (now Lockheed Martin) moving into the suburbs, and a naval training center opening in 1968. In conjunction with the population explosion, downtown's urban renewal programs changed the skyline of Orlando. Skyscrapers sprouted in the 1960s in the wake of the CNA Building, and now the tallest tops 30 stories.

Outside of downtown, city neighborhoods sprang up around social and economic centers. **Parramore** was the heart of swing in the 1950s, when giants like Count Basie and Ella Fitzgerald stopped in to play at the South Street Casino. **College Park**, a very distinct community within the city, arose during the 1920s land boom as the city of Orlando's limits were extended to Par St. After Edgewater High School opened in 1952, the area saw another big growth boom. Streets perpendicular to north–south Edgewater Dr (the community's "Main Street") are named for major universities.

On the south shore of Lake Eola, **Thornton Park** has undergone recent revitalization to become the city's tony place to live, dine, and shop. **North Orange Ave** and **Virginia Dr** define the cultural and antiques districts within the city; cultural offerings cluster around Loch Haven Park as well. Since the 1980s, Hispanic immigrants from South America and the Caribbean have been moving into the southeastern neighborhoods of the city, redefining them with businesses and cultural events that reflect the lifestyles of their homelands.

GUIDANCE In advance of your trip, get general information from the **Orlando/Orange County Convention & Visitors Bureau** (407-354-5586; www.orlandoinfo.com), 6700 Forum Dr, Suite 100, Orlando 32821; they can also help with hotel bookings and provide the free Orlando **Magicard** (1-888-799-1425), a passport to discounts on attractions, accommodations, transportation, and shopping throughout the region.

For directions to city neighborhoods, parks, and downtown sites, as well as information on the city's culture and history, visit the **City of Orlando** web site (www.cityoforlando.net). For a full calendar of downtown Orlando's festivals and special events, contact the **Downtown Development Board** (407-246-2555; www.downtownorlando.com), 100 S Orange Ave, 32801.

For tickets to events held at the Florida Citrus Bowl, Bob Carr Performing Arts Centre, and TD Waterhouse Centre, contact the **Centroplex Box Office** (407-849-2020; www.orlandocentroplex.com).

GETTING THERE *By car*: Two major arteries bisect the heart of Orlando: **I-4** and **FL 408** (a toll road also known as the East-West Expressway).

By air: To the south, the **Greater Orlando International Airport** (407-825-2001; www.state.fl.us/goaa) serves the world with hundreds of flights daily on 89 different carriers; check their web site for contact information on the many airlines servicing Orlando. To the north, **Orlando Sanford International Airport** (407-322-7771; www.orlandosanfordairport.com) hosts many foreign charters and offers regular commuter service on Pan Am.

By bus: **Greyhound** (1-800-229-9424; www.greyhound.com) has a major terminal on John Young Parkway between FL 408 and FL 50.

GETTING AROUND *By car*: The **Orange Blossom Trail** (US 441, US 17-92) and **Colonial Dr** (FL 50) are the major thoroughfares through the city; expect wall-to-wall strip malls and traffic lights along both. **Edgewater Dr**, off West Colonial Dr, forms the main road through College Park, which can also be reached from I-4 off Par St or Princeton Ave. Keep in mind that most downtown Orlando streets are one-way; **Orange** and **Magnolia Aves** and **Central Blvd** and **Pine St** are the major crossroads through downtown.

By bus: Downtown, **Lymmo** is a free bus service on a 3-mile loop, with no longer than a 5-minute wait at the sheltered stations. It operates Mon–Thu 6 AM–10 PM, Fri 6 AM–midnight, Sat 10 AM–midnight, Sun 10–10. Beyond, **Lynx** (407-841-8240; www.golynx.com) offers 56 routes throughout the tricounty area; fare is $1.25.

By bicycle: To step back in time to the neighborhoods that show the true character of Orlando, leave the main roads and amble down the slower routes like Central Blvd. College Park in particular is bike-friendly, with a bike lane running down Edgewater Blvd. A network of bicycle paths runs throughout the city; see *Bicycling* for details.

By pedicab: In the evenings, free pedicabs roam downtown looking for "fares" (they rely on tips to survive, so be generous).

By taxi: You'll rarely be able to hail a taxi along the street, but you will find taxi stands outside major hotels and restaurants. To summon a taxi, call **National Cab** (407-678-8888) or **Yellow Cab** (407-699-9999).

By rental car: Primarily located at Orlando International Airport—though rentals can be arranged through some hotels—rental agents include **Alamo** (1-800-327-9633); **Avis** (1-800-831-2847); **Budget** (407-850-6700); **Enterprise** (1-800-736-8222); **Hertz** (1-800-654-3131); and **National Car Rental** (1-800-227-7368).

PARKING You won't find much in the way of street parking in downtown Orlando; your best bet is to hit one of the nine downtown garages, such as the **Market Garage** at 60 W Pine St, **Church Street** at 150 S Hughey, or the **Library Garage** at 112 E Central and 119 Pine St. There is limited 2-hour metered parking on downtown streets. At Mills and Colonial, the shops have parking behind them. In the **Virginia** and **Mills** antiques districts, some shops have lots and street parking is free; along **N Orange Ave**, you'll find some short-term spaces, but the shoppers well outnumber the spaces. Instead of fighting for street parking, look for the P sign at Orange and Highland; turn on Alden Rd and leave your vehicle at the Lake Highland Sports Complex for unlimited free parking. **College Park** has free 2- and 3-hour on-street parking, and some of the businesses have parking lots behind them, accessed via alleyways.

MEDICAL EMERGENCIES The region is well staffed for medical emergencies. Within city limits, you'll find **Florida Hospital East Orlando** (407-303-8110), 7727 Lake Underhill Rd; **Florida Hospital Orlando** (407-303-6600), 601 E Rollins St; and **Orlando Regional Medical Center** (407-841-5111), 1414 S Kuhl Ave—the only Level 1 Trauma Center in Central Florida.

* To See

ART GALLERIES

Downtown

Gallery at Avalon Island (407-992-1200; www.avalonisland.cc), 39 S Magnolia Ave, inside the historic Rogers Building (see *Historic Sites*), features public interaction with modern impressionism, with new shows opening each month and **Guinevere's** coffeehouse to keep things humming (chai chiller, hooray!). I added my wistful two-line dream to a "poetry line" strung across the gallery one fine autumn evening, and several months later I'm all smiles—it came true. Free.

Orlando City Hall Galleries (407-246-2221), Orange Ave and South St. Rotating exhibits in the ground-floor gallery and the third-floor gallery outside the mayor's office have selected works from their permanent collection. Mon–Fri 8–9, Sat and Sun noon–5; free.

Oval on Orange (407-648-1819; www.ovalorlando.org), 29 S Orange Ave. Co-op gallery and working space for the Orlando Visual Artists League, where there's always something new on the walls; monthly shows include juried exhibitions. Open Thu 11–2, Fri 11–10, Sat 3–10; free.

At the **Westin Grand Bohemian** (see *Lodging*), the **Grand Bohemian Gallery** (see *Selective Shopping*) showcases regional and national artists; wander

Sandra Friend

THE GALLERY AT AVALON ISLAND, IN THE HISTORIC ROGERS BUILDING

upstairs (check at the front desk first) for a look at the fifth-floor galleries, including rotating single-artist exhibits in one meeting space and the Orlando Room, with its paintings of the city's mayors and the city skyline.

Orange Ave
Fredlund Gallery (407-898-4544), 1219 N Orange Ave, features five permanent Florida artists such as Dee Smith (who paints roseate spoonbills in Audubon's style) and Peter Pettigrew with his oils of Florida waterways, as well as other changing exhibits.

Maria Reyes Jones Gallery (407-893-9878), 1810 N Orange Ave, has her vivid pop art palm trees and florals that just scream *Florida*—I can't wait to own one!

Virginia Dr
Gallery on Virginia (407-898-8343), 1003 Virginia Dr, is a cooperative representing the works of the Artist League of Orange County, with 23 artists displaying their creative pottery, art glass, batik, turned wood, jewelry, and paintings in a bright gallery space.

HISTORIC SITES

Downtown
To know the real Orlando, walk the city streets (see *Walking Tours*) in search of historic sites. The core of old Orlando dates back to the late 1800s, typified by the **Rogers Building**, 39 S Magnolia Ave, circa 1886, a former British tearoom and performance venue that is the oldest remaining building downtown. Stamped tin decorates the building inside and out; the building is considered the best example of preserved sheet-metal construction in the state. Just down the street is the city's first doctor's office, the **Dr. McEwen Building** at 108 E Central Blvd. When it was constructed between 1921 and 1923, competing for customers with the grand San Juan Hotel (demolished 1981), the **Angebilt Hotel** (now an office complex with an incredible atrium) on Orange Ave was, at 11 stories, Orlando's first skyscraper. The **Downtown Historic District** stretches from Magnolia Ave toward I-4, containing buildings dating back to the early 1900s, including the **Bumby Arcade** on Church St and the **Orlando Railroad Station** (see *Railroadiana*) circa 1900.

Overlooking Lake Lucerne, the 1893 painted lady Victorian **Dr. Phillips House** is now part of the Courtyard at Lake Lucerne (see *Lodging*), but stands on its original location and is one of Orlando's oldest homes; the city's oldest home, the 1883 **Norment-Parry House**, is part of the complex as well, which falls within the **Lake Cherokee Historic District**, encompassing a neighborhood of stately homes between Lake Lucerne and Lake Cherokee.

The **Lake Lawsona Historic District**, with its beautifully canopied brick roads and 1920s homes, is bounded by Summerlin Ave, South St, Hampton Ave, and Robinson Ave, and includes historic **Fern Creek**, which was a stopping point for cattle drovers to water their herds. Three other residential historic districts within city limits also celebrate the city's classic architecture, from the late 1800s to the 1930s: the **Lake Copeland Historic District**, which centers on Lake Copeland; the **Lake Eola Heights Historic District**, which sits between Lake Eola and E Colonial Dr and encompasses more than 480 buildings of historic merit; and the **Colonialtown South Historic District** between Concord St, Ridgewood St, and Shine Ave.

Built in 1927 with a facade mimicking the New York Public Library (minus the lions), the **Orange County Courthouse** hosted the infamous trial of Ted Bundy; his initials can be seen scratched into the courtroom table. With the opening of a new courthouse, the building now hosts the Orange County Regional History Center (see *Museums*).

South Orlando

The Fort Gatlin Monument is on Gatlin Ave just a few feet east of the intersection of Summerlin St in south Orlando, commemorating the location of the 1838 U.S. Army fortress that attracted settlers to the region.

College Park

Dating back to 1882, the **Erricsson-Harper House**, 19 W Princeton St, was built by a Union soldier who received a homestead land grant for his military service. Orlando's own astronaut, **John Young**, is commemorated with a plaque outside his birthplace along Princeton Ave; he grew up in College Park. There is no plaque outside the **Kerouac House** (www.kerouacproject.org) at 1418 Clouser Ave, but literature buffs make the pilgrimage anyway to pay homage to Jack Keroauc. Sleeping under the stars beneath the grand old live oak tree in the front yard when the mood struck him, Keroauc spent a year in an apartment in the back of his mother's house penning *The Dharma Bums*. This 1920s cottage now serves as a writer's retreat, with a memorabilia exhibit in the back room; the home is open for tours during the annual **Central Florida Book & Music Festival** (see *Special Events*).

MURALS Look for the **Orlando** mural hidden behind the trees on Pine St at Orange Ave, and a colorful mural of **lizards and flowers** climbing up a picket fence on the side of the parking garage at Central Blvd and Rosalind Ave. A **Wyland** sea life mural graces the side of a shop along East Colonial Dr near Mills Ave, and a mural commemorating the **history of the telephone** is on the side of the AT&T building across from the historic Orange County Courthouse. A historic **Coca-Cola advertising mural** graces the side of the redbrick building housing Parky's Deli at 71 E Church St.

MUSEUMS

Downtown

🖉 ♿ **Orange County Regional History Center** (407-836-8500; www.the

historycenter.org), 65 E Central Blvd, in the historic Orange County Courthouse, uses bold graphics and engaging interactive displays to tell the story of Orlando. Start your tour with the multimedia presentation in the Linda W. Chapin Theatre and move on to ancient cultures and geology; I loved the human-sized Winter Park Sinkhole that you can stand in and examine closely. Sounds and aromas bring the outdoors inside, with tactile exhibits like logs, cowhide, and mattresses stuffed with Spanish moss. Walk through the history of the cattle and citrus industries and on to the kingdoms—those of Henry Sanford, the Florida land boom, and Disney. $7 adults, $3 ages 3–12, $6.50 students and seniors.

Orlando Fire Museum (407-898-3138), 814 E Rollins St. Built in the 1920s to house horse-drawn steamer trucks, this historic firehouse is now a newly renovated museum showcasing antique fire equipment such as ladder trucks, steamers, and pumpers. Free.

Wells' Built Museum of African American History (407-245-7535), 511 W South St. Dr. William M. Wells was a prominent African American musician and owner of the South Street Casino, where Count Basie, Ella Fitzgerald, Cab Calloway, and hundreds of other regulars played during segregation. The Wells' Built Hotel opened next door to house acts and visitors. The museum traces the history of Orlando's African American community and displays African art on loan. Open Mon–Fri 9–5; free.

Mills Ave

Loch Haven Park is the one-stop cultural center of Orlando, the up-and-coming Alden Arts District, with the Orlando Science Center, Shakespeare Festival, Folk Art Museum, Mennello Museum, Orlando Museum of Art, and Civic Theatre Complex. Whimsical art is scattered along the winding paths throughout the park; brightly colored Adirondack chairs invite you to stay and sit a spell along the lakes.

Mennello Museum of American Folk Art (407-246-4278; www.mennellomuseum.com), 900 E Princeton St, shows off the city's collection of southern folk art and the lifework of Maine sea captain Earl Cunningham (1893–1977), whose nautical folk art oils on Masonite simply glow; look carefully to note the tremendous depth of detail on each piece. Some of the museum's galleries are dedicated to rotating exhibits on world folk art. Open Tue–Sat 11–5, Sun noon–5; fee.

Founded in 1924, the **Orlando Museum of Art** (407-896-9920; www.omart.org), 2416 N Mills Ave, covers a broad spectrum of art, from American classics to African, ancient Americas, and exhibits by contemporary artists. Open Tue–Sat 10–5, Sun noon–5; $6 adults, $5 seniors and students, $3 children 4–11.

✐ ♿ Kids can be kids at the four-story **Orlando Science Center** (407-514-2000 or 1-877-208-1350; www.osc.org), 777 E Princeton St, where interactive fun rules in themed areas like Science City, Body Zone, and Kidstown (where you must be under 48 inches to enter). At 123 Math Avenue, exhibits make it easy to understand how math works at home, and Physics Park lets you build bridges and roller coasters. On the bottom floor, NatureWorks focuses on Florida habitats, with alligators swimming across a cypress swamp, mangroves marching along a shoreline, and sinkholes forming (as they do) in Orlando roads. There were lines out the door for a peek through the observatory telescope when Mars drew close to the earth, and the eight-story Dr. Phillips CineDome offers one of the top IMAX experiences in the state. Be sure to stop in the Science Store for the coolest toys and books for kids. The "Unlimited Ticket" offers admission to the exhibit halls, planetarium, observatory, and CineDome films for one price: $14.95 adults, $13.95 seniors, $9.95 ages 3–11. Open Tue–Thu 9–5, Fri and Sat 9–9, Sun noon–5.

RAILROADIANA At the **Orlando Railroad Station**, 76–78 Church St, see the original brick South Florida Railroad depot dedicated Jan 14, 1900. Built in the Queen Anne style, it was part of the Plant System. To add to the picturesque view, a steam train has been parked here for years—it was part of the show at the now-defunct Church Street Station.

SPORTS The **Orlando Predators** (407-447-7337; www.orlandopredators.com) are an arena football team playing in the TD Waterhouse Centre, 600 W Amelia St, downtown. Sharing the space during basketball season is the popular **Orlando Magic** (1-800-338-0005; www.orlandomagic.com), playing Nov–Apr; their female counterparts, the **Orlando Miracle** (407-839-3900; www.orlando miracle.com), dominate the court May–Aug, and the **Orlando Seals** hockey team takes to the ice during winter.

Originally built in 1936, the **Florida Citrus Bowl Stadium** (407-849-2001; www.orlandocentroplex.com/citrusbowl.shtml), 1610 W Church St, has been revamped several times over the decades, and hosts the annual New Year's football bowl game, the Florida Citrus Bowl, plus events like the Superbowl of Motorsports and UCF Knights football. Adjoining **Tinker Field**, 287 S Tampa Ave, is a 5,500-seat baseball stadium hosting amateur and semipro baseball games; it's used as an alternate site for some major-league spring training.

✷ To Do

BICYCLING Explore the city via the **Orlando Bikeway System** (www.cityoforlando.net/planning/transportation/bikeways/default.htm), a network of dedicated bicycle paths and bike routes that includes the popular **Cady Way Trail** (see *Greenways*). In College Park you can rent a bike from **Orange Cycle** (407-422-5552), 2204 Edgewater Dr.

BOAT EXCURSIONS Drift across downtown's **Lake Eola** under the twinkle of city lights in a romantic gondola with **GondEola**

THE ORLANDO RAILROAD STATION ON CHURCH ST

Sandra Friend

(407-658-4226 or 1-866-658-4226), where your appropriately dressed gondolier will croon a romantic ballad or simply power the boat while you and your love cuddle; $45 for 40 minutes, including a keepsake photo. If you're up for more of a physical challenge, paddle across the lake in a showy **swan boat** (407-839-8899), the signature craft of Lake Eola, with rentals at Lake Eola Café—$7 per half hour, Mon–Thu 11–5, Fri–Sun 11–9, three people per boat.

DINNER THEATER The **Orlando Broadway Dinner Theatre** (407-843-6275 or 1-800-726-6275; www.themarktwo.com), 3376 Edgewater Dr, long known to locals as the Mark Two, provided my first dinner theater experience years ago with a date—*Guys and Dolls* was a real treat. I've returned since to enjoy the best live musicals in Central Florida, all featuring Screen Actors Guild actors. In addition to the show, the preshow buffet (showcasing prime rib and a huge salad bar) shines. Desserts aren't included in the ticket price ($29–43 matinees, $31–49 evenings), but it's nice to spend the intermission enjoying coffee and a slice of cheesecake.

FAMILY ACTIVITIES For a big list of fun family things to do in the city of Orlando, visit the City of Orlando Recreation Bureau web site (www.cityoforlando.net/cys/recreation/index.htm), where you can pull up lists of activities that you and the kids can do together in parks around the region. One specialized park is **Orlando Skate Park** (407-898-9600; www.actionparkalliance.com/orlando.htm), Central Blvd near Primrose Dr, which offers fun for skateboarders in a flow course and giant bowl, a virtual swimming pool without water; bring your own safety gear or rent theirs. It costs $6 for a 3-hour session. Nearby **Colonial Lanes** (407-894-0361), 400 N Primrose Dr, is a great place to take the family out bowling; open daily 9 AM–midnight or later.

FISHING Thanks to a partnership between Orange County Parks and Recreation and the Florida Fish and Wildlife Conservation Commission known as Fish Orlando! (407-317-7329; www.floridafisheries.com/fishorlando), some city parks are stocked with top-quality channel catfish and largemouth bass; get a copy of their brochure for a list of more than 50 regional destinations. At **Shadow Bay Park** (407-296-5191), 5100 Turkey Lake Rd, you can borrow fishing equipment and teach the kids to fish at Lupine Pond; catch-and-release encouraged, limit one catfish over 30 inches per day. **Turkey Lake Park** (see *Parks*) offers fishing in a fully rigged Tracker Bass Boat sponsored by Bass Pro Shops, available Thu–Sun 7–11 AM, $5 for four to six people per boat.

GHOST TOURS **Orlando Hauntings** (407-992-1200; www.orlandohauntings.com). Starting off from Guinevere's in the historic Rogers Building (see *Historic Sites*), a period-dressed (for my group, a Cracker cowman) guide leads you through the streets of downtown Orlando, recounting chilling tales of mayhem and murder with a solid basis in historical fact—though you'll get a rise out of the number of haunted elevators downtown. Fun and informative, tours take 2 hours and cost $13 adults, $10 ages 9 and under; meet the ghoulish crew on Fri and Sat at 8 PM. Reservations a must.

GOLF **Boggy Creek Golf Club** (407-857-0280), 3650 8th St, offers golfing on a mostly flat nine-hole public course with wide-open fairways and small greens; a driving range and putting green are available.

For a taste of the genteel Old South, visit the historic **Dubsdread Golf Course** (407-650-9558), 549 W Par St, established in 1924 by Carl Dann Sr. "in the middle of nowhere." The city grew to encompass the course, which is now a ribbon of green shaded by ancient live oaks, stretching from College Park toward Winter Park. During World War II the facility became the unofficial officers' club, and it retains that proper feel; the Tap Room at Dubsdread (see *Dining Out*) is a fine place for a special meal. Green fees run under $20 for the 18-hole course.

HIKING Enjoy more than a mile of hiking at **Turkey Lake Park**, where you'll walk through oak hammocks and along wetlands fringing the lakeshore. Other brief nature walks can be taken in a semi-wilderness setting at **Dickson Azalea Park** and **Langford Park**. See *Parks*.

SCENIC DRIVES For a real taste of old Orlando, follow Central Blvd east out of downtown toward the Orlando Executive Airport, where grand old live oaks dwarf modest 1920s homes along brick streets in the **Lake Lawsona Historic District** (see *Historic Sites*). Past Fern Creek and Langford Park, turn left on Mills Ave to return to the endless strip mall that is E Colonial Dr (FL 50).

SPAS **The Urban Spa** (407-481-8485; www.eoinn.com) at Eo Inn (see *Lodging*) provides a full menu of delightful pampering, from indulgence packages including facials and full-body massage to couples massage, aromatherapy wraps, salon services, and waxing. Services start at $10 for waxing and pedicures, $40 for skin treatments and reflexology massage.

WALKING TOURS

Downtown

Pick up a copy of the *Historic Downtown Orlando Walking Tour* brochure at the **Orange County Regional History Center** (see *Museums*), where your 13-point tour of downtown history begins. Presented by the Historical Society of Central Florida, each of the ***Orlando Remembered*** exhibits along the route depicts city history with a montage of paintings, period photographs, and artifacts like doorknobs and tambourines. Interested in knowing more about **Orlando City Hall**? Call the office of the city clerk (407-246-3308; www.cityoforlando.net), 400 S Orange Ave, to arrange a tour. The **Orlando Parks Bureau** (407-246-2827), 195 N Rosalind Ave, can set up tours of Lake Eola Park and historic sites within the city.

College Park

An annual **College Park Neighborhood Association Historic Homes Tour** (407-898-2946; www.collegeparkorlando.org), typically held in Dec, opens up the doors of College Park's most interesting homes, which are nestled in oak-canopied subdivisions dating back to the 1920s. Donation.

✷ Green Space

BEACHES **Warren Park** (407-858-3289), 3406 Warren Park Dr, north of FL 528 on Daetwyler Rd. A small sand beach along the lake is a perfect place to take the tots to build sand castles. Open 8–8 summer, 8–6 winter.

BOTANICAL GARDENS ♿ **Harry P. Leu Gardens** (407-246-2620; www.leugardens.org), 1920 N Forest Ave. Nestled along Lake Rowena in a residential area shaded by grand old live oaks, the nearly 50 acres of botanical gardens are broken up into themed areas such as Native Wetlands, Rose Garden, Annual Garden, and the North and South Woods, with more than a mile of paved paths meandering through the gardens. My favorite place is the Tropical Stream Garden, completed in 2000, lush with banana trees, ginger, ferns, palms, orchids, and bromeliads along burbling streams. Opened in 1962, Leu Gardens owes its spectacular collection of camellias (one of the largest in the country) and tropical plants to Harry P. Leu, a businessman and horticultural enthusiast who traveled worldwide to collect seeds and plants; the Leus' 1880s home, now the **Leu House Museum**, is open to the public for tours as part of the garden's admission. Civic and cultural groups meet regularly at the Garden House, where you might catch folk musicians or the Orlando Symphony; this is one of the most popular venues in the region for weddings. The gift shop at the Garden House offers an excellent selection of books on botany, gardening, and Florida history. Open 9–5 daily; Leu House closed in July. Fee.

GREENWAYS ♿ **Cady Way Trail** (407-836-6160), 1360 Truman Rd, is a 3.8-mile urban greenway with a paved bicycle path connecting the Fashion Square Mall on E Colonial Dr with the Cady Way Pool in Winter Park; you'll find trailhead parking at both ends of the trail.

PARKS The city of Orlando has 83 public parks, mostly small neighborhood playgrounds and green space with picnicking. If you love the outdoors, here are some you shouldn't miss:

Tiny **Big Tree Park**, 930 N Thornton Ave, protects a live oak more than 500 years old; its branches shade almost the entire park.

Dickson Azalea Park (407-246-2283), 100 Rosearden Dr, between Central Blvd and Robinson Blvd, is a linear park that follows historic Fern Creek, crossing the winding tree-shaded waterway several times on bridges. Park your car at the Langford Park Neighborhood Center and walk along the creek to enjoy hundreds of azaleas dripping pink and magenta blooms in February.

Lake Eola Park (407-246-2827), 195 N Rosalind Ave, dominates downtown Orlando and enjoys special protection as part of a land grant left to the city by Florida cattle baron Jacob Summerlin, who settled here in 1873. The lake is the site of the first encampment by U.S. Army troops entering the area during the Second Seminole War, and is encircled by beautifully landscaped grounds and a paved walking trail. Stop to enjoy a bench in the shade, catch a play at the Walt Disney Amphitheatre, or feed the ducks and swans at the Chinese "Ting" gazebo. Elegant swan boats ply the waters; to rent one, stop by the Lake Eola Café (see *Boat Excursions*).

Lake Fairview Park (407-246-2288), 2200 Lee Rd, provides access to Lake Fairview with a boat ramp and public beach, picnic and playground facilities, and athletic fields.

Major Carl T. Langford Park (407-246-2150), 1808 E Central Blvd, has playgrounds, ball fields, boardwalks over marshes, and winding paths under the old oak trees; don't miss the swinging bridge across Fern Creek. It's one of the few places in the city you'll see wildlife—I encountered a Florida box turtle along my walk.

At **Turkey Lake Park** (407-299-5594), 3401 Hiawassee Rd, take the family out for a picnic, kayak on the lake, get out your bike and take on more than 2 miles of trails, or hike around the 300-acre preserve. Kids will love the Cracker farm with its barnyard animals, and you can even rent a fully equipped bass boat (see *Fishing*) to try your luck on the lake.

In addition, the city owns and maintains **Orlando Wetlands Park** (see "Orlando North") near Christmas.

✱ Lodging

BED & BREAKFASTS

Downtown 32801
The Courtyard at Lake Lucerne (407-648-5188; www.orlandohistoricinn.com), 211 N Lucerne Circle E. Few cities let you sleep with their history, but at the Courtyard, you can relax in Dr. Phillips's bedroom and mull over his contributions to Florida's citrus industry. The Dr. Phillips House is a masterpiece of grand Victorian architecture circa 1893, faithfully restored by owner Charlie Minor and tastefully decorated with period furnishings and Charlie's special touches. Guests especially enjoy the two romantic turret rooms—Room 405, with a sleigh bed and brick fireplace, and Room 406, with a fireplace and Jacuzzi—for their sweeping views of Lake Lucerne. Four historic buildings make up the complex, centered on a garden courtyard popular for weddings. $150–225.

Thornton Park 32801
The Veranda (1-800-420-6822; www.theverandabandb.com), 115 N Summerlin Ave. With 12 lavish rooms ($99–159), a cottage ($199), and a honeymoon suite ($139) arranged around a large oak-canopied courtyard, this is a fabulous place to stay right in the middle of Thornton Park. Every room is unique. Two of the more modern rooms, the Magnolia and Washington, feature four-poster bed and Jacuzzi, and overlook bustling Pine St. Breakfast is served family style in the dining room adjoining the office.

HOTELS AND MOTELS

Downtown 32801
Courtyard by Marriott (407-996-1000; www.courtyard.com/mcoma), 730 N Magnolia, is a pleasant new property geared toward business travelers, with executive work desk, two dataport telephones, and voice mail in every room. But the traveler on vacation can also kick back and enjoy their outdoor pool, indoor spa with hot tub, mini gym, and hydromassage tubs in selected rooms, $120 and up.

Embassy Suites (407-841-1000;

www.embassysuites.com), 191 E Pine St. A seven-story indoor atrium lends light to 167 two-room suites ($125–160), each with separate bedroom and living room; the hotel is in the thick of the action, within walking distance of all downtown Orlando. Guests receive a cooked-to-order breakfast as part of their room rate.

From the ebony pillars and gilded moldings to the textured Italian smelted tile underfoot, the grandeur of the Renaissance meets the sleek lines of today at the **Westin Grand Bohemian** (407-313-9000 or 1-800-WESTIN-1; www.grandbohemian hotel.com), 325 S Orange Ave, named "Best in Brand" for the Westin chain of hotels. Marvel at more than 150 original paintings and sculptures handpicked by owner Richard Kessler and showcased throughout the hotel—from the formal art gallery off the lobby to the pieces (all for sale, just ask) hanging on the walls of your room, in the common areas, and even in the public rest rooms. Each spacious guest room ($190–260) extends the luxury of the traditional Westin Heavenly Bed (pillow-topped bed, fluffy duvet, and piles of pillows) and Heavenly Bath to in-room Starbucks coffee, a CD player, a mini bar, high-speed Internet access, and surroundings appealing to the artist within. Every room has an evening view of the city lights, and you're right in the thick of the action in the Orange Ave club district. At night patrons pack the hotel's **Bösendorfer Lounge** and **Klimt Rotunda** for martinis, jazz, and conversation; the richly appointed Bösendorfer piano is one of only two in the world.

Thornton Park 32801

Eo Inn (407-481-8485 or 1-888-481-8488; www.eoinn.com), 227 N Eola Dr. Formerly a youth hostel, this restored 1923 boutique hotel has sleek lines and simple hues that resonate with art lovers like myself. Its 17 rooms ($99–219) are a delight for working travelers—each has a built-in cubbyhole work space for setting up your laptop. Some rooms come with Jacuzzi or garden tub, or a balcony overlooking a shady courtyard. On the rooftop you'll find an exclusive urban spa (see *Spas*); downstairs, a **Panera Bread**. The complex is an easy walk around Lake Eola from downtown, and just up the street from fine dining in Thornton Park.

✷ Where to Eat

DINING OUT

College Park

The Tap Room at Dubsdread (407-650-0100), 549 W Par St. Talk about an Orlando classic. Steve Allen performed here. Folks still come in and tell the manager, "We got married in the dining hall 58 years ago. Mind if we take a look?" Warm wood walls accent this comfortable restaurant with its fabulous view of the Dubsdread Golf Course. The menu offers Orlando's best burger (according to the *Orlando Sentinel*), $7, and creative salads ($7–9) at lunch, with entrées like filet mignon, shrimp scampi, and pot roast moving to the menu in the evening ($10–19).

Downtown

♿ Off the lobby of the Westin Grand Bohemian (see *Hotels and Motels*), **The Boheme** offers intimate four-star dining in a favorite venue for city hall power lunches. Their eclectic cuisine mixes French and Asian influences, with entrées starting around $25.

Reservations are suggested; appropriate dress is a must. Voted "Best Hotel Restaurant in Orlando" for 2003 by readers of *Orlando Magazine*.

For a romantic candlelight dinner, head for **Lee's Lakeside** (407-841-1565), 431 E Central Blvd, where you can soak in the sweep of Lake Eola with its grand fountain and the Orlando skyline casting twinkling reflections across the water as the sun sets. Entrées start around $20; the piña colada muffins are a must. Serving Sun–Fri 11–10, Sat 5–11.

Considered one of the country's top restaurants, **Louis' Downtown Restaurant** (407-648-4688; www.louisdowntownrestaurant.com), 116 W Church St, provides intimate dining spaces in a renovated 1884 building that's an architectural delight transporting you to Orlando's frontier days—with its original stained glass, rich mahogany accents, and vaulted ceilings. Savor bacon-wrapped fillet of beef, downtown chicken potpie, and other delicious entrées, $12–36. Every Wed, enjoy wine tastings in the well-stocked wine cellar. Reservations are recommended, and you'll feel out of place without appropriate dress. Dinner Tue–Sun (until 11 PM Fri and Sat), lunch on Fri 11:30–2; live music Thu–Sun.

Manuel's on the 28th (407-246-6580), 390 N Orange Ave. On the 28th floor, you expect an excellent view of the city skyline—and you're not disappointed. Manuel's is a favorite of the late-night crowd, serving dinner entrées like fennel-roasted rack of lamb and steamed lobster, $17 and up, 6–10 PM.

East Colonial

Barney's Steak and Seafood (407-896-6864; www.barneyssteakhouse.com), 1615 E Colonial Dr. Sometimes I get a major craving for steak, and if I'm nearby, I seek out Barney's, an Orlando landmark since 1975. Their New York strip smothered in mushrooms is simply delightful, and with a huge salad bar and fast service, it rivals its competitors for the money. Open for lunch and dinner; entrées $14–28.

Orange Ave

La Coq Au Vin (407-851-6980), 4800 S Orange Ave. I can forever thank my former boss for taking the staff here for a Christmas party; we had my farewell party here, too. Owners Louis and Magdalena Perrotte are used to hosting private parties, as well as most of their competitors—this is the place that area chefs come to dine. It's fabulous and unpretentious French cuisine, from their signature *coq au vin* to the scrumptious chocolate mousse; entrées start around $12. Lunch served Tue–Fri 11:30–2, dinner Tue–Sat 5:30–10 and Sun 5–9.

Thornton Park

Like its counterpart in Winter Park, **Dexter's** (407-648-2777; www.dexwine.com), 808 E Washington Ave, is a place to see and be seen, with food worth waiting for. Hang out on the patio and enjoy the view.

It's pricey, but **Hue** (407-849-1800; www.huerestaurant.com), 629 E Central Blvd, is the hip and happening place in Thornton Park, where jazz and modern art meet over pan-Asian fusion food like oven-roasted Chilean sea bass with Asiago tapenade ($34) and wok-seared ahi tuna with a sesame ginger glaze ($28). At lunch try the CAB sirloin burger ($8) or lemon pappardelle pasta ($9).

Downtown

♿ **Ichiban Japanese Restaurant** (407-423-2688), 19 S Orange Ave. In an upscale urban atmosphere dropped right in from Tokyo, this snazzy Japanese restaurant offers sushi and traditional bento box lunches (a great bargain) for $5 and up; open for dinner, too.

There are no yachts at the **Lake Eola Yacht Club** (407-841-0333; www.lakeeolayachtclub.com), 407 E Central Blvd, but you can daydream about sailing while enjoying a view of the lake that complements entrées ($10–22) like Florida black grouper, coconut shrimp, and wild mushroom ravioli. Lunch sandwiches and salads ($7–13) daily, and breakfasts served Sat and Sun ($5–9) include bagels and lox and Lakeside Blintzes.

College Park

When I worked nearby, one of my old lunch standards was the **Princeton Diner** (407-425-5046), 3310 Edgewater Dr, where meat loaf and mashed potatoes went great with a freshly made chocolate milk shake; serving breakfast and lunch for under $6.

Shakers (407-422-3534), 1308 Edgewater Dr. Vintage salt and pepper shakers crowd shelves and tabletops in this great family restaurant, where the breakfast selections ($2–7) include goodies like almond pancakes and Greek omelets, and lunch salads, quiches, and specialty sandwiches ($4–9) include Mom's Meatloaf, spinach salad, and the tasty Orlando Grill with spinach, mushrooms, tomatoes, and provolone grilled on pumpernickel, topped with a special dressing. Yum!

West Colonial

Johnny Rivers Smokehouse and BBQ Company (407-293-5804), 5370 W Colonial Dr. An old lunch favorite for me and the tech writing crew—upscale barbecue with dressy southern sides like sweet-and-sour key lime corn bread and collard greens; lunch and dinner, $7–12.

O'Boys Real Smoked Barbecue (407-425-OBOY), 924 W Colonial Ave. Serving up mounds of real smoked barbecue (starting around $5) to an overflowing lunch crowd, O'Boys is an institution in the Edgewater area. If you're wary of ribs but want to give the taste a try, their riblets will tickle your fancy. My top pick: the overly generous chef salads topped with your choice of barbecue beef, pork, or chicken, laced with a heaping helping of homemade barbecue sauce and your choice of dressing.

East Colonial

An Orlando classic that my generation grew up on, **Beefy King** (407-894-2241), 424 N Bumby Ave, serves up roast beef sandwiches fit for a king, chicken sandwiches with the slaw on top, and thick orange shakes: It's what fast food *ought* to be. Grab a meal for $3 and up.

With its distinctive bit of roadside Americana (the giant fork), **Hot Dog Heaven** (407-282-5746), 5355 E Colonial Dr, beckons with all-beef hot dogs: Try the southern-style dog with slaw, the New York–style with onions and mustard, or the Chicago-style with onions, peppers, and relish. Great root beer floats, too!

Little Saigon (407-423-8539), 1106 E Colonial Dr. When I worked nearby, this was a great lunch stop with a menu made up of photographs—if you don't know Vietnamese food, it certainly helps! Their hearty noodle-thick soups ($6–7) can't be beat, and I would often make an inexpensive meal of their massive summer rolls (spring rolls with a twist—wrapped in rice paper rather than fried), served with tasty peanut dipping sauce ($2.50).

Mama B's Giant Subs (407-422-7353), 692 N Orange Ave. A favorite of downtown workers, especially for the folks across the street at the *Orlando Sentinel*, Mama B's serves up massive New York subs hot and cold.

Viet Garden (407-896-4154), 1237 E Colonial Dr. Wrapped in wall murals of Asia, this is a Thai and Vietnamese restaurant I've patronized time and again. At either lunch or dinner ($6–20), settle back and enjoy fresh garden rolls ($2.50), chicken cashew nut ($8), and a tall glass of Thai iced tea ($2).

Orange Ave

At **Cecil's Texas Style Barbecue** (407-423-9871), 2800 S Orange Ave, you dish your own side dishes—pile it on! Hickory-smoked BBQ ($4–10) is the centerpiece of the meal. I'm partial to the pork, and won't miss the cheesy au gratin potatoes. U-serve soft serve ice cream included with every dinner!

Sit on the patio at the **Tiramisu Café** (407-228-0303), 1600 N Orange Ave, and enjoy the breeze off Lake Ivanhoe while feasting on sandwiches ($6–8) like vegetable mezzaluna with snazzy sides like capellini pesto salad or lemon-cilantro coleslaw; dinner entrées run $8–10. Live jazz livens things up on Thu–Sat evenings.

White Wolf Café (407-895-9911), 1829 N Orange Ave. Step into this classy antiques-bedecked bistro with its marble-slab tables and savor some of the best salads Orlando has to offer, served up with unique fresh breads. My favorites: the White Wolf Waldorf, the Greek salad with real kalamata olives, and the vegetarian plate with mango-almond tabouli and black bean hummus. They serve lunch and dinner (except Sun), with entrées $8–10, and daily flatbread pizzas $10.

Semoran Blvd

I love Thai food, and **Royal Thai** (407-275-0776), 1202 N Semoran Blvd, never disappoints, no matter whether I'm ordering spring rolls and *tom yum goong* or a full entrée like *pa-nang* or drunken noodles. If you order your entrée ($6–12) hot, it will be fiery.

Virginia Dr

In the antiques and arts district, snazzy **Logan's Bistro** (407-898-5688), 802 Virginia Dr, offers tasty quesadillas ($7-plus), daily quiches ($9), and entrées ($10–23) like free-range chicken and Veal Shank Redemption.

Thornton Park

Coffee House of Thornton Park (407-426-8989), 712 E Washington St, showcases local art and its specialty desserts like the "Charlie Brownie Häagen-Dazs Ice Cream Pie" (try walking away from *that* one) in a 1922 bungalow. They also make key lime milk shakes and vanilla chai smoothies, and serve lunch (11–3) items like Cuban sandwich and veggie focaccia, $5–6.

Wildfires BBQ (407-872-8665), 700 E Washington St, is an upscale barbecue and grill where they take 'gator bites and drizzle them with roasted garlic aioli ($7); oak-grilled sandwiches ($8–10) and house-smoked barbecue ($7–8, served with a colorful side of tortilla chips and watermelon) make great lunch choices, and it's fun to sit on the patio and watch the world go by.

✷ Entertainment

FINE ARTS The **Dr. Phillips Center for the Performing Arts**, 1111 N Orange Ave, hosts performances of the **Orlando Ballet** (407-426-1739; www.orlandoballet.org) Sep–May, and the **Orlando Opera Company** (1-800-336-7372; www.orlandoopera.org), with three main-stage and four minor productions each year.

Southern Ballet Theatre (407-426-1733), for two decades Central Florida's only professional troupe, performs seasonally at the Bob Carr Performing Arts Centre, as does the **Orlando Philharmonic Orchestra** (407-896-6700; www.orlandophil.org) and its guest symphonic orchestras during the annual **Festival of Orchestras** (407-896-2451; www.festivaloforchestras.com).

THEATER **Bob Carr Performing Arts Centre** (407-849-2001; www.orlandocentroplex.com), 401 W Livingston St. From Broadway shows to symphony performances, high-ticket entertainment stops here on its tours.

In the historic 1886 Bumby Arcade, the **Church Street Theatre**, 110 W Church St, hosts the **Orlando Youth Theatre** (407-254-4930; www.orlandoyouththeatre.com) and **Orlando Black Essential Theatre** (407-491-9762).

At the **John and Rita Lowndes Shakespeare Center** (407-477-1700), 812 E Rollins St, the play's the thing! It wasn't until I started attending the **Orlando-UCF Shakespeare Festival** (www.shakespearefest.org) that my background in English lit actually meant something . . . to see Shakespeare performed means so much more than just reading the words. I was blown away by the *Taming of the Shrew*. The venue's the thing, too—what an incredible location, with the old John Young Science Center renovated to provide three different theaters for various-sized plays. And if you'd rather enjoy the Bard outdoors, try **Shakespeare in the Park** under the bandshell along Lake Eola every Apr.

Mad Cow Theatre (407-297-8788; www.madcowtheatre.com), 105 E Pine St, presents off-off-Broadway versions of modern classics and contemporary plays in an intimate downtown venue with regular productions.

Orlando Theatre Downtown (407-841-0083; www.theatredowntown.net), 2113 N Orange Ave. During *A Streetcar Named Desire* chills went down my spine when Stanley threw his meal at Stella; they were so close I wanted to scream at him for treating her that way. Great shows and an intimate setting (125 seats) surrounding the stage make this an outstanding venue. **Studio Theatre** (407-872-2382; www.orlandotheatre.com), 398 W Amelia St, provides another intimate theater experience with seats right next to the stage.

Plaza Theatre (407-228-1220; www.theplazatheatre.com), 425 N Bumby Ave. Primarily featuring *The Rock and the Rabbi*, a sleek off-Broadway production that brings together the talents of a dozen singer-musicians (featuring an extensive percussion section), including the commanding performance of Gary Richardson as the biblical Peter telling the story of Jesus through his eyes, this Orlando landmark from the 1960s (the former Rocking Chair Theatre) draws appreciative crowds for its variety of shows.

UCF Civic Theatre (407-896-7365; www.icflorida.com/community/groups/civic), 1001 E Princeton St, offers theater productions on three stages throughout the year, as well as classes for children and adults.

COMEDY ✐ **SAK Theatre Comedy Lab** (407-648-0001; www.sak.com), 398 W Amelia St. Orlando's longstanding hot spot for improv is hot—just ask Wayne Brady, an alumnus who moved on to bigger and better things with ABC. These folks are serious about perfecting their craft, not selling drinks: They put on a PG-only show, and no alcohol is served.

NIGHTCLUBS I dare say no other city in Florida is as packed with nightclubs at its core. It's not my scene, but I know they're out there, catering mainly to a college-age crowd. You'll find wall-to-wall bars and clubs along Orange Ave near Wall St and Church St, and they do come and go; among the more crowded on the Sat night I strolled by were **Zinc Bar** (407-246-1755), 13 S Orange; **Tabu** (407-648-8363), 46 N Orange; and **Big Belly Brewery** (407-649-4270), 33 W Church St. Take a late-night stroll through the district; with more than 30 choices, you'll find one to suit your tastes.

✷ Selective Shopping

College Park

At **Acacia Collectibles** (407-872-2374), 1313 Edgewater Dr, look for fuzzy blueware, antique pottery, and costume jewelry.

Sandra Friend

WALL STREET IS A HAPPENING PLACE.

Beyond Words (407-316-8622), 1315 Edgewater Dr, offers a fabulous selection of children's books, plus home decor items like wreaths and candles.

The original dress shop on this block a decade ago, **Bijou's Boutique** (407-841-9728; www.bijousboutique.com), 2501 Edgewater Dr, features fancy purses and dressy clothing with a French flair.

Step into the soothing world of **Drema's Gallery of Dreams** (407-236-7878), 2525 Edgewater Dr, for delightful works of art and decor items in a melding of New Age and Asian influences, where you'll find frogs and mermaids, angels and fairies, pillows cloaked in Rajasthani fabrics, and soap-bubble-like witch balls; ask about their drumming circles and yoga classes.

The new **Gold Finales Chocolatiers** (407-650-8203), 2122 Edgewater Dr, is a don't-miss stop for chocoholics, with gourmet handcrafted kosher chocolates, pastries, and lollipops.

My Secret Garden (407-246-1975),

2300 Edgewater Dr, carries floral soaps and gift items.

Truffles and Trifles (407-648-0838), 711 W Smith St, is a fine gourmet kitchen shop that will tempt you in with gourmet foods in the window; it's a great place to look for cookbooks.

Downtown

Grand Bohemian Gallery (407-581-4801), 325 S Orange Ave. Befitting the grandeur of its setting in the Westin Grand Bohemian (see *Lodging*), this gallery showcases massive works by local artists, including Yuri Maiorov, the ribbon-clad flier of Cirque du Soleil who photographs his fellow performers in black and white, and Todd Lundeen, with his haunting images of Nepal. In addition to photography, enjoy the grand oil paintings, soapstone carvings, art glass, and a fine selection of handcrafted jewelry.

Mills Ave

Colonial Photo & Hobby (407-841-1485), 634 N Mills Ave, is where I head for consultations on camera equipment and for next-day slide developing; they also carry a large stock of professional films. Half the store is devoted to models (airplanes, trains, cars, boats), so it's fun for the kids, too.

Iron Gate Antiques, Inc. (407-896-0181), 1722 N Mills Ave. You can't miss this massive red warehouse just south of Loch Haven Park; inside, 4,000 square feet of antique furnishings, paintings, and large home decor items are just waiting to be browsed.

Ritzy Rags (407-897-2117), 928 N Mills Ave, is your glam stop for funky clothing, be it vintage duds or dress-up for a masquerade party.

Inside **Tara II** (407-894-2411), 1416 N Mills Ave, step into a 1960s dining room and pore over home decor from the 1940s through the 1960s; you'll find yourself humming "Tijuana Taxi" as you check out the back room for additional antiques, mostly larger pieces.

Orange Ave

Fun and funky, the **Antique Arcade** (407-898-2994), 1806 N Orange Ave, deals in kitsch—think love beads, mood rings, disco balls, 1970s lamps, and tulips big enough to take shade under.

At **Boom-Art** (407-281-0246; www.rainfall.com/boom-art), 1821 N Orange Ave, artists Glenn and Sandy Rogers create "recycled art," vibrant and affordable pop art pieces with a comic-book flair; they'll keep you in touch with your inner child.

At **The Fly Fisherman** (407-898-1989), 1213 N Orange Ave, shop for upscale outdoor clothing and fishing tackle in a relaxed atmosphere.

In the green brick house, **Golden Phoenix Antiques** (407-895-6006), 1826 N Orange Ave, melds the exotic and commonplace, with garden wicker and floral-print dishes next to brass trays from Turkey.

Humbug's Antiques (407-895-0155), 1600 N Orange Ave, focuses on fine furnishings with Asian and European influences.

Sleek lines and classic woods characterize **Restoration** (407-895-1800), 1800 N Orange Ave, featuring the finest of fine antique furnishings in vintage oak and mahogany.

Step back into the 1960s at **Rock & Roll Heaven** (407-896-1952), 1814 N Orange Ave, and browse through Orlando's largest collection of vintage vinyl, cassettes, and eight-tracks.

Sandra Friend

SHOPPING'S GREAT IN THE ORANGE AVE ANTIQUES DISTRICT.

Tim's Wine Market (407-895-8463; www.timswine.com), 1223 N Orange Ave, had that rare Inniskillin ice wine I've been on the lookout for, plus hundreds of other options at reasonable prices. Tim hosts regular wine tastings and seminars; call for reservations.

Thornton Park

Dish & Dat (407-426-9696), 716 E Washington St, has a neat mix of old and new housewares and gourmet foods.

🐾 **Happy Tails** (407-841-3100), 819 W Washington St, is one of the more offbeat stores I've encountered, where metal and ceramic "pet art" go hand in hand with dog cookies. Pet lovers will go ga-ga!

🐾 **Urban Think! Bookstore** (407-650-8004; www.urbanthinkorlando.com), 625 E Central Blvd, plays off its name with mod surroundings decked out with fine art from local artists, a coffee bar with comfortable chairs, and urban glamour mags. In an age where independent booksellers truly struggle, I salute Jim Crescitelli for providing his city's literati a place to hang out and discuss philosophy or pore over the newest in literary fiction.

Virginia Dr

Atlantis Art Glass Studio, Inc. (407-896-9116), 809 Virginia Dr. Creative multilayered stained-glass pieces decorate the front room of this studio, where you can pick up supplies and take classes on the art.

Designer's Emporium (407-898-5393), 1109 Virginia Dr. This large, open showroom features antiques and home decor that appeal to the world traveler—safari lamps, European paintings in baroque frames, Victorian fringe and feather lamps, even a French inlay mahogany coffee table.

Flag World (407-895-9245), 1119 Virginia Dr. If you need a flag—any flag—this is the place. Pick your country and size; they sell seasonal house banners and pennants, too.

FARMER'S MARKETS The **Downtown Farmer's Market** on Church St (under I-4) happens every Sat morning 7–1; amble through and follow your nose to tasty baked goods and fresh-cut flowers. Streets are blockaded so residents can browse fresh produce at the weekly **College Park Farmer's Market**, downtown College Park along Edgewater between Princeton and Smith, Thu 6:30–7:30 PM.

✱ Special Events

February: **Central Florida Fair** (407-295-3247; www.centralfloridafair.com), 4603 W Colonial Dr, is the region's big traditional county fair, with rides, music headliners, and more, at the Orange County Fairgrounds.

February–April: **Firelight Fridays at Lake Eola Park**. Sunset, second Sat. Savor the city skyline at sunset while listening to live jazz, opera, and classical music as you stroll with your sweetheart around Lake Eola.

March: **Festival of Speed** (www.festivalofspeed.org), second weekend. One of the country's top cycling events brings nearly 500 cyclists into town for 2 days of racing. On Sat enjoy live entertainment, food, arts, and games; see the web site for location and times.

April: The **Central Florida Book & Music Festival**, College Park, features live concerts, tours of the Kerouac House (see *Historic Sites*), arts and crafts, and a huge book sale.

Spring Fiesta in the Park, first weekend, Lake Eola Park. Browse through 175 booths of regional arts and crafts during this spring arts festival, which includes live entertainment and food vendors.

May: **Orlando International Fringe Festival** (407-648-0077; www.orlandofringe.com), 398 W Amelia St. Ten days in May devoted to nearly 500 performances of street theater, performance art, and cabaret, creatively pulled together in downtown Orlando noon–midnight. $5 cover charge; most performances held indoors.

October: **Festival Calle Orange**, last Sat, wraps 10 blocks of downtown Orlando in festive Latino music, dance, and arts, with more than 50,000 participants flocking to the city to salsa and merengue in the streets.

October–April: At the **Downtown Arts Market** (407-356-8626; www.orlando.arts), Florida artists display their creations in a juried arts show on the second Sat of every month Oct–Apr. It's held on Wall St adjacent to the Orange County Regional History Center (see *Museums*).

ORLANDO NORTH

When I moved to northern Orlando some years ago, I was delighted to discover its shady avenues and sparkling cypress-lined lakes, its garden areas and thickly forested wilderness places—a stark contrast to the not-so-appealing overdeveloped open prairies that characterize the south end of the metro area, which I'd always assumed was what all of the Orlando metro looked like. Not so. The original communities of this region have deep roots, harking back to territorial Florida, when eager families came by steamboat and train to eke out a life on a new homestead.

Seminole County, established in 1913, follows the meandering course of the St. Johns River. Its towns reflect Florida's pioneer and boomtown history. **Oviedo** is Old Florida, settled in the 1870s, its quaint downtown now surrounded by a sea of suburbia spreading from Orlando. Although they're rapidly vanishing under developers' bulldozers, you can still find citrus groves and cattle ranches toward **Geneva** and **Chuluota**. Perusing an 1890 map of the region, I was surprised to see Crane's Roost Lake and **Altamonte Springs** listed; while there are plenty of restaurants and mall-type shopping spots in the area, you won't find anything left of the original settlement. But drive a few miles north, and it's a delight to discover the picturesque historic district of **Longwood**, established in 1878, just off FL 434. Incorporated in 1877, **Sanford** grew out of 1830s Mellonville, a settlement around Seminole War–era Fort Mellon; founder Henry Sanford developed a planned community with green space, and today most of the residential neighborhoods are fully canopied by ancient live oaks. Sanford envisioned the town as the gateway city for South Florida, where rail and river transportation converged.

Orange County (which includes the city of Orlando) was once the heart of Florida's citrus industry. The settlements of **Oakland**, **Winter Garden**, **Ocoee**, **Apopka**, **Zellwood**, and **Tangerine** around the shores of Lake Apopka date back to the late 1800s and early 1900s, founded along the rail lines during the industry's heyday. Although the town of **Christmas** is best known for its busy post office, it picked up its name from Fort Christmas, completed on Dec 25, 1837, as a U.S. Army outpost during the Second Seminole War. Similarly, **Maitland** sprang up around Fort Maitland and adjacent **Eatonville**, the nation's first free black community, incorporated in 1887. And then there's cosmopolitan

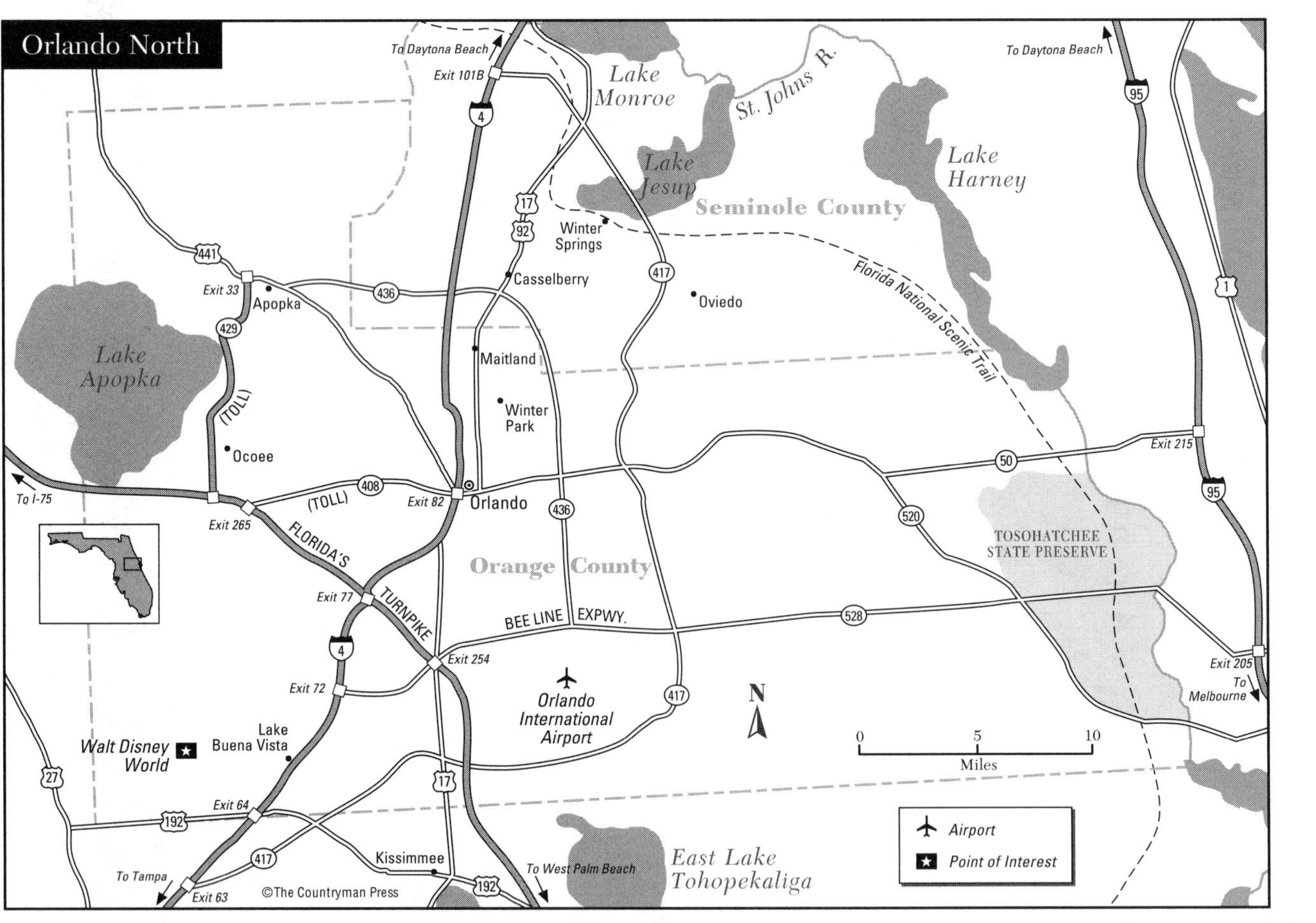

Orlando North
To Daytona Beach
Exit 101B
Lake Monroe
St. Johns R.
Lake Jesup
Seminole County
Lake Harney
To Daytona Beach
Winter Springs
Casselberry
Oviedo
Florida National Scenic Trail
Exit 33
Apopka
Lake Apopka
(TOLL)
Ocoee
Maitland
Winter Park
Exit 215
To I-75
Exit 265
(TOLL)
Exit 82
Orlando
FLORIDA'S TURNPIKE
Orange County
TOSOHATCHEE STATE PRESERVE
Exit 77
BEE LINE EXPWY.
Exit 254
Exit 72
Orlando International Airport
Exit 205
To Melbourne
N
0
5
10
Miles
Walt Disney World
Lake Buena Vista
Exit 64
Kissimmee
To Tampa
Exit 63
©The Countryman Press
To West Palm Beach
East Lake Tohopekaliga
Airport
Point of Interest

Winter Park, founded in 1882 and so much a little city that I almost included it in the "City Neighborhoods" chapter. But it's staunchly outside the Orlando city limits and proud of it. Although its downtown is a shopper's delight, with Ann Taylor, Williams-Sonoma, and the Pottery Barn jostling for space with local art galleries and liberal arts Rollins College, Winter Park still finds the time and space for a Sat-morning farmer's market.

GUIDANCE

Seminole County

Seminole County Convention & Visitors Bureau (407-665-2900 or 1-800-800-7832; www.visitseminole.com), 1230 Douglas Ave, Suite 116, Longwood 32779.

Orange County

Orlando/Orange County Convention & Visitors Bureau (407-354-5586; www.orlandoinfo.com), 6700 Forum Dr, Suite 100, Orlando 32821.

GETTING THERE *By air*: Not just one, but two international airports cover the region. **Greater Orlando International Airport** (407-825-2001; www.state.fl.us/goaa) serves the world with hundreds of flights daily; check their web site for contact information on the many airlines servicing Orlando. **Orlando Sanford International Airport** (407-322-7771; www.orlandosanfordairport.com) hosts many foreign charters but also offers regular commuter service on Pan Am.

By car: The region is bisected by **I-4** and **FL 417** (the Greeneway, a toll road) and bounded on its southern edge by **FL 50** (Colonial Dr) and **FL 408** (the East-West Expressway, another toll road).

By train: The southern terminus of the **Amtrak** (1-800-USA-RAIL; www.amtrak.com) Auto-Train is in Sanford.

By bus: **Greyhound** (1-800-229-9424; www.greyhound.com) has a major terminal on John Young Pkwy between FL 408 and FL 50.

GETTING AROUND *By car*: Everyone uses I-4 to access the northern and eastern suburbs, which is why it's a parking lot in rush hour. But **US 17-92**, **Semoran Blvd** (FL 436), and the **Orange Blossom Trail** (US 441) make great alternative routes: Despite the traffic lights, traffic usually moves at a steady clip. E Colonial (US 50) takes you out past the University of Central Florida, while W Colonial heads to Winter Garden. Paralleling this busy road are the two toll roads on which you can make great time through the middle of Orlando: FL 408 between Ocoee and Goldenrod, and FL 417, which connects the UCF area with Oviedo and Sanford.

By bus: The Orlando metro area is served by the **Lynx** bus system (407-841-8240 in Orange County; 407-628-2897 in Seminole County), with 56 routes; look for the paw-print bus stop signs. Exact change $1.25 fare. Service runs 5:45 AM–10 PM or later.

By taxi: To summon a taxi, call **National Cab** (407-678-8888) or **Yellow Cab** (407-699-9999).

By rental car: Primarily located at Orlando International Airport—but rentals can be arranged through some hotels—rental agents include **Alamo** (1-800-327-9633); **Avis** (1-800-831-2847); **Budget** (407-850-6700); **Enterprise** (1-800-736-8222); **Hertz** (1-800-654-3131); and **National Car Rental** (1-800-227-7368).

PARKING Most of Orlando's outlying communities have free surface lots and street parking, although you'll find vast metered parking lots (2- to 3-hour time limits) and parking garages just a block off Park Ave in Winter Park.

PUBLIC REST ROOMS You'll find public rest rooms in Maitland, adjacent to the Maitland Art Center at Lake Sybelia, and in Lake Lily Park next to the Garden Club.

MEDICAL EMERGENCIES There are many major hospitals in the region, including **Health Central** (407-296-1000), 10000 W Colonial Dr, Ocoee; **Florida Hospital Apopka** (407-889-1000), 201 N Park Ave, Apopka; **Central Florida Hospital** (407-774-0455), 916 N FL 434, Longwood; and **Florida Hospital Altamonte** (407-303-4321), 601 E Altamonte Dr, Altamonte Springs.

✷ To See

ART GALLERIES

Maitland

Maitland Art Center (407-539-2181; www.maitartctr.org), 231 W Packwood Ave. From the street it looks like a Mayan temple complex, perfectly fitting for its setting under fern-draped live oaks and lush greenery around Lake Sybelia. And indeed, a maze of outdoor courtyards leads you past works of art across the street from the art gallery and classroom space designed in the late 1930s by artist Andre Smith; the gallery showcases rotating exhibits of works of art from the permanent collection, and there's an excellent art shop. Open Mon–Fri 9–4:30, Sat and Sun noon–4:30; free.

Sanford

Sanford OVAL (407-324-1577), 508 Sanford Ave, is the premier exhibit space in town for the Sanford/Orlando Visual Artists League, featuring themed monthly exhibits in all media. Free.

UCF

University of Central Florida Art Gallery (407-823-5203), 4000 Central Florida Blvd. Rotating exhibits with a focus on local and student artists. Free.

Winter Park

Creadle School of Art (407-671-1886), 600 St. Andrews Blvd. Founded in 1965, this nonprofit school of the arts incorporates several indoor and outdoor gallery spaces with a collection of lakeside studios. Follow the path through the sculpture gardens to the Jenkins Gallery, and check out the rotating exhibits. Classes are offered on a regular schedule; call for details. Open Mon–Thu 9–5, Fri and Sat 9–4; free.

The **Jeanine Taylor Folk Gallery** (407-740-0991; www.jtfolkart.com), 2800 Corrine Dr, curates four to eight shows per year, showcasing contemporary folk artists from the Deep South.

HISTORIC SITES

Eatonville

Follow the walking trail through the Eatonville Historic District, circa 1887, when Joseph E. Clarke purchased the land from Josiah Eaton and established the nation's first incorporated black community. Interpretive markers trace the history of buildings such as the **Hungerford School** and the **St. Lawrence AME Church**.

Longwood

With more than 30 historic buildings, the Longwood Historic District showcases what the villages of Central Florida looked like during Reconstruction. The walking tour brochure (see *Walking Tours*) touches on such gems as the 1873 **Inside-Outside House**, 141 W Church Ave, probably the oldest prefabricated house in the United States—and it was put together wrong when reassembled in Altamonte Springs. It was moved to its present site in 1973. The **Clouser Cottage**, 218 W Church Ave, is an original board-and-batten pioneer home from 1881. But two structures dominate the old village—the **Longwood Hotel**, 300 S CR 427, opened as the Waltham in 1886, and the **Bradlee-McIntyre House** (407-767-1636), 130 W Warren St, lovingly restored to its 1885 glory; the Central Florida Society for Historic Preservation offers tours through the house the second and fourth Wed and Sun 11–4, $3 donation.

Maitland

In 1915 Orange County paved the old military road between Fort Mellon in Sanford and Fort Gatlin in Orlando, creating **the first grouted brick road in Florida**. In 1925 the road became part of the Dixie Highway; walk the restored highway at Lake Lily Park past the historic **Waterhouse Residence**, built 1883, and its adjoining carpentry shop; both are open as museums (see *Museums*).

Ocoee

Built in 1884, the **Withers-Maguire House**, 16 E Oakland Ave, is a two-story Frame Vernacular home built by Kentuckian William T. Withers, who wintered in Ocoee. Restored to a house museum, it's open to the public Sat and Sun 2–4. Free.

Oviedo

Settled by northerners looking for a winter haven, the **Lake Charm District** (centered on Lake Charm) dates back to the late 1800s. The **Lawton House**, 200 W Broadway, built in 1890, houses the Oviedo Chamber of Commerce and the Oviedo Historical Society.

Sanford

Downtown Sanford is loaded with historical structures dating to 1877–1924, well worth a walking tour (see *Walking Tours*) to catch highlights like the **Whalers Saloon** and the **Pico Hotel**, built in 1877 for Henry Plant's railroad. A separate **residential historic district** lies south between Magnolia and Park Aves. Circa 1913, the **St. James AME Church**, 819 Cypress Ave, is an anchor structure for **Georgetown**, an African American community created by Henry Sanford with its own commercial district. During the early 1900s, Sanford gained fame as "Celery City" because of the abundant crops shipping from its port. A stone marker at Mellonville Ave and 2nd St marks the site of **Fort Mellon**, constructed during the Second Seminole War. Florida's first Swedish community, **New Upsala**, was established in 1871 with Swedish immigrants who worked in Henry Sanford's orange groves; the cemetery on Upsala Rd remains. The Orlando Sanford International Airport occupies the grounds of the former **Sanford Naval Air Station**, an operational base 1942–1968; historical exhibits and vintage aircraft are on display at the airport.

Winter Garden

The recent completion of the West Orange Trail, a bicycle corridor, has revitalized historic **downtown Winter Garden**, where Plant St is now lined with cozy coffeehouses, arts and antiques shops, and several historic museums. Don't miss its Italianate fountain with mosaics depicting citrus-packing labels.

Winter Park

Established in 1885 on the site of a former sawmill, **Rollins College** (407-646-2000; www.rollins.edu), 1000 Holt Ave, is the oldest independent college in Florida. Stroll the campus and discover architectural gems like the **Knowles Chapel**, designed by Ralph Adams Cram, the renowned Gothic architect whose work also graces Rice University, West Point, and Notre Dame, its entrance topped with a scene of the Spanish landing at St. Augustine; a piazza connects the chapel with the Anne Russell Theatre, circa 1931. Don't miss the state's top art collection at the **Cornell Fine Arts Museum** (see *Museums*). At the north end of Park Ave, **Casa Feliz** is undergoing restoration with an eye to becoming a house museum. Two blocks west of Park Ave, the **Hannibal Square District** is Winter Park's historic African American neighborhood.

WINTER GARDEN MOSAIC DETAIL

Sandra Friend

MUSEUMS

Apopka

Museum of the Apopkans (407-703-1707), 122 E 5th St. A slab of limestone shot through with solution holes and an old red tractor sit outside a new log cabin in downtown Apopka that houses more than a century's worth of historical artifacts and records. In terms of presentation and depth of material, it's one of the best local history museums I've seen. A research library with hundreds of scrapbooks and historical documents will soon house genealogical material as well. Free; donations appreciated.

Christmas

✐ ♿ **Fort Christmas Historical Park and Museum** (407-568-4149), 1300 Fort Christmas Rd. Housed in a replica of Fort Christmas (the original Seminole War–era log fortress sat less than a mile north on Christmas Creek), this historical museum covers regional history 1835–1940. Seven historic structures around the park are open during daily guided tours—check out slices of Florida frontier history like the **Beehead Ranch House**, circa 1917, a hunt lodge formerly in Tosohatchee State Reserve, and the **Yates** and **Simmons Houses**, excellent examples of rural Cracker homesteads. Museum open Tue–Sat 10–5, Sun 1–5; park open daily.

Eatonville

Zora Neale Hurston National Museum of Fine Arts (407-647-3307; www.zoranealehurston.cc), 227 E Kennedy Blvd. From her searing novel *Their Eyes Were Watching God* to her 1940s work with the WPA collecting oral history and folktales throughout Florida, Zora Neale Hurston's contributions to African American literature and culture are inestimable. In her honor, this small gallery provides a space for rotating exhibits from artists of African American descent, and sells copies of her many books. Donation.

Geneva

Geneva Museum (407-349-5697), 165 1st St. This small historical society museum covers life in Geneva during its periods of cypress logging, citrus growing, turpentining, and cattle ranching. Open the first Sun of the month, May–Oct, 2–4.

Goldenrod

Goldenrod Station & Museum (407-677-5980; www.goldenrodchamber.org), 4755 Palmetto Ave. In the 1890s settlers started a thriving orange industry; the Florida land boom brought "suburban homes" to Aloma Ave. Learn this and more at this museum of local history, housed in a former fire station.

Maitland

Holocaust Memorial Resource & Education Center (407-628-0555; www.holocaustedu.org), Jewish Federation of Greater Orlando Community Campus, 851 N Maitland Ave. The sculpture *The Deportation* at the entrance to this important memorial touched me deeply, and my education continued as I walked along the museum's permanent exhibit wall, a time line of the history of the Jews in Europe, the Nuremberg Laws, the ghettos, the concentration camps, complete with photos and video of the horror. As a Gentile unschooled in the Holocaust, I walked away with tears in my eyes and a deeper appreciation of the Jewish struggle. Open Mon–Thu 9–4, Fri 9–1, Sun 1–4. Free; donations appreciated.

✐ **Maitland Historical Museum** (407-644-2451; www.maitlandhistory.com), 221 W Packwood Ave. Rotating exhibits showcase facets of Maitland's long history, from its role in the Seminole Wars of 1838 to its settlement in 1872 as a citrus grove community around Lakes Faith, Hope, and Charity to today. Behind the main building is the **Telegraph Pioneers Museum**, with the largest exhibit of historic telephone equipment in Florida. Best of all—the switching equipment works! The docents have fun showing off how rotary phones kick off the switches, and how the first magneto telephones (no dial, just a speaker) connected to the switchboards. Central Florida's first telephone service began in 1909 when the Galloway family of Maitland had telephone lines installed so their customers could place orders. Everyone had a three-digit phone number. The company grew and evolved into the Winter Park Telephone Company, then continued as a rare family-owned operation until 1976. Open Thu–Sun noon–4; donation.

Historic Waterhouse Residence and Carpentry Museum (407-644-2451; www.ourfrontporch.com/osi/mhs), 820 Lake Lily Dr. The scent of roses drifts from a nearby garden as you walk up Florida's first brick road (see *Historic Sites*) to this 1883 home, restored to 1884 with period furnishings as a house museum. Open Thu–Sun noon–4; donation.

Sanford

✐ **Sanford Museum** (407-302-1000), 520 E 1st St. Did you know that Henry Sanford was a the head of the U.S. Secret Service in Europe during the Civil War? You'll uncover this and a lot of other unique facts about the town's founder and the region as you explore the exhibits in this waterfront museum, from sports and agricultural history to artifacts from Fort Mellon. Talk to the curator for the full story, including Sanford's extensive archives and library. Open Tue–Fri 11–4, Sat 1–4; free.

Housed in the "poor farm" circa 1926, the **Museum of Seminole County History** (407-665-2489; www.co.seminole.fl.us), 300 Bush Blvd, illuminates this county's extensive history in a rambling expanse of exhibit rooms. Learn about iceman John Wesley Woods's role in establishing the Sanford Zoo, view 1920s antiques in the period rooms, and see relicts from Fort Mellon circa 1837. Open Tue–Fri 9–noon and 1–4, Sat 1–4; free.

✐ **Student Museum** (407-320-0520), 301 W 7th St. The oldest school building in the region (circa 1902) is a working educational center and museum exploring pioneer Florida, the Timucua, and life in the early 1900s. Open weekdays 1:30–4.

UCF

Exhibits and artifacts at the **National Vietnam War Museum** (407-273-0201; www.nvwm.info), 3400 N Tanner Rd, commemorate our country's military representatives in Vietnam. Open Fri and Sat 11–5, Sun 1–5; donation.

Winter Garden

Central Florida Railroad Museum (407-656-0559; www.cfcnrhs.org), 101 S Boyd St. Perhaps the finest collection of railroad memorabilia—including a renowned collection of dining car china—in Florida is tucked away inside the former Tavares & Gulf railroad depot, managed by the Central Florida chapter of the National Railway Historical Society.

Winter Garden Heritage Museum (407-656-5544), 1 N Main St. Inside the 1918 Atlantic Coast Line passenger depot, exhibits recount the history of this vibrant citrus-packing town. Outside, kids can pose with a Ford F-750 pumper truck and a 1907 citrus spray wagon, or the Chessie caboose parked on a siding. Daily 1–5; free.

Winter Garden History Center (407-656-3244), 32 Plant St. Exhibit cases and walls of photos tell the story of Winter Garden's rise to citrus fame, with a stronger focus on local people and places than the heritage museum. Free.

Winter Park

Albin Polasek Museum and Sculpture Gardens (407-647-6294; www.polasek.org), 633 Osceola Ave. A Czech-born sculptor of the human form whose heyday spanned the 1920s through the 1940s, Polasek retired to this 3-acre estate along Lake Osceola in 1949 and established working studios and a gallery. Docent-led tours take you beyond the art gallery to walk through Polasek's home and chapel, which contain treasures like the A.D. 100 bust of a centaur from Pompeii and a late-18th-century icon of St. Spiridon; enjoy a stroll through the beautifully landscaped outdoor sculpture gardens, with his whimsical multiheaded Slavic gods and soaring religious images. Open Tue–Sat 10–4, Sun 1–4; fee.

Cornell Fine Arts Museum (407-646-2546; www.rollins.edu/cfam), 100 Holt Ave. One of Florida's true art treasures hides on the campus of Rollins College, where rotating and permanent exhibits showcase the college's incredible collection of European and American art of more than 6,000 pieces dating back to 1380. On a leisurely stroll through the galleries, I found myself lost in the details of paintings like *A Mosque in China* (Alberto Pasini, 1882) and *Moonlight Seascape* (Thomas Moran, 1892). Open Tue–Fri 10–5, Sat and Sun 1–5; free.

Morse Museum of American Art (407-645-5311; www.morsemuseum.org), 445 Park Avenue N. A private museum founded in 1942 with collections built over 50 years by the McKean family, this incredible celebration of art glass features the world's most comprehensive collection of the works of Louis Comfort Tiffany; the showpiece is the Glass Chapel that Tiffany installed at the 1893 World's Columbian Exhibition in Chicago. It's a don't-miss stop for art lovers; you'll see works from Maxfield Parrish and others. Open Tue–Sat 9:30–4, Sun 1–4, and until 8 on Fri Sep–May; fee (free on Fri after 4).

A CHESSIE CABOOSE RESTS IN FRONT OF WINTER GARDEN'S HERITAGE MUSEUM.

Sandra Friend

The **Winter Park Historical Association Museum** (407-647-8180), 200 W New England Ave, provides an overview of this old Florida boomtown, its architecture and its growth, with a photographic time line of early Winter Park. Open Thu–Fri 11–3, Sat 9–1, Sun 1–4. Free, donations appreciated.

RACING Prepare to be shaken up at **Speed World** (407-568-5522; www.speedworlddragway.com), 19442 E Colonial Dr, Bithlo, a real contrast to the cultural offerings of suburban Orlando. Home of the Crash-o-rama, Florida's only school bus demolition derby, Speed World hosts stock car racing on Fri evenings at 8 and drag racing 3 nights a week. The adjacent **Orange County Raceway** (407-568-6693), 19444 E Colonial Dr, has several different earthen tracks, hosting motocross, BMX, and mud-bogging. Admission runs $10 and up; call for a schedule of events.

RAILROADIANA One of Florida's last local short lines, the **Florida Central Railroad**, has its shops and yard along US 441 at the north end of Apopka at the **Seaboard Air Line Railway Depot**, 36 E Station St, circa 1918. Driving past, you'll see both rolling stock and engines; the Orlando–Mount Dora Railroad stores its passenger cars here. In Winter Garden the town's two original passenger depots are now historical museums—railfans shouldn't miss the **Central Florida Railroad Museum** (see *Museums*) and the **Chessie caboose** parked along Plant St. At the Seminole County Museum in Sanford, see railroad relics like switches and signs. Along Lake Virginia at Rollins College (see *Historic Sites*), the **Dinky Dock** marks one terminus of the narrow-gauge **Dinky Line**, circa 1888, that brought cypress cut in Oviedo to a sawmill on this site.

ZOOLOGICAL PARKS AND WILDLIFE REHABILATION

Bithlo

With a mission of rehabilitating and releasing animals back to the wild, the nonprofit **Back to Nature Wildlife Refuge** (407-568-5138; www.btn-wildlife.org), 18515 E Colonial Dr, takes in more than 2,000 animals every year, primarily birds. Stop and tour their roadside zoo of exotic animals and permanent residents; free admission, donations appreciated. Open daily 9–4, closed major holidays.

Christmas

Jungle Adventures (407-568-1354; www.jungleadventures.com), 26205 E Colonial Dr. Don't let the roadside-attraction exterior fool you: Jungle Adventures is about conservation. Yes, you enter through the maw of Florida's largest alligator sculpture, a true piece of old-time kitsch that was the original owner's home. But once inside this nearly 40-year-old former alligator farm, now a 20-acre preserve, I walked the Jungle Nature Trail and met some of the most knowledgeable guides I've ever encountered at a commercial attraction, as they wowed their guests with extraordinary detail on Florida habitats, endangered species programs, and Native culture. In the floodplain of the St. Johns River, the park offers several pleasant boardwalk loops, a boat ride, and some of the largest alligators I've ever seen, as well as four daily wildlife shows featuring endangered Florida panthers. Open daily 9:30–5:30; $16 adults, $12.50 seniors, and $8.50 ages 3–11.

Maitland

Audubon Birds of Prey Center (407-644-0190; www.audubon.org), 1101 Audubon Way. Centered on a 1924 bungalow along 2.5 acres on Lake Sybelia, this special refuge is dedicated to the rehabilitation and release of injured raptors, with a large raptor trauma clinic, a walking trail around aviaries with birds unable to be released to the wild, and a small research library and gift shop. Home to the state's Eaglewatch program, the facility has rehabbed and released more than 200 bald eagles since it opened in 1979. Open Tue–Sun 10–4; fee.

Sanford

Central Florida Zoo (407-323-4450; www.centralfloridazoo.org), 3755 NW US 17-92. The entrance road to this acclaimed zoological park tells the story: You're stepping into a place that blends perfectly with its natural surroundings, the floodplain forests of Lake Monroe. Visitors utilize a series of boardwalks to connect the buildings and enclosures; past alligators and bald eagles, a Florida nature walk meanders through the forest. The key focus, of course, is conservation and the reproduction of endangered species like Grand Cayman rock iguanas and wreathed hornbills. A herpetarium shows off Florida's venomous snakes as well as endangered species like the Aruba Island rattlesnake, king cobra, and Amazonian palm viper. But the kid in you (or your kids) gets to play, too. At Zoofari Outpost, feed and pet llamas, goats, zebu, and cows; a hand-washing station is thoughtfully provided. And I was almost tempted by the retro "make your own souvenir" plastic injection Mold-A-Rama, with its aroma pulling me back to the 1960s. Ever conscious of its audience, the zoo hosts special kids' events like the Zoo Boo Bash, a gentle trick-or-treat for youngsters. Spend an afternoon and get to know the 300-plus animals hidden throughout the 116-acre park; it's a great retreat. Open daily 9–5; $8 adults, $5 seniors, $4 children 3–12. New "Behind the Scenes" tours offer encounters with cheetahs and elephants for an additional $5, with reservations required.

✷ To Do

AIRBOAT RIDES With the St. Johns River making a mazy meander along the eastern edge of the region, this is prime airboat territory. My first-ever airboat outing was with **Bill's Airboat Adventures** (407-977-3214; www.airboating.com), where Captain Bill Daniel takes you on a truly educational journey through the marshes where the river flows toward Lake Monroe, pointing out Indian mounds and cypress swamps while giving you background about Florida's unique aquatic habitats. Fares run $25–35 depending on length of tour, less for children under 14; by appointment only. In Christmas, **A-Awesome Airboat Rides** (407-568-7601; www.airboatride.com) departs from the St. Johns River bridge on FL 50 just east of Christmas to take you on a spin up through Puzzle Lake or down along the fringe of Tosohatchee Reserve, where Captain Bruce points out the region's wildlife. At **Black Hammock Fish Camp** (see *Eating*

Sandra Friend

TRAVELING THE ST. JOHNS BY AIRBOAT

Out) in Oviedo, hop **Gator Ventures** (407-977-8235) for a spin around the alligator-rich Lake Jesup.

BICYCLING Orlando's suburbs boast numerous dedicated paved bicycle trails, as well as marked routes for bicycles in both urban and rural areas. While the eventual intent is to have the **Cross Seminole Trail** cross the entire county, it presently has paved segments open between Oviedo and Winter Springs and Lake Mary and Longwood, including a fancy suspension span carrying the trail across I-4. Hikers on the Florida National Scenic Trail share this route through suburban Orlando. Look for green BIKE ROUTE signs in other parts of the county for quiet back-road trips.

If you're interested in biking the popular **West Orange Trail**, which passes right through downtown Winter Garden, check out the rentals at **West Orange Bike** (407-877-8884), 6 E Plant; **Abbott's Bicycles** (407-654-0115), 36 E Plant; and **Bikes & Blades** (407-877-0600), 17914 FL 438 ($5 per hour or $25 per day). Most shops are closed Sun.

BIRDING The region's top spot for birding is **Orlando Wetlands Park** (see *Parks*), where vast human-made wetlands filter treated water flowing into the St. Johns River floodplain. Walk the Berm Trail for an eagle's-eye view of the marshes and the many wading birds that call it home. Looking for eagles in the wild? Stop at **Black Hammock Trailhead** (FL 434 at FL 417) on the **Cross Seminole Trail** (see *Greenways*) and walk in to the trail junction (left fork); look up and to your left. This eagle pair has been nesting in the pines for nearly a decade. Of course, you'll find herons and egrets hanging out at most regional parks.

BOAT EXCURSIONS Step back into another era with a boat trip from Sanford, the **Rivership *Romance*** (407-321-5091 or 1-800-423-7401; www.rivership romance.com), 433 N Palmetto Ave, on a delightful cruise along the St. Johns River. Sanford was the last port of call up the St. Johns for turn-of-the-20th-century steamships, which brought tourists and settlers to Central Florida until the railroads gained a strong foothold in the 1920s. Your ship is a refurbished 1940s Great Lakes steamer, which glides across Lake Monroe and up the St. Johns with ease. Of course, what would a cruise be without dining? The dining room, all red velvet and windows, feels like an elegant palace, and your choice of five entrées includes prime rib and roasted herb-crusted grouper. The helpful wait staff will make suggestions on meals and drinks, and your "cruise director" lines up activities (like dancing and a narrated ecotour) on the 2- to 3-hour cruise. Tickets $36.75 or $47.25; $52.50 for moonlight dining and dancing cruise held Fri and Sat evenings.

Drift across Winter Park's placid lakes on a 12-mile, 1-hour excursion you won't forget: the famed **Winter Park Scenic Boat Tour** (407-644-4056; www.scenicboattours.com), 312 E Morse Blvd. I knew about the lakes, the gardens, and many of the homes of the wealthy gentry who settled in Winter Park in the 1920s, but I was surprised and delighted at the passages between the lakes—the canals are narrow and shaded. The captains know their stuff, and will give you a great history lesson while talking about the backgrounds of local families and their historic upscale homes. Tickets $8 adults, $4 for ages 2–11.

ECOTOURS With pontoon boats departing from Sanford, **Toon Tours** (407-314-2954), 4255 Peninsula Point, guides you on narrated nature cruises along the floodplain forests of the St. Johns River. Departing from Gator's Riverside Grill (see *Eating Out*) in Sanford, the **St. Johns River Cruise** (407-330-1612) takes you on a lazy pontoon journey on a quiet electric boat, a 2-hour shallow-water ride with interpretive information about the region and its natural inhabitants; adults $14, children $8, seniors $12. **Seminole Safari** (1-877-387-4452; www.allseasonscommerce.com) sets up multistop ecotours in the woods and on the rivers with pickup and drop-off at your hotel; lunch is provided.

FAMILY ACTIVITIES Play mini golf at **Congo River Golf** (407-682-4077), 531 W Semoran Blvd, Altamonte Springs, where you can feed the live 'gators out front! At **Flea World** (see *Selective Shopping*) on US 17-92, Sanford, you'll find **Fun World**, offering carnival rides and shows; when I drove by, a Chinese acrobatic troupe was strutting their stuff. Open Fri–Sun 10–7. Stop by the **RDV Sportsplex** (407-916-2442), 8701 Maitland Summit Blvd, to see the **Orlando Magic** (www.nba.com/magic) and other teams practice.

GAMING **Orlando Jai-alai** (407-331-9191), US 17-92 and FL 436, Casselberry. Wager on players' performance in this high-speed cousin to lacrosse, where athletes hurl the ball back and forth at speeds up to 150 mph. They offer horse racing telecasts as well. For more racing, just up US 17-92 is the **Sanford-Orlando Kennel Club** (407-831-1600), 301 Dog Track Rd, Longwood, with greyhound racing.

GOLF **Casselberry Golf Club** (407-699-9310; www.casselberrygolf.com), 300 S Triplet Lake Dr, Casselberry, is an interesting 18-hole public course—built in 1947, the par-69 course winds like a slender ribbon through residential communities. It's a local favorite, and it doesn't hurt that green fees (including golf cart) run $15–28.

Winding along the edge of Wekiwa Springs State Park (see *Parks*), the **Sabal Point Country Club** (407-869-4653; www.sabalpointgolfclub.com/sabalpoint), 2662 Sabal Club Way, Longwood, is a naturally landscaped semiprivate 18-hole course, par 72; its signature 13th hole is a grassy island nestled in the state park.

HIKING Hikers on the eastern side of Orlando are blessed with an almost infinite array of trails to choose from; an explanation of them all would merit another book. Is it any wonder that the largest Florida Trail Association chapter (the Central chapter) meets in Orlando? Pick up a flyer from Seminole County (see *Parks*) for an excellent sampling, or thumb through the St. Johns River Water Management District recreation guide (available online at sjr.state.fl.us/programs/outreach), and get yourself a copy of *50 Hikes in Central Florida* (Backcountry Guides), which covers more than a dozen hikes in this region in extreme detail. My top picks that are *not* in the first edition: the **Florida Trail** between Chuluota and Oviedo, a scenic segment following the Econ River, and the trails at **Spring Hammock Park** (fun for kids), which lead out to some of the oldest cypresses in Florida along Lake Jesup.

PADDLING **Kings Landing** (407-886-0859), 1014 Miami Springs Rd, rents canoes and kayaks for paddlers to head down Rock Springs Run to the Wekiva River, as does **Wekiva Adventures** (407-321-7188; www.wekivaadventures.com), which also does guided trips. You'll find these waterways busy on summer weekends; a good alternative is the Econ River from Bithlo to Oviedo. Check with **Hidden River Park** (407-568-5346), 15295 E Colonial Dr, where they not only rent canoes and kayaks but also run guided paddling trips of 9 to 12 miles; some include overnight camping. **Riverquest Kayaks** (407-834-4040), 4099 Orlando Ave, Casselberry, rents kayaks-to-go and does free demos in Lake Katherine behind the store. **Travel Country Outdoors** (see *Selective Shopping*) runs kayak clinics, leads guided trips, and rents kayaks and canoes. For a unique urban paddle past million-dollar homes and down the scenic canals of **Winter Park**, check in at the Winter Park Scenic Boat Tour (see *Boat Excursions*) for canoe rentals.

SAILING **Fun Maritime Academy** (1-866-320-SAIL; www.funma.com), 531 N Palmetto Ave, A Dock, offers sailing instruction and boat rentals on vast Lake Monroe. Instructional courses start at $125 ("Learning the Ropes") and range up to $500 for a 2-day basic keelboat course for craft 25 feet or smaller. The American Sailing Association certifies their instructors.

SCENIC DRIVES In such an urban setting, you wouldn't expect much in the way of scenic drives, but there are a few beauty spots worth noting. Heading east of Sanford toward the coast, **FL 46** parallels the sprawling wetlands of the St. Johns River, with expansive views. **CR 427** between historic Longwood and Lake Mary has a pretty section through Spring Hammock Preserve, and even **US 17-92** cleans up nicely as it rounds the bend at Sanford, heading north as **Lakeshore Dr** along the oceanlike expanse of Lake Monroe. For a beautiful historic district trip, drive **Oak St** west from downtown Sanford, or check out beautiful old homes tucked under a canopy of ancient live oaks on **Park Ave** between US 17-92 in Maitland and Winter Park.

SWIMMING Swim within sight of Lake Apopka at **Farnsworth Pool**, a community swimming pool in Winter Garden, or jump into the icy fresh springwater of

Rock Springs Run at Kelly Park and **Wekiwa Springs** at Wekiwa Springs State Park (see *Parks*).

TRAIL RIDING Visit **Devonwood Stables** (407-273-0822), 2518 Rouse Rd, between FL 50 and University Blvd, for horseback riding lessons and trail riding.

TUBING Head out to **Kelly Park** (see *Parks*) for Central Florida's only tubing experience. Rock Springs Run gets its start as the spring splashes out of a rocky cliff, forming a crystal-clear stream flowing toward the Wekiva River; the tubing run starts right in front of the caves from which the river flows, and continues along a gentle crystalline course for a mile. Tubes must be rented outside the park; several vendors on Park Ave will let you take tubes with you, and they'll pick up the tubes at the park each evening.

WALKING TOURS Pick a copy of the *Sanford Historic Downtown Walking Tour* at the Sanford Museum (see *Museums*) for a stroll through Sanford's historic business district, where several of the downtown blocks date back to 1887. The Longwood *Historic District Walking Tour* touches on 33 points of interest; pick up a brochure at city hall. Pick up *A Walking Tour of Eatonville, Florida* at the town hall or the Zora Neale Hurston National Museum of Fine Arts (see *Museums*), with details on 10 significant sites in the town's history, and *Historic Properties of Maitland Florida*, a booklet from the Maitland Historical Society, to check out homes dating back to the 1880s.

✵ Green Space

BOTANICAL GARDENS Behind a screen of cypresses fringing the shore of Lake Maitland, **Kraft Azalea Gardens** (407-599-3334), Alabama Dr (off Palmer Ave), Winter Park, has spectacular fragrant blooms Jan–Mar. According to local legend, if you stand in the circle of columns in the replica Parthenon and whisper at the wall, your voice will echo back.

Part wilderness, part formal gardens, **Mead Gardens**, S Denning Dr, Winter Park, offers 1.5 miles of gentle walking trails (including a Braille Trail) around well-groomed natural areas along a clear creek linking lakes in Orlando and Winter Park; slip away to this lovely urban oasis for a quiet walk in the woods. Named for pioneer Florida horticulturalist Dr. Theodore L. Mead, the 55-acre former botanical garden opened to the public on Jan 14, 1940.

University of Central Florida Arboretum (407-823-3146), UCF campus. This little-known tranquil oasis encompasses gardens of both native and exotic plants. Follow the 30- to 45-minute trail through the bromeliad sanctuary, cycad garden, and palm collection, or wander for an hour through Florida's natural habitats of pine flatwoods, oak hammock, cabbage palm strands, marshes, and scrub. Park next to the Stockyard Conservatory Greenhouse; open sunrise–sunset daily. Free.

GREENWAYS Greenways (primarily old railroad beds converted to paved trails) crisscross the entire Orlando metro area, providing miles of comfortable biking.

Kelly Park (407-889-4179), 400 E Kelly Park Rd, Rock Springs. Picture a grotto where ferns and mosses dangle over the dark entrance, where a glassy stream emerges from the earth and flows away over ancient slabs of limestone. Rock Spring is a magical place, a water park as designed by Mother Nature (with a little help from her friends)—the natural spring run twists and winds through the forest under a heavy canopy of trees before reaching an island buttressed with concrete; the waterway splits in two. Take your choice; both sides of this lazy river spill out into a broad pool that serves as the park's main swimming area. Bream and killifish sparkle in the depths as you float over aquatic gardens of tapegrass. Caught up in the gentle flow, you leave the busy swimming hole and float back into the forest to reach the take-out point after a mile. Yes, the park can be overrun on weekends—the trouble with many of our natural places is they're loved to death. Better to visit on a quiet afternoon or early morning, when you can slowly snorkel or tube (see *Tubing*) with the current without bumping into anyone else. In addition to its watery wonders, Kelly Park has extensive shady picnic grounds, several generations of playgrounds, pleasant pathways paralleling the run, and a campground (see *Campgrounds*). Paddlers can launch their craft just down the road at Kings Landing (see *Paddling*) for a trip down this wild and scenic river, one of the few unspoiled waterways in Central Florida. Open 9–7 in summer, 8–6 in winter. Fee.

DRIFTING DOWN KELLY PARK'S ROCK SPRINGS RUN

Sandra Friend

The **West Orange Trail** (407-654-5144; parks.onetgov.net/index.htm) runs 22 miles from a trailhead near Monteverde to its terminus in downtown Winter Garden, with another disconnected segment heading east out of Apopka toward Sorrento. The **Little Econ Greenway** (407-249-4586), 2451 Dean Rd, links the UCF area with the **Cady Way Trail** coming out of the city of Orlando, and the **Cross Seminole Trail** (407-665-2093) connects Oviedo with Winter Springs, Longwood, Lake Mary, and Heathrow, with parts still under construction. Efforts are actively under way to link together Orlando's network of greenways with those in adjoining Lake and Polk Counties to eventually provide hundreds of miles of protected cycling throughout Central Florida.

PARKS The northern Orlando metro is blessed with a large number of urban parks, far too many to cover here. Enjoy a walk around **Lake Lily Park** in Maitland, where you can watch turtles from the boardwalk. Sedate **Lake Lotus Park** (407-293-8885) off FL 414 provides an immersion into a sliver of wilderness along the Little Wekiva River. Several pleasant community parks provide scenic views of and boat ramp access to Lake Apopka, like **Trimble Park** in Tangerine and **Loughton Park** in Winter Garden. On the Winter Springs–Longwood border, **Big Tree Park** on General Hutchinson Pkwy protects the South's elder statesman, an ancient bald cypress known as The Senator, thought to be more than 2,000 years old. **Crane's Roost Park** behind the Altamonte Mall, FL 436, appeals to the urban Altamonte Springs crowd as a place to see and be seen while power walking and jogging around the lake. For full information on the region's parks, contact **Orange County Parks & Recreation** (407-836-6200; www.orangecountyparks.net), 4801 W Colonial Dr, Orlando 32808, and **Seminole County Parks & Recreation** (407-665-7352), 264 W North St, Altamonte Springs 32714, for their respective brochures.

Clarcona Horseman's Park (407-886-6255), 3535 Damon Rd, is a unique 40-acre public equestrian facility off CR 435 with dressage show rings, judging towers, and horse stalls. Connects to the West Orange Trail's equestrian path; RV camping available.

Orlando Wetlands Park (407-246-2213), 25155 Wheeler Rd, Christmas, provides miles of biking and hiking trails around human-made impoundments where nearly 2,000 acres of wetlands naturally filter treated wastewater before it is released to the St. Johns River. Rest rooms and picnic tables at trailhead; closed Oct–Jan 20. Free.

✐ Encompassing nearly 8,000 acres along the wild and scenic Wekiva River, **Wekiwa Springs State Park** (407-884-2008), 1800 Wekiwa Circle, Apopka, has a crystalline spring for swimming, more than 10 miles of hiking and off-road biking trails, canoe rentals for launch, and a large family camping area with electric and water hookups, dump station, and rest rooms. Fee.

NATURE CENTERS **Oakland Nature Preserve** (407-656-1117), FL 438. With 95 acres of wetlands and uplands along Lake Apopka, this living laboratory has a boardwalk down to the lake and interpretive trails winding through the woods; an environmental center and Cracker homestead are under construction. Free.

WILD PLACES Despite being one of Florida's most densely populated counties, Seminole County offers excellent wilderness getaways thanks to the **Seminole County Natural Lands** program (407-665-7352; www.co.seminole.fl.us/natland). Wilderness areas include the **Chuluota Wilderness Area**, 3895 Curryville Rd, Chuluota, with 625 acres of densely wooded hammocks and floodplain forest with hiking trails; the **Econ River Wilderness Area**, 3795 Old Lockwood Rd, Oviedo, protecting shoreline along the scenic Econlockhatchee River and a corridor through which the Florida Trail passes; the **Geneva Wilderness**, 3501 N CR 426, Geneva, where you can take a short hike through scrub and flatwoods around ponds dotted with lilies; the **Lake Jesup Wilderness**, 5951 S Sanford Ave, Sanford, 490 acres with wetlands along vast Lake Jesup, part of the St. Johns River chain of lakes; **Lake Proctor Wilderness**, 920 E FL 46, Geneva, with its beautiful ponds amid the sand pine scrub; and **Spring Hammock Preserve**, FL 419, Winter Springs, one of my favorite places in the region for its ancient cypress stands along the edge of Lake Jesup. For maps and directions to all of these natural areas, visit the county's web site. Free.

The **St. Johns Water Management District** (407-893-3127; sjr.state.fl.us) also does its part to preserve wild lands along the St. Johns River floodplain, with hiking and equestrian trails, seasonal hunting, fishing, and paddling permitted in their conservation areas in the region. **Hal Scott Preserve**, Dallas Rd off FL 520, offers hiking and trail riding through vast palmetto prairies along the Lower Econlockhatchee River; **Lake Jesup Conservation Area** in Oviedo and Lake Mary encompasses several wetland areas along Lake Jesup, with some picturesque but soggy hiking trails; **Lake Monroe Conservation Area** off FL 46, Sanford, includes hiking and camping in the Kratzert Tract, and canoe-in campsites on Brickyard Slough; **Seminole Ranch Conservation Area** in Christmas, adjoining Orlando Wetlands Park, includes a portion of the Florida Trail running through jungle-like hydric hammocks dense with cabbage palms; and the **Wekiva River Buffer Conservation Area** in Longwood has the Sabal Point Trail, a hiking trail along a cypress-logging tramway that takes you into the floodplain forest without getting your feet wet.

The **Little-Big Econ State Forest** (407-971-3500; www.fl-dof.com/state_forests/LB_Econ.htm), CR 426, Oviedo, protects the floodplain of the Econlockhatchee River, with its palm hammocks and sandy beaches; the Florida Trail and a series of bike trails run through the forest. Fee.

Off FL 46, the truly wild **Lower Wekiva River Preserve State Park** (407-884-2008; part of Wekiva Basin Geo Park) has only one short nature trail intruding into the landscape, which protects the confluence of Blackwater Creek and the Wekiva River. Several Timucuan shell mounds sit along the river's edge. Free.

South of FL 50 at Christmas, the 28,000-acre **Tosohatchee State Reserve** (407-568-5893), 3365 Taylor Creek Rd, stretches along 19 miles of the St. Johns River floodplain, providing vast marshes for wintering birds and hammocks of ancient oaks enjoyed by backpackers on the reserve's two loop trails and the Florida Trail; deer and turkey hunters share the woods. Fee.

Lodging

BED & BREAKFASTS

Oviedo 32765

Step back into genteel old Oviedo at **Kings Manor** (407-365-4200; www.kingsmanorbb.com), 322 King St, a two-story Victorian with a classic Florida dogtrot design, built in 1884 by George Browne, Florida's Speaker of the House. Hosts Roberta and Paul McQueen restored this beauty to its full glory, with five original fireplaces and their mantels accented by period furnishings; the light-button system is also original to the house. Three massive guest rooms ($99) feature romantic appointments like sleigh beds and soft white robes as well as practical amenities like Internet access. Sit on the front veranda of Master John's Green Room and soak in the grandeur of the live oak canopy, or enjoy the common area, including the large screened back porch. Full breakfast served.

Maitland 32789

Thurston House (407-539-1911 or 1-800-843-2721; www.thurstonhouse.com), 851 Lake Ave. Innkeeper Carole Ballard has one of the best-kept secrets in metro Orlando: a beautiful 1885 Victorian overlooking Lake Eulalia, convenient to everything and yet privately tucked away, surrounded by several acres of gardens and forests. Mingle with other guests on the porch, relax in the spacious parlor, or simply enjoy one of four spacious rooms ($140–160) with reading area, desk with phone and dataport, and comfortable bed. Expanded continental breakfast weekdays and full breakfast on weekends; popular with business travelers.

Sanford 32771

Higgins House (407-324-9238; www.higginshouse.com), 420 S Oak Ave. Steeped in history, this 1894 Victorian home of the first railroad superintendent in Sanford has a 1902 Kimball piano dominating the grand parlor; guests partake of a full three-course breakfast (dietary restrictions honored) overlooking the "Secret Courtyard" backyard. A two-bed masculine-themed room and The Pub, a TV lounge with stocked fridge, make this B&B popular with the guys, but there's also a romantic bridal suite with a country feel. Three rooms, $105–125.

HOTELS AND MOTELS There is no lack of lodging in the northern Orlando metro area. At every exit off I-4, you'll find a variety of major chain hotels with a wide range of amenities, such as **Springhill Suites by Marriott** (407-995-1000) in Sanford 32771, **Homewood Suites Orlando North** (407-875-8777) in Maitland 32751, and the **La Quinta Inn & Suites** (407-805-9901) in Lake Mary 32746. The newest options are clustered around the business parks at Lake Mary and UCF.

Maitland 32751

♿ **Lake of the Woods Resort** (407-834-7631 or 1-800-544-1266; www.lakeofthewoodsresort.net), 8875 S US 17-92. Newly renovated by local owners, this 38-unit motel complex with banquet center offers pleasant, spacious rooms, kitchenettes, and suites ($60–95) overlooking the placid waters of Lake of the Woods, with a beautiful lakeside pool.

Sanford

The Best Western Marina Hotel (407-323-1910), 530 N Palmetto Ave,

Sanford 32771, has a commanding waterfront on Lake Monroe, adjacent to the marina; you could cast a line right out your front door. The rooms ($59) have the usual amenities but show a little wear thanks to their proximity to the water. The swimming pool overlooks the massive lake, and there's always a breeze.

At the 1950s **Slumberland Motel** (407-322-4591), 2611 S Orlando Dr, Sanford 32773, Lee and Yong Li offer clean nonsmoking efficiencies ($38–40) with older furnishings and paneled walls; a sparkling pool sits outside the appealing exterior.

UCF

♿ **Comfort Suites** (407-737-7303; www.comfortsuites.com/hotel/fl061), 12101 Challenger Pkwy, Orlando 32826. These roomy suites ($69–119) add a sofa and dedicated work space for road warriors to the traditional motel room layout. In-room amenities include fridge, microwave, and free high-speed Internet access; convenient to UCF and FL 50, with a small pool, business center, and large common breakfast area.

♿ **Hilton Garden Inn** (407-992-5000; www.orlandoeastucf.gardeninn.com), 1959 N Alafaya Trail, Orlando 32826. Less than 3 years old, this pleasant chain hotel adjacent to UCF hums on the weekdays but is quiet on the weekends. In addition to the usual in-room amenities you'd expect at a Hilton, like refrigerator, microwave, coffeemaker, and high-speed Internet access in each room, enjoy the pool and hot tub outside; kids stay free with adult guests.

Winter Park 32789

Enjoy 1920s elegance in an intimate setting at the **Park Plaza Hotel** (407-647-1072 or 1-800-228-7220; www.parkplazahotel.com), 307 Park Ave S, where an old-fashioned elevator takes you up to a series of high-ceilinged rooms and suites ($100–225) with original pine floors and classy touches like sleigh beds and writing desks; the tiled bathrooms are original. In the popular Balcony Suites, guests can enjoy their coffee in an outdoor balcony garden overlooking Park Ave.

WORKING RANCH

Chulota 32766

Big Oaks Ranch (407-629-1847; www.bigoaksranch.com), 615 Grand Chenier Cove. Relax in the shade of an oak hammock in a gorgeous two-story log cabin along the banks of Mills Creek on this 720-acre working beef cattle ranch, where longhorns and Herefords roam the fields in the distance. Featuring five uniquely decorated rooms, including a children's room, the spacious cabin is popular for on-site wedding packages but can also be rented for $100 per couple plus $25 per child, minimum of 2 nights, no credit cards; reservations required.

CAMPGROUNDS

Apopka 32712

Kelly Park (see *Parks*) has a well-shaded 24-site campground with electric hookups ($15 per site plus $3 electric) within walking distance of Rock Springs, with resident rangers on site.

Christmas 32709

Christmas Airstream RV Resort (407-568-5207), 25525 E Colonial Dr. With deeply shaded sites tucked under a canopy of tall cabbage palms and pines, and a sparkling swimming pool out front, this is one *very* appealing campground, with three meeting halls with kitchen facilities. Electric and water hookups, on-site dump station; rates start at $15. No tents.

Winter Garden 34787

The appealing **Stage Stop Campground** (407-656-8000), 700 W FL 50, offers easy access to the theme parks, and features full-hookup spaces ($25) with concrete patios and picnic tables, a game room with pool tables, and an Olympic-sized swimming pool; tent campers welcome.

✷ Where to Eat

DINING OUT

Altamonte Springs

♿ **Maison & Jardin** (407-862-4410), 430 Wymore Rd. It's not a dinner, it's an experience. As you sip wine and look out across the French country garden, soft classical music fills the air. Set in an elegant country manor house with 8 acres of beautifully landscaped grounds, it's *the* special-occasion restaurant in the region, a place to impress a date or to take Mom on Mother's Day. When I lived nearby, we called it the "Mason Jar" and my friends joked about stuffy waiters, but when I arrived for dinner, I found all of the wait staff pleasant and knowledgeable, eager to make recommendations. And you'll want them, too—with 1,600 bottles of wine in their cellar, Maison & Jardin boasts the most extensive wine list (38 pages) in Florida, with vintages in every price range. Ah, and then there's the food, artfully presented by executive chef Hans Spirig. The foie gras came decorated with an orchid, and a palate-cleansing mango sorbet was offered between each course—the First Course, $8–55 (yes, for caviar crêpes), covers appetizers; the Second Course, $6–8, salads; and the Main Course, $22–33, entrées. My hot, flaming spinach salad was prepared in a tableside display, and a feather of rosemary capped the beef Wellington, which came with chunky baby vegetables. Their broad range of desserts ($7–11) includes a mousse of the day, bananas Foster prepared tableside, and a mocha java pie perfect for a chocolate lover like me. Open Tue–Sat 6–10; reservations recommended.

Casselberry

♿ **Enzo's Italian Restaurant on the Lake** (407-834-9872), 1130 S US 17-92, in a class by itself, is the crème de la crème of Italian restaurants in this region, where dresses and suits are de rigueur and the prices match the atmosphere; expect to drop $15–26 on refined Italian entrées like veal scaloppine sautéed with capers, artichokes, tomatoes, and white wine.

Cypriana Greek Restaurant (407-834-8088; www.silveroid.com/cypriana.htm), 505 Semoran Blvd, is a little slice of Greece, with murals wrapping the dining area in scenes of the islands, blue-and-white-checkered wicker chairs, and Greek newspapers at the counter. Enjoy a fine dining menu that extends beyond ordinary Greek specialties to entrées ($8–14) like shrimp Mykonos, lamb chops, and chicken Aegean, or stop in at lunch ($5–7) for a shish kebab or marinated Greek sausage.

Longwood

Ali Baba (407-331-8680), 1155 W FL 434. It's like stepping into a temple complex in Basra, the vast space decorated with tiles and tapestries. Ali Baba is Orlando's only Persian restaurant, and your best bet here is to hit the daily buffets. In addition to offering a great sampler of Middle Eastern cuisine (entrées $8–15), the buffet is a fabulous deal. On weekends expect entertainment from belly dancers. A small shop at the cashier's station offers Middle Eastern imports, including quite an array of exotic foods.

Mona Lisa Ristorante (407-265-8246; www.monalisaristorante.com), 135 W Jesup Ave. The aromas of Italy permeate this comfortable bistro, which serves up Italian country entrées like *maccheroni alla chitarra*, *penne amatriciana*, and *veal saltimbocca alla romana* ($11–23). Lunch ($6–9) and dinner, reservations recommended.

Maitland

Antonio's La Fiamma Trattoria (407-645-5523), 611 S Orlando Ave. Enjoy fine dining above Antonio's Café (see *Eating Out*), with refined Italian entrées like *penne al forno*, *bistecca tagliata*, and *pollo carciofi*, $7–16.

Bucco di Beppo (407-MACRONE), 1351 S Orlando Ave. Adopt your very own Italian family at this Italian comfort-food haven, where the food comes in platters serving a crowd (singles beware!)—pasta $10–24, entrées $18–30, and dinner for two, $25. For greatest fun, reserve the Kitchen Table, a booth right in the middle of the action, where you can watch the chefs at work.

Sam Snead's Tavern (407-622-8800), 1801 Maitland Blvd. It's a natural for sports fans visiting the RDV Sportsplex, with decor honoring golfer Sam Snead. And the food is superb: I enjoyed the best-ever steak sandwich of my life at this particular location; steaks at other locations in this growing chain have never disappointed me. They serve lunch and dinner in a cozy tavern atmosphere, with sandwiches and burgers starting around $7, steak and seafood entrées $15 and up.

UCF

Michael's Italian Restaurant (407-273-3631), 12309 E Colonial Dr. There aren't a lot of restaurants that have been on this strip for 20-plus years, but Michael's keeps the customers coming back with good Italian home cooking for a fair price. Pleasant surroundings and excellent service (where staff are quite willing to explain the entrées to you) accent classy Italian dishes like *pollo vitello* and *zuppa di pesce*, prepared to order ($13–18); choose your *carne*, *pollo*, or *pesce* alla *cacciatore*, *Parmigiana*, or *Milanese*. My grilled vegetable ravioli was perfect, with a hint of herbs and plenty of garlic dressing up the fresh marinara sauce.

Winter Park

Del Frisco's Steakhouse (407-645-4443; www.delfriscosorlando.com), 729 Lee Rd. It's a classy old-fashioned steak house with a refined 1940s feel, where you'd expect Frank Sinatra to step out of the shadows. Serving some of the region's best USDA prime steaks and seafood for dinner, including filet mignon, porterhouse, swordfish, and salmon (entrées, $19–33). Appropriate dress and reservations suggested—it's a popular date-night spot with live music on weekends.

Dexter's On the Square (407-629-1150; www.dexwine.com), 558 W

New England Ave. Great wine, great art: That's the theme at Dexter's, a classy corner bistro where I've enjoyed many a party with friends. I'm partial to the jambalaya, but their chicken tortilla pie is tasty, too. Lunch and dinner entrées start around $10.

EATING OUT

Altamonte Springs

♿ **Bahama Breeze** (407-831-2929), 499 Altamonte Dr. It looks a little incongruous, this breezy beachfront-style restaurant parked in the front lot of the Altamonte Mall. And normally I wouldn't list a chain restaurant—this is part of the Darden's family (Red Lobster, Olive Garden, and the like). But it started here at the mall, and this place is fun, with "Floribbean" offerings like paella, coconut curry chicken, and piña colada bread pudding; it'll tickle your taste buds like it did mine. Serving dinner, with entrées $10 and up.

♿ The fun and festive **Don Pepe's Cafe** (407-682-6834), 937 W Semoran Blvd, serves heaping plates of authentic Cuban food (entrées $7 and up), spicy and heavy (think *ropa vieja*, fried plantains, and roast pork in *mojito* sauce), and some of the most creative-looking mixed drinks I've ever seen.

A standout amid the sea of chain restaurants around it, 🏵 **Kohinoor** (407-788-6004), 249 W Semoran Blvd, hides in a strip mall behind TGI Fridays. Having visited India, I appreciate this restaurant's authenticity, particularly for the kormas and chicken biryani, with almonds and raisins mixed into the aromatic rice, and tandoori specialties like chicken tikka masala. Open for lunch and dinner, with buffet specials; entrées start around $11.

♿ **Too Jays** (407-830-1770), 515 E Altamonte Dr. Got a craving for pickled tomatoes? A real Reuben? This is as close as Central Florida gets to a New York deli, and this successful small chain has since spread across neighborhoods of displaced New Yorkers all over southeast Florida. Have some potato pancakes, authentic blintzes, or herring in cream sauce; they serve the best Reubens around (sandwiches $6–8, dinner entrées $8–12). And don't forget dessert—the baked goods at the checkout will have you salivating. My fave: the Mounds Cake, a heady concoction of chocolate and coconut with a rich chocolate icing.

It doesn't look like much more than a little roadside shack along Semoran Blvd, but looks can be deceiving. **Uncle Jones Bar-B-Que** (407-260-2425), 1370 E Altamonte Dr, offers up some of the best ribs in the region.

Apopka

🏵 **Roma Ristorante** (407-886-2360), 730 Orange Blossom Trail. Since 1964, Maria and her family have created Italian specialties for the pleasure of patrons, and patrons and owners pass into a second generation with the founder's children running the business. Featuring homemade egg noodle pastas, including fettuccine, lasagna, and spaghetti, as well as Italian classics like veal marsala and shrimp scampi; dinners $9–15.

Casselberry

Dinner in a cozy Aspen lodge—that's the theme at the **Colorado Fondue Company** (407-767-8232; www.coloradofondue.com), corner of Red Bug Rd and Semoran Blvd, where you cook your own meal in a fondue pot or atop a sizzling hot rock while relaxing in a slice of the Rocky Mountains. Appetizers (primarily fondues) $8–9, entrées $11–19, fixed price "Colorado Fondue for Two," $38. Melted chocolate desserts, too!

Customers keep coming back to **Rolando's** (407-767-9677), 870 E Semoran Blvd, where Cuban art in a bistro atmosphere accents hearty Cuban food like *papas rellena* (stuffed potatoes), *ropa vieja* (shredded beef), and *arroz con pollo* (chicken and rice). Lunch and dinner served daily, $4 and up.

Lockhart

Where city meets suburbs near the Lockhart Post Office, **Thai Cuisine** (407-292-9474), 5325 Edgewater Dr, surprised me when they opened a few years ago—hidden behind an Oriental store, you could hardly tell they were there. But I stopped in when I saw the sign, and discovered authentic Thai curries and entrées ($7–9) that are fabulous and inexpensive. If you order it hot, it will be *hot*!

Longwood

Kobe (407-389-1888), 1231 Douglas Ave. There's something about the spectacle of having a Japanese chef prepare dinner in front of you that I just adore—it's creative *and* it's fun. I've always enjoyed my visits to Kobe, where as much as I love their sushi (rolls $4–8) I always have to have something prepared on the table, usually Tori Chicken Teriyaki or Sirloin & Shrimp. Entrées ($13–26) and tempura ($11–19) come with salad and rice.

Korea House (407-767-5918), 977 FL 434 (at Rangeline Rd), was Central Florida's first authentic Korean restaurant, and my friends who've traveled in Korea vouch for the food, especially the kimchi; lunch and dinner entrées $7–27.

Lake Mary

I love the **Easy Street Café** (407-320-8100), 3590 US 17-92, for its great sandwiches and salads ($5–8) served up in a relaxed country atmosphere in open, airy rooms; their soups are made from scratch, and their meats are fresh. I'm partial to the Sunshine Salad, with blue cheese, fresh orange slices, walnuts, cucumber, sunflower seeds, tomatoes, and grapes on a bed of green leaf and iceberg lettuce. In the evening enjoy pasta, steaks, barbecue ribs, and chicken, $9–16.

Maitland

Antonio's Café (407-645-1039; www.antoniosonline.com), 611 S Orlando Ave. On the lower floor of this restaurant complex, enjoy a bustling casual atmosphere amid an Italian store and deli, where the aroma of baking from the wood-burning oven will have you salivating for classic Italian calzones and pizza topped with portobello mushrooms and fresh tomato slices; lunch and dinner $6–17.

A Maitland landmark, **Kappy's** (407-647-9099), US 17-92, is an old-fashioned drive-in with all-beef hot dogs, Philadelphia hoagies, New York heroes, and "super rich & thick" jumbo shakes; grab lunch or dinner (except Sun) for $2–5.

Ocoee

Positano (407-291-0602), 8995 W Colonial Dr. It's an Italian restaurant with a twist: Order a sub or pizza at the counter, or sit down in one of the spacious booths for a more upscale meal. Most folks come here for their excellent daily lunch buffet ($9), which gives you a sampling of entrées like veal scaloppine, ravioli, and several types of salad; entrées $8–28.

Oviedo

Bill's Elbow South (407-365-2435), 1280 Oviedo Marketplace Blvd. Imagine this concoction: a biscuit topped with cinnamon and sugar, a dollop of vanilla ice cream, more cinnamon and sugar, and cornflakes. It's called the King of Oviedo, and according to the gal who met me at the door of this popular Oviedo landmark, she and her friends would drive miles just to split one of these desserts. Bill's recently moved into spacious accommodations at the Oviedo Marketplace Mall, but they still have the same fabulous food (lunches $4–5, dinners $8–24), and paintings by local artists decorate the walls—including the famous free-range Oviedo roosters that hang out by Popeye's Fried Chicken, go figure!

Black Hammock Fish Camp (407-365-2201; www.theblackhammock.com), 2536 Black Hammock Fish Camp Rd. Only Glenn Wilson could stroll through the Sanford Airport security checkpoint with an alligator on a leash and not raise any eyebrows. A fixture in Oviedo, Glenn is the heart and soul behind this funkiest of fish camps, where you can watch baby 'gators crawl around in an aquarium and get your picture taken with one while chowing down on the best catfish and farm-raised alligator in Central Florida (entrées $6–13). This is the place I take *my* friends for a taste of authentic Orlando. Before dinner, you can grab an airboat ride on Lake Jesup; afterward, hang out at the waterfront bar and listen to the house band jam.

Toucan Willie's (407-366-6225; www.toucanwillies.com), 829 Eyrie Dr. Taking on the popular "Floribbean" theme seen commonly in South Florida, Toucan Willie's does a nice job with atmosphere, from the faux Key West front porch dining room with rattan furnishings to the Caribbean and Jimmy Buffett music drifting through the air. While appetizers ($5–9) such as fried mushrooms or coconut shrimp may tease you, leave room for the seafood gumbo ($4), a spicy, thick, and creamy rendition with an almost gravy-like texture. Served with a side of mustard dipping sauce, the fried oysters ($11) have a subtle breading and are honest-to-God fresh. Nice and flaky, the crabcakes ($15) boast much more crab than breading. The top value on the menu is Willie's Deal Meals, satisfying smaller portions at $11 with veggies, side, and salad included. The dining room stays open until 10 most evenings, 11 Fri and Sat.

The Town House Restaurant (407-365-5151), corner of Central and Broadway. Sip your morning coffee and watch the town of Oviedo come alive through the picture windows in this local institution, the pride of an Athenian family with attention to detail. Enjoy a great breakfast value with a stack of fluffy pancakes with bacon (one of two daily specials at $3), or give the corned beef hash ($4) a whirl. Lunches include Greek favorites like gyros and Greek salad as well as more traditional fare from BLTs to burgers.

Sanford, downtown

The Colonial Room (407-323-2999), 115 E 1st St, has been the town's favorite breakfast ($3–6) spot for more than 25 years, serving up home-style southern cooking like the big Country Breakfast (where stewed apples or grits or potatoes come with your eggs, toast, and meat). Serving lunch and dinner ($3–9), too; no credit cards accepted.

Divine Deli (407-268-4884), 106 S Park Ave, offers sandwiches, wraps, and salads, $3–6; with a quiche of the day and breakfast items, $1–3.

Hollerbach's Willow Tree Café (407-321-2204), 205 E 1st St, specializes in authentic German cuisine like schnitzels and strudels, cheesecake, and freshly baked German breads, but they also have an incredible array of salads and deli sandwiches ($4–10); serving lunch Mon–Sat, dinner Wed–Sat.

Rose Cottage Tea Room (407-323-9448; www.rosecottageinn.com), 1301 Park Ave. It's so impeccably British you can pick up the *Union Jack* at the door. A traditional Victorian tearoom serving an assortment of luncheon and dinner specials ($10–12), and of course, Victorian tea ($10) with finger sandwiches, scones, European pastries, and fresh fruit. Open until 3.

Sanford—riverside

Gator's Riverside Grill (407-688-9700), 4522 Peninsula Pt. Overlooking the St. Johns River, this cozy seafood shack offers snook (a rare find on a menu) as well as 'gator bites, tuna bites, grouper sandwiches, and other seafood goodies in baskets and sandwiches; $4–12, serving lunch and dinner.

Otter's Riverside (407-323-3991; www.otters-riverside.com), 4380 Carraway Place at Hidden Harbor Marina. Tasty seafood—smoked fish dip, baskets of catfish and 'gator bites, oyster po'boy—complements steak and pasta entrées ($10–20) in a dining room with a waterfront view; this is also the first restaurant I've seen that sports its own pool. Bring your bathing suit, and call for directions first—this one's tough to find, but worth it. Live entertainment on Sat and Sun afternoons!

Sanford, US 17-92

Colorado's Prime Steaks (407-324-1741), 3863 Orlando Ave. Step into a virtual Aspen eatery for a taste of Colorado beef: My girlfriends brought me here for the "Dark Horse Saloon" steak sandwich ($8), which was certainly tender, but I think the fire-grilled burgers ($6–8) are a better lunch choice.

UCF

Greeted by a 'gator and a pink pig, you know you'll have fun at **Bubbalou's Bodacious BBQ** (407-423-1212; www.bubbalous.com), one of the area's best for barbecue ribs and pork. I used to live around the corner from their original Winter Park location; this spacious restaurant seems downright upscale by comparison. But the great food hasn't changed one bit. Bodacious platters, combos, and dinners, $9–13; try a fried pickle on the side.

Maharajah (407-384-8850), 12239 University Blvd. Some of the tastiest vegetarian Indian cuisine I've encountered in this region comes from this unassuming little restaurant in a strip mall across from UCF. The lunch buffet ($8, 11–2) is great for busy folks, but the à la carte items ($2–5) are wonderful, too—I savored *batata vada* and *samosa chaat* with my *dosa iddy*. Serving lunch and dinner Mon–Sat, dinner Sun.

Winter Garden

Downtown Brown's (407-877-2722),

126 W Plant St. A real soda fountain with retro seats and the original floor, where you can enjoy "eats & sweets" like fresh fruit salads, Belgian waffles, stuffed baked potatoes, and, of course, sundaes. Breakfast $2–5; daily blue plate lunch special $6. It's a popular hangout for bikers on the West Orange Trail.

J. R.'s Daily Jolt (407-877-0266), 28 W Plant St. Comfy sofas invite you to settle in and thumb a well-worn novel while sucking back that cup o'joe; in addition to a fine selection of coffees, J. R.'s sells eclectic gift items and makes a mean ice cream shake.

Winter Park

Bakely's Restaurant and Bakery (407-645-5767), 345 W Fairbanks Ave, has weekday breakfast specials starting at $3, but what draws the crowds is their fresh baked goods and comfort foods, including hand-dipped shakes. Sparkling blue and yellow tile sets a French country atmosphere, but the food is Mom and apple pie. Serving breakfast ($2–7), lunch and dinner ($4–14), with entrées like meat loaf, country-fried steak, and sautéed baby clams.

At **The Briarpatch Restaurant** (407-628-8651), 252 Park Ave N, order shakes at the old-fashioned marble-topped ice cream counter, or settle back in the casual country setting for a Park Avenue Salad with mandarin oranges, praline pecans, Gorgonzola, and grilled chicken on a bed of romaine. Breakfast omelets include sage sausage frittata and pear and Gorgonzola, $7–10; lunch salads and sandwiches $4–11; dinner entrées like pesto-crusted salmon $10–13.

Chapters (407-644-2880), 358 Park Ave N. It's a restaurant, it's a bookstore, *and* it's a performance space—it's one of my favorite places in Orlando, recently moved from College Park to this roomier locale, a fine bistro within an extensive library of new and used books. The crabcakes in my Crab Cake Salad tasted like they were 99 percent fresh crab, and the Taco Salad was just plain huge! Salads, quiches, and pastas run $7–10, while entrées are $14–19. One-man shows like *An Evening with Thomas Jefferson* play on the open second-floor stage, where you can catch jazz and blues bands Thu–Sat evenings. Dinner reservations suggested.

I know of no place in Orlando better than **Fiddler's Green Irish Pub & Eatery** (407-645-2050), 544 Fairbanks Ave, to nab a steaming bowl of potato leek soup and a shepherd's pie; entrées $8–17. Most evenings, you'll catch an entertainer or two strumming in the front room.

Winter Park—Semoran Blvd

Greek Flame Taverna (407-678-2388), 1560 N Semoran Blvd, is my old local favorite for just plain good Greek food—*moussaka*, *dolmades*, and gyros; lunch and dinner $5–7. Leave room for one of the great pastries in the front case.

Lacomka Bakery & Deli (407-677-1101), 2050 N Semoran Blvd, is a unique Russian grocery with authentic lunch offerings ($1–7) like *pirozhok*, *blinchiki*, *pelmeni*, and *borsh*; the napoleon with traditional Russian cream is an incredible delight.

Old Germany Restaurant (407-657-6800), 2054 N Semoran Blvd, offers old-fashioned German dinners

($6–20) like *leberkase*—finely ground oven-baked German meat loaf—goulash, rouladen, sauerbraten, and 17 types of schnitzel, plus six types of brats. For a real delight, try their hot onion cake ($4) as a starter.

Winter Park—US 17-92

At **Chamberlin's Market & Café** (407-647-6661), expect top-quality vegetarian and organic offerings from this hometown health food grocer; the café (open for lunch and dinner during store hours) is fun to dine in, and serves up great hummus, veggie pitas, and a tasty vegetarian chili, $5 and up.

Fuji Sushi (407-645-1299), 1449 Lee Rd. Booths gracefully decorated with Japanese paintings accent this classic sushi bar that my friends agree is the best in Orlando. Choose from vegetarian rolls, spicy rolls, house special rolls, and Fuji's exclusive rolls, $4–11. Not into sushi? Happy Cat still smiles down on you. Have a hot teriyaki entrée ($9–17), kettle dish, or curry. Lunch served Mon–Fri, dinner daily.

Thai Place (407-644-8449), 501 N Orlando Ave. When I lived nearby, I stumbled across this restaurant en route to the movies and have been coming ever back since. The owners treat you like family, and the intimate setting makes it a perfect place to meet a friend for a meal. I love the house peanut dressing, and recommend the *pad med mamuang*, made with cashew nuts. House specials include Siamese duck, grouper, chicken, and shrimp in several choices of preparations; entrées $10–14, lunch $6.

Winter Springs

Villa Capri (407-388-7766), 5661 Red Bug Lake Rd. My friends highly recommend this comfortable Italian bistro where "family size" portions are the norm; the attentive wait staff will recommend their favorites, like the tomato and mozzarella Caprese Salad. Expect to take some of your massive lunch or dinner ($10–19) entrée home.

✷ Entertainment

Maitland

With indie films every evening at 7:30 and 9:30, the **Enzian Theatre** (407-629-0054; www.enzian.org), 1300 S Orlando Ave, is Orlando's hot spot for film buffs. The best part? Dinner *and* a movie in one seating.

Sanford

The **Helen Stairs Theatre** (407-321-8111), 203 S Magnolia Ave, is a revitalized theater from 1922, the Milane, where Rachmaninoff performed in 1928 and Tom Mix delighted kids in 1933. Restored in 2000, it's again showcasing live acts as diverse as Lee Greenwood, *The Marriage of Figaro*, and *The Nutcracker*. **Children's Theatre Arts of Florida** (1-800-684-0091; www.ctftheatre.com), 120 S Park Ave, presents outreach shows at various city locations and main-stage shows like *Charlie and the Chocolate Factory* at the Helen Stairs Theatre; theater classes are offered during the summer for children of all ages.

Kick up your heels while line dancing at **The Barn** (407-324-2276), 1777 S French Ave, with country music at its foot-stomping finest; opens 7 PM Wed–Sun, $5 cover.

Orlando Theatre Project (407-328-2040; www.otp.cc), Seminole Community College, 100 Weldon Blvd. This small Actors' Equity group presents American classics like *Death of a*

Salesman and *Grapes of Wrath*, as well as original plays by local playwrights. Three plays presented Nov–May.

Winter Park

A walk though the bistros of Winter Park will yield plenty of weekend entertainment, primarily live jazz and blues at places like **Chapters**, **Dexter's**, and **Fiddler's Green** (see *Eating Out*).

At the **Annie Russell Theatre** (407-646-2145; www.rollins.edu/theatre), 1000 Holt Ave, enjoy dance and theater events as well as the **Bach Festival Society** (407-646-2182; www.bachfestivalflorida.org), which holds an annual concert series that spans the gamut from piano recitals and philharmonic orchestras to African drumming and dance.

✱ Selective Shopping

Altamonte Springs

Travel Country Outdoors (407-831-0777 or 1-800-643-3629; www.travelcountry.com), 1101 E Semoran Blvd. Being an outdoorsperson, this is one of my frequent stops in the Orlando area, the most extensive backpacking and paddlesports outfitter in the region.

Christmas

Country Craft Christmas (407-568-8084), 25250 E Colonial Dr. What would Christmas be without Christmas? This large new shop represents more than 20 area crafters with country craft items, a Victorian room, and, of course, a room brimming with Christmas ornaments and home decor. Open daily.

Lockhart

3 Flea Market, US 441 at Overland Rd. Right at the county line, this small flea market is a gathering place for folks who are emptying their attics and garages, selling their wares off tables behind their trucks. You'll wade through a lot of stuff, but there's always the chance of an excellent bargain! Sat and Sun, rain or shine.

Longwood

The Apple Basket (407-332-1700), 218 W Church Ave. Primitive furniture, country chic, vintage china, and collectibles like Dept 56 in a home more than a century old.

Beth's Gifts and Accessories (407-834-1077), 1000 N CR 427. Nearly 20 years ago Beth Williams opened a pottery and African violet shop; her son carries on the family tradition of fine customer service with furniture at excellent prices, fine art—including many Florida-themed pieces—and home decor items.

Culinary Cottage (407-834-7220), 141 Church Ave. Gourmet food, gift items, and reasonably priced art glass fills the 1870 Inside-Outside House (see *Historic Sites*), where each room offers up new gift ideas.

Judy's Dolls (407-332-7928), 280 W Warren Ave. Featuring a popular "newborn nursery" (one of only two in Florida) and "create a doll," plus a doll repair "hospital," this cute little shop is the perfect place to pick out the perfect doll.

Legible Leftovers Books & Bottles (407-339-4043; www.legibleleftovers.com), 706 US 17-92, is a browser's delight, with room after room filled with well-organized used books. Plenty of paperbacks (trades welcome) and nice depth in areas like philosophy, travel, and cooking. Open daily at 9:30. The **Cat's Meow** gift shop takes up a tiny corner of the store with crafts and home decor items; don't let the cats out!

Sweet William Antiques (407-831-1657), 216 W Warren Ave. Inside a historic home, you'll find beautiful stained-glass windows along with Victorian antiques, books, dolls, and jigsaw puzzles. Outside, a landscaped garden of young plants and pottery (all for sale) fill the space between this shop and the adjoining **Enchanted Cottage**.

Maitland

Cram-packed with antiques and collectibles, **Bestnwurst Antiques** (407-647-0533), 145 S Orlando Ave, has delighted customers for nearly 20 years with great finds in glassware, furnishings, silver flatware, and costume jewelry.

At **Cranberry Corners Antiques** (407-644-0363), 203 E Horatio Ave, country primitives fill the rooms, mingling antiques like restored quilts from the 1880s with home decor such as quilted pillows, homemade soaps by Granny Greer, jam and chutney, and scented candles.

With more than 85 dealers, **Halley's Antique Mall** (407-539-1066), 475 S Orlando Ave, has an excellent diversity in stock—from fine china and paintings to vintage ads and books—and reasonable prices. Open daily.

Voted "Best in Florida," the **Orange Tree Antiques Mall** (407-622-0600), 150 Lake Ave, has been around for more than a decade, filled with rooms of collectibles, antiques, and fine art, with a heavy emphasis on glassware and art glass. In the Highwaymen Room, I saw paintings by Sam Newton I wished I owned, and found a classic streetcar sign in another corner. Take your time; you'll browse for hours!

Oakland

J&M Antiques and Collectibles (407-654-1663), 6 E Oakland Ave. Shopping for glass? Check out this well-displayed collection of Fenton, Carnival, Imperial, Depression, and more; I took home an original piece of Florida art. Glad my girlfriends turned me on to this one!

Ocoee

The Book Rack (407-253-0020), 421 N Clarke Rd, features stacks of gently used paperbacks at half retail, with trade-ins encouraged.

Oviedo

The Artistic Hand (407-366-7882), 353 N Central Ave. Dwarfed by an ancient live oak tree, this little purple house with white trim holds a fairyland of treasures created by artisans all over Florida. Established in 1992 by Barbara Walker-Seaman, the Artistic Hand overflows with the works of more than 200 artists in an appealing variety of media, from fine art paintings to collage, sculpture, traditional pottery, textiles, glass, and so much more. Browse the bright rooms and you're sure to come up with a suitable gift for the art lover in your family, since the prices range right on down to downright reasonable.

Sanford, downtown

Downtown Sanford is an antiques mecca, definitely worth a full day for browsing; there are plenty of dining options, too. Shops and bookstores line 1st Ave; these are just a few of the many.

Music from the 1940s permeates **Arts and Ends** (407-330-4994), 116–118 E 1st St, where glass is the focus (think jet black, amethyst, and art deco), as well as fine art and gift items; you'll find Highwaymen paintings here!

Heritage House (407-321-2680), 228 E 1st St, features dealer booths with glass and dishes—a huge selection of Mosser glass, sparking iridescent in reds and greens, as well as Imperial, L. G. Wright, Fenton, and Westmoreland.

Magnolia Square (407-322-7544), 201 E 1st St, is the oldest antiques shop in town, and it has a special draw—an ice cream parlor serving locally made homemade ice cream. The owners take several buying trips a year, filling the large, open rooms with a fresh stock of collectibles, jewelry, and dishes.

Maya Books & More (407-321-6504), 309 E 1st St, displays its Florida books and a good selection of used tomes in comfy digs; if you're looking for record albums, you'll find them here, too.

Miss Libby's Antique Emporium (407-324-4009), 102–104 E 1st St, has more than 5,000 square feet of dealer booths filled with lamps, photo cards, beaded purses—heck, even an ice cream parlor table-and-chair set.

Molly and Me (407-321-3166), 210 E 1st St, features top-notch primitives—think meat grinders, iron kettles, antique tools, and pulleys—and a lot of classic furnishings.

Bibliophiles gather at **Our House Books & Coffee** (407-324-0054), 308 E Commercial St, where you can sip java while thumbing through a cheap paperback or regional magazine; there's Internet access, too, for $3 an hour.

A nicely arranged library of books and albums makes it **Something Special** (407-323-5332), 105 E 1st St, where you'll also find glassware, jewelry, toys, and home decor.

The Victorian Rose (407-330-2232), 1307 S Park Ave, adjoins the Rose Cottage Tea Room (see *Eating Out*), selling imported European antiques—tea sets, saltcellars, and cutlery from England, France, and Germany—as well as vintage jewelry and Depression glass.

At **Yesteryears** (407-323-3457), 205 E 1st St, Victoriana is the theme, with a large selection of Vaseline glass, salt dips, cups and saucers, and vintage lace dresses.

Sanford, US 17-92

Flea World (407-330-1792, ext 224; www.fleaworld.com), US 17-92. This massive 1,700-booth complex claims to be the largest flea market in the world, although the one in Webster (see "Nature Coast") gives them a run for the money. Nonetheless, you'll find everything you're looking for and a lot of stuff you're not. Open Fri–Sun 9–6.

Winter Garden

More than a frame shop, **Miss Jane's Custom Framing** (407-877-1097), 28

DOWNTOWN SANFORD'S ANTIQUES DISTRICT

Sandra Friend

W Plant St, features the colorful, playful works of local artists in pottery, linens, art glass, and photography.

Trailside Antiques (407-656-6508), 12 W Plant St. Local handicrafts, Victorian furniture, classic advertising, and a whole lot more—this place is packed with goodies.

Webb's Antique Mall (407-877-5921; www.webbsantiquemalls.com), 13373 W Colonial Dr, hidden in a strip mall next to the Kmart, provides a dizzying array of dealer booths and row upon row of display cases showcasing gems like antique pottery, fine art, and jewelry. Disney collector note: This store's proximity to the source means tons of Disney-employee-only goodies showing up on the shelves.

Winter Park—downtown

Like its New York counterpart, Park Ave is where tony Orlando comes to shop. In addition to upscale chains, you'll find plenty of local gems along this elegant thoroughfare, including a nice selection of consignment art galleries. Don't forget to stroll down East Morse Ave, which is also crowded with shops.

In Grenada Court look for **Brandywine Books** (407-644-1711), 114 Park Ave S, for used, rare, and out-of-print titles.

✐ At **Fairy Tales** (407-539-0374), 102 Park Ave S, you'll find ideal gifts for the small fry in your life—toys with bold graphic designs; storybook characters like Pooh, Clifford the Big Red Dog, and Curious George; and a fine selection of children's books.

Replica Tiffany lamps and other fine pieces of American art glass will entice you into **Favrile** (407-647-3777), 208 B Park Ave S; continue to the back of the gallery to enjoy fine art paintings by Florida artists.

Ferris-Reeves Galleries (407-647-0273), 140 Morse Blvd. Established in 1949, this antiques gallery contains real historical gems like a brass coal-fired bed warmer; peek inside for primitives, fine art, glassware, and silver.

Kathmandu (407-647-7071), 120 Morse Blvd, deals in imports like ceremonial masks, Rajasthani tapestries, and jewelry as well as incense and New Age items.

Since the 1960s, the **Miller Gallery** (407-599-1960), 348 Park Ave S, has displayed exceptional fine arts from around the globe, with one-of-a-kind pieces of art for your home; one section always focuses on Florida artists.

Olive This, Relish That (407-644-1966), 346 Park Ave N, is a fun pair of gourmet food shops with goodies like imported olive oil from small producers in the Mediterranean, tapas, stuffed olives, and martini glasses.

The **Park Avenue Gallery** (407-644-1545), 136 Park Ave N, features Paul Crumline's images of Winter Park, plus art glass, crystal, candles, and home decor items.

In addition to the most extensive collection of handcrafted jewelry in the United States, **Timothy's Gallery** (407-629-0707; www.timothysgallery.com), 212 Park Ave N, has inspirational and playful art pieces like turned wood bowls, kaleidoscopes, and vibrant art glass from more than 350 nationally renowned artists.

Winter Park—US 17-92

Like its sister shop in Maitland, the **Orange Tree Antiques Mall** (407-839-2863), 853 S Orlando Ave, has an incredible array of vintage items to explore. Take your time!

Chocoholics will delight in **Schakolad Chocolate Factory** (407-677-4114), hidden in Winter Park Village at 480 N Orlando Ave, where third-generation chocolatier Edgar Schaked presents fine handmade chocolates and truffles beyond description.

FARMER'S MARKETS AND FRESH PRODUCE

Goldenrod
Visit the Goldenrod Station (see *Museums*) for the **Goldenrod Farmer's Market** (407-677-5980), every Sat 8–1, for fresh produce, baked goods, candles, honey, and plants from local farmers and vendors.

Maitland
Hollieanna Groves (407-644-8803 or 1-800-793-7848), 540 S Orlando Ave. While Maitland's famed orange groves have vanished under the developers' bulldozers, Hollieanna, an old family operation, still offers ready-to-ship citrus during the growing season.

Oviedo
Pappy's U-Pick Strawberries, Fruit and Produce (407-366-8512) is one of the last remaining farms in what used to be a busy celery-growing district. Follow the signs from FL 434 along De Leon Ave to Florida Ave.

Sanford
The **Farmer's Outlet** adjacent to the wholesale state farmer's market on US 17-92 carries whatever's fresh that day. A new retail component to the state farmer's market is presently under construction.

Winter Park
Every Sat morning 7–1, stop in Winter Park for the **Winter Park Farmer's Market** (407-599-3358), corner of Lyman and New York Ave, where you'll find exotic spices and freshly baked pies next to ferns and flowers, homemade jellies, and, of course, farm-fresh produce.

Zellwood
Farm Fresh Produce, Laughlin Rd and US 441, sells sweet Georgia peaches and produce from local farms (including the famed Zellwood corn, in-season) at a permanent roadside stand.

Long & Scott Farms (352-383-6900; www.longandscottfarms.com), CR 448A, is the last remaining grower of Zellwood corn; many farmers' fields have turned to housing developments throughout this area. Stop here in springtime for their fun Corn Maze and to pick up a bushel of the sweetest corn in Florida.

✳ Special Events

January: **Central Florida Scottish Festival and Highland Games** (407-I-AM-SCOT; www.flascot.com), third Sat, Central Winds Park, Winter Springs. After 27 years, those men in kilts are still tossing sabers and throwing hammers, dancing Highland dances and playing the pipes. Join in the fun as a participant or spectator!

Zora Neale Hurston Festival of the Arts and Humanities (407-647-3959 or 1-800-972-3310; www.zoranealehurstonfestival.com), 227 E Kennedy Blvd, Eatonville, last week. Celebrating the legacy of Eatonville's best-known resident, this renowned African American festival, now 15 years old, focuses on the arts and humanities, featuring a juried street festival of the arts, live music, film screenings, and more.

March: The **Florida Film Festival**, held mid-Mar and centering on the Enzian Theatre in Maitland (see *Entertainment*), features the finest in independent filmmaking from Florida studios, with at least 150 films screened in four regional venues, plus informative seminars from the filmmakers. Free.

Fort Christmas Militia Encampment (407-568-4149), late Mar and Nov. Soldiers in 1840 U.S. Army regalia demonstrate life during the Seminole Wars.

Thousands flock annually to the **Winter Park Sidewalk Art Festival** (407-647-5557), one of Florida's largest arts festivals, encompassing the downtown district. In addition to juried competitions, arts vendors, and food, enjoy live music all day and jazz headliners at night.

April: **Rajuncajun Crawfish Festival**, Oviedo, at Black Hammock Fish Camp (see *Eating Out*), third Sat. In its 15th year, this fun Cajun food festival raises money for the Central Florida Children's Home and presents live Cajun and zydeco performers like the Porchdogs. All-you-can-eat buffet and entertainment, $30 advance, $40 at the gate; kids 7–12 are $15, under 7 free.

In its 16th year, the **Maitland Festival of the Arts** (407-644-0741), third weekend, Maitland Civic Center, brings in renowned artists in all media.

A Taste of Oviedo (407-365-6500; www.oviedochamber.org), fourth Sat. After a decade of treating participants to the best food that Oviedo restaurants have to offer, this annual festival is going strong.

May: Love corn-on-the-cob? Then don't miss the **Zellwood Sweet Corn Festival** (407-886-0014; www.zellwoodsweetcornfest.org), 4253 W Ponkan Rd, an annual event that celebrates this rural community's best-known export. Marvel at the boiler Big Bertha—cooking 1,650 ears of corn every 9 minutes in 350 gallons of boiling water. Arts and crafts vendors, live music, and more.

November: **Fort Christmas Militia Encampment**. See *March*.

ORLANDO SOUTH

CELEBRATION, HOLOPAW, KENANSVILLE, KISSIMMEE, ST. CLOUD, AND YEEHAW JUNCTION

Osceola County was created in 1886 with sections of Brevard and Orange Counties and was named in honor of Seminole chief Osceola. Only 18 miles from downtown Orlando and less than an hour's drive to the Atlantic Ocean, the area has long been known as an important crossroads. Kissimmee, the county seat, was once Central Florida's largest shipping port. As headwaters to the Florida Everglades system, Lake Tohopekaliga still serves as the launch point for boats, which travel through a series of locks to Lake Okeechobee and onward to either the Atlantic or Gulf. Trains have been rolling through with supplies since the shipbuilding heyday with the Florida East Coast, Seaboard, and Amtrak Railroad systems still in operation.

Before the area became the gateway to Disney and other Central Florida attractions, the cattle industry dominated the land. Osceola County's rich cattle history still has not diminished. Except for the northwest quadrant, the area remains one of the largest cattle-producing counties in the state, which is why you'll see so many steak houses around town. Large acres of open land also provide an excellent habit for wildlife. The rich forests, vast prairies, and clear lakes are home for many endangered species, as well as some of the best fishing in the world. The Kissimmee Chain of Lakes is where you'll find world-class bass fishing and the largest concentration of nesting bald eagles in the continental United States.

GUIDANCE **Kissimmee–St. Cloud Convention & Visitors Bureau** (407-847-5000; www.floridakiss.com), 1925 E Hwy 192, Kissimmee 34742.

St. Cloud Chamber of Commerce (407-892-3671; www.stcloudchamber.cc), 1200 New York Ave, St. Cloud 34769.

GETTING THERE *By air*: **Greater Orlando International Airport** (407-825-2001; www.state.fl.us/goaa/).

By bus: **Greyhound Lines** (407-847-3911; www.greyhound.com), 103 E Dakin Ave, Kissimmee, has service near the historic district, just off US 192.

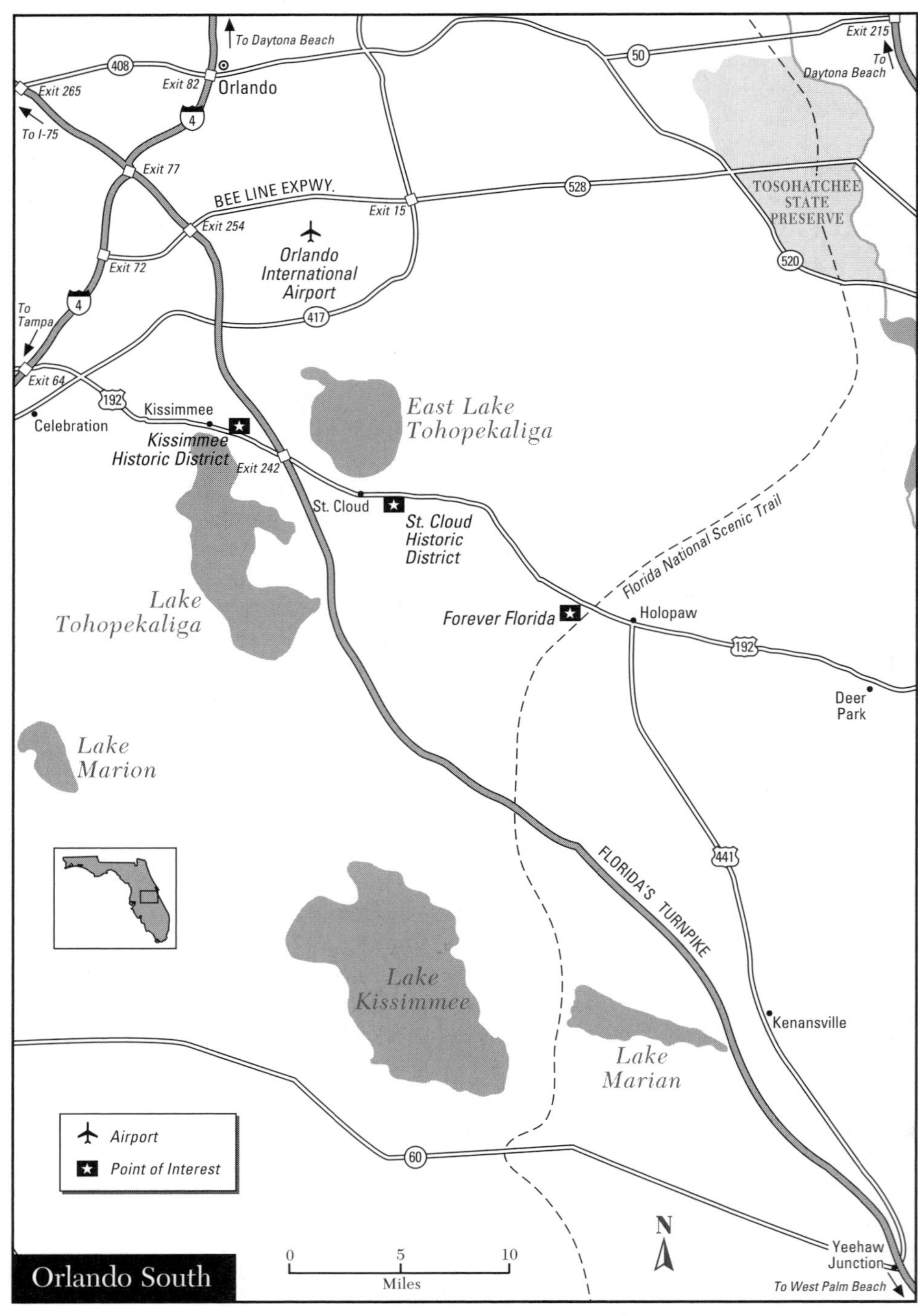
To Daytona Beach
408
Exit 82
Orlando
Exit 265
To I-75
4
Exit 77
BEE LINE EXPWY.
528
Exit 15
Exit 254
Orlando International Airport
Exit 72
To Tampa
4
417
Exit 64
192
Kissimmee
Celebration
Kissimmee Historic District
Exit 242
East Lake Tohopekaliga
St. Cloud
St. Cloud Historic District
Lake Tohopekaliga
Forever Florida
Holopaw
Florida National Scenic Trail
192
Deer Park
50
Exit 215
To Daytona Beach
TOSOHATCHEE STATE PRESERVE
520
Lake Marion
441
FLORIDA'S TURNPIKE
Lake Kissimmee
Kenansville
Lake Marian
Airport
Point of Interest
60
N
0
5
10
Miles
Yeehaw Junction
To West Palm Beach
Orlando South

By car: **Florida's Turnpike** and **I-4** both have exits to US 192 and the Osceola Pkwy. **US 192** runs though the heart of Osceola County, with plenty of shops, restaurants, and lodging—but traffic jams are common. For a faster east–west connection, use the Osceola Pkwy, **US 522** (toll), then get off on either **John Young Pkwy** or **Orange Blossom Trail**. Both run north to south, with the Orange Blossom Trail making a pass through the Kissimmee historic district before connecting to the parkway.

By train: **Amtrak** (1-800-872-7245; www.amtrak.com) provides regularly scheduled service to Kissimmee, near US 192 and the historic district, and metro Orlando, just north of the theme parks. **Coach USA** vans will take you from the station directly to your hotel.

GETTING AROUND **US 192** weaves through the heart of the tourist area, from Holopaw and St. Cloud, through Kissimmee, past Disney, and out to FL 27. Once you reach Kissimmee, the road is also known as the Irlo Bronson Hwy and is marked with brightly lit guide markers at about 1-mile intervals. These markers coincide with businesses listed in the *Kissimmee–St. Cloud Resort Area Map of US 192 Guidemarker Locations*; you'll find a long stretch of chain restaurants, economy motels, and fast-food and dine-in eateries here. On US 192, you know you've entered the "Disney Zone" near the main gate when the lampposts turn purple. Jump off I-4 (exit 26C) or Florida's Turnpike (exit 249) to the Osceola Pkwy, **US 522** (toll), for a direct route into Disney without the stop-and-go traffic. John Young Pkwy also connects to US 522 and will take you directly into the heart of Kissimmee.

MEDICAL EMERGENCIES **Florida Hospital Celebration Health** (407-764-4000), 400 Celebration Place, and **Florida Hospital Kissimmee** (407-846-4343), 2450 North Orange Blossom Trail, Kissimmee, are located near Disney and the US 192 attractions.

✷ To See

ART GALLERIES The **Osceola Center for Arts** (407-846-6257; www.ocfta.com), 2411 E Irlo Bronson Hwy (US 192), Kissimmee, provides great Broadway productions for about $15. The art gallery features local and national artists and is host to several special events. Open Mon–Fri 10–6, Sat 10–4.

HISTORIC SITES

Kissimmee

Bataan-Corregidor Memorial (407-846-6131), Lakeshore Blvd. This memorial in honor of the Americans and Filipinos who fought in World War II depicts scenes from the 1942 Bataan Death March.

The 1916 **Colonial Estate** at 240 Old Dixie Highway is worth a drive by just to see the colossal Ionic columns supporting a full entablature. But don't knock on the door—it's a private residence.

Makinson's Hardware Store, 308 Broadway Ave. Opened in 1884 by W. B.

Makinson Sr., this is the oldest operating hardware store in the state of Florida. A glorious mural depicting a bygone era is on the south side of the building.

The Monument of States, Monument Ave. Built in 1943, this impressive 50-foot tower, representing every state and 20 foreign countries, contains over 1,500 stones, meteors, and stalagmites, as well as petrified wood, teeth, and bones. Conceived by Dr. Bressler-Pettis, the monument soon received national attention; tourists, governors, and even a U.S. president furnished stones for its inclusion. The tower also contains fragments from the original Washington Monument's base. Dr. Bressler-Pettis's ashes are buried at the site.

Old Holy Redeemer Catholic Church, 120 N Sproule Ave. A single-story Gothic Revival facility, circa 1912, with a battlemented entrance porch and stained-glass windows. Originally Catholic, it now serves the Hispanic community as a First United Methodist church.

Osceola County Courthouse, 1 Courthouse Square. One of the state's oldest courthouses (circa 1886), and the only one in daily use, the Osceola County historic courthouse continues to retain its architectural integrity and is listed on the National Register of Historic Places. Dedicated May 6, 1890, it once had a cow pen in front of it, where lost cows were held until their owners claimed them.

St. Cloud

Mount Peace Cemetery (407-957-7243), 755 E 10th St. Final resting place for more than 300 Civil War Union veterans set amid the serenity and grandeur of centuries-old live oak trees.

Yeehaw Junction

Desert Inn (407-436-1054), 5570 South Kenansville Rd. It's worth taking a peek inside this late-1800s watering hole on the National Register of Historic Places (see *Eating Out*).

MUSEUMS

Kissimmee

♿ **Flying Tigers Warbird Restoration Museum** (407-933-1942; www.warbirdmuseum.com), 231 N Hoagland Blvd. These restored vintage planes are meant to fly and do! You'll see planes like a 1944 B-17 Flying Fortress or P-40 Warhawk in various stage of restoration, and fully functional planes like the 1928 OX-5 Bird and 1947 DeHavilland Vampire DH-100 reach for the skies on test flights. Fly one of these warbirds or a Bell 47 helicopter at **Warbird Adventures** (see *Aviation*). Throughout the working museum, a guide explains the restoration stage from start to finish along with the history of each aircraft on site. The museum PX displays memorabilia from World War II and Hollywood movies. Ground support is covered in the **Military Vehicle Museum**. If it doesn't fly, then it's in this collection of military transportation. Part of the Pastport Flight of Four. Open Mon–Sat 9–5:30, Sun 9–5.

Osceola County Historical Museum & Pioneer Center (407-396-8644), 750 N Bass Rd. Genealogy library of Osceola County residents, pioneer display, and nature preserves with trails and boardwalk. Open Thu–Sat 10–4, Sun 1–4.

St. Cloud

The Cannery Museum (407-892-3728), 901 Virginia Ave. Take a tour of a Depression-era cannery, blacksmith shop, and one-room schoolhouse. Call for hours.

G.A.R. Museum (407-892-6146), 1101 Massachusetts Ave. Built in 1914, this building, on the National Register of Historic Places, houses Civil War items and GAR memorabilia. Guided tours available. Open Mon, Tue, and Thu 10–4.

♿ **Historical Museum of St. Cloud & Osceola County, Florida** (407-892-3671; www.stcloudchamber.cc), 1200 New York Ave. Artifacts, photographs, and collectibles housed in St. Cloud's oldest commercial building, the First National Bank, circa 1910. Also home to the St. Cloud Chamber of Commerce. Open Mon–Fri 9–4.

REPTILE VIEWING 🏵 ✎ ♿ **Reptile World Serpentarium** (407-892-6905), 5705 E Irlo Bronson Hwy (FL 192). Since 1972, this working research facility, operated by George Van Horn and his wife, Rosa, has supported over 400 research labs and supplies venom proteins for three antivenin companies. The facility houses 600 to 700 snakes, of which 50 or so are on display. From the enormous anaconda to the camouflaged Madagascar leaf nose, the natural history of reptiles is displayed in clean, indoor exhibits. Daily, at approximately noon and 3, you can watch George and Rosa milk venomous snakes such as albino monoclid cobras, eastern diamondback rattlesnakes, and Florida's cottonmouth, while you are safely outside the glass enclosure. Call for exact times. Those too squeamish to watch the venom milking can spend time outside with the turtles and gopher tortoise, green iguanas, American alligator, and various birds. Best value at only $5.75.

GEORGE VAN HORN MILKS AN EASTERN DIAMONDBACK AT THE REPTILE SERPENTARIUM

Kathy Wolf

RODEO ♿ **Kissimmee Sports Arena & Rodeo** (407-933-0020; www.ksarodeo.com), 1010 Suhl's Lane, Kissimmee. Heart-pounding, foot-stomping action in the traditional rodeo style. Every Fri 8–10 PM. Call for additional dates.

✳ To Do

AIRBOATS ♿ Hop on one of **Boggy Creek Airboat Rides** (407-348-4676; www.bcairboats.com). West location on Lake Tohopekaliga, 2001

Warird Adventures

WARBIRD ADVENTURES' FIGHTER TRAINERS FLYING IN FORMATION

AVIATION

Just off US 192, **Orlando Helitours** (407-397-0226) flies air-conditioned 206 Jet Rangers, which seat up to four people. If you've never ridden in a helicopter, this one is like a Land Rover for the air. You'll want to take this one for an aerial view of the Disney properties; Blizzard Beach looks like Santa's village from the air. A "ride" ($15) is barely worth it, as you'll go up, bank a turn, and come back down in 2 or 3 minutes. So opt for the $35 tour, which gets you over part of Disney and back in 7 to 9 minutes, or—for the ride of your life—go for 12 to 15 minutes ($65) and see all of Disney. Charter flights can take you anywhere you want for as long as you want.

Stallion 51 (407-846-4400; www.stallion51.com), 3951 Merlin Dr, Kissimmee. I watched as a man in his mid-80s climbed into the cockpit of the Crazy Horse, his wife waving him good-bye as he closed the bubble canopy. This former P-51 pilot had flown this aircraft for real in World War II and now, as a birthday gift, he was taking it up again. For about an hour he took to the skies and performed maneuvers like he did so long ago. His hands were still steady; it all came back to him high up in the clear blue skies. As he taxied

E Southport Rd, Kissimmee; east location on East Lake Tohopekaliga, 3702 Big Bass Rd, Kissimmee. Continuous 30-minute guided airboat tours in 18-passenger airboats around the marshy edges of the Toho lakes. Custom and night rides on six-passenger boats available. Open daily 9–5:30. $18 adults, $13 ages 3–12.

Take an entire afternoon with **Cypress Glade Adventure Tours** (407-855-5496; www.gatorland.com). This exceptional tour gives you a taste of real Florida's natural beauty. You'll be picked up at Gatorland (see "Theme Parks"), where back to the hangar and deplaned, he burst into tears. This had been his dream, and his loving wife had made it a reality. Off they went for parts unknown after what I suspect was his best birthday gift ever.

If you mention *P-51* to anyone who knows planes, they will immediately say *Ohhh!* and get starry-eyed. Only a few of these "Cadillacs of the Skies" were ever made, and even fewer are still in operation. The rare Crazy Horse at Stallion 51 is one of only 12 dual-control Mustangs in the world. This highly maneuverable warbird delivers heart-stopping performance with exceptional vertical and horizontal capabilities. The half-hour or 1-hour orientation tour will have you flying the plane 90 percent of the time. No flight experience is necessary, but this trip will cost you. Still, it's worth every penny for those who dream to fly the very best.

♿ Forget the simulators; slip into the front cockpit and take to the skies in a real World War II fighter at **Warbird Adventures, Inc**. (407-870-7366 or 1-800-386-1593; www.warbirdadventures.com), 233 N Hoagland Blvd, Kissimmee. Take your "wingmate" with you in another plane and do some formation flying. Yes, you can fly tip to tip and experience all the aerobatic maneuvers used by the aces. Loop, dip, roll, fly upside down, and capture every screaming bit of it on video with their three-camera system. No flying experience is necessary; your instructor will walk you through each maneuver as *you* fly a real T-6/SNJ/Harvard. $160 for 15 minutes (no aerobatics); $270 for half hour (aerobatics option, $30); $490 for an hour (includes aerobatics and positive-g maneuvers). Add-ons: three-camera video $40 VHS, $50 DVD. Stills $20.

If you'd rather fly a helicopter, take the controls of a real Bell 47 MASH chopper and get a great view from up front in the bubble. Learn to fly turns, low-low level, autorotation, and even hover. With the aerobatic option you'll learn all the positive-g maneuvers. $80 for 15 minutes (basics); $150 for 30 minutes (includes hover); $280 for 60 minutes (includes low-low, hover, positive-g maneuvers, off-field landing/takeoff, and autorotation). Add-ons: one-camera video $30 VHS, $40 DVD. Stills $20. Open daily 9–sunset. No flying experience necessary.

you'll be taken to Lake Toho for a half-day adventure. Then you'll glide across the marshy waters in a six-passenger airboat. Let the wind blow through your hair as you experience several hours of Florida's natural beauty. Pass through one of the Chain of Lakes locks to a remote lake, where there are more bald eagles than boaters. Hunt for baby 'gators and see one of the oldest known cypress trees in its natural habitat. Lunch included on a secluded shore. Night tours also available. Call for current prices and get a combo pass, which includes a half day at Gatorland.

TJ Airboats at Richardson's Fish Camp (407-846-6540), Lake Tohopekaliga at 1550 Scotty's Rd, Kissimmee, will take your breath away in 40 minutes as they glide along the edges of Lake Toho and places beyond in the smaller six-passenger airboats. Open daily. Night rides by reservation only. $20 adults; $16 ages 12 and under. Charter fishing, too!

Richardson's Fish Camp (407-846-6540) and **Southport RV Park** (407-933-5822) also offer airboat rides (see *Fish Camps, RV Parks, and Marinas*).

DINNER SHOWS The longest-running dinner show in the area, **Medieval Times Dinner & Tournament** (407-239-0214, 407-396-1518, or 1-800-229-8300), 4510 W Irlo Bronson Hwy (US 192), is an institution. Arrive early and go back in time to the 11th century at the Medieval Life Village, where you'll walk through buildings and exhibits of the Middle Ages. The extra $2 to see the medieval torture room is worth it and a real eye-opener—each historical artifact is explained in full, graphic detail (it's not for the squeamish or little ones). Over at the castle, enter the great hall where you'll meet the royal court prior to the show and shop for costumes and accessories, dragon goblets filled with grog, and souvenir collectibles. As noble lords and ladies you will be assigned a brave knight who will fight on your behalf while defending the kingdom. Experience the adventure and romance as stunning Andalusian stallions perform amazing displays of horsemanship, much like the great Lipizzaners, while valiant knights compete in tournament games and jousting matches until only one knight remains. $47 adults; $31 ages 3–11.

Set in a 1930s speakeasy, **Capone's Dinner & Show** (407-397-2378 or 1-800-220-8428), 4740 W Irlo Bronson Hwy (US 192), comes alive in Gangland Chicago with comedy and Broadway-style musical productions. Surrounded by mobsters and dames at Al Capone's secret hideaway, you'll dine on Mama Capone's Italian American buffet during song and dance performed by some of the area's best professionals. Don't be surprised if the "Feds" raid the place. The buffet has more food than you can load on your plate—and you can go back for seconds. You'll also enjoy unlimited beer, sangria, rumrunners, and soft drinks served by your very own mobster. No preshow. $40 adults, $24 ages 4–12.

ECOTOURS

Kissimmee

Aquatic Wonders Tours, Inc. (407-846-2814; www.natureboat.com), Big Toho Marina. This is the one the locals recommend! Captain Ray will take you deep into the headwaters of the Everglades on this informative and entertaining wildlife tour, in the comfort of a smooth-sailing pontoon boat. This knowledgeable captain also offers a true hands-on experience (the only one I know of) where you will dip your net and examine its contents under a microscope. Largemouth bass fishing (see *Fishing*) is also available. Call ahead for reservations. $21 for a 1½- to 2-hour ecotour; $35 for the 3-hour exploration tour.

Cypress Glade Adventure Tours (407-855-5496) will take you by airboat (see *Airboats*) deep into the natural waterways of Kissimmee's Chain of Lakes in search of alligators, bald eagles, and roseate spoonbills in this remote wilderness.

St. Cloud

Forever Florida (407-957-9794 or 1-866-854-3837; www.foreverflorida.com and www.floridaeco-safaris.com), 4755 N Kenansville Rd. This working cattle ranch and nature preserve is a loving tribute to the owners' son, Allen Broussard. This enthusiastic naturalist who successfully battled cancer, but lost the fight to heart disease at 29, is remembered in a moving tribute and 4,700 acres protected in part by The Nature Conservancy. The *un*touched, *un*spoiled wilderness is *un*surpassed for seeing the way the Real Florida used to look. You'll travel through nine ecosystems by either elevated swamp buggy or horseback (see *Trail Riding*), through the Broussards' Crescent J. Ranch and the Allen Broussard Conservancy, where you'll see Cracker cattle, longhorn steer, alligators, eagles, and more. The knowledgeable guides will tell you all about the local flora and fauna, and discuss land management—including the effects of lightning and the necessity of controlled burns—in this informative and entertaining adventure. Kids will like the petting pen near the main lodge, and hikers will enjoy the natural paths; 6 miles of the Florida National Scenic Trail stretch through the heart of the property. Two-hour Swamp Buggy Tour ($28) includes lunch. Two-hour Swamp Buggy Heritage Safari Tour ($35) includes lunch and cattle round-up. Open daily 9–6. Reservations suggested.

FISHING

Everywhere

Champion Pro Guide Services Central Florida (407-935-9344; www.championbass.com), 2317 Emperor Dr, offers fly-fishing, trophy bass fishing, and saltwater flats fishing for redfish, tarpon, snook, and trout.

Florida Guidelines (321-777-2773 or 1-888-800-9794; www.flguidelines.com), covering the state of Florida. Rodney Smith, a Florida native and outdoor photojournalist, will help you plan a memorable fishing excursion. Sight-fish the lagoons for redfish and snook, fish for big bass in lakes and rivers, cast your line inshore for tarpon, kingfish, and shark, or wield fly rod or light spin tackle for pompano, snook, and spotted sea trout. This consortium of experienced guides will help you locate the trophy fish of your dreams. Sightseeing trips also arranged. Inshore fishing $275 half day, $375 full day. Offshore fishing $550 half day, $700 full day.

Kenansville

♿ **MFCTOO at Overstreet Landing** (407-436-1966 or 1-800-347-4007; www.mfctoo.com), 4500 Joe Overstreet Rd. Boat ramp, RV sites, guide service, wildlife tours, and bait-and-tackle shop.

Kissimmee

♿ The following professional guides offer handicapped assistance: **A 1 Bass Guide Service** (1-800-707-5463; www.a1bassguideservice.com). The first-class professional guides at **A+ Tom & Jerry's Bass-N-Flats Fishing** (407-935-9801; www.tomandjerrys.net) will help you locate saltwater tarpon, redfish, and snook. Learn the proper techniques from professional anglers at **First Strike Service** (407-935-1257 or 1-888-937-6843).

Aquatic Wonders Tours, Inc. (407-846-2814; www.natureboat.com), Big Toho Marina. With the only fishing boat in the area that takes six people, not only will this captain help you land a trophy bass, but he's also knowledgeable about the area's various flora and fauna. Families and budding ecology majors will want to check out his unique hands-on ecotours (see *Ectours*). Call ahead for reservations. $200 for half day, $350 for full day.

One of these exceptional guides is sure to fit your personality and fishing expertise: Premier bass fishing on central Florida's lakes is found through **Bass Guides** (407-932-3446 or 1-877-274-8433; www.bassfishingguideflorida.com). Experience trophy bass fishing with **Captain Bob's Lunker Bass Guide Service** (407-931-3118 or 1-888-847-6424; www.anglersinfo.com/charters/lunkerbass and www.cyberangler.com/guides/lunkerbass) with free pickup to and from Disney-area hotels. **Fish with Robbie** (407-847-9157; www.kissimmeefishing.com), in the Kissimmee Chain of Lakes, offers free pickup to and from your hotel.

St. Cloud

♿ **Jay's Bass Bustin' Guide Service** (407-892-9582) offers full- and half-day charters for individual or group trips. All gear provided to catch the big one!

Captain Chuck takes you in search of trophy-sized largemouth bass with **A-Action Professional Bass Guide Services** (407-892-7184; www.centralfloridabassfishing.com).

GOLF **Omni Orlando Resort at ChampionsGate** (321-677-6664; www.omnihotels.com), 1500 Masters Blvd, Orlando (see *Lodging*). Two phenomenal 18-hole, par-72 championship golf courses designed by Greg Norman are set amid the natural beauty of Florida. Special care was taken to create a natural environment. You'll tee off while hot-air balloons soar overhead nearby, and then chip one in on the green while a pair of sandhill cranes honk their approval. The challenging international course resembles the great links of Scotland, and also boasts the highest course rating in Florida—76.3! Before you tee off, perfect your swing with lessons from the **David Leadbetter Golf Academy**; you might just find David himself wandering the grounds.

MASSAGE THERAPY When your feet are worn out from shopping and theme parks, call **Barbara Cox** (407-847-0984 or 407-948-2505) for a Swedish, geriatric, or deep tissue massage. This talented and knowledgeable masseuse will find all those knots and knead away the stress of the day. Couples or girls-night-out packages bring several massage therapists to your home or hotel, so there's no waiting.

PARASAILING ♿ **Boggy Creek Parasail** (407-348-2700; www.boggycrkparasail.com), 3702 Big Bass Rd, Kissimmee. Parasailing is the calmest of the air adventures; try this first if the others make you nervous. Sit in the sturdy harness and gently float off the back of the boat, gliding up to 800 feet over East Lake Tohopekaliga. The 360-degree panoramic view around the lake, all the way to Disney and beyond, is unsurpassed. Unlike ocean parasailing, there is no crosswind, and the feeling is one of peace and quiet, with just a light rustle of the gigantic colorful canopy. Your landing is just as gentle, right on the back of the boat, but if you want a taste of adventure, ask Captain Joe to dip your toes on the way down. Friends and family of nonfliers ride for free so they don't miss the action. Open daily 9–5:30.

SPA Slip into luxury at the **Celebration Day Spa** (407-303-4400), 400 Celebration Place, Celebration. Enjoy the fitness facilities, indoor lap pool, sauna, and steam rooms before or after your treatment. The Aromatherapy Massage ($80) takes you through a botanical journey with essential oils extracted from healing herbs and oil. The Warm Stone and Paraffin Massage ($130) removes all your tension as warm paraffin coats your entire body, softening your skin; then warm stones glide over your body, melting away your stress. For the best buy after walking through the theme parks, opt for the Anti-Fatigue Leg Treatment ($30). A full menu of day-spa treatments, like facials, sea scrubs, manicures, and pedicures, awaits you.

TRAIL RIDING

Kissimmee

For years I wondered where I could go horseback riding near Orlando—and there was a great stable just down the street! Get off US 192 and head a few miles down Orange Blossom Trail, where a sign will point you to **Horse World Riding Stables** (407-847-4343; www.horseworldstables.com), 3705 S Poinciana Blvd, with over 700 acres of wooded trails tucked back off the road. Wildlife appears on cue in this natural environment; ducks, alligators, eagles, and deer don't seem to mind the horses. Depending on the time of year, you may even see a newborn foal with its mom. Three levels of riding are offered: Nature Trail (walk) is a relaxing ride along gentle sandy trails and is great for families with kids or those with no prior riding experience; the Intermediate Trail (walk/trot) will take you under a beautiful canopy of live oaks and contains a *lot* of trotting. You'll want to have some riding experience for the Advanced Trail (walk/trot/canter), which is a great workout, lasting about 1½ hours. These horses are well groomed and well behaved. I selected the Intermediate ride, and when my horse got to the "canter" section, her ears perked up waiting for my guide's signal. When none was given, she continued on with the trot, but I felt like I had dashed her hopes—she would have responded if I'd asked for more. Such control is a testament to exceptional horses; where you often find trail ponies racing for the barn, you'll see none of this here. Special thanks to my guide, Austin Roberts, who took me on an incredible ride through a magical land. Nature Trail: $35 adults and children 6 and over; $15 ages 5 and under, riding double with adult. Intermediate: $42 adults and children over 10. Advanced: $59 adults and children over 10. Children's pony ride around property $6. Weight limit 250 pounds for trail rides; 50 pounds for pony rides. Open daily 9–5.

St. Cloud

Forever Florida (407-957-9794 or 1-866-854-3837, www.floridaeco-safaris .com), 4755 N Kenansville Rd. See the real Florida while riding several hours on horseback through nine ecosystems. You can take your choice of the 1-hour ($35), 2-hour ($55), or—if your seat can take it—the longer 3-hour ($70) tour; all rides are walk only. Ask for the tour through Bull Creek, where your horse will go belly deep crossing this beautiful wetland wilderness. You might even pass a sunning alligator—but don't worry, the horses are used to them. For an adventure you'll never forget, join the City Slickers Roundup ($150), where you'll be part of a working cattle drive as they move their herd across the Crescent J. Ranch. Or go for the half-day Rawhide Roundup ($90). Trail rides include lunch. For those who don't ride, take an elevated swamp buggy ecotour (see *Ecotours*). Open daily 9–6.

WALKING TOURS **Saddle Rack's Historic Walking Tour** (407-847-5364), 811 W Verona St, Kissimmee. Travel back in time and relive the history of the Florida "cow hunter." Learn about the influence of the steamboat. Old buildings come alive with every tale spun by your guide **Earl Evans** on this custom walking/riding tour through Kissimmee's historic district by a native. By appointment only. Call and leave a message and he'll call you right back.

WATER SPORTS **Buena Vista Water Sports** (407-239-6939; www.bvwater sports.com), located on Lake Bryan on FL 535, Lake Buena Vista. Come on in, the people are friendly and the water is clean and warm. This is the place to go for waterskiing, Jet Skis, and wakeboarding. Rentals and rides from $40. Need to learn? You'll be up skiing in no time with only one lesson ($50) at **Dave's Water Ski School**. Dave teaches you on land then skis beside you in the water. Open daily.

✷ Green Space

BEACHES **Ralph V. Chisholm Park** (407-892-2397), 4700 Chisholm Park Trail, off Narcoossee Rd (FL 15), St. Cloud. Set along the shoreline of Lake Narcoossee, this large county park provides a pleasant public beach and boat ramp for fishing access plus vast acreage for trail riding; walk the open fields, and you'll see sandhill cranes. Free.

NATURE CENTERS **Osceola County Schools Environmental Study Center** (407-870-0551), 4300 Poinciana Blvd, Poinciana. Protecting 200 acres of the Reedy Creek Swamp, this environmental center opens your eyes to the beauty of the cypress forest; walk the boardwalk out to Reedy Creek to see several ancient cypresses, one topped with a bald eagle nest. The Indian Mound Trail leads through a floodplain forest to a midden along the creek. Open Sat 10–5, Sun noon–5; free.

PARKS At the north end of Lake Tohopekaliga, **Kissimmee's Lake Front Park** features a lighthouse, fishing pier, boat ramp, picnic tables, playground, and children's water play area.

Moss Park (407-273-2327), 12901 Moss Park Rd, Orlando, is a 1,500-acre Orange County park popular for camping and picnicking. A hiking trail through a wetlands area good for birding connects this park with Split Oak Forest Mitigation Park (see *Wild Places*). Fee.

Peghorn Nature Park (407-957-7243), Peghorn Way, St. Cloud. Two hiking trails wind through a variety of ecosystems in this 58-acre urban park.

WILD PLACES **Bull Creek Wildlife Management Area** (407-436-1818), Crabgrass Rd off US 192, Holopaw. The Florida Trail creates a 17-mile loop through this vast wilderness of pine flatwoods and prairies along Bull Creek, with several primitive campsites; take a scenic drive through the forest on the 8-mile Loop Rd. Trail riding and hunting are also permitted. Free.

Disney Wilderness Preserve (407-935-0002), 2700 Scrub Jay Trail, located off Poinciana Blvd. Administered by The Nature Conservancy, this 12,000-acre preserve along pristine cypress-lined Lake Russell protects vast pine flatwoods, bayheads, and cypress domes. Walk the 4.5-mile outer loop for the big picture, or take an easy stroll on the interpretive trail. Sep–June, take a swamp buggy ride (fee) out into the boggy ecosystems.
Open daily 9–5; fee.

Lake Lizzie Nature Preserve (407-892-2397), Midland Dr, St. Cloud, is a 918-acre nature preserve with a network of hiking and equestrian trails that lead through the pines to Lake Lizzie and Trout Lake. From US 192, follow Pine Grove Rd to Bass Hwy to find Midland Dr. Free.

Makinson Island (407-892-2397), in the northern third of Lake Tohopekaliga, Kissimmee, is a 132-acre island preserve accessible only by boat, with a 3.5-mile hiking trail. Free.

Prairie Lakes Wildlife Management Area (407-436-1818), 1231 Prairie Lakes Rd off Canoe Creek Rd, Kenansville. Protecting wet prairies along the southern edge of Lake Kissimmee, this preserve offers a figure-8 loop of the Florida Trail with 12 miles of hiking; an observation tower gives a bird's-eye view of the Kissimmee prairies. Trail riding and hunting also permitted. Free.

THE KISSIMMEE LIGHTHOUSE

Kathy Wolf

Split Oak Forest Mitigation Park (407-892-2397), located on Clapp-Simms-Duda Rd just north of the intersection of FL 15 and Boggy Creek Rd, Narcoossee. Protecting acreage along Lake Hart for sandhill crane habitat, this massive wilderness park centers on a significant botanical feature, an ancient oak tree that split in two and continued to grow. A network of 7 miles of hiking trails encircles the park: The North Loop passes through scrub, flatwoods, and oak hammocks along the lake, while the South Loop meanders through vast, open, wet prairies. Day use only, no camping permitted; visit adjacent Moss Park (see *Parks*), connected via the Swamp Trail, for camping. Free.

Three Lakes Wildlife Management Area (407-436-1818), US 441, 13 miles south of Holopaw. A 7-mile section of the Florida Trail crosses this wilderness of pine flatwoods, open prairies, and scrub; the forest roads are popular for biking and trail riding. Seasonal hunting permitted. Fee.

✷ Lodging

HOTELS AND MOTELS

Celebration 34737

Celebration Hotel (407-566-6000 or 1-888-499-3800; www.celebrationhotel.com and www.kesslercollection.com), 700 Bloom St. One of the wonderful Kessler Collection properties (see "Theme Parks"), this small hotel has only 115 rooms and suites, so you'll feel like you're in a country inn or bed & breakfast. Richard Kessler personally selects many outstanding pieces of art: You can't miss the bronze life-sized alligator sculpture in the lobby, and you'll want to see if you can find Chief Osceola in the mural. Staff treat you not like guests, but like family. Literally steps from the shopping and dining establishments, you won't need your car. When you want some privacy, you'll enjoy sunning and swimming at the heated pool overlooking a lovely lake and miles of walking trails. High-season rates start at $225 rooms, $305 suites; low-season (June–Sep) start at $175 rooms, $255 suites. Thirty percent discount for Florida residents.

Kissimmee 34736

The charming **Wonderland Inn** (407-847-2477; www.wonderlandinn.com), 3601 S Orange Blossom Trail, is an oasis not far from all the area's attractions. This former 1950s roadside motel has been lovingly restored by its gracious host, Rosemary O'Shaughnessey. Reminiscent of a more relaxed time, you will comfortably settle into your cozy room with hand-painted garden murals. Rosemary is a loving caretaker and will often think of your needs before you do. When I arrived "home" after a long day researching, she had left an encouraging note beside a glass of red wine. On another day, I found fresh orange juice in the refrigerator, "for vitamin C." The on-site gardener keeps the landscape meticulous with over 30 different types of flowers and flowering trees. Sit in the garden and take in the aromatic jasmine while watching butterflies or the all-white squirrels. Make your own breakfast in your room or enjoy the full complimentary breakfast with new friends in the Main House. Rooms and suites $80–160.

Kenansville 34739

✐ **Heartbreak Hotel** (407-436-1284 or 407-436-0208; www.heartbreakhotelkenansville.com), 1350 S Canoe Creek Rd. Well off the beaten path, this old-fashioned hotel along the railroad tracks in Kenansville charms with its historic exterior and four nicely appointed, roomy suites ($100–125), each with wooden floors, a full kitchen, and a porch with rocking chairs.

RESORTS **Omni Orlando Resort at ChampionsGate** (321-677-6664; www.omnihotels.com), 1500 Masters Blvd, Championsgate 33896. I got a preview of this new luxury resort and can't wait for the opening, slated for Oct 2004. The Mediterranean-style resort features top-notch luxury and lavish natural landscaping. There's plenty of relaxation here, with nature and jogging trails, a 10,000-square-foot European Spa, a formal heated pool, a family activity pool with water slides, and my personal favorite—an 850-foot lazy river that winds through a tropical paradise.

VACATION HOMES **Alexander Holiday Homes** (407-932-3683 or 1-800-621-7888; www.floridasunshine.com), 1400 W Oak St, Kissimmee 34744. These luxury condos and vacation homes have up to seven bedrooms, so bring the family or your closest friends. The privacy makes a peaceful escape from the resort areas and an ideal way to relax and soak up the Florida sunshine.

American Vacation Homes (407-847-0883 or 1-800-901-8688; www.americanvacationhomes.us), 1631 E Vine St, Kissimmee 34744, offers more than 250 fully furnished individually owned homes scattered through several housing developments; capacities of 6 to 14 guests make these rentals an ideal option for families on vacation. Pick your size and amenities (high-end rentals include pools), and they'll figure out the rates.

One of the largest suppliers of fully furnished homes, the folks at **ResortQuest Orlando** (407-396-2262; www.resortquestorlando.com), 7799 Styles Blvd, Kissimmee, can select which home will be right for you, from condos in resort-style settings to portfolio homes with private pools. By the day, week, or month.

FISH CAMPS, RV PARKS, AND MARINAS

Kenansville

Cypress Lake RV and Sports Club, LLC (407-957-3135), 3301 Lake Cypress Rd, Kenansville 34739. Restaurant, bait and tackle, RV sites, cabin rentals, and airboat rides.

Lake Marian Paradise Marina (407-436-1464), 901 Arnold Rd, Kenansville 34739. Bait and tackle, RV sites, and cabin rentals.

♿ **MFCTOO at Overstreet Landing** (407-436-1966 or 1-800-347-4007; www.mfctoo.com), 4500 Joe Overstreet Rd, Kenansville 34739. Boat ramp, RV sites, guide service, wildlife tours, and bait-and-tackle shop.

Kissimmee

Big Toho Marina (407-846-2124; www.kissimmeefishing.com), 101 Lake Shore Blvd, Kissimmee 34741. This full-service marina rents out boats, tackle, bait, rods, and reels so that you can explore Lake Tohopekaliga on your own, or ask about the many fishing charters and professional bass fishing guide services available in the area. Open daily from 5:30 AM.

East Lake Fish Camp (407-348-2040), 3705 Big Bass Rd, Kissimmee 34744. Complete camping and fishing resort complex. Enjoy the natural surroundings with modern conveniences. Restaurant, live bait, fishing licenses and tackle, dock, boat rentals, shaded and paved RV sites, air-conditioned cabins with maid service, tent sites with shelter, Olympic-sized swimming pool, tennis court, children's play area, Laundromat, showers, and rest rooms. Restaurant on site.

Richardson's Fish Camp (407-846-6540), 1550 Scotty's Rd, Kissimmee 34744. Full RV hookups and campsites, trailer and cabin rentals, bait-and-tackle shop, boat ramp, wet and dry storage with covered slips. Airboat rides.

Southport RV Park, Campground, Marina & Fishing Guide Service (407-933-5822; www.southportpark.com), 2001 E Southport Rd, Kissimmee 34746. Full RV hookups, campsites, and cabin rentals. Picnic pavilions, general store, bait and tackle, boat ramp. Wet and dry storage. Airboat rides.

St. Cloud

St. Cloud Fishing Pier and Marina (407-957-7243), 1106–1108 Lakeshore Blvd; send mail to 3001 17th St, St. Cloud 34769.

✷ Where to Eat

DINING OUT

Celebration

The atmosphere at **Café Dantonio** (407-566-CAFE), 691 Front St, is fun and relaxed. The meals—Italian! Sample the dozen pasta dishes ($11–20) with meats, seafood, lobster, and fresh herbs, or entrées ($13 and up) where the main course is *pollo*, *scaloppine*, or *pesce*. Pizza ($11–17) is also on the menu.

Dark rich wood and New England hospitality surrounds you at **Celebration Town Tavern Bostonian** (407-566-2526), 721 Front St. They actually fly in all of their seafood, as well as their secret breading. You'll get to taste Ipswich clams (dinner is $17) and real clam "chowdah"—which passed this Mainer's test ($4 cup, $6 bowl). One- and 2-pound lobsters are reasonably market priced; those who are just too tired to fight the hard-shell crustacean can try the Lazyman's Lobster Casserole, which has all the meat from a 2-pounder. Complete your meal with none other than a Boston cream pie ($5).

Kissimmee

Kissimmee Steak House (407-847-8050), 2047 E Irlo Bronson Hwy (US 192). They grow 'em big in cattle country, and this family-owned steak house serves up the biggest with a 32-ounce porterhouse ($25) and 24-ounce top sirloin ($19). Smaller appetites will want the 7-ounce fillet ($17) or the 12-ounce New York strip ($16). If you must have fish in a steak house—they have that, too. Casual dress. Open for dinner Tue–Sat.

One of America's Top 10 Steak Houses, **Charley's Steak House** (407-239-1270), 2901 Parkway Blvd, uses only USDA prime and choice beef, aged 4 to 6 weeks. An extensive wine list complements your meal. Open for dinner nightly.

EATING OUT

Celebration

Stop by the **Market Street Café** (407-566-1144), 701 Front St, for sandwiches and burgers ($8–9); dinner specialties ($11–13), including prime rib ($15); and fabulous desserts like Ultimate Chocolate Cake ($5) or a hot fudge sundae ($4).

For that afternoon cup of tea, check out **Sherlock's** (407-566-1866; www.sherlocksofcelebration.com), 715 Bloom St, which has an extensive selection of traditional exotic teas, coffees, wines, and imported beers.

Kissimmee

East Lake Fish Camp on East Lake Tohopekaliga (407-348-2040), 3705 Big Bass Rd. Located next to Boggy Creek Airboats (east location). This restaurant serves up a tasty Florida platter of 'gator tail, frog legs, and catfish ($14), along with fresh salads ($3–7), steak and seafood dinners ($7–15), beer and wine in a rustic setting. Don't miss the all-you-can-eat Fri-night buffet ($10), Sat-night seafood buffet ($12), Sun breakfast buffet ($7), and Sun-night prime rib buffet ($15). Breakfast and lunch.

Flipper's Pizza (407-397-9509), 5770 W US 192. Located in Old Town, this old-fashioned pizza shop will even deliver! Terrific pizza with special sauce and fresh ingredients makes this spot a crowd pleaser. Having tried them up on I-Drive near SeaWorld, I went back to sample their Neapolitan-style Sonoma pizza with sun-dried tomatoes, red onions, artichoke hearts, and spinach ($11–15). My friends loved the penne pasta with meatballs topped with mozzarella cheese ($6).

My Family's Pizza (407-346-6747), 3297 S John Young Pkwy, tucked inside the Citgo station. This local favorite is located near the Wonderland Inn (see *Lodging*) and serves up 20-inch pizzas ($10–15), calzones and strombolis ($8), and subs and gyros ($5). Best bargain is a pizza burger for $2. Call ahead and Alex can customize your order, going way beyond pizza.

Signature by the Lake (407-931-1303), 220A E Monument Ave. Fresh food with a gourmet flair. "Winedown" Fri.

Susan's Courtside Café (407-518-1150), 18 South Orlando Ave. Friendly country atmosphere in a historic home. Light breakfast fare, with fresh coffee roasted on the premises and sold by the pound. Lunch includes a selection of salads ($4) and sandwiches ($5–6), personal-sized gourmet pizza ($4–6), homemade cakes, pies, and cookies. Hot cappuccino and cool iced mocha, smoothies, and slushies ($3–4). Open Mon–Fri for breakfast, lunch, and dinner.

St. Cloud

Cypress Restaurant at Forever Florida (407-957-9794), 4755 N Kenansville Rd. Whether you're here to explore the working cattle ranch or just passing through, stop by for a quick lunch of 'gator bites ($8), chicken fingers ($6), Cypress Burger ($6), or fresh garden salad ($3). That's the entire menu, but you'll enjoy it either inside a beautiful lodge or outside on the porch surrounded by the natural landscape. Wine and beer available. (Also see *Ecotours* and *Trail Riding*.)

For a taste of fresh Florida fish, head to **Fred's Lakeside Grill and Marina** (407-892-1954), 4715 Kissimmee Park Rd.

Yeehaw Junction

For some down-home cookin' Florida style, step inside the **Desert Inn** (407-436-1054), 5570 South Kenansville Rd, just west of exit 193 off Florida's Turnpike. You'll note right off that this is not your typical listing on the National Register of Historic Places. This late-1800s watering hole served railroad workers, moonshiners,

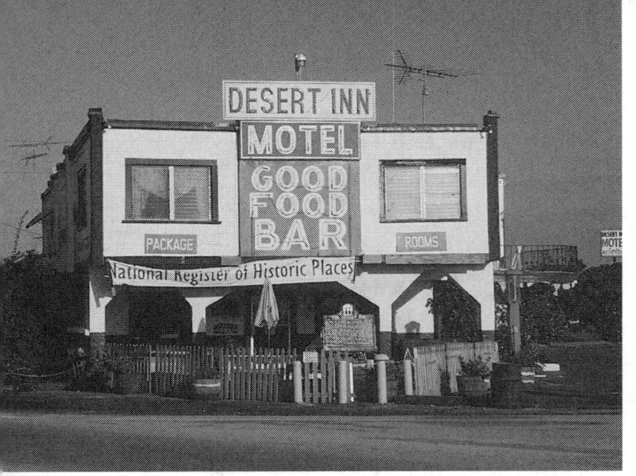

Kathy Wolf

THE DESERT INN, YEEHAW JUNCTION

traders, cowboys, and Indians—some of whom are still here today. Dig into such home-style dishes as Italian meat loaf ($7), spicy chili ($3), or slow-baked roast beef or pork ($8) with gravy. The adventurous will want to try half a pound of deep-fried frogs, gatorburger ($5), or turtleburger ($6). Open 7 days for breakfast, lunch, and dinner.

✷ Selective Shopping

Celebration

The whole town of Celebration is one great place to shop, with quaint streets like Market, Bloom, and Front winding along the lake. But my favorite place was **Day Dreams** (407-566-1231; www.daydreamsdollsandbears.com), 603 Market St. And I couldn't get out without a big dent in my credit card. This is the place all grandmothers should go for that oh-so-special grandchild—and they are all that special. All the old favorites are here, along with few new ones, like Madame Alexander, Susan Wakeen, and Lee Middleton. You'll find bunnies and bears from Boyd and Hermann, and other creatures from one of the best Steiff collections around. The collection of quality books is outstanding, with selections from Wise and Lang that I just couldn't put back once I had them in my hand.

Kenansville

The ground floor of the historic **Heartbreak Hotel** (see *Lodging*) features a great gift shop with gourmet foods, Yankee candles, Christmas ornaments, and a selection of nicely priced antiques in the back room.

Kissimmee

Remember when you could walk into a clothing store and get unsurpassed personal service at a great price? Well, you still can at **Shore's Men's Wear** (407-847-4747), 201 Broadway. Manager George Cross will help choose from a selection of quality clothing and Florsheim shoes; he'll even rent you a tuxedo for that special night out. Ladies will receive the same quality products and service next door at **Shore's Town and Country for Ladies** (407-846-6922), 203 Broadway. For over 30 years, **Lewis Music** (407-847-6397), 117 Broadway, has offered musical instruments and an extensive selection of sheet music with lots of old American favorites.

ANTIQUES AND COLLECTIBLES

Kissimmee

The best way to approach antiques shopping in Kissimmee's downtown historic district is to go with Earl Evans (see *Walking Tours*). He knows everyone in town, and just walking in on his arm will get you a great deal.

A fine selection of folk and country can be found at **Aaron's Amish Store** (407-518-9544), 109 Broadway, and **The Cottage Gifts & Collectibles** (407-847-2299), 106 Broadway. **Bryan's Attic Antiques** (407-933-2263), 12 E Darlington Ave, will have your grandmother's favorites. Superheroes will want to stop by **Comic Books & Collectibles** (407-870-0400), 17 W Monument Ave. The hottest wheels are at **Diecast Cars of Orlando** (407-932-3343), 16 Broadway. For antiques, jewelry, and fine furniture, go to **Lanier's Historic Downtown Marketplace** (407-933-5679; www.laniersantiques.com), 108 Broadway—if you can't find it there, then you're not looking.

St. Cloud

Forget Me Not Antiques (407-892-7701), is on 10th. On New York Ave, you'll find **Caesar's Treasure Chest** (407-892-8330); **Chime & Time Clock Repair** (407-892-9633); **Simple Pleasures** (407-957-9569); and **Quarter Moon Antiques** (407-957-0399). Over on Pennsylvania Ave, look for **Copper Kettle Antiques** (407-892-7099); **St. Cloud Antiques** (407-957-2060); and **The Olde Woodshed** (407-957-3400).

CAMERAS You'll find great cameras, accessories, and, of course, film at **Cameras Unlimited** (407-787-3535), 5039 W Irlo Bronson Hwy (US 192), and **Camera Outlet** (407-397-9800), Parkway Pavilion, 2901 Parkway Blvd (across from Celebration off US 192), which also has European PAL systems. **192camera.com Outlet Store** (407-390-1220) offers free pickup from your hotel.

FARMER'S MARKETS **Osceola Flea and Farmer's Market** (407-846-2811), 2801 E Irlo Bronson Hwy (US 192). Over 900 booths of antiques, collectibles, new and used merchandise, Florida souvenirs, and local produce. Free admission, parking, and entertainment. Open Fri–Sun 8–5. **Weekly Farmer's Market**, 201 E Dakin Ave. Selections of locally grown fruits, vegetables, herbs, and baked goods are marketed in the downtown historic district on Thu morning 7–1 in the civic center parking lot.

FISHING TACKLE You'll need the right equipment to catch Florida's big bass. The folks at **Florida Fishmasters Pro-Guide & Tackle, Inc**. (407-892-5962 or 1-800-424-5090), 3325 13th St, will help you select the right gear and tell you how to use it.

✷ Special Events

February: One of nation's oldest (since 1944) and top rodeos, **Silver Spurs Rodeo of Champions** (407-847-4052; www.silverspursrodeo.com), literally rides into town (down US 192) in this semiannual event at the new 2003 Silver Spurs Arena in Osceola Heritage Park. The precision skills coupled with an incredible air-conditioned indoor arena make this the largest rodeo east of the Mississippi and a must-see for everyone—from all walks of life. You'll witness 60 of the top cowboys and cowgirls from all over the world compete for over $50,000 in prizes and accolades while performing everyday ranching tasks, from tie-down calf roping to Xtreme Bulls, in this nationally televised event. One of the more beautiful displays is the popular Silver Spurs Quadrille Team, riding a type of square dance on horseback and performed by eight couples decked in their western finest.

For those who think this can't be good for the animals, let me set the record straight. As a staunch defender of animal rights, I entered the world of cowhunters and bullwrestlers with hesitation and an open eye. So down on the arena floor I went to get up close and personal with the wranglers of today in this exhibition of ranch skills. What I found was that the bulls and horses, and even the calves, are treated better than the family dog. A closer inspection revealed animals with rich shiny coats comparable to champion thoroughbreds at the Kentucky Derby. When not being ridden (for 8 seconds or less), even the bulls were social. Any why shouldn't they take good care of these animals? Training is lengthy, and the championship livestock is expensive—even the equipment to transport them (in air-conditioned comfort) rivals a recreational RV. A different world? Yes. But one that is full of emotion and excitement, with no evidence of animal abuse and sanctioned by the Professional Rodeo Cowboys Association.

April: **The Great American Pie Festival** (407-566-2200; www.celebrationfl.com), Celebration. A weekend all about pies.

Spring Art Festival (407-566-2200; www.celebrationfl.com), Celebration. Fine art festival on Market, Front, and Bloom Sts.

Celebration's **Semi-Annual Yard Sale** (407-566-2200; www.celebrationfl.com), throughout the town of Celebration. The whole town participates in this spring and fall cleaning of garages and attics. One day only in both Apr and Oct.

🐾 *May*: The **Posh Pooch Celebration** (407-566-2200; www.celebrationfl.com), for dogs and their human companions, features live music, demonstrations and doggy info, contests, and even dog weddings! Great food includes special menu items just for dogs.

October: **Celebration of Fall Festival** (407-566-2200; www.celebrationfl.com), Celebration. Leaves fall on Market St, live entertainment and hayrides. For Celebration's **Semi-Annual Yard Sale**, see *April*; for the **Silver Spurs Rodeo**, see *February*.

November: **Now Snowing Nightly** (407-566-2200; www.celebrationfl.com), Celebration. Snow falls, with carolers and holiday merriment throughout the town. Kids and pets can take photos with Santa.

The **Annual Osceola Art Festival** in historic downtown Kissimmee features local and nationally known artists, live entertainment, food, and more. Free.

November–December: Get your handcrafted holiday gift at the **Annual Osceola Crafter's Holiday Gift Gallery**, Osceola Center for the Arts.

THEME PARKS

It seems like the theme parks have been here forever, but my generation remembers a Florida when Orlando was a sleepy citrus and cattle town and the state's tourist attractions centered on its springs, beaches, and lakes. That changed forever in 1971, when Walter Elias Disney unveiled the Magic Kingdom and a handful of truly different themed resorts, ushering in the phenomenon that is **Walt Disney World**. As vacationers shifted to this new take on entertainment, businesses followed: Hotels mushroomed along US 192 and in Lake Buena Vista, restaurants moved in to feed the steady stream of visitors, and other large entertainment entities took note and opened their own attractions, bringing **SeaWorld** and **Universal Studios Orlando** to life over the late 1970s and early 1980s. The 1990s saw explosive growth along International Drive (referred to locally as I-Drive) with the creation of the massive **Orange County Convention Center** complex and the establishment of **Celebration**, a planned-by-Disney residential community. From a playful re-creation of Disneyland in the rural prairies southwest of downtown Orlando, the theme park region has taken on a life of its own, pushing Orlando to the crest of the tourism wave, a top destination for travelers from around the world.

GUIDANCE Before your trip, get in touch with the **Orlando/Orange County Convention & Visitors Bureau** (407-354-5500; www.orlandoinfo.com), 6700 Forum Dr, Suite 100, Orlando 32821. **Walt Disney World** (407-WDW-INFO; www.disneyworld.com) offers an extensive web site for trip planning, as do **Universal Studios Orlando** (1-800-711-0080; www.univacations.com) and **SeaWorld** (1-800-224-3838; www.seaworldvacations.com). You'll want the ***International Drive Resort Area Official Visitors Guide*** (407-248-9590; www.internationaldriveorlando.com), 7081 Grand National Dr, Suite 105, Orlando 32819, which will direct you to all the wonders along this curvilinear stretch of touristville.

GETTING THERE *By air*: **Greater Orlando International Airport** (407-825-2001; www.state.fl.us/goaa) serves the world with hundreds of flights daily; check their web site for contact information on the many airlines servicing Orlando.

By bus: **Greyhound Lines** (407-292-3440; www.greyhound.com), 555 N John

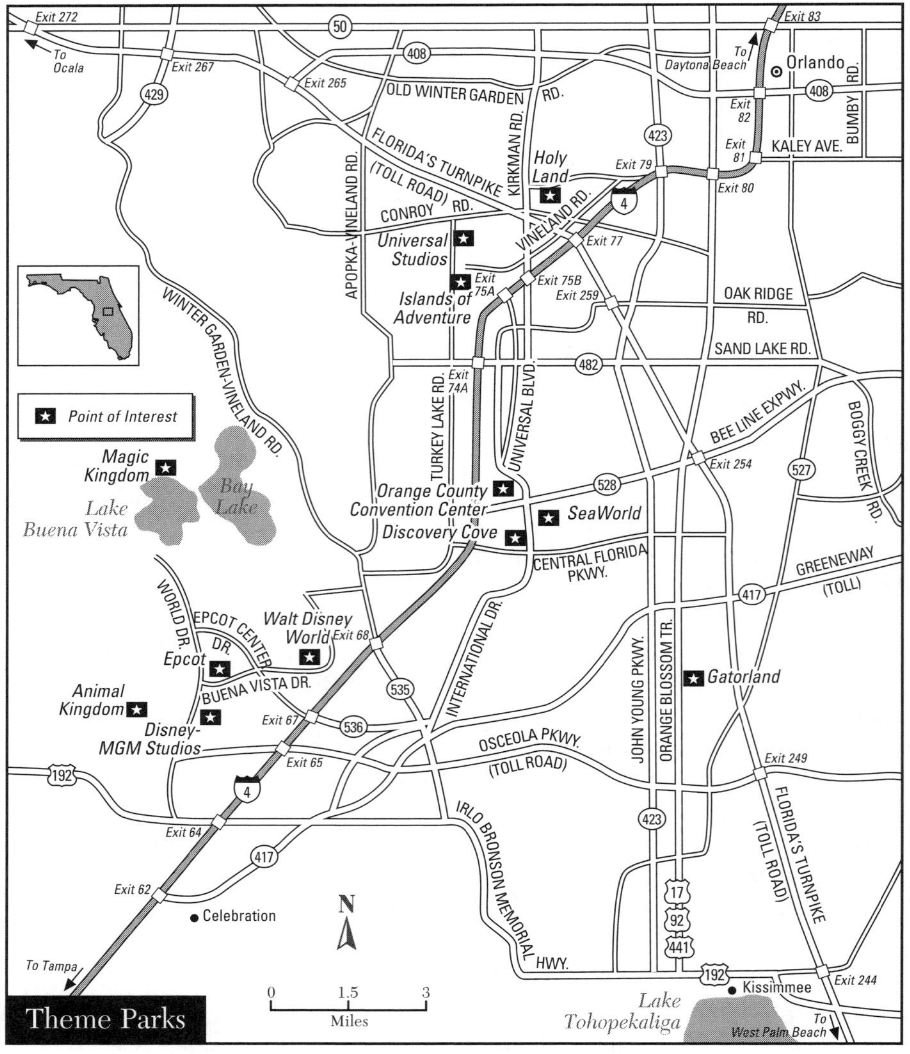

Theme Parks

Young Pkwy, Orlando, drops you in the heart of the theme park area. **Coach USA** (407-826-9999) provides door-to-door shuttle van service from Amtrak's Orlando station.

By car: **I-4** runs though the heart of the theme park district, with plenty of signs to instruct you as to where to exit. However, it's Orlando's busiest highway. From the Orlando International Airport, the **Beeline Expressway** and **FL 417** (toll) provide quick access to the area. Use the **Osceola Pkwy** (toll) to drive straight into Walt Disney World, with easy access to Wide World of Sports, Downtown Disney, but be aware that the speed limit drops to 45 mph the moment you hit the Disney property; pay attention to signage, which instead of standard highway green turns purple.

By train: **Amtrak** (1-800-872-7245; www.amtrak.com) provides regularly scheduled service to metro Orlando, just north of the theme parks. **Coach USA** vans will take you from the station directly to your hotel.

GETTING AROUND **I-Drive** parallels I-4 between Universal and Lake Buena Vista and is "Entertainment Row," with hundreds of restaurants, shops, hotels, and small attractions lining the busy street; look for pedestrian traffic. Worth noting is that I-Drive connects to S I-Drive by way of FL 536. S I-Drive will take you straight to US 192. On **US 192** you know you've entered the "Disney Zone" near the main gate when the lampposts turn purple; Black Lake Rd provides a back entrance to the Animal Kingdom area. **Turkey Lake Rd** and **Palm Pkwy** provide an alternate to I-Drive on the north side of I-4, a quiet way to slip between the theme parks. **FL 535** runs north–south through Lake Buena Vista.

♿ **I-Ride Trolley** (407-354-5656; www.iridetrolley.com) travels through the International Drive resort area. The easy-to-use 10-foot-high markers along both sides of the road designate trolley stops. The Main Line route serves the I-Drive resort area north and south every 20 minutes. The Green Line serves Universal Blvd every 30 minutes. There are only a few spots to transfer between the lines: Main Line (32 N, 32 S, 14 N) and Green Line (10 N, 10 S, 2 N). Fares: single 75¢, senior 25¢. Exact change required. Unlimited ride passes are not sold on trolleys and must be purchased at any of the 90 locations along I-Drive. One-day $2, 3-day $3, 5-day $5, 7-day $7, and 14-day $14. Kids ride free with a paying adult. Handicapped accessible with an ADA-specified hydraulic lift system.

PARKING The theme parks sock you for a hefty parking fee ($6 and up), which is what makes staying "on property" and using their free transportation a huge allure. Disney hotels charge only for valet parking; Universal's hotels charge $6 daily for self-parking, double that for valet, as do many of the luxury hotels. Parking garages provide the only parking for I-Drive attractions. There are no parking fees at area malls. Parking fees run $8 daily for Disney's four major theme parks; free parking at Downtown Disney and the water parks and for self-parking guests at the resorts (valet parking extra). Parking at Universal Orlando is in a state-of-the-art parking garage, complete with moving sidewalks. Their fee is also $8, with valet at $16. Parking at SeaWorld will also cost you $8, but at their Discovery Cove it's free.

MEDICAL EMERGENCIES **Florida Hospital Orlando** (407-303-5600), 601 E Rollins St, **Florida Hospital East Orlando** (407-303-8110), 7727 Lake Underhill Rd, and **Sand Lake Hospital** (407-351-8500), 9400 Turkey Lake Rd, cover the metro area and I-Drive. **Florida Hospital Celebration Health** (407-764-4000), 400 Celebration Place, and **Florida Hospital Kissimmee** (407-846-4343), 2450 N Orange Blossom Trail, Kissimmee, are located near Disney and the US 192 attractions. For minor emergencies, stop by the **Main Street Physicians Walk-In Emergency Clinic** (407-370-4881), 8324 International Dr.

DISCOVERY COVE ♿ **Discovery Cove** (407-370-1280 or 1-877-4-DISCOVERY; www.discoverycove.com), 6000 Discovery Cove Way. If you've been wondering if it's worth the $129 admission to visit SeaWorld's little sibling, let me do the math for you. First there's admittance to an amazing paradise set among white sandy beaches, blue lagoons, and grottoes and filled with dolphins, rays, tropical fish, and exotic birds. Then there's a freshly prepared lunch that rivals any of those at the fancy resorts. After that, they give you not 1 but 7 days' entrance to SeaWorld or Busch Gardens Tampa Bay. My calculator couldn't take it! This has got to be the best bargain around, but the real bonus is how you'll feel after spending a day there. I can only describe it as having been to a spa and experiencing all that it might have to offer.

Each day, only 1,000 guests are permitted to enter this oasis, so you won't find the usual rushing-to-get-there-first dash from the parking lot—which is so small, you won't need the valet, but they have one anyway. And there's no need to arrive any more than 15 minutes before the park opens. It's just not necessary. Check-in is a breeze inside the exotic open-air lodge. Then, instead of squeezing through turnstiles, you'll walk out onto a terrace where you'll sip Florida orange juice and hot coffee. Pet the drowsy-eyed sloth and take a hint from this furry creature—this is the place to chill out and relax. Meander down a winding tropical path while a guide explains all the wonderful amenities. Slip on a wet suit and grab a towel and snorkel gear, then stow your extra items in the locker rooms stocked with fluffy towels, toiletries, and hair dryers. You won't even need your camera, as staff photographers discreetly wander the property taking reasonably priced photos.

So what's to see and do? Swim as long as you want in the **Coral Reef**, where you'll be surrounded by tropical fish, leopard rays, and even barracudas as they hover from under a sunken shipwreck. Spend hours floating down the heated **Tropical River** discovering ancient artifacts. If you time it just right, you'll get to feed the *sting-less* rays in the **Ray Lagoon**, while they'll tickle your body begging for more food. For the best experience, snorkel motionless in the water and let these gentle water pilots come to you. Those having a **Dolphin Experience** will have an assigned time period with a group of about six or eight other swimmers. During the 45-minute adventure, you'll spend time getting to know your dolphin by doing some behavioral training; when you and your dolphin have bonded, hang on and take an unforgettable ride around the lagoon.

A MOTHER AND DAUGHTER TAKE PART IN THE DOLPHIN EXPERIENCE, DISCOVERY COVE.

Discovery Cove

A fabulous meal starts around 11 and continues to about 3, so there's no rush here, either. The lavish selection includes salads (from greens to macaroni), entrées (from giant burgers and steak fries to baked fish with steamed veggies), desserts (from pudding to red velvet cake), and soft drinks, iced tea, and coffee. There's a small fee for tropical drinks, beer, and wine. After lunch, take in some sun or shade while lounging around on comfy beach chairs, cabanas, or secluded hidden hammocks. Walk through the tropical free-flight **Aviary** and get acquainted with toucans, hornbills, or hundreds of other exotic birds. You'll want to slide your feet so as not to step on these little feathered friends.

The beauty of this place will astound you, and you'll remember the feeling long after you're gone. Open daily 8:30–5:30. Tickets to Discovery Cove follow a fixed price structure and are dependent on season and subject to change without notice:

	All Ages	**Comments**
1-day admission without dolphin swim	$149 in-season; $129 off-season	Includes 7 consecutive days to SeaWorld or Busch Gardens Tampa; must be taken before or after visit
1-day admission without dolphin swim	$179 in-season; $159 off-season	Includes 14 consecutive days to both SeaWorld and Busch Gardens Tampa; must be taken before or after visit
1-day admission with dolphin swim	$249 in-season; $229 off-season	Includes 7 consecutive days to SeaWorld or Busch Gardens Tampa; must be taken before or after visit
1-day admission with dolphin swim	$279 in-season; $259 off-season	Includes 14 consecutive days to both SeaWorld and Busch Gardens Tampa; must be taken before or after visit
Trainer for a day	$419 in-season; $399 off-season	

DISNEY The epicenter of Florida tourism, **Walt Disney World** (407-WDW-INFO; www.disneyworld.com) consists of a 47-square-mile complex of theme parks, resorts, shopping centers, and wilderness, a city onto itself with its own police force, fire rescue, and transportation system. From Walt Disney's original vision in the 1950s, the world-renowned entertainment complex has grown in directions that Walt probably never expected, hosting baseball spring training,

THEME PARK TIPS

Take it from a lifelong hiker—you will do a *lot* of walking while visiting the theme parks. While I've been tempted to carry a GPS to clock it, rest assured you will walk between 2 and 10 miles a day, from crossing the massive parking lots to the tram that whisks you to the gates to wandering across the vast acreage encompassed by each park. Prepare accordingly, just as if you were going on a hike. Wear comfortable shoes, go lightweight (leave as much baggage as you can in the car; it will be faster through the new security checkpoints), wear sunscreen and a hat, and carry water bottles! Water fountains are tough to find, and bottled water is especially pricey once you enter the park gates. It's far too easy to dehydrate when you're outdoors in the Florida sun, so you need to make a point of drinking water frequently while strolling around and standing in line. Carry energy bars as emergency food; it's too tempting to skip meals when you're caught up in parades, rides, and the like. And don't forget raingear—you'll be glad you brought that cheap plastic poncho along when Central Florida's daily afternoon thundershowers hit, June–Oct.

• **Beware of bottlenecks**. You'll stand in three lines at each park's gate unless you buy tickets in advance: one for a security check (try not to carry a purse or backpack unless you truly need one), one for a ticket purchase, and one to get through the gate. And then there are the lines for the rides, some of which can take an hour or more. At Disney, use the Fastpass, and at Universal, the Express, to nab fixed-time tickets for the more popular rides; that'll cut your wait down to 10 minutes or less. Traveling solo? Take advantage of the "singles" line on rides such as Test Track and Mission: Space at Epcot; it'll give you a big jump ahead of the crowd. Keep alert for parade routes, as daily parades can block access to certain parts of the park!

MAIN STREET IN THE MAGIC KINGDOM Sandra Friend

- **Don't try to fit it all in**. It's just not possible. To see all the attractions in the Orlando area, you'd need literally 67 full days. The major theme parks are designed so it'll take you 2 or 3 days *per park* to see and do every little thing. Make a plan beforehand and stick to it. Despite the popularity of Park Hopper passes at Disney, the single-day Park Hopper isn't worth your time and effort unless you're spending the morning at one park and then heading to Epcot for some fine international cuisine for dinner. You'll eat up a lot of time in transportation between the parks when you try to switch venues midday. Alternatively, if you're staying at or near a park, remember that this is a *vacation*. Take the opportunity to nip out to your hotel or B&B during the heat of the day for a siesta, or take a leisurely boat tour before plunging back into activities in the evening. At the Walt Disney World Resort, guests staying "on property" have access to free transportation via buses, monorails, and boats; however, the buses are time consuming. Plan an hour or more each way from your room to the park gate.
- **Have a plan**. If your group decides to split up, pick a specific place and time to meet—and stick to it. These parks are vast, and it's easy to lose a toddler or a teen left alone for a few seconds. I've seen families utilize walkie-talkies and cell phones to keep track of each other. If you make meal reservations, stick to them precisely, since Disney will charge you $10 or more if you don't show up.
- **Outfit your kids with a journal** to serve as an autograph book—they'll have plenty of photo ops with theme park characters, so have each character sign a blank page, and paste the child's photo into the book after the trip as a special bit of memorabilia.
- **Bargain hunting?** Despite billboards you'll see around Florida, park admission prices are non-negotiable; those operators are selling you tickets at a discount in exchange for something, usually your presence at a time-share presentation. However, if you're looking for a bargain on hotel rates or package details at Disney, stop at the **Disney Information Center** (352-854-0770) at FL 200 and I-75 in Ocala (see "Marion County"), where if you *ask* for the best rate on a particular hotel or date, you'll get it with a smile—but they won't volunteer the information; open 9–6 daily. Rates here beat anything you'll be quoted online or on the phone; if you're a Florida resident, identify yourself (photo ID required) for rock-bottom rates and discount seasonal passes. For the best prices on rooms, shoot for the low-attendance times: Feb, Sep, and between Thanksgiving and Christmas. Most of the time you can get the best hotel rates by contacting the hotels directly and not through the kiosks peppered around town or off the highway. These visitors info centers have great maps, but again will want you for a time-share presentation. If you have the extra 4 hours or so to go to a presentation, you *will* get the freebies they have offered, and some of the time-shares are well worth the investment. The only "official" visitors centers are the ones listed in this book.

race car driving, and one of the world's best circus performances. Each of these "on property" venues is discussed under the appropriate categories for this chapter.

Hours vary daily at the Disney theme parks. When you arrive, request the current 2-week calendar that shows park hours, parades, and special events. In general, Animal Kingdom closes the earliest (5 PM) and Epcot the latest (9 PM), but there are often exceptions for special events; the parks generally open at 9 AM, but guests staying in the Walt Disney World Resort hotels are offered earlier entrance to certain parks on a rotating basis. Tickets to the four major parks follow a fixed price structure (subject to change without notice):

	Ages 10+	Ages 3–9	Comments
1-day admission	$54.75	$43.75	
4-day Park Hopper	$219	$176	
5-day Park Hopper plus	$282	$226	Includes water parks and Pleasure Island
Theme park annual pass	$379	$322	
FL resident theme park annual pass	$299	$254	
Premium annual pass	$499	$424	Includes water parks and Pleasure Island
FL resident premium annual pass	$399	$339	Includes water parks and Pleasure Island

Disney's Animal Kingdom

Education about conservation with a side of entertainment—that's **Animal Kingdom**, the 500-acre theme park that staunchly claims it's "not a zoo" but nevertheless presents animals in natural habitat enclosures, melding nature *and* art. Themed regions radiate from **Safari Village**, where art is everywhere: more than 1,500 hand-painted wooden folk art animal carvings crafted in Bali decorate the buildings, and the enormous Tree of Life dominates the skyline. It's an incredible work of art, with 325 animals carved into the structure, and houses the 3-D film ***It's Tough to Be a Bug***—a performance that'll get a rise out of you. In the surrounding garden, animals like axis deer and green peafowl roam, each identified with an interpretive sign adorned with a poem about the creature, information on the animal, and a map of its habitat. **Camp Minnie Mickey** presents live shows—most notably the *Festival of the Lion King*, a grand Broadway-style performance of artistic pageantry that you won't want to miss—and offers kids chances for character photos and autographs. The din of the crowd in **Harambe** mingles with live music and echoes off the buildings, creating an atmosphere like a busy African village, gateway to **Kilimanjaro Safaris**, a popular bumpy ride through re-created African forests and savannas where herds of antelope, rhinos, and elephants roam. I enjoy strolling down the **Pangani Forest Trail**, watching the troupe of lowland gorillas wander through their habitat. **Rafiki's Planet Watch** requires a train ride out to the complex; en route, you'll see the animals from a different perspective, including within their nighttime digs. The complex is Animal Kingdom's nerve center, with veterinarians looking after rare species and a nursery for new additions to the animal families. In **Anandapur** stroll the **Maharajah Jungle Walk**, where a 900-pound Malayan tapir lazes beneath the bamboo, Rodrigues fruit bats and Malayan flying foxes dangle from the trees, and female Bengal-Sumatran tigers loll about beneath flapping prayer flags in the temple ruins. **Kali River Rapids** is the thrill-seeker's destination for this section of the park, and you *will* get wet on this ride. A new thrill ride, **Expedition EVEREST**, will whisk you down the Himalayas on a runaway mountain railway; it opens in 2006. At **DinoLand USA**, step into campy 1950s fun with the giant **Boneyard** for kids to dig through, **Chester & Hester's Dino-Rama**, a midway carnival/amusement park with the popular **Primeval Whirl**, and **Dinosaur!**, a bumpy time-travel trip past marauding dinosaurs as meteors fall to earth. Tie it all together by watching the artsy daily parade at 4 PM, with beautifully costumed critters stealing the show from Minnie and Mickey.

Disney-MGM Studios

Moviegoers shouldn't miss **Disney-MGM Studios**, where you're whisked away to the back lots and studios of Tinseltown, Disney style, with 1940s art deco setting the tone. It's full of feel-good movie-themed rides and shows like **The Great Movie Ride** and **Jim Henson's Muppet Vision 3D** (where I can never get enough of Statler and Waldorf bickering in the balcony), but many of the themes reveal the 1989 opening of this park, like **Star Tours** and the **Indiana Jones Epic Stunt Spectacular**. I encourage you to walk through **Walt Disney: One Man's Dream**, a multimedia museum of Walt's life and the evolution of his empire from the *Wonderful World of Disney* to the Walt Disney World of today; it's a great primer on what Walt was all about. **The Magic of Disney Animation** introduces you to the artists who make movie magic happen, with a tour of their working studios. Thrill-seekers gravitate to the **Twilight Zone Tower of Terror**, a 13-story sudden drop, and the **Rock 'n' Roller Coaster**, where Steven Tyler and Aerosmith lead you through a recording studio into a parking garage for a blastoff from 0 to 60 mph in 2.8 seconds followed by a blitz through the dark—think Space Mountain on a caffeine buzz. Live theater shows that will captivate the kids include *Beauty and the Beast*, *Voyage of the Little Mermaid*, and *Bear in the Big Blue House*; *Fantasmic!* draws upon Mickey's performance in *Fantasia* with a limited-seating outdoor light and sound show to close out each evening.

Epcot

It's extraordinary the influence that **Epcot** had on my family: One year, my sister joined in a street performance in Morocco; the next, she was braving her way to

Marrakech for real. It's a theme park for adults, a virtual trip around the world for those who haven't yet set foot outside the United States, very much like the world's fairs of my youth—with shopping! With their focus on future technologies, the pavilions of **Future World** remind me of those old world's fairs, right down to the corporate sponsorship. Ride beneath a 5.7-million-gallon artificial reef in **The Living Seas**, or take a guided boat trip through working greenhouses in **The Land**; let the kids play in **ImageWorks** and **Innoventions**. In **Wonders of Life**, a script straight from *Fantastic Voyage* comes to life in **Body Wars**, a high-speed trip through the immune system. You'll need the Fastpass for the top two rides in the park—**Test Track**, the mile-long General Motors simulator that speeds you through automobile tests, and the impressive **Mission: Space**, which uses NASA technology to propel you and your team into space, where you feel like you've left earth's gravitational pull. My usual reason for visiting Epcot, however, is to stroll around the 4-acre **World Showcase Lagoon** to shop and eat. Movies and rides in the country pavilions add to the fun, but I enjoy the cultural exhibits the best, like the Animales Fantásticos "spirits in wood" from Oaxaca at Mexico, and the Gallery of Arts and History in Morocco, a reverent mosque-like museum filled with treasures from their national museum. Of course, I still get chills when I see Ben Franklin walking through **The American Adventure**, and it's hard to pass up the beauty of **Impressions de France**, but visiting World Showcase is about soaking up atmosphere. I've seen and done it all many, many times, but I'll always come back for dinner and the unique imports filling the shops, especially during the annual October **Food & Wine Festival** (see *Special Events*).

Magic Kingdom

With the top theme park attendance in the world, the **Magic Kingdom** is the core of the Disney empire, encompassing Walt's original vision of bringing fantasy and imagination to life. Start off with a walk down Main Street USA to reach the statue of Walt and Mickey, around which all of the themed areas radiate. I've always loved **Adventureland**, with its funky Caribbean atmosphere; laugh your way down the classic **Jungle Cruise**, slip down into the dark watery corridors of **Pirates of the Caribbean**, or sing along with the birdies in the **Enchanted Tiki Room** (albeit under new wisecracking management; I miss the 1960s feel). In adjoining **Frontierland**, motorized rafts float visitors to **Tom Sawyer Island**, one of the most fun "natural" attractions in the park, where kids can play in Fort Langhorn—a frontier fort that looks suspiciously like Fort Christmas—and sneak through catacomb-like caves. My favorite thrill rides at the park are **Big Thunder Mountain Railway**, a runaway train, and **Splash Mountain**, a dressed-up log flume that'll have you whistling *zip-a-dee-doo-dah* through vignettes populated by critters from the Uncle Remus stories of Joel Chandler Harris. **Liberty Square**'s big draw is the ever-creepy **Haunted Mansion**, while behind the Bavarian facades of **Fantasyland** lie the busiest rides in the park—make sure you get a Fastpass for **Peter Pan's Flight**, the new 3-D **Mickey's PhilharMagic**, and the incredibly popular **Many Adventures of Winnie the Pooh**, where you drift through scenes of the A. A. Milne books in a giant honey jar. **Tomorrowland** is a campy 1950s sci-fi version of the future dominated by **Space Mountain**, but families stand in even longer lines for **Buzz Lightyear's Space Ranger Spin**, a mobile shooting gallery based on the *Toy Story* movies. I still love the **Carousel of Progress** ("Now is the time . . . now is the best time . . . now is the best time of your life"), a vision of the future from the past—I first saw it at the 1965 New York World's Fair. The newest part of the Magic Kingdom, **Mickey's Toontown Fair**, is a cartoon village and county fair rolled into one, with Minnie and Mickey's houses, the **Barnstormer at Goofy's Wiseacre Farm** (a gentle roller coaster), and lots of opportunities for character photos and autographs at the **Toontown Hall of Fame** tent. Tie it all together with a ride around the world on the **Walt Disney World Railroad**, featuring classic steam engines that were model railroader Walt's pride and joy.

SEAWORLD **SeaWorld Adventure Park Orlando** (407-363-2613; www.seaworldorlando.com), 7007 SeaWorld Dr. Founded in 1964 by four graduates of the University of California—Los Angeles (UCLA), SeaWorld began as a small 22-acre marine zoological park along the shores of San Diego. The larger Orlando park opened in 1973, but was still small compared to the other Central Florida theme parks. Working with other marine facilities, SeaWorld maintained its focus on its founding principles of conservation, research, education, and entertainment, eventually growing into the most respected marine zoological collection in the world and accredited by the American Zoo and Aquarium Association (AZA). In 1989 Anheuser-Busch Companies, Inc., purchased the parks to complement their Busch Gardens attractions, bringing with them state-of-the-art adventure rides. SeaWorld Adventure Parks is still based primarily on educational exhibits and ecoconservation shows, but now you'll experience thrills and chills from furry polar bears in the frigid waters of the Arctic to dicey drops on Kraken.

One of the things I noticed first at SeaWorld was shade, lots of it. Fully mature trees create a cool, breezy canopy over most of the pathways, leaving you refreshed throughout the day. For further refreshment, take your seat in the "Soak Zone" at any show that involves salt water. These zones are clearly marked and should be avoided unless you really want to be doused by a wall of water. Even sitting near this area you'll get a bit of a splash, so protect your camera.

SeaWorld is set up so you can wander and explore. Take your time; there's a lot to see and do. And while they'll tell you it can be done in 1 day, you'll want to schedule 2 to really see it properly. At the **Key West at SeaWorld** you can feed dolphins in **Dolphin Cove** or touch stingrays at **Stingray Lagoon**. See the newest calves and their moms at the **Dolphin Nursery** and learn how these mammals are born. Over at the **Key West Dolphin Fest** you'll be entertained surfside by Atlantic bottle-nosed dolphins and *Pseudorca crassiden* (false killer whales) as they perform spectacular behaviors to a tropical beat. See the endangered **Manatees: The Last Generation** and learn of their plight. Six thousand pounds of snow fall daily inside the **Penguin Encounter**, where the temperature is a chilly 30 degrees. Over 200 penguins, like the 3-foot-tall king penguin and rockhopper, sporting a yellow crest of feathers, romp with puffins in the icy waters of the Antarctic. Go to the north end of the globe at **Wild Arctic**, where a simulated jetcopter takes you on a fast and bumpy expedition over the frozen tundra, then under the sea, in search of beluga whales and polar bears. Experience the same show without the ride in the walk line. Check your show schedule for **The Shamu Adventure**, SeaWorld's famous killer whale, and hang around late for the last show as Shamu shakes to a rock-and-roll beat. **Clyde and Seamore Take Pirate Island** is a high-seas buccaneer adventure. Laugh to the crazy antics of sea lions, otters, and an adorable walrus, as their swashbuckling high jinks unfold.

Don't miss **Pets Ahoy,** where the animals not only steal the show, they run it. Watch while pets rescued from local animal shelters perform amazing and hilarious skits. Then go home and train your pet to do the same. For more feline antics, head to the **New Waterfront** for **Kat 'n' Kaboodle**, and watch exotic cats, like the Bengal, Sphynx, and Siamese, demonstrate incredible feats. The intimate show is streetside, so get there early to find a good spot. Stop by the **Clydesdale Hamlet** to pet the world-famous Budweiser Clydesdales. Touch tropical fish, sea urchins, and starfish at the **Caribbean Tidepool**. Denizens of the deep surround you as you pass through a 60-foot underwater tunnel in **Shark Encounter**. Take a break and pedal around the lake in your own pink **Flamingo Paddleboat**.

For high-adventure thrills, take a trip over to **Journey to Atlantis,** where sirens fight to keep their city, and then ride the mythical sea creature **Kraken**. Make sure you tie your sneakers tight, as Kraken has no floor. This intense roller coaster is one of the world's highest and fastest. You'll climb 149 feet, then drop down 144 feet and go through seven inversions at speeds of up to 65 mph—only for those with guts of steel. The unique water coaster **Journey to Atlantis** is one of the best rides around and not to be missed! This water ride through the lost city of Atlantis has spectacular special effects, and then plunges everyone down one of the steepest flume drops in the world. Just when you think the ride is over, you hear a voice say, "Leaving so soon? I don't think so . . ." and the boat becomes a roller coaster, dipping and curving then plunging you back in the water.

Learn about the realm of the shark at an add-on close encounter, as you snorkel or scuba inside a real shark cage. The 2-hour **Sharks Deep Dive** is limited to two guests. While you can swim with dolphins at Discovery Cove, SeaWorld lets you swim with whales! Conduct animal training sessions in this one-on-one **Whale Swim Adventure**. The 2-hour program is limited to four guests. You'll need to get up before dawn to work alongside marine mammal experts. The 8-hour **Marine Mammal Keeper Experience** is perfect for those thinking about a career in marine fields or for those who want an unforgettable adventure. Your adventure doesn't have to end when the park closes, either: Have dinner over at the **SeaFire Inn** as the **Makahiki Luau** (see *Dinner Shows*) entertains you with a celebration of the ancient customs of the Pacific Islands.

SeaWorld opens at 9 AM year-round, with extended hours during summer, holidays, and special events. Tickets to SeaWorld follow a fixed price structure (subject to change without notice):

	Ages 10+	Ages 3–9	Comments
1-day admission	$54	$45	Take 10 percent off when ordering an E-ticket at least 7 days in advance
Combo pass	$90	$81	Includes 1 day each at SeaWorld and Busch Gardens Tampa Bay
14-day/four-park Flex	$180	$146	Includes Universal Studios, SeaWorld, Islands of Adventure, and Wet & Wild; must be consecutive days
14-day/five-park Flex	$215	$180	Includes Universal Studios, SeaWorld, Islands of Adventure, Wet & Wild, and Busch Gardens Tampa; must be consecutive days
Marine Mammal Keeper	$389		Includes lunch, T-shirt, career book, souvenir photo, and 7-day pass to SeaWorld
Sharks Deep Dive with scuba	$150		Includes T-shirt, shark info booklet, and poster; park admission is not included, and is required
Sharks Deep Dive with snorkel	$125		Includes T-shirt, shark info booklet, and poster; park admission is not included, and is required

UNIVERSAL **Universal** (407-363-8000; www.universalsorlando.com). So popular was the Universal Studio Tour in Hollywood, California, that Universal pioneers decided to duplicate it in Orlando's growing entertainment center. The working studio and theme park was pitched as a partnership to Paramount, where none other than Michael Eisner was acting studio chief. Paramount passed on the project, and it was a few more years before Universal was ready to set up shop. Then they got lucky and landed Academy Award–winning producer-director Steven Spielberg as creative consultant. The king of family action-adventure films, Steven was a perfect fit for the motion-picture-themed park. Opening in 1990, only a year after Eisner's launch of MGM Studios, the modest action-adventure park had some problems and took a few more years to get its bearings. Almost from the beginning, though, the concept of Islands of Adventure was being developed. In 1999 the adrenaline-pumped adventure park, the entertainment complex CityWalk, as well as on-site resorts, became a reality. And they're not done yet! Two more parks, resorts, and a golf course are in the making. What used to take 1 day to visit now takes 3.

The 2,300-acre resort and amusement complex is all in one neat geographic area, making navigation a snap. And the close proximity means there's no need for monorail or bus transfers. Once you park your car at Universal, you'll travel on moving sidewalks, then enter the exciting CityWalk, where you'll find restaurants, nightclubs, cinemas, and lots of shops. The Islands of Adventure Port of Entry is just a few more steps to your left, while Universal Studios is equidistant to your right.

These are no kiddie parks. At Universal Studios things blow up, sharks lunge at you, and laser guns zap nasty aliens. At Islands of Adventure most of the rides are for extreme thrill-seekers, making it a great place for teens bored with the warm and fuzzy parks. But for high-speed thrills, 3-D excitement, and nonstop adventure, this is the place to get pumped up.

DUELING DRAGONS AT UNIVERSAL'S ISLANDS OF ADVENTURE

Universal Orlando

Universal opens at 9 AM, with earlier access if you're staying at one of the on-site resorts (see *Hotels and Motels*). Both adventure parks close at the same time, with CityWalk (see *Eating Out* and *Entertainment*) staying open to the wee hours. In winter the parks can close as early as 6 PM or as late as 8 PM, with summer hours extending to 9 or 10 PM. Make sure to call in advance, as closing times seem to change depending on the season, special events, or during spring break. Special events, such as Halloween Horror Nights, will have additional admission fees. Tickets are as follows (subject to change without notice):

	Ages 10+	Ages 3–9	Comments
1-day admission/one park only	$54	$45	
2-day/two-park unlimited access	$100	$89	
14-day/four-park Flex	$180	$146	Includes Universal Studios, SeaWorld, Islands of Adventure, and Wet & Wild; must be consecutive days
14-day/five-park Flex	$215	$180	Includes Universal Studios, SeaWorld, Islands of Adventure, Wet & Wild, and Busch Gardens Tampa; must be consecutive days
Theme park preferred annual pass	$170	$170	Includes Universal Studios, Islands of Adventure, free parking, and other discounts; no blackout dates
Theme park power annual pass	$110	$110	Includes Universal Studios and Islands of Adventure; blackout dates apply
CityWalk Party Pass	$9		Includes 1-night club-to-club access
CityWalk Party Pass + movie	$12		Includes 1-night club-to-club access and one movie
FL resident preferred annual pass	$170		Same price as nonresidents, but you can pay it over 12 months

Islands of Adventure

This is where the rides are! At the Port of Entry, on the far left side of CityWalk, you'll enter five islands set along exotic coastlines, where you might enter a comic-book city full of superheroes and old favorites, or a strange architectural land full of Seussian characters, then continue on to a jungle where dinosaurs rule and a mythical island full of legendary gods and dragons. If you collected comic books as a kid or were first in line for such movies as *Jurassic Park* and *Spiderman*, then this is the place for you. If you don't like adrenaline thrill rides, then head back over to Universal Studios, where there's still plenty of excitement without the white-knuckle chills. On **Marvel Super Hero Island**, the **Amazing Adventures of Spider-Man** takes you on a 3-D adventure while you help fight the Sinister Syndicate in your transport vehicle. Beware: The action-packed simulator may move along a track, but the drops will feel real. On **Doctor Doom's Fearfall** the 150-foot drop *is* real. For more even more heart-pounding action, the **Incredible Hulk** launches you out of a purple tunnel at 40 mph, then immediately inverts and plunges 105 feet toward the lagoon—only to loop around and do it again. On **Jurassic Park River Adventure**, you will take a water ride back 65 million years through the jungles of the Jurassic period; then the velociraptors escape and anything can happen. You'll be refreshed (and wet) after being plunged 85 feet into total darkness while escaping the *T. rex*. The little ones will enjoy **Pteranodon Flyers** soaring high above the prehistoric jungle and **Camp Jurassic** playground. Make sure to walk down the **Triceratops Discovery Trail** to see what's in the veterinary paddock. Over on the **Lost Continent**, twin serpents, Fire and Ice, pass within *inches* of each other during their roller-coaster dogfight on **Dueling Dragons**. My daughter still hasn't forgiven me for chickening out. So for the timid there's **The Flying Unicorn**, a junior roller coaster set in an enchanted forest. Sounds tame, but this one still had enough twists and drops to tickle my belly. The walk-through **Poseidon's Fury** showcases the king of the sea's power with water and fire explosions, including an impressive wave tunnel.

Get your towel out for the wacky water rides in **Toon Lagoon**. Help Popeye save Olive Oyl at **Popeye & Bluto's Bilge-Rat Barges**, a white-water adventure, then take care of Snidely Whiplash once and for all on **Dudley Do-Right's Ripsaw Falls**. The two-step waterfall near the end is one of the steepest of any flume ride adventures anywhere. The young and young-at-heart will enjoy **Seuss Landing**, complete with a spin on **The Cat in the Hat**, and an odd variety of Seuss characters on the **Caro-Seuss-El** that even the adults will want to ride. More Seussian characters can be found at **If I Ran the Zoo**, a great place for parents to sit while kids climb around the interactive play area. As you head out of the park you'll still be exhilarated, so hang around CityWalk for dinner, movies, or nightclub action. The day has only just begun.

Universal Studios Florida

♿ If you just can't get enough of Steven Spielberg's productions *Jaws*, *E.T.*, *Men in Black*, *Shrek*, *Twister*, and *Back to the Future* (yes, they were all his), then turn right at CityWalk and "ride the movies." The old standbys, **Jaws** and **Earthquake**, are still here (and still just as exciting), along with new 3- and 4-D shows, rides, and adventures. Universal's rides are without a doubt thrilling, but you won't need nerves of steel to go on anything at this park. Some rides will jolt you around a bit, though thankfully not one of them features death-defying drops; *those* rides are over at Islands of Adventure. But hold on: Just when I thought it was safe to wander around, I find out **Kong's Penn Station** is being turned into **Revenge of the Mummy**, a screaming roller-coaster ride with pyrotechnics, computer animation, Egyptian sets, and space-age robotics—all indoors and slated for a late-2004 opening. That said, you can safely step into any of the other movies around the park.

Go **Back to the Future** in your own time-travel vehicle. This simulator ride jolts you left, right, up, down, back, and forth while you hurtle through the past, present, and future in this Sensurround adventure. Board your own rocket and blast off on a wild chase on **Jimmy Neutron's Nicktoon Blast**. The individual simulators make this ride even more realistic in its out-of-control cartoon adventure. I waited for over an hour to see **Shrek 4-D**, and it was worth it. I just can't give away the 4-D part—it would spoil the adventure. Don't wait until the end of the day to see this one, or Jimmy Neutron, both on the exit path. **Terminator 2: 3-D Battle Across Time** merges live action and actors with 3-D special effects. Don't forget to take your 3-D glasses off during the live-action sequences. You'll have to fight off aliens in the interactive **Men in Black Alien Attack**. And you'll want to do it again and again, as the ending is different, depending on how many aliens you terminate while spinning around and at times moving backward—it's one of the most unusual rides in the park. You'll need to brace yourself during the intense seismic activity on **Earthquake—The Big One**. Ceilings collapse, pyrotechnics explode, and a wall of water rushes toward you as the authentic quake measures 8.3 on the Richter scale. If want more natural disasters, head over to **Twister**. To get the most out of this walk-on adventure, get into the story line, and then hold on as a real vortex whips into town. It's even got cows! Take a trip back to 1975 on a boat ride through Amity, but be warned: You'll never know when **Jaws** will charge the boat. You'll want to bring a change of clothes for the kids, and then head over to **Woody Woodpecker's Kid Zone** for water-based fun where **Curious George Goes to Town**. Climb the 30-foot spiderweb or twist and turn down the 200-foot water slide at **Fievel's Playland**. Jump into a crate and hang on for a wild and nutty roller-coaster ride through a nut factory on **Woody Woodpecker's Nuthouse Coaster**.

You'll need to arrive at least 15 minutes before showtimes for *Beetlejuice's Rock 'N' Roll Graveyard Revue*, *Blues Brothers*, *Extreme Ghostbusters*, *Animal Planet Live!*, *Universal Horror Make-up Show*, and the *Wild Wild West Stunt Show*. Make sure you pick up a show schedule, as some shows have only two performances a day.

Don't forget that Universal Studios is a working studio. You never know what show may be shooting on the day you arrive, or what celebrities may be wandering about. Stroll through the **Street Sets** in the New York and Hollywood sections, where an exhibit honoring America's favorite redhead is at **Lucy—A Tribute**. For studio soundstages, head over to **Production Central** for a peek at Stage 54 and Nickelodeon Studios, then discover the cinematic tricks of **Alfred Hitchcock: The Art of Making Movies**.

If you love anything on film, Universal Studios is the place to be. Toward the end of the day, I had just enough time to slip into the **E.T. Adventure**. And I'm so glad I didn't miss it. After taking a walk through tall woods, I boarded my "bike" and flew off to the stars to help E.T. save his world. This gentle, rolling ride is full of great scenes and not to be missed. After all, it was one of Spielberg's own favorites.

✷ The Other Parks

The smaller theme parks can be viewed in less than a day and are worth just as much attention. **Gatorland** is a must when visiting Florida; for a bit of serenity and biblical history check out **Holy Land Experience**. I am sorry to report that **Splendid China** closed at the end of 2003 and hope that at some point they will return.

GATORLAND ✐ ♿ How can you come to Florida and not go to **Gatorland, Alligator Capitol of the World** (407-855-5496 or 1-800-393-JAWS; www.gatorland.com), 14501 S Orange Blossom Trail? Let me dispel any myths that this is just a cheesy roadside attraction—it's not! The 110-acre theme park has been around for over 50 years, and has wisely grown with the times from a 1950s alligator farm to an amazing ecofriendly wildlife preserve. You can cover the park in just a few hours or stay all day enjoying the natural environment and educational shows and exhibits. Walk around the shockingly clean walkways past massive 'gators and crocodiles set in a natural environment. Gatorland wants you to learn about these prehistoric beasts, so four great shows get you up close and personal. Find out about the parts and personality of the alligator, and then cross over a bridge and sit on a real 8-footer at the **Gator Wrestling Show**. Watch trainers interact with a rare collection of crocodiles at **Jungle Crocs of the World**. Discover "what's in that box" at the **Up Close Encounters**, and don't miss the headliner show, **Gator Jumparoo**, where alligators and the most enormous crocodile you'll ever see (his name is Alf) will jump to new heights.

For hands-on fun, you can pet and feed deer, tortoises, emus, llamas, goats, and exotic birds at **Alligator Alley**. For more birds, enter the **Aviary** to feed the colorful and curious lorikeets. Kids will want to cool off at **Lily's Pad**, a mini water park. To get a bird's-eye view of over 100 'gators in their natural habitat, climb the three-story observation tower and look over the 10-acre breeding marsh and bird rookery—part of the Great Florida Birding Trail. Gatorland doesn't stop there. **Cypress Glades Adventure Tours** (see *Airboats*) picks you up at the park, and takes you deep into wild areas on airboat excursions. This half-day adventure takes you into the heart of the Florida wetlands and marshes, where you'll see even more 'gators. Open daily 9–5. Gatorland admission $20 adults, $10 children ages 3–12.

HOLY LAND EXPERIENCE Bringing a little piece of the Middle East to Central Florida, the **Holy Land Experience** (407-367-2065 or 1-866-872-4659; www.holylandexperience.com), 4655 Vineland Rd, reflects the devotion of Robert and Judith Van Kampen, who wanted a place to display their growing collection of biblical and archeological artifacts. Entering through a traditional Middle Eastern medina, visitors encounter large-scale replicas of **Christ's tomb at Calvary**, the **Temple of Jerusalem**, and other biblical sites, with regularly scheduled plays and pageants bringing the pages of the Bible to life. Interpretive signs explain the biblical significance of plantings in the lush gardens. At the scale model of **Jerusalem AD 66**, expect an entertaining talk on biblical history.

The centerpiece of the park is the **Scriptorium**, through which you'll walk on a 1-hour "guided" tour (at the pace of the museum's narrative and lighted sets) through five exhibit areas featuring the world's largest private biblical collection, with pieces dating back to cuneiform tablets from the city of Ur, 2000 B.C. In chronological order, each of the themed areas ushers you through an era of the history of the Bible, from its origins on papyrus to hand-copied scriptoria from the 12th through 15th centuries, through the Wyclif gospels and Gutenberg press to today. It's a fascinating walk through history, with only a little bit of sermonizing along the way. At the end of the tour, the **Ex Libris bookshop** has an excellent selection of Bibles and historical and religious tomes. There are thematic food stands and gift shops scattered throughout the park. Admission $29.75 adults, $19.75 ages 6–12, $5 parking; Jerusalem Gold Pass $69.75 provides annual admission. Modest dress (no shorts, please) is expected of guests; the park is popular with church groups.

✷ More Things to See

BASEBALL Catch the **Atlanta Braves** during spring training at **Disney's Wide World of Sports** (407-828-FANS; www.disneyworldsports.com) Feb–Apr 1. The "on property" sports training complex includes the Sports Experience multiskill playground for kids, offers weight-training facilities, and hosts ongoing amateur and professional training and competition year-round; general admission is an affordable $10 for ages 10-plus, $8 for those 3–10. During the season, the Class AA **Orlando Rays** call the complex home.

MARCHING DUCKS **Famous Peabody Ducks at the Peabody Orlando** (407-352-4000 or 1-800-PEABODY; www.peabodyorlando.com), 9801 International Dr. A Peabody tradition since 1930, the world-famous Peabody Mallard Ducks march to much pomp and circumstance from their "penthouse," down the elevator, and across a red carpet into the hotel's beautiful lobby fountain, where they spend the day splashing and grooming. Young and old alike will enjoy the antics of the drake and his four ladies-in-waiting as official Duckmaster Eric Anderson and the Honorary Duckmaster (or -mistress) escort them to their place of honor. Kids and famous celebrities have enjoyed being honorary Duckmasters, and you can, too. Call Eric well in advance of your trip if you would like to be one. Daily at 11 and 5. Free.

MUSEUMS ♿ If you thought the movie was phenomenal, then sail on over to **Titanic—The Exhibition** (407-248-1166), 8445 International Dr, now permanently docked at the Mercado. This captivating, and at times emotional, hourlong tour takes you through re-created sections of the ship and is cleverly narrated by actors in period costume. As I began my tour, I was told that each ticket bore an actual passenger's name, and that at the end of the voyage my class distinction—and, more importantly, whether or not I survived—would be revealed. I held a gentleman's ticket as Mr. Charles Chapman, which eerily enough was also my uncle's surname; my daughter was to be Mrs. Lizzie Faunthorpe. As we entered the Ship of Dreams, a young lad with thick Irish brogue told us of the vessel's architecture and escorted us throughout the various rooms recounting that fateful night. Passing through watertight doors, we entered a room kept at the same temperature as it was back on that evening in April 1912. After touching the "iceberg," we were ushered to the deck (also freezing), and the male passengers were asked to stay behind as the women continued on to the "lifeboats." The emotion was overwhelming. Even the men around me couldn't help but show their feelings, realizing that we would never see our loved ones again. Once through the doors, we learned our fate on the memorial wall; both my daughter and I were second-class passengers and did not survive. After the tour you are free to walk back through the exhibit for a closer look at photographs, a millionaire's suite, the grand staircase, recovered artifacts, and costumes from the movie. The gift shop tastefully displays books, tapes, music, crystal, jewelry, and RMS *Titanic* logo items. Open daily; first tour at 10, last at 8.

An indoor garden, waterfalls, and 12-foot-high mountains set the scene for 14 model railroad trains and over 30 trestles and tunnels at the **Trolley & Train Museum** (407-363-9002), 8990-A International Dr. Climb aboard a California Victorian-style trolley or small replica of an 1880 locomotive. Open daily. $6 for the museum, $3 for a trolley ride.

The very best of rock-and-roll memorabilia is locked in the **Hard Rock Vault** (407-599-7625; www.hardrock.com), 8437 International Dr. Guided tours take you through a stash of over 1,000 pieces, a kick-butt listening room, an art gallery, and superstar dressing rooms, from Elvis, the Beatles, and Clapton to heavy metal and punk. Daily 9 AM–midnight. $15 adults, $9 children 6–12.

SHRINE **Mary, Queen of the Universe Shrine** (407-239-4010; www.maryqueenoftheuniverse.org), 8300 Vineland Ave, was built to accommodate the spiritual needs of the vast number of visiting Catholic tourists. Completed in 1986, the 2,000-seat church and 22-acre sanctuary are open to all and a welcome respite after a day spent shopping or at the theme parks. At the center of the tranquil Rosary Garden, overlooking a small pond, sits an 1875 statue of Mary holding the divine infant; in the Mother and Child Chapel, a bronze statue honors the universal symbol of motherhood; and the shrine's museum houses many Marian art treasures, including a 17th-century oil painting of *The Assumption of the Blessed Virgin* by Spanish artist Bartolome Murillo. The extensive gift shop displays a fine selection of quality religious gifts. Shrine open daily. Gift shop open Mon–Fri 8:30–5, Sat and Sun 8:30–8.

✳ To Do

AIRBOATS **Cypress Glades Adventure Tours** (407-855-5496) picks you up at Gatorland (see *The Other Parks*) and takes you deep into natural Florida on an

BALLOONING Visitor interest in ballooning has, well, ballooned substantially over the last decade, leading to stiff competition among a large number of operators who'll take you up, up, and away to see the Disney property gleaming from the air. However, one operator stands head and shoulders above the crowd. Since 1983, the pilots at **Orange Blossom Balloons** (407-239-7677; www.orangeblossomballoons.com) have taken off at daybreak daily (weather permitting) to drift across the Orlando skies. I'd never been in a balloon before, and was a bit frightened at the concept—I don't do well with heights. So it amazed me to find that we were several hundred feet in the air and I'd never felt us lift off. There is no sensation of movement, except the breeze blowing through your hair; you look down, and it's as if you're walking on air—or as Captain Jeff put it, "It's like standing above the earth and having it moved below you." The duly promised spectacular sunrise over the Magic Kingdom and downtown Orlando was soon eclipsed by the beauty of watching our two sister balloons in colorful flight below and above us. Captain Bob skimmed the treetops to put a spin on our descent so we'd end up in an open space after the hour-long flight, which was soon followed by a traditional champagne toast and all-you-can-eat breakfast buffet. Cost? $150, including breakfast and postflight champagne.

ORANGE BLOSSOM BALLOONS DRIFTING OVER ORLANDO

Sandra Friend

intimate trip through lakes and locks. See Florida where there are no houses and very few other boats. Lunch included. Half day $55, $45 for ages 3–12; night rates $38 and $28.

AVIATION **Air Florida Charter** (407-888-4114; www.airfloridacharter.com) operates small aircraft out of the Orlando Executive Airport near downtown but specializes in 45-minute aerial tours over the theme parks, with souvenir photo.

Air Florida Helicopters (407-354-1400; www.airfloridahelicopters.com), 8990 International Dr, is one of the longer-standing helicopter ride operators in the area, operating from their oh-so-visible helipad on I-Drive. Now flying Robinsons, one of the safest choppers around.

BICYCLING At **Walt Disney World** rent old-fashioned tandem bikes at **Disney's Boardwalk** and **Port Orleans Resort** (see *Resorts*), or grab a standard road bike or mountain bike at **Fort Wilderness** (see *Campgrounds*) to hit the many miles of paved trails under the pines.

BIRDING Visit **Tibet-Butler Preserve** (see *Nature Center*) to listen to the ospreys cry over Lake Tibet; keep alert to identify warblers in the palmetto scrub.

BOATING **Walt Disney World** (407-WDW-PLAY) boasts the world's largest fleet of rental watercraft, more than 500 boats ranging from mini Watermouse powerboats (safe for teens) to pontoon boats. Skim the surface of Bay Lake or paddle down miles of canals; check in at the Polynesian Village Resort, Contemporary Resort, or Fort Wilderness for details.

DINNER SHOWS

I-Drive area

♿ The only show that doesn't serve alcohol, **Dolly Parton's Dixie Stampede** (1-866-443-4943; www.dixiestampede.com), 8251 Vineland Ave, is an American extravaganza. In the fabulous preshow, Australia's Electric Cowboy Greg Anderson and his horse Starstruck light up the night as he weaves through the crowd all the way up to the balcony! In the main arena, the arrival of the American buffalo will take your breath away. There's lots of Dolly's southern hospitality as the story of young America unfolds through friendly rivalry between North and South. You'll see cowboys, Union soldiers, southern belles, and Native Americans perform magnificent horsemanship and lots of hometown American singing and dancing. This is one of the best dinner show banquets; the eat-with-your-hands four-course feast boasts a whole Cornish game hen, hickory-smoked barbecue pork, vegetable soup, roasted potatoes, corn-on-the-cob, a yummy buttery biscuit, and an apple turnover. Stop by to see the horses; they're housed out front in a beautiful open-air stable every day from 10 AM to showtime. One to two shows every night. $44 adults, $19 ages 4–11.

Pirate's Dinner Adventure (407-248-0590; www.piratesdinneradventure.com), 6400 Carrier Dr. The preshow opens with an appetizer buffet set in an old seaport village. You'll have plenty of time to visit the local merchants or stop by the Pirate's Maritime Museum. Developed by Mel Fisher, the museum portrays pirate life through historical artifacts and examples of pirate crimes and punishments. The main show features a full-sized replica of an 18th-century Spanish galleon set in a large lagoon. Ship's mates defend the vessel with special effects, swashbuckling swordplay, and aerial acrobatics from 70-foot masts. This show is full of loud explosions and pyrotechnics, so it may be too much for the little ones. The feast includes salad, roast chicken, tender beef or shrimp, rice or red potatoes, mixed vegetables, and apple cobbler. Complimentary beer, wine, soft drinks, and coffee are offered only during the main show. Stay around for the Buccaneer Bash immediately following. One show nightly. $47 adults, $28 ages 3–11.

♿ Not quite up for a full-scale extravaganza with more crowds? The **Outta Control Magic Show** is just the place to unwind. This intimate dinner show is 90 minutes of high-energy comedy and improvisation. You'll wonder how only two guys can keep you so entertained. They are fabulous and funny! There's no preshow, but lots of audience participation. A simple dinner of unlimited hand-tossed pizza, popcorn, beer, wine, and soda will more than satisfy you. $18 adults, $15 ages 4–12 and seniors. Magic Combo package ($32) includes dinner show and admission to Wonderworks (see *Funhouses*).

♿ Who did it? That's the question you'll be asking yourself all night. **Sleuth's Mystery Dinner Theater** (407-363-1985 or 1-800-393-1985; www.sleuths.com), 7508 Universal Blvd, offers nine different comedy-mysteries, so you can come back again and again and never really know whodunit. Put your investigative talents to the test while interacting with cast members to solve the crime. Listen carefully, take notes, and ask questions—you might be chosen for a cameo role. Full-course dinner is served with hors d'oeuvres; salad; a choice of Cornish hen and baked potato, lasagna and meatballs, or prime rib and baked potato; vegetables; a delicious "mystery" dessert; and unlimited beer, wine, soft drinks, coffee, and iced tea. Nightly. No preshow. $42 adults, $24 ages 3–11.

🖍 **Merry Mystery Dinner Theatre** (407-363-1985 or 1-800-393-1985; www.sleuths.com), 7508 Universal Blvd, offers two different shows geared for the kids. In the comedy-mystery *The Faire of the Shire*, discover the clues to save the Shire and outwit the evil baron. The *Magical Journey of Juniper Junior* takes you into a Harry Potter–like realm of supernatural imagination to foil an evil wizard. Part of Sleuth's Mystery Dinner Theater group. Call ahead; shows are sporadic throughout the month. $28 adults, $16 children.

Lake Buena Vista

♿ Saturday nights are just deadly at **MurderWatch Mystery Dinner Show** (407-827-6534; www.murderwatch.com) at the Grosvenor on the mezzanine level, 1850 Hotel Plaza Blvd. Dreamland Productions has been putting on interactive murder mysteries for over 15 years, and only on Sat night. The variety of scripts, written and directed by members of Mystery Writers of America, keeps well-cast professional actors fresh and audiences begging for more. This total immersion in interactive theater has nonstop action. You'll need to pay attention—all is not what it seems. Just when you think the murder has been solved, think again; there just might be a twist! In *Mystery Mayhem and the Mob*, you'll meet members of the Thomasino "family"—Italian mobsters out on the town celebrating Don Thomasino's daughter's engagement to a famous race-car driver. A dozen or so guests are selected as special operatives to help the FBI protect them as they wander about the gorgeous banquet hall "tawkin'" to guests. Will the FBI be successful? Or will rival families, or maybe one of their own, rub them out once and for all? This is your chance to sport your nicer clothes, unlike the other shows; this one is in an elegant ballroom, and hands down the best

THE INSIDE DISH ON DINNER SHOWS Themed dinner shows have their own special appeal, and each production is unique. From the comedy of vaudeville revues, to interactive detective mysteries where you solve the crime, to full-scale productions with horses and pyrotechnics, you'll love them all. After a long day at the parks, you might think that a late night out may be too much for the kids, or for you, but much to my surprise everyone remained wide awake throughout the entire show. I like the idea that I didn't have to wait in line, my seats were reserved, I didn't have to order anything, and in some shows beer and wine were free, and free flowing.

There is an order to the way things work at dinner shows. First, unless noted, there is a preshow about an hour before the scheduled performance. This gives you a chance to arrive on time, and for them to hawk their souvenirs. For whatever you paid for your ticket, plan at least half that for trinkets and memorable goblets and mugs. Not that you should come late; the preshows are as entertaining as the main event, and help set the mood. Once inside you will sit with other guests—at long benches facing the action at the larger shows, and around community tables at the mystery and comedy shows. Except for buffet dinners, your meal will come in stages and you'll have no control over what it is or when it appears, although all the shows handle serving seamlessly.

Depending on the show, expect to spend anywhere from 90 minutes to 3 hours being entertained; all shows require reservations, although last-minute tickets can often be purchased. Admission fees can range from $16 upward to a whopping $50. Almost all the shows have discount coupons on their web sites with additional coupons in flyers and kiosks around town—some as much as half off. The admission does not include gratuity, and the servers expect one, as it's really their main paycheck. So do you tip on the full ticket price or what you think the food portion would cost? Most servers are happy with $5 per adult and $2–3 for each kid. Guests with allergies to hay and animals should take the necessary precautions at live animal shows.

food of any dinner show. The lavish buffet is prepared by Disney resort chefs and includes everything you'd expect from a top resort, including roast prime rib of beef and desserts to "die" for. Quality wine, beer, soda, and coffee are complimentary and unlimited, with mixed drinks available for a fee. Two shows on Sat night only. No preshow. $40 adults, $11 ages 9 and under.

SeaWorld

♿ **Makahiki Luau in The Waterfront at SeaWorld—Seafire Inn** (407-363-2613; www.seaworldorlando.com). Enter the exotic South Seas at this exciting luau celebration of ancient rituals, and rhythmic music and dance, presented on stage in authentic costumes of Native islanders. At the preshow, the island chief arrives amid lots of dancing and drumming. Here you'll get a complimentary drink; inside, you'll have to pay for beer, wine, and tropical drinks. Soft drinks, coffee, and tea are free and unlimited. The Polynesian fare is more than you could ever eat, and the pause in entertainment while the meal is served is well thought out, so you have time to enjoy your family's company. Adults will enjoy tropical salad, Hawaiian chicken, sweet-and-sour pork, mahimahi in piña colada sauce, fried rice, stir-fried vegetables, and dessert—all served family style with extras on request. Children will get a meal of chicken fingers or hot dogs in a souvenir bucket. You'll need to pay the adult fee if your kids will be eating the adult meal. This is one of the earliest dinner shows, with the preshow starting at 6 and your meal hitting the table around 7:15. You'll be out by 9, and directly after the show you can enjoy a brief admission to SeaWorld during extended hours. $43 adults, $28 ages 3–11.

Universal

Participate in an extravagant Hawaiian feast and dinner show at the **Wantilan Luau** (407-503-DINE) at the Royal Pacific Resort (see *Resorts*). Suckling pig roasts in a pit in the midst of a tropical garden; Hawaiian dancers perform as servers bring around tropical fruit salad, tropical fruitcake, and ahi tuna poke salad. Sat night, $50 adults, $29 children 12 and under; reservations required.

US 192

A family business for more than 15 years, **Arabian Nights** (407-239-9223; www.arabian-nights.com), 6255 W Irlo Bronson Hwy, presents a breathtaking performance: 60 horses and 30 performers in a dazzling area of magical scenes. I kept forgetting to eat my dinner while riders and horses swept past for nearly 2 hours, weaving together the story of a royal wedding while showcasing the talents of 16 different breeds and one extra-special horse, Walter Farley's Black Stallion, who performs "at liberty"—no rider! The three-course dinner includes unlimited beer and wine. $44 adults, $27 ages 3–11. For an extra $15, the VIP tour provides an extra hour of interaction with the horses on the arena floor and a private tour of the stables, plus preferential seating in the first three rows. Reservations recommended; although the arena holds 1,300 guests, it does sell out!

The other two shows on US 192—**Medieval Times Dinner and Tournament** and **Capone's Dinner & Show**—are farther east and have full reviews in "Orlando South."

FAMILY ACTIVITIES Beyond the attractions, the family can unwind with a round of miniature golf in any one of many venues. The popular **Fantasia Gardens**, with its scale replicas of renowned golf holes, is in the Epcot resort area. **Disney's Winter Summerland** course, with a North Pole theme, adjoins Blizzard Beach. **Congo River Golf** follows the footsteps of African explorers, while swashbucklers will want to head to **Pirate's Cove Adventure**, both on I-Drive.

Many midway attractions offer just good wholesome fun. Drive go-carts the old-fashioned way, on elevated wooden racks, at **Magical Midway**. The Avalanche track has a 30-degree drop off the top of the arcade building. Experience free fall from the Space Shot Tower, then face off against your friends on the bumper boats and cars. Over at **Fun Spot Action Park** you'll drive go-carts around twists and turns on a concrete track. The park also offers an arcade and small selection of midway rides. Down off US 192, **Old Town** is a great place to hang out after the parks have closed, especially on Fri and Sat nights when classic cars cruise the strip. Stroll down brick streets browsing 75 specialty shops, eight restaurants, and an assortment of midway rides, including the world's tallest slingshot. The **Windstorm** roller coaster with 80-degree banked turns and a g-force of 4.7 gives thrills as good as the coasters at the big parks.

FISHING Yes, you can cast for bass in the shadow of Cinderella's Castle at **Walt Disney World** (407-WDW-PLAY) on a 2-hour guided trip on Bay Lake, with all tackle and cold drinks provided. Catch-and-release only; no fishing license required.

FUNHOUSES

Downtown Disney

DisneyQuest is Florida's ultimate funhouse, with five floors of interactive fun and games. Yes, you can plunk the kids down in front of skee-ball and other classic arcade games, or play Space Invaders until midnight. But I got hooked on virtual reality: Design your own roller coaster, then ride it in a simulator on Virtual Space Mountain—and if it isn't hard-core enough for you, the attendant will conjure up a wild ride! Or grab a paddle and go white-water rafting on the Virtual Jungle Cruise, dodging dinosaurs and lava flows while the waves splash your face. It's a perfect rainy-day destination (complete with restaurants and snack bars), or you can spend your entire evening having a blast; $32 adults, $26 ages 3–9.

I-Drive

Ripley's Believe It or Not Odditorium (407-345-0501; www.ripleysorlando.com) stays open late to catch the curious with displays of Robert Ripley's international finds that made the phrase *believe it or not!* famous. Like its original St. Augustine counterpart, the walk-through 16-gallery attraction has its bizarre displays strung together by funhouse favorites like spinning tunnels and warped mirrors. Of course, I love the fact that it's slipping into a sinkhole. Open daily 8 AM–1 AM; $16 adults, $11 ages 4–12.

Skull Kingdom (407-354-1564; www.skullkingdom.com), 5931 American Way. Before 5 the monsters are sleeping, and this haunted house of ghouls and the macabre is available for tours. After 5 anything goes. You'll have 15 minutes to run for your life—and you'll want to run. Not for the timid or squeamish. Beware: Near the witching hour, the monsters are wide awake. Day show $9 all ages. Night show $14 and strongly recommended for ages over 14 only.

✐ **Wonderworks** (407-351-8800; www.wonderworksonline.com), 9067 International Dr. It first catches my eye as I drive up I-Drive. It looks as though a secret laboratory, housed in a three-story ancient structure, has crash-landed upside down! I cautiously enter through a rising mist as the building creaks and moans. My first clue that this is no ordinary funhouse comes when I pass over a bridge while an optical illusion spins around the walls and ceiling. I actually have to hang on and close my eyes to get across. Stepping off the bridge, I enter the laboratory where testing is being done on earthquakes and hurricanes. Hang on tight, real tight, in either of these experiments. The 1989 San Francisco earthquake, measuring 5.3 on the Richter scale, is re-created at your kitchen table, while over in a subway car, winds rip through at 65 mph. Heading up to the second floor, enter a scientific world of imagination. Over 100 interactive exhibits range from realistic to virtual reality. Design your own roller coaster and then ride it. Dance like you've never danced before as your psychedelic shadow grooves with you. Find out what you will look like in 25 years with computer aging, or try out the many "face-lifts." Strike a pose and leave your shadow behind. Climb a rotating wall. Stand your hair on end on the Bridge of Fire. Play a tune on the *big* piano keyboard. Challenge a 7-foot basketball player as you are immersed into a virtual-reality court, or avoid the sharks and barracudas as you swim under the sea. Optical illusions are everywhere. I was told to allow 2 hours for the experience, but I stayed for 5! The time flew by so fast I missed the laser tag and arcade games on the third floor. Open daily 9 AM–midnight. $17 adults, $13 ages 4–12. Magic Combo package ($32) includes Wonderworks and admission to the Outta Control Magic Show dinner show (see *Dinner Shows*).

US 192

You'll have chills running up your spine in the three-story **Grimm Haunted House in Old Town**. This old-fashioned fright house, with lots of stairs and hallways, is customized to your fright level, so it's okay for adventurous young ones. Open daily. Sun–Thu noon–11, Fri and Sat noon–midnight. $8 adults, $6 ages 10 and under.

GOLF Central Florida is a golfer's paradise, with more than 100 courses radiating out from the theme park area. Without driving all over creation, how can you choose the one for you? Contact **Tee Times USA** (1-888-465-3356; www.teetimesusa.com), a free golfer's matchmaker service, if you will, that helps you pick a course and make reservations. Disney's courses (407-WDW-PLAY) include **Eagle Pines**, **Osprey Ridge**, and **Lake Buena Vista**, where you might rub elbows with Tiger Woods and other top golfers taking on their 99 holes of golf.

MOTORCYCLING I know you were Born to Ride! At **Harley-Davidson Real Riding Adventure** (407-423-0346 or 1-877-740-3770; www.orlandoharley.com), 3770 37th St, you'll first learn important safety instructions and then gradually get to know the Harley-made 500cc Buell Blast. This personalized 1½-hour course teaches you how to shift gears, turn corners, slalom, and then come to a rolling stop. The one-on-one course is offered twice a week, and you get a really cool certificate at the end. No motorcycle license necessary, but you'll need further instruction to get one. Reservations are a must. Wear hard shoes and bring a long-sleeved shirt. $149. Have your own bike? Orlando Harley also teaches basic and experienced courses and offers official examinations for the Florida DMV.

PARASAILING Glide with grace above Bay Lake at **Disney's Contemporary Resort** (407-939-0754), with a bird's-eye view of the Magic Kingdom as you rise to 600 feet. The unique launch boat allows you room for takeoff and landing without getting your feet wet.

RACE-CAR DRIVING Learn to handle a 600-horsepower stock car on the three-corner track of the **Richard Petty Driving Experience** (1-800-BE-PETTY) at Walt Disney World, where professional race-car drivers offer you experiences ranging from a three-lap ride-along ($89) to three hands-on training sessions of 30 laps ($1,199). Overheard from one satisfied customer: "The car sticks to the track like glue!" Open daily 9–5, reservations suggested.

Rev your engines while the lights count down red–yellow–green, then *go*. Strap into the life-sized race cars at **G-Force** (407-397-2509), next to SkyCoaster (see *Skydropping*) off US 192, and hold on for one wild ride. You and your passenger will race on a straight track alongside another car. Once you hit the pedal, the car launches like a jet fighter, and in less than 2 seconds you'll reach 120 mph. It's all over in less than 2 seconds, but you'll feel the adrenaline for hours. Make sure to get the video for instant replays. Open daily 10–midnight. $27 for driver, $10 for passenger.

SPA **Canyon Ranch Spa at Gaylord Palms** (407-586-205; www.gaylordhotels.com), 6000 W Osceola Pkwy. Your journey begins with a eucalyptus steam bath and shower, and then you'll relax in the waiting room while cool cucumbers soothe your eyes. An attendant escorts you to your private sanctuary for personalized body treatments like their signature Euphoria for the best in stress relief, with warm sage and geranium oils, or the Endless Energy Pedicure for those tired feet. Avoid end-of-the-day appointments so that when your treatment is over, you'll have time to relax in the coed tearoom with a cup of selected herbs, lunch in the Everglades Atrium, or enjoy a swim in Gaylord's outdoor pool. Open daily 8–9.

SCUBA DIVING AND SNORKELING At The Living Seas pavilion in **Epcot**, visitors will wave and point as you drift through a 6-million-gallon saltwater aquarium, getting to know the loggerheads and sergeant majors on the coral reef. Certified divers are welcome to dive on the twice-daily **DiveQuest** programs (407-WDW-PLAY); rates include equipment, so leave your dive gear at home. On the **Epcot Seas Aqua Tour**, snorkelers without scuba certification use scuba-assisted snorkeling equipment to explore the reef.

Visitors to **Disney's Typhoon Lagoon** (see *Water Parks*) snorkel above leopard and nurse sharks and schools of tropical fish at Shark Reef, included in the park's admission.

SKATEBOARDING Skaters from beginners to advanced take to the 31,000-square-foot **Vans Skate Park** (407-351-3881), 5220 International Dr, in the Festival Bay Outlet Mall. The wood-and-concrete bowl reaches depths up to 8 feet, with ramps surfaced in Finland birch. Skateboards and safety equipment available for rent for $5–10 per 2-hour session.

SKYDROPPING Just off US 192 next to Old Town, two vertical columns reach toward the sky. Then you notice something dropping from them. What's going on here? Sometime back in the early 1990s, bungee jumping morphed into a safer version of the vertical drop, and **Skycoaster** (407-397-2509), 2850 Florida Plaza Blvd, Kissimmee, became an instant hit among thrill-seekers around the globe. The newest version tops out at 300 feet, the tallest of all the skycoasters. It's so high, in fact, that it requires aircraft beacons. Fitted with an FAA-approved flight suit and skydiving harness, I was attached to a cable and then winched backward and upward. Climbing to 100 feet, you'll get a great view with Disney just off to the northwest. At 200 feet, uh . . . what did I get myself into? At 300 feet my head began to spin and I just wanted to get down. A pull of the cord accomplished that, and I dived headfirst *screaming* as I raced toward the pond below. At 76 mph I leveled out and swung back and forth, skimming the treetops. At night you'll get an amazing view of city lights and area attractions. Single rider $37, two riders $64, three riders $81. Don't forget the $16 video. You'll want to capture this one for the grandkids.

SURFING Surf's up with **Craig Caroll's Cocoa Beach Surf School** (407-WDW-PLAY) every Tue morning at **Typhoon Lagoon** (see *Water Parks*), where for an additional fee over park admission participants learn how to "hang 10" in a safe non-shark-infested environment—the wave pool. School runs 6:30–9 AM, prior to the park's opening.

SWIMMING In addition to the water parks, all of the area's resort hotels feature elaborate swimming pools, from the 750,000-gallon mini water park with shipwreck at **Disney's Yacht Club Resort** to the intimate winding stream with cozy little nooks for sipping a piña colada at the **Hyatt Regency Grand Cypress**. No matter where you're staying, expect the pool to be a focal point of activity on hot afternoons.

TRAIL RIDING **Disney's Fort Wilderness** (407-WDW-PLAY) offers trail rides ($35) on mellow Paso Finos, quarter horses, and others gentle enough for the kids, following a beaten track for 45 minutes through a remnant of pine flatwoods where you will almost always see deer. At **Grand Cypress Equestrian Center** (407-239-1938 or 1-800-835-7377; www.grandcypress.com/equestrian), 1 Equestrian Dr (off FL 535, 4 miles northwest of I-4 at Lake Buena Vista), participate in a riding academy approved by the British

SKYDIVING That funky blue building towering off Universal Blvd and I-Drive beckons you to come inside for the ride of your life. I wish I had gone to **Sky Venture Skydiving Wind Tunnel** (407-903-1150; www.skyventure.com), 6805 Visitors Circle, before actually taking the plunge from 13,500 feet. Knowing then what I know now would have enhanced the experience, and taken away some of the tenser moments. You'll still feel real skydiving flight, but this time from only a few feet off the ground. And you'll get an incredible workout. It's amazing just how many muscles it takes to balance on a column of air pushing 120 mph winds at you. After only two 1-minute flights, I was sore for several days.

Check in with Ron Landon at the office and get a taste of what's to come on the live-feed monitors, then head up the steps for a preflight briefing where flight instructors, like Ron Henderson and Dan Perry, tell you how to hold your body and what hand signals you'll need while in the tunnel. Then you'll gear up in a real flight suit, goggles, and helmet and head to the observation room, where you might see real skydiving teams practicing their routines. Once inside the tunnel you'll sit comfortably in a waiting area with about 12 other fliers. When it's your turn, you'll come to the door of the tunnel and just fall in. It's that easy. The air immediately catches you, and you're airborne. You'll have a real-time flight of about 1 minute while your instructor helps you position your body for turns and higher altitude, but more importantly keeps you from banging into the wall. Depending on your body position, you fly about 4 to 6 feet off the wire mesh base. Don't worry, the fans won't suck you up, but if you catch the wind just right you can get as high as 15

Horse Society, with leisurely Western-style wilderness trail rides starting at $45.

WATER PARKS **Disney's Blizzard Beach**. Native pine trees poke out of snowcapped faux Rocky Mountains, giving the place a surreal Colorado feel; even the bathhouses, gift shops, and restaurants look like they belong at an Aspen ski resort. The ski theme extends to a chairlift that carries you up to the highest peak with the most intense water slides. Open daily 10–5; $32 adults, $25 ages 3–9. Free parking.

Disney's Typhoon Lagoon. If I could pick only one water park to visit in all of Florida, this would be the one. Lush tropical plantings usher you in to a world of watery fun, centering on a massive wave pool with sporadic waves. Secret trails lead up and over rocky mountains, across swinging bridges, and through caves; visitors can snorkel across Shark Reef, or grab a tube and drift down a lazy river under the blooming raintrees all day. Open daily 10–5; $32 adults, $26 ages 3–9. Across from Downtown Disney; free parking.

feet. Wildman Dan showed me just how high, as he caught the air, shot upward, did a few somersaults, dived, and flipped into a sitting position.

Two minutes are all you'll need. I sent my daughter back in again and again for photos, and after the fourth minute she was done. With the recent upgrades of bigger motors and wind controls, wind speed can now be changed in 2 to 3 seconds to accommodate any size or skill of fliers. And instead of tiny windows, your friends and family can now watch you through 9-foot acrylic panels from the comfortable observation area. Whether you plan to do a real skydive or not, you should at least try this Peter Pan experience. Adults need to be in relatively good shape and under 250 pounds. Kids can fly, too—sometimes better than the adults. The little ones I saw there had the time of their life. Open weekdays 2–midnight, weekends noon–midnight. Reservations strongly recommended. $39 adults, $34 ages 5–12. Videos available for $16.

SHERRI LEMON RECEIVES FLIGHT INSTRUCTIONS AT SKY VENTURE.

Kathy Wolf

✐ You'll have something to scream about at **Wet 'n Wild** (407-351-3200; www.wetnwild.com), 6200 International Dr, with exciting thrill rides down a water pipeline, through a twisting dark tunnel, down a 76-foot vertical drop, or "flushed" around and around in a giant bowl. When it's time to take it easy, float down the Lazy River or splash around the ocean-like beach. Open daily. $33 adults, $27 ages 3–9.

WATERSKIING Learn to ski, kneeboard, or wakeboard at **Sammy Duvall's Water Sports Centre** (407-939-0754) at **Disney's Contemporary Resort**, where you can book a tournament-level ski boat and learn to ski with a professional instructor; sessions last 1 hour.

✷ Green Space

NATURE CENTER ✐ Hiding just beyond touristy Lake Buena Vista, **Tibet-Butler Preserve** (407-876-6696), 8777 CR 535, protects a precious 440 acres of pine flatwoods, bayheads, and scrub along the shore of Lake Tibet; 3.5 miles of well-maintained interpretive hiking trails wind through the forest. Kids and adults alike will enjoy the exhibits at the environmental center.

PARK At **West Beach Park**, 9227 Winter Garden–Vineland Rd (FL 535), shaded picnic pavilions overlook the sweep of cypress-lined Lake Tibet, and the playground has a big canopy over it—great shelter from those afternoon rains! Open 8–7 daily.

✷ Lodging

BED & BREAKFAST

Lake Buena Vista 32836

Perrihouse (1-800-780-4830), 10417 Vista Oaks Court. Sixteen acres of solitude just 10 minutes from Disney—that's the big secret that is Perrihouse, a quiet retreat near Lake Tibet. Owners Matt and Becky Manganella pride themselves on creating a comfortable nest for their guests. Each room ($105–150) has its own bath and exterior entrance; guests share a warm den lined with birdhouses and filled with books and videos, a pool and hot tub, and gardens designated a backyard urban bird sanctuary. I couldn't ask for a more perfect place to kick back with a novel and take a break poolside between hours on my feet at Disney.

HOTELS AND MOTELS

Lake Buena Vista 32830

Most major motel chains are represented on Palm Pkwy, which is a quieter and less congested place to stay than the entertainment complex that is I-Drive; most of the properties are new or newly refurbished, and an easy drive to Disney's "back door" via Downtown Disney. Here are a few I recommend:

From the road, it looks like an apartment complex, and indeed, **Clarion Suites** (407-238-1700 or 1-800-423-8604; www.clarionflorida.com), 8451 Palm Pkwy, provides the amenities of home for short-term stays; their one-bedroom units have more square footage than most Orlando apartments. Each time-share is individually owned but collectively rented out at standard prices through the front desk. The complex includes a swimming pool, whirlpool, playground, workout room, basketball court, and billiards room. From $67–74 for a hotel room up to $150–169 for a two-bedroom deluxe villa sleeping 10, it's a great bargain for families.

I have it on the best authority (my sister, a former Hilton employee) that the **Hilton in the Walt Disney World Resort** (407-827-4000), 1751 Hotel Plaza Blvd, rocks. Just as at the Disney Resort hotels, you're treated to an early entrance to the theme parks, and it's an easy stroll to Downtown Disney. The spacious four-star accommodations include top-notch amenities like dual-line telephones, mini bar, coffeemaker, and double vanities in the bathroom. Rates start at $149; family suites and multiday package deals available.

Since 1996 **Holiday Inn Family Suites** (407-387-5437 or 1-877-387-KIDS; www.hifamilysuites.com), 14500 Continental Gateway, has been dedicated a kid-friendly and safe environment. This all-suite hotel features themed **Kid Suites** that gives kids their own special space complete with entertainment center and bunk beds. Choose natural settings like Jungle,

Manatee, and Endangered Species Birds; food themes like Camp Kellogg, A&W All American, and Coca-Cola Polar Bears; or science and history rooms like Space Exploration, Choo Choo and Historical Trains, and Hot Air Balloons. There's certainly a theme to satisfy your little one's imagination. Parents can stretch out in their own king- or queen-bedded room, and the whole family will enjoy the family room and full kitchen. Take the kids down to the train-themed playground and zero-depth-entry pool, making it great for toddlers. Play miniature golf at Putt Putt Junction or take a train ride around the property. Girls will want to stop by **Sugar & Spice** kids salon for a Manigirl ($20), Pedilady ($32), Fantasy Facial ($35), or Jamaican braids. The boys aren't left out, either; they'll experience the spa from a guy's point of view as a Pirate, Commando, or rock star Celebrity ($15). The complimentary full breakfast buffet has different items each morning, so you won't get bored. The resort takes great interest in the safety of your children. From the moment you enter your room, your television provides an entertaining safety show aimed at both kids and parents. High gates surround all the pools, so even the best climbers can't scale them. And resort security staff are clearly identified, making a safe haven for a lost youngster. An adorable place for families, this resort has a lot of excitement; nonfamily travelers may find it overwhelming at times. Two- and three-bedroom suites range $152–400 a night, with special rates about $50 less.

✐ The **Sheraton Safari Hotel** (407-239-0444), 12205 Apopka-Vineland Rd, just looks like fun—walk inside, and you're immersed into an African theme. Spacious, comfortable rooms provide in-room safe, coffeemaker, dataport, and more. The kids will love being spit out of the mouth of a 79-foot python into the swimming pool, and you'll love relaxing with a cool tropical drink at the **Zanzibar** lounge. The 489 family-priced units include standard rooms ($89–109) and large suites ($109–169).

I-Drive 32819

Richard Kessler (www.kesslercollection.com) just doesn't own any bad hotels. Each of the Kessler Collection includes his special touch with designer interiors and gracious service. Throughout the properties you'll find hand-selected fine art and sculptures equivalent to those seen in galleries and museums. Kessler's properties on I-Drive are the pink **Doubletree Castle** with towering spires, decorated with European art and complemented by Renaissance music, and the **Red Horse Inn** with hand-sawn old-growth cypress accented by lots of hammered and polished copper with a southwestern flair. The Doubletree Castle (407-345-4511 or 1-800-95-CASTLE) has rooms and suites with king and queen beds; $99–229. The Red Horse Inn (407-351-4100) has rooms and studios with double and queen beds; $65–100.

The **Peabody Orlando** (407-352-4000 or 1-800-PEABODY; www.peabodyorlando.com), 9801 International Dr, is only one of two hotels in the Orlando area receiving the Mobil 4-Star Award, and it gets my vote as well. From the very moment you drive up under the covered entrance you'll be greeted with the friendly valet staff, most of them longtimers with tenures of up to 18 years. What makes this group so special is that they are direct employees of the hotel and not a vendor concession. I hope they don't change that. Once inside, the staff continue to generate southern hospitality. Don't miss the famous Peabody Marching Ducks (see *Marching Ducks*) as they parade down the red carpet at 11 and 5 each day. Rates are a steep $395–485, but travelers will find bargains as low as $149 during the holiday season when conventions wane.

Universal Studios 32819
Hard Rock Hotel (407-503-ROCK), 5800 Universal Blvd. Want to rub elbows with a rock star? So does most of Orlando, making this themed Loews Hotel—a virtual "Hotel California"—a favorite hangout on the last Thu of each month during "Velvet Sessions," when members of world-renowned bands like Cheap Trick, Twisted Sister, and the Lovin' Spoonful stop in for a jam. Rock and roll permeates the grounds, even underwater in the swimming pools! Bedecked with memorabilia, it's one sizzling place. Rates start around $189.

ERIC ANDERSON AND THE FAMOUS PEABODY MARCHING DUCKS

Kathy Wolf

RESORTS

Disney
With 30 uniquely themed resorts, **Walt Disney World** (407-W-DISNEY; www.disneyworld.com) has nearly 28,000 rooms scattered across their property, separated into several tiers of pricing: value (from $77), moderate (from $133), deluxe (from $194), and home-away-from-home (from $214). As my family has discovered over the years, you can wrangle a much better deal (see *Theme Park Tips*), but it takes some work. The most popular resort groupings are clustered near Animal Kingdom, Epcot-MGM (within walking distance), Magic Kingdom (travel by monorail or boat), and Downtown Disney (travel by boat). An extensive bus system links the resorts and theme parks. Room sizes range from very small (at the **All Star Resorts**, $77–124) to extremely spacious (**Polynesian Resort**, $299–575). If you plan to stay "on property," here are my top picks from personal visits, all with enough room for a family of four:

Resort	Price	Why?
Animal Kingdom Lodge	$199–610	Rooms surround an African savanna with live animals; fabulous African decor in common areas
Boardwalk Inn	$289–675	Surrounded by nightlife; walk to Epcot and MGM
Contemporary Resort	$239–675	Right in the middle of the action, with a monorail down the middle; great views of Bay Lake
Coronado Springs Resort	$133–209	Sprawling complex centered on a large lake, with an Aztec pyramid dominating the swimming area
Grand Floridian Resort & Spa	$339–840	Genteel Old Florida beach atmosphere with spectacular lake frontage
Polynesian Resort	$299–575	Immerse in a tropical wonderland, complete with splashing waterfalls; walk to monorail transportation
Port Orleans Riverside	$133–209	Lazy bayou feel with natural landscaping; boat to Downtown Disney
Shades of Green	Varies	Official U.S. Armed Forces Recreation Center; vacationing servicemen and -women pay according to their rank
Wilderness Lodge	$199–475	Patterned after national park lodges of the Pacific Northwest, with a faux Yellowstone swimming area; boat transportation to Magic Kingdom

I-Drive 32837

Grande Lakes Resort Orlando (www.grandelakes.com), home to both Ritz-Carlton and J. W. Marriott, features the 18-hole Greg Norman championship golf course, three tennis courts, a 40,000-square-foot spa with 40 treatment rooms, a 6,000-square-foot fitness center with private lap pool, hydrotherapy pools, arcade room, executive business center, gift shops, and world-class restaurants. Relax in the lazy river pool, and then dine at Primo (see *Dining Out*), both at the **J. W. Marriott** (407-206-2300), 4040 Central Florida Pkwy. **The Ritz-**

Carlton at Grande Lakes Resort Orlando (407-206-2400), 4012 Central Florida Pkwy, is where you'll find Norm Van Aken's new restaurant—Norman's (see *Dining Out*).

I-Drive S 34746

Once you arrive at the **Gaylord Palms Resort & Convention Center** (407-586-2000; www.gaylord hotels.com), 6000 W Osceola Pkwy, you'll forget about the outside world. The stately resort, situated on 63 acres and visible from I-4, is centrally located to all the area attractions. Step inside; you'll be greeted with the ambience of an Old Florida mansion. Experience the unique geographic areas of Florida under the resort's 4.5-acre atrium, where the climate is always a perfect rain-free 72 degrees. The resort's showpiece is a replica of the Castillo de San Marcos, the historic Spanish fort in St. Augustine. Climb up the stairs and wander through archways, or drink from the "fountain of youth" in this smaller version of the famous stronghold. In the Key West section you'll find a 60-foot sailboat sitting in a coral reef surrounded by a re-creation of Mallory Square, including a nightly sunset celebration. On the west side of the atrium, the "river of grass" comes to life in the Everglades, where swamp walkways take you through misty fog in search of animated alligators—or are they? Emerald Bay is a boutique hotel within the resort and offers upscale amenities and services.

Like the atrium, each geographic section is mirrored in the guest rooms and suites. The Key West rooms are bright and colorful, capturing the festive island spirit. Nature enthusiasts will like the Everglades rooms saturated with earthy colors, wicker furnishings, and flora and fauna, including whimsical dragonflies. St. Augustine accommodations evoke old-fashioned elegance with rich sepia tapestries and authentic artifacts. I loved the 18th-century map design in the bedskirts. Each evening your turndown service includes a bedside Florida Fact card, giving you something to ponder before dropping off to sleep. This doesn't feel like your typical cookie-cutter resort. The architectural and interior designers brought out their very best when they fashioned each room, right down to the custom carpets. You'll be impressed with the employees at this resort as they greet you with friendly smiles and take care of your needs at lightning speed. I still can't get over how fast my maid straightened my bathroom while I sat typing at my computer. You'll feel like you're at a bed & breakfast, and you'll love it! Rates from $319.

Lake Buena Vista 32836

At the **Hyatt Grand Cypress** (407-239-1234; www.hyattgrandcypress .com), 1 Grand Cypress Blvd, it's not a hotel, it's an experience. With 1,500 acres to roam and an incredible list of on-site activities, it's a wonder that anyone ever leaves to go to a theme park. Swim in a waterfall-fed canyon, bike along tropical nature trails, or visit the world-class equestrian facility for riding lessons. Four on-site restaurants offer fabulous cuisine: Coquina (see *Dining Out*) is one of Orlando's top fine-dining choices. Amenities include what you've come to expect from top-notch hotels: dataport, mini bar, in-room movies, and a private balcony. Luxury doesn't come cheap: Rates start around $200.

Universal 32819

Portofino Bay Resort (407-503-1000), 5601 Universal Blvd. Drifting into this Italianate resort for a corporate Christmas dinner, I felt as if I'd stepped into a Mediterranean village—the scene is a ringer for the real Portofino, with luxurious villas spilling down to the edge of the harbor. Dine at one of the many romantic restaurants, or retreat to your room and savor a sensual evening with the pampering only Loews provides. Rates start around $150.

Royal Pacific Resort (407-503-3000), 6300 Hollywood Way. The newest entrant to the Loews family of hotels at Universal is lavishly themed around post–World War II South Pacific travel, when arriving by airplane or steamship was an experience unto itself. I walked around under the Balinese umbrellas feeling like I'd bump into Bob Hope, Bing Crosby, and Dorothy Lamour; 1940s music pervades the on-site restaurants. Subtle touches such as high-thread-count sheets, dimmer switches, and free postcards that look like old steamship trunk stickers add to the comfort of each well-appointed room, which comes standard with a coffeemaker, ironing board, hair dryer, Playstation, Wayport high-speed Internet access, safe, and mini bar. In the Loews tradition, the hotel also lets you borrow comfort or necessity items from two long lists of choices, including a down pillow, an air purifier, a sound machine, personal exercise equipment, or even travel guides. If you're looking for a place to relax amid the hubbub of the theme parks, this is it. Rates start around $159, with deep discounts for Florida residents.

US 192

American Vacation Homes (407-847-0883 or 1-800-901-8688; www.americanvacationhomes.us), 1631 E Vine St, Kissimmee 34744, offers more than 250 fully furnished individually owned homes scattered through several housing developments; capacities of 6 to 14 guests make these rentals an ideal option for families on vacation. Pick your size and amenities (high-end rentals include pools), and they'll figure out the rates.

CAMPGROUNDS

Disney

Fort Wilderness Resort and Campground (407-824-2727), 4510 N Fort Wilderness Trail, Lake Buena Vista 32830. For $34–82, pitch your tent or pull up the trailer under the shade of Florida pines in this back-to-nature campground, where you can walk for miles on pleasant footpaths or grab a bus or rent a golf cart if you're in a hurry. The best deals for families on Disney property are the Wilderness Cabins, essentially upscale park models that sleep up to eight (or more, if the kids are small) and have a full kitchen and outdoor grill, with rates starting in the $120s.

US 192

Encore SuperPark Orlando (863-420-1300 or 1-888-558-5777; www.rvonthego.com), 9600 US 192 W, Clermont 34711. It's a massive campground with paved pads and patios, full hookups, pull-through sites perfect for your big rig, sunny spaces amid pleasant landscaping. This park offers great on-site amenities, including two swimming pools, recreation center, and tennis courts. Thirty- and 50-amp service; rates start at $32.

✷ Where to Eat

DINING OUT AT DISNEY Most Walt Disney World restaurants do not have individual phone numbers. For priority seating, call 407-WDW-DINE.

Downtown Disney

♿ **Fulton's Crab House** (407-934-2628), Pleasure Island. On the paddle-wheeler *Empress Lily*, Dungeness crabcakes ($28) and Fulton's seafood boil ($33) come accompanied by unexpectedly exquisite breads and salads; every nuance of my meal here was sheer perfection, including the impeccable service. I'd choose this place for a date anytime. Entrées $20–44; reservations recommended.

Epcot

♿ Always humming with activity, the **Chefs de France** are a perennial favorite, serving specialties like salade Niçoise and slowly braised leg o' lamb, with dinner entrées $15–26. For a savory, inexpensive treat, stop in for an appetizer—the tomato and goat cheese tart is divine. Hidden upstairs, the intimate **Bistro de Paris** appeals for a quiet romantic dinner, with pan-seared lobster, filet mignon, and a spectacular wine list. Dinner entrées $28–32; reservations recommended.

♿ **Coral Reef Restaurant**, The Living Seas. Seafood with an aquarium view: Immersed in The Living Seas, diners stare out over the faux reef as they chow down on blackened catfish, grilled ahi tuna with ginger puree, and roasted-garlic-marinated tofu. Serving lunch and dinner, $16–27.

♿ **L'Originale Alfredo di Roma Ristorante**, Italy. Yes, *that* Alfredo—as in fettuccine—with sparkling Italian chandeliers setting an atmosphere to transport you to Venice. Savor their signature fettuccine, or the *gnocchi al Gorgonzola* sprinkled with walnuts. *Magnifico!* Dinner entrées run $18–34; reservations suggested.

♿ **Restaurant Akershus**, Norway. In the past 20 years I've dined at most of the World Showcase restaurants, and I think none holds a candle to the uniqueness of this traditional Scandinavian smorgasbord in Norway. Since I'm of Scandinavian descent, it could be a genetic attraction to the cuisine, but prior to my visit, I'd never before had pickled herring or mashed rutabagas. I was smitten by the array of seafood and potato-based salads. Dinner buffet $19 adults, $8 ages 3–11, cheaper at lunchtime; character breakfast featured every morning.

♿ **Restaurant Marrakesh**, Morocco. Hidden in the warren of alleyways that make up the souk at Morocco, this truly exotic restaurant offers fare ($17–30) you're not about to find elsewhere—shish kebab, couscous, roast lamb, and more; for an introduction to the cuisine, I suggest the Marrakesh Feast ($28) or Royal Feast ($30), each a sampler of exotic delights. Belly dancing and Moroccan music accent the experience.

♿ **San Angel Inn**, Mexico. Now, this is a place for romance: a dimly lit virtual movie set of Mexico inside a giant Aztec pyramid, with a cantina looking over a waterway and jungle along the edge of a bustling village, where mariachi bands stroll by. Granted, it's a fantasy, but a pleasant one, and the food offered here—from one of Mexico City's finest restaurants—is genuine Mexican cuisine like *mole poblano* (chicken in a bitter chocolate and hot pepper sauce) and *camerones* *con fideos* (grilled shrimp on angelhair). Serving lunch and dinner, $10–23.

Magic Kingdom

♿ ✐ **Cinderella's Royal Table**. What princess wouldn't want to feast in Cinderella's castle? Mornings offer a character breakfast; for lunch and dinner, savor roast prime rib ($23–26), beef tenderloin ($26), or a less regal but nonetheless tasty smoked turkey breast focaccia sandwich ($12). Kids will appreciate the Bibbiddi Bobbiddi Brew smoothie ($8) served in a collectible castle.

Disney-MGM

♿ A replica of the famous Tinseltown celebrity hangout, **The Hollywood Brown Derby** is all about glamour; caricatures of the famous grace the walls, and you can arrange lunch with an animator (Mon–Wed, $61 ages 12 and up) from the adjoining studio. Center-stage entrées ($19–27) include the creative Thai noodle bowl with coconut-crusted tofu, grilled Atlantic salmon, and sesame-seared tuna mignon. For lunch, don't miss their signature Brown Derby Cobb Salad, $13.

Disney resorts

♿ **Artist's Point**, Disney's Wilderness Lodge. I love the name and the memories it evokes: of standing on the "Artist Point" rock ledge at Colorado National Monument, overlooking vast red-rock canyons. Capturing nature's artistry each evening, this restaurant has a Frank Lloyd Wright feel and adventuresome offerings (entrées $19–30) like grilled buffalo sirloin and savory rabbit sausage, as well as a wine list showcasing Pacific Northwest vintages.

♿ **California Grill**, Disney's Contemporary Resort, 15th floor. Featuring a show kitchen so you can watch the chefs prepare market-fresh beef and seafood, this classy restaurant has great offerings for vegetarians and is the ultimate spot to catch fireworks exploding over the Magic Kingdom. Enjoy sushi (deluxe platter $23), Sonoma goat cheese ravioli ($9), and more; entrées $20–34.

♿ **Kimonos Sushi Bar** (407-934-1621), Walt Disney World Swan. This authentic Japanese restaurant soothes with bamboo, black lacquer, and rice paper lanterns setting the ambience. Sushi rolls ($5–11), à la carte selections ($4–13), and tempura and salads with a side of—yes!—karaoke.

♿ **Shula's Steak House**, Walt Disney World Dolphin. Classic Sinatra tunes set the tone for what critics call the top steak house in Orlando, serving choice cuts of certified Angus beef ($21 and up)—prime rib, porterhouse, filet mignon, New York strip—and succulent fresh seafood. My goodness, they even have a linebacker-worthy 48-ounce porterhouse ($70).

♿ **Victoria & Albert's** (407-939-7707), Disney's Grand Floridian Beach Resort. Elegant and intimate, it's Disney's top restaurant, and more an experience than a dinner. Expect to drop at least $100 per person for an ever-changing prix fixe menu of the finest gourmet food, with extra for wine pairings. The Chef's Table in the kitchen is booked up to 6 months in advance.

MORE DINING OUT OPTIONS

Universal

Business is brisk at **Emeril's Tchoup Chop** (407-503-CHOP; www.emerils.com) at the Royal Pacific Resort (see *Resorts*), the second of

Emeril's Orlando restaurants. Looking out over lush tropical gardens, diners enjoy the "kick it up a notch" choices like banana-leaf-steamed fish of the day and Kiawe smoked oyster stuffed quail. Lunch choices $5–20, dinner entrées $18–32.

Memories of India (407-370-3277), Bay Hill Plaza, 7625 Turkey Lake Rd. In my former corporate life, the engineers and I descended on this authentic Indian restaurant for lunch, when you can pick up any of 18 different thalis—entrées with basmati rice, nan, raita, pickle, papad, and dessert—for a song ($5–9). My fave: dal makhani; the guys would always go for vindaloo, the hotter, the better. Prices climb at dinner ($9–21), but the quality remains superb. Even though my old office moved 10 miles north, they still call here for take-out. A most excellent standout among Indian restaurants in Orlando: nay, in all of Florida. Don't miss it.

I-Drive

Norman's (407-392-4300; www.grandelakes.com) at the Ritz-Carlton at Grande Lakes Resort (see *Resorts*). Chef Norman Van Aken (I knew him when . . .) of Key West and South Florida fame brings his Floribbean cuisine to Orlando. Van Aken, a pioneer of the New World Cuisine, has been waking up our taste buds ever since. Prix fixe dinner around $55.

Primo by Melissa Kelly (407-393-4444; www.grandelakes.com) at the J. W. Marriott at Grande Lakes Resort (see *Resorts*). When Melissa Kelly's staff called me I just about dropped the phone! Melissa is known all over my home state, Maine, with her original restaurant, **Primo** in Rockland. So when they asked me to dinner I couldn't find a date fast enough. The folks over at J. W. Marriott found a real gem when they convinced Kelly to re-create her concept of "Italian sensibility" here in Florida. And now she and partner Price Kushner, Primo's pastry chef and co-owner, split their time between Maine and Florida. I missed her by a delayed flight, but got to meet her chef de cuisine, Kathleen Blake, who with grace and style balances her culinary career with four children, and general manager Suzanne Bonham, who will knowledgably pair your dining selections with the appropriate wines. This talented group of women really do it all in a culinary world long dominated by men. The trendy restaurant lacks the "attitude" prevalent in other upscale restaurants, and while nice clothes are a good idea, you don't need to dress to the nines. Presentation is everything at Primo, with tables set comfortably apart and a sound system that will make you think live musicians are around the corner. Food is prepared with not only fresh ingredients, some grown on the property, but also as many organic ingredients as possible. Start with a salad of roasted organic beets wrapped around fresh goat cheese ($9); your entrée selection might be seared Maine scallops with caramelized Vidalia onion vinaigrette, morels, and summer truffles ($24). Finish off your meal with a trio of crème brûlée: black-and-white, lemon verbena, and lavender ($9), which had me calling take-out later that same night.

You'll want to check out these other fine-dining establishments around I-Drive: **Cafe TU TU Tango** (407-248-2222), 8625 International Dr; **Chaparral Steakhouse** (407-298-7334), 6129 Old Winter Garden Rd;

Charley's Steak House (407-363-0228), 8255 International Dr; **Palio** (407-934-1609), 1200 Epcot Resorts Blvd in the Swan Hotel; **Stonewood Tavern and Grill** (407-297-8682), 5078 Doctor Phillips Blvd; **Seasons 52** (407-345-1020), 7700 West Sand Lake Rd.

EATING OUT AT DISNEY Most Walt Disney World restaurants do not have individual phone numbers. For priority seating, call 407-WDW-DINE.

Animal Kingdom
From the pot stickers at **Charkrandi Chicken Shop** (Anandapur) to fresh fruit and juices at the **Harambe Fruit Market**, Animal Kingdom provides a nice variety of good food in their snack bars and chow wagons; it's possible to nab food and a drink for under $10.

✐ **Rainforest Café** (407-938-9100). Strategically placed at the front entrance, this chain restaurant provides tasty food and naturally themed entertainment for the kids. It's noisy once the crowds show up—with gorillas grunting, elephants trumpeting, and a faux rainstorm every 15 minutes or so, and the din of diners around you, you won't be able to hold a conversation—but it's the less crowded option of the two locations at Disney, especially in the midafternoon. I'm partial to the huge seafood salad, Cyclone Crab Cakes, and Tribal Salmon, and Dad loves the mushroom-shaped juice bar with its fresh carrot juice. Open 11–5, $10–40; reservations taken at the door.

Creative fare makes dining a pleasure at **Tusker House**, Harambe, where you can feast on grilled salmon, rotisserie chicken, and turkey wraps, $7–8. My pick—the grilled vegetable sandwich with hummus spread and fresh fruit.

Disney-MGM Studios
On Sunset Blvd, **Anaheim Produce** has fresh fruit displayed in big produce bins, with a side of frozen lemonade. Adjoining the Hollywood Brown Derby, the **Starring Rolls Bakery** offers fresh tasty treats ($3–4) like cream puffs, tiramisu, and, my favorite, the Bavarian fruit tart with blueberries, mandarin orange, kiwi, and strawberries atop Bavarian cream.

50's Prime Time Café (near the Indiana Jones show). Most restaurants don't have a waitress nagging you like Mom did—"Eat your vegetables!"—but that's part of the charm of this cozy café that takes me back to my childhood, right down to the tables and flour bin from my family kitchen. It's a meat-and-potatoes menu of meat loaf, pot roast, and the like complemented by gourmet dishes like grilled shrimp salad and pan-seared salmon; $12–19, lunch and dinner.

Mama Melrose Restaurant Italiano (near Muppets 3-D). A comfortable Italian family restaurant infused with the aroma of their wood-fired oven. Choose from flatbread pizzas or main courses like oak-roasted salmon or eggplant Parmesan with sun-dried tomatoes. Lunch and dinner, $12–22.

Downtown Disney
Bongos Cuban Café. Savor the salsa of South Beach at this restaurant created by Emilio and Gloria Estefan, where the food goes beyond Cuban sandwiches to encompass lunch and dinner favorites like *paella de mariscos* (seafood paella) and *ropa vieja*, $14–20.

Ghirardelli's Soda Fountain & Chocolate Shop. Hey, it's chocolate and ice cream—how can you pass this one by? I certainly can't. World-famous hot fudge sundaes and enough varieties of ice cream that you'll find something you'll love; I'm nuts about the chocolate-and-raspberry Fog Horn sundae. It's open late, too, with fancy creations for $4–7, not counting the insane eight-scoop Earthquake mega banana split for $20.

House of Blues. Dan Aykroyd's dream restaurant serves up tasty Cajun cuisine, with Louisiana crawfish, Southern Voodoo shrimp étouffée, Creole seafood jambalaya, and homemade banana bread pudding in a bayou atmosphere pulsing with Mississippi Delta music; serving lunch and dinner, $9–24, with frequent live music inside and on the patio. A special Sunday gospel brunch ($30 adults, $15 ages 3–9) includes all-you-can-eat southern fixin's followed by a foot-stompin' church meeting.

Rainforest Café (407-827-8500). My favorite casual eatery in Downtown Disney—it's fun, and the portions are huge. Set inside a giant smoking volcano that rumbles and belches a column of smoke, this is a place to take the kiddies, not a quiet getaway, as the cavernous setting echoes every sound. The wait to get in can be ridiculously long, but if you plan to do some shopping, no big deal. Just like the venue at Animal Kingdom, a large retail store with a rain forest theme shares the space; the menus are identical as well.

Epcot

What fun to graze around the World Showcase, sampling ethnic foods and tasty treats. First stop: a wet burrito ($7) and frozen margarita ($7) at **Cantina de San Angel**, where ibises try to steal the food off your table. Move on to Norway's **Kringla Bakeri Og Kafe** for some lefse or a berry tart ($2–4), or the **Lotus Blossom Café** in China for a crystal noodle salad ($5) and ginger ice cream ($2)—a tough choice over the massive mint chocolate chip soft serve ice cream cones ($3) at **Refreshment Outpost**. Grab a Tokyo sushi roll ($6) or udon noodles ($5) at **Yakitori House** in Japan, and shawarma sandwich platters ($7–11) at the **Tangierine Café** in Morocco. And it's impossible to walk past the **Boulangerie Patisserie** in France without peeking in at the elegant tarts, chocolate mousse, and meringues ($2–4). Slosh through real slush and snow to wash it all down with freebie foreign Coca-Cola products at **Ice Station Cool**; I'm partial to Smart Watermelon from China.

Biergarten, Germany. Pile on the sauerbraten and Wiener schnitzel at this all-you-can-eat German buffet, with one of my favorite desserts—Black Forest cake—included. Lunch costs $6 children, $15 adults; dinner $8 children, $20 adults.

The Garden Grill Restaurant, The Land. Home cooking served family style, with heaping mounds of grilled flank steak, country-style catfish, and a never-ending bowl of home-grown salad; vegetarians will appreciate the zesty roasted vegetable stew. The restaurant rotates as you eat, and Disney characters come to call, making this a fun experience for the kids at lunch and dinner. Children 3–11, $10; adults $20 lunch, $22 dinner.

Rose & Crown, Britain. I've savored many a shepherd's pie out on the patio of this unpretentious offering from the British Isles, where the accents are authentic and the food knocks the stuffing out of the old stereotypes about English cooking. Meat and potatoes are the strong points here—my mom loves the prime rib—along with Harry Ramsden's famous fish-and-chips. Reserve ahead if you want to sit inside, but you'll catch the best view in the park of parades and fireworks from the shaded patio. Serving lunch and dinner, with entrées $11–20; leave room for a sticky toffee pudding or lemon posset, $4.

Magic Kingdom

The Magic Kingdom is full of delightful little places for casual eating, if you know just where to look. Unfortunately, my favorites seem to shut down whenever attendance sags, but they serve (in my opinion) the best fare. At **Aunt Polly's Dockside Inn** on Tom Sawyer Island, munch on peanut butter and jelly sandwiches ($4) and sip lemonade while watching the riverboats steam by from the comfort of a shaded rocking chair—it's heaven for those wanting to get away from the crowds. **El Pirata y el Perico** in Adventureland offers beef empanadas, tacos, and nachos ($4–6) in the Plaza del Sol Caribe. For fresh fruit, fruit juice, and frozen fruit swirls, try **Aloha Isle** (near the Swiss Family Treehouse), **Sunshine Tree Terrace** (adjoining the Enchanted Tiki Birds), the **Enchanted Grove** (by the Mad Tea Party), and the **Toontown Farmers Market**. Grab an ice cream at the **Plaza Ice Cream Parlor** on Main Street, where they serve up my dad's favorite, butter pecan.

Liberty Tree Tavern. Sit in a slice of New England and enjoy hearty lunch fare like a Pilgrim's Feast of turkey and mashed potatoes ($14); I'll always savor the Colony Salad ($12) I had here a lifetime ago. Characters come to greet the kids for a special fixed price buffet dinner ($22, $10 ages 3–11) of carved beef, smoked pork loin, macaroni and cheese, and more.

Disney resorts

Boatwright's Dining Hall, Disney's Port Orleans Riverside. A shipbuilding theme permeates this comfortable family restaurant, where I've never been disappointed by a meal, especially the heaping helpings served up at breakfast. Try the banana-stuffed French toast ($8) or their signature sweet potato cakes ($7). Serving all day, $7–20; at dinner, the summer vegetable stack with smoked cheddar grits ($14) is exquisite.

Boma, Disney's Animal Kingdom Lodge. Expand your culinary horizons: Immerse yourself in the colors and aromas of an African marketplace, where you'll find quinoa porridge, brioche, pap, and bobotie next to the bacon and eggs at this serve-yourself set of buffet stations. Breakfast buffet $15, $8 ages 3–11.

'Ohana, Disney's Polynesian Resort. When my family stayed here in the 1970s, the Papette Bay Verandah was one of our favorites around Bay Lake, where I learned what South Seas cooking entailed. The all-you-care-to-eat 'Ohana replaces this old favorite, with skewers of chicken, beef, and veggies grilled over flaming open pits; desserts extra. $24 adults, $10 ages 3–11.

Spoodles, Disney's Boardwalk. I

love Spoodles. When I brought my brother-in-law (who's an executive chef) here, even he was impressed by the tasty selection of breads and spreads brought to our table while we decided on exactly what sort of Mediterranean cuisine tickled our fancy. Try a handful of tapas (tiny appetizers) and pass them around, or order one of the big bowls of pasta. A little bit of everything, from Portuguese and Spanish to Moroccan, North African, and Greek, teases your taste buds. Serving breakfast and dinner, $15–25.

Trail's End Buffeteria, Fort Wilderness. A family favorite for many years, this rustic-themed buffet next to the Hoop-de-Doo Musical Revue offers all-you-can-eat breakfast, lunch, and dinner, with barbecued chicken and ribs, salad bar, and tasty cobblers. Prices top out at $16 adults, $7 ages 3–11.

Whispering Canyon Café, Disney's Wilderness Lodge. Whoop it up under the grand rafters of this western-themed lodge with wait staff who urge you and the kids out of your seats for rocking horse races and other madcap fun, while they bring out platter upon platter of barbecue and chicken in the all-you-can-eat Canyon Skillet ($22); you may also order à la carte items like meat loaf and vegetarian pasta ($16–27). Serving breakfast, lunch, and dinner.

MORE EATING OUT OPTIONS

I-Drive

Adobe Gilas of Orlando (407-903-1477), 9101 International Dr, Pointe Orlando. Wake up your taste buds! Create your own drink with over 65 brands of tequila, and enjoy gargantuan nachos, thick tortillas, and Tabasco-riddled Mexican food inside this hot tamale. Live bands Wed–Sun.

B-Line Diner (407-352-4000; www.peabodyorlando.com), Peabody Hotel, 9801 International Dr. Open daily 24 hours. Stop by this 1950s diner inside the Peabody Hotel before or after watching the Peabody Duck March. At this unusual diner, it feels like the dining car just drove in: Gray booths, cream walls, checkerboard floor, and lots of sleek chrome take you back in time. For breakfast try the gingerbread-like sweet potato pancakes served with pure maple syrup, chicken-apple sausages, and spiced pecans ($8.95); or the tropical stuffed French toast with pineapple, strawberries, mango, and macadamia nuts ($8.25). Soups ($3.95), salads ($6.95–10.25), pasta ($10.95–11.95), burgers and sandwiches ($8.25–9.25). For a lean burger, try the farm-raised ostrich burger ($11.95) served on cranberry sage focaccia with sun-dried cherry and cranberry relish and fruit cup. Hearty selection of main entrées from the smoked half chicken ($15.95) to filet mignon ($25.95). "Feelin' Ducky" menu items offer up healthy selections low in cholesterol, fat, and sugar, but high in fiber. Just don't expect to find duck served here!

Boston Lobster Feast (407-248-8606; www.bostonlobsterfeast.com), 8731 International Dr. This place is always packed, so come early. Features all the lobster, sushi, crab legs, and prime rib you can eat. Take advantage of the early-bird specials until 6 PM.

Cold Stone Creamery (407-226-2259), 5250 International Dr. In 1988 Arizonians Donald and Susan Sutherland made their own version of smooth and creamy ice cream, custom-blending each serving on a frozen granite stone (the "Cold Stone"), served up in a fresh-baked waffle cone. You'll find such blendings as Cookie Doughn't You Want Some, Fruit Stand Rendezvous, and Nights in White Chocolate, but don't even look at the fat grams. Yum!

Flipper's Pizza (407-351-5643), 7480 Universal Blvd near Wet & Wild, and (407-345-0113) at 6125 Westwood Blvd near SeaWorld. Eat in or call for delivery. This old-fashioned pizza shop makes terrific pizza with special attention to fresh ingredients and home-style sauces. My favorites are the Bianca, an all-white pizza with ricotta, Romano, mozzarella, fresh garlic, olive oil, and oregano ($8–12); and the Ravioli Florentine, with chicken, spinach, and Asiago cheese ($9). Their hand-thrown pizzas are made in the traditional style, or ask for Neapolitan (a thinner version) or Chicago. Also at Old Town in Kissimmee.

Kitty O'Sheas Irish Pub (407-238-9769; www.kittyosheaspub.com), 8470 Palm Pkwy. Gather around the big-screen TV for Mon-night football, or sink the eight-ball in the billiards tables. This comfortable Irish-gone-sports pub with deep booths still serves up a great shepherd's pie, bangers and mash, and beer-battered fish-and-chips ($9). The full bar features such Irish drinks as the Leprechaun and Irish Car Bomb. Oh, and yes—they have plenty of Guinness.

Pizzeria Uno Chicago Bar & Grill (407-351-UNOS), 8250 International Dr. You just can't go wrong here if you're craving Chicago's original deep-dish pizzas. I keep coming back for the white one.

Owned by several racing legends, **Race Rock International** (407-248-9876), 8986 International Dr, is the pit stop for fans and celebrities of fast-action motor sports. You'll find 30 video monitors and lots of race memorabilia depicting the world of racing from motorbikes to NASCAR. Try out the interactive simulators before fueling up with burgers, pizza, and entrées, $7–23.

Founded in 1981 by Frank Crail in Durango, Colorado, **Rocky Mountain Chocolate Factory** (407-465-1002), 8200 Vineland Ave, has become one of the fastest-growing companies satisfying sweet teeth all over the world. With over 250 locations, they still don't have a shop near me. Come on, Frank! So I make regular trips to the Orlando Premium Outlets location (see *Selective Shopping*) and watch Brian and the gang whip up some fudge in copper kettles, then mold the creamy mixture on cool marble slabs. After which they let me sample the pralines—and you can, too. Also at the other end of town at Festival Bay (407-352-1023).

Sonic, America's Drive-In (407-352-0016), 5399 International Dr. Order drive-in style and have your food delivered by roller-skating wait staff. Best BLT on Texas toast for only $1.99. The large root beer floats are sure to wet your whistle and are almost a meal in themselves.

Other great spots just off I-Drive are **Bonefish Grill** (407-355-7707), 7830 W Sandlake Rd; **Cariera's Cucina Italiana** (407-351-1187), 7600 Doctor Phillips Blvd; and **Rick's Oyster Bar** (407-293-3587), 5621 Old Winter Garden Rd.

Lake Buena Vista
Crab, crab, and more crab—that's the menu at **The Crab House** (407-239-1888), 8496 Palm Pkwy, where they serve up crab nine different ways ($17–31) and offer an all-you-can-eat seafood-and-salad bar ($21) with snow crab, blue crab, smoked salmon, and more. Lunch and dinner, $12 and up.

Pebbles (407-827-1111), 12551 FL 535, one of several locations in town, offers creative California cuisine for lunch and dinner at moderate prices, $8–28. Expect outrageously sized portions—I wish I could have taken the other half of my wild mushroom and pesto pasta ($13) home.

Universal Studios
Islands Dining Room, Royal Pacific Resort. Looking out over the sparkling pool, with palm frond paddle fans slowly rotating overhead, you can sink back and imagine yourself in the South Pacific in the 1940s while choosing from a pan-Asian menu that'll tickle any gourmet's taste buds. The attentive wait staff bring out a virtual bouquet of creative breads as you wait for your salad or entrée ($12–25), with choices that include ahi tuna ($22); gently fried potato rounds complement the subtle smoky flavor. Save room for dessert—when the fellow across the room received his plateful of java brownie sundae, I thought he'd faint contemplating the size of the task in front of him. Open for breakfast, lunch, and dinner, with daily specials and a children's section; live entertainment, including Universal character breakfasts.

You'll have a hard time choosing among the great eateries at **CityWalk at Universal Orlando** (407-363-8000; www.universalsorlando.com). At **Emeril's Restaurant Orlando** you'll find a sophisticated menu with a New Orleans twist; lively Florida fare at **Jimmy Buffett's Margaritaville**; steaks, chops, and BBQ at **NASCAR Café**; and rockin' burgers at the largest **Hard Rock Café**.

US 192
Angel's Diner and Buffet Lobster & Seafood Feast (407-396-7300), 7300 W Irlo Bronson Hwy. The gleaming chrome in Angel's Diner evokes the 1950s, and Elvis impersonators occasionally drift through; the adjoining buffet draws a steady crowd with its all-you-can-eat lobster and prime rib. The early-bird special runs 4–6 PM, $20; $27 thereafter. You'll stand in a long line to pick up copious portions of seafood, sushi, steak, and lobster, but it's an excellent bargain. Expect a constant hubbub similar to eating in any of the theme park food courts. Adjoining '50s diner open 6:30 AM–11:30 PM daily. Located in the Holiday Inn Nikki Bird Resort on US 192.

✷ Entertainment

Downtown Disney
Run, do not walk. Get yourself a ticket to the **Cirque du Soleil** show **La Nouba** now. If you do nothing else at Disney, you *must* see this show. It's simply the most whimsical, artistic performance you'll ever experience. Yes, there are acrobats and clowns and high-wire acts, but it's not a traditional circus; it transports you to another dimension. It's also not cheap—tickets (407-939-7600) start at $59 adults, $39 ages 3–10. Skip a day at a theme park, if you must, to fund your expedition.

Top rock, blues, and country artists play the music hall at the **House of Blues** (407-WDW-2NITE); enjoy live blues in the restaurant Thu–Sat starting at 11 PM.

Since my high school days, **Pleasure Island** has been a gathering place for young adults to strut their stuff on the dance floors at 8Trax and Mannequins Dance Palace. These days, the smooth sounds of the **Pleasure Island Jazz Company** are more my speed, though I find the **Adventurers Club** a fun hangout, too—I just wish those masks would stop picking on me. One cover charge ($21) lets you into nine clubs.

I-Drive
The three entertainment venues in Pointe Orlando (see *Selective Shopping*) will keep you up past midnight. You'll dance in a stunning surreal world in **Matrix** (407-370-3700), featuring futuristic techno and hip-hop beats. **Metropolis** (407-370-3700) has all the glitz and glamour of a Victorian parlor, but they still kick it up to contemporary sounds of the 1980s and 1990s. Cover varies nightly, but includes access to both clubs. Go to the extreme at **XS Orlando** (407-226-8922) in the land of virtual reality. Game cards $20 for 1 hour, $25 for 2 hours. 25 percent discount for Florida residents.

Universal Orlando
The nightlife at **CityWalk at Universal Orlando** (407-363-8000; www.universalsorlando.com) will keep you hopping long after the parks close. You'll be jammin' to live reggae at **Bob Marley's—A Tribute to Freedom**. At **Pat O'Brian's** you'll experience Mardi Gras 365 days a year. **City Jazz** brings you high-energy funk, R&B, blues, soul, and jazz, and at **The Groove** you'll be dancing to hits from the 1970s and 1980s.

✱ Selective Shopping

Disney—Animal Kingdom
As you sweep clockwise around the park, look for **Creature Comforts** near the Tree of Life, with a nice selection of stuffed animals. In Harambe, Mombasa Marketplace has several booths and a great shop, **Ziwani Traders**, with intriguing African wood chimes, straw baskets, ornamental masks, sculptures, and figurines in clay—a wonderful variety of art. In Safari Village, **Outfitters Gift Shop** brings it all together, setting an artistic tone with tapestries, copper art, and carved totem poles surrounding all the bits and pieces of unique art from around the park.

Disney-MGM Studios
At the Animation Studios, stop in the **Animation Gallery** for art books, posters, paintings, prints, and framed numbered cels; one gallery room displays art (not for sale) with scenes from *Mary Poppins*, *Winnie the Pooh*, *Peter Pan*, and more. On Sunset Boulevard, **Legends of Hollywood** has a focus on Winnie the Pooh, with perfect gifts for toddlers and fans of Pooh Bear. The **Muppet Stuff Shop** next to Muppets 3-D sells Kermit and friends, including videos and DVDs of the classic *Muppet Show* and movies. And of course, I had to stop in **The Writer's Stop** at Stage 14, a snazzy little coffee shop lined with books—not just Disney titles, but best-sellers and local interest, too!

Downtown Disney
Whimsical gifts abound at **Hoypoloi**, where fun art glass jostles for space with pottery and ceramics that just cry out to come home with me.

If you're obsessed with refrigerator magnets, then **Magnetron** is the store for you—that's all they stock. Finish off that state magnet collection, or start a new egg-shaped one.

Looking for an exotic Barbie, or a set of Lincoln Logs? Check out **Once Upon a Toy**, where they stock our childhood classics in addition to the usual Disney stuff.

Commander Data's uniform takes center stage at **Starabilias**, a movie memorabilia extravaganza dealing in everything from posters of classic flicks to clothes worn by the stars.

Thank you, Richard Branson, for bringing the **Virgin Megastore** (www.virginmega.com) to Orlando, elevating our music and movie choices to world-class standards. I love being able to pick up a new release from my favorite Greek pop artist, or finding a complete selection of Peter Sellers movies on DVD. With two stories of music, movies, and books to choose from, you *will* walk out with something!

Epcot

At Epcot's **World Showcase**, it's more a matter of where *not* to shop—you'll find enchanting gifts under every roof. Bargain hunters will find inexpensive exotic gifts in the **Yong Feng Shangdian Shopping Gallery**, China, where you can pick up fragrant soaps for a dollar; it's also a great place for books on philosophy, elegant silks, and fine furnishings. I've found warm fleece jackets at the **Puffin's Roost**, Norway, and delicate glass ornaments in **Glas und Porzellan**, Germany. Pause as you pass **Village Traders** to watch African artists carving original art in soapstone and wood; the unique musical instruments demand attention as well. At **Morocco**, slip into a maze of alleyways to browse authentic metalworking, rugs, and clothing in the souk. But my favorite shopping stop is **Mitsukoshi** in Japan, where I get lost in the artistry of rice bowls and sushi trays.

Magic Kingdom

I love the **Zanzibar Trading Company** in Adventureland—it's set up like a Moroccan souk, broad and meandering, selling safari wear, oil lamps, turned wood, handwoven baskets, Moroccan drums, bullwhips, and other exotica. On Main St, the **Market House** features glassblowing and Austrian crystal glasses and vases, and it's tough to pass by the **Main Street Confectionary**, with its copper-kettle fresh-fudge kitchen. Right next to City Hall, the **Main Street Gallery** showcases fine Disney art, including animation cels and limited-edition bisque figurines.

I-Drive

Any toy enthusiast will want to pay homage to the world-famous toy emporium **FAO Schwartz** (407-352-9900; www.fao.com) in Pointe Orlando. The adventure begins with a 33-foot Raggedy Ann at the door, and you won't miss 32-foot "Truffles" the Bear at the Pointe Orlando entrance. And yes, they have the Big Piano.

Stop by **Global Camera Gallery** (407-477-0089), 11025 International Dr, for NTSC and European PAL conversions.

You're a long way from the ocean, but don't let that stop you. The surf is up 24/7 at **Ron Jon Surf Shop** (407-481-2555), 5160 International Dr.

Orlando Harley-Davidson Historic Factory Dealership, 3770 Harley Davidson Dr. This is the one place to stop for any motorcycle enthusiast. The largest Harley dealership in Florida showcases the company's history, including a replica of the original building. Take a tour of the real factory and watch them assemble your very own "hog."

MALLS AND OUTLETS If the attractions are the number one tourist destination here, then number two is shopping. So get out your credit cards: Orlando offers every type of shopping experience, from discount outlets to upscale malls. Here are some of the major players worth checking out.

Belz Factory Outlet World (407-352-9611; www.belz.com), 5401 W Oak Ridge Rd, and **Belz Designer Outlet Centre** (407-354-0126), 5259 International Dr, have over 170 stores full of name-brand and designer clothing, housewares, jewelry, shoes, toys, books, CDs, camera equipment, and restaurants.

Factory Stores at Lake Buena Vista (407-238-9301; wwww.lbvfs.com), 15591 FL 535, offers factory-direct pricing on name brands commonly found at your local mall.

Festival Bay (407-351-7718; www.belz.com), 5250 International Dr. This Belz conglomerate makes its mark by merging shopping and entertainment in one complex. Look for Bass Pro Shops Outdoor World, Vans Skate Park (see *Skateboarding*), Ron Jon Surf Shop, Cinemark 20 Theatres, Sheplers (westernwear), and Steve and Barry's, the largest college and pro sports apparel store in Florida.

Mall at the Millenia (www.mallatmillenia.com), 4200 Conroy Rd. New in 2003, this is Central Florida's only Bloomingdale's, Macy's, and Neiman Marcus. Features upscale shops and boutiques, including Tiffany, Chanel, Hugo Boss, Lladro, Louis Vuitton, Gucci, and such U.S. staples as Gap, Banana Republic, Tommy Bahama, and Crate and Barrel. Not an outlet, but bargains can be found in this classy atmosphere. Seven full-service restaurants provide fine-dining options. Free live music on First Fridays. Valet, foreign currency exchange, and multilingual concierge available.

Orlando Premium Outlets (407-238-7787; www.premiumoutlets.com), 8200 Vineland Ave. A Mediterranean-style village of 110 upscale outlet stores: Coach, Escada, Kenneth Cole, Burberry, and Polo Ralph Lauren, to name just a few. Stop by the Rocky Mountain Fudge Factory (see *Eating Out*) for some of the best fudge and pralines in town!

Pointe Orlando (407-248-2838; www.pointeorlando.com), 9101 International Dr. The open-air shopping, dining, and entertainment environment is in the heart of I-Drive. You can't miss the gigantic Raggedy Ann in front of FAO Schwartz, which also has a famous piano keyboard. Mall-type shops with Muvico theaters, XS Orlando, and Matrix and Metropolis nightclubs (see *Entertainment*).

✷ Special Events

April–June: One of the best times to see Epcot is during the **Annual Epcot International Flower & Garden Festival**. Colorful blooms, elaborate gardens, and topiaries are shown at their best throughout the park. Take a tour or go behind the scenes and learn how they do it at gardening workshops where guest speakers with the greenest of thumbs share their secrets.

Mid-October–mid-November: **Epcot Food & Wine Festival**. Nibble on ethnic goodies as you stroll around the World Showcase, trying foods and wines from more than 25 countries (*not* just the ones represented permanently at the park). Prices start as low as $1 for a taste, so it's a cheap way to graze. All month long, the festival includes special seminars on wine and beer, exhibits on regional foods, and temporary marketplaces selling wine and gourmet foods.

November–January: **ICE!** at the Gaylord Palms Resort (see *Lodging*) showcases a whimsical winter wonderland with interactive displays and over 5,000 blocks of carved ice. Different types of ice are carved with hand tools (no chain saws for these elves) and look like either flawless crystal or compacted snow. The larger-than-life frozen sculptures depict scenes from the North Pole and Nativity in the coolest attraction in town. This incredible 41-day event sells out fast, so make your reservations early (407-586-0000). $17 adults, $13 seniors, $9 ages 12 and under.

Central Florida 2

POLK COUNTY

LAKE COUNTY

NATURE COAST

MARION COUNTY

OCALA NATIONAL FOREST

Kathy Wolf

POLK COUNTY

Built on citrus, cattle, and phosphate mining, Polk County owes its legacy to hardy settlers who followed the military trails south through Florida's 1820 frontier to rolling hills and wide-open prairies. The ancient spine of Central Florida, the Lake Wales Ridge has the peninsula's highest hills, up to 300 feet; these high, dry relict sand dunes seemed ideal for the cultivation of citrus. Flat prairies around its 554 lakes were perfect for cattle. And thus grew settlements like **Fort Meade**, Polk County's oldest town (circa 1849), which also has the unusual distinction of being the geographic center of the population of Florida (circa 2003). **Lake Alfred** sprang up around Fort Cummings, a Second Seminole War fortress. As the South Florida Railroad pushed south in 1911, speculators created towns like **Dundee**, **Haines City**, and **Lake Wales**. When a devastating freeze trashed citrus groves across Florida in 1896–1897, a small area was uniquely insulated; this was appropriately named **Frostproof**. As Florida's fourth largest county, it's a whopper—its landmass is equal in size to Delaware.

The 1920s Florida land boom transformed the region forever, bringing a broad brush of elegance and culture to the emerging towns of **Bartow**, **Winter Haven**, **Auburndale**, and **Lakeland**. Nowhere is this reflected better than downtown Lakeland's classy promenade around Lake Mirror, and the world's largest collection of Frank Lloyd Wright buildings at Florida Southern College. A cosmopolitan art scene permeates Lakeland's elegant downtown district.

Take a spin down US 27 or US 17-92 to discover the magic of this landscape of orange groves and cattle ranches, of homes clinging to steep slopes above picturesque lakes, of historic downtowns brimming with antiques and art, a patchwork of agriculture and settlement less than an hour from metro Orlando.

GUIDANCE **Central Florida Visitors & Convention Bureau** (863-298-7565 or 1-800-828-7655; www.sunsational.org), P.O. Box 8040, Cypress Gardens 33884. For maps and materials, stop in the storefront at the former entrance to Cypress Gardens, or at the Lakeland Center.

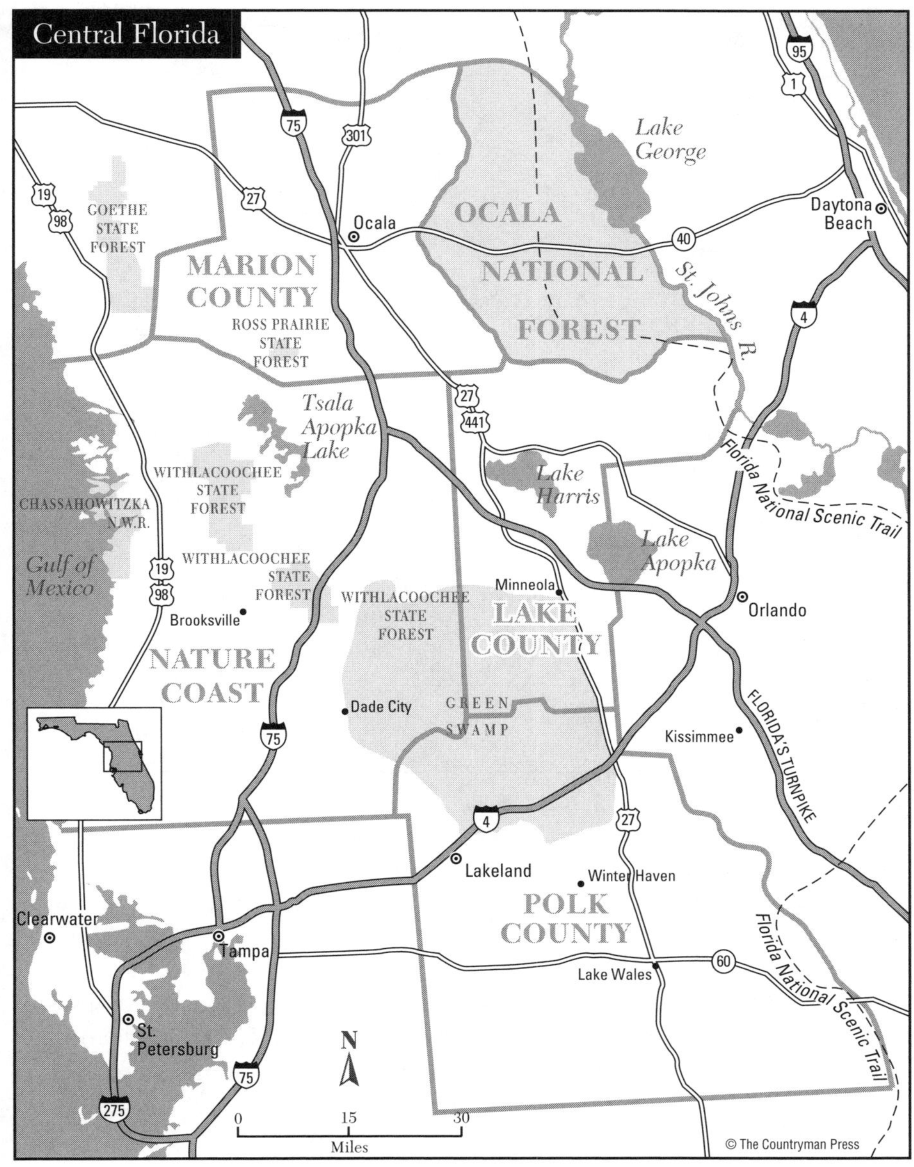

GETTING THERE *By air*: Polk County lies equidistant from the **Orlando International Airport** and **Tampa International Airport**.

By bus: **Greyhound** stops in Bartow (863-553-2774), Winter Haven (863-293-5935), and Lakeland (863-682-3107).

By car: **I-4** runs along the northern edge of the county, and **SR 60** runs close to the southern border. Use **US 27** and **US 17-92** to drive north and south through major population areas. A network of twisty, windy county roads circles the

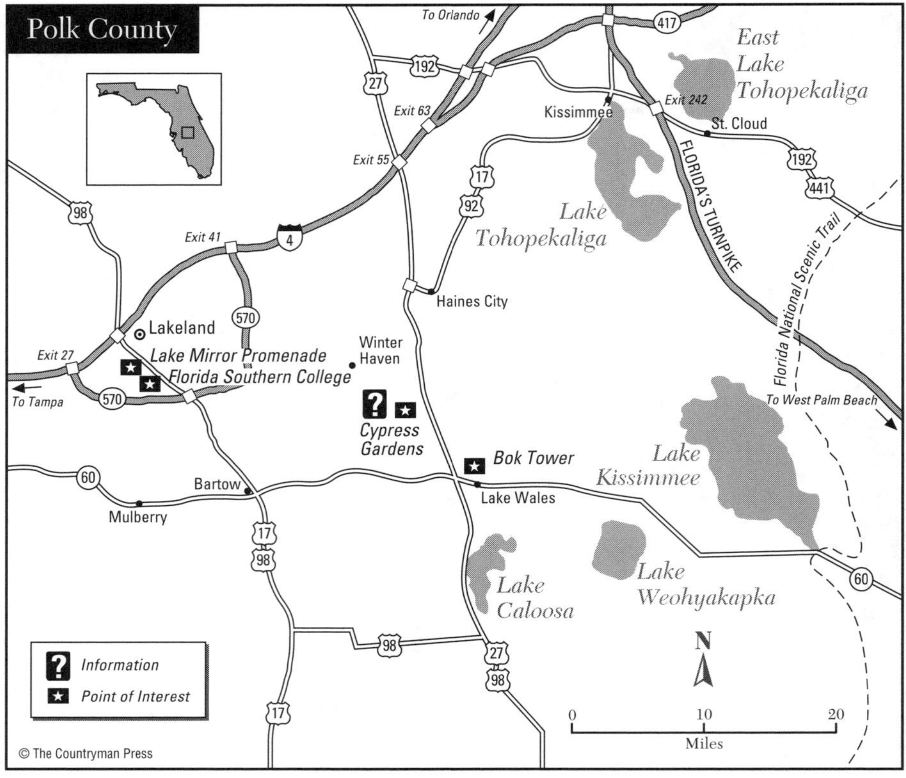

hundreds of lakes to connect communities. More than 80 percent of visitors to Polk County drive their own vehicles, as rural areas have limited bus service.

By train: **Amtrak** (1-800-USA-RAIL) stops in Winter Haven (863-294-9203) and Lakeland (863-683-6368).

GETTING AROUND The **Citrus Trolley** (863-688-RIDE) provides free transportation through downtown Lakeland, running from Lake Morton to the free Oak Street Park & Ride lot north of the antiques district, Mon–Fri 7:30–6. On Sat, 11–3, the route expands to include Hollis Gardens and the Polk Museum of Art.

PARKING **Winter Haven** has free on-street parking, 2-hour limit; **Lakeland** offers the same but also has metered municipal lots and one small free 4-hour parking lot on Kentucky between Pine and Trader's Alley in the antiques district, plus the Oak Street Park & Ride. All of the smaller towns offer unlimited free parking in their downtowns.

MEDICAL EMERGENCIES **Bartow Memorial Hospital** (863-533-8111), US 98, Bartow; **Heart of Florida Regional Medical Center** (863-422-4971), 40100 US 27, Davenport; **Lakeland Regional Medical Center** (863-687-1100), 324 Lakeland Hills Blvd, Lakeland; **Lake Wales Medical Center** (863-676-1433),

410 S 11th St, Lake Wales; **Winter Haven Hospital** (863-293-1121), 200 Ave F NE, Winter Haven.

✷ To See

ART GALLERIES

Davenport
Professional artist **Lori Sanchez** (863-424-0070), at Wallaby Ranch (see *Hang Gliding*), creates awesome hang-gliding art using the techniques of the Old Masters. Bright blue and red gliders pepper the sky in the whimsy of Miró, a hang glider crosses a valley in the beautiful style of Van Gogh, and even Picasso's cubism is represented. You'll find these extraordinary artworks on posters, T-shirts, and notecards, and maybe, just maybe, she'll part with an original. Whether or not you're a hang-gliding enthusiast, you'll be sure to appreciate Lori's humor and style.

Frostproof
The tiny **Frostproof Art League & Gallery** (863-635-7271), 12 E Wall St, is home to over 50 local artists' creations featuring Florida wildlife, landscapes, and floral paintings in oil, acrylic, and watercolor. Classes scheduled throughout the year are open to the public. Open Mon, Tue, Thu, and Fri 9–4.

Lakeland
Arts on the Park (863-680-2787), 115 N Kentucky Ave. Sculpture, Florida landscapes, and wildlife art dominate this Lakeland Creative Arts Center with monthly receptions and six annual juried shows; this nonprofit arts organization also manages the annual Fall Festival of Art. Open Tue–Sat noon–4; free.

Imperial Art Gallery (863-603-4663), 128 S Kentucky Ave, is a cooperative of Lakeland artists working in all media, like Jeanne Barker's watercolors of trilliums and lady's slippers, and Madeline Lay's acrylics of swans drifting across Lake Morton, a favorite theme for local artists. Gift cards and postcards are an inexpensive way to take home an original design. Closed Sun.

♂ ♿ **Polk Museum of Art** (863-688-7743; www.polkmuseumofart.org), 800 E Palmetto St. Nine galleries, two floors: hundreds of pieces of art. A permanent pre-Columbian collection includes hands-on activities for kids; a brick waterfall dominates the eclectic sculpture garden. If you're looking for whimsical educational gifts for the kids, don't miss the Museum Shop. Open daily, closed major holidays. Free.

Lake Wales
The Lake Wales Arts Center (863-676-8426; www.lakewalesartscenter.org) or www.cityoflakewales.com), 1099 SR 60 E. Built in 1927 as the Holy Spirit Catholic Church, this Spanish Mission–style facility was named to the National Register of Historic Places in 1990 and is open to the public Mon–Fri 10–4 for musical performances, tours, lectures, classes, art exhibitions, and an annual arts show. Local and national artists' work can be purchased in the fine arts and crafts gift shop (see *Selective Shopping*).

Original art from local artists can be found at **The Gallery and Frame Shop**

(863-676-2821), 249 E Stuart Ave, which also offers limited-edition prints and artist supplies. Open Mon, Tue, Thu, and Fri 9:30–5:30, Sat 9:30–noon.

Winter Haven

Ridge Art Association (863-291-5661; www.ridgeart.org), 210 Cypress Gardens Blvd. More than 50 years old, this nonprofit fine arts organization has monthly juried and invitational art exhibitions. Open 12:30–4.

ATTRACTIONS ♿ **Fantasy of Flight** (863-984-3500; www.fantasyofflight.com), 1400 Broadway Blvd, Polk City. Aviation takes on a new sparkle at this unique attraction that bills itself as the "World's Greatest Aircraft Collection" but is much, much more. It's an immersion in the history of flight; the skillful use of multimedia, mirrors, and movie makes you feel part of the action. Free fall over Polk County's farms and fields, participate in a B-17 bombing mission, or take off in a flight simulator for a dogfight over the Pacific. The walk-through history lesson and hands-on simulators are so entertaining, they're well worth the price of admission. Of course, there's the museum component, too, with two hangars of classic aircraft to explore, including a Martin B-26 Marauder, a P-51 Mustang, and a flying boat, the Short Sunderland. All of the planes displayed are airworthy, which makes many of them one-of-a-kind. Grab a bite at the retro Compass Rose restaurant (see *Eating Out*), and browse the aircraft models in the gift shop. Open daily 9–5 (closed Thanksgiving and Christmas), $24.95 adults, $22.95 seniors, $13.95 children; part of the Pastport Flight of Four program. For an additional fee, take a Backlot Tour through the restoration shops, take off in a hot air-balloon (see *Ballooning*), or fly the friendly skies in a 1930s biplane (see *Aviation*).

BASEBALL Spring means the return of the **Cleveland Indians** (941-291-5803) to Chain O' Lakes park in Winter Haven and the **Detroit Tigers** (941-686-8075) warming up at Joker Marchant Stadium in Lakeland. Teams play their exhibition games in March, and tickets range $5–25, depending on the team and location.

HISTORIC SITES

Bartow

The Colonial Revival **A. A. McLeod Residence**, 395 S Central Ave, circa 1922, is now a law office. The story goes that city officials wanted to cut down an old oak tree on the south side of the house. The elderly Mrs. McCleod sat bearing a shotgun and refused to have her stately tree cut down. The city acquiesced, and the tree remains to this day.

The two-and-a-half-story neo-Gothic **Associate Reformed Presbyterian Church**, 205 E Stanford St, was built in 1926 and is one of the largest churches in Bartow.

One of the most architecturally significant homes today is the **Benjamin Holland Residence**, 590 E Stanford St. The 1895 home was placed on the National Register of Historic Places in 1975. Benjamin Holland's son, Spessard L. Holland, became governor of Florida and is a U.S. senator.

First Methodist Church, 310 S Broadway. One of the first two churches in Bartow, this stunning representation of Richardson Romanesque architecture was built in 1906 for only $16,000.

L. B. Brown (863-534-0100), 470 2nd Ave. Home of the Neighborhood Improvement Corp. of Bartow, Inc. Born into slavery around 1856, Lawrence Bernard Brown rose above his roots and settled in Bartow, building a meticulously crafted two-story structure in an unusual Z layout. The circa-1892 home has leaded-glass transoms, gingerbread trim, turned posts, unique picturesque millwork, and a Palladian window. The foundation rests on 13 brick piers and 18 huge pine tree trunks and showcases a superior level of craftsmanship indicative of the late 19th century.

One of the oldest African American churches, the 1893 **Mount Gilboa Missionary Baptist Church**, 1205 Martin Luther King Blvd, is one of the oldest churches in Polk County. The current two-and-a-half-story building was constructed in 1928.

Swearington-Langford Residence, 690 E Church St. The neoclassical brick building was built in 1925 for John J. Swearington, a state senator and prominent attorney. Placed on the National Register of Historic Places in 1982, it has served as location for a movie and several commercials.

The two-story **Windsweep** home at 935 Oak St was featured in the movie *China Moon*, which starred Madeleine Stowe and Ed Harris.

The 1908 **Thomas Lee Wilson Residence**, 555 E Stanford St, was used in another movie, *My Girl*, staring Jamie Lee Curtis, Dan Aykroyd, and Macaulay Culkin. The two-and-a-half-story wood frame residence is now open to guests as the Stanford Bed and Breakfast.

CLASSIC AIRCRAFT ON DISPLAY AT FANTASY OF FLIGHT

Sandra Friend

The **Wonder House**, 1075 Mann Rd, was featured in a Ripley's Believe It or Not cartoon. The unique 1925 residence has a natural air-conditioning system and a system of mirrors that allows the residents to see who is at the front door from several locations throughout the house.

Homeland

Once a farming community centered on the Bethel Methodist Church, the town of Bethel was renamed in 1885 by a young Irishman who felt the area looked like his native Ireland. Several pioneer buildings sit on the 5-acre **Homeland Heritage Park** (863-534-3766), dedicated to preserving educational, religious, and cultural history and located at the intersection of Church Ave and 2nd St. Go 4 miles south of Bartow on SR 60 to SR 17 S, then FL 640 W; turn south on Hibiscus Ave to the intersection. The one-room Bethany School, built of cypress wood in 1878, was the first building rescued. Initially enrolling only 5 children, the school grew to 75 pupils within the first year, becoming the county's largest at that time. The 1887 Homeland Methodist Church was moved from across the street, and during restoration in 1987, beautiful stained-glass windows were discovered hidden by a dropped ceiling. Two 19th-century Polk County economic stations are depicted: an original log cabin, and the typical rural homestead of an affluent family. This park often hosts events, such as the Cracker Story Telling Festival each Oct (see *Special Events*). Open Mon–Sat 9–5. Tours available. Free, except for special events.

Lakeland

Frank Lloyd Wright Buildings at Florida Southern College (863-680-4110), 11 Lake Hollingsworth Dr. Architecture aficionados should not miss the largest collection of Wright buildings anywhere on earth—18—clustered on the campus of Florida Southern College. Stop by the Frank Lloyd Wright Visitor Center and Esplanade Gift Shop (closed Mon) for a walking tour brochure before starting your walk around campus. Some of the characteristic Wright designs easily stand out, like geometric forms, colored-glass accents, and clerestory windows. But you'll be surprised at how pervasive the Wright touch was across this campus—including the planetarium, the only one Wright ever designed. Open daily; free.

Lake Mirror Promenade & Park, off E Main, Orange St, and Lake Mirror Dr. Modeled after the 1893 Columbian Exposition Court of Honor, this restored 1928 gem designed by Charles Wellford Levitt looks as sparkling new as the day it opened. An ornate balustrade lined with lamps makes this a comfortable, romantic stroll well into the evening.

Pick up a walking tour brochure (see *Walking Tours*) for a detailed explanation of downtown's architectural landmarks, from the 1927 **Polk Theatre** (see *Entertainment*) to the 1903 **Clonts Building**, a Romanesque former dry goods store at 228 E Pine St, and **Munn Park**, established in 1884 as Lakeland's downtown square.

Lake Wales

A stroll through **Historic Downtown Lake Wales** (www.historiclakewales.com) will remind you of the exciting 1920s. Browse through the quaint collections of shops and galleries in one of Florida's Main Street cities, placed on the National Register of Historic Places in 1990. You find fascinating architecture, vintage charm, and fun nightlife along Central, Stuart, Park and Orange Aves, Scenic Hwy, Market St, and N 1st St. Pick up a self-guided walking tour at the Depot Museum (see *Museums*), which also lists the many beautiful murals depicting the bygone era. On Fri 8–2 stop by the farmer's market in the MarketPlace between Park and Stuart (see *Selective Shopping*).

Pinewood Estate at Historic Bok Sanctuary (see *Botanical Gardens*). Step into the 1930s Mediterranean Revival mansion and you'll want to move right in. The 20-room home of C. Austin Buck features antique furnishings, Latin-inspired tile, intricate woodwork, awe-inspiring architecture, and a secret staircase. The best time to see this home is during the holiday season for **Christmas at Pinewood** (see *Special Events*). Open daily and included with Bok Sanctuary admission. Tours ($5 adults, $3 children) are offered Mon–Sat at 11:30 and Sun at 1 except for 3 weeks in Nov.

Loughman

In 1930 the **Old Tampa Highway** opened, connecting Orlando with Tampa through Lakeland. A mostly forgotten chunk of the original brick-and-cypress highway remains intact off Ronald Reagan Pkwy at the eastern border of the county; look closely at the imposing concrete POLK COUNTY boundary marker along the old brick highway for a sculptor's faux pas.

HOCKEY The **Lakeland Loggerheads** (863-834-7825; www.lakelandloggerheads.com) pro hockey team plays in the Lakeland Center Nov–Apr; game tickets run $7–17.

MUSEUMS

Bartow

Polk County Historical Museum (863-534-4386; www.polk-county.net/museum), 100 E Main St. Learn about the early pioneers and Seminole Indians though exhibits depicting stories of the cattle, citrus, and phosphate industries, as well as local military history and a children's discovery room. Tours available. Open Tue–Fri 9–5, Sat 9–3; free.

Dundee

The **Dundee Depot** (863-439-1312), 103 Main St, features the history of Dundee and the Atlantic Coast Line railroad, since the town attributes its establishment to the rail line. Artifacts date back to 1911. Open Thu and Sat 10–3; free.

Fort Meade

At the **Fort Meade Historical Museum** (863-285-7474), Broadway and Tecumseh, browse through 1800s newspapers and marvel at artifacts from the pioneer settlers of Florida's frontier; the region marked the northern boundary of Seminole Tribal Lands in the 1840s. Open 9–11 Tue, 10–2 on first and third Sat; free.

Frostproof

Frostproof Historical Museum (863-635-7865), 210 S Scenic Hwy, shares the early years of this citrus town through the memorabilia of pioneer families—clothing, photos, books, vintage household items, and other ephemera. Open 9–noon Mon, Wed, Thu; free.

Lake Alfred

The **Lake Alfred Historical Museum** (863-956-3937) at the chamber of commerce contains exhibit cases with historical photos and ephemera, such as an 1839 map of the region's original wagon roads; Mon–Thu 10–2. Across the street, the fire station has vintage pieces of firefighting equipment.

Lakeland

♂ ♿ **Florida Air Museum** (863-644-0741; www.sun-n-fun.org), 4075 Doolittle Rd, adjoining Lakeland Regional Airport, is the center stage for the annual Sun 'n Fun Fly In (see *Special Events*), showcasing more than 45 vintage and exotic aircraft like a 1912 Sopwith Camel and a Pitts S-1 special stunt plane with tooled leather seats; the variety of methods used to mount wings and engines testifies to the creativity of aircraft designers. A newly christened exhibit space pays homage to Howard Hughes's contribution to aviation; Hughes's personal memorabilia were given to the museum for a permanent display. Mon–Fri 9–5, Sat 10–4, Sun noon–4; donation of $8 adults, $6 seniors, $4 ages 8–12. Part of the Pastport Flight of Four.

Lake Wales

Lake Wales Depot Museum & Cultural Center (863-678-4209; www.cityoflakewales.com), 325 S Scenic US Alt 27. Since the extension of the Atlantic Coast Line Railroad in 1911, the Lake Wales junction played an important role in the town's early development. Providing easy access from north, south, east, or west, the railroad soon brought pioneers seeking new lifestyles. Listed on the National Register of Historic Places, the restored 1928 Atlantic Coast Railroad station features a 1916 Pullman car, a 1926 Seaboard Air Line caboose, and assorted railroad memorabilia. Several exhibits display the history and early industries of Lake Wales, including a beautiful collection of quilts. Test your trivia knowledge by trying to identify over 70 dolls on display in the Celebrity Doll Challenge. Don't miss the Annual Pioneer Days and quilt show in the fall (see *Special Events*). Open Mon–Fri 9–5, Sat 10–4. Donations appreciated.

Florida's Natural Grove House Visitor Center (863-676-1411 or 1-800-237-7805; www.floridasnatural.com), 20160 US 27, is a half-mile north of SR 60. Central Florida's Polk County produces more citrus crops than the entire state of California. This is as close to the groves as you can get (tours in the actual groves are no longer offered), and Florida's Natural is as fresh as it gets. This "not-from-concentrate" company is owned entirely by local growers. Learn about Florida orange growers at this educational visitors center. The short film on the citrus industry is well worth watching. Sample juices while browsing the citrus-themed gift shop or sit at the picnic tables under several varieties of orange trees. Open Mon–Fri 10–5, Sat 10–2.

Mulberry

Mulberry Phosphate Museum (863-425-2823), 101 SE 1st St. Florida's mineralogical wealth is phosphate, used in products ranging from hair color and dog food to fertilizer. Housed in a historic railroad depot and railcars, the museum explores phosphate mining and use, the spectacular fossil record uncovered by phosphate mining, and Florida's railroad history. Rockhounds and kids alike will delight in digging through the freshly mined pile of limestone outside in search of fossils and phosphate nuggets. Open Tue–Sat 10–4:30; donation.

Polk City

♿ **AWSEF Water Ski Experience** (863-324-2472; www.waterskihalloffame.com), 1251 Holy Cow Rd. From the early days of waterskiing (1922, Lake Pepin, New York) through Esther Williams and Corky the Clown at Cypress Gardens to the U.S. Water Ski Team, this one-of-a-kind museum and hall of fame covers it all; interactive displays (including a special exhibit on disabled waterskiing) show you what happens when you're out on the water. Educational clinics and exhibitions are held in the lake out back. Fee.

RACING **USA International Raceway** (1-800-984-RACE; www.usaspeedway.com), along FL 33 north of Lakeland, is a 0.75-mile high-banked oval stock car racing track, home of the Hooters Stock Car Series. Need I say more? Racing events are held nearly every week; check the web site for a schedule.

RAILROADIANA In Haines City the 1923 **Seaboard Coast Line passenger station** with a couple of vintage baggage carts out front adjoins Railroad Park. Built in 1912, the **Dundee Passenger Depot** was the first depot on the Haines City–Sebring line of the Atlantic Coast Line; it remained active until 1975. An ACL caboose sits outside the small historic museum. The 1899 **ACL freight and passenger depots** in Mulberry house the Mulberry Phosphate Museum (see *Museums*), with several pieces of historic rolling stock on site.

ZOOLOGICAL PARKS AND WILDLIFE REHABILITATION **Genesis Zoological & Wildlife Rehabilitation Center**, behind the International Market World (see *Selective Shopping*) flea market on US 17-92. This small rehab center hosts full-grown white Bengal tigers, the type popularized by Siegfried & Roy in Las Vegas. Despite the entertainers' claims, white tigers are not a separate breed but a genetic abnormality, and all white tigers in the United States are descendants of a single male Bengal tiger trapped in India in 1951. Volunteers at the center care for privately donated tigers suffering from physical defects related to inbreeding.

✱ To Do

AVIATION At **Fantasy of Flight** (see *Attractions*), hang on to your hat on a 20-minute flight in the world's oldest New Standard 1929 open-cockpit biplane. Pilot and proud owner Rob Lock of Waldo Wright's Flying Service (www.waldowrights.com) takes you airborne in a special sky ballet befitting this grand old barnstormer, the only antique D-25 capable of carrying four passengers. Flights run Nov–Apr, $55.

Jack Brown's Sea Plane Base (863-956-2243; www.gate.net/~seaplane), 2704 US 92 W, Winter Haven. What better way to get your seaplane license than while learning on Florida's "Land of 1000 Lakes"? In just 2 days you'll be able to take off, land, and sail, along with mastering techniques necessary for rough or glassy waters. Land license required.

BALLOONING **Fantasy of Flight** (see *Attractions*) offers crack-of-dawn balloon trips with one of their local pilots, who also lifts off from **Town Manor B&B** (see *Lodging*) for romantic getaway flights.

BICYCLING In Dundee ride a pleasant 1.8-mile paved loop, the **Lake Marie Bike Path**, overlooking rolling hills topped with citrus; for a longer ride, hit the **Van Fleet State Trail** (see *Greenways*), which starts in Polk City and heads north into Sumter County, providing nearly 30 miles (each way) of on-pavement cycling.

BIRDING Surprisingly, the **Eagle Ridge Mall** retention ponds on US 27 are a popular stop for birders, but you'll also find fabulous birding in most of the region's parks, especially **Lake Kissimmee State Park** (see *Parks*), where I've spotted Florida scrub-jays, crested caracaras, sandhill cranes, wild turkeys, and bald eagles all in one day's visit. **Lake Morton** is where you'll find Lakeland's famed swans (wings are clipped, so they don't fly away) and hundreds of other waterfowl; nearby **Lake Hollingsworth Municipal Park** has a more natural community of wading birds passing through. **Pine Ridge Nature Preserve Trail** at Historic Bok Sanctuary (see *Historic Sites*) is home to 126 wild bird species.

BOATING With 554 lakes in Polk County, imagine the possibilities; you'll find public boat ramps off every major road and along quite a few minor roads as well. The county's largest lakes include Lake Kissimmee, Lake Hatchinhea, and Lake Pierce, all extremely popular destinations for anglers. **Cherry Pocket** and **Jennings Resort** (see *Fish Camps*) are just two of many fish camps catering to anglers with bait and tackle, boat ramps, and live wells.

DRIVING TOURS Solve the mystery of **Spook Hill** (863-676-3445), N Wales Dr, as you defy gravity. Early settlers traveling around Lake "Wailes" noticed their mule-drawn wagons struggling with their loads as they moved downhill. Years later, residents noticed that their cars would roll uphill in this same spot—all by themselves. Test this phenomenon for yourself. I did, and it worked! Drive to the white line at the base of the hill, put your car in neutral, and watch it roll backward, uphill. Watch for cars behind you, as this is a one-way road. Free.

FAMILY ACTIVITIES ✐ **Admiral's Cove** (863-326-5588), 5665 Cypress Gardens Blvd, in front of Admiral's Best Western in Winter Haven (FL 540), offers miniature golf on a challenging little course with a pirate theme, replete with waterfalls and a replica pirate ship. **Family Fun Center** (863-644-1728), 4825 S Florida Ave, Lakeland, also has miniature golf and arcade games; right up the street you can take the family bowling at AMF Lakeland Lanes. **Gator Family Park** (863-648-0567), 4685 US 98, has go-carts, bumper carts, batting cages, and a game room.

Explorations V Children's Museum (863-687-3869; www.explorationsv.com), 109 N Kentucky Ave, Lakeland, offers small children one of the most fun hands-on experiences I've encountered in Florida. Kids play dress-up with clothing and props that let them be a television weather forecaster, a policeman, a fireman, a construction worker, and various other professionals. A miniature Publix supermarket lets the tots get the hang of shopping, and they can withdraw play money from an ATM. In the basement, older kids will enjoy internationally themed sets with challenging puzzles. Open 9–5:30, closed Sun and major holidays; children 2–15 $4, adults $2.

Pottery by the Park (863-687-0405), 105 N Kentucky Ave, Lakeland. Pick your bisque, pick your colors, and sit at the counter to design the platter, mask, or creature of your dreams! Painting fee $6 adults, $4 children (not including bisque purchase); a couple of days after you paint, pick up your completed creation.

FISHING In addition to hundreds of sparkling lakes shimmering with sunfish and bass, you'll find two excellent stocked venues for fishing near Lakeland: **Tenoroc Fish Management Area** (863-499-2421), 3829 Tenoroc Mine Rd, and **Saddle Creek Park** (see *Parks*). Both provide managed impoundments with plenty of bank fishing and special fishing opportunities for youngsters and the disabled.

GENEALOGICAL RESEARCH **Polk County Historical and Genealogical Library** (863-534-4389; www.polk-county.net/library.html), East Main St, in the east wing of the 1908 neoclassical courthouse. This comprehensive research facility stocks family history for residents of the southeastern United States, with full-time staff on site for assistance. Open Tue–Sat 9–5.

GOLF **LekaricA Golf Course in Highland Park Hills** (863-679-9478; www.lekarica.com), 1650 S Highland Park Dr, Lake Wales. The par-72, 18-hole golf course, built by Stiels and VanKleek in 1927, was designed for the way golf was meant to be played: relaxed and uncrowded. The sweeping, rolling hills have a challenging elevation change of 111 feet. Fees: 7–1, 18 holes $30, 9 holes $15; 1–close, 18 holes $26, 9 holes $15, including cart. Walking is allowed 3–close for only $14.

For computerized swing analysis and lessons, stop by **GQ Golf, Inc**. (863-676-8628), Eagle Ridge Mall, 468 Eagle Ridge Dr, Lake Wales, which also carries golf accessories and apparel.

HANG GLIDING Thought you needed mountains to hang glide? Not so! On 200 secluded acres of field and forest, just a few miles south of the theme parks, you'll find a relaxed community of hang gliders at **Wallaby Ranch** (863-424-0070 or

1-800-WALLABY; www.wallabyranch.com), 1805 Dean Still Rd, Davenport. Sample a tandem flight, or learn to fly solo or how to tow gliders with an ultralight at this full-service flight park. Owner and USHGA-certified tandem instructor Malcolm Jones will take you up to 2,000 feet so that you can soar just like the birds. Arrive early while the air is still and calm, as most tandem flights end by 10 AM. After your flight, hang around and grab a cup of coffee and cool conversation in the screened-in rec barn, or wander the property's many hiking trails. Stop by the gift shop, for posters and T-shirts of Lori Sanchez's whimsical Fine Art of Hang Gliding series, depicted in the style of such classic masters as Miró and Picasso (see *Selective Shopping*). Open 7 days, 7:30–sunset, dependent on weather. A 15-minute tandem flight costs $95; package of 10 flights, $650. Observers free.

HIKING I'm amazed at the rapid growth of the Polk County Environmental Lands Program (863-534-7377; www.polk-county.net) over the past several years, as I've watched hiking trails open up on newly acquired public lands that still

Kathy Wolf

SHERRI LEMON READY FOR TAKEOFF AT WALLABY RANCH

FLYING HIGH AT WALLABY RANCH At some time in our lives we have all dreamed that we were flying—soaring high in the sky like Superman. Given any excuse to take to the skies, I'm there. Researching every possible air venue, I found that you can hang glide in the flatlands of Florida, and subsequently made a call to Wallaby Ranch (see *Hang Gliding*). So at the crack-o-doodle-dawn, my daughter Sherri and I headed down US 27 toward Davenport. A short drive down a country road brought us to the entrance of retain a rustic wilderness feel: A parking lot (and maybe a portable toilet) is all you get, but the trails are well marked with a map at the trailhead. Recent additions to the program include the **Lakeland Highlands Scrub**, at the south end of Lakeland Highlands Rd, and **Hickory Lake Scrub** along CR 17 south of Frostproof. You'll also find trails in places like **Saddle Creek Park** (see *Parks*) or in Nature Conservancy and state forest lands along Lake Wales Ridge. Backpackers have several great options, including the **Florida Trail** along the Kissimmee River south of River Ranch and the loop trail systems at **Lake Wales State Forest (Lake Arbuckle Tract)** and **Lake Kissimmee State Park** (see *Parks*).

PADDLING Starting at the Fort Meade Outdoor Recreation Area (see *Parks*), the 67-mile **Peace River Canoe Trail** is a serene float trip down a slow-moving tannic river with sand bluffs, floodplain forests, and dense pine forests. Contact the Canoe Outpost (863-494-1215 or 1-800-268-0083; www.canoeoutpost.com)

the ranch, and there stretching out across the open field, the mist still lingering, we were greeted by a pair of sandhill cranes honking their hellos. Barefoot and smiling, owner Malcolm Jones sauntered over and proclaimed it an awesome day for flying. "You going up? Well, let's go!" We filled out a few papers and got our official hang-gliding card, then headed out to the center of the 45-acre field.

Malcolm instructed us in flight safety, and we snuggled into the comfortable horizontal harness, which looked much like a sleeping bag. As the aerotug started to pull us along, I got a dog's-eye view of the grassy field. Then we were airborne, just a few slight feet off the ground. A deer raced alongside us until we were well above the trees. Climbing higher and higher, I breathed in the view of the 250-acre ranch below. At 2,000 feet, Malcolm released the tugline and we were flying on our own. Really flying! Searching out rising air, he had me pull the bar toward my hip, shifting my weight, and we banked a turn. I had wings—real wings that worked exactly like the ones in my dreams! Slowing the glider by slightly pushing the bar out and shifting my weight again, we circled around and around; I spotted the deer now ambling down a trail.

The time went by much too fast, and soon we were setting up our approach. I felt a rush of adrenaline as we increased our speed heading toward terra firma. And then we were skimming just inches above the field, touched down, and gradually rolled to a stop. Of all the air sports, this is the one that keeps you up the longest. The ranch record is 6½ hours. It's also the least expensive for those who want to learn solo and pilot their own bird. So guess what's on my Christmas list?

in Arcadia for shuttles; the state Office of Greenways and Trails (850-245-2052 or 1-877-822-5208; www.dep.state.fl.us/gwt) can provide specific details and a map of the route.

SKYDIVING **Lake Wales Skydiving Center** (863-678-1003; www.skydivelakewales.com), Lake Wales Airport, 440 Airport Rd. This drop zone is host for many world-record skydiving events and the best novice training center around, with a stadium-seat theater where you can review tapes of teams or get critiques on your own video-recorded flight. A Twin Otter takes you 2.5 miles in the air for a tandem free fall at 120 mph, relative work, accelerated free fall (AFF), or free flying, capturing it all with professionally edited video and photographs. Not quite ready to jump? Sit in the hangar on an eclectic selection of comfy couches and watch the experts pack chutes. Bring your sunscreen, lawn chair, and binoculars and watch pros from around the world gather for the Annual Easter, Thanksgiving, and Christmas Boogies. **Jump 'N' Jacks** is right there in the hangar for after-jump snacks and light meals. First tandem jump $155, and if you want to go back up the same day it's only $104. Video and stills $79. Tandem jumpers must be 18 and less than 230 pounds.

SWAN SPOTTING The swan motif you see around **Lakeland** commemorates the city's long history of swans drifting across its lakes; the original pair lived on Lake Bonny in 1926. In 1954 the queen of England presented two mute swans to Lakeland, descendants of a pair presented from Queen Beatrice to Richard the Lion-Hearted during the Crusades. You'll see several generations of swans gliding across Lake Morton, as well as elegant swan sculptures that are part of "Swansation," a project encompassing 62 unique works of art scattered around the region.

WALKING TOURS

Bartow

You'll find hundreds of beautifully restored historic homes and commercial buildings throughout the city of Bartow. A map reveals 36 of these homes in a self-guided walking tour from the visitors center at 510 N Broadway (or call 1-800-828-7655).

Lakeland

Check with the City of Lakeland Community Development Department (863-834-6011), 228 S Massachusetts Ave, for *A Walking Tour of Downtown Lakeland*, a brochure that leads you past 44 sites of historic and cultural interest around Lake Mirror, Munn Park, and the antiques district. *Touring the City of Haines City: Walking Guide to Historic Downtown* details 24 historic sites of this citrus industry boomtown, established in 1883.

Lake Wales

Roam around downtown Lake Wales (see *Historic Sites*) and stop by the Lake Wales Depot Museum (see *Museums*) to pick up a map of historical and cultural

Sandra Friend

SWAN SCULPTURES DOT DOWNTOWN LAKELAND.

sites, including several well-executed murals.

WATERSKIING Polk County's 500-plus lakes are one of the nation's hot spots for waterskiing; if you're game to try it, talk to an instructor like **Ski Way** (941-326-1754), US 92, Auburndale.

✷ Green Space

BOTANICAL GARDENS ♿ The National **Historic Bok Sanctuary** (863-676-1408; www.boksanctuary.org), 1151 Tower Blvd, is set in the middle of 128 acres on the highest point in peninsular Florida. At 298 feet the view of surrounding areas, including the phosphate pits around Mulberry, is breathtaking. You'll want to see the informative video first to truly appreciate the grounds and tower. Then open your senses. The sanctuary and tower were dedicated as a gift to the American people in 1929 by Pulitzer Prize–winning author Edward W. Bok, a Dutch immigrant and humanitarian, as a place of enjoyment. The world-renowned 60-bell carillon, the largest weighing 12 tons, rivals those heard in Europe and performs for 45 minutes typically around 3 PM. The gift shop offers a wide variety of gifts and books relating to gardening, nature, and Florida topics. Look for the children's hidden garden arbor nearby. Open daily 8–5. Call ahead for exact concert times. $6 adults, $2 ages 5–12. Motorized personal mobility cart available.

Like a formal English garden, Lakeland's small but beautiful **Hollis Garden** (863-603-6281), 702 E Orange St along Lake Mirror, is sectioned off into themed "rooms" that grow increasingly ornate and manicured as they flow downhill toward the lake. Rocky grottoes with lily ponds yield to serene presentations of red, yellow, and green flora around sod centers. Pieces of sculpture and fountains accent the formal gardens. Open 10–dusk, closed Tue. Free.

I remain hopeful that Florida's classic botanical garden, Winter Haven's **Cypress Gardens**, will reopen this fall as announced. The 60-year-old attraction with its lush tropical gardens folded in spring 2003 after a consortium of developers took control of the property. A statewide outcry caused the Florida legislature to purchase part of the property to preserve the gardens. For updates on the park's status, watch the Friends of Cypress Gardens (www. cypressgardens.com) web site.

GREENWAYS Running for nearly 30 miles along a former railroad bed, the **Gen. James A. Van Fleet Trail State Park** (352-394-2280) provides a ribbon of pavement for bikers, in-line skaters, and hikers to traverse rural Polk, Lake, and Sumter Counties. Four trailheads provide access; the Polk City Trailhead is near the junction of FL 33 and CR 665.

NATURE CENTERS **Babson Park Audubon Center** (863-638-1355), FL 17 in Babson Park, protects 3.5 acres of longleaf pine sandhill on the Lake Wales Ridge and offers educational programs for all ages, but especially the kids—they can dress up as the creatures of the ridge and put on puppet shows. You'll also find a bookstore and library in the center. The Caloosa Nature Trail circles the building, giving you a personal introduction to "Florida's desert," the scrub.

Street Audubon Nature Center (863-324-7304; www.lakeregion.net), 115 Lameraux Rd, Winter Haven. Centered on the Mabel Howe House, which has a library with interpretive information on Florida habitats, this 42-acre tract is crisscrossed with nature trails that lead out through hardwood forests to the "Window on Lake Ned" bird blind.

PARKS **Fort Meade Outdoor Recreation Area** (863-285-9562), US 98 east of the bridge, provides access to the Peace River for anglers and canoeists, a short nature trail along the river, sports facilities, and picnic pavilions; it also hosts a country music jamboree (fee) the second Sat of every month.

Lake Kissimmee State Park (863-696-1112), 14248 Camp Mack Rd. On the western shore of Lake Kissimmee, this vast state park encompasses prairies and oak hammocks, pine flatwoods and scrub, and is one of the top places for wildlife-watching in the state: In a single weekend here, I counted 26 deer, two caracaras, a box turtle, a flock of turkeys, alligators, several sandhill cranes, and numerous wading birds. Set up base camp at the campground (water and electric hookups) or hit the backpacking loops (16 miles of trail) for primitive camping. Boat access to Lake Kissimmee, marina and camp store, and a unique living history 1876 **Cracker Cow Camp** open on weekends. Fee.

West of Lakeland on US 92, **Saddle Creek County Park and Campground** (863-665-2283) has a chain of former phosphate pits heavily stocked with fish to attract area anglers; tent and trailer campers will appreciate the simple but peaceful surroundings of the small campground. A 1.2-mile hiking trail follows Saddle Creek along the eastern edge of the park.

WILD PLACES Despite its name, the **Green Swamp** is not an extraordinarily wet place. Covering 860 square miles (including a large chunk of northern Polk

County), it's the headwaters of four major rivers and a crucial natural resource for Central Florida, a place where rainfall percolates through flatwoods, sandhills, and cypress domes to replenish the Floridan Aquifer, the state's primary freshwater resource. Along US 98 north of Lakeland, **Gator Creek Preserve** provides a place for a short walk out into this interesting mélange of habitats; follow Rock Ridge Rd north from US 98 to **Green Swamp West WMA** for access to backpacking along the Florida Trail.

When the rest of Florida was under a few feet of water in Miocene times, long, thin dune-capped islands stood well above the waves—the **Lake Wales Ridge**. As a result, strange and unusual plant species evolved; the ridge has the highest concentration of rare and endangered plants in the continental United States. These are the "mountains" of peninsular Florida, rising up to 300 feet. Several preserves permit access on foot via hiking trails; tread gently. **Lake Wales Ridge State Forest** (863-635-7801), 452 School Bus Rd, includes nearly 14,000 acres around Frostproof, including the **Arbuckle Tract** with its 20-mile Florida Trail backpacking loop; several Polk County Environmental Lands provide access off CR 17, and The Nature Conservancy (863-635-7506) manages **Tiger Creek Preserve**, with trails off Pfundstein Rd in Babson Park and CR 630 south of Lake Wales.

✱ Lodging

BED & BREAKFASTS

Auburndale 33823

Town Manor on the Lake (863-984-4008), 585 FL 559. Live R. J. Straw's 1930s life of luxury in his historic home, where relaxation comes easy in the hammock on the screened back porch overlooking Lake Juliana, or swaddled in a soft robe in an even softer feather bed. Period furnishings and original fixtures accent the imported Brazilian hardwood floors and Italian tiled baths. Innkeeper Nandy makes you feel right at home with fresh lemonade and pastries on arrival; sit by the pool and watch the ducks waddle past, or keep an eye on the lake as a fellow guest comes in for a seaplane landing. I rate this as one of the top B&B experiences in Florida; I started referring my friends here the day after I arrived. The five rooms run $99–179, with romantic getaway, honeymoon, and ballooning packages available.

Bartow 33830

The Stanford Inn (863-533-2393; www.thestanfordinn.com), 555 E Stanford St. Located in the historic district, this charming turn-of-the-20th-century neoclassical home was featured in the movie *My Girl* and is within a short walking distance of all the downtown shops and restaurants. Four rooms, a cottage, and a carriage house, decorated with antique beds, plush quilts, fireplaces, and romantic details, are available for $125–165 a night. The Victorian Rose Room features an 1855 wood-carved Victorian queen-sized bed, private bath, separate shower, and Jacuzzi. The carriage house and cottage have full kitchens. This is one of the few B&Bs with a pool, which is surrounded by a sundeck and lush tropical landscaping, so bring your beach towel.

Lakeland 33801

Shaw House (863-687-7120), 605 E Orange St. With a broad veranda overlooking Hollis Park (see *Botanical Gardens*) and Lake Mirror, this relaxing getaway (circa 1900) is right in the middle of the action. It's a quick stroll along the Lake Mirror promenade to Main St and just a few blocks to Florida Southern College. Each of the four rooms is a small suite with bedroom and sitting room. The baths have an interesting mix of original built-ins and new tile and artsy washbasins. Guests gather on the comfortable porches or in the common living and dining areas downstairs. $89, including full breakfast.

HOTELS AND MOTELS Older motels with budget prices cluster around the "Baseball City" interchange of US 27 and I-4 (outside rural Davenport) and at US 98 and I-4 in Lakeland. Around many of the region's lakes, you'll find old-fashioned 1940s–1960s cottages and family motels along the major highways; they vary greatly as to quality.

THE FRONT DOOR OF THE SHAW HOUSE
Sandra Friend

Lake Wales 33898

LekaricA Country Inn and Golf Course in Highland Park Hills (863-676-8281; 1-888-676-8281; www.lekarica.com), 1650 S Highland Park Dr. Bob and Nancy Weaver have the best-kept secret in town with this 1927 lakeside inn. The minute you walk through the doors you step back to a simpler time of Old Florida elegance and warm family values. The spirit of a bygone era is found everywhere from the friendly staff to the quaint accommodations. The country inn has 23 guest rooms, nine suites, and five spacious apartments with full kitchen and private deck overlooking the lake. Continental breakfast is included. On Tue–Sat the full-service restaurant serves lunch and dinner, and on Sun a fabulous brunch. The extensive and creative menu features such treats as the famous Bok Tower dessert (see *Dining Out*). Outside, relax under the twin live oaks, swim in the lakeside pool, try your skill on the three official Wimbledon cricket courses, or play golf among the pine and citrus trees (see *Golf*). The inn's unique name, LekaricA, was created using a combination of the Weaver children's names—Lesley, Kara, and Eric. The Weavers are still on site, but Kara now runs the dining room and Eric has taken the helm as general manager.

Lakeland 33811

LeMans Suites (1-800-647-7929; www.lemanssuites.com), 1501 Shepherd Rd. Furnished one-story apartments with all linens and housewares, south of downtown. Rates run $35–85, depending on size, amenities (whirlpool tubs available), and length of stay (2-day minimum).

The Lakeland Terrace Hotel (863-688-0800 or 1-888-644-8400; www.terracehotel.com), 329 E Main St. In 1924 this high-rise hotel overlooking Lake Mirror was at the top of its class—a year-round destination, a rarity in those days. Extensively renovated in 1998 to showcase its 1920s charm, the hotel offers 73 comfortable rooms and 15 suites ($149–169), each with a spacious desk with dataport, in-room safe, ironing board, and hair dryer, and what I truly needed after several days on the road: a soft robe and the best set of aromatherapy lotions and potions I've encountered in my travels, perfect for unwinding with a nice soak in the tub.

Winter Haven 33384

Although it's an older motel, the **Lake Roy Beach Inn & Suites** (863-324-6320; www.lakeroybeachinn.com), 1823 Cypress Gardens Blvd, has serious curb appeal—it overlooks sparkling Lake Roy and has a pool right on the lake. The spacious rooms are in great shape and have nice furnishings, with your choice of suites or single rooms for $68–128, including continental breakfast.

RESORTS

Haines City 33844

✐ **Westgate Grenelefe** (1-866-422-7511; www.westgateresorts.com), 3200 FL 546. Once a premier golfing destination, this 1970s resort awaits updating under the new management of Westgate. Only one of the three courses is open, but the greens and their surrounding condos ($69–89 for a hotel room, $89–109 for a spacious villa) blend beautifully into a natural woodland setting that you rarely find in today's resort complexes. Well off the beaten path, it's a quiet destination for relaxing at the pool, playing a round of golf, or reading a book under the shade of a live oak; guided fishing trips available.

River Ranch 33867

Westgate River Ranch (1-800-785-2102; www.westgateriverranch.com), 24700 SR 60 E. Situated on 1,700 pristine acres on the Kissimmee River, this new and improved resort has recently received a face-lift. New individual cabins, waterfront town homes, and golf villas are currently in development. Airboat and swamp buggy rides, horseback riding, barbecue and hayride Fri and Sat nights, American Championship Rodeo Sat night featuring bull riding, barrel racing, and a kids calf scramble, river cruise/pontoon boat rides, trap and skeet range, petting farm, tennis and basketball courts, nine-hole golf course, swimming pool, pony rides, bike and golf cart rentals, catch-and-release fishing, guided nature walks Fri and Sat afternoons. The resort also has a 5,000-foot lighted runway with future plans for airport houses and private hangars. **Fisherman's Cove Restaurant** serves breakfast, lunch, and dinner 7 AM–9 PM. The western saloon features one of Central Florida's top county-and-western bands every Fri and Sat night. The marina has access to both the Atlantic Ocean and Gulf of Mexico.

VACATION HOMES 🐾 ✐ ♿ **Sunsplash Vacation Homes** (863-287-

5846; www.sunsplash.com), off CR 54, Davenport. One of the cheapest ways to take the family on vacation is to rent one of the nearly 3,000 vacation homes in Central Florida. Sunsplash homes are individually owned and decorated by host families, who rent out these spacious, airy houses when they're not living in them. Each has a large full kitchen with all utensils and linens. Some include a screened pool, and smokers and pets can be accommodated. Rates start at $500 per week for a three-bedroom house, and the 75 units on this property are within a 30-minute drive of Disney World.

FISH CAMPS

Dundee

Jennings Resort (863-439-3811), 3600 Jennings Rd, off Canal Rd east of Dundee, Haines City 33844. Anglers will love this century-old beauty spot with RV and tent spaces ($15–20) and concrete block cottages ($62–68) tucked under cabbage palms and oaks on the edge of sparkling blue Lake Pierce; a brand-new screened pool overlooks the expanse of the lake. On-site bait and tackle, fish-cleaning house, and camp store. Cottages have two beds, a small bath, and kitchenette, plus outdoor seating and grill. Book well in advance if you plan an in-season (Jan–Apr) visit.

Cherry Pocket (863-439-2031; www.cherrypocket.com), Cherry Pocket Rd, off Canal Rd east of Dundee, Lake Wales 33898. A 1947 classic on Lake Pierce, with 55 RV spots (mostly booked in snowbird season), eight old-time cabins, a marina, bait and tackle, and one of the best Old Florida restaurants (see *Eating Out*) you'll ever set foot inside.

River Ranch

Westgate River Ranch RV Park (1-800-266-2927; www.westgateriverranch.com), 24700 SR 60 E, 33867. Dude ranch (see *Resorts*).

CAMPGROUND

Davenport 33836

Deer Creek RV Golf Resort (1-800-424-2931), 42749 US 27, is a massive campground with its own golf course and pleasant landscaping preserving natural pines. Paved spaces ($35 summer, $40 winter) have full hookups, and most winter visitors use golf carts to zip around the property. One- and two-bedroom park model units available, $55–75.

✱ Where to Eat

DINING OUT

Lakeland

Antiquarian (863-682-1059), 211 E Bay St. Fine art, smooth jazz, and good food, all set in a bold and playful former Studebaker showroom with changing exhibits from Florida artists. Chef Gary Schmidt's French influence coaxes forth delightful entrées ($22–24) like shrimp and blue crab in caper-dill mayonnaise, Bay Street gumbo, salmon of the day, and roast duck confit in a raspberry-chili sauce with caramelized onion cilantro reduction; a pre-fixed three-course dinner runs $28, including appetizer, soup or salad, and entrée. Leave room for a slice of lemon chess cake, two-layer chocolate torte, or any of the six dessert choices of the evening. Lunch portions cost $9–10. Enjoy live jazz Sat evenings.

Terrace Room (1-888-644-8400),

329 E Main St. Gourmet taste buds will delight at the creative entrées ($19–32) like seared ahi tuna loin and porcini-dusted sea bass, which come accompanied by your choice of three different salads. Try the goat cheese salad, as I did, for an unexpected taste sensation of caramelized bananas and nuts with the baby greens and fried ball of cheese. Five entrées, including two steaks, are straight off the wood grill, the enticing aroma of which pervades the hotel's lobby. Finish off your meal with a delicate chocolate mousse served in a chocolate cup, or a house-special key lime pie. Befitting the elegant surroundings, proper dress is required. Serving all meals daily; dinner reservations recommended.

Lake Wales

Chalet Suzanne Restaurant, Country Inn, and Cannery (863-676-6011 or 1-800-433-6011; www.chaletsuzanne.com), 3800 Chalet Suzanne Dr. Astronaut Jim Irwin, a regular here, first brought their "Moon Soup" aboard Apollo 15, and it has been a staple on several flights since. The Hinshaw family has been creating an aura of romance and culinary delights since 1931. Sit and relax while you gaze across Lake Suzanne as several varieties of turtles amuse you with their water "ballet." Classical music plays in the background, seemingly to their movements. Only two dishes are served at breakfast, but it was still hard to decide—they were both so good. Scrambled eggs were touched with a bit of chives and accompanied by delicate Swedish pancakes served with real maple syrup, or in true Scandinavian style with wild lingonberries. A choice of baked ham or sausage patties completes this dish ($16). Or you can have perfectly poached eggs Benedict with thinly sliced ham and homemade hollandaise, served on a puff pastry ($18). Four-course luncheon entrées ($31–39) and traditional six-course dinners are an event in themselves ($59–78). Check the web site for coupons. Open 7 days.

Refresh yourself at the horseshoe bar, then step through the inviting entry into **LekaricA Restaurant** (863-676-8281 or 1-888-676-8281; www.lekarica.com), 1650 S Highland Park Dr. The private dining room with high ceiling, greenery, and white lattice chairs is reminiscent of the genteel elegance of a time long forgotten. The pink and white tablecloths await the breathtaking presentations of such creative delights as the Golden Gate sandwich, served with sashimi-style tuna, cucumbers, alfalfa sprouts, spinach, onion, lettuce, and wasabi-sesame aioli ($9); the Rum Butter Chicken, a boneless breast grilled and served over angelhair pasta with a rum butter sauce ($16); Tobago Trinity Pasta, served with currants, diced pineapple, and mandarin orange wedges, tossed with sun-dried tomato fettuccine with rogan josh curry cream sauce and topped with skewered jumbo jerk prawns ($17); or Bush Hawk Delmonico, the finest cut of beef grilled the way you like it ($22). Don't forget to save room for dessert. LekaricA is the only restaurant authorized to serve a chocolate replica of the Bok Tower (see *Historic Sites*), which you can have filled with either chocolate or strawberry mousse. Open for lunch, dinner, and Sunday brunch.

Auburndale

The Peacock Tea Room (863-965-1684), 212 Howard St, is a local favorite serving sandwiches, quiches, and homemade desserts, Mon–Fri for lunch.

Joe's Italian Deli & Sicilian Restaurant (863-967-4305), 213 E Lake Ave, features a full line of subs and traditional Italian dishes ($6–8) like baked ziti, eggplant Parmesan, and manicotti florentino for lunch and dinner, Mon–Fri.

Bartow

A sign posted inside **The Cookie Jar Bake Shop** (863-519-3333), 305 E Main St, proclaims that A BALANCED DIET IS A COOKIE IN EACH HAND, and they have a great selection available, including snickerdoodles and First Lady Laura Bush's own cowboy cookies. But they are most famous for their wedding and specialty cakes. Try a slice of the red velvet or lemon coconut with lemon curd ($2). The attractive retro café, with the large mural of Main St on the back wall, also serves a light lunch. Try the croissantwiches in two sizes ($3–5), or chicken or ham and cheese in spinach or sun-dried tomato wraps ($6–7). Barnie's coffee coolers, cappuccino, and flavored coffees are also offered. Open Mon–Fri 7–4.

Take a break from the heat at the popular **Cool Shoppe Ice Cream** (863-533-1635), 135 S Central Ave.

Catfish Country (863-646-6767), 2400 E. F. Griffin Rd, offers relaxed seafood dining with a Cajun flair.

Davenport

The Hotel Tea Room & Flower Corner (863-421-0827), 301 W Maple St. The Flower Corner is full of gifts and collectibles, home to ladies' Red Hat teas, and soon to be a bed & breakfast. The Hotel Tea Room offers an ever-changing menu. Lunch includes a selection of salads, an entrée, sourdough rolls, beverage, and dessert of the day for $9. Reservations recommended.

Dundee

❀ At **Cherry Pocket** (see *Fish Camps*), Old Florida meets gourmet chef: When chef Rich Eten's father bought a funky 1947 fish camp, he convinced his Prudhomme-trained son to come along for the ride. And what a ride it is! Pull in the drive, and you'd assume it's a biker bar; the atmosphere is pure fish camp with a few dressy touches hidden inside. Dinner specials might include frog legs, mahimahi, or grouper, all prepared in Creole fashion with lots of starches and sauces; my plate of Key West grouper held enough food for several meals. Entrées run $9–18, and it's not just seafood: You'll find filet mignon and steak Oscar on the menu, as well as lemon-pepper chicken and fettuccine dishes. My next trip back, I'll order the Jack Attack Platter ($16), with half a pound of crab legs, fried catfish fillet, beer-battered shrimp, oysters, coleslaw, french fries, and hushpuppies. It's hard to find, you'll wait for an hour or two on weekends, and the rest rooms are up on the hill, but it's an experience you won't want to miss.

Melonie's Cafe (863-439-5416), 209 Main St. Open since 1987, this local establishment displays an eclectic bit of roadside Americana. And although there is no white-water rafting near Dundee, that won't stop Melonie or her stepsons from talking about their trips. Photos of their adventures—along with a kayak hung from the ceiling—encourage discussion. Soups ($2–3), salads ($4–6), burgers and sandwiches ($5). Top the meal off with Natahalla Crunch ($2), a hot fudge ice cream delight. Breakfast and lunch Mon–Sat.

Haines City

Magnolia Memories Gourmet Restaurant and Tea Room (863-421-7764), 1100 Polk City Rd. Enjoy gourmet lunch specials and afternoon tea with signature mushroom delights, tea cookies, tea sandwiches, and scones, served in a gracious old southern home 11–2, Tue–Sat. Afternoon tea by appointment (see *Selective Shopping*).

No tall tales here, just mouthwatering seafood at **Fish Tales, Inc**. (863-421-3474), 35510 US 27. All-you-can-eat catfish ($12), or try some frog legs ($14). You'll also find such veggies as okra, turnip greens, and black-eyed peas. Catch the dinner theater during the summer months. Open daily for lunch and dinner.

Lake Alfred

Part of **Barn & Stable Antiques** (see *Selective Shopping*), the **Backporch Restaurant & Tea Room** presents a delightful picnic lunch 11–3 daily. Fill your basket with your choice of soup or salad, sandwich, and dessert for $7, and you'll be served in the elegant garden room or outdoors on a porch overlooking a lily pond.

Gary's Oyster Bar & Seafood House (863-956-5055), 670 E US 17-92, is the oldest oyster bar in Polk County, where you can pick up a dozen raw or steamed shucked oysters for $6. The house-special platter ($18) represents Florida's aquatic bounty—fried catfish, shrimp, scallops, oyster, turtle, 'gator tail, and frog legs; I'd go for the broiled seafood sampler ($18) with snow crab, petite lobster tail, Gulf flounder, and sautéed scallops. Dinner served daily, $9–18.

Remember When Café (863-956-0299), 148 Haines Blvd W. Salad lovers take note: This sandwich shop has a signature salad with mandarin oranges, strawberries, red onion, pineapple, pecans, raisins, and blue cheese on a bed of mixed greens. Now that's a *garden* salad! Serving lunch, $4–6.

Lavender & Lace Tearoom and Gift Shop (863-956-3998), 430 N Lakeshore Way, is a proper Victorian tearoom serving upscale lunches ($8–12). It's decorated in grape and hyacinth arbors; one entire room is lined floor to ceiling with tea sets. But what caught my attention was the choice of eight desserts (starting at $4), including a three-layer Hummingbird Cake with bananas, nuts, pineapple, and cream cheese. Yum! Mon–Sat 11–3:30.

Lake Hamilton

Gift Mill Food, Fun 'n Factory Store (863-439-5075), 823 US 27. Grab a bite to eat at the Bread Bowl Café. It's a shop, it's a restaurant—and what a restaurant, serving fresh food fast in a nostalgic setting. Massive salads, stews, and soups are served in freshly baked bread bowls; sandwiches come with your choice of fresh side and a crisp dill pickle. Order up a bottomless root beer from the old-fashioned soda fountain, and don't forget a scoop of homemade ice cream, like peppermint chocolate chip or sugar-free butter pecan. Lunch bowls and sandwiches cost

$5–7; the menu is expanding to include steak and seafood dinners soon. One of the few places in the area open till 7:30!

Lakeland

Lakeland is where it all began for **Crispers** (863-682-7708; www.crispers.com), 217 N Kentucky Ave, a new Florida chain that's a gourmet extension of Publix Supermarkets. Creative soups, sandwiches, and salads like Thai fusion, Niçoise, and Greek are freshly made ($3–8); don't miss the tasty fresh-baked mile-high carrot cake and specialty cheesecakes. Open daily, lunch and dinner.

The new **Garden Bistro** (863-686-3332), 702 E Orange St, feels like an extension of adjacent Hollis Gardens, with hand-painted ivy on the interior walls, garden tables and benches to dine at, and outdoor seating overlooking Lake Mirror's promenade. Open for breakfast ($3–5) and lunch ($3–7), the restaurant's menu reflects creativity and simplicity, with selections like Belgian waffles, sushi salad, hummus pita, and pretzel-wrapped franks.

Harry's Seafood Bar & Grille (863-686-2228), 101 N Kentucky Ave, is one of those perennial Florida chains you'll find in five other downtowns; in Lakeland, the New Orleans party atmosphere is infectious. I was unable to finish a heaping order (three!) of pan-seared crabcakes with creamy smashed potatoes, but I still had to try a slice of Lulu's Louisiana Mud Pie: It was heaven for this chocoholic. Open for lunch and dinner, entrées and platters $7–9.

The aroma will lead you straight to **Jimbo's Pit BBQ** (863-683-3777), 1215 E Memorial Blvd (US 92), serving Lakeland since 1964. Savor tender real pit barbecue for reasonable prices, lunch and dinner—if you don't fill up on the free kosher dills and hot cherry peppers first!

JJ's Café (863-683-5267), 132 S Kentucky Ave, offers fresh salads, chargrilled sandwiches, burgers, quesadillas, subs, wraps, and panini in a relaxed downtown atmosphere, $3–7. Stop in for a muffin and coffee in the morning, or enjoy a fresh steak sandwich (neatly trimmed sirloin tips, no less!) for lunch. Open 7–3 daily, 4–10 Fri and Sat.

Kick back at **Mitchell's Coffee House** (863-680-2944), 235 N Kentucky Ave, with a cup of coffee and a muffin in the morning, or a "create your own" deli sandwich in the afternoon ($4–6, 11–2). Specialty coffees include Almond Joy and I Dream of Jeannie; try one with a slice of Coca-Cola cake.

Olde Curiosity Shoppe & Tea Room (863-802-0064), 133 Palmetto Ave. An antiques shop stocked with British imports sets the stage for traditional British fare like ploughman's lunch and beans on toast, as well as afternoon tea.

At the **Rib House** (863-687-8260), 2918 S Florida Ave, it's like eating with family—the waitresses know the regulars, and everyone banters about what's up with whom. I stopped in for breakfast and was blown away by their creative rendition of stuffed French toast (a special that day). The extensive breakfast menu runs $2–7 for eggs, omelets, scramblers, sandwiches, and pancakes and French toast; lunch and dinner focus on barbecue and deli favorites. Open daily at 7 AM.

Lake Wales

While shopping in the downtown historic district, stop by **Stuart Avenue Café** (863-676-9000), 216 E Stuart Ave—a small place with big taste.

Polk City

Compass Rose, at Fantasy of Flight (see *Attractions*), takes you back to a 1940s airport commissary, with a display case full of tempting pies and the availability of fresh milk shakes affecting your menu choice right off the bat: Will it be burgers, salads, or sandwiches, with your choice of fries or soup? Open 8–4 daily, $3–7.

Winter Haven

No matter what you choose at **El Norteno** (863-298-0993), 1925 6th St NW, it'll be great; I loved the enchiladas here. Serving authentic Mexican food and drinks in a casual atmosphere: burritos, enchiladas, tacos, and platters for $6–14 (dinner) and $4–6 (lunch).

Tsunami Sushi (863-293-2395), 317 W Central Ave, is a five-star downtown sushi bar with a bistro feel. Order sushi rolls, or try sashimi and tempura platters; items can be ordered à la carte. Open for dinner.

✷ Entertainment

One of the last remaining themed theaters in the United States, the **Polk Theatre** (863-682-7553), 127 S Florida Ave, Lakeland, has that grand cinema magic lacking nowadays in the multiscreen cineplex: After all, the Munchkins danced here on the 50th anniversary of the *Wizard of Oz*! Seats slope gently down to the red-velvet-curtained stage; the balcony section has twinkling stars overhead. Films, primarily independent productions, are shown on weekends ($5.50 adults, $3.75 students), with a slate of live performances running Nov–Apr, where you can catch performers like Roger Williams, Bea Arthur, the Coasters, and the Royal Shakespeare Company.

Theatre Winter Haven (863-294-SHOW) at Chain O'Lakes Park offers at least six quality stage productions—musicals, plays, and dramatic readings—every season. Performances run Thu–Sun evenings; individual tickets $18 musicals, $16 nonmusicals.

Lake Wales Little Theatre, Inc. (863-676-1266), 411 N 3rd St, Lake Wales. Since 1978 this little theater has been in continuous operation, bringing high-quality entertainment to patrons near and far away. Call for schedule.

Affordable quality live theater can be found at the **Pied Piper Players** (863-603-7529; www.piedpiperplayers.com), Lake Mirror Center Theatre, 121 S Lake Ave, Lakeland. Now entering its 19th season, seven productions feature musicals, comedies, and Pulitzer Prize–winning dramas. $12–14.

✷ Selective Shopping

Bartow

The two-story circa-1893 brick structure at 125 S Central Ave houses **Chinoiserie Antiques** (863-534-8534), but it was used as Lovett's Grocery for 20 years, then Lizzie Epperson's Millinery from 1913 until 1939. Interior design service is also available.

Flower Cart (863-533-8861), 1425 N Broadway. Just because you're on vacation doesn't mean you can't have fresh flowers in your inn or timeshare. Take out fresh handpicked flowers for half price at the Flower Happy Hour every Fri, 3:30–5:30 PM.

There's lots of antiquing up and down Main St. Start at **Yates Antiques**

(863-533-7635) for fine quality antiques. **Thom Downs Antiques** (863-519-0395) has garden accessories and fountains. Go to **Apple Seeds** (863-533-6400) for country gifts, furniture, and a great Christmas display. **Century Room Antiques & Gifts** (863-533-6274) has everything from small collectibles to large furniture. **Mr. & Mrs. Mac's Farm Antiques** (863-534-8282; www.primitivesand collectibles.com) is known for primitives and Amish-made jams. You'll find military items and banks at **Nelson's Nostalgia, Antiques & Collectibles Mall** (863-533-2365). Located inside an old department store, **Phillips' Antiques** (863-533-2365) offers a wide range of items. And for Roseville pottery, try **Yesterday and Today Collectibles** (863-533-0290).

Dundee
Southern Comfort Antiques (863-439-4944), 29119 US 27 N, houses a couple of dozen antiques and collectibles dealers in 4,000 square feet of air-conditioned comfort.

Eagle Lake
Earl's Trading Post (863-294-5389), 371 FL 17 N, just north of Bartow. Nice assortment of better-quality used furniture, antiques, and collectibles.

Haines City
South by Southwest Innovations (863-419-1056; www.sbyswest innovations.com), 600 E Hinson Ave. When Jan Bowen moved back to Florida from Taos, she brought the Southwest she loved with her. Native American originals—hand-painted pottery, sculpture, ceremonial rattles—fill the nooks of this expansive shop, the largest southwestern outlet in Florida.

Lake Alfred
Barn & Stable Antiques (863-956-2227), FL 557 at FL 557A. Since 1970, this rambling collection of red buildings on a family ranch has housed one of the best-kept shopping secrets in Florida—the quality antique furnishings here are cheaper than buying new from most furniture stores! In addition to chairs, tables, love seats, and armoires, you'll find classic stained glass, two gift shops with home decor items (one seasonal, the other Far Eastern in tone), a nursery, and the Backporch Restaurant & Tea Room (see *Eating Out*). Take your time and browse a while; this is one place I'd drive out of my way for.

At **Biggar Antiques** (863-956-4853), 140 W Haines Blvd, everything is bigger—this 40-year-old family business is the home of huge advertising items, like Pop-Tarts boxes you could crawl into and giant Bayer Aspirin bottles. Great selection of advertising signs and posters, too!

International Market World (941-665-0062), 1052 US 92 W, an enormous flea market and auction at the US 17-92 junction, has a large covered building bustling with excitement every weekend as hundreds of vendors set out their wares. Fri–Sun 8–3.

Lake Alfred Antique Mall (863-956-2488), 155 E Haines Blvd, is full of tiny treasures like thimbles, cameos, and saltcellars; I had fun browsing through stacks of classic Florida postcards.

Gourmet goodies abound at **Potpourri Antiques** (863-956-5535), 142 W Haines Blvd, where seasonal gift items accent glassware, dishes, and home decor.

You can't miss **Sherman's** (863-956-8058), with its antique playground equipment outside; inside, it'll delight the inner child with toys from your past (or mine, at least) like tin cars, windup walkers, Chatty Cathy, and Holly Hobbie; some of the wares are displayed on a 200-year-old ox yoke table.

Lake Hamilton

In the two small cottages at **Century Cottage Antiques & Gifts** (863-439-0203), 29890 US 27, browse through the well-kept rooms for great prices on blue lace glass, Victorian lamps, jewelry, and furnishings.

Gift Mill Food, Fun 'n Factory Store (see *Eating Out*). It's hard to believe this place started as a clothing manufacturing company's outlet store. Since 1992, the shop has exploded in size, and is stocked with everything from fur coats to wind chimes, chocolate-covered blueberries, creative cookbooks, and, yes, Exclusively Pegi Goff clothing, with the original design appliqués still manufactured on site.

Clown Rushmore (863-439-8928), 29600 US 27. Where are the clowns? You won't have to beep your red nose, as this museum/gift shop has one of the most extensive clown collections anywhere, with over 20,000 on display. Open Tue–Sun 10–5.

Lakeland

At **Brooke Pottery** (863-688-6844; www.brookepottery.com), 223 N Kentucky Ave, I was swept away by the sensual shapes and bold colors of this functional art—but then, I'm a sucker for pottery. This fine craft shop is the cornerstone of the downtown shopping district, a mainstay for 15 years, filled with beautiful items like raku fish, witch balls, and spoons carved from wild cherry.

Tucked away in Traders Alley, **Caseylynn Antiques & Books** (863-682-2857), 214 Traders Alley, has rare and collectible books, used books, and paper ephemera.

Lloyds of Lakeland (863-682-2787), 301 N Kentucky Ave, offers two floors stuffed with antiques and collectibles, including an incredible collection of glass: Fenton, cobalt, ruby, pressed, and more.

The fine mahogany tables at **Peacock Antiques** (863-686-7947), 234 N Kentucky Ave, look like they've been set for dinner, with curios, tea sets, and classic glassware.

East of downtown Lakeland, look for **Second Hand Rose** (863-665-0755), 600 S Combee Ave, where dealer booths contain retro toys, old Florida postcards, glassware, and other ephemera; radio-controlled model airplanes take up one corner of the first floor.

🐾 Since 1977, Suzanne Merritt of **Benson's Canine Cookies** (863-647-0851; www.bensonscaninecookies.com), 4525 S Florida Ave #6, has been cooking up gourmet delights for the canine crowd. Named for her fluffy companion, Benson, who puts his "paw of approval" on every batch of cookies. There must be something to it, as this little dog just celebrated his 18th birthday! Every package contains over 3 ounces of real meat, wheat germ, chopped garlic, and brewer's yeast with no fillers, salt, sugar, by-products, preservatives, or artificial coloring. Shipping available.

Lake Wales

Local and national artists' work can be purchased in the fine arts and crafts gift shop at the **Lake Wales Arts Center** (863-676-8426;

www.lakewalesartscenter.org); see *Art Galleries*.

It's at **Chalet Suzanne Restaurant, Country Inn, and Cannery** (863-676-6011 or 1-800-433-6011; www.chaletsuzanne.com), 3800 Chalet Suzanne Dr, that you'll find ceramicist Boz, creating colorful ceramic soup dishes in the Norwegian style. The famed "Moon Soup" is served on his creations in the restaurant (see *Dining Out*). Wander around the grounds; many famous celebrity autographs can be found in the sunken Autograph Garden. Browse through the gift shop inside the inn's lobby or stroll down the brick walkway to the soup cannery, where you can go on a free guided cannery tour, complete with soup and sauce sampling. Open daily.

Spook Hill (see *Historic Sites*) isn't the only haunted site in Lake Wales. The spirit of a previous owner supposedly haunts the two floors of the 1928 country store and gas station, **Antique Mall Village** (863-293-5618), 3170 US 17 N. The local landmark has been a favorite for antiques shoppers since 1977. You name it. It's here.

Historic Downtown Lake Wales (www.historiclakewales.com) (see *Historic Sites* and *Special Events*) will take you back to the 1920s with several vintage shops and eclectic eateries. The **MarketPlace** is home to the weekly farmer's market Fri 8–2. Victorian, primitive, shabby chic, and retro antiques are found at **Ageless Accents** (863-679-8686), 118 E Stuart Ave. You'll find a nice variety of antiques and collectibles at **Inglenook Antiques** (863-678-1641), 3607 N Scenic Hwy (FL 17), which also sells herbal products and alternative health books in a quaint pre-1920s home. Wander over 4,000 feet of space at **Once Upon a Tyme Antiques** (863-676-0910), 201 N Scenic Hwy. Once you've selected your treasure, go to **Bruce's Antiques** (863-676-4845), located behind Once Upon a Tyme, for any needed antique restoration. For rare books or forgotten decorating accents, stop by **Bittersweet Memories** (863-676-4778), 247 E Park Ave. Pick out a new bauble at **B S D Galleries** (863-679-2787), 208 E Stuart Ave, or **Gallery on Park** (863-679-3932; www.historiclakeswales.com/galleryonpark), 16 W Park Ave, which both offer their own style of handcrafted gold and silver jewelry and blown glass.

Winter Haven

Andy Thornal Expedition Outfitter (863-299-9999 or 1-800-499-9890; www.andythornal.com), 336 Magnolia Ave SW. Whether you're planning a backpacking trip on the Florida Trail or looking for technical clothes and lures for your next fishing trip, this is the place to come: Their selection encompasses all outdoor sports, and they run fly-casting and fly-tying schools.

What to do with an old five-and-dime? **The Antique Connection** (863-294-6866), 270 W Central Ave, fills it up with dealer booths and an ice cream parlor in the back corner. Furnishings, glassware, and dishes dominate the stock.

Filling two floors of a 1928 country store and gas station, **Antique Mall Village** (863-293-5618), 3170 US 17 N, is a local landmark, a favorite for antiques shoppers since 1977 and complete with its own haunt: the ghost of an owner who died while counting the day's receipts. Mountains of saltshakers, piles of paintings, brass and tin and aluminum items, advertising signs, record albums—you name it, it's here. Closed Sun.

Classic Collectibles & Antiques (863-294-6866), 279 W Central Ave, is a sprawling complex of dealer booths with a nice selection of art glass and collectible glassware (Carnival, Fenton, Depression, and ruby) as well as unique furnishings like a circa-1790 deacon's bench in English oak.

Perfect Elements (863-294-2279), 329 W Central Ave. A fun and whimsical shop of home decor: art with bold faces and bright colors, fairies and candles, Silvestri items, and funky teapots.

CITRUS STANDS, FARMER'S MARKETS, AND U-PICK During the winter citrus season, expect to see roadside fruit sellers along US 27 and SR 60 with temporary stands and pickup trucks.

Auburndale

Walker Groves (1-800-887-1253), 580 FL 559. With citrus groves and pine forests perched above Lake Juliana, the Walker family has one of the most historic orange stands in the state: They've been handing out samples of fresh-squeezed orange juice since 1884. Stop by for a sample and walk away with a bagful of fresh fruit.

Davenport

Webb's Candy (863-422-1051 or 1-800-289-9322; www.citruscandy.com), 250 US 27 S. Open daily 9:30–6:30. Call for tour information. Florida's oldest citrus-packing and candy factory was started in the 1920s by two friends, Miss Blogett and Miss Stilman, who still live nearby. Their unique recipe for "citrus candies" is the same one used today by the Webb family. Paul and Nadine Webb, no strangers to candy making, brought with them over 100 chocolate and fudge recipes, including their silky goat's-milk fudge. Take a tour of the candy factory, where the yummy confections are still made by hand in the original copper kettles and water-welled cooled tables. Free gift wrapping. Shipping available.

Dundee

Davidson of Dundee (863-687-3869; 1-800-654-0647; www.davidsonofdundee.com), US 27. Open daily. Watch while citrus candy, chocolates, marmalades, and jellies are made right in the factory kitchen. Then sample such fresh delights as pecan orangettes, creamy nougat, and key lime truffles. Shop the enormous gift store for fresh citrus (in-season), attractive candy baskets, and marmalades. Shipping available.

Fruitree Fruit Shop (863-439-1396), US 27. Fruits, candies, and Florida souvenirs all at a great price. This is the place for authentic cypress-knee crafts. Cypress roots can no longer be harvested, so these will soon become rare to own. Beautiful cypress clocks $10–150.

Haines City

At the **Haines City Farmers Market** (863-421-3773), amble around Railroad Park on Wed 8–5 to choose from fresh local produce, baked goods, and craft items. **The Orange Ring** (863-422-1938), 35969 US 27, featuring Indian River citrus, has been a local fixture since the 1970s.

Gifts and antiques are for sale amid gracious southern charm at **Magnolia Memories** (863-421-7764), 1100 Polk

City Rd. Gourmet lunch and afternoon tea served Tue–Sat (see *Eating Out*).

Lakeland

Selling produce from a little green shed since 1979, **Pam's Fruit Stand** (863-647-3695), 434 Pipkin St, carries seasonal regional fruits and veggies like collard greens, pumpkins, and strawberries from nearby Plant City.

Lake Wales

Local produce farmers and students from Roosevelt School offer quality fruits, vegetables, and herb plants at the MarketPlace in **Historic Downtown Lake Wales** (see *Historic Places*) each Fri 8–2.

Winter Haven

Pinecrest Farms (863-293-6518), 2750 US 17 N, sells fresh organic produce and herbs.

✷ Special Events

The "Polkpourri" of festivals and events throughout the county include several art exhibitions, antiques shows, and heritage festivals.

January: **Festival of the Buffalo Pow Wow** (863-665-0062; www.intlmarketworld.com), International Market World, 1052 W US 92, Auburndale. Experience the heritage and culture of Native Americans at this 3-day celebration of traditional food, arts, crafts, dance, drumming, dancing, storytellers, and live buffalo. Special events for children on Fri 9–2. Fee.

Alafia River Rendezvous—Visitor Days (863-965-0386; www.floridafrontiersmen.org), Homeland. Just south of Bartow, where mountain men once met to trade wares, this pre-1840 living history event features food vendors, shooting competitions, knife throwing, and more. $6.

February: **Annual Mardi Gras Festival** (863-638-2686; www.lakewalesmardigras.com), Lake Wales. This annual event is on the Sat prior to Fat Tuesday and features musical entertainment, gala balls, and a colorful parade through Historic Downtown Lake Wales.

Annual Lake Wales Fine Arts Show, the Lake Wales Arts Center (863-676-8426; www.lakewalesartscenter.org), 1099 SR 60 E. This annual arts show is in its 34th year with more than 24,000 visitors. Fine art and entertainment on the shores of Lake Wales.

April: **Bloomin' Arts Festival** (863-644-4907 or 863-533-2600; www.bartowchamber.com), 1240 E Main St, Bartow. One of Florida's premier arts shows, drawing some of the finest artists throughout Florida and the Southeast. Brought to you by the Bartow Art Guild, this spring arts and flower show exhibits the works of 175 artists and craftspeople and offers a student art exhibit, quilt show, antique car show, food, and more.

More than 30 years old, the weeklong **Sun 'n Fun Fly In** (863-644-2431; www.sun-n-fun.org) held in early Apr at the Florida Air Museum, Lakeland (see *Museums*), is the second largest general aviation event of its kind in the world. Expert aviators and eager participants fly in from more than 80 countries to exchange information via more than 400 forums, seminars, and workshops on aviation. Some 500 commercial exhibitors strut their wares, and daily air shows entertain the throng of more than 600,000 visitors during the week. If you love aviation, everything you ever wanted to learn is here—don't miss it!

May: **Historic Bok Sanctuary Concert** (863-688-3742), presented by the Imperial Symphony Orchestra.

October: **Crickette Club Annual Halloween Parade & Carnival** (863-534-0120; www.bartowchamber.com), IMC Park, Bartow. This old-fashioned fall event has been around since 1941 and is one of the largest costumed events in Central Florida.

Fall Festival (863-421-3773), Historic Railroad Park, Haines City. Crafts, food, entertainment, children's costume contest, and auction.

Cracker Story Telling Festival (863-284-4268), Homeland Heritage Park, Bartow. Polished storytellers weave tall tales of Florida history at this fun and educational event. Walk the grounds while local musicians fill the air with Florida folk music. Food vendors and crafters. Cracker whip contest on Sat. $6 adults, $4 children.

Pops in the Park (863-688-3743), IMC Agrico Outdoor Stage, Bartow. Concert presented by the Imperial Symphony Orchestra.

Annual Pioneer Days (863-678-4209). A celebration of Lake Wales history at the Depot Museum and around Lake Wales. Historical reenactments and antique car parade along S Scenic Hwy (US Alt 27), with lots of crafts, artisans, food, and entertainment.

Annual Downtown Bartow Winter Craft Fair (863-533-7125 or 863-534-4030; www.bartowchamber.com). This outgrowth of the Bloomin' Arts Festival has over 160 craft booths, produce, plants, children's activities, and food, helping you get an early start on holiday shopping.

Quilts and Tea (863-419-4797), Davenport Historic District. Throughout the historic district, the Heart & Sew Quilters of Davenport features more than 100 antique quilts and their history. Certified quilt appraiser on site. Call in advance for tickets ($7) to the afternoon tea or brunch.

The **Lake Wales Ridge Folk Art Festival** (863-676-4778), the MarketPlace in Historic Downtown Lake Wales (see *Historic Sites*), celebrates American music with live bluegrass, country, and gospel music. You'll find traditional crafts, food, and old-fashioned children's games, and at night everyone joins in the fun at the Evening Circle Dance.

November–January: **City Lights—Cypress Nights**, a countywide holiday lighting festival, is an annual tradition throughout Polk County. Each town has its own lighting theme. Auburndale is the city of wreaths; Bartow, the city of nostalgia; Davenport, the city of holly; Dundee, the city of friends; Eagle Lake, the city of mistletoe; Fort Meade, the city of trees; Frostproof, the city of snowflakes; Haines City, the city of angels; Lake Alfred, Toyland; Lake Wales, the city of bells; Lakeland, the city of swans; Mulberry, a winter wonderland; Polk City, the city of deer; and Winter Haven, the city of poinsettias. Take in the lights in Bartow from a 42-seat horse-drawn wagon or play in the snow in Haines City.

Christmas at Pinewood (863-676-1408; www.boksanctuary.org), Historic Bok Sanctuary, 1151 Tower Blvd (see *Historic Sites*). Tour includes Bok Sanctuary admission: $14 adults, $8 children. All 20 rooms in the 1930s Mediterranean Revival mansion are lavishly decorated in the spirit of Christmas.

December: **Seasonal Carillon Music** (863-676-1408; www.boksanctuary.org), Historic Bok Sanctuary, 1151 Tower Blvd, Lake Wales. Holiday songs played on the 60-bell carillon at half-hour intervals. $8 adults, $3 children, includes admission to Bok Tower Sanctuary (see *Historic Sites*).

Life of Christ Passion Play (863-676-9300), Lake Wales. The birth of Jesus Christ, the baptism of John the Baptist, and more is performed live with spectacular costumes, lighting, and special effects on one of the largest sets in the country. Order tickets early, as this one sells out fast. $20 adults, $15 children. Group rates available.

Parade of Trees (863-533-7125), Polk County Historical Museum, Old Courthouse Bldg, Bartow. $1 adults, free to children 12 and under. Visitors—not trees—parade down Candy Cane Lane among beautifully decorated Christmas trees. Vote for your favorite themed tree by placing "A Penny for Your Thoughts" in the jingling penny jar in front of each tree.

Jingle Bell Jaunt (863-439-5083 or 863-438-0697), Bartow. $9 adults, $6 children; those under 3 can ride for free on your lap. Horses dressed in their Christmas finery and jingling sleigh bells pull a 42-seat wagon past 150 lighted homes. The easy-entry steps with handrails make this a nice ride for all ages. Early reservations are recommended.

Glitter, Glisten and Snow (863-421-3773), Historic Railroad Park, Haines City. The city transforms into a magical winter wonderland, including a mountain of snow to play in! This flurry of an event is free and features chestnuts, cider, cookies, entertainment, and Santa.

LAKE COUNTY

Central Florida's sparkling lakes provide a natural backdrop to small towns and villages scattered across the gently rolling Central Highlands. The name is no misnomer: Lake County has more than 1,000 lakes, many renowned for their bass fishing. During the post–Civil War Reconstruction period, settlers streamed into Central Florida, eager to nab land grants. Named the seat of Lake County in 1872, **Astatula** was founded on the shores of Little Lake Harris. But the subsequent shift of population to the railroad corridor forced the county seat to move to its present location, **Tavares**, on the western shore of Lake Dora. Established on a knoll on the eastern shore of Lake Dora, the 1880s village of Royellou became **Mount Dora**, named for Dora Ann Drawdy, its first permanent homesteader. Its growth, fueled by early steamboat traffic, accelerated after the first steam train pulled into town. Known as Florida's antiques capital, Mount Dora retains that turn-of-the-20th-century feel—and has hilly streets reminiscent of a New England village. Unexpectedly hilly thanks to ancient sinkholes turned to lakes, **Clermont** saw its first residents in 1884; the historic district is now off the beaten path off FL 50 at 8th St. **Leesburg** dates back to 1853, and its history is reflected in its charming downtown.

As in much of Florida, developers shaped the modern landscape. After devastating freezes in the 1980s, the sweet fragrance of orange blossoms in spring as you drive down US 27 was replaced by a carpet of nearly treeless subdivisions and landscaped retirement villages along US 27 around Clermont and **Lady Lake**. In the early 1900s, developers in on the Florida land boom created genteel lakeside communities like **Howey-in-the-Hills** and **Eustis**. While Eustis is small, it has a gorgeous turn-of-the-20th-century downtown, accentuated by the beauty of lakeside Ferran Park; Magnolia Ave forms the core of its downtown district. **Umatilla** shows off its heritage as a citrus town—not only are the lakes still surrounded by orange groves, but a large citrus-packing plant dominates the town as well. Umatilla is the gateway to the Ocala National Forest. To the west of Clermont, the towns of **Groveland** and **Mascotte** grew up around cattle ranching; Groveland retains a frontier-town feel.

GUIDANCE The **Lake County Visitor's Center**, 20763 US 27, sits on the west side of US 27 between Leesburg and Clermont, near Florida's Turnpike; open

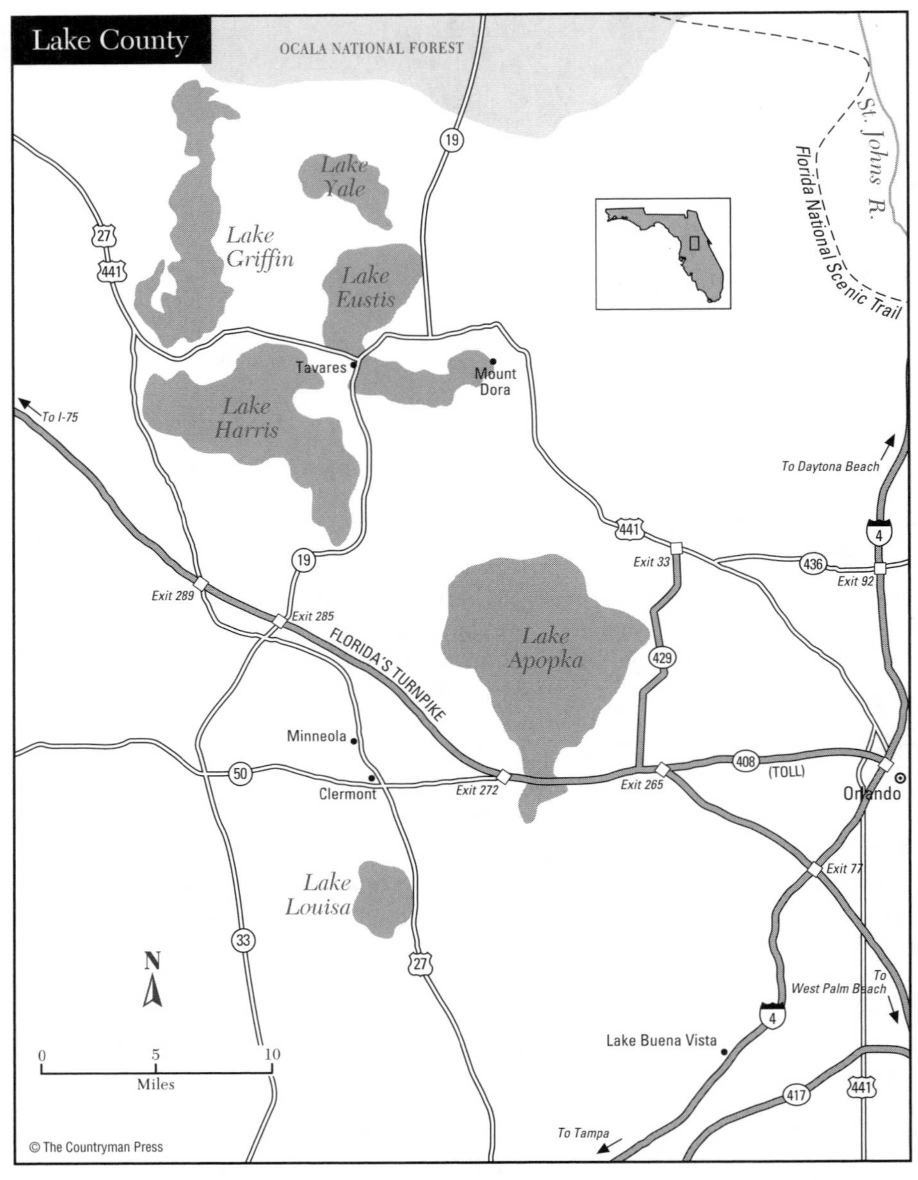

8–5 daily, offering free orange juice and lots of helpful information. In Mount Dora, stop in the old ACL railroad station, now the **Mount Dora Chamber of Commerce**, for flyers on local accommodations and shops. You may also contact **Lake County Economic Development & Tourism** (1-800-798-1071, www .lakecountyfl.com), 315 W Main St, Tavares 32778.

GETTING THERE *By car*: **US 441**, **US 27**, **FL 19**, and **FL 33** provide north–south access through most of Lake County's communities; Florida's Turnpike has two Lake County exits near Leesburg and Clermont.

By air: **Orlando International Airport** provides the closest commuter service for Lake County.

By bus: **Greyhound** (352-787-4782) stops at 1006 S 14th St and US 27 in Leesburg.

PARKING In addition to plenty of street parking and small municipal lots throughout **Mount Dora**, there's covered parking at the end of Donnelly St by the railroad tracks; all free and unlimited in time. **Clermont** offers free street parking with 2-hour limits, as does **Eustis**; find one of the small surface lots if you want to park longer.

PUBLIC REST ROOMS A rare find in Florida, but Lake County has them. In **Mount Dora**, they're in Childs Park, adjacent to the railroad depot; in downtown **Clermont**, at the corner of Minneola and 8th St.

MEDICAL EMERGENCIES Major hospitals include **Florida Hospital Waterman** (352-253-3388; www.fhwat.org), US 441, Tavares, and **Leesburg Regional Medical Center** (352-323-5762), 600 E Dixie Ave, Leesburg.

✷ To See

ART GALLERIES

Eustis

Lake Eustis Museum of Art (352-357-4952), 113 N Bay St. Local artists shine in this public venue that hosts traveling art exhibits, showcases fine arts from its permanent collection, and holds quarterly juried art competitions. Open Mon–Sat noon–4.

Mount Dora

Europa Gallery (352-385-9450; www.europagallery.com), 351-A N Donnelly St. Rotating exhibits of regional art with stunning realism that captures Florida's hidden places.

Mount Dora Center for the Arts (352-383-0880), 138 E 5th Ave. Regional art and cultural center presenting rotating monthly exhibits in the gallery and an annual arts festival. The center sponsors **4th Thursdays** May–Aug, with tastings, live music, and artistic demonstrations in the evenings.

The Red Door Studio (352-383-8004), 109 E 4th Ave. Original art by Rudy Drapiza on massive canvases; vases and watercolors by fellow artists.

ATTRACTIONS The **Citrus Tower** (352-394-4061; www.citrustower.com), 141 N US 27, still stands high above Clermont, but the view just isn't what it was when I first took the elevator to the top in the 1960s. On a clear day, you have great vistas of Lakes Apopka, Louisa, and Minneola, but the rolling sandhills topped with blossoming orange trees are now carpeted in rooftops of subdivisions; $3.50 adults, $1 children 3–15. At the base of the tower, the **House of Presidents** (352-394-2836), 123 N US 27, showcases the "White House in Miniature," a scale model, and rooms thickly packed with presidential paraphernalia for $9.95 adults, $4.95 children.

GHOST TOWNS Five miles east of Eustis, the town of **Seneca** once had hotels, churches, a sawmill, and orange groves. During the Seminole Wars, an army payroll was supposedly hidden near the springs and never recovered.

HISTORIC SITES Most of Lake County's cities are historic districts—visit downtown Clermont, Eustis, Leesburg, Mount Dora, and Tavares for a taste of Florida between the 1890s and 1920s. In Mount Dora the **McDonald Stone House**, circa 1883, is a beautiful home on the corner of 7th Ave and McDonald St. The **Community Congregational Church** is Mount Dora's oldest place of worship, dating back to 1887. In 1893 Pittsburgh native John P. Donnelly moved to Mount Dora and built an imposing Queen Anne Victorian (Donnelly St, between 5th and 6th Aves) that now houses the Masonic Temple.

HISTORIC TOURS Departing the Lakeside Inn (see *Lodging*), the **Mount Dora Road Trolley** (352-357-9123) offers narrated 1-hour historic tours, $8 adults, $6 children. Closed Sun.

MUSEUMS **Austin Carriage Museum** (352-750-1763; www.austincarriagemuseum.com), 3000 Marion County Rd, Weirsdale. Learn about more than two centuries of the horseless carriage through over 175 opulent historic and reproduction carriages displayed in three large galleries. Narrated tours offered Tue–Fri at 2 PM ($10) explain the history of these vehicles, which range from Victorian carriages to a replica stagecoach.

McTureous Homestead and Museum, FL 19, Altoona. This little Cracker homestead called Aunt Bessie's Place was the childhood home of Private Robert McTureous Jr., who received a USMC Medal of Honor during World War II. The adjacent park has picnic tables and a playground.

Mount Dora Museum of Speed (352-385-1945; www.classicdreamcars.com), 206 N Highland St, showcases a private collection of automobile memorabilia and classic muscle cars. Open 10–5 Tue–Sat, $8.50 admission; tours available for groups of four or more.

At the **Royellou Museum** (352-383-0006), 450 Royellou Lane, learn the history of Mount Dora, as presented in the old city jail by the local historical society. Fri–Sun 1–5; $2.50 adults, $2 children. Other regional-history museums (all free) include the **Lake County Historical Museum** (352-343-9600), 317 W Main St, Tavares (Mon–Fri 8:30–5); the **Leesburg Heritage Society and Museum** (352-365-0053), 111 S 6th St (Thu 2–4); the **Lady Lake Historical Society and Museum** (352-753-1159), 107 S Old Dixie Hwy (Sat 11–3); **Eustis Historical Museum** (352-483-0046), 536 N Bay St (Tue–Fri 1–4); and the **Tavares Historical Museum** (352-343-7252), 121 Alfred St (Thu 1–4).

POLO One of the state's few polo stadiums is at the **Villages Polo Club** (352-

750-POLO; www.thevillagespoloclub.com), with spring and fall polo matches. Call for their schedule.

RAILROADIANA In 1886 the **Jacksonville, Tampa & Key West Railway** first steamed into Mount Dora; active rail service continued until 1973 under the auspices of the Seaboard Coast Railway. Remnants of the town's railroad heyday remain: several quaint low-clearance **Florida Central Railroad trestles**, and the **ACL passenger depot** (now the chamber of commerce), a narrow building on Alexander St adjoined by All Aboard South (see *Selective Shopping*). Stop in for information about the **Mount Dora Railroad** (352-735-4667; www.mountdoratrain.com), Florida's only steam rail excursion train, which runs between Orlando and Mount Dora (see *Railroad Excursions*). In Umatilla a bright orange **SCL caboose** sits on a siding outside the public library along FL 19.

WINERY At **Lakeridge Winery & Vineyards** (1-800-768-WINE), 19239 US 27 N, guided tours begin every 15 minutes with a video on the winemaking process, then move out to a catwalk over the barrels and tanks. As the tour takes you outside, you overlook 75 acres of grapes, both hybrids and muscadine. Finish off with tasting four types of wine. In addition to house-label items, the winery store has gourmet foods and gift items. Check the calendar for monthly special events like free jazz and blues festivals out on the green hillsides. Open Mon–Sat 10–5, Sun 11–5. Free.

ZOOLOGICAL PARKS AND ANIMAL REHABILITATION ✐ Show the kids some real barnyard critters at **Uncle Donald's Farm, Inc.** (352-753-2882), Griffin Ave, Lady Lake, where they can milk a goat, pet a horse, feed the chickens, bounce around on a hayride, and visit with rehabilitating wild animals and birds. Admission $7 adults, $6.75 children, includes animal feed and hayrides; pony rides extra. Open Feb–Apr, Oct–Nov: Thu–Sat 10–4, Sun noon–4.

✐ For the wilder side of life, visit **Amazing Exotics** (352-821-1234; www.amazingexotics.com), 17951 SE CR 452, Umatilla, a working zoological education center, exotic animal rescue facility, and retirement home for animal actors. Just weeks after I watched one of the trainers petting and feeding a white-faced gibbon, the gibbon and other primates appeared with Jay Leno on the *Tonight Show*. Fifteen tigers and a complement of chimpanzees go about their paces in large enclosures on the hillside, while the lower section of the compound features lemurs, white wolves, a clouded leopard, and other rare and interesting animals. Visitors on the daily tour cover the 100-acre ranch by foot and tram with a knowledgeable guide; tours run $34–94, depending on the amount of hands-on time with the larger mammals. Reservations are required. The facility also offers hands-on classes for students learning exotic-animal management.

✷ To Do

BALLOONING Since 1978, **Hot Air Balloon Tours** (352-243-7865), 21432 CR 455, has taken passengers up, up and away on champagne flights over the Clermont area.

BIRDING Thousands of migrating birds stop at the impoundments of **Emeralda Marsh Conservation Area** between Lake Yale and Lake Griffin in Umatilla, between CR 42 and 44. Looking for rare birds? It's the place to go. On a single day I counted several bald eagles, more than a dozen limpkins, and numerous purple gallinules. For casual birding, you won't go wrong in **Mount Dora**; all of the lakeside parks offer excellent birding, especially at dusk. Check *Green Space* for more opportunities; every lakefront park has its resident egrets, ospreys, and herons. Ospreys nest in the tall cypresses along the **Dead River**, and are best seen on an ecotour (see *Ecotours*).

Sandra Friend

AT AMAZING EXOTICS

BOAT TOURS **Dead River Vic's Dora Canal & River Cruises** (352-742-5000) depart from behind the restaurant (see *Dining Out*) for sightseeing tours on a mock riverboat, the *Contessa*. At the Mission Inn (see *Resorts*), **Lake Harris Cruises** (352-324-3101) runs an elegant antique yacht, *La Reina*, on the Harris Chain of Lakes. In addition, numerous operators run ecotours (see *Ecotours*) along the Harris Chain.

CARRIAGE RIDES **A Hitch In Time** (352-394-8851; www.ahitchntime.com), 20301 Sugarloaf Mountain Rd, takes you on tours by horse and carriage around the streets of Mount Dora.

DIVING **C&N Divers & Snorkeling** (407-735-5040) in Mount Dora can set you up with gear to snorkel nearby Kelly Park or explore Wekiwa Springs, just over the border in Orange County (see "Orlando North").

ECOTOURS ♿ Departing from Palm Gardens along US 441 at the Dead River Bridge, Capt. D. J. Hollander and his wife, Lynne, have spent more than a decade showing off what they love so well—the creatures that inhabit the rivers, Chain of Lakes, and Dora Canal on **Heritage Lake Tours** (352-343-4337). Lynne does a great job of pointing out alligators hidden in the lilies, otters slipping off riverbanks, and ospreys nesting in the tall cypresses along the Dead River. And that narrow, jungle-like channel that the quiet boat barely fits through? That's the Dora Canal—a tight passage brimming with wildlife. The year-round 90-minute excursions cost $12.50; call for departure times. Closed Sun.

Docked at the Lakeside Inn (see *Lodging*), the pontoon ***Captain Doolittle*** (386-736-7707; www.nuwproducts.com/doolittle) runs lazy Sunday shoreline cruises to the Apopka Canal and Lake Beauclaire, as well as Dock & Dine

AVIATION Seminole-Lake Gliderport (352-394-5450; www.soarfl.com), P.O. Box 120458, Clermont 34712. As the towrope dropped off our glider, I felt a sudden pang of fear: At more than 3,000 feet, I'd never been this high before without the assistance of an engine. Knut Kjenslie, owner/pilot/flight instructor, asked if I wanted to take the controls. "I'll let you drive," I said, and settled back for the ride. With a bubble of Plexiglas around my head, I could see as far as the birds could—and could see what the birds were up to. Chasing after climbing hawks, Knut had us rising up a column of air in a lazy spiral. "Do you like roller coasters?" he asked. I nodded. Within moments, he had us plunging on a trackless ride with serious g-forces—what a blast! I expected the quiet, but I'd never imagined gliders to be so maneuverable. Now *this* was an experience I'll never forget. Rides and instruction starts at $80; rentals for certified pilots at $25 per hour.

AUTHOR SANDRA FRIEND SAVORS THE PERFECT LANDING.

Sandra Friend

cruises that hopscotch along the Chain of Lakes (for groups of six or more). Daily Dora Canal Cruises cost $15; Champagne at Sunset Cruises cost $20 single, $35 couple, Fri and Sat 7:30–9.

Wekiva Falls Resort (see *Campgrounds*) runs hour-long narrated "jungle cruises" along the wild and scenic Wekiva River. Enjoy the peaceful journey in a quiet electric boat through the most natural stretch of river in the Orlando metro area. Daily 9–4 on the hour; $15 adults, $10 ages 2–11.

At **Showcase of Citrus** (352-394-4377; www.showcaseofcitrus.com), 5010 US 27, near US 192, ride a monster 4x4 across a 2,500-acre cattle ranch in search of deer and sandhill cranes; $20 adults, $10 children 3–10.

FISHING With two lengthy chains of lakes offering up some of the best trophy bass in the state, you can bet fishing is on the mind of many visitors to Lake County. There are more than a dozen fish camps on the lakes (see *Fish Camps*) and plenty of public boat ramps to launch your own craft. In addition to largemouth bass, you'll find the Harris Chain of Lakes (which includes Lake Griffin, Lake Harris, Little Lake Harris, Lake Eustis, and Lake Dora) brimming with bream, shellcracker, and bluegill. Grab bait and tackle and put in your boat at **Banana Cove Marina** (352-343-7951), on FL 19, Tavares, or **Florida Angler's Resort** (see *Fish Camps*), south of Leesburg on US 441. Fishing along Lake Louise and Lake Minneola is more laid back; you won't find as many powerboats on the water.

GOLF Golfing is big in Lake County, where the rolling greens make for challenging courses. Most of the county's 26 courses are semiprivate, such as the renowned **El Campeón** at the Mission Inn (see *Resorts*). One of the top 25 courses in the state, it's the third oldest resort golf course in Florida, established in 1926, and features rolling hills along cypress-lined lakes. The public **Clerbrook Resort** (see *Campgrounds*) has green fees starting at $18; watch out for the sandhill cranes! Check with the visitors center (see *Guidance*) for a brochure outlining all public golf courses in the county.

HANG GLIDING **Quest Air Hang Gliding** (352-429-0213; www.questairforce.com), 6548 Groveland Airport Rd, Groveland, offers hang-gliding training with certified instructors; flights start 2,500 feet above the ground.

HIKING The **Florida Trail** crosses Lake County through Seminole State Forest, heading into the Ocala National Forest. But Lake County also offers great day hikes: Try Lake Louisa State Park, Flat Island Preserve, Hidden Waters Preserve, Tavares Nature Park, and Mason Nature Preserve (see *Green Space*).

PADDLING Both of the major chains of lakes are more suitable for motorized craft than kayaks and canoes, due to the sheer size of the lakes—but don't be shy about paddling around the edges, where there's plenty of wildlife to be seen. Rent canoes from the livery at **Lake Griffin State Park** (see *Green Space*) or at **Lake County Canoe & Kayak** (352-357-4900), 121 N Bay St ($45 per day including paddle and PFD) in Eustis. If you take to the Dora Canal under your own power, do so either early or late on a weekday to avoid the messy motorboat congestion that occurs every weekend.

RAILROAD EXCURSIONS ♿ A great day for railfans—the **Mount Dora & Lake Eustis Railroad** (352-383-8878; www.mtdorarailway.com), 150 W 3rd Ave, Mount Dora, is up and running! I'm glad to see another comeback of this historic route, just in time for this book. Enjoy an elegant dinner excursion ($45 adults, $43 seniors) on the Orange Blossom Dinner Train in a vintage-1928 M-201 self-propelled car, with entrées like grilled Pacific salmon, prime rib, and Georgia bourbon chicken, or take the family on the Dora Doodlebug, a 1930 Brill, on an 8-mile trip ($9 adults, $8 seniors, $5 for 12 and under).

SCENIC DRIVES For a look at Old Florida, drive along CR 42 (County Line Rd) at the northern edge of the county, and scenic CR 561, which winds south from Astatula through Minneola and Clermont, looping around the lakes before it ends south of Groveland on FL 33.

SPORTS TRAINING Training for a marathon or more? Visit the campus at the **USA Triathlon National Training Center** (1-888-841-7995; www.usat-ntc.com), 1099 Citrus Tower Blvd, Clermont, where athletes can evaluate their abilities in the Human Performance Lab, work out in a state-of-the-art fitness center, and practice at the aquatic center with its 70-meter heated pool, plus a track-and-field complex with a 400-meter track.

TRAIL RIDING **Rocking Horse Stables** (352-669-9982), 44200 FL 19, Altoona, offers trail riding into the southern portion of the Ocala National Forest, and accepts overnight campers with horses, as does **Fiddler's Green Ranch** (see *Ocala National Forest*). Bring your own horses to ride the trails in Rock Springs Run Reserve State Park, Seminole State Forest, and Lake Louisa State Park (see *Green Space*).

WATER SPORTS With all its lakes, Lake County draws international attention for its water sports. Learn to water ski at several accredited schools—**Hansen Ski/World Wakeboard Center** (352-429-3574), Groveland; **Sunset Lakes Tournament Skiing** (1-800-732-2755; www.jacktravers.com), Okahumpa; and **Swiss Ski School** (352-429-2178; www.swissskischool.com), Clermont. Wakeboard enthusiasts can also opt for **P. J. Marks Wakeboard Camp** (352-394-8899; www.wakeboardcamp.com), a popular training spot in downtown Clermont that's fun to watch from the waterfront parks.

✷ Green Space

BOTANICAL GARDENS **Discovery Gardens** (352-343-4101; www.discoverygardens.ifas.ufl.edu), 30205 FL 19, Tavares. Roam 20 themed gardens in this educational resource supporting hands-on gardener training, including a special Children's Garden, colonial brick Courtyard Gardens, and a formal rose garden. Mon–Sat 9–4; free.

GREENWAYS Rail-trail corridors under development in Lake County include the **Lake Minneola Trail**, which presently has a ribbon of pavement ideal for biking from downtown Clermont through Minneola; the **Fruitland Park Trail**, which will run from Griffin Rd to Lake Ella Rd in Fruitland Park; and the **Tav-Lee Trail**, planned between Tavares and downtown Leesburg.

NATURE CENTER Just east of Eustis, **Trout Lake Nature Center** (352-357-7536), 520 E CR 44, offers interpretive exhibits and nature tours Oct–Apr, Fri and Sat 9–4, Sun noon–4. Free.

PARKS At the end of 3rd St, **Clermont Waterfront Park** has a playground, sheltered picnic benches, and a fishing pier, all for a daily parking fee of $2.

Lake Louisa State Park (352-394-3969), 12549 State Park Dr, Clermont, protects 4,500 acres around Lake Louisa, the largest of the Palatlakaha Chain of Lakes, fed by the Green Swamp, with paddling, hiking, and a developed campground. Active restoration is turning abandoned citrus groves back into natural longleaf pine and wiregrass habitat.

The green expanse of **Ferran Park** along Lake Eustis is the southern terminus of the Eustis Lake Walk, a 0.25-mile boardwalk providing a great lakeside stroll.

In a shady hammock sloping down toward the lake, **Lake Griffin State Park** (352-360-6760), 3089 US 27-441, Fruitland Park, provides access for paddlers (on-site rentals) and boaters out to the Chain of Lakes through a marsh filled with floating islands of vegetation. Hikers can amble the short nature trail; a pleasant campground is tucked under the oaks.

In Howey-in-the-Hills, **Griffin Stormwater Park** on S Lakeshore Dr follows the shoreline of Little Lake Harris, offering a paved lakeside walking and biking trail, picnic area, playground, fishing pier, and a connecting walk in the woods to nearby **Mason Nature Preserve**, with boardwalks out to the lake. **Hickory Point** (352-343-3777; www.lcwa.org), a Lake County Water Authority recreational facility off FL 19 on Little Lake Harris, has a swimming beach, fishing pier, and nature boardwalk; fee.

LAKE DORA AT SUNSET

Sandra Friend

Venetian Gardens, off FL 44 in Leesburg, is a pleasant family park along Lake Harris with marina, boat ramp, fishing, and a public swimming pool. **Herlong Park**, off US 441 on Lake Griffin, has a picnic area and boat ramp with fishing opportunities.

A ribbon of green runs along Lake Dora's eastern shore: **Gilbert Park** encompasses a landscaped version of Alexander Creek, which burbles downhill into the lake at **Grantham Point**, where the "Port of Mount Dora" and **Mount Dora Lighthouse** are located. Next door is the wonderfully wild **Palm Island Park**, with a mile of trails along lakeside boardwalks out to wooded Palm Island. To the north, a lakeside walking and fitness trail leads around to **Evans Park**, another grassy spot for picnicking.

Running between the railroad and Lake Dora in downtown Tavares, **Wooten Park** provides a gentle waterfront walking trail, picnic facilities, fishing platforms, and a playground for the kids.

WILD PLACES **Sunnyhill Restoration Area** (386-329-4404), CR 42 at the Ocklawaha River. Overlooked by many because it's just a little off the beaten path, this wilderness tract (once a cattle ranch) protects 9 miles of the Ocklawaha River floodplain, encompassing vast marshes along the scenic Lower Ocklawaha as well as uplands of scrubby flatwoods and scrub. Trails cater to hikers, bikers, and equestrians; the Levee Trail provides your best birding opportunities.

Surrounded by the vast Okahumpa Marsh, two deeply forested islands create the biological haven that is **Flat Island Preserve**, CR 25A, Leesburg, where orchids and colorful fungi flourish beneath ancient live oaks. A 4-mile trail with backpacking campsite circles the preserve, and you can rent canoes to paddle out into the marsh. This wilderness area is best visited during winter—the mosquitoes can be vicious the remainder of the year. **Sawgrass Island Preserve**, off CR 450, Umatilla, appeals to equestrians with its miles of trails along Lake Yale; hikers and birders can also amble the 1,100-acre preserve with its vast sawgrass marsh. Both preserves are managed by the Lake County Water Authority (352-343-3777), 107 N Lake Ave, Tavares.

At the southeastern tip of the county, **Rock Springs Run Reserve State Park** (352-383-3311), FL 46, protects 9,000 acres of prime bear habitat at the confluence of Rock Springs Run and the Wekiva River. Hiking, biking, and equestrian trails crisscross the preserve, and seasonal hunting is permitted. Adjacent **Seminole State Forest** (352-360-6675; www.fl-dof.com/state_forests/Seminole.htm) encompasses more than 25,000 acres along the Wekiva River Basin, forming an important greenway connector for bear migration to the Ocala National Forest. The **Florida Trail** runs through the forest, and paddlers can enjoy a rugged trip on Blackwater Creek.

✻ Lodging

BED & BREAKFASTS

Clermont 34471

Mulberry Inn (352-242-0670), 915 Montrose St. Dating back to 1890, this grand home has three Victorian rooms and a shared bath on its second floor. Add the clink of dishes downstairs and soft murmur of conversation when you step out into the hall—this isn't your everyday B&B. What was once the common area downstairs is now the trendy Bistro Safran (see *Dining Out*), but as proprietor Alain Wolf says, this is your home—don't be shy about wandering through the kitchen, or relaxing in the grassy yard. Of the three rooms, the popular Mulberry Suite has a private balcony in the trees shading Montrose St; another room features an en-suite clawfoot tub. Enjoy melt-in-your-mouth croissants and fresh fruit at breakfast. While the new owners have focused their efforts on their restaurant, they promise remodeling of the rooms within the next year. $70–95.

Mount Dora 32757

Christopher's Inn (352-383-2244; www.mountdora.com), 539 Liberty Ave. Just up the street from Mount Dora's beautiful lakeside parks, hospitality awaits in an 1887 home with beaded pine walls and ceilings. Decorated in a lush Victorian style with an eye to antiques lovers (note the 1940s *Reader's Digests* and saltshaker collection in the parlor), Christopher's offers four cozy rooms with bath. $85–110, including full breakfast.

Coconut Cottage Inn (352-383-2627; www.coconutcottageinn.com), 1027 McDonald St. World traveler? Here's a place to bring back the memories! From the Zen Den with its serene Japanese furnishings to the Arabia Room, Coconut Cottage features the decor of faraway lands, inspired by the innkeepers' travels. $139–149, including expanded continental breakfast.

♿ **Darst Victorian Manor** (352-383-4050), 495 Old US 441. Something old, something new: Antique furnishings dress up spacious rooms and suites within a decade-old three-story house built to look like a Victorian manor, down to the gingerbread trim. Overlooking Lake Dora, this busy six-room B&B serves gourmet breakfasts and an afternoon tea (4 PM daily), and has an outdoor hot tub for guests. $134–230.

Farnsworth House (352-735-1894), 1029 E 5th Ave. Off the beaten path but attracting a regular clientele, this Superior Small Lodging dates back to 1886, offering three very spacious, well-decorated suites with kitchen and bath, plus two themed efficiency apartments in the detached Carriage House. Relax outdoors on the porch swing, or take a soak in the hot tub. $105–145, including expanded continental breakfast.

Mount Dora Historic Inn (1-800-927-6344; www.mountdorahistoricinn.com), 221 E 4th Ave. In a cozy, convivial setting, Lindsay and Nancy Richards showcase their love of antiques in their 1886 home on the edge of the shopping district, with four lavishly decorated rooms and a full gourmet breakfast. $95–135.

Nelson Manor (352-735-5288; www.nelsonmanor.com), 1355 Donnelly St. With sumptuous Victorian decor and gracious charm, this 1922 Arts & Crafts Victorian offers three tasteful rooms and a warm welcome from innkeeper Kathleen Nelson Daughtry, whose motto is, "The whole house belongs to my guests." Relax on the screened porch, stroll through the formal gardens, or kick back in the lower-level living room next to the fireplace. $95–155.

Simpson's (352-383-2087; www.simpsonsbnb.com), 441 N Donnelly St. Formerly the historic Simpson Hotel, this vibrant B&B sits right in the center of the action, in the heart of the shopping district. Each of the six comfortable and roomy suites ($95–115) has a small kitchen and private bath. You'll find a continental breakfast of fruit and bread, presented with a bouquet of roses, inside your refrigerator, but you can always graze the snack tray of chocolate chip cookies, peanuts, and popcorn if you can't wait until morning.

HOTELS AND MOTELS

Clermont 34771

♿ **Holiday Inn Express** (352-243-7878), 1810 S US 27. A busy new property with a large continental breakfast; rooms are outfitted for business travelers, including ample-sized desk with dataport. $80–100.

Leesburg 34748

Microtel Inn & Suites (352-315-1234; www.microtelinn.com), 9700 US 441. A pleasant new motel with spacious rooms ($59–79) and a swimming pool, near the historic downtown.

Mount Dora 32757

♿ **Lakeside Inn** (1-800-556-5016; www.lakeside-inn.com), 100 N Alexander St. Step back in time to a peaceful place, where guests play cards in the spacious lobby and sit out on the rocking chairs on the front porch, taking in the view of Lake Dora. Since 1883, the Lakeside Inn has been catering to those looking for a quiet getaway—including guests like President Calvin Coolidge, who wintered here in 1930. Built to accommodate tourists coming by steamboat and buggy, the original 10-room hotel consisted of a portion of the main building, which now includes the lobby, guest rooms, and two eateries: the **Tremont** (a classy lounge) and the Beauclaire (see *Dining Out*). It's quintessential Florida—as evening falls, a lone osprey cries from its perch above the swimming pool; couples stroll out on the dock to watch the shimmering lake turn to silver. Expanded several times through the 1930s to take advantage of the increasing tourist traffic via steam trains, this historic hotel now consists of five separate guest lodges, all with the graceful ambience of that period. Seasonal rates start at $119, including continental breakfast; a variety of room types and package deals available. Canoes and paddle boats available for rent; lake cruises depart from the adjacent dock. Within an easy walk of downtown and the lakeside parks.

Tavares 32778

Inn on the Green (352-343-6373 or 1-800-935-2935; www.innonthegreen.net), 700 E Burleigh Blvd. Beautifully situated on the edge of a

THE LAKESIDE INN

Sandra Friend

lake, this independent motel has the atmosphere of a golf resort, from its poolside putting greens and pleasant landscaping to the white-and-green motif of the buildings. Guests gather in a large, comfortable room overlooking the greens for continental breakfast. The spacious rooms have a touch of class and are a real value for the price, $65 and up; golf packages available.

Umatilla 32784
Fox Den Country Inn (352-669-2151), FL 19. Featuring 10 units in a classic 1950s motel plus a 1925 home and a 1909 five-bedroom home for rent, this small family operation has pleasant small rooms outfitted with antiques; guests can wander through the orange groves down to Lake Umatilla. $54–160; reservations required, as the office is staffed part time.

RESORTS

Howey-in-the-Hills 34737
♿ The **Mission Inn** (1-800-874-9053; www.missioninnresort.com), 10400 CR 48, pitches itself as a "Golfer's Paradise," and with 36 holes they can certainly back up that claim. But golf isn't the only game at this resort, run by the same family for more than three decades. Spanish colonial architecture, replete with formal courtyards and fountains, accents the well-landscaped grounds with its many facilities: eight tennis courts, a full-service marina with rental boats, cruises, and fishing guides, and five restaurants and lounges, including **La Hacienda**, with its expansive breakfast buffet, and **El Conquistador**, serving intimate fine dinners in a luxurious setting, with a focus on prime steaks and wines. With 176 spacious standard rooms and suites, there are lodgings to fit every preference and budget. Rates start at $84, with numerous golfing and fishing packages available; on-site bicycle rentals.

WORKING RANCH

Weirsdale 32195
Continental Acres Equine Resort (352-750-5500; www.continentalacres.com), 3000 Marion County Rd. On the county line, this 365-acre working horse farm opens its doors to visiting equestrians, with paddocks for your horses and pleasant cottages for you and your family, $61–300 (depending on size; check the web site for full details). Riding lessons start at $65 (with your horse) or $85 (with theirs), or just kick back and relax on casual rides around the farm. Grassy RV sites with water and 30- or 50-amp hookups cost $15. The ranch is also home to the Austin Carriage Museum (see *Museums*).

FISH CAMPS

Leesburg 34788
Florida Anglers Resort (352-343-4141), 32311 Angler's Ave (along US 441), hosts major bass tournaments on Lake Harris. Kick back with the kids in a rustic cottage ($75–130) and enjoy the swimming beach and playground while the family angler is out casting for bass.

Tavares 32778
Palm Gardens (352-343-2024), 11801 N US 441, features a little bit of everything along the Dead River, from full-hookup RV sites ($20) and cottages ($55–65) to live bait, pontoon rentals, and an on-site restaurant serving breakfast.

Umatilla 32784
Nelson's Fish Camp (352-821-3474), on the Ocklawaha River, CR 42. Providing prime access to this scenic river basin for anglers and paddlers, Nelson's offers campsites and rustic cabins under a canopy of grand old live oaks; full-service marina with slips, gas pumps, boat rentals. A small grill room inside the camp store serves up the basics.

CAMPGROUNDS

Clermont 34711
The Bees Resort (352-429-2116; www.thebeesresort.com), 20260 US 27. Pick your spot, shade or sun, and set up your tent, pop-up, or trailer for a relaxing stay, $14–20; enjoy the swimming area and recreation hall, nine-hole miniature golf, and on-site nature trail.

Clerbrook Golf and RV Resort (1-800-440-3801), 20005 US 27. With more than 1,200 full-hookup spots on 287 acres, this is one whopping campground, and a favorite of many snowbirds—the natural landscaping attracts wintering flocks of sandhill cranes. Nab an RV space ($29) or tent site ($26) or go upscale with villa rentals ($75). On-site 18-hole golf course with resident golf pro, three swimming pools and four spas, beauty salon and barbershop, and even its own post office.

Citrus Valley Campground (352-394-4051), 2500 US 27 S. Particularly popular because of its proximity to Disney World (just 9 miles), this massive campground has 372 sites—a mix of full hookup ($24) or water and electric ($17–22), park models ($89), and permanent sites. Busiest Nov–Mar, with lots of organized snowbird activities.

Leesburg 34748
Holiday Travel Resort (1-800-428-5334), 28229 CR 33. Ah, the life: an indoor pool and spa, a nine-hole golf course, shuffleboard and tennis courts, and a marina. Focused on long-term stays (but with room for vacationers), this massive campground has large pull-through sites ($26) with full hookups, on-site groceries, and three recreation halls managed by a social director.

Sorrento 32776
Extraordinarily convenient to northern Orlando, **Wekiva Falls Resort** (407-830-9898) isn't just about camping; it's a destination, on the wild and scenic Wekiva River, with canoe rentals, a swimming area, and guided ecotours along with more than 800 sites, from tent camping to full RV hookups, starting at $20.

✱ Where to Eat

DINING OUT

Clermont
The popular **Bistro Safran** (www.bistrosafran.com), occupying the ground floor of the **Mulberry Inn** (see *Bed & Breakfasts*), lends a *special* touch of class to downtown Clermont. Massive porch windows bring the greenery in; the dessert tray sits by the front door, tempting you the moment you arrive. In this Parisian-style bistro managed by chef Fredric Le Pape and Alain Wolf, patrons can't help but break into their high school French as they order up entrées ($18–27) like *Le Canard* and *Le Boeuf*, complemented by more than 20 varieties of wine. My choice of *Le Cabilland*—a tenderloin of cod with mixed provincial vegetables and homemade mashed potatoes—was

superb; the cod simply melted into the fresh tomatoes, onions, and pureed potatoes, providing a light, healthy meal. I made up for the calories with crème brûlée, its delicate caramelized crust stretched thin over rich vanilla custard. If you enjoy fine dining, dress for the occasion and savor the experience. Lunch and dinner; reservations recommended.

Eustis

Caffe Capri Ristorante (352-483-1112; www.restaurant.com/caffecapri), 31 E Magnolia Ave. Dive into Italian specialties like *farfalle al salmone*, *penne Boscaiola*, and *gnocchi alla Sorrentina* on a menu that'll have you licking your lips—salmon and crabmeat pizza, mmm. Lunch 11–2, $6–9; dinner 4:30–10, $10–13. Closed Mon.

Leesburg

Vic's Embers (352-728-8989), US 441, takes you back to the 1950s with supper-club ambience; you'll expect Dean Martin to step out of the shadows. Whereas their sister restaurant likes to tease, the entrées here are straightforward classics, from 12-ounce blackened prime rib rubbed in Creole seasonings to filet mignon with crab legs. Prices are upper crust, too: $11–33, with two "steak for two" options, $39–50.

Mount Dora

Beauclaire (352-383-4101), 100 N Alexander St. Step back into the 1920s at the Lakeside Inn's classy dining room, where wait staff drift through the room to fill your glasses and take your orders in an atmosphere with a Great Gatsby feel. Breakfast $4–6, lunch $7–10, dinner $17–27; the tasty Maryland crabcakes come with Zellwood corn fritters from the famed nearby farming district. Open for all meals daily. Dress for dinner, and make a reservation!

Goblin Market (352-735-0059), 331-B Donnelly St. Classical music drifts through the dining rooms, where you're surrounded by shelves lined with books—as an author, I felt right at home. And the food is fabulous. Lunch is a bargain for the quality: Try the Irish whiskey onion soup ($5) for a twist on an old favorite, or the potato-crusted grouper sandwich ($9) at lunch. Return at dinner for fine-dining choices like raspberry-glazed duck ($23) or North Atlantic salmon roulade ($23). This is the "in" place in Lake County; reservations highly recommended.

Tavares

Angelo's (352-343-2757), 2270 Vinedale Rd, appeals with fine dining in a relaxed atmosphere. Traditional Italian dishes like stuffed shells, shrimp scampi, and baked ziti comprise their menu ($5–8), with the addition of more refined entrées in the evenings such as chicken Sorrento and flounder al forno ($7–14).

Dead River Vic's (352-742-5000), 3351 W Burleigh Rd, has a great view of the cypress-lined Dead River and is always hopping with customers on the weekends, eager to chow down on their fish with a Florida flair—creations like Chef Richey's Backwater Gator Wings ($6-plus) and Sorrento shrimp scampi ($10). Lunch and dinner $7–12; and yes, that's swamp cabbage in the chef salad!

EATING OUT

Clermont

The Daley Dog (352-243-2844), 12914 US 27, celebrates Chicago-style dogs with 14 choices ($2–6) and a handful of sandwiches in a bistro atmosphere with beer and wine; lunch and dinner, closed Sun.

The **Chef's Table** (352-242-1264; www.clermontchefstable.com), 796 W Minneola Ave, is a busy lunchtime stop for deli sandwiches, salads, and ice cream delights. Sandwiches come in heaping baskets; chef's signature specialties include the country meat loaf sandwich, homemade hot sausage, and muffuletta. Lunch $4–7; closed Sun.

The Corner Seafood Grill (352-394-6911), W Montrose St, is one of the area's cornerstones since 1993, serving up excellent deep-fried whole belly clams, stone crab, and stuffed Florida whole lobster with a Key West flair. Menus change regularly, but expect burgers, sandwiches, salads, and entrées like chicken Cozumel at lunch ($6–11) and a focus on seafood at dinner ($15–29).

Clermont Pier House (352-242-4569), 528 8th St, serves seafood and sandwiches in a nautical atmosphere. Lunch and dinner run $6–29 (for the special seafood boil for two); live entertainment Thu–Sat, including a comedy club.

Eustis

The funky hometown **Eustis Street Grill** (352-223-7087), 1 N Eustis St, serves fabulous fluffy old-fashioned pancakes and the signature Eustis Deluxe Omelet, with breakfast and lunch daily ($2–5) and dinners on weekends, when the Eustis Street Blues takes the front window stage Fri and Sat evenings.

Laurabelle's Rose Room (352-483-0300), 51 W Magnolia Ave. With the best view in town—a wall of windows overlooking Lake Eustis—and tasteful Victorian decor, this dainty lunchroom appeals with offerings like their chicken salad supreme amandine, served with fresh fruit and accompanied by a muffin. Don't miss the signature chocolate mousse with a touch of raspberry sauce. Sandwiches $6.45–7.45, salads $5.95–6.95; open 11–2.

Strawberry's Dessert Parlor (352-589-2313), 24 E Magnolia Ave. Ice cream and lunch specials, fresh cookies, and eight kinds of hot dogs. Open until 5 weekdays, 9 weekends; closed Sun.

Groveland

Choctaw Willies (352-429-4188), 214 W Broad St. The delicious aroma of hickory smoke permeates this family restaurant with a western feel, where "unusually fine barbecue" is the centerpiece of the menu. Lunch and dinner entrées ($8–10) like baby back ribs, southern-fried catfish, and, of course, heaping plates of chicken, beef, or pork barbecue come with two sides, with choices that include sweet potatoes and Choctaw stew. It's barbecue just the way I like it—thin slabs with a red ring and a subtle smoky taste. Open 11–8, closed Sun.

Leesburg

C&H Smokehouse Grill (352-315-9700), 951 N 14th St. Flavorful slabs of ribs and mounds of barbecue make this a local favorite.

Joni's Café (352-787-4330), 412 W Main St, provides a pleasant downtown lunch experience on weekdays, with healthful sandwiches (including the "Healthwich") and salads, $4–5.

Mount Dora

Al E. Gators Pub (352-735-5203), 3rd Ave Alley. Follow the garden path off S Donnelly to find this spacious bar and grill with outside deck, a comfy place to kick back a few beers and top it off with a burger or burrito; serving lunch and dinner, $5–7.

For a quick snack, stop at **Chew Chew Express** (352-735-9300), 112 W 3rd St, adjoining the railroad tracks, for BBQ pork sandwiches, Hawaiian shaved ice, or a scoop of Grumpy's homemade ice cream.

With its broad doors open to the street, **Eduardo's Station** (352-735-1711), 100 E 4th Ave, reminds me of a Caribbean sidewalk café, where Latin music spills out into the antiques district. Spicy Tex-Mex favorites dominate the lunch and dinner menu, $7–16.

At the **Frosty Mug Icelandic Restaurant & Pub** (352-383-1696), 411 N Donnelly St, descend into a European rathskeller with tables arranged around a bar right out of the Old World. Never mind the choice of imported beers on tap: The food is just plain heavenly to a Nordic gal like me. Appetizers include gravlax (Icelandic cured salmon), *sveppa strimlar* (beer-battered portobello), and crunchy stuffed olives, $8–9. The pan-seared Icelandic haddock is their signature dish, but other artfully presented entrées ($12–22) like schnitzel and Atlantic salmon will surely tempt. And for dessert . . . can you imagine Icelandic fried ice cream? It's called *saet fjalla brie* ($9), and it's fabulous. Live jazz piano and creative sculptures by local artists add to the very different atmosphere; it's an unexpected treat in the heart of Florida, serving lunch and dinner daily.

Watch the world wander past at **The Gables Restaurant** (352-383-8993; www.mtdora.org), 322 N Alexander St, where tasty salads, burgers, and creative entrées ($8–10) like coconut-crusted grouper and Cajun seafood ragout complement daily soups and dessert specials. My pick: the Maryland-style crabcake with garlic lime mayonnaise, presented with a perfect potato salad on baby greens. The comfy dining room is filled with antiques, and the fresh bread at your table (different every day: I had kalamata and feta, and sunflower wheat) comes from the adjoining **Sunshine Mountain Bakery**, 115 W 3rd Ave.

Garden Gate Tea Room (352-735-2158), 142 E 4th Ave. Duck through the arbor to enter this lacy, frilly bower of femininity and sample an asparagus sandwich (asparagus, Jack cheese, purple onion, fresh Thousand Island dressing on grilled pumpernickel) or the quiche of the day, $7–8.

Mount Dora Kringle Company (352-735-5754), 3985 N FL 19. This Scandinavian bakery features authentic Danish kringles that take 2 days to make. Open Mon–Sat 7–4:30.

Palm Tree Grill (352-735-1936), 351 N Donnelly St. A street-corner Italian restaurant with a patio atmosphere, accentuated with gorgeous murals inside; large windows let you watch the passersby. The menu encompasses both traditional Italian dishes and more creative endeavors like eggplant rollatini and stuffed shells florentine, with salads starting at $9, pasta entrées at $10; serving lunch and dinner.

Windsor Rose Tea Room (352-735-2551), 142 W 4th Ave. A proper British tearoom in the heart of Mount Dora, serving full English tea ($20, or $8 for one) all day, with fresh-made trifles, tarts, and cakes ($2–4) that you'll find hard to pass over. For lunch, try British favorites like cottage pie, Cornish pasty, Scotch eggs, and ploughman's lunch ($7–8, with salad). Open 10–6, Sun 11–6.

Tavares

Magoo's (352-253-0475), 390 W US 441. I grabbed a hearty country-style breakfast for under $5 at this family restaurant one Sat morning, glad that I'd ordered the short stack of pancakes because they were so filling! Serving breakfast and lunch (under $6), 5:30–3.

Twist-tee Treat (352-343-6177), 397 N US 441. Shaped like a giant ice cream cone, it's your quick stop for a cold treat. There's an additional location in Clermont off US 27 near FL 50—just look for the outrageously large cone!

Umatilla

The Mason Jar (352-589-2535), 37534 FL 19. I've been driving past here for years, and rare is the day I don't see the massive parking lot packed at mealtime. Serving up good old-fashioned country cooking like fried chicken, cheese grits, and yams, the Mason Jar provides fast, friendly service in a comfortable family atmosphere. Sandwiches $3–5, dinners $5–8. Open daily for breakfast, lunch, and dinner.

Old Crow Real Pit BBQ (352-669-3922), 41100 FL 19, came recommended from several barbecue lovers before I had a chance to try them myself, and I was very impressed with their smoked ham. Open Thu–Sat evenings.

Yalaha

Yalaha Country Bakery (352-324-3366; www.yalahabakery.com), 8210 CR 48. From the loving hands of pastry chefs straight from the Black Forest, these fresh-baked breads and incredible pastries are made with springwater; no preservatives. Visitors arrive by the busload to walk away with authentic olive bread, napoleons, and Bavarian custard tarts ($1–3) from the two-story Bavarian building gaily painted with flowers and trees. On Sat the complex bustles with activity thanks to free folk music concerts out on the lawn. In addition to the luscious baked goods, the bakery serves up sandwiches, salads, and pizza for lunch. Open Mon–Sat 8–5; shipping baked goods worldwide!

Entertainment

Clermont

At the **Pier Restaurant** (see *Eating Out*) catch the weekly comedy club, Fri and Sat; for a funky jam session, head to **2 Dog Café**, 550 West Ave, where live music rocks the coffeehouse starting at 7 PM Fri, 10 PM Sat.

Mount Dora

Hankering for Broadway musicals? Check out the **Bay Street Players** (352-357-7777), 109 N Bay St, Eustis, a 30-year-old repertory group presenting six musicals each season in a playhouse reminiscent of a small London theater. The **Mount Dora Theatre Company** (352-383-4616; www.icehousetheatre.com) presents Shakespeare, cutting-edge plays, and old standbys. In the evening stop in at the **Frosty Mug** (see *Eating Out*) for live jazz piano (except Mon).

Yalaha

Bring your lawn chair down to **Yalaha Country Bakery** (see *Eating Out*) on Sat at 10 AM to enjoy free folk, blues, acoustic rock, and the occasional oompah band. For a monthly list of performances, check www.edelweiss music.net or call 352-324-3366.

✵ Selective Shopping

Clermont

Collectibles & More (352-242-6631), 836 W Montrose St. Antiques and vintage furniture, costume jewelry, Depression glass, and pottery. Closed Sun.

Shannon's Books & Things (352-243-3232), 791 W Montrose St. A cozy family-owned bookstore with new and used tomes, and a great selection of children's books. Closed Sun.

The Vintage View (352-243-9977), 763 W Montrose St. It's like browsing Grandma's house, with 14 dealers showcasing dishes, vintage clothing, glassware, and more. Closed Sun and Mon.

Wendimere's Herb Shoppe & Day Spa (1-888-568-HERB; www.herb pantry.com), 702 W Montrose St. I went in for flaxseed and booked a same-day appointment for a long-overdue massage. Natural foods, vitamins, massage therapy, and an aromatherapy bar.

Westwind Antiques (352-243-0806), 719 West Ave. For those seeking the immaculate period dining room: fine china, tea sets, and the linens and furniture to set them on.

Yesterdazes Antiques (352-242-6370), 517 West Ave. Expect the unusual at this eclectic antiques emporium, where you can browse through the garage for ornamental architecture or poke through themed rooms inside the house for collectible toys, primitives, and vintage clothing—everything from tin toys and feather boas to Rubik's cubes. Closed Sun and Mon.

Eustis

The Book Rack (352-589-0400), 2862 David Walker Dr. Tucked away in the Eustis Village Shopping Center, this used-book store has thousands of titles on hand.

Old South Stained Glass & Antique Mall (352-357-5200), 320 S Grove St. Where better to house a stained-glass studio than in a former church? But the studio, with its elegant artwork, supplies, and classes, is just one facet of the business—every themed room brims with antiques, from primitives to Coca-Cola.

Peddler's Wagon (352-483-2797), 25 E Magnolia Ave. Enticing fragrances fill this home decor shop, from sprays of flowers, dried flower wreaths, and candles; regional art graces the walls.

Porter's (352-357-2540), 120 E Magnolia Ave, is an independent camera shop with professional-grade film and processing, international electrical adaptors, and other important necessities for photographers on the road; don't miss their back corner gallery of fine art photography of local subjects.

Fruitland Park

North Lake Flea Market (352-326-9335), 2557 US 27-441. Busy weekend flea market with a garage sale atmosphere.

Lady Lake

South Wind Trading Post (352-753-0500), 835 US 27. I have to list this one—I remember stopping here as a kid in the 1960s. It has all the touristy stuff like citrus candies, T-shirts, and alligator heads, plus quite a range of Native American items.

Leesburg
Leesburg has a pleasant historic downtown with a nice selection of shops. You'll find most businesses on Main St and the town square, where a fountain burbles in front of city hall. All downtown shops are closed Sun.

The Corner Nook Antiques (352-360-0091), 606 Main St, has glassware, lamps, and vases displayed on fine antique furnishings.

In addition to its gifts and home decor, **Distinct Innovations** (352-365-1717), 706 Main St, serves up lattes and espresso in their snazzy little coffeehouse; pick up some gourmet goodies to take home.

Grace's Books & Records (352-315-0867), 309 W Main St. Dealing in used books and records, with an excellent selection to browse through. Open Tue–Sat.

Victoria's Antique Warehouse (352-728-8668), 113 N 7th St, focuses on antique furnishings and garden accessories spread throughout a large warehouse; look here for large items.

Victorian Rose (352-728-8388), 600 Main St, is a large, neatly arranged store specializing in Victoriana, including furnishings and jewelry.

South of downtown, **Morning Glori Antique Mall** (352-365-9977; www.morningglori.com), 111 S 14th St, has more than 60 dealers with quilts and primitives, coins and postcards, and plenty of fine antique furniture. Open daily.

Mascotte
Po' Robbi's Antique Village (352-429-5994), 856 W Myers Blvd. Huge vintage advertising signs, gas pumps, wagons, and other large pieces of ephemera fill the front yard of this eclectic dealer.

Minneola
Uncommon Market (352-242-4699), 200-B S US 27. Gourmet foods, European imports, specialty meats (ostrich, buffalo, rabbit, and the like), and a fine selection of wines; weekly wine tasting Fri evening, $5. Closed Sun and Mon.

Mount Dora
The corner of 5th Ave (Old US 441) and Donnelly St marks the epicenter of Mount Dora's renowned shopping district, which stretches on for several blocks in all directions. From pottery to books, antique furnishings to gourmet foods, you'll find it here! Here's a sampling of Florida's largest selection of shops in one small downtown:

All Aboard South (352-735-1245), 115 W 3rd Ave. Along the old Mount Dora Railroad tracks, this train shop features HO&G-scale rolling stock, tracks and kits, software simulators, and home decor items.

Barbara B's (352-385-7207), 411 N Donnelly St #107. Eclectic home decor, featuring playful Indonesian wood carvings, wooden spoons and masks, and animal carvings.

Dickens & Reed (352-735-5950), 140 W 5th Ave. Inside and out, it feels like one of the little bookshops on Charing Cross Road, London, with a thoughtful collection of new and used books, including a nice section on Florida topics, and the **Leaky Cauldron Café**, a coffeehouse abuzz with conversation.

Double Creek Pottery (352-735-5579), 430 N Donnelly St. For more than 30 years, the mother-daughter team of Joanne and Betty Barwick, graduates of the art festival circuit, have created whimsical floral pottery—one look and you'll be right in the door.

Noni Home Imports (352-383-1242), 112 E 5th Ave. Proprietor Lori Davis wanders the world for folk art like Rajasthani wall hangings, Thai daybeds, and "vegetable ivory" carvings; Lonely Planet guidebooks and world music transport you to the Far East.

Old Towne Bookshop (352-383-0878), 127 W 5th Ave. From floor to ceiling, books line the walls of this tiny shop filled with rarities and nostalgia.

Oliver's Twist Antiques (352-735-3337), 404 N Donnelly St. Always busy, with a wide selection of antique furnishings, glassware, and large home decor items.

Princess Antique Mall (1-800-637-2394), 130 W 5th Ave. Explore this mini mall with two stories of collectibles and antiques in dealer booths, plus a café and fudge shop.

Purple Pineapple Antique Mall (1-888-735-2190), 317 N Donnelly. Full of fun niches to explore, these dealer booths contain a little bit of everything, from stained glass to Red Hat items.

Southern Exotics (352-735-2500), 116 W 5th Ave. Orchids peeping out from behind beaded Victorian lampshades: an antiques shop with a floral twist.

Summerfield Lane (352-735-6800), 237 W 4th Ave. Featuring bath and body products, including Pre de Provence soaps; April Cornell linens.

Uncle Al's Time Capsule (352-383-1958; www.sign-here.com), 140 E 4th Ave. Music from the 1940s drifts through this memorabilia shop, setting the tone for the movie collectibles inside.

Yada Yada Pottery (352-735-1328; www.yadayadapottery.com), 822 N Donnelly St. Coffee shop kvetching meets creativity: Stop in for a latte and paint yourself a ceramic figurine. Selling fine art in the adjoining gallery; regular art classes available as well as just drop-in-and-paint sessions.

Yesterday, Today, and Tomorrow (352-735-1887), 427 N Donnelly St. Floral paintings spill across the storefront and down the sides, inviting you to step inside and browse through showy vintage clothing and jewelry.

South of downtown, don't miss **Renninger's Antique and Flea Market** (352-383-8393), 20651 US 441. Open weekends only, this expansive complex has a split personality. Hang a right, and you drive down to the sedate ambience of antiques dealers with permanent booths inside a large air-conditioned mall as well as a village of permanent shops around the edge of the complex. Turn left and drive up the hill to the busy buzz of thousands of people combing through hundreds of flea market stalls selling everything from inexpensive used books to antique reproduction signs, live birds, local produce, and garage sale items. Renninger's also holds huge special events, like a motorcycle and car swap meet on the second Sun of every month, and an annual Civil War reenactment. This is a don't-miss stop if you enjoy spending hours and hours browsing, and the flea market prices are pretty darn good.

Sorrento

Cypress Things (352-383-3864), 28625 FL 46. The cigar-store Indian on the porch startled me, it was so lifelike. Joe, Shane, and Ethel Chavis carve cypress and other woods into works of art, from life-sized bears and fine furnishings to totem poles.

Umatilla

Umatilla Antique Markets (352-669-3202), 811 N FL 19. Sift through dealer tables for antiques and flea market items. Open Thu–Sat 9–4.

CITRUS STANDS, FARMER'S MARKETS, AND U-PICK

Clermont

Del-Don Florida Market (352-394-6555), 2049 US 27. It's not just a produce stand, it's a step back to pre-Disney tourism, with an adjoining shop stuffed with goodies like Florida citrus candy, carved coconuts, citrus jellies, and scented orange balls ("use as a sachet!") for 40¢. Carries Yalaha Bakery products in winter.

R&R Fruit (352-394-6281), 2700 US 27. Permanent citrus stand with fresh local fruit near the border with Polk County.

Showcase of Citrus (352-394-4377; www.showcaseofcitrus.com), 5010 US 27. With a yellow-and-black-striped safari swamp buggy parked in front, you can't miss this seasonal citrus stand that boasts a citrus museum, live trees for sale, swamp buggy rides through the groves, and, of course, citrus for sale.

Eustis

Buy your food direct from the source at the **Lake County Farmers Market** (352-357-9692), every Thu (except legal holidays) at the Lake County Expo Grounds, FL 19 N.

Mount Dora

Hutchinson & Sons Produce (352-589-6612), 4600 Old CR 19. Stop in for seasonal vegetables and fruit including fresh mangos and citrus; open 9–6.

May Brothers OJ Groves (352-357-2636), US 441 and Eudora, behind the Wal-Mart. Selling fresh citrus under a big tent.

Tavares

Hammock Gift Fruit (352-343-3117), 30238 FL 19. A seasonally open citrus grower's outlet store that will ship your selections home.

✷ Special Events

February: **Thunder Road Cruiser Show** (352-357-7969), first Sat, Ferran Park, Eustis. Annual vintage car show with a 1950s theme, food vendors, and awards for "best in show."

Georgefest (352-357-3434), last weekend, Ferran Park, Eustis, is the state's oldest continuous festival (since 1901), celebrating George Washington's birthday with a parade, fun events like a citrus squeeze and pie-eating contest, and patriotic fireworks over the lake. Free.

March: **Leesburg Art Festival** (352-787-0000; leesburgartfestival.com), last weekend. Nearly 30 years old, this annual festival brings in more than 100 fine artists and craftspeople.

April: **Mount Dora Regatta** (352-383-3188), first weekend. Every Apr, the Mount Dora Yacht Club hosts the Mount Dora Regatta, a showy display of yachtsmanship across Lake Dora.

October: ✐ **Umatilla Black Bear Festival** (www.flblackbearfestival.org), first Sat. An educational festival celebrating Florida's endemic bruin with environmental presentations and field trips into bear habitat. Bring your injured teddy bear to the Bear Repair Clinic! Free.

December: **Eustis Art League Winter Art Show** (352-357 5031), first weekend, at the Eustis Art League, downtown. Approaching its 50th year, this celebration of the arts features the talented members of the local art league.

Florida Whips Carriage Festival (352-750-5500), Lady Lake. For those intrigued by the days before the horseless carriage, this annual carriage festival celebrates two centuries of craftsmanship with a promenade of carriages and parade of breeds. Held the second weekend of December at Continental Acres Equine Resort (see *Resorts*); fee.

Venetian Gardens Light Up (352-365-0053), Leesburg. More than half a million twinkling lights in this waterfront public park create one of the most delightful Christmas displays in the region; open 6 PM nightly all month.

NATURE COAST

CITRUS, HERNANDO, PASCO, AND SUMTER COUNTIES

Encompassing the most accessible part of the Gulf Coast in Central Florida, the counties of the Nature Coast provide unparalleled outdoor recreation opportunities amid Old Florida towns (dating back to the 1840s) that provide quiet respite from their bustling neighbors to the south and east. Where the Withlacoochee River winds northward from the Green Swamp, its floodplain forests and feeder lakes define the interior of the region; vast estuaries along the Gulf of Mexico fringe its western border. Roam through hundreds of square miles of the Withlacoochee State Forest and adjoining public lands, paddle the Withlacoochee River, or bike the Withlacoochee State Trail, which runs the length of the region. Kick back at **Lake Panasoffkee**, where you can catch an 11-pound largemouth bass right off a dock, or kayak the maze of estuary waterways from **Hernando Beach** to **Crystal River**. Seek out busy little **Webster**, home of the state's largest farmer's and flea market, or head for the antiques shops of **Inverness**, **Brooksville**, and **Dade City**. Steeped in history, the region was a battleground during the Seminole Wars and the Civil War. Get off the beaten path and wander the back roads to connect with the people and places that make up this fascinating and beautiful region of rivers and coastal estuaries.

GUIDANCE Look for the giant manatee on US 19 in Homosassa to find the **Greater Nature Coast Visitor's Center** (352-621-7200; www.swimwithamanatee.com) in Citrus County. Other regional contacts include the **Hernando County Tourist Development** (1-800-601-4580; www.co.hernando.fl.us/visit), Brooksville; the **Pasco County Office of Tourism** (1-800-842-1873; www.visitpasco.net), 7530 Little Rd, New Port Richey; and the **Sumter County Chamber of Commerce** (352-793-3099; www.gosumter.com), 225 US 301 S, Sumterville.

GETTING THERE *By air*: For the quickest access to the Nature Coast region, fly into **Tampa International Airport** (with a wide selection of carriers) and drive up the new **Suncoast Pkwy** (FL 589), a toll road cutting through the heart of the region to reach the coast at Chassahowitzka.

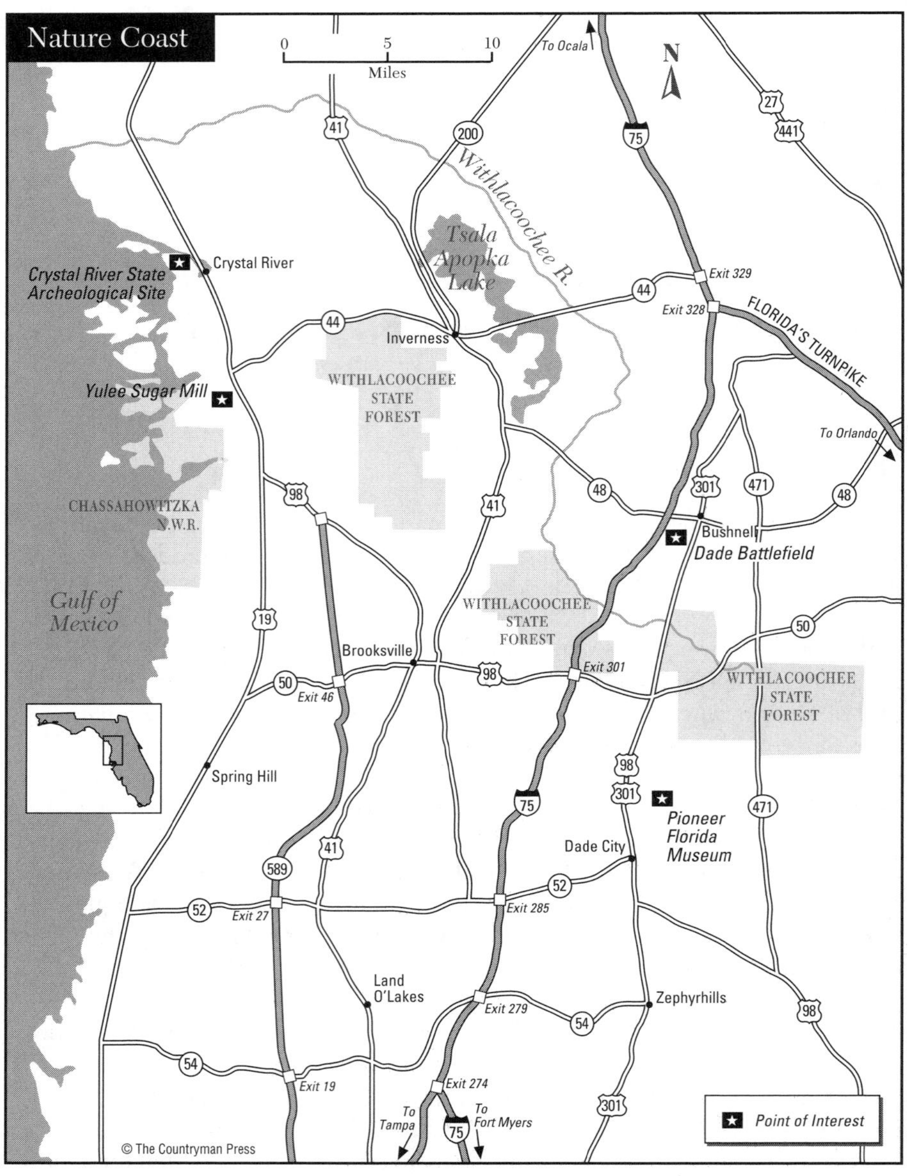

By car: Both the **Suncoast Pkwy** and **I-75** provide quick access to the region; use **FL 52**, **FL 50**, and **FL 44** to make east–west connections with **US 301**, **US 41**, and **US 19**.

By bus: **Greyhound** (1-800-229-9424; www.greyhound.com) runs through Brooksville, Crystal River, Dade City, New Port Richey, and Spring Hill.

By train: **Amtrak** Silver Service/Palmetto (1-800-USA-RAIL; www.amtrak.com) stops in Wildwood and Dade City en route to Tampa daily.

PARKING You'll find free public parking in all of the towns along the Nature Coast; some spaces are limited-term.

PUBLIC REST ROOMS Look for them in **Dade City** at the chamber of commerce building off Church Ave.

MEDICAL EMERGENCIES Two major regional hospitals are **Seven Rivers Community Hospital** (352-795-6560), 6201 N Suncoast Blvd, Crystal River, and **Pasco Regional Medical Center** (352-521-1100), 13100 Fort King Rd, Dade City.

✷ To See

ARCHEOLOGICAL SITES At the **Crystal River State Archeological Site** (352-795-3817), 3400 N Museum Pointe, a paved interpretive trail winds around a ceremonial mound complex built more than 2,500 years ago; evidence of human use of this site dates back nearly 10,000 years, encompassing four cultural periods in Florida's history. A tour boat at the site provides birding tours along the Crystal River. Fee.

The **Fort Island Beach Archeological Site**, a Weeden Island culture site, adjoins the public beach (see *Beaches*); explore via unmarked footpaths. Another Weeden Island site, the **Oeslner Mound**, Sunset Blvd, New Port Richey, is all that remains of a village settled around A.D. 1000 and occupied for several hundred years; Smithsonian archeologists analyzed the site in 1879.

ART GALLERIES **Brooksville City Art Gallery** (352-596-2443), 201 Howell Ave, features rotating exhibits from local artisans in quilting, photography, painting, and more, and is the permanent home of the Hernando County Historical Quilt.

Pasco Fine Arts Center (727-846-7322), 5744 Moog Rd, Holiday. Galleries showcase the works of locally and nationally renowned artists in all media, with an adjoining artists' co-op shop. Open Mon–Sat 9–4; free.

ATTRACTIONS ✐ **Boyett's Citrus Grove and Attraction** (352-796-2298 or 1-800-780-2296), 4355 Spring Lake Hwy, Brooksville. In the tradition of old-time Florida roadside attractions, Boyett's will thrill the kids with its wildlife park, 14,000-gallon saltwater fish tank, touristy gift shop, and ice cream parlor. Peek through the windows (in-season) and watch citrus being packed! Open daily 9–5; free.

Weeki Wachee Springs (352-596-2062), corner of US 19 and FL 50, Weeki Wachee. What little girl wouldn't be awed by real live mermaids? I know I was back in 1968, and that was well before Disney cornered the attraction market. Newt Perry's classic 1947 roadside attraction still centers on underwater choreography à la Esther Williams in sparkling Weekiwachee Spring, where the gals can never have a bad hair day. Relying on specialized air hoses, the mermaids hold their breath for up to 3 minutes at a time. A bird-watching cruise on the quiet electric *Princess Wondrous* will introduce you to one of the most beautiful rivers in Florida as hungry pelicans tap dance on the canopied roof, and a walk down the Tranquility Trail immerses you in the native hardwood hammock on the river's edge. Now owned by the tiny city of Weeki Wachee (with a former mermaid as mayor), the attraction is taking steps to correct years of neglect by prior owners. $13.95 adults, $10.95 ages 3–10. Prices rise to $18.95/14.95 during the summer months, and include admission to adjoining **Buccaneer Bay** (see *Water Park*). Open Thu–Fri 11–3, Sat and Sun 10–3.

GHOST TOWNS One of the largest sawmills in Florida operated in busy **Centralia** between 1910 and 1921, until loggers depleted the virgin cypress stands. Abandoned in the 1930s, the remains of the town hide under vegetation along US 19 in Chassahowitzka National Wildlife Refuge.

HISTORIC SITES

Brooksville

Chisnegut Hill (352-796-6254), CR 481, is a grand mansion that was once the center of a 2,080-acre plantation owned by Colonel Raymond Robins, a founding father of Brooksville. It now serves as a nature center, retreat, and conference center for the Florida Fish and Wildlife Conservation Commission.

Bushnell

The Second Seminole War began amid the longleaf pine flatwoods at **Dade Battlefield Historic State Park** (352-793-4781), 7200 CR 603, where in Dec 1835 Major Francis Dade led his troops on their march to Fort King into an unexpected trap: 180 Seminole warriors waited, angered by the federal Indian removal policy. After 6 hours and two waves of attacks, more than 100 soldiers lay dying; only 3 escaped.

THE FAMOUS WEEKI WACHEE MERMAIDS

Sandra Friend

Dade City

Downtown Dade City dates back to the 1890s; a walking tour (see *Walking Tours*) of historical sites introduces you to Victorian dwellings like the **McIntosh** and **Starr** houses as well as neoclassical and Florida boom architecture, all within a few city blocks along Meridian Ave.

Elfers

Baker House (727-849-1628), 5740 Moog Rd. The centerpiece of Centennial Park, this is the oldest Florida Cracker home in western Pasco

County, constructed in 1882 in a traditional dogtrot style, with a center corridor separating the living areas. Open for tours Sat 11–3.

Inverness

Fort Cooper State Park (352-726-0315), 3100 S Old Floral City Rd, marks the site of another page in the history of the Seminole Wars, where a bedraggled battalion of sick and injured soldiers walking to Tampa stopped to regroup and recuperate after a monthlong battle at the Cove of the Withlacoochee; they hastily built a wooden fort to defend themselves in Apr 1836 when the Seminoles attacked. An annual reenactment relives the event.

New Port Richey

Explore the revitalized 1920s downtown (see *Walking Tours*) for a look at landmarks like the 1926 **Meighan Theater**, a former movie theater named for a silent film great and reborn as the Richey Suncoast Theatre, and **The Hacienda**, a 55-room 1927 hotel that attracted the crème of the Hollywood film industry.

St. Leo

St. Leo College dates back to 1890, and its grounds hold some interesting treasures. Built from local stone, **Our Lady of Lourdes Grotto** (across FL 52 from the St. Leo Abbey) was completed in 1916. Florida coral rock and stained glass make up the adjoining **Garden of Gethsemane Grotto** from 1938. The distinctive Romanesque-style **St. Leo Abbey Church** has beams of cedar from trees harvested at the college; it opened for worship in 1948. The oldest building on campus is the **St. Leo Abbey**, originally dedicated as a Benedictine monastery in 1902.

MEMORIALS At the **Florida National Cemetery** (352-793-7740), 6502 SW 102nd Ave, west of Bushnell, you'll find the **Memorial Trail**, a paved footpath running past memorial plaques honoring veterans of the U.S. armed forces. This is the only national cemetery for veterans in Florida.

MUSEUMS

Brooksville

Hernando Heritage Museum (352-799-0129; www.hernandoheritagemuseum.com), 601 Museum Court. A 12-room Victorian home built in 1856 on an original land grant, the May-Stringer House boasts more than 10,000 regional-history artifacts on display. Open Tue–Fri noon–3 for 45-minute guided tours; fee.

Crystal River

Coastal Heritage Museum (352-795-1755), 532 Citrus Ave. Tucked inside the original town hall, a WPA project from 1939, this small museum is crammed with little-known historical facts about the maritime towns of Citrus County. An award-winning diorama depicts downtown Crystal River in 1927; displays cover such offbeat topics as school boats used to reach island schoolhouses, the oyster-canning industry, and the cedar pencil industry. Open Tue–Fri 11–3, closed July; free.

OLD HOMOSASSA Yulee Sugar Mill Ruins Historic State Park (352-795-3817), Yulee Dr. In the 1850s David Levy Yulee had already made quite a name for himself. Born in St. Thomas, he was brought to the Florida Territory in 1817 by his family and attended law school in St. Augustine. After attending Florida's first constitutional convention, he was elected a territorial delegate to the U.S. Congress, and became Florida's first U.S. senator when Florida achieved statehood in 1845. All the while he managed businesses ranging from the Atlantic & Gulf Railroad to his 5,100-acre sugar plantation, Margarita, on the Homosassa River. By 1851 the sugar mill had 1,000 workers, primarily slaves. Yulee joined the Confederate Congress when Florida seceded, and used his mansion at Tiger Tail Island in the Homosassa River as a storehouse for ammunition and supplies. So it was no great surprise that the Union Blockading Squadron targeted the plantation. In May 1864, after a failed attempt at ambushing Yulee on the road from Homosassa to Archer, a Federal naval detachment burned the mansion to the ground. The mill, standing inland, escaped damage but fell into ruin as the plantation was abandoned. Now partially restored, the original machinery stands in place; walk through the complex to learn the historic process of turning sugarcane to sugar, which Yulee adapted from his Caribbean birthplace.

THE YULEE SUGAR MILL AT OLD HOMOSASSA

Sandra Friend

Dade City

Starting in 1961 with a donation of 37 antique farm vehicles, the collection of the **Pioneer Florida Museum** (352-567-0262), 15602 Pioneer Museum Rd, has grown to cover 20 acres. Eight historical buildings typical of early pioneers are spaced for leisurely exploring. Check out the Trilby Depot, circa 1896, complete with a 1913 Porter steam engine; pretend to shop in the 1920s C. C. Smith General Store; and go back to school in a 1930s one-room schoolhouse. Don't miss the First Ladies of Florida doll collection, or the doctor's room outfitted with memorabilia from an office of a local doctor and dentist, in the Main Building. Open daily 1–5. Fee. Nearby, Withlacoochee River Park (see *Parks*) hosts living history events in its replica Creek Indian and Florida Cracker villages.

Hernando

Ted Williams Museum & Hitters Hall of Fame (352-527-6566), 2455 N Citrus Hills Blvd. Baseball fans shouldn't miss this triumphant tribute to one of the Hall of Fame's top hitters, where you walk through the bases of a baseball diamond to review this legend's career. Eighteen galleries contain collectibles, scrapbooks, a research library, and actual game footage from the 1940s. Open Tue–Sun 10–4; $5 adults, $1 children.

Homosassa

Olde Mill House Gallery and Printing Museum (1-888-248-6672; www.chronicle-online.com/printmuseum.htm), 10466 W Yulee Dr. An unusual museum devoted to a vanishing art—typesetting. In addition to its displays of letterpresses and movable type, this museum offers hands-on experience with its antique machines, under the tutelage of curator Jim Anderson. Open Mon–Sat by appointment only; cost ($25 per hour) depends on size of group.

Inverness

Museum of Citrus County History (352-637-9928), 1 Courthouse Square. From the outside, it looks like a prop from *Back to the Future*, and it was featured in Elvis's *Follow That Dream*. But this 1912 courthouse is authentic, and exhibits inside tell the story of Citrus County. Free.

New Port Richey

In what was once a two-room schoolhouse from 1916, the **West Pasco Historical Society** (727-847-0680), 6431 Circle Blvd, contains artifacts and papers on early area businesses and local history, including genealogical records; the Indian Gallery contains artifacts from Seminole and Timucua sites. Open Fri and Sat 1–4; free.

Zephyrhills

The **Zephyrhills Depot Museum** (813-780-0067), 39110 South Ave, inside the restored 1927 Atlantic Coast Line railroad depot, opened in 1998. Four exhibit rooms emphasize the history of trains with artifacts from the original depot. Genealogists will want to check out the Family Room for local family history. Open Tue–Sat 10–2. Free.

RAILROADIANA In addition to the **Zephyrhills Depot** (see *Museums*), look for the **Seaboard Coast Line** freight station in Inverness along the Withlacoochee Rail Trail, down Apopka Ave east of the Old County Courthouse. The **Crystal River Railroad Depot**, with Seaboard Air Line rolling stock, adjoins Crystal St one block south of Citrus Ave. The **Citrus County Model Railroad Association** maintains a public display of their model-railroad layouts at the Citrus County Fairgrounds (US 41, south of Inverness), open Sat during flea market hours.

WINERIES **Florida Estates Winery** (813-996-2113; www.floridaestateswines.com), 25241 FL 52, Land O'Lakes. Set on a 3,600-acre working cattle ranch, this newcomer to the winery business shines with an intriguing array of specialty and dessert wines such as strawberry port, key lime, and orange; I was impressed by the tasty Plantation Spice wine ($12), which pairs well with chocolate. Most of their products are fermented and bottled at their sister winery, Eden Vineyards, but all contain some Florida grapes. Open Mon–Sat 11–5, Sun 1–5; small fee for tasting their full range of wines.

ZOOLOGICAL PARK AND WILDLIFE REHABILATION **Homosassa Springs Wildlife State Park** (352-628-5343; www.homosassasprings.org), 4150 S Suncoast Blvd, Homosassa. It's a blast from my past—a former roadside attraction now serving as a zoological park featuring Florida's native wildlife (excepting Lucifer the hippo, who was made a citizen of Florida to legally remain in his longtime home). Stroll the forested grounds and enjoy the rambling and slithering of Florida's wildlife; many of the animals are here for rehab or because they cannot be reintroduced into the wild. In the Fish Bowl, you descend into an inside-out aquarium, where you look through plate-glass windows at swirls of fish and manatees drifting by around the first-magnitude, 45-foot-deep crevice of Homosassa Springs. $7.95 ages 12 and up, $4.95 children 3–12. Daily 9–5:30, ticket counter closes at 4.

✻ To Do

AIRBOATING At **Wild Bill's Airboat Tours** (352-726-6060; www.wildbillsairboattours.com), FL 44, take a 10-mile spin up the Withlacoochee River for a look at this wild, twisting waterway edged by dark floodplain forests. $20 adults, $10 kids 10 and under.

BICYCLING Bike rentals are available at two **Suncoast Bicycles Plus** (1-800-296-1010; www.suncoastbikes.com) locations, each convenient to a trail: 1 mile from the **Fort Island Beach Trail** at 471 NE 1st Terrace, Crystal River; 1 block west of US 19; and 332 N Pine St, Inverness on the **Withlacoochee State Trail** (see *Greenways*), where you'll also find rentals at **Hampton's Edge** (352-799-4979), trailside in Istachatta, and **Nobleton Boat Rental** (see *Paddling*). Bikers have more than 12 miles of trail to roam at the **Crystal River State Buffer Preserve**, just north of Crystal River, and can bike a couple of miles on the **Pepper Creek Trail** at Homosassa Springs (see *Zoological Park*). The two long-distance trails in the region are the Withlacoochee State Trail and the **Suncoast State Trail**, connecting the Nature Coast to the Tampa Bay area (see *Greenways*); for off-road fun on 32 miles of forested trails, visit the **Croom Off-Road Bicycle Trails** off Croom Rd, north of Brooksville off US 41, in Withlacoochee State Forest (see *Wild Places*).

BIRDING Birders will delight at whooping cranes at **Chassahowitzka National Wildlife Refuge** (see *Wild Places*), but birding must be done by boat. Flocks of black skimmers often hang out at **Fort Island Beach** (see *Beaches*); at **Fort Island Trail Park** (see *Parks*) on Crystal River, watch for wading birds. Great blue herons roost in the trees at **Homosassa Springs Wildlife State Park** (see *Zoological Park*); the park's free Pepper Creek Trail attracts birders looking for warblers. Bird-watching is also superb at **Weeki Wachee Preserve**, off Shoal Line Rd in Hernando Beach, where more than 230 species have been recorded, including a nesting colony of least terns. All of the *Green Space* entries will net you great birding, but one of the region's newest parks, **Key Vista Nature Park** (see *Parks*), is a top site for ospreys and bald eagles. For many more sites, visit the Citrus Birding Trail at www.citrusbirdingtrail.com.

DINOSAUR SPOTTING More than a decade ago an Istachatta sculptor named Herwede created life-sized dinosaur sculptures to populate a park. Look for his remaining **half a brontosaurus** along CR 476 west of Nobleton. On US 19 in Spring Hill, a monstrous **1960 Sinclair Oil gray dinosaur** houses Harold's Auto, and a **pink dinosaur** stands roadside a few miles farther south.

DIVING

Crystal River

Bird's Underwater Dive Center (1-800-771-2763; www.birdsunderwater.com), 320 NW US 19, is a certified PADI five-star dive center with 4-day open-water class (minimum age 10), $225. **Crystal Lodge Dive Center** (352-795-6798; www.manatee-central.com), 525 NW 7th Ave, at the **Best Western Crystal River Resort** (see *Lodging*), is a full-service dive shop with on-site instructors, offering guided snorkeling or sightseeing tours on **Crystal River** and the nearby **Rainbow River** (see "Marion County"). **Crystal River Manatee Dive & Tour** (352-795-1333; www.manateetouranddive.com), 267 NW 3rd St, has cold air, boat, and equipment rentals; diving or snorkel tours $25. **Plantation Dive Shop** (352-795-5797; www.crystalriverdivers.com) at the Plantation Inn and Golf Resort (see *Resorts*) takes divers out on guided trips, offers instruction, and rents boats and gear; popular King Spring, 75 feet deep, is just a few hundred yards from their back door.

New Port Richey

Sunny Seas Scuba (727-849-2478), 7115 US 19 S, runs full- and half-day expeditions into the Gulf, and has rentals, sales, instruction, and nitrox; **Super Sports & Scuba** (727-848-7122), 7129 US 19, takes divers out into the Gulf for dives of 45 to 75 feet, with classes from open water to dive master available.

Weeki Wachee
Yes, you can dive **Weekiwachee Spring** when the mermaids are off-duty; contact one of the above dive centers for details, as most run trips to this crystal-clear spring.

ECOTOURS The **J. B. Starkey's Flatwood Adventure** (813-926-1133 or 1-877-734-WILD; www.flatwoodsadventures.com), 12959 FL 54, Odessa, is a true working cattle ranch, dating back to 1899. Discover five different ecosystems on a comfortable 2-hour Range Buggy tour ($17). Keep your eyes peeled for wild Osceola turkey and white-tailed deer. You may even need to stop for a gopher tortoise sunning on the trail. Listen for alligators as you a walk along an elevated 450-foot boardwalk through a real cypress swamp. To get a taste of the true Florida landscape and the way life used to be, take a 1-hour ($35) or 2-hour ($65) narrated horseback riding tour through terrain rarely traveled by humans. Full-moon hayrides ($25) and horse rides ($49) include a delicious BBQ, roaring bonfire, marshmallows, and s'mores; lower rates for seniors and children.

River Safaris and Gulf Charters (1-800-758-FISH; www.riversafaris.com), 10823 Yulee Dr, Homosassa. Offering narrated cruises on the Homosassa River ($15–25), airboat rides into the estuaries ($22–50), and swimming with manatees ($30) in winter, as well as boat rentals (canoes and kayaks, $20–30), it's your one-stop shop for exploration of the natural wonders of the Homosassa River and its surrounding estuaries.

Susan Davis (352-628-5707), a certified ecoguide, leads custom-tailored paddling trips down the Homosassa River and out into the Gulf estuary. Susan has a private camp on Little Tiger Tail Island, and her basic trip circles historic Tiger Tail Island, the site of David Yulee's plantation, Margarita, which was once connected to the mainland by a plank road.

Also running out of Homosassa, Captain Mike's **Sunshine River Tours** (352-628-3450 or 1-866-645-5727; www.sunshinerivertours.com) take you out on a pontoon boat to go snorkeling with the manatees at Bluewater Springs; birding trips, scalloping trips, and custom-tailored ecotours are also available.

In addition to being a dive center, **Bird's Underwater Dive Center** offers winter tours of manatee habitats, as well as guided dives and snorkeling trips on the Crystal River and the Rainbow River, as does **Crystal Lodge Dive Center** (see *Diving* for both).

FAMILY ACTIVITIES **Adventureland** (352-726-7001), US 41 between Floral City and Inverness, has a nicely landscaped miniature golf course and adjacent driving range. On US 19, **Crazy Eddie's Go-Karts** (352-563-1167) isn't just about go-carts: Let the kids try out the bumper boats, mini golf, and water balloon stations as well. For indoor fun on a rainy day, try the **Sportsmen's Bowl** (352-726-2873; www.sportsmensbowl.com), 100 N Florida Ave in Inverness, the **Roller Barn** (352-726-2044), 1740 US 41 north of Inverness, or **Jimmy's Skating Center** (352-793-3570), 5260 US 301 between Sumterville and Bushnell.

FISHING In addition to world-class bass, you can reel in a steady stream of panfish from **Lake Panasoffkee** for your evening repast—the lake is so clean, there's no limit. See *Fish Camps* for places to cast. Inshore and flats fishing is big all along the Nature Coast, with snook, tarpon, cobia, and Spanish mackerel. Charters run $300 and up for a full day, and you'll find eager guides all the way from **Crystal River** down to **Holiday**; stop in and ask around at the marinas. Anglers who want a taste of old-time Florida fishing shouldn't miss **Aripeka**, a historic fishing village off US 19 at the Pasco-Hernando county line, and **Old Homosassa**, at the end of Yulee Drive.

GOLF

Crystal River

Plantation Inn Golf Resort (see *Resorts*) has 27 holes of championship golf on a Mark Mahanah–designed course that's stood the test of time for nearly 50 years. Flowing around naturally landscaped water holes, it's also a haven for alligators and wading birds, a pleasant spot for nongolfers to take a stroll.

St. Leo

Lake Jovita Golf & Country Club (352-588-2233; www.lakejovita.com), 12900 Lake Jovita Blvd, features an extraordinary challenge—the longest natural drop of any golf course in Florida, 94 feet from tee to green on the 11th hole. The undulating landscape is reminiscent of the Carolina foothills; the course was designed by PGA pro Tom Lehman.

The 18 holes of **St. Leo Abbey Golf Course** (813-588-2016), 33640 FL 52, are great for beginners. Spread over 80 acres of rolling countryside, the open fairways and fast greens are sure to add just the right challenge. Full pro shop on site; rental clubs available.

Sumterville

From US 301, you can see the expanse of **Shady Brook Golf & RV Resort** (352-568-2244), 178 N US 301, a public 18-hole course (par 72, $14–16) adjoined by an RV park of grassy sites under a smattering of pine trees; the park is frequented by snowbirds, but you can inquire at the pro shop regarding overnight and weekend stays. Each hole has an interpretive sign giving the lay of the land. After a round, golfers gather at the **Shady Brook Grille**, just outside the pro shop.

Wesley Chapel

Challenge your skills amid tall cypress trees and tranquil lagoons at **Saddlebrook Golf and Tennis** (813-973-1111), 4750 Fox Hunt Dr. Located on 480 acres of rolling terrain, this semiprivate course provides two 18-hole championship courses designed by Arnold Palmer.

You'll learn the four basics—swing fundamentals, the scoring zone, course strategy, and how to practice like a pro—at the **Arnold Palmer Golf Academy** (813-907-4653 or 1-800-729-8383; www.saddlebrookresort.com), 5700 Saddlebrook Way. Palmer personally selects professional instructors—many former tour champions. Several packages available, including a 30-minute individual lesson or a personal analysis of your swing, which includes a take-home video of your performance.

HIKING Although you'll stumble across signs for great little hikes like **Crystal River Ecowalk** and **Churchfield Hammock Trail** off US 19 at Crystal River State Buffer Preserve (352-563-0450), hiking opportunities on the Nature Coast mainly center on the many tracts of **Withlacoochee State Forest** (see *Wild Places*). The 43-mile **Citrus Trail** and 26-mile **Richloam Loop**, both part of the Florida Trail, are the best places to backpack; day hikers shouldn't miss the **Croom Hiking Trail** (off FL 50 at Ridge Manor) and the **Johnson Pond Trail** (off CR 33 south of Citrus Springs).

MANATEE-WATCHING The Nature Coast prides itself on being Manatee Central, where hundreds of these gentle giants come to winter in the many warm springs along the coast. A permanent population resides in rehab at **Homosassa Springs State Wildlife Park** (see *Zoological Park*), but if you're up for a little adventure, **Crystal River National Wildlife Refuge** (see *Springs*) is the place to take to the water in a kayak or with snorkeling or diving equipment. In Crystal River ask your outfitter for a map or directions to some of the area's sweet spots for manatee sightings, like **Magnolia Springs**, **Three Sisters**, **Mullet Spring**, and **Kings Springs**. Stay outside the roped boundaries of the manatee preserves along the river and do not touch or chase these massive creatures: Harassment of a manatee is a felony. Ecotour operators (see *Ecotours*) can also take you up close to the wintering manatee population.

PADDLING The Nature Coast is a top paddling destination in Florida, thanks to its many winding channels and extensive estuaries. Paddling is the best way to explore **Chassahowitzka National Wildlife Refuge**; the main put-in is at the **Chassahowitzka River Campground and Recreational Area** (see *Campgrounds*), where they also rent canoes and kayaks. For exploration of the crystalline **Homosassa River**, grab your rentals at either the **Marguerita Grill** (352-628-1336), 10200 W Halls River Rd, **Riversport Kayaks** (1-877-660-0929; www.flakayak.com), 2300 S Suncoast Blvd, or **River Safaris** (see *Ecotours*). Reservations are suggested for rentals to paddle the popular and pristine 8-mile route along the **Weekiwachee River**; stop in at **Weekiwachee Canoe & Kayak Rental** (352-597-0360; www.floridacanoe.com), behind the Weeki Wachee attraction, for rentals, $22–31. At **Crystal River** all the dive shops (see *Diving*) rent canoes and kayaks. My personal experience on the river says go for a kayak: It can slip into tight spots between the islands and yet stays perfectly stable when you're out in the broad river channel, where you'll meet a lot of motorized boaters. Navigable just north of Dade City, the **Withlacoochee River** flows north through the region and provides a fabulous multiday trip for paddlers. Rent canoes and kayaks at **Nobleton Boat Rental** (1-800-783-5284; www.nobletoncanoes.com), CR 476, where owners Charlie and Bob Meers hold a barbecue and music festival the third Sat of each month.

PARAGLIDING **FlyByRanch Paragliding School** (1-888-727-2868), CR 237 in Oxford, outside Wildwood, offers lessons in paragliding over the rural countryside near I-75.

ALONG THE HOMOSASSA RIVER

Sandra Friend

SCENIC DRIVES There are plenty of quiet back roads throughout the Nature Coast, so it all depends on the scenery you're looking for. For a taste of the Old South, head up **Istachatta Rd** (CR 39) from Nobleton to Floral City, driving through tunnels of live oaks, passing farms and colorful floodplain forests. Turn left on **FL 44** and continue into Floral City, marveling at the ancient oaks shading the town. For a drive through the Gulf estuary, follow the **Fort Island Trail** from Crystal River west to its terminus at Fort Island Beach; enjoy the vast expanse of salt marsh broken up by islands of cabbage palms. Through rolling hills topped with cattle ranches and horse farms, **US 41** passes through small-town Florida on its route through the Nature Coast, as does **US 301**: You'll see few strip malls and chain restaurants along these routes, and US 41 traces the route of Spanish explorer Hernando de Soto through the region.

SKYDIVING Take the jump and get in with a whole new league of people at **ZHills Skydive City** (1-800-404-9399; www.skydivecity.com), 4241 Skydive Lane, Zephyrhills, where the thrills start at 13,500 feet. Let the wind whip past you as you fly at 120 mph, then deploy your parachute and glide into the drop zone for a perfect landing. This is one of the best places for tandem jumps. If you want to learn more, the experienced instructors will teach you how to fly by starting with either static line deployment or instructor-assisted deployment. Weight limit for tandem jumps is 220 pounds. Tandem free fall $169, video and photo $80.

SPAS Step into paradise at **The Spa at Saddlebrook Resort** (813-907-4419 or 1-800-729-8383; www.saddlebrookresort.com). Your attendant will escort you to the dressing room, where you wrap yourself in luxury with a spa robe and slippers. Take an aromatherapy steam, sauna, or whirlpool before (or after) your services, then relax over a cup of tea. Your therapist will then take you to a private oasis for your personally selected body treatment. Choose a Relaxation on the Rocks stone massage, or revive and rejuvenate with a Citrus Herbal Body Scrub or a Wild Lavender Body Facial topped off with a unique glycolic peppermint crème. Products from the Spa Salon are available to continue your experience at home. Spa and salon open daily 9–8.

LEAP OF FAITH AT ZHILLS Always my adventure child, Sherri convinced me to do a mother-daughter jump for part of my research. "How can you write about it if you don't experience it?" So I found myself on a cool spring morning pulling on a brightly colored jumpsuit at **ZHills Skydive City** (see *Skydiving*). As the instructors attached our harnesses, we nervously listened to the necessary instructions for a safe jump. Sherri now wore a somber look, but neither one of us was backing out. We boarded the Twin Otter aircraft, stripped of its seats, and took a seat on the floor; the instructor attached us to a rail inside the plane. Looking around, I noticed that everyone had a parachute—except us. Ours, it would appear, were attached to our tandem instructors. I double-checked my connection to the railing. As we climbed to over 13,000 feet we both grew increasingly quiet. The adrenaline-pumped jumpers were rooting for us, shouting "Redheads Rule!" Then one by one they left the plane and shot toward the earth at alarming speed. I leaned against JC as he attached the tandem harness in four places, checked it, and then checked it again. "Are you ready?" he yelled, as we toddled toward the open door. I nodded, as there wasn't a drop of spit in my mouth left for vocalizing. As we hung on the door I was thinking only one thing—*Don't scream; it's all on camera!*

We counted one—two—three and then we were airborne. And I was free. The fear left me instantly and it was awesome. A surreal feeling enveloped me and I was surprised that I had no sense of falling, just a lot of wind in a very large open space. Pure freedom. We flew up to and probably over 120 mph for what seemed like minutes, but was just shy of 60 seconds. Then we deployed the parachute and I found myself gently sitting in my harness like a swing with JC still securely attached. It was so quiet, and you could see for miles. The ground still didn't look any closer. I breathed in the cool air as we glided in the remaining 5,000 feet. Not once did I get vertigo, and not once did my fear return. Both Sherri and I felt safe the entire time—tandem accidents are rare. The gear was checked and rechecked several times, and we were instructed clearly and repeatedly in not only what we needed to do, but also what was going to happen at each stage so there really were no surprises. Were we scared? Yeah, the video doesn't lie. Would we do it again? Race you to the drop zone!

SWIMMING See *Beaches* for saltwater swimming throughout the region. For freshwater fun, hit **Hernando Beach** off US 41 in Hernando, with sandy shores on Lake Tsala Apopka, and Lake Holathlikaha at Fort Cooper State Park (see *Historic Sites*), or Buccaneer Bay (see *Water Park*).

TRAIL RIDING **Just Horsin' Around** (352-637-2206), on FL 44 west of the Withlacoochee River, offers trail rides on the shady forest roads in Flying Eagle

WMA along the river. **Rymar Ranch** (352-382-4761) in Lecanto leads trail rides into Withlacoochee State Forest's Citrus Tract; by appointment only. And if you just plain enjoy being around horses, sleep above the stables at **Cypress House** (see *Lodging*), where guests can join in on guided trail rides, $25 for a 2-hour trip.

WALKING TOURS *Citrus County's Heritage* introduces visitors to historic sites on walking tours of downtown **Crystal River**, **Inverness**, and **Floral City**; an overview map spotlights additional sites throughout the county. Contact the Citrus County Office of Historical Resources (352-637-9929) for a copy. *Historical New Port Richey* from Greater **New Port Richey** Main Street Inc. (727-842-8066; www.newportricheymainstreet.com) showcases the 1920s boomtown established by Hollywood bigwigs; Gloria Swanson and Alfred Hitchcock maintained seasonal residences here. *Visit Dade City* outlines a walking tour of historic sites from the 1880s through 1926; contact the Greater **Dade City** Chamber of Commerce (352-567-3769; www.dadecitychamber.org) for a copy. **Brooksville** also offers a walking tour of historic homes; pick up a brochure at the chamber of commerce or check the web site www.brooksvillemuralsoc.org.

WATER PARK With water slides and swimming in one of the clearest rivers in Florida, **Buccaneer Bay** at Weeki Wachee Springs (see *Attractions*) is included in summer ticket prices to the park; open from the end of March through Labor Day weekend.

✷ Green Space

BEACHES Fringed with estuaries, the Nature Coast isn't known for its beaches. But at **Fort Island Beach**, west of Crystal River at the end of Fort Island Rd, you can stretch out on the sand and enjoy the sun, or dive into the Gulf for a swim. At **Pine Island Park**, east of Weeki Wachee at the end of CR 550, enjoy Hernando County's only sandy strand, open 8–7 and perfect for sunset-watching, with Willy's Tropical Breeze Café providing munchies; fee. **Hudson Beach**, off US 19 south of Hudson, provides a small sandy shore (limited swimming) on the Gulf at **Robert A. Strickland Memorial Park**, and **Robert K. Rees Park** in Port Richey has 45 acres of shell-fringed beaches. Both parks are off US 19; follow the BEACH signs. If you have a boat, head for **Anclote Key Preserve State Park** (727-469-5942), 1 Causeway Blvd, Dunedin, off Anclote, where paradise awaits along 4 miles of the most secluded beaches on the coast.

BOTANICAL GARDENS **Nature Coast Botanical Gardens** (727-684-2125), 1489 Parker Ave, Spring Hill. This peaceful 3.5-acre retreat has seven themed spaces, including a butterfly garden, herb garden, and waterfall. Open daily; free.

GREENWAYS With its northern terminus at US 98 near Chassahowitzka and its southern terminus at Lutz, the **Suncoast State Trail** (1-800-749-PIKE; www.floridasturnpike.com) is one heck of a long ride. Built in conjunction with the

Suncoast Pkwy, the 42-mile ribbon of pavement parallels this new highway right into suburban northern Tampa. Occasional rest stops have rest rooms; benches are scattered along the route. There's little to no shade, but I still see more bikers on the trail than cars on the highway when I drive to Tampa. The **Withlacoochee State Trail** (352-726-0315), 3100 S Old Floral City Rd, stretches 46 miles between Trilby, north of Dade City, to Dunnellon, ending just before you reach the Marion County line. It's a favorite of long-distance bicyclists, with lodgings in Hernando and Inverness plus several campgrounds along the way.

NATURE CENTERS North of Brooksville off US 41, **Chisengut Nature Center** (352-796-6524; www.auxsvc.usf.edu/chisengut) at Chisengut Hill (see *Historic Sites*) has six interpretive trails radiating out from an educational center operated by the Florida Fish and Wildlife Conservation Commission. Open daily.

PARKS In addition to the parks mentioned under *Beaches*, coastal parks along the Nature Coast include **Fort Island Trail**, a small park along its namesake road, with a boat ramp and fishing pier where you can watch manatees swim past in Crystal River; **Jenkins Creek Park**, Shoal Line Rd in Hernando Beach, with boat ramps, a boardwalk, and an observation tower overlooking fabulous sunsets over the Gulf estuary; and **Key Vista Nature Park**, 2700 Bailey's Bluff Blvd, Holiday, where nature trails provide wildlife-watching opportunities along the Gulf of Mexico.

In Pasco County (727-847-2411, ext 1260), 14 miles of backpacking, biking, and equestrian trails span a vast wilderness between the Pithlachascotee and Anclote Rivers at **Starkey Wilderness Park**, Wilderness Rd, which also has picnic pavilions and a developed campground. Get out into the wilds at **Crews Lake Park**, 16739 Crews Lake Dr, on a mile-long nature trail with special migratory bird and butterfly observation areas. **Withlacoochee River Park**, 12449 River Rd, has camping, hiking, and replicas of an 1800s Florida pioneer settlement and a 1700s Native American village.

Hernando County has **Lake Townsend Regional Park**, providing picnic facilities and trailhead access to the Withlacoochee State Trail in Nobleton at CR 476. In Sumter County, off CR 470, **Marsh Bend County Park** provides anglers a place to cast off an old railroad bridge on the Outlet River.

SPRINGS Thirty springs protected by **Crystal River National Wildlife Refuge** (352-563-2088; www.nccentral.com/fcnwr.htm) in Crystal River serve as critical wintering grounds for nearly 20 percent of the nation's manatee population. Stop by the **Manatee Education Center** on US 19 next to Homosassa Springs Wildlife State Park (see *Zoological Park*) for interpretive information; if you're paddling into the refuge (it's made up of river bottom and a handful of islands), tie off at the pontoon anchored near Banana Island.

WILD PLACES I'll never forget the image of whooping cranes following an ultralight airplane from Nebraska to **Chassahowitzka National Wildlife Refuge** (352-563-2088; www.nccentral.com/fcnwr.htm), one of the wildest places the Nature Coast has to offer. You can't get there on foot: Most of the refuge is the fringe of estuary along the Gulf Coast. Grab a paddle and head out on the water from the **Chassahowitzka River Campground and Recreational Area** (see *Campgrounds*) for bird-watching and spectacular scenery, like the cabbage palm hammock at Seven Cabbage Cut. **St. Martin's Marsh Aquatic Preserve** (352-563-0450) and **Crystal River State Buffer Preserve** also protect a broad swath of the Gulf Coast estuary at Crystal River. The region has several wildlife management areas and water management areas that encompass floodplain forests along the Withlacoochee River, such as **Half Moon**, **Flying Eagle**, and **Lake Panasoffkee**; when it's not hunting season, the forest roads provide a place for exploration of these jungle-like forests. But the largest wild region along the Nature Coast is the **Green Swamp**, the birthplace of the Withlacoochee, Ocklawaha, Hillsborough, and Peace Rivers, accessed via hiking trails and forest roads west of Ridge Manor and Dade City in Pasco County.

The Nature Coast is also home to Florida's most expansive state forest, **Withlacoochee State Forest**, which is broken into a smattering of separate tracts scattered across the region. In addition to being a popular destination for deer hunters each winter, the forest has a little something for everyone. Campers flock to several developed camping areas, including the beautiful **Hog Island** and **River Junction** recreation areas in the **Croom Tract**, and **Holder Mine** and **Mutual Mine** campgrounds in the **Citrus Tract**. Most equestrians head for **Tillis Hill**, a horse camping area in the heart of the trail system in the Citrus Tract. Stop at the **Withlacoochee State Forest Recreation and Visitors Center** (352-754-6896), 15003 Broad St, Brooksville, for maps and information on all of the tracts.

✱ Lodging

BED & BREAKFASTS

Brooksville 34605

Claflin House (352-799-5034), 133 S Brooksville Ave. A classic southern belle, this columned 1908 Greek Revival beauty offers the genteel grace of Old Brooksville. Relax on the formal veranda, play pool in the game room, or wander up the brick street for some antiques shopping. Three rooms, $85–95, each with original fireplace; the roomy Coogler Room, with its pre–Civil War bedroom suite and private bath with clawfoot tub and bidet, especially impressed me. A gift shop in the foyer sells antiques and items pertaining to regional history; owners Keith and Linda Claflin serve up a tasty breakfast. No alcohol permitted on premises.

♿ **Farmer Browns** (352-799-9996; www.bbonline.com/fl/farmerbrowns/index.html), 456 Myers Rd. Relax on a working Florida farm, surrounded by orange groves, pine plantations, and livestock. Hosts Fred and Marcia Brown are living their retirement dream on a 45-acre farm where they serve up their own fresh-squeezed orange juice and farm-fresh sausage and bacon for your breakfast. Common spaces include a screened porch overlooking the pines, a great room with a large-screen television, and acres of land to roam on nature trails that lead down to wetlands and burbling little waterfalls. The three guest rooms ($55–95) include a basement suite (great for families) with its own patio looking out on the pines, and two top-floor rooms with their own private balconies, four-poster high bed, and desk built into each dormer—perfect for writers on the road. It's off the beaten path (call for directions), but if you want to introduce the kids to agriculture or just get away from it all, it's an ideal slice of rural Florida.

Green Gables Inn & Tea Room (352-754-9923; www.bnbfinder.com/bedandbreakfast/level3/16500), 202 E Liberty. Step into Donald and Mamron Warner's home and you won't be able to take your eyes off the woodwork—the dark, rich wainscoting, moldings, cabinets, and doors are the handiwork of the former owner, a cabinetmaker. It's the perfect accent to this Victorian home, making the common areas feel formal yet comfortable. Themed guest rooms ($65–110) include the Friendship Garden, French Country Suite, and African Safari; guests enjoy a full breakfast. Mamron also runs a tearoom, noon–2:30, and holds a unique "travel supper" on the second Sat of each month—bring photos of your favorite travel destination to discuss and share; meals by reservation only.

Bushnell 33513

Cypress House (352-568-0909 or 1-888-568-1666; www.bbonline.com/fl/cypresshouse), 5175 W 90th Blvd. If you love the outdoors, you must visit this very special B&B in the rural rolling hills of Sumter County, where Jan Fessler caters to folks looking for outdoor recreation—whether it be a trail ride with her horses, bicycling on the Withlacoochee State Trail, kayaking down the Withlacoochee River, or hiking the Florida Trail in Withlacoochee State Forest. Set under ancient live oaks, the lodge has five country-themed rooms and suites, $60–110; they'll board your horses (space permitting) for an additional fee.

Chassahowitzka 34448

♿ **Chassahowitzka Hotel** (1-800-807-7783; www.chazhotel.com), 8551 W Miss Maggie Dr. From the outside, you'd never suspect this hotel dated back to 1910—that's how thorough David Strickland's renovations have been. His grandfather ran this as the area's premier resort for anglers, and David reopened it in 2001 to cater to those heading out on the water; a boat ramp and canoe livery are just down the street. It's classy for the outdoor recreation crowd: seven beautifully refinished rooms long on practicality, with multiple beds and common multiple-stall, multiple-shower bathrooms at either end of the upper floor. The ground-floor room is fully wheelchair accessible. A den with an overflowing toy bin will keep the kids busy, and there's a television in the large living room, or you can sit out on the quiet porch and lose yourself in a book. Room rates ($50–75) include a continental breakfast; cooked breakfast or your catch prepared for dinner for an additional charge. Dinner available 3 days a week; call ahead for reservations, and ask about their fishing guide service.

Dade City 33525

Lark Inn (352-521-3289; www.thelarkinn.com), 37438 Meridian Ave. When Bob and Jo Larkin found the grand 1890 Mobley House, they couldn't resist the challenge of restoring it to its original grandeur—three stories of elegant hardwood floors, glassed-in sunporches, and cozy, warm rooms with high ceilings and period furnishings. It's a delightful place within an easy walk of the downtown antiques district; rooms cost $100 and include a full gourmet breakfast.

Floral City 34436
Morning Glory Country Chalet (352-341-0043; www.bbonline.com/fl/morning), 12296 S Turner Ave. Step into the whimsical award-winning gardens and home of Cathy and Gene Foley, who envisioned—and created—a retreat worthy of the Swiss Alps. Cathy's floral art decorates the walls of the guest room ($70–85); the ample bath includes a mini fridge and shower. Breakfast comes in a basket to be savored at the sitting table overlooking the forest. Topping off the fairy moonlight garden, the gazebo above the goldfish pond serves as a site for intimate weddings. Gene is a notary, and can perform your service: Ask for the Honeymoon Special. Don't forget to visit with Mrs. Goodcow, who enjoys being fed by the guests.

Inverness 34450
Inverness Place (352-637-3104; www.invernessplace.com), 811 Zephyr St. Two spacious rooms ($110–125) with roomy private bath open onto a broad porch in one of the "grand old dames" of Inverness; each room is invitingly decorated with antiques and period reproductions. Downstairs, a cozy sunporch awaits readers, or curl up in the warm parlor with a good book. Full breakfasts include such delights as skillet frittatas and French toast.

San Antonio 33576
St. Charles Inn (352-588-4130; stcharlesinnbedandbreakfast.com), 12503 Curley Rd. Built as the St. Charles Hotel in 1913, this charming B&B adjoins an orange grove. You'll want to spend as much time outside as in, tempted by the rocking chairs on the wraparound porch overlooking a garden shaded by an ancient cedar. Choose from two bright, airy rooms (one with twin beds) or a suite, $85–125.

HOTELS AND MOTELS

Homosassa 34448
McRae's of Homosassa (352-628-2602), 5300 S Cherokee Way. Kick back on a rocking chair overlooking the Homosassa River, or wander down to the marina to enjoy live music at the tiki bar. It's your choice at laid-back McRae's, a perfect launch point for boaters headed out to the Gulf, with large, clean, basic rooms. $50–90, kitchenettes available.

THE MORNING GLORY COUNTRY CHALET NEAR FLORAL CITY

Sandra Friend

Hudson Beach 34667

Inn on the Gulf (1-877-840-8321; www.innonthegulf.com), 6330 Clark St. This family-owned motel has one of the best views in Pasco County, overlooking the Gulf of Mexico and several marinas. Eighteen kitchenette suites, $55–85, with older furnishings; caters to smokers, with all rooms permitting smoking, although the Sunset Room (see *Eating Out*) does not.

Inverness 34450

Central Motel (1-800-554-7241; www.centralmotel.com), 721 US 41 S. One of the nicest family motels in the region: Each enormous room sports a desk and a table (phones have dataports) as well as a coffeemaker and small refrigerator; there's a popular pool area and easy access to the Withlacoochee State Trail (pedal right on out of the back of the parking lot!). Reservations recommended, especially on weekends. $42–60.

Crown Hotel (352-344-5555; www.thecrownhotel.com), 109 N Seminole Ave. Step into London in the heart of downtown Inverness: 34 small but charming rooms in an early-1900s landmark, themed with a British flair, complete with replica Crown Jewels in the lobby. A swimming pool and patio are tucked away behind the building, and guests enjoy both a pub and a fine-dining restaurant on site. Rooms range from $45 for a twin bed to $129 for the penthouse suite.

Port Richey 34668

Comfort Inn (1-800-533-1157), 11810 US 19. This Gold Award–winning motel is a pleasant stop in a relentlessly urban stretch of US 19. Sparkling new rooms ($62–83) feature coffeemaker, hair dryer, ironing board, and 25-inch television with 50 cable channels. The lobby's continental breakfast room has a charming garden bistro feel, and the heated outdoor pool looks appealing.

RESORTS

Crystal River 34428

Best Western Crystal River Resort (1-800-435-4409; www.crystalriverresort.com), 614 NW US 19. While the rooms sparkle with the cleanliness you'd expect from a major chain, this is not your typical chain motel. Guests enjoy complimentary cruises around Kings Bay every afternoon from the on-site marina, and have free use of the boat ramp and dock. The swimming pool and hot tub overlook Kings Bay, and are adjoined by Crystal Lodge Dive Center (see *Diving*)—a full-service dive shop that offers instruction, rental equipment, and guided trips—and Cravings on the Water (see *Eating Out*), a comfy waterfront tiki bar and restaurant. Spread out over four buildings, the smartly decorated rooms ($79–106) include a coffeemaker, ironing board, and hair dryer; efficiencies available. Adjoining the lobby, the **Sea Treasures** gift shop includes a broad selection of fishing rods and reels. Small, attended pets permitted.

Plantation Inn Golf Resort (1-800-632-6262; www.plantationinn.com), 9301 W Fort Island Trail. Its roots go back to a 1950s hunting and fishing lodge, expanded upon to meet family needs. Now the Plantation Inn is a major destination; most of the guest rooms are housed in grand structures with a southern plantation feel, overlooking Crystal River. Extras include a marina and dive shop with instruction, manatee tours, and an 18-hole golf course with a guaranteed 'gator in every water hazard. Don't worry, they're friendly—and if you stay in the two-story golf course villas ($99–175, sleeps six, full kitchen, two baths), you'll be tempted to amble the fairways for some prime bird-watching: coots and herons on the water, sandhill cranes on the greens.

Old Homosassa 34448
Homosassa Riverside Resort (1-800-442-2040; www.riversideresorts.com), 5297 S Cherokee Way. It's a place I enjoyed as a kid, watching monkeys play on an island in the Homosassa River; our endangered manatees weren't too common then. Now that the resort is more than 40 years old, it's undergoing another renovation, this time to create condo rentals (each with kitchen, $55–85 standard, $150–210 suites). Enjoy large, clean, pleasant rooms, many overlooking the river—where you now can see a manatee drift past your room. Riverside swimming pool, shops, boat rentals and tours, boat ramp and trailer parking, fishing guides, restaurant, lounge, and tiki bar.

Wesley Chapel 33543
Saddlebrook Resort (1-800-729-8383; www.saddlebrookresort.com), 5700 Saddlebrook Way. What I found at this impeccably groomed resort was six-star service. Yes, *six stars*! From the bellman to the front desk to housekeeping to the gift shop attendant, no matter where I went I was greeted with the best service I have ever received—*anywhere*. The courteous, professional staff are what makes this place so special. Once you check into your spacious suite ($130–352, including breakfast and dinner), take a stroll through the **Walking Village** where you can stop for a bite to eat at the **Terrace on the Green**, listen to live music at the **Polo Lounge**, perfect your backhand at the **Tennis Shop**, relax in the **Spa**, or take a dip in the 500,000-gallon **SuperPool**. Greet each morning with a lavish buffet breakfast in the **Cypress Restaurant**, where you'll find the best Belgian waffles and hearty scrambled eggs with cheese. I loved the granola yogurt and fruit served in a martini glass. And coffee to go is a nice touch. When the day winds down, you'll want to dine at the richly appointed **Dempsey's Steak House** or watch your favorite sporting event on oversized screens at **TD's Sports Bar**. Whatever you do at Saddlebrook, you won't need your car.

CABINS

Homosassa 34448
Nature's Resort (see *Campgrounds*), offers beautiful waterfront A-frame chalets as well as park models that are basic and clean, with full kitchens and room to sleep 4; $90.

Lake Panasoffkee 33538
Tracy's Point Fish Camp (352-793-8060; www.qsy.com/tracyspoint), CR 437, has very pleasant "brand new rustic" cabins, all within a few feet of the lake. Grab your bait and tackle from their shop, rent a boat ($35–85), and hit the water for some serious bass fishing. $44–65; 2-night minimum stay.

In addition to lakeside camping, **Werda-Hecamiat** (see *Campgrounds*) has several units that impressed the heck out of me: a duplex with two spacious rooms, each with full kitchen and all new appliances, perfect for families; and the Banana, a little old fish-camp-style cabin renovated to a T. $85, with a 2-night minimum.

CAMPGROUNDS

Chassahowitzka 34448

Run by Citrus County, the **Chassahowitzka River Campground and Recreational Area** (352-382-2200), 8600 W Miss Maggie Dr, offers both full-hookup ($18) and primitive ($14) campsites surrounded by the jungle-like floodplain forests of the Chassahowitzka River. There's a camp store and canoe livery; daily charge ($1.50–2) for noncampers to park at the boat ramp/put-in.

Crystal River 34428

Lake Rousseau RV Park (352-795-6336; www.lakerousseaurvpark.com), 10811 N Coveview Terrace. Hidden along a quiet cypress-lined cove of Lake Rousseau, prime bass fishing territory, this snowbird retreat gets busy in winter, with more than 100 sites and two sets of boat docks; full hookup, $16–22; no tents.

Quail Roost RV Campground (352-563-0404; www.quailroostcampground.com), 9835 N Citrus Ave. Ten acres of camping with 72 full-hookup sites ($25), sparkling heated swimming pool and recreational hall with fireplace; nice mix of sunny and shady sites.

Homosassa 34448

🐾 ✐ **Camp N' Water RV Resort** (352-628-2000), 11465 W Priest Lane. Follow the signs from Yulee Dr to find this campground tucked away on the Homosassa River, with well-shaded full-hookup sites with picnic tables, $24. Nice riverside swimming pool, dining area, and lounge; dockage and boat ramp available to guests.

🐾 ✐ **Nature's Resort** (1-800-301-7880), 10359 W Halls River Rd. Campsites along the entry road are bounded on both sides by thick forest, and large hardwoods provide a shady canopy overhead. Prefer the waterfront? Full-hookup sites ($28) face the estuary, with easy access for paddlers; tie a motorboat up right in front of your camper. Their on-site marina has a waterfront bar and grill with pool tables, and rents canoes and kayaks as well as pontoon boats. A large clubhouse provides a gathering place for the camping community, with swimming pool and shuffleboard. Bathhouse provided for tent campers ($21); small nondenominational church near the camp store and office.

Turtle Creek Campground (352-628-2928), 10200 W Fish Bowl Dr. Nestled in the river hammock floodplain of the Homosassa River, this expansive campground (part shade, part sun) includes full hookups, heated swimming pool, and air-conditioned recreation hall. RVs, trailers, and tents welcome, $24; convenient to Homosassa Springs Wildlife State Park (see *Zoological Park*), boat ramps, and restaurants.

Hudson 34467

Sunburst RV Park (727-868-3586 or 1-877-287-2757; www.rvonthego.com), 9412 New York Ave. A pleasant park with large, level campsites optimized for RVs ($21.50 and up) with 30- and 50-amp service, partial and full hookups, phone and cable available.

Inverness 34450

Riverside Lodge & RV Resort (1-888-404-8332; www.riversidelodge

rv.com), 12561 E Gulf to Lake Hwy. In a shady hammock on the Withlacoochee River, this pleasant resort offers RV campsites ($20–25) and cabins ($59–69) with easy access to the water for boating and fishing.

Lake Panasoffkee 33538
Werda-Hecamiat RV Park & Marina (1-877-793-8137), 965 CR 439. Sunrises and cool breezes off the best panfish lake in the region: That's what you'll find at this great little "where the heck am I at?" family campground with sunny grassy spots and spontaneous fish fries, a proper camp store, and a covered boat slip.

DIVE RESORTS

Crystal River 34429
Port Hotel & Marina (1-800-443-0875), 1610 SE Paradise Circle. Elvis slept here. Honest! In 1959 he filmed *Follow That Dream* in and around Citrus County, and this was his home away from home. The basic rooms at the Port Hotel show their age; new owners have renovation plans. Meanwhile, it's a great venue for water sports enthusiasts—every room faces the Crystal River Aquatic Preserve, where manatees gather en masse each winter seeking the warmth of the springs. Push your kayak right in from the grassy lawn outside your room, or grab a snorkel and swim out to the ropes to watch these gentle giants feeding. On-site dive shop, boat rentals, boat ramp, swimming pool, waterfront bar, and Ale House restaurant.

FISH CAMPS

Lake Panasoffkee 33538
Idlewild Lodge and RV Park (352-793-7057), 4110 CR 400. Providing great access to the wild spaces of Lake Panasoffkee's northern shore, this fish camp has shady RV spaces with paved pads and full hookups ($19), modest cottages ($62–81), and a pool for the kids to hang out at while the family angler is out chasing bass. Launch fee waived if you're a guest, and all guests have access to a nice boardwalk out on the lake to a fishing platform. Cottages slated for renovation this year.

Pana Vista Lodge (352-793-2061; www.qsy.com/panavista/index.html), 3417 CR 421. One of Florida's oldest fish camps, dating back to the 1880s, Pana Vista attracts folks looking for peace, quiet, and fishing. Situated on the Outlet River between the lake and the Withlacoochee River, it's an ideal place to plunk down your RV or tent under the tall magnolias and cabbage palms before prepping for a day on the water. Looking for more amenities? Try the modest fish-camp-style duplex cottages ($50-plus) with air-conditioning and heating; linens and utensils furnished. Pontoon boat rentals, full-service bait-and-tackle shop, live well, fishing guides available.

✷ Where to Eat

DINING OUT

Brooksville
Victoria's Steak House & Lounge (352-799-8985), 11738 Broad St. An emphasis on hand-cut prime rib, porterhouse, filet mignon, New York strip, and T-bone, accentuated with more than a dozen seafood entrées, forms the meat of this local favorite—and the meat is excellent! Open daily for lunch and dinner, entrées $9–17; sandwiches and salads

$5–8. Adjoining lounge hosts live country music on weekends.

Crystal River
Charlie's Fish House Restaurant (352-795-3949), US 19. Perched on the edge of Kings Bay, Charlie's is an old standard in town, a family-run operation for more than 40 years. You won't be disappointed with any selection from the menu; I'm partial to the local mullet, escalloped oysters, and grouper. Sandwiches start at $2.50; entrées, $8 and up. Stop in their adjoining fish market to nab smoked mullet and mullet dip. Lunch and dinner served; great specials Mon–Fri 11–3.

Dade City
Lunch on Limoges (352-567-5685), 14139 7th St. I've never seen a place with so much southern pizazz—waitresses in sparkling white uniforms bring you tall glasses of iced tea, and the daily menu is on a chalkboard carried from table to table. The tall cakes rival any you'd find in a fine bakery. It's the place to see and be seen at lunchtime, serving sandwiches, salads, and entrées ($9–12) like shrimp salad, pecan grouper, and Tuscan shrimp with pasta. The YaYa sisterhood would find it just divine; I sure did!

Hernando Beach
Bare Bones (352-596-9403), 3192 Shoal Line Blvd. Tom and Karen McEachern preside over this intimate fine-dining experience noted for its classy tableside preparation of fresh seafood and steaks ($9–19), and daily Sunset Dinners (3–5:30), a bargain at $7. Closed Mon and Tue, serving dinner with lunch added on Sun.

Homosassa
Misty River Seafood House (352-628-6288), 4135 S Suncoast Blvd, features fresh seafood in tasteful preparations such as shrimp imperial, lemon-pepper fish, and coconut shrimp (entrées, $9 and up), as well as several selections of steak, pork, and chicken for landlubbers. Watch for stone crab claw specials! Open for lunch ($5–7) and dinner; daily Sunset Specials 3–6 PM, $7–9.

Inverness
Chateau Chan Sezz (352-344-9900), 206 N Apopka Ave. Chef Keith Chances takes French cuisine seriously, offering delights that have won the top "Taste of Citrus" awards for fine dining, presentation, and desserts. Served inside intimate dining spaces within the historic McLeod House, appetizers ($2–6) run the gamut from crabcakes and escargots to baked Brie with apricots. Lunch diners appreciate the quiche of the day ($5) and a variety of hearty salads ($5–7), including Waldorf Salade and Salade Chateau Maison. Dinner entrées (to $12) showcase the chef's specialty sauces and seafood, such as pistachio-crusted salmon fillet with dill crème. Leave room for dessert ($5–6)—the smooth and creamy crème brûlée sports a thin caramelized crust.

Lake Panasoffkee
Harbor Lights Restaurant (352-793-7058), CR 470. Well off the beaten path, this restaurant has a fabulous view of the lake and has been a local fixture since 1982, featuring all-you-care-to-eat buffets with crab legs, sirloin steak, roast beef, baked ham, and more. Open for dinner Thu–Sun; lunch on Sun.

Ozello
Pecks Old Port Cove (352-795-2806), W Ozello Trail (CR 494). At the end of a 9-mile drive leading to the Gulf of Mexico, Pecks's specialty

is crab—garlic, soft-shell, snow, stone, and steamed—and plenty of it, thanks to their crab farm out back. But you'll find all the seafood fresh, not frozen, from the scallops and oysters to the calamari appetizers. Expect monster portions for a reasonable price. Entrées start at $7.93, sandwiches $2.93–9.53, with daily all-you-can-eat specials. Bring cash—no credit cards accepted. Open daily 11–10; reservations suggested.

Port Richey

Catches (727-849-2208), 7811 Bay View Ave. Perched above the Pithlachascotee River, this roomy restaurant with a New England feel features more than a dozen types of seafood, including coconut shrimp ($15) and giant Caribbean lobster tail (market price); lunch and dinner, $12–20.

EATING OUT

Bayonet Point

Soup to Nuts Diner (727-861-1467), US 19 at Division St. You'll find a 1950s diner theme and prices to match: Breakfast (1 egg, home fries or grits, and toast) starts at 89¢! Serves steakburgers and sandwiches ($4–7), too; breakfast until 2 PM. Open daily 6 AM–8 PM.

Brooksville

Amy's Diner (352-848-0661), 4 N Broad St. Breakfast is served all day in this busy country kitchen with a touch of Greece—the menu includes a feta and gyro omelet, and the potato salad comes crowned with a proper kalamata olive. Breakfasts start under $2. Open daily, breakfast and lunch.

Main Street Eatery (352-799-2789), 101 N Main St. The Buzzard Breath Chili tempted, but I settled on Bill's Special, piled high with ham, bacon, and three cheeses, with black beans and yellow rice on the side. Borrowing from several cuisines, this friendly local favorite lunch stop ($3–5) shines. Closed Sun.

Crystal River

Café on the Avenue (352-795-3656), 631 N Citrus Ave. At Heritage Village, an artful presentation of salads, sandwiches, and entrées in a country garden atmosphere. Their signature dish is a Greek salad ($7) piled high with shrimps and anchovies; I was impressed by the fresh mini sweetbreads and smooth mushroom-crab bisque. Lunch favorites $5–8, dinner entrées $12 and up.

Serving up Cuban favorites from Grandma Mimi's special recipes and seafood fare at the Best Western Crystal River (see *Resorts*), **Cravings on the Water** (352-795-2027), a casual open-air dockside restaurant and bar, is a great place to kick back and enjoy a drink while watching the ospreys dive into Kings Bay. Enjoy black beans and rice ($5), picadillo ($7), or any of several other Cuban favorites. Open 7–9, serving breakfast, lunch, and dinner; entertainment on weekends includes live music and Parrothead parties.

Dockside Ice Cream Shoppe (1-800-844-0867), 300 N US 19. In addition to an excellent selection of flavors (cookie dough and coconut are two favorites), the venue is superb: Step outside onto the deck for a sweeping vista of Kings Bay and watch the marina traffic putter by. You might even spy a manatee during the winter months!

Grannie's Country Cookin' (352-795-8884), corner of US 19 and Fort

Island Trail. This place is hopping every time I stop by—park in the strip mall behind it if you can't find a space. Expect the waitresses to call you "sweetheart" and "darlin'" as they dish up southern comfort food at prices that date back to the 1960s: You can grab a full meal for under $5. Breakfast served all day; breakfast, lunch, and dinner specials are posted on the board. The strawberry biscuit (for dessert *or* breakfast) is a real gem. Open 5 AM–9 PM daily.

Dade City

A Matter of Taste Café & Tea Room (352-567-5100), 14121 7th St. A family favorite with huge sandwiches ($5–7) and creative salads (shrimp chef, California cool plate, their famous Pineapple Boat, and more) served in large baskets, $4–7. Open for lunch Mon–Sat, 11–2:30.

Kafe Kokopelli (352-523-0055), 37940 Live Oak Ave. My friends rave about this unique restaurant that melds the best of the Southwest with traditional southern hospitality. Sample the chicken curry ($11), or go for the cedar-planked salmon ($17); daily house specials include homemade spaghetti and meatballs and pot roast. Serving lunch and dinner, with entrées $7–17.

Floral City

Shamrock Inn (352-726-6414), 8343 E Florida Ave. "Good friends, good food, good times" is their motto, and as you step through the doorway painted with a giant leprechaun into this Irish-themed bar and grill, you'll feel at home. In addition to great American standbys like burgers, salads, and the best wings in the area, you'll find some offbeat items like Wiener schnitzel ($8) and spinach dip with chips ($5). Breakfast served 6–11, $1–6 or $3 for AYCE specials; lunch items ($3–6) and dinner plates ($6–16) until closing.

Hernando

Frank's Family Restaurant (352-344-2911), Hernando Plaza, US 41 at FL 200. Think real blueberry pancakes, waffles with fruit, and omelets all the way. Frank's has on-the-ball service, good food, and bargain prices, attracting a steady local clientele. Breakfast $1–6, lunch $2–6, dinner entrées $5–9.

Right along the Withlacoochee State Trail, **Sabina's Hernando Diner** (352-637-1308), 2400 N Florida Ave, is a classic old-fashioned diner with red cushioned seats, a great place to stop for an ice cream cone or a banana split when you're out on a long bike ride. Open for breakfast, lunch, and dinner ($2–8); breakfast served all day.

Homosassa

Dan's Clam Stand (352-628-9588), 7364 Grover Cleveland Blvd. It's small and off the beaten path, but for those who love freshly fried fish, Dan's serves up heaping helpings ($4.95 and up). The top attraction: whole belly clams ($12.95), with much more clam meat than clam strips. Open for lunch and dinner; no credit cards. A second, roomier location is in Crystal River on FL 44 E.

Old Homosassa

Charlie Brown's Crab House (352-621-5080), 5267 S Cherokee Way. My dad stops at Charlie Brown's for calamari; I like the fresh Gulf shrimp and locally caught blue crabs ($11 and up). Tempting seafood salads, seafood pasta, and po'boys; if you love seafood (entrées $8 and up), it's a great venue to chow down while watching for manatees out in the Homosassa River. Steak lovers choose from prime rib, New York strip, Delmonico, and top sirloin ($12–16). Located on the grounds of Homosassa Riverside Resort (see *Resorts*).

Dunbar's Old Mill Tavern & Eatery (352-628-2669), 10465 W Yulee Dr. For Florida fare with a Greek flair, stop in at the Old Mill Tavern, adjacent to the Yulee Sugar Mill (see *Historic Sites*). Don't let the rough exterior fool you—the food is great. Try the Country Green Salad ($6–9), authentic with its lack of lettuce and reliance on tomatoes and cucumbers, or snag a gyro sandwich ($4–6). Seafood also dominates the menu. Open for lunch ($2–9) and dinner ($6–13); karaoke Fri and Sat.

Museum Café (352-628-1081), 10466 W Yulee Dr. Adjacent to the Yulee Sugar Mill (see *Historic Sites*), the Museum Café serves up authentic Ybor City Cuban sandwiches piled with salami, ham, spiced pork, and Swiss cheese ($6). Stop in to see the restored 1924 Model T in the middle of the dining room, and peek into the Olde Mill House Gallery and Printing Museum (see *Museums*), which shares the building.

Old Homosassa Smokehouse (352-628-6663), W Yulee Dr. There's hardly enough room inside to swing a mullet, but the aroma will draw you right in. Grab some ribs or a smoked meat sandwich ($4 and up) with sides and retreat to the picnic table outside for a feast, or choose the house specialty—smoked mullet (and smoked mullet dip, yum), $4–6 depending on size of fish.

Hudson

Sunset Room at Inn on the Gulf (see *Hotels and Motels*). Never mind the killer sunset view: I've found the ultimate chocolate cake at this seaside local favorite. It's called Double Chocolate Ecstasy, and it looks like a million heavy calories but melts on your tongue like the foam atop an ice cream soda. Seafood is the standard here, with a side of Hellas: *Saganaki*, calamari, and traditional Greek village salad show up on the menu. Sandwiches $6–8, entrées $8–27.

Inverness

Al's Italian Restaurant (352-726-9094), 804 US 41 S. Since 1977, Al's has served up pizzas and pasta made the old-fashioned way, from scratch, in a bright open dining environment. Order up a sub ($3–6) or slice of pizza ($2.50), or delve into their broad range of entrées ($4–12), which go beyond the traditional Italian favorites to encompass chicken cordon bleu, stuffed flounder, liver and onions, and other selections. Vegetarians will appreciate the special meatless entrées section with choices like broccoli and cheese manicotti and spinach-stuffed shells. Open for lunch and dinner; closed Tue.

Cinnamon Sticks Restaurant and Bakery (352-726-7333), 2120 W FL 44. Boasting the "Best Breakfast in Citrus County," served all day, this local family-run favorite is always humming. In addition to traditional favorites and omelets, you can order several types of crêpes or a fruit blintz, as well as skillet breakfasts piled high atop seasoned home fries ($3–9); you won't go away hungry! Dinners include down-home favorites like meat loaf, southern-fried country steak, and Thanksgiving dinner with all the trimmings ($6–11).

🏵 **Cockadoodles Café** (352-637-0335), 206 W Tompkins St. From cheese blintzes with strawberries to an 8-ounce rib eye with eggs, this downtown café (open 7–2) serves one heck of a breakfast ($1–6). Lunch includes house-special platters like meat loaf, open-faced roast beef sandwiches, and chicken livers ($2–5). Great food, great service!

🏵 **Fisherman's Restaurant** (352-637-5888), 12311 E Gulf to Lake Hwy. Don't drive too fast: You might miss this tiny cottage along FL 44 near the Withlacoochee River. But stop for a taste of chef Bob Root's seafood, and he'll reel you in for good. Their massive fried shrimp are lightly breaded with a delicate hint of pepper, and their lime pie is one of the best I've had. Choose from a nice range of fresh seafood entrées, including grouper, scallops, and oysters, or from several prime cuts of steak. Serving lunch and dinner: seafood $6–27, platters $22–30, steaks $11–24; closed Mon.

Happy Dayz Diner (352-860-1957), 727 US 41 S. Adjacent to the Central Motel (see *Hotels and Motels*), it's a fun stop harking back to the days when Elvis roamed US 41 making movies. Daily specials, $6 or two for $10, include home-cooked favorites like stuffed green peppers, meat loaf, and pot roast. Live 1950s entertainment Thu–Sat 6–9; gift shop with nostalgic items.

Kimberly's (352-344-4222), 840 US 41 S. A diner with an emphasis on the most important part of the meal: Two pages of desserts dominate the menu, with specialty sundaes like the Dusty Road, Hawaii 5-0, and Mounds Delight competing with ice cream sodas, malts, and floats ($1–4). Of course, you can opt for a real meal, too ($4–7): Try the catfish sandwich or smothered chicken. Open 7 AM–10 PM daily.

🏵 **Stumpknockers on the Square** (352-726-2212), 110 W Main St. Like its sister restaurant in Marion County, Stumpknockers delivers excellent seafood dinners ($9–15) and the best freshly fried mushrooms in Florida (monster portion served with dipping sauce, $5). Housed in a historic building, the downtown location makes it a great lunch stop when you're browsing the shops. Open for lunch and dinner; closed Mon.

Istachatta

The **Istachatta Country Store** (352-544-1017), 28198 Magnon Dr, along the Withlacoochee State Trail, offers simple country breakfast and lunch items 7–2 daily. On Wed the community gets together for pasta night, 5–6:30, and there's a fish fry 4–7 on Fri evening.

Lake Panasoffkee

Catfish Johnny's (352-793-2083), CR 470, looks like a BBQ place but, hey, this is Lake Panasoffkee—fish dominates the menu, in baskets, grilled, and fried. Lunch served 10:30–4, $3–7; dinner specials include home-cooked entrées like country-fried steak and catfish, or choose a seafood platter for two, $8–20. Homemade desserts like coconut cake and peanut butter pie will tempt, $2 a slice. All-you-can-eat catfish served Fri.

New Port Richey

Garden Gate Café (727-844-5400), 5546 Main St. Faux grape arbors set a garden atmosphere in this riverside café that serves not just a classy tea party ($13 per person) but also a full range of salads, soups, and sandwiches ($3–9). Leave room for the stellar desserts ($4): Black Forest crêpes filled with brandy-soaked cherries and Toasted Snowball with ice cream rolled in toasted coconut are just two of the tempting possibilities. Open Mon–Sat 11–3.

Spring Hill

Pit Boss BBQ (352-688-BOSS; www.pit-boss.com), 2270 US 19. In a gambling mood? This Vegas-themed open-pit barbecue smells delicious, and the food is as good as the aromas off the fireplace—I was impressed by the freshly made burger on a toasted bun with thick-cut fries on the side. Ribs are their specialty, and you'll be tempted by banana split cake for dessert. Serving lunch and dinner, $4–12.

✷ Entertainment

Weekends bring live music to many area restaurants, including **Casey's Pub** and the **Happy Daze Diner** (see *Where to Eat*) in Inverness, and **Sam's Hudson Beach Bar** (look for the miniature village on the roof!) on the Gulf. For large live concerts, check the schedule at **Rock Crusher Canyon** (352-795-1313; www.rockcrushercanyon.com), housed in a former quarry west of Inverness.

Show Palace Dinner Theatre (727-863-7949), US 19, Hudson, features Screen Actors Guild players in fabulous comedies and musicals like *Guys and Dolls* and *Mame*; I was impressed by the roomy stage setup, and the food certainly satisfied. Reservations required.

Whether you are looking for Las Vegas song stylings, light comedy and magic, or a full all-out Broadway musical or American play such as *Nunsense* or *Steel Magnolias*, **Angel's Cabaret** (727-847-0019; www.angelcabaret.net), 5201 US 19, Southgate Shopping Center, New Port Richey, is sure to have your entertainment pleasure. Don't miss this professionally produced venue directed by Broadway alumni Jimmy Ferraro and his talented wife, Dee Etta Rowe. Since 1977, Jimmy has consistently presented fabulous productions to the West Pasco area and has no plans to stop anytime soon. Before the show a buffet dinner is served in the intimate 150-seat theater. There's something for everyone at the lavish buffet, laid out with such offerings as Swedish meatballs, Greek salad, beef stroganoff, stuffed shells, chicken marsala, and baked scrod. A chocolate éclair tops the meal. $34 adults, $20 children 5–12 for dinner and show; $22 for show only.

✷ Selective Shopping

Brooksville

Antique Sampler Mall (352-797-9330), 31 Main St. Victorian furniture, glassware and china displayed on vintage dining room tables, and a lot of jewelry—offers free antique jewelry appraisals second Sat monthly. Closed Sun.

The Broken Mold (352-796-6979), 100 Brooksville Ave, has themed rooms of home decor items—nautical, Native American, Far East, and more.

The Purple Cow (352-796-5530), 5 Main St. Purple doors usher you into this room full of country chic antiques, with an emphasis on glassware. From a cast-iron Yorkie to a plaster mermaid, you'll find funky home decor here!

Rogers' Christmas House & Village (1-877-312-5046; www.rogerschristmashouse.com), 103 S Saxton Ave. Step into Christmas any time of year in this beautiful complex of homes in downtown Brooksville, with its Storybook Land cast of characters, Christmas villages, and pretty gardens under the oaks. Daily 9:30–5.

Bushnell

Jacobik Antique Gallery (352-793-2466), 224 S Main. Collector dishes, paintings, glassware, and furnishings tastefully displayed in a roomy gallery; Mon–Sat 10:30–5, or by appointment.

Chassahowitzka

Naber's Doll World (352-382-1001; www.naberkids.com), 8915 S Suncoast Blvd. In a building reminiscent of the Black Forest, German-born Harald Naber displays more than three decades of craftsmanship with his collection of hand-carved wooden collectible dolls. Popular with doll collectors around the world, new limited-edition one-of-a-kind creations ($200–250, with summer clearance specials as low as $99) are also produced here; the fine wood grain shows beneath each realistically painted face. A former bush pilot, Naber started his carving in Alaska, and returns to those roots with at least one Eskimo doll series annually. An on-site doll hospital can restore your aging antiques to their original glory, and if you've ever wanted a miniature of your grandkids, a local porcelain doll artist affiliated with Naber creates lifelike portrait dolls ($289).

Howards Flea Market (1-800-832-3477 or 352-628-3532; www.howardsfleamarket.com), 6373 S Suncoast Blvd. Featuring Mr. Ed's Books and a bunch of other weekend vendors, this roadside flea market on US 19 attracts a lot of browsers. Open Fri 7–2, Sat–Sun 7–3.

Coleman

Bobby's Antique Village (352-330-2220), US 301, a collection of late-1800s and early-1900s buildings, has plenty to delight antiques aficionados, from the classic exteriors to the bottles, tools, and ephemera packed inside.

Crystal River

Crystal River Antiques (352-563-1121), 756 NE US 19. Glassware and dishes pack the windows of this antiques shop along busy US 19.

Dockside Trading Company (1-800-844-0867), 300 N US 19. A shop featuring nautically themed gifts and souvenirs: seashells, carvings of manatees, T-shirts with Guy Harvey's excellent artwork, and a nice selection of children's books.

Heritage Village, 631 N Citrus Ave. A collection of shops that meet a variety of interests, from clothing to home decor, in a village of historic buildings along Citrus Ave; free parking. My favorite is the playful **Manatee Toy Company** (352-795-6126; www.manateestore.com), which features a little bit of everything fun about maritime Florida, from books and stuffed animals to T-shirts and Jimmy Buffett music. A new bookstore, **Poe Books**, has opened in the complex, but I haven't been able to catch them in—yet.

Lil's Candy Shop & Antique Annex (352-563-1993), 425 N Citrus Ave. Who can pass up a fresh chunk of cashew bark, or an exquisite truffle? Come for the handmade chocolates, and poke around the antiques in the back.

Magical Senses (352-795-9994), 560 N Citrus Ave. In addition to incense, cleansing candles, and aromatherapy, this decidedly offbeat shop features a full wall of packaged herbs for potion making, and books with a Wiccan theme. Closed Sun and Mon.

Otter Creek Trading Company (352-564-0001; www.ottercreek tradingco.com), 406 NE 1st St. Hidden away on a back street across from the post office, Jim Smith's delightful shop features one-of-a-kind foreign imports ranging from African masks, Chinese vases, and Indian hand-beaten copper to giant sculptures and stuffed animals. No matter who you're shopping for, you will find a unique gift here.

The Shoppe for Something Else (352-795-2015), 650 N Citrus Ave. Stroll through an exotic wonderland of home decor with a touch of Africa and the Far East, just across from Heritage Village.

Dade City

Downtown Dade City boasts an extraordinary antiques district, with more than 20 thriving shops catering to a full range of tastes. It's a shopper's getaway for the Tampa crowd, and I guarantee you'll be hooked the first time you visit. Park once, walk everywhere. Here's a sample of what caught my eye; most shops are open Mon–Sat.

At **Annetta's Antiques** (352-567-5809), 14136 8th St, I stumbled across a kewpie doll and a rhino made from elephant skin, and noticed the Currier & Ives prints on the walls. There's a little bit of everything collectible here, with more in their walk-up attic.

Classic toys like a Flash Gordon propeller pop up in **Antiques on the Main Street** (352-523-0999), 14122 7th St, where you'll also find folk art, country primitives, and classic books.

I walked out of **Bea's Antiques and Sweets** (352-523-0019), 37912 Church Ave, with a huge stack of books; other gals in line were more concerned with the homemade chocolates. It's a warren of dealer booths with everything from handicrafts and primitives to collectible books and Pez dispensers.

The Book Shack (352-567-5001), 14407 7th St, carries a nice stock of used titles.

Church Street Antiques (352-523-2422), 14117 8th St, has a great selection of vintage jewelry, tea sets and fine china, and a bargain room in the back.

The Corner Emporium (352-567-8966), 37838 Pasco Ave, isn't really on the corner, but it's full of Far Eastern home decor, Fenton glass, and gourmet goodies, with a bargain attic upstairs.

Distinctive crystalline copper-toned pottery fills the window at **Glades Pottery and Gallery** (352-523-0992), 14145 7th St, where they showcase art from more than 20 American artists.

The Olive Branch (352-458-9243), 14123 7th St, has pillows and purses emblazoned with retro-Florida postcard motifs; they deal mainly in collectibles and home decor.

Ivy Cottage (352-523-0019), 14110 7th St, boasts an entire wall of Little Golden Books as well as architectural and farmstead antiques, beads, and Civil War ephemera.

South of downtown, **Ms. Charlotte's Antiques** (352-567-6717), 11124 US

98, is a multidealer antiques mall with primitives, furniture, glassware, vintage clothing, and more. Open Thu–Sat.

Floral City

Cabin Clutter Country Decor (352-344-4711), 7785 S Florida Ave. In a historic three-story building, this eclectic collection of mostly country-themed and primitive antiques and crafts is a delight to explore; you'll find something new around every corner. More than a dozen dealers are spread out through roomy booths, and the prices are fantastic.

Suzanne's Antiques and Collectibles Corner (352-344-4711), 8294 E Orange Ave. Although there's a heavy emphasis on antique glassware and small curio items, you'll also find shelves of books to browse, vintage clothing and furnishings, and accoutrements worthy of the Red Hat Ladies.

Sweeter Charity (352-341-0137), 8305 E Orange Ave. The antique pottery in the window caught my eye; inside, I found imported clothing, wall hangings, and beautifully decorated boxes from India, as well as a large selection of antique pottery—a truly unique find—displayed in glass cases.

Hernando

The Art of Fishin' (352-637-3316), 2780 N Florida Ave, Hernando Plaza, US 41 at FL 200. In addition to a nice selection of fishing tackle, this little shop showcases colorful hand-tied flies.

Awesome Books and Gifts (352-637-1182), 2780 N Florida Ave, Hernando Plaza, deals mostly in paperback trades, but I found some nice travel narratives on the shelves. Open Tue–Sat.

Denny-Lynn's Fudge Factory (352-637-3438), 2780 N Florida Ave, Hernando Plaza. Stuffed with shelves floor to ceiling, overflowing with several hundred selections of goodies, this family-run store aims to please with plenty of homemade creations, including their signature old-fashioned seafoam candy. Try freshly dipped fruits, fresh fudge, sugar-free candies, a rainbow of Jelly Belly flavors, and an amazing array of chocolates; you scoop from penny candy jars.

Hernando Beach

Wolding Fine Art Gallery & Gifts (352-597-9422; www.woldingstudios.com), 3410 Shoal Line Rd. A little bit nautical, a little bit jungle: the bold, bright colors of acrylics, stained glass, and metal art will draw you right into this vibrant display of more than a dozen local artists, where sea turtles, lizards, and manatees cavort on the walls.

Homosassa

Howards Flea Market (352-628-3437), along US 19, south of Homosassa Springs, open weekends, has 50 acres of vendor space with a garage sale atmosphere: You will find bargains here!

Mason Bleu Uni-ques (352-682-6676), 8445 W Homosassa Trail. The stagecoach outside this bright blue house will catch your attention; inside, shelves filled with antiques and collectibles.

River Safaris Gallery (1-800-758-FISH; www.riversafaris.com), 10823 Yulee Dr. Although the store serves as a storefront for their brisk ecotour business (see *Ecotours*), it also displays fine arts: The owner is a potter; her husband, a sculptor. From pottery and glasswork to copper sculpture, their art (and that of many other local artists showcased in the gallery) explores natural maritime themes.

Inverness

Book Worm (352-726-9141), 105 Dampier St. I'd never realized the connection between book cover design and genre until I saw the walls of paperbacks filling this popular used-book store. The romance section gleamed in pastels; the suspense and horror section looked foreboding in shades of red and black. Closed Sun; closed Mon in summer.

The Exchange (352-726-4550), 101 N Seminole Ave. Tucked away in the south wing of the Crown Hotel, this small antiques store features furniture at reasonable prices, glassware, dishes, books, and general ephemera. Coin collectors will appreciate the small coin shop within the store.

Maine-ly Antiques (352-637-3133), 1259 S Elmwood Dr. Their sign will surely catch your eye: a Victorian lady astride a giant lobster! "Recycled history" is the name of the game here, where spacious dealer booths gleam with goodies; a heavy emphasis on items from 1900 to 1940, from Coca-Cola tins and jewelry to an unexpectedly large stock of 1940s hardcover novels. Jewelry repair shop on site.

Rainy Day Editions (352-637-3440), 202 Tompkins St. A tall bookcase filled with new books on Florida greets you when you enter this mostly used-book store with an excellent selection of hardcover and paperback by genre; dig through, and you'll find some real treasures.

Ritzy Rags & Glitzy Jewels, Etc. (352-637-6333), 105 Courthouse Square. The sign says it's the ROLLS ROYCE OF CONSIGNMENT SHOPS, and the owners tell me they're the "theme park of Inverness . . . people stop here *before* they visit with relatives!" The 1940s music, funky flamingos, and a giant high-heeled chair say it all: classy yet eclectic. In addition to a fine selection of vintage clothing and jewelry, you'll find unusual home decor items and playful paintings from local artists.

San Gabriel Pottery, Plants, and Gifts (352-341-1444), 310 W Main St. In addition to the Mexican pottery, porch swings, and plants displayed outside, this cozy shop contains southwestern art. Open daily 10–5.

Sandy Bottom Bayou (352-341-2171), 101 W Main St. Delightfully different, this store melds antiques with art, featuring antique furniture hand painted by local artists, as well as offering a nice selection of children's books.

Vanishing Breeds (352-726-6614), 105 W Main St. Featuring a nice selection of beautiful wildlife art, from classy copper sculptures to limited-edition carvings of birds, as well as conservation-minded gift items, cards, puzzles, games, T-shirts, and wildlife books.

New Port Richey

Looking for a gift? **Karen's Gifts** (727-841-0207), 6232 Grand Blvd, has choices large and small, from a mountain of stuffed bears to Christmas ornaments and Heritage Lace.

Odessa

Step into the **Palmetto Patch** (813-926-9954) at **J. B. Starkey's Flatwood Adventure** (see *Ecotours*) for such gifts as handcrafted apple or pine needle baskets; learn how to weave your own in just few hours with

Marsha Starkey. Don't forget to ask about a "boondoggle" to protect your home from lightning. Classes are once a month on Sat morning, $30.

Webster
Webster Flea Market/Sumter County Farmer's Market (352-793-2021; www.sumtercountyfarmers market.com), 516 NW 3rd St, off CR 478; use I-75 exit 309. No other flea market in Florida tops this bonanza of 4,000 vendors spread out over 40 acres. In peak season it's a madhouse, with more than 10,000 people buzzing around. But the bargains at Webster are legendary: Pick up cheap produce, pore over antiques, buy a classic car, beat the prices on Asian imports, and catch some excellent crafts. From poodles to Porsches, you'll find it at Webster—and don't be shy about haggling over prices. Open Mon only, 6–3; closed on Christmas.

Wildwood
Bobbie's Collectibles, 103 S Main St. A small shop stuffed with collectible glassware, knickknacks, comic books, and other collectible ephemera; reasonable prices.

Russell Stover Factory Outlet (352-748-6282), 950 Industrial Dr, off FL 44 just east of I-75. It's every kid's dream come true—step into a grocery store, and the shelves are lined with nothing but gobs of candy. At the "world's largest candy outlet," you'll find a fabulous selection of cut-rate candy (seconds, seasonal, and slightly discounted standards), from traditional fancy chocolates to jelly beans, licorice sticks, and jellies.

Wildwood Antique Mall and Auction House (352-748-0788), 101 S Main St. Open at 12:30 PM for browsing the second and fourth Sun of each month, it's an auction house with a wide range of estate items: Auctions start promptly at 1:30 PM.

CITRUS STANDS, FARMER'S MARKETS, FRESH SEAFOOD, AND U-PICK

Bushnell
Halls Produce and Seafood (352-568-2498), corner of CR 476 and US 301, has fresh fruit *and* seafood, by the bushel or pound. Don't miss their smoked mullet!

Crystal River
Charlie's (see *Eating Out*) has an adjoining fresh seafood outlet with smoked mullet dip, and **Real Crystal Seafood** (352-795-3311), Citrus Ave, offers huge Gulf shrimp, mullet, and grouper.

Dade City
Browse an array of the freshest local produce, jams, and baked goods at the **Dade City Farmer's Market** (352-521-0766) on the second Sat of each month, Oct–Apr, in downtown around the courthouse.

Floral City
Both **Sparracino's Produce** (352-637-2001) and **Ferris Groves** (352-860-0366) on US 41 north of town offer just-picked citrus and other regional fruits.

Hernando
The **Farmer's Market** (352-637-5323), US 41 S, sells "quality produce at reasonable prices," with shipping available.

Homosassa
Stormans Produce (352-628-3766), 3862 S Suncoast Blvd, proffers the freshest stuff under the tarps of their permanent stand on US 19; stop at the **Old Homosassa Smokehouse**

(see *Eating Out*) for succulent smoked fish.

Inverness
Buzbee's Farm Fresh Produce (352-726-3867), 850 N US 41. Check out their nursery items, herbs, and plentiful local produce at reasonable prices.

Land O'Lakes
Fresh Market at Florida Estates Winery (see *Wineries*), held the second and fourth Sat, Dec–Feb. Enjoy live music while browsing vendor booths with fresh fruit, baked goods, crafts, and spices; don't miss the wine tasting!

Oxford
Brown's Country Fresh Produce, corner of CR 102 and US 301, is a popular local stop for farm-fresh produce—peppers, potatoes, tomatoes, beans, and other crops in-season—right on the county line. **Jennings Citrus Packers** (1-800-344-2531), on US 301, wholesales but is open to the public (in-season) for sales of Indian River citrus fruit and juice; will ship.

Webster
The **Sumter County Farmer's Market** (see *Selective Shopping*) brings in the crowds every Mon morning; shop early for the freshest produce and baked goods.

✷ Special Events

January: **Florida Manatee Festival**, Crystal River. Attracting manatee enthusiasts from around the country, this massive first-weekend event celebrates the Nature Coast's signature mammal with manatee-sighting trips, arts and crafts vendors, and fun activities for the entire family.

Dade's Battle Re-enactment, first weekend at Dade Battlefield Historic State Park (see *Historic Sites*). Massive Seminole War reenactment held at 2 PM each day, encampments and trade fair all weekend. Fee.

Brooksville Raid (352-799-0129, www.brooksvilleraid.com), Hernando County, third weekend. Relive the Civil War during one of the top reenactments in the state, including a full encampment, sutlers, Blue/Gray Ball, and a re-creation of the Brooksville Raid.

Annual Quilt and Antique Shoe and Sale, which is held in conjunction with the **Dade City Kumquat Festival** (352-567-3769; www.dadecitychamber.org) on the Pioneer Florida Museum grounds, last Sat. Taste dishes made from this small, tangy citrus fruit and experience the beauty of small-town life when you watch the kids vie for Kumquat Princess and Best Kumquat Costume; adults can participate in the recipe contest and 5/10K runs.

February: **Annual Heritage Day Festival**, May-Stringer House, Brooksville. Living history demonstrations of weaving and crafts, Native American dance, and country music.

Pasco County Fair, FL 52, third week. Approaching its 60th year, this traditional county fair celebrates local produce, livestock, arts and crafts, and is the proud host of the Heart of Florida Folk Festival.

March: **Fort Cooper Days**, Inverness. Reenactment of Second Seminole War battle between the Seminoles and the ambushed federal troops who hastily constructed Fort Cooper for protection; a weekend's worth of living history demonstrations.

Strawberry Festival, Floral City. Held at Floral Park along US 41, this popular festival celebrates the incoming strawberry crop with fun activities and the State Fiddling Championship.

Swamp Fest, Weeki Wachee, first weekend. Entertainment, swamp foods, and an excellent display of local arts.

The **Will McClean Music Festival** (352-465-7208; www.willmclean.com), mid-Mar, Sertoma Youth Ranch, Brooksville, provides a weekend's worth of the finest Florida folk music along with poetry, storytelling, and workshops on songwriting, guitar, banjo, and dulcimer. Bring your lawn chairs! Weekend tickets $20 in advance, $25 at the gate; children under 12 free.

April: **Hernando County Fair**, fairgrounds. A weeklong traditional county fair with rides, games, food, informative displays, musical entertainment, and the judging of local crafts and livestock.

Jump into the **Spring Magnolia Festival and Garden Show** on the grounds at Pioneer Florida Museum (352-567-0262), where you will find many vendors of various subjects connected to gardening and landscaping.

May: **Cotee River Seafood Festival and Boat Show**, New Port Richey. At Sims Park in the historic district, this festival features fresh Gulf seafood and regional artists.

September: Travel back through time at the annual Labor Day weekend **Pioneer Days Festival** at Pioneer Florida Museum, where you can experience Civil War battle reenactments and see craft demonstrations, pioneer exhibits, antique cars, even pony rides for the kids. Adults $6, children $2; free parking.

October: **Rattlesnake Festival** (www.rattlesnakefestival.com), San Antonio, third Sat. Dating back to 1967, this scary-sounding festival celebrates Florida's reptiles with snake shows, gopher races, reptile demonstrations, and more. There's barbecue and games to boot . . . and no, they don't round up rattlesnakes anymore.

November: **Old Homosassa Arts & Crafts Seafood Festival**, second weekend. Now three decades old, this extravaganza of art and food brings in fine artists from around the country to share the limelight with some of the Nature Coast's top wildlife artists.

MARION COUNTY

Lakes, forests, and farms define the landscape of Marion County, the center of Florida's thoroughbred industry, with more than 600 horse farms scattered across the county. Established in 1827, Fort King served as a trading post and outpost for the U.S. Army. Several months after General Wiley Thompson, the U.S. Army agent responsible for removing the Seminoles from Florida, embarrassed Chief Osceola by placing him in leg irons at the fort for "insolent remarks," Osceola shot and killed Thompson and another man walking past Fort King. Along with an attack on Major Francis Dade's troops along the military trail between Fort Brooke and Fort King, these incidents sparked the lengthy Second Seminole War.

Incorporated in 1844, the county saw a steady stream of settlers in response to the Armed Occupation Act. Dubbed Brick City when it was rebuilt in brick after a devastating fire, **Ocala** is a modest-sized city, established in 1846, radiating from a quaint downtown. Nearby **Silver Springs**, home of the world's largest freshwater spring, has attracted tourists since the late 1800s; today's tourists enjoy glass-bottomed boat rides along the crystalline stream, where schools of fish whirl around the many spring vents. At the south end of the county, **Ocklawaha** and **Weirsdale** sit on the edge of scenic Lake Weir; Ocklawaha lives in infamy as the home of Ma Barker and her gang. Historic **Belleview**, founded in 1884, is the county's second largest city, with quite a few excellent restaurants. In **Dunnellon**, settlers arrived in droves in the 1890s in Florida's equivalent of the gold rush—the boom sparked by the first discovery of phosphate in Florida by Alburtus Vogt in 1889.

Heading north from Ocala on US 301 or US 441, you'll encounter small-town life in villages like **Citra**, **Orange Lake**, **Irvine**, and **Reddick**. Victorian **McIntosh** turns on the charm with narrow paved streets shaded by grand old moss-draped oaks. Home of the annual 1890s Festival, this former railroad and citrus packing town is a peaceful place to explore.

GUIDANCE **Ocala/Marion County Chamber of Commerce** (352-629-8051; www.ocalacc.com), 110 E Silver Springs Blvd, Ocala 34470, is downtown on the square, open 10–4 daily. Stop in to pick up maps and brochures and to see their regular fine-art displays.

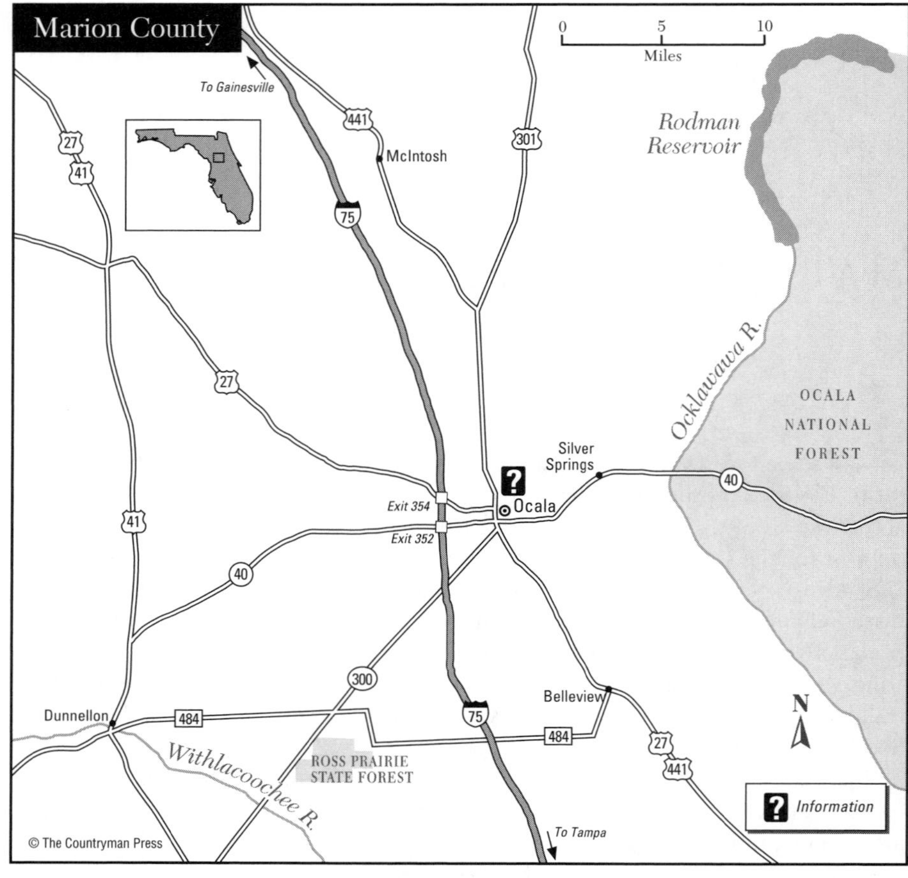

GETTING THERE *By air*: Ocala is 1½ hours north of Orlando International Airport via **Florida's Turnpike** and **I-75**, and 40 minutes south of Gainesville Regional Airport.

By bus: **Greyhound** (1-800-229-9424) stops in Ocala.

By car: Six exits off **I-75** provide access to Marion County's communities. **US 27**, **301**, and **441** all meet in the middle of Ocala, passing north–south through the county; **FL 40** ties together the east–west corridor.

By train: **Amtrak** (1-800-USA-RAIL) stops in Ocala.

PARKING All of Marion County's communities have free street parking. In downtown Ocala there are time limitations (normally 2 hours) on many of the spaces.

MEDICAL EMERGENCIES Several Ocala-area hospitals serve Marion County and its surrounding rural neighbors: **Munroe Regional Medical Center** (352-351-

7200), 131 SW 15th St; **Ocala Regional Medical Center** (352-401-1000; www.ocalaregional.com), 1431 SW 1st Ave; and **West Marion Community Hospital** (352-291-3000; www.westmarion.com), 4600 SW 46th Court.

✷ To See

ART GALLERIES

Belleview

All About Art (352-307-9774), 5162 US 441. Tucked behind B. D. Bean's Coffee Co. (see *Eating Out*), this cooperative represents local artists in media ranging from oils and acrylics to photography, textiles, and pottery, offering an excellent selection of fine arts as well as regular art classes. Open Tue–Sat 11–5. Free.

Ocala

Appleton Museum of Art (352-236-7100; www.appletonmuseum.org), 4333 E Silver Springs Blvd. Based on a foundation of industrialist Arthur I. Appleton's large personal collection of Oriental art, the Appleton Museum is a work of art itself in Italian marble. One gallery features European masterworks from the 1800s, including the *The Knitter* by William Adolphe Bouguereau and *Daphis and Chloe* by his wife, Elizabeth Jane Gardener, both circa 1888. The Victor DuBois Collection of West African Art, with its many intriguing masks and figurines, adjoins a pre-Columbian exhibit of bowls, pendants, vessels, and other artifacts. Upstairs, galleries feature changing exhibits of national significance. At 1 PM weekdays, enjoy a docent-led tour of the galleries. Admission $6, free for students.

Brick City Center for the Arts (352-840-9521), 23 SW Broadway. Exhibit space for local artists affiliated with Central Florida Community College; features regular juried shows, special events, and art classes, as well as a small gift shop. Open Tue–Fri 10–4, Sat 11–2. Free.

Florida Thoroughbred Breeders' and Owners' Association (352-629-2160), 801 SW 60th Ave. View original art and artifacts from Florida's horse industry inside the offices of this busy equine business complex; Mon–Fri 8:30–4:30. Free.

Gallery East (352-236-6992), 4901 E Silver Springs Blvd. A nonprofit artists' cooperative with exhibits by member artists, who also teach regular art classes. Exhibited items in various media are for sale. Open Tue–Sat 10–5. Free.

CFCC Webber Exhibit Center (352-873-5809), 3001 SW College Rd. Featuring rotating exhibits ranging from an annual model railroad display to environmental education to presentations by local artists. Open Mon–Sat 11–5. Free.

McIntosh

Ice House Gallery (352-591-5930), US 441 and Ave C. Enjoy fine arts and sculpture by regional artists, displayed in the town's historic icehouse; antiques collectors will find the vintage tools interesting. Open Fri–Sun 10–5. Free.

Sandra Friend

THE VIEW IS INCREDIBLE THROUGH SILVER SPRINGS'S GLASS-BOTTOMED BOATS.

SILVER SPRINGS ♿ **Silver Springs** (352-236-2121; www.silversprings.com), 5656 E Silver Springs Blvd. In the 1960s this was my family's top Florida vacation destination, Florida's first real tourist attraction. It started in 1878 with the invention of a new device called a glass-bottomed boat, used to ferry visitors down the crystalline waters of the Silver River to observe one of the world's largest springs. Real Florida lurks around every bend. Alligators sun on the grassy garden slopes, raccoons slink between the cypress knees, and millions of fish swim in swirling schools around the river's many spring vents. Beautiful formal gardens line the northern shore of the river, tucked beneath grand old cypresses and oaks. Jazz drifts through the trees from hidden speakers. Wander through the gardens to discover treats like the **World**

ATTRACTIONS **Don Garlits Museums** (1-877-271-3278; www.garlits.com), 13700 SW 16th Ave, Belleview. The famed funny car driver with a place in the Smithsonian Museum of American History shows off his personal drag-racing and classic car collections, totaling nearly 200 vehicles. Open daily 9–5, closed Christmas. $12 adults, $10 seniors and ages 13–18, $3 ages 5–12.

HISTORIC SITES Stop in at the Ocala Chamber of Commerce (see *Guidance*) for the *Marion County Historical Tour Sites* booklet, which provides a map with locations of the county's most significant historic sites. The towns of **Citra**, **McIntosh**, and **Reddick** date back to 1881 and 1882, with architecture to match; **Belleview** and **Weirsdale** hide 1885 Victorian districts in their downtowns. But one of the region's most significant sites is **Fort King**, SE Fort King St east of SE 36th Ave, a major stop on the military trail in 1827 and the sparking point of the First Seminole War.

of Bears, the only place in Florida to see Kodiak and grizzly bears; the **Jeep Safari**, a ride through wildlife habitats with giraffes, zebras, and lemurs; and the **Lost River Voyage**, a cruise along the river's floodplain forests. Kids will enjoy the **Kids Ahoy! Playland**, which includes a small petting zoo and a wild animal carousel.

In recent years one of the biggest draws for the park has been the concerts held at **Twin Oaks**, an outdoor amphitheater with a faux southern mansion stage, where top baby boomer favorites like Frankie Vallee, Loretta Lynn, and the Smothers Brothers play to overflowing crowds between Jan and Apr; lights twinkling in the live oaks and cabbage palms create a fairyland atmosphere after dark. On Ross Allen Island, boardwalks neatly fitted around the trees of a natural floodplain forest lead you through habitats inhabited by native Florida reptiles and amphibians as well as species from around the world. Florida's most critical endangered species, the Florida panther, rates its own large exhibit. From Fort King Landing, the Jungle Cruise takes you down a natural waterway through more wildlife habitats.

Silver Springs has changed ownership many times since I modeled an indigo snake at the Ross Allen Reptile Institute, but some things haven't changed. A kid can still walk into the Dockside Emporium and buy a seashell for a dime, you can still sit on the lucky horseshoe cabbage palm under the watchful gaze of Chief Osceola, and the alligators continue to crawl up onto the neatly manicured lawns to sun themselves. Retaining its unspoiled natural appeal, Silver Springs remains one of my favorite places. $32.99 adults, $29.99 seniors, $23.99 ages 3–10, with many discounts and affordable multiday passes available, plus a combination ticket with Wild Waters; $6 parking fee.

MUSEUMS **Marion County Museum of History** (352-629-2773), 307 SE 26th Terrace in the McPherson Government Complex, Ocala. This museum features artwork and artifacts from early Marion County, including a 1,500-year-old canoe, farming equipment, and historical photos. Open Fri and Sat 10–2; fee.

Silver River Museum and Environmental Education Center (352-236-5401), 1445 NE 58th Ave. In Silver River State Park (see *Parks*), this classy natural and cultural history museum shows off the bones of prehistoric creatures, Seminole artifacts, Spanish cannons, and more; outside, roam a replica Cracker village and see an original glass-bottomed boat used at Silver Springs. Open weekends and holidays 9–5; fee.

RAILROADIANA It's hoped the old **Dunnellon Depot** will someday be a museum and visitors center, but in the meantime at least the turn-of-the-20th-century building has been preserved—it's along US 41 across from city hall. The **McIntosh Depot** houses the local historical society museum.

✷ To Do

BICYCLING Built by the Ocala Mountain Biking Association, the wild rides of the **Santos Biking Trails** are geared for high-speed pedaling on singletrack through the lush forests of the Cross Florida Greenway. Choose from rides like the Canopy Trail, under the shade of massive live oaks, or the Sinkhole Trail, which loops around a giant sink. Blazes denote three levels of difficulty: gentle (yellow), moderate (blue), and oh-my-God (red), which includes the quarry drops. Don't forget the helmet! Rent bikes at the nearby **Santos Trailhead Bicycle Shop** (352-307-2453; www.santosbikeshop.com), 8900 S US 441, or **Streit's Cyclery Ocala** (352-629-2612), 1274 E Silver Springs Blvd.

The **Ross Allen Loop** at **Silver River State Park** (see *Parks*) runs 5 miles along old forest roads near the campground. Just south of **Dunnellon**, the **Withlacoochee State Trail** heads south through the Nature Coast region for a 42-mile ride ending at Dade City, passing through Old Florida towns with plenty of facilities.

CARRIAGE TOURS **Ocala Carriage Tours** (1-877-99-OCALA; www.ocala carriage.com), 4776 NW 110th Ave. For a refined visit to Ocala's horse farms, enjoy a formal horse-drawn carriage tour along the back roads of horse country.

DIVING **Paradise Springs** (352-368-5746), 4040 SE 84th Lane Rd, a privately owned spring, combines dive training with a picture-perfect window into the Floridan Aquifer. Pick up your open-water and cave certifications in their classes, or stop by to dive the springs. For open-water diving, try a drift dive on the **Rainbow River** from the KP Hole (see *Swimming*) or on the **Silver River** (put in at Ray Wayside Park on FL 40). Certified cave divers will want to check out **Hal Watts Forty Fathom Grotto** (352-368-7974) for practice in technical deep diving, open by reservation only; the cavern is more than 100 feet deep in places.

ECOTOURS **Captain Mike's Lazy River Cruises** (352-637-2726; www.lazy rivercruises.com), departing from Stumpknockers on the Withlacoochee (see *Eating Out*) and the Dunnellon City Boat Ramp at US 41 and the Withlacoochee Bridge. Enjoy a leisurely float on a pontoon boat with a certified eco-heritage guide along the cypress-lined Withlacoochee and Rainbow Rivers. Call for reservations; specify length of trip (1–5 hours), number of participants, and any activities you'd like to concentrate on (diving, snorkeling, birding, swimming). These three factors will determine price ($10–30 per person).

FAMILY ACTIVITIES ✐ Located in front of the Market of Marion (see *Selective Shopping*), **Marion Nature Park** (352-347-7800), 12888 S US 441, a tiny teaching zoo, lets kids get up close and personal with barnyard animals, reptiles, and birds. At Brick City Park, the **Discovery Science Center** (352-401-3900) has hands-on science and nature exhibits for the kids, including an outdoor dinosaur "bone dig," fun physics activities, and scavenger hunts; open Tue–Fri 9–4, fee. At **Easy Street Family Fun Center** (352-861-9700), on Shady Rd near the Paddock Mall, play mini golf and race go-carts until the wee hours. At the **Ocala Drive In** (352-629-1325), S Pine Ave, drive-in theater makes its last stand; bring the kids and catch an inexpensive double feature (first film always family-oriented) every weekend. Flea market and antiques mall open weekends.

FISHING **Angler's Family Resort** (352-489-2397), US 41, Dunnellon, caters to anglers heading out on the **Withlacoochee River**; visit **Carney Island** (see *Parks*) for access to Lake Weir. **McIntosh Fish Camp** (352-591-1302), 5479 Ave H, is a great place to launch an expedition on **Orange Lake**, with boat rentals, bait and tackle, and basic lodging.

GAMING Next to the racetrack at Ocala Breeder's Sales, **Champions Restaurant & OTB Facility** (352-237-4144), SW 60th Ave, has parimutuel wagering, harness racing, and off-track betting in the ITW Teletheatre. Open at 11 daily; free after 6 PM. **Ocala Jai-alai** at Orange Lake presents a high-speed lacrosse-like sport with wagering on players.

GOLF The granddaddy of public courses is the **Ocala Municipal Golf Course** (352-622-8681), 3130 E Silver Springs Blvd, which opened in 1920; at the 18th hole tee, you'll encounter a granddaddy live oak closing in on the millennium mark. **Golden Ocala Golf and Country Club** (352-622-2245), 7340 N US 27, a semiprivate course, stakes its reputation on popular replica holes from top courses around the world, and the nearby **Golden Hills Golf & Turf Club** (352-629-7980) on US 27, a par-72 championship course, is owned in part by golf architect Rees Jones.

HIKING Enjoy more than 30 continuous miles of the **Florida Trail** along the **Cross Florida Greenway** (see *Greenways*), where you hike with history along the relict remains of the Cross Florida Barge Canal, reforested over the past 70 years. The 2-mile Land Bridge Loop (off CR 475A, north of CR 484) is a popular day hike along the route.

HORSE FEVER With all the horses in Marion County, there's a fair chance you'll want to track some down. In addition to checking out the listings under *Carriage Tours* and *Scenic Drives*, grab a copy of the *Visitor's Guide* from the chamber of commerce for a driving tour of **Horse Fever** locations, where you can spot (and pose with) 27 life-sized horse sculptures remaining in the county after a fund-raising auction for the arts.

PADDLING In addition to popular canoe routes on the **Rainbow River** (put in either at Rainbow Springs State Park or at the FL 484 bridge, 6 miles downstream) and **Silver River** (put in at Ocala Boat Basin, Ray Wayside Park, FL 40), the nearby **Ocala National Forest** (see the next chapter) offers beautiful wilderness paddling. To paddle on the beautiful Rainbow River, rent canoes and kayaks at **Rainbow Springs State Park** (see *Springs*). In Dunellon both **Dragonfly Watersports** (1-800-919-9579; www.dragonflywatersports.com), 20336 E Pennsylvania Ave, and **Rainbow River Canoe and Kayak** (352-489-7854; rainbowrivercanoeandkayak.com), 12121 Riverview Dr, handle rentals and shuttling along the Rainbow and Withlacoochee Rivers. At **Brasington's**, Ocala (see *Selective Shopping*), you can rent a kayak and take it with you to explore area rivers and lakes.

RETREAT CENTER **Crone's Cradle Conserve** (352-595-3377), P.O. Box 535, Orange Springs 32182, is a unique private preserve 6.4 miles west of Citra off CR 318. Watch for the sign along the highway and turn north on an unpaved road that leads you into the woods, emerging at a grassy area along a lake, a tranquil spot with meandering pathways, gardens, a playground, and porch swings. It's a tranquil retreat center focusing on women's issues, and an active organic farm with a large shop offering garden items, seedlings and herbs, seasonal produce, and books for nurturing the soul. Open until 3 daily.

SCENIC DRIVES Head into the country west of I-75 to enjoy Marion County's many horse farms. While you'll see quite a few between Ocala and Dunnellon on FL 40, getting off the beaten path is more fun. **CR 225** and **CR 326** provide excellent routes through the heart of Horse Country.

SWIMMING For a splash in cold but clear water, visit the popular swimming area at **Rainbow Springs State Park** (see *Springs*). Downstream, swimmers go with the flow at **KP Hole County Park** (352-489-3055), 9435 SW 190 Ave Rd. Warmer waters wait in Lake Weir at **Carney Island** (see *Parks*), which is also a favorite launch point for water skiers.

TRAIL RIDING To the north of Ocala, **Young's Paso Fino Ranch** (352-867-5305; www.youngspasofino.com), 8075 NW FL 326, has trail riding, farm tours, and riding lessons. **Ocala Foxtrotter Ranch** (352-347-5551; www.ocalafoxtrotter.com), 11800 S CR 475, offers riding lessons and trail riding along the extensive equestrian trail system of the **Cross Florida Greenway** (see *Greenways*), while **North Star Acres** (352-489-9848) provides guided trail rides of 1½ and 3 hours along some of the state's most beautiful riding trails in Goethe State Forest.

RIDERS AND HIKERS SHARE THE CROSS FLORIDA GREENWAY.

Sandra Friend

TUBING **Dragonfly Watersports** (see *Paddling*) supports 4-hour tubing trips down the crystal-clear Rainbow

River from KP Hole County Park to the CR 484 take-out, and **Rainbow Springs State Park** (see *Springs*) will soon offer tubing trips at the head spring.

WALKING TOURS Check with the Marion County Chamber of Commerce (see *Guidance*) for dates and ticket fees for its annual **Heritage Tour of Homes**, which allows public access to homes in **Ocala's** historic districts. In **Dunnellon** (www.dunnellon.org), take a walk around the Historic Village (see *Selective Shopping*), where interpretive markers explain the history of homes dating back to 1902.

WATER PARK **Wild Waters** (1-800-234-7458; www.wildwaterspark.com), corner of FL 40 and CR 35, adjoining Silver Springs. A densely knit canopy of live oaks shades four speeds of rides on eight very different slides in one of Florida's original water parks. Let the kids run wild in Cool Kids Cove, squirting, splashing, and pouring water through a complex of pipes and wheels, or grab a raft and hit the wave pool. Open Memorial Day–Labor Day, $23.99 adults, $20.99 guests under 48 inches, kids 2 and under free, plus a combination ticket with Silver Springs available; $6 parking fee.

WATERSKIING Lake Weir is Water-Ski Central for the region, where many a barefoot skier has gotten his or her training; access via **Carney Island** (see *Parks*).

✷ Green Space

GREENWAYS **The Marjorie Harris Carr Cross Florida Greenway** is a 110-mile corridor cutting across Marion County into adjoining Putnam and Levy, from the St. Johns River to the Gulf of Mexico. Florida's premier greenway project owes its existence to the failed Cross Florida Barge Canal, a 1920s project resurrected in the 1960s and fought off by environmentalists. The mile-wide corridor provides separate hiking, biking, and equestrian trail systems as well as access for anglers to prime fishing in Lake Rousseau and Rodman Lake; there are numerous trailheads along the corridor. For maps and information, contact the Office of Greenways and Trails Ocala Field Office (352-236-7143), 8282 SE CR 314, or stop in weekdays; the office adjoins the Marshall Swamp Trailhead.

PARKS In **Brick City Park** (352-401-3900), 1211 SE 22nd Rd, Ocala, a boardwalk trail loops around a historic limestone quarry laced with caverns. **Carney Island Recreation and Conservation Area** (352-288-8999), 13275 SE 115 Ave, offers Lake Weir access for swimming, boating, picnicking, and hiking. **Silver River State Park** (352-236-7148), 1425 NE 58th Ave, has one of the nicest campgrounds in the region, with brand-new upscale cabins and one of the busiest hiking trail systems in Florida.

SPRINGS **Rainbow Springs State Park** (352-489-8503), US 41 north of Dunnellon, protects the first-magnitude spring and hundreds of smaller bubblers that make up the headwaters of the Rainbow River. Unusually rugged slopes around the river are due to 1890s phosphate mining tailings; this former theme park still sports its botanical gardens with azalea-covered slopes (visit in late Feb for optimum blooms) and tall artificial waterfalls. Canoeing and kayaking (on-site outfitter), swimming, hiking, and picnicking are all part of the fun; a shady campground downriver provides river access.

WILD PLACES Encompassing more than 500,000 acres, the **Ocala National Forest** (see the next chapter) takes up most of the eastern half of Marion County. **Ross Prairie State Forest** (352-732-1201) adjoins the Cross Florida Greenway off FL 200 south of CR 484, with new hiking and horse trails opening to the public via the Ross Prairie Trailhead. West of Dunnellon, **Goethe State Forest** (352-447-2202), 8250 SE CR 336, spills across the Marion-Levy border, with 50,000 acres of longleaf pine forests open to hunting, horseback riding, and hiking.

✷ Lodging

BED & BREAKFASTS

McIntosh 32664

Merrily (352-591-1180), Ave G. Built in 1888, this beautiful Victorian home has been open to guests for more than 12 years. "I'm not going to heat it for just me and my dog," says Margie Karow, the energetic owner, "so I'm happy to visit with people." There are three rooms ($70) with shared sitting rooms and bath, each tastefully decorated; the room with twin beds is popular with ladies traveling together. Period furnishings downstairs accent the polished hardwood floors. A light breakfast is served in the grand dining room, featuring muffins and fresh fruit. Relax on the spacious porch in a rocker or on the swing and take in the lush landscaping under the ancient oak trees.

BIRTH OF A RIVER: VIEW OF THE HEADSPRING AT RAINBOW SPRINGS

Sandra Friend

Ocala

♿ Set in the heart of Horse Country, **Heritage Country Inn** (352-489-0023; www.heritagecountryinn.com), 14343 W FL 40, Ocala 34430, has six rooms ($99) with unique Florida themes, from an 1800s plantation to Florida's springs, and features wood-burning fireplaces, single Jacuzzis, and separate private entrances.

The Inn at Jumbolair (352-401-1990; www.jumbolair.com), 1201 NE 77th St, Ocala 34479, in a fly-in community, has five luxurious apartment-sized suites ($225 and up) named for prize steeds, a pool and fitness center, and an equestrian facility.

Weirsdale 32195

Shamrock Thistle and Crown (1-800-425-2763; www.shamrockbb.com), P.O. Box 624, CR 42. You'll delight at this quiet three-story Victorian (the 1887 Thomas B. Snook house), once the manor house for an orange grove empire. Owners Brantley and Anne Overcash infuse the residence with a Scots-Irish theme, where each comfortable suite tells a story. A romantic cottage overlooking the pool makes a great honeymoon getaway. Whirlpool suites with fireplaces are available; TV and VCR are provided in every room. Full breakfast served. Rates range $89–200, depending on season and amenities; modest dress requested.

HOTELS AND MOTELS

Dunnellon 34432

Two Rivers Inn (352-489-2300; www.tworiversinn.com), 20719 W Pennsylvania Ave. An old-fashioned motor court resurrected as a snazzy little inn—what a treat! And what a storied history. Originally built as officers' quarters for the Dunnellon Air Field (where glider pilots trained) during World War II, these cottages were moved into town after the war to become Davis Motor Court. J. R. Lang (of nearby J. R.'s Pub and Grille) bought the disheveled place in 1991 with plans for renovation. Each of the 15 spacious rooms and suites ($50–60) is fully updated and decorated with an interesting theme—the Safari, the River, the Savannah—and each has a fridge, microwave, toaster, and coffeemaker.

Ocala 34481

Numerous small chain motels cluster at Ocala's I-75 exits; those on US 27 offer rates as low as $29.95 for a single. The upscale choice at this intersection is the **Yankees Ramada Inn** (352-732-3131 or 1-800-272-6232), 3810 NW Blichton Rd, owned by George Steinbrenner, a longtime Ocala-area snowbird with his own horse farm. Baseball fans will love the Yankees memorabilia throughout the common spaces and a chance to see George or some of his players who pop in during winter; $59–139.

Amid the choices at the FL 200 exit of I-75, the **Ocala Hilton** (352-854-1400 or 1-877-602-4023; www.hiltonocala.com), 3600 SW 38th Ave, Ocala's only themed hotel, shines. Visit the paddock out back, and you'll feel a part of Florida's thoroughbred capital. Enjoy the Fri-night poolside garden parties (AYCE $5), weekly comedy club (see *Entertainment*), and Arthur's (see *Dining Out*), one of Ocala's top-rated restaurants. Rates vary from $79 and up; packages available for trail rides, horseback lessons, hayrides, horse farm tours, and boarding your horse.

Looking for romance? In a class by itself, the **Ritz Historic Inn** (1-888-382-9390; www.ritzhistoricinn.com), 1205 E Silver Springs Blvd, offers 32 designer-themed suites clustered around a formal walled courtyard and an on-site jazz club. Rates start at $70 for a two-room suite.

CAMPGROUNDS

Irvine 32686

Under a heavy canopy of tall hickory and elm trees, the **Encore RV Resort Ocala** (1-877-267-8737; www.rvonthego.com), 16905 NW CR

225, is a truly relaxing camper's destination, with a sparkling pool to share with your fellow campers, a pleasant recreation hall with big-screen TV, and big spaces ($23–28) that allow you room to kick back, fire up the grill, and enjoy your home away from home.

Ocala 34474
KOA Ocala (352-237-2138; www.koa.com/where/fl/09258.htm), 3200 SW 38th Ave. Nestled in a pleasant wooded setting (albeit along I-75), this full-service campground has camping cabins, hot tub, and a swimming pool plus full-hookup sites. Tents welcome.

Ocala Ranch RV Park (1-877-809-1100; www.ocalaranchrv.com), 2559 SW CR 484. A family-owned and -operated park with top ratings from Woodall's; more than 150 spaces including large pull-throughs. Full hookups, heated swimming pool, clubhouse under construction. Fills up quickly for the winter months, but a handful of overnight spots are reserved for drop-in guests during the snowbird season. $25, no tents permitted.

Silver Springs 34488
With 618 spaces, **The Springs RV Resort** (352-236-5250), 2950 NE 52nd Court, caters to snowbirds but has a daily rate of $23 for full-hookup RV sites. The grassy open area is anchored by a large picnic pavilion and clubhouse with pool; two bathhouses provide hot showers.

* Where to Eat

DINING OUT

Dunnellon
Flexing a little creative muscle near the Rainbow River, **Rusty Pontoon's Grille** (352-489-4010), 20049 E Pennsylvania Ave, offers a menu that is anything but average. My friends rave about "The Magnolia," a salad of mandarin orange, dates, and hearts of palm over greens ($5), and the grilled crabcakes ($11) that are mostly crab. My own favorite is the Withlacoochee Catfish ($11), a take on "catfish cordon bleu" with bits of ham scattered through a velvety shrimp and cream vermouth sauce ladled over a heap of fried catfish. All food is presented with the chef's special touch. The relaxed atmosphere and down-to-earth prices add to a diner's delight. Daily dinner specials $10–16.

Ocala
Amrit Palace (352-873-8500), 2635 SW College Rd. While most patrons come by for the daily lunch specials (reasonably priced at $6), the Amrit Palace offers the best Indian cuisine in the region. Of special note are the vegetarian entrées, including a proper mushroom bhajee.

Arthur's. Tucked away inside the Ocala Hilton (see *Hotels and Motels*), this classy restaurant (open for breakfast, lunch, and dinner) serves traditional food with an artistic flair. The menu changes frequently; my meal included lightly breaded fried green tomatoes, a smooth and rich bisque-like clam chowder, and a Cajun-spice-rubbed sirloin garnished with fresh oysters, onions, and peppers. Watch you don't fill yourself up on the fresh bread—the brown bread with citrus butter was virtually a dessert. Your best buy: "Dinners at Dusk," $12 for nightly gourmet specials 4:30–6:30.

Carmichael's (352-622-3636), 3105 NE Silver Springs Blvd, hosts a regular clientele in a comfortable "bring the outdoors in" setting—wood floors, brick walls, large windows, and a veritable forest of plants setting the stage for a fine-dining experience. Every breakfast kicks off with a complimentary basket of their trademark hot fresh orange-glazed buns, mouthwatering flaky pastries with a hint of orange zest. Lunch and dinner reservations suggested.

Felix's (352-629-0339), 917 E Silver Springs Blvd. Most fine restaurants feature a dessert tray. But Felix's catches your attention streetside with signs touting their DESSERT ROOM! They're best known for their buckhead beef, and are one of the few restaurants around that let you order a half serving. Dine in classy surroundings in a Victorian gingerbread home, for lunch Tue–Fri, dinner Tue–Sat.

Tony's Sushi Japanese Steakhouse (352-237-3151), 3405 SW College Rd. From traditional bento box lunches to perfect sashimi, Chef Tony presents Asian favorites that please both your artistic and culinary senses. Enjoy tableside preparations, or sit down at the bar to watch sushi chefs at work. Sushi $3–11 per roll, platters $15; dinners $9–25.

McIntosh

Kismet Café (352-591-3188), 5590 4th St. Delicious fresh foods served up in a funky folksy Florida atmosphere: Sip on a house-specialty ginger-honey lemonade (or BYOB) while making your entrée ($9) selection from such delights as shepherd's pie, spinach-walnut quiche, or feta chicken with yellow rice, each served "Chicago style" with salad and homemade bread on the plate. This is the local library, too—how can you not love a restaurant with an entire wall devoted to books? Features live music on weekends. Open Thu–Sun 11–2:30 for lunch, 6–9:30 for dinner.

EATING OUT

Belleview

B. D. Beans Coffee Co. (352-245-3077), 5148 SE Abshier Blvd. Fun and funky, playful and painted, B. D. Beans sparkles with artistic flair in both its surroundings and its menu selections: creative and healthful quiches, salads, and sandwiches, $4–7, with daily specials; smoothie lovers will rejoice at the wide selection, including coconut, toasted almond, and chai. Java junkies have their day, too, with nearly a dozen choices. When I'm in a veggie mood, I go for the succulent portobello mushroom sandwich or the tasty veggie melt; the grilled Havarti sandwich is one of my favorites. Serving coffee and muffins at breakfast, lunch items until 5. Closed Sun. Don't miss the rest rooms!

La Casa Del Pollo (352-307-0555), 10819 SE Abshier Blvd. Known locally as "Chicken Time," this authentic Cuban restaurant is tops in the region, going well beyond the mainstays of Cuban sandwiches and chicken, black beans and rice, to offer numerous hot pressed sandwiches ($4.95–6.25) such as the Puerto Rican Tripela, a house specialty, with roast pork, deli ham, Swiss cheese, seasoned Cuban steak, and pickles; empandillas, homemade soups, vegetarian options, and delicious entrées ($5–25) like chicken Caribe, lobster Creole, and picadillo à la Cubana. Never tried Cuban food? Your best bet is the Cuban Classic Sampler for two ($19), a combination platter with a little bit of everything. Lunch and dinner; closed Sun and Mon.

Ms. Steve's Dairy D Lite, corner of FL 484 and US 27-301-441. A busy drive-through (or walk-up, but parking is nearly impossible) family ice cream shop with hot dogs ($1.35) and a wide variety of dessert selections: cones $1–2, sundaes $2, shakes $2–3.

Lassie's Restaurant (352-245-4318), 5068 SE Abshier Blvd. It's rare these days to find a 24-hour nonchain diner, but that's Lassie's, with basic home-cooked fare like stuffed cabbage, hot roast beef and mashed potatoes, ravioli, and grilled cheese. Prices range from $1 for a hot dog to $18 for the all-you-can-eat stone crab claws, so there's something for everyone, especially with breakfast served any hour of the day.

Dunnellon

The Front Porch Restaurant and Pie Shop (352-489-4708), 12039 N Florida Ave. Murals bring the outdoors in at this popular family-owned restaurant, a local fixture since 1986, offering up regional favorites like Ybor City Cuban sandwiches, 'gator tail, fried yam sticks, chicken gizzards, cheese grits, and okra. Serving breakfast, lunch, and dinner, but the capper is dessert—their famous piled-high pies, $2 a slice. Closed Mon.

Old Fashioned Sweet Shoppe (352-489-0503), 20669 W Pennsylvania Ave. Small-town ice cream parlor with hand-dipped homemade ice cream, big salads ($6), and an array of sandwiches ($2–6). Closed Sun.

Stumpknockers on the River (352-854-2288), FL 200 at the Withlacoochee River Bridge. Barely an evening goes by when the parking lot isn't packed—except on Mon, when they're closed. Featuring seafood of all stripes, Stumpknockers sits right on the cypress-lined Withlacoochee River. Giant portions make it tough to take on the appetizers, but don't miss the fried mushrooms ($5), freshly battered and served in an overflowing basket with accompanying dipping sauces. Nightly specials feature local seafood, such as grouper amandine ($12) or lobster Newburg ($14), but hearty appetites won't go wrong with the all-you-can-eat catfish ($11), the crabmeat-stuffed flounder ($10), or the seafood platter ($15). If you haven't tried alligator yet, here's the place, with three different preparations of 'gator steaks ($11–13) or crispy 'gator nuggets ($6). Serving dinner Tue–Sat, lunch and dinner on Sun.

McIntosh

Antique Deli (352-591-1436), US 441 and Ave G. Stop in for the sweet tea, stay for a sandwich ($2–5) or fresh-made salad and a great southern dessert like old-fashioned banana pudding ($1) or a frozen Mississippi mud pie ($2). Features root beer floats ($2) and ice cream ($1), too! Gift and craft items and a smattering of antiques line the walls. Open for lunch and dinner.

Jim's Pit BBQ (352-591-2479), I-75 and CR 318. You might not assume it's a restaurant from the gas pumps, citrus stand, and selection of touristy gifts near the cashier, but head to the back of the building for some real pit barbecue, served up in this locale by Jim for more than 20 years. In addition to barbecue dinners ($7–13, with barbecue beans, coleslaw, and garlic bread) and sandwiches ($2–6), they serve up breakfast ($3–5) and ice cream as well.

Ocala

Abio's Italian Restaurant (352-629-4886; www.abiospizza.com), 2377 SW College Rd. For a green olive fanatic like me, tiny Abio's hits the spot with their New Jersey Joy calzone: mozzarella, ricotta, sausage, onion, green peppers, and green and black olives stuffed into a pizza crust and baked with sauce. Subs, baked Italian dishes, and pizza, $4–6. Closed Sun.

Champions (352-237-4667), 1701 SW 60th Ave. Dine while watching the thoroughbreds step through their paces at the Ocala Breeder's Sales track; lunch, $6–8, in an off-track betting facility.

Charlie Horse Restaurant (352-622-4050), 2426 E Silver Springs Blvd. It's a casual place to gather with friends, with a sports-bar atmosphere, and the appetizers are great (potato skins, yum!), with more than a dozen choices; the burgers, wings, and Charlie's specially topped steaks are the reason to stop here. Entrées $4–20; stick around after 9 for open-mike karaoke!

Crossroads Country Kitchen (352-237-1250), 7947 FL 40, is a great country breakfast stop ($3–8) with tasty pancakes in five flavors; they do lunch and dinner, too (entrées under $10), with daily specials and live music on Fri evenings 5–9.

Cyber Grind (352-62-CYBER), 36 S Magnolia Ave. Ocala's first Internet café shines with European sophistication, offering panini sandwiches ($5–9), salads, and gourmet pastries and bagels as a sidebar to the coffee and smoothies nursed while you surf on a DSL connection. Get your java fix 7 AM–10 PM Mon–Fri, 10 AM–11 PM Sat.

On the square, **Harry's** (352-840-0900; www.hookedonharrys.com), 24 SE 1st Ave, feeds Ocala's need for a vibrant downtown. Popular with the late-night crowd, this upscale Florida chain bar and grill serves up pan-seared crabcakes thick with blue crabmeat, red beans and rice Cajun style, and tasty Gulf Coast oysters among its many entrée choices ($6–9), lunch and dinner.

Huckleberry Finn's (352-402-0776; www.huckleberryfinns.org), 3821 NW Blitchton Rd. Whipping an old ex–Howard Johnson's restaurant into shape takes a lot of guts and creativity, especially when a string of prior owners failed to make a go of it. But Huckleberry Finn's is going strong, serving up Florida food with a Caribbean flair, from thick slabs of their house-specialty Sugar Cane French Toast to funky salads like the Kiwi Fruit Salad, a carved pineapple stuffed with exotic fruit and served with sorbet. Even the everyday food shines: When British tourists compliment the fish-and-chips, you know it's good. Entrées start at $7.

Magnolia Bakery (352-629-5533), 1412 N Magnolia Ave. Since 1948, this hometown bakery has provided fresh bread and delectable desserts to the people of Ocala; stop by at lunchtime for sandwiches and salads.

Mango's (352-402-9822), 20 SW Broadway. Open Mon–Fri 9–3, this newcomer to downtown features Caribbean cuisine, vegetarian specialties, and fabulous old-fashioned homemade root beer floats—free root beer refills! Try the beach quesadilla, a tasty mix of cheeses and veggies with fresh salsa, or the sunshine salad, piled high with fresh fruit, carrots, and almonds and topped with creamy strawberry-mango dressing. Most of the offerings contain mango. Subs, salads, and sandwiches, $6–7.

Veranda Gallery and Tea Room (352-622-0007), 416 SE Fort King St. Enjoy a quiet weekday lunch in genteel Old Ocala, with sandwiches and salads $8–10.

Wolfie's (352-622-5008), 2159 E Silver Springs Blvd. An Ocala tradition since the 1960s, Wolfie's attracts a crowd of regulars. The servers know their patrons well, and you'll swear they can read your mind. Offering daily specials such as all-you-can-eat fried fish, spaghetti, pot roast, and meat loaf dinners. Bountiful salads run $4–8. Sandwiches include New York classics like kielbasa, Reuben, club, and pita ($3–5), plus burgers and dogs "grilled to order." Breakfast served all day. Open Mon–Sat 6–9, closed Sun.

Ocklawaha

Gator Joe's Beach Bar & Grill (352-288-3100), 12431 SE 135th Ave. Riding the coattails of Ma and Pa Barker's infamous shootout with the FBI in 1937 (see *Special Events*), the restaurant takes its name from Old Joe, a massive alligator who lived along this shoreline and was mentioned in one of the Barkers' letters. This funky Florida seafood restaurant is perched on Johnson's Beach with walls of windows overlooking the grand sweep of Lake Weir, serving up huge lunch sandwiches ($6–8), and dinner entrées ($9–13) like Joe's Kickin' Frog Legs, Barker's Ribeye, and grouper nuggets. Special kids' menu and live calypso music on Sat 2–6; closed Mon.

Summerfield

Sam's St. Johns Seafood (352-307-7387), 17860 SE 109th Ave. Migrating down from the Jacksonville area, this family-owned and -operated seafood chain packs a punch for your lunch dollar—the $5.99 all-you-can-eat specials keep the place hopping. Sam's serves up tasty dishes in an undersea diner atmosphere, with walls lined with mock coral reefs and fish surrounding standard diner booths, tables, and chairs. Try the flaky fresh grouper sandwich ($6), or one of their seafood salads served in a giant shell-shaped bowl ($5). Dinner entrées ($8–15) run the gamut from golden fried trout to surf and turf. Two other Ocala locations: in the Winn-Dixie plaza at the corner of FL 326 and US 301, and along FL 200 at Heath Brook Plaza.

Entertainment

The **Marion Cultural Alliance** (352-369-1500), 110 E Silver Springs Blvd, Suite B, Ocala, represents such cultural offerings as the **Central Florida Symphony Orchestra** (352-351-1606), 416 SE Fort King St, with a season of Oct–Apr; the **Central Florida Master Choir** (1-877-996-2252), performing at regional venues in Oct and Nov; and the **Central Florida Philharmonic Orchestra** (352-873-4347), with performances in three venues Oct–Apr. The **Ocala Civic Theatre** (352-236-2274), 4337 E Silver Springs Blvd, is more than 50 years old (I saw *Dial M for Murder* here as a teen), and presents a broad repertoire of plays during its Sep–June season.

At the **Ocala Hilton** (see *Hotels and Motels*), enjoy **The Comedy Zone** on Fri and Sat evenings, with national acts bringing out the laughs; reservations are a must, as engagements are frequently sold out.

The **Silver Springs Concert Series** (see *Attractions*) features major country acts like Loretta Lynn, Lee Greenwood, and Alan Jackson, and baby boomer favorites like Frankie Vallee and the Smothers Brothers. Concert price is included in admission on concert dates, and is part of the price of the annual pass.

Orange Blossom Opry (352-821-1201; www.obopry.com), 13939 CR 42, Weirsdale, is an old-fashioned foot-stompin' country music mall set amid the orange groves around Lake Weir, with its own opry cast and visiting headliners like Bobby Bare and the Blackwoods. Shows are Thu–Sat evenings at 7; Thu is always a country jam session (bring your own instrument!). Tickets $13–15 for headliners.

✷ Selective Shopping

Belleview

Market of Marion (352-245-6766), 12888 SE US 441. More than 1,000 vendors keep this massive flea market one of the busiest in the region, with great buys on produce, clothing, and garage sale items; they host special events, too. Open Fri Oct–Apr, Sat and Sun all year.

Mossy Oaks Antique Mall (352-307-0090), 6260 SE 118th Place. Off US 301 just south of town, this classy antiques mall represents 25 dealers. It's a joy to browse through the neatly arranged displays of art glass, saltcellars, quilts, and furnishings; I was delighted to find a good selection of books on Florida. You'll find the eclectic here, too: One dealer specializes in refurbished antique gas pumps, another dealer shows off retro chairs and stools, and a custom furniture maker takes up the back of the place. Closed Sun.

Citra

The Orange Shop (1-800-672-6439; www.floridaorangeshop.com), US 301. Step into the wayback machine and take a trip back in time to when fresh-squeezed orange juice flowed free for every tourist cruising through Florida. Opened in 1936, the Orange Shop still has that old-time appeal with lots of scented and kitschy souvenirs and, of course, oranges ready to ship nationwide.

Dunnellon

Spread across several blocks of the 1890s boomtown district in downtown Dunnellon, the **Historic Village Shops** occupy classic Victorian and Cracker houses bursting at the seams with antiques, fine arts, and gifts. With more than 15 shops to choose from, leave yourself plenty of browsing time! Some you shouldn't miss:

Nooks & Crannys (352-489-2774), 20613 W Pennsylvania Ave. In addition to featuring excellent values on ceramics, turned wood, and other fine arts on consignment from local artists, Nooks & Crannys offers regular 1-day arts and crafts classes—learn to weave a pine needle basket, or to create cast paper.

Linda William's Past & Present Shoppe (352-489-9366), 20643 W Pennsylvania Ave. From the outside, it looks like an old hardware store, not at all in step with the surrounding chic storefronts. But after 15 years, owner Linda Williams still deals in the basic antiques that folks are looking for—books, collector plates, saltshakers, and the like. Check the back corner for a selection of used vinyl and player piano rolls, and don't miss the huge mural depicting Dunnellon circa 1909, its centerpiece the digging of the Cross Florida Barge Canal (see *Greenways*).

✐ **Our Florida Bookstore and Art Gallery** (352-489-3114), 20709 W Pennsylvania Ave. It's the perfect place to immerse in what's so special about Florida—an entire bookstore devoted to the subject. From mysteries by Carl Hiaasen and Randy Wayne White to history tomes by Michael Gannon and yours truly, Sandra Friend, this Florida-centric bookstore covers the state in every possible way. There's even a room for the kids, entirely devoted to children's literature on the Sunshine State. Truly a one-of-a-kind place, decorated with fine Florida art, including the primitive folk art of Ruby C. Williams, as well as fossils gathered by the owner's husband.

Two Sisters Antique and Gift Gallery (352-465-6982), 20721 W Pennsylvania Ave. When the shopkeeper hands you a glass of icy pink lemonade, how can you *not* keep browsing? Feathered with fine furniture, linens, jewelry, and more, this friendly feminine nest screams *girl stuff* and is an ideal place to find the perfect gift for Mom or Sis.

Grumbles House Antiques & Specialty Shops (352-465-1460; www.grumbleshouseantiques.com), 20799 Walnut St. In this showy southern mansion, rooms overflow with a mix of old and new. Step down the breezeway to its sister shop, **The Barracks**, which places an emphasis on antique glassware.

Green Wagon Collectibles (352-489-9446), 20775 Chestnut St. Authentic antiques at reasonable prices, from postcards and glassware to fine furniture and a bathroom filled with classic dolls.

The Gingerbread House (352-489-0647), 20781 Chestnut St. Museum curators take note: *This* is where you need to shop. Celebrating more than 30 years in the antiques business, the Gingerbread House offers eclectic items snapped up at estate sales, from mortars and pestles purchased from indigenous Panamanians during the building of the Panama Canal to historic objects picked up by wreckers off the Gulf Coast.

McIntosh

Historic Harvest Village Shops, 22050 US 441 N. Open only on weekends, this mini mall of antiques shops at the north end of town attracts collectors from around the state. Stop in at **O'Brisky's Book Barn** (352-591-2177) for a sampling of the massive book collection available at his main store in nearby Micanopy; browse **Victorian Rose Antiques** (352-591-6980) for that perfect antique trunk, desk, or armoire.

Dianna Van Horn Antiques (352-339-6864), US 441 and Ave B; (352-591-1185), Ave G and 3rd St. At her US 441 storefront, the focus is on glassware and pottery and other small collectibles. Head back to Dianna's second location in the large tin-roofed barn (the old packing house) across from the McIntosh Depot, and you'll find a little bit of everything and a lot of classic furniture, with a heavy turnover of items weekly.

Ocala

All That Art (352-368-6841), 18 SW Broadway. Directly across from the Brick City Center for the Arts (see *Art Galleries*), it's much more than a frame shop, featuring paintings, sculpture, and gift items from 18 local and regional artists, with prices to suit every budget.

Brasington's Adventure Outfitters (1-888-454-1991; www.brasingtons.com), 2801 SW 20th St (moving soon to a new location on E Silver Springs Blvd). Getting ready for a big adventure in the Ocala National Forest, on the Cross Florida Greenway, or on one of Ocala's many scenic rivers? Gear up at Brasington's, where you'll find Florida-appropriate outdoor clothing, camping supplies, and kayak rentals amid a flood of technical equipment. Located just off FL 200.

Fletchbilt Handbag & Shoe Outlet (352-629-0134; www.handbag-factory.com), 1927 SW College Rd, offers discounts up to 50 percent off retail for leather purses in every style imaginable; their fine stock of shoes includes sandals for $10 and moccasins for $25.

Frazier Coal Company (352-368-7678), 3970 S Pine St. Primitives, from painted furniture and window frames to shipping labels and antique tools, to fit your country decor.

Golden Tymes (352-622-7660), 805 SE Fort King St, focuses on baskets and primitives, including cypress clocks; offers traditional basket-weaving classes.

I-75 Super Flea Market (352-351-9220), 3132 NW 44th Ave. Open on weekends and popular with locals, this flea market is fun to browse; you'll find garage sale items, permanent booths with collectibles, and the usual array of cheap gimcracks and gadgets imported from Asia.

Nina's Antiques (352-629-7051), 3415 E Silver Springs Blvd. From a neoclassical 1860 Egyptian desk clock to 1960s jack-in-the-boxes, Nina has quite a collection, especially for those looking to establish a classy dining room: Her Fenton glass, Depression glass, Carnival glass, and others are displayed on beautiful antique wooden tables, sideboards, and china closets.

Ocala Antique Gallery (352-622-4468), 3700 S US 441. A bevy of dealers with a little bit of everything: Information overload will develop after you browse a while! Philatelists delight in the sheer volume of postcards and postal history, book lovers find brimming shelves, and if stereoscopic pictures are your thing, well, there aren't too many places in Florida that have more of a selection. You *will* find something here you'll like—just keep looking. Closed Sun.

Paddock Room Galleries (352-629-3723), 226 E Silver Springs Blvd. The only shop in Horse Country solely dedicated to equine-related gifts, from fine art to casual throws. Closed Sun.

Potosi Mexican Arts (352-622-4099), 1218 E Silver Springs Blvd. Imagine a bathroom sink with a conch spout pouring water into a copper washbasin—it's unusual, artistic, and functional. That's what Potosi is about, marrying art to function via the craftsmanship of noted Mexican artists. Closed Sun.

Orange Lake

Orange Lake Trading Post (352-591-0307), 19063 N US 441. Bulging with ephemera, this funky shop along US 441 has everything from architectural pieces and farm tools to nuts and bolts.

Silver Springs

✐ **Silver Springs Curio Shop** (352-236-2673), 5472 E Silver Springs

Blvd. Occupying the corner of FL 40 and FL 35 since 1952, this gift shop epitomizes old-time Florida tourism, where they still sell lamps and dolls made from seashells as well as T-shirts, beach towels, and chunks of coral. One of my favorite childhood haunts, it's a great place for kids to spend their dimes on seashells.

FARMER'S MARKETS AND U-PICK

Belleview

Frank's Fruit Shoppe (352-245-2370), 5625 SE Abshier Blvd, carries fresh citrus (they will ship!) and the best fresh veggies in-season.

Silver Springs

Two long-standing and popular fruit and vegetable stands are on FL 35 (Baseline Rd) near its intersection with FL 40: an unnamed stand next to the Silver Springs Post Office, just north of the intersection, and **K&L Produce** (open daily), an air-conditioned indoor market, south of the intersection near the exit from Silver Springs.

✷ Special Events

January: **Mustang/Ford Roundup** (352-236-2121), Silver Springs. In a town like this, you'd think it was a horse gathering, but no—it's a roundup of more than 400 classic Fords, a mecca for serious antique-auto buffs. Held second weekend of January at Silver Springs. Fee.

Ma Barker Day (352-288-3751), Ocklawaha. Meet Marion County's historic terrorists: Ma Barker and her gang, who had their little shootout with the FBI in the sleepy village of Ocklawaha in 1937. Everyone wakes up with a bang on the second Sat, with three reenactments of the classic gun battle.

February: **Taste of Ocala** (352-237-1221), Ocala. Looking for a quick way to sample Ocala's wide range of dining? This annual benefit fund-raiser for Central Florida Community College is just the ticket. Diners gather at the Paddock Mall on the last Sat of the month for an evening's worth of grazing. Fee.

April: **Boomtown Days** (352-489-2320), Dunnellon, third week. Celebrating its roots as a turn-of-the-20th-century phosphate boomtown, Dunnellon kicks up its heels in mid-Apr with pageantry, music, crafts, and canoe races down the Rainbow River.

May: **African-American Arts Festival** (352-629-8051), Webb Stadium at Dr. Martin Luther King Jr. Blvd, Ocala. First weekend. This 3-day celebration of the African American community is still going strong after a dozen years.

August: **Ocala Shrine Club Rodeo** (352-694-1515), Ocala, weekend before Labor Day. In some cities, they ride funny cars. Not here in Ocala. Here, it's a wild ride around the Southeast Livestock Pavilion as the Shriners take on the meanest cattle this side of Kissimmee.

October: **McIntosh 1890s Festival** (352-591-4038), McIntosh, last Sat. Step into yesteryear with a visit to McIntosh during the annual 1890s festival, now in its third decade of all things Victorian: arts, crafts, and food booths.

FAFO Images in Art (352-622-7263), Ocala, last Sat. Without a doubt the largest annual display and sale of fine arts in Marion County, featuring 250 juried artists, at the McPherson Government Complex, SE 25th Ave.

November: **Ocklawaha River Raid** (352-288-3751), Lake Weir, first weekend. Although Marion County saw its fair share of Civil War skirmishes, only one true battle raged: The local militia, the Ocklawaha Rangers, fought off a Union army invasion. Step into the Union and Confederate camps, or visit the sutler's village for an old-time treat.

Ocala Scottish Games and Irish Feis (352-347-2873), Ocala, second Sat. A gathering of the clans from which the region's original European settlers came, with Highland and Irish step dancing for all; stop by for the pipers, stay for the caber toss. Events held at the Ocala Regional Sportsplex, 3500 SW 67th Ave.

December: **Festival of Lights** (352-236-2121), Silver Springs. Of the many special events held at Silver Springs (see *Attractions*), the annual Festival of Lights delights the most—millions of twinkling lights illuminating the gardens along the Silver River. Fee; holiday buffet available.

OCALA NATIONAL FOREST

When President Theodore Roosevelt designated 160,000 acres of the Big Scrub as the Ocala National Forest on Nov 24, 1908, he created the first national forest east of the Mississippi River. To those of us who live nearby and cross it often, it's simply "the Forest." But this is a forest unlike any other. Encompassing parts of Lake, Putnam, and Volusia Counties, and most of eastern Marion County, it has grown to more than half a million acres in the past century. It protects the world's largest continuous scrub forest, a desert-like environment of ancient sand dunes capped with vegetation adapted to a lack of water. Yet within these rolling hills hide vast wet prairies and crystalline springs that pour forth millions of gallons of fresh water from the Floridan Aquifer. On his explorations of the St. Johns River, botanist William Bartram wrote about **Salt Springs** in 1774, describing the spring with its 52-million-gallon-per-minute flow as an "amazing crystal fountain." The Ocala National Forest is the stronghold of the Florida black bear, and the home of the largest Florida scrub-jay population in the world. Its communities predate the establishment of the national forest, when settlers moved into the region in the 1840s to homestead in frontier towns like **Astor**, ideally situated as a trading post along the St. Johns River; **Paisley**, not far from Alexander Springs, and **Fort McCoy**, established during the Seminole Wars.

GUIDANCE After you preplan your trip via the extensive Ocala National Forest web site (www.southernregion.fs.fed.us/florida/recreation/index_oca.shtml) presented by the USDA Forest Service, you'll find helpful and accommodating staff at four visitors centers throughout the Ocala National Forest. The busiest and easiest-to-access location (just east of Silver Springs off FL 40) is the **Ocklawaha Visitors Center** (352-236-0288), 3199 NE CR 315. If you're headed south from Palatka on FL 19, stop at the **Buckman Lock Visitors Center**, open Mon–Wed 7–5, Thu–Sun 9–5. Coming north from Altoona on FL 19, the **Pittman Visitors Center** (352-669-7495) is inside the Seminole District Ranger Station. The **Salt Springs Visitors Center** (352-685-3070), 14100 N FL 19, is centrally located within the Forest at Salt Springs. Detailed maps of the entire Forest and its recreation areas are available for $7 at each center.

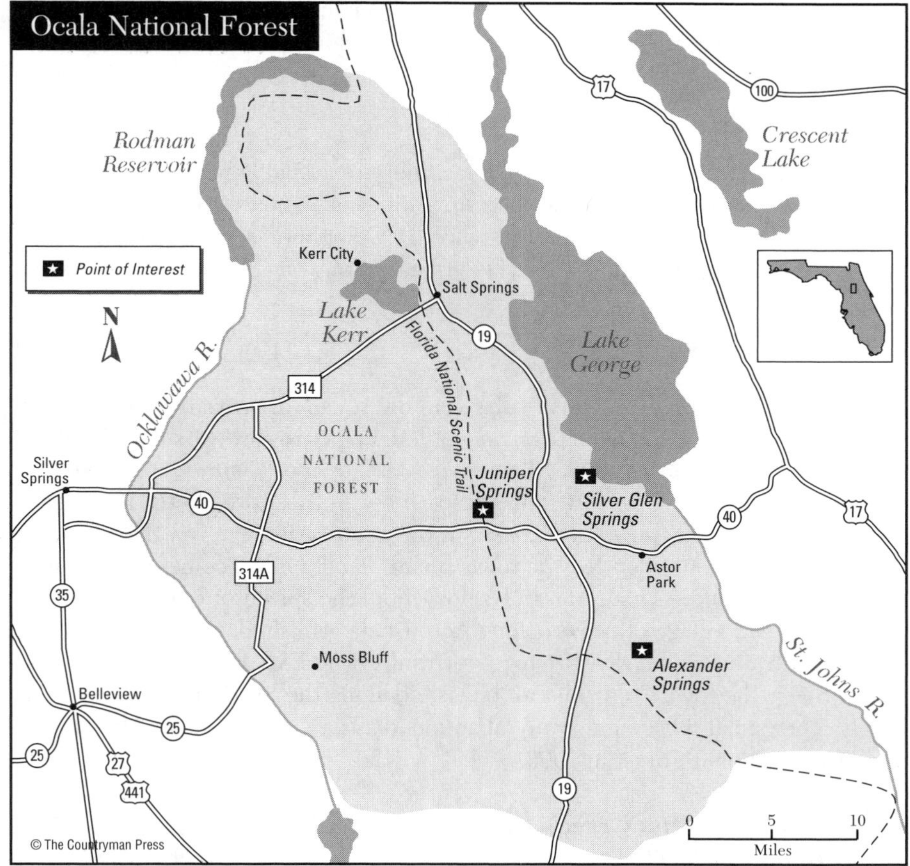

Most communities in the area do not have their own post office but rely on postal service from outside the Forest (such as Ocklawaha and Silver Springs), which makes finding a place based on its address confusing. To help ease this confusion, I've grouped services under their communities rather than their mailing addresses.

GETTING THERE *By car:* **FL 40** runs east–west from Ormond Beach to Silver Springs, and is considered the main route through the Ocala National Forest. This is a heavily trafficked two-lane road (with sporadic passing zones) through large stretches of wilderness; drive carefully. **FL 315** runs north from FL 40 west of the Ocklawaha River to Fort McCoy and Orange Springs. **FL 314** runs north from FL 40 at Nuby's Corner (just east of the Ocklawaha River) to **FL 19** at Salt Springs. FL 19, designated the "Backwoods Trail" scenic drive as it passes through the heart of the Big Scrub, is the primary north–south road through the area, heading north from Altoona to meet Palatka above the northern edge of the Forest. **CR 42** provides another scenic drive along the southeastern edge of the Forest, connecting a string of small Lake County communities like Deerhaven and Paisley.

MEDICAL EMERGENCIES No medical facilities are available within the confines of the Ocala National Forest and its communities. The nearest hospitals are in Ocala (to the west) and Palatka (to the north). Cell phone service is sporadic to nonexistent throughout the Forest: Do not count on your phone to summon help for an emergency.

✷ To See

GHOST TOWNS Numerous small villages in the region disappeared shortly after the deep freeze of 1889, which convinced fledgling citrus growers that the Big Scrub was too far north to grow their crops. The town of **Kismet**, complete with a hotel, sawmill, tavern, and school, attracted northern settlers to the area near **Alexander Springs** (see *Green Space*) in the 1880s. After the freeze, the hotel's relocation to Altoona sounded the town's death knell. Only a cemetery remains along CR 445, where Duke Alexander, for whom the springs are named, still rests. The 1875 village of **Acron** along Acron Lake vanished with the end of steamboat traffic, as did the thriving riverfront town of **St. Francis** along the St. Johns River; the town's remains can be visited along the St. Francis Hiking Trail. Many other small settlements were abandoned as part of the establishment of the Ocala National Forest in 1908.

MUSEUMS Inside **Miss Grace's Emporium** (see *Selective Shopping*), the **Paisley Museum** displays the region's settlement and history in the original post office, featuring artifacts and ephemera from the Parkers, who developed the town of Paisley. Free.

WORKING LOCK An integral part of the 1960s development of the Cross Florida Barge Canal, the **H. H. Buckman Lock** (386-329-3575) now provides a portal for anglers headed from the St. Johns River to Rodman Reservoir. Operations are visible from parks on both sides of the lock, but an overlook on the north side lets you get the best view; access via FL 19 and Buckman Lock Rd.

✷ To Do

BICYCLING Making a 22-mile loop between trailheads at Paisley and Alexander Springs, the **Paisley Woods Bicycle Trail** provides an excellent off-road experience for mountain bikers looking to get out into the sand pine scrub, rolling sandhills, and hardwood swamp of the southern portion of the Forest. Marked with yellow diamonds, the trail has an option of a shorter loop at the halfway point.

BIRDING You'll see and hear birds everywhere along hiking trails and the edges of lakes in this vast wilderness, but my top pick for bird-watching goes to the

Ocklawaha Prairie Restoration Area (352-821-2066) at Moss Bluff, CR 314A, where thousands of blue-winged teals and hundreds of sandhill cranes spend each winter. For sightings of Florida scrub-jays, head to the **Florida Trail** through Juniper Prairie Wilderness or through the scrub north of CR 314.

BOATING Rent pontoon boats ($85–145) and fishing boats ($20–60) at the south end of the Forest at **Nelson's Fish Camp** (see *Fish Camps*), or at the north end at **Salt Springs Run Marina** (352-685-2255; www.onf.net/saltrunmarina), where pontoon boats run $70–110, powerskiffs $27.50–45 (plus gas). If you're running under your own power, tie up and stay a while at the **Astor Marina** (see *Motels*) with its 68 wet slips along the St. Johns, or put your own boat in at one of the many boat ramps throughout the Forest. Check the official national forest map for boat ramp locations.

ECOTOURS **Guided Tours with Captain Peggy** (352-591-1508; www.goldenimages-photo-scuba.com). Outdoor photographer Captain Peggy Goldberg leads custom-tailored photo safaris (surface and scuba) and tour charters on the Silver and Ocklawaha Rivers, as well as kayak trips along Juniper and Alexander Runs. Tours start at $15 per person, per hour, for a minimum of four participants.

FERRYBOAT Since its first incarnation in 1856, the **Fort Gates Ferry** remains the only crossing of the St. Johns River between Astor and Palatka. It runs 7–5:30; closed Tue. The western terminus is 7 miles east of Salt Springs on a rough dirt road nearly impassable during the rainy season; the ferry runs to Welaka on the eastern shore of the St. Johns River.

FISHING Where better to cast a line than the **St. Johns River**? Lake George has some of the best bass fishing in the state; ask around at the **Astor Marina** (see *Motels*) for fishing guides. There are dozens of sparkling lakes throughout the Forest, just waiting for quiet bank fishing—places like Hopkins Prairie, Halfmoon Lake, Grasshopper Lake, and Lake Kerr beckon. Pull out the national forest map and pick yourself a sweet spot!

DANCE OF THE SANDHILL CRANE

Sandra Friend

HIKING Hiking trails established by the USFS within the national forest include the **Yearling Trail** (off FL 19), which loops around historic Pat's Island, where Marjorie Kinnan Rawlings met the family who became the basis of her Pulitzer Prize–winning novel; the **Lake Eaton Trails** (off CR 314), showcasing a giant sinkhole in the scrub; and the **Salt Springs**

THE FLORIDA TRAIL When Jim Kern and friends painted their first blaze at FL 42 in Paisley in 1966, they brought a new concept to the Sunshine State: backpacking in Florida. Envisioned by Kern as a southern counterpart to the Appalachian Trail, the Florida Trail now runs more than 1,300 miles from the Big Cypress Preserve on the edge of the Everglades north to Fort Pickens on Pensacola Beach. Established in the late 1960s, the "Ocala Trail" was the first hiking trail blazed by the Florida Trail Association, and still draws more backpackers than any other part of the Florida Trail. It runs more than 70 miles straight through the heart of the Ocala National Forest. Starting at Clearwater Lake Recreation Area in Paisley, it passes within hike-in distance of Alexander Springs Recreation Area, Juniper Springs Recreation Area, and Salt Springs Recreation Area before reaching Buckman Lock at the north end of the Forest. Backpackers seek out beauty spots like Farles Prairie, Hidden Pond, Hopkins Prairie, and Grassy Pond to settle down for the night. For maps and guidebooks, contact the **Florida Trail Association** (1-877-HIKE-FLA; www.floridatrail.org), 5415 SW 13th St, Gainesville 32608.

Loop (off FL 19), taking you through the scrub down to beautiful Salt Spring. Four of the national forest recreation areas (see *Recreation Areas*) also have don't-miss hiking and nature trails. The Florida Trail Association maintains a 7.7-mile loop trail, the **St. Francis Hiking Trail**, through the Alexander Springs Wilderness. Access is from FL 42 just west of FL 44 at River Forest Campground. For more hikes in this bountiful wilderness region, see *50 Hikes in North Florida* and *50 Hikes in Central Florida*.

HUNTING The Ocala National Forest remains one of Florida's most popular hunting grounds during deer hunting season in fall and turkey hunting season in spring. For information on hunting seasons and regulations, check the Florida Fish and Wildlife Conservation Commission web site at www.floridaconservation.org. Several times a year, the commission offers classes to introduce ladies to activities in the great outdoors at their Hunter Education Training Center on Lake Eaton. Dubbed Becoming an Outdoors Woman, the program presents such diverse offerings as archery, backpacking, birding, and fly-fishing; call 561-625-5126 for details, or visit the web site.

PADDLING **Juniper Run** is one of Florida's most beautiful waterways, winding nearly 6 miles through the scenic Juniper Prairie Wilderness with a single takeout rest stop along the way. Rent a canoe at the concession at Juniper Springs Recreation Area (see *Green Space*) and they'll pick you up at the end of the trip. The concessionaire at Alexander Springs Recreation Area is similarly accommodating, and the spring run is very different: Where Juniper Run is mostly a shallow, narrow, winding channel canopied by overhanging trees, **Alexander Run** is a broad, slow-moving, and deep waterway with islands creating side channels. At

Silver Glen Springs Recreation Area (see *Green Space*), rent canoes or kayaks for an out-and-back paddle down crystalline **Silver Glen Run** to **Lake George**; Salt Springs Recreation Area (see *Green Space*) provides rentals for you to paddle **Salt Springs Run**, retracing the route of William Bartram as he explored this wilderness channel flowing into Lake George; also check in at Salt Springs Run Marina (see *Boating*) for rentals. Canoe and kayak rentals at Colby Woods RV Resort (see *Campgrounds*), $20–25, allow you to put in along the wild and scenic **Ocklawaha River**, with easy access to the **Silver River** upstream, as do those at Ocklawaha Canoe Outpost & Resort (see *Cabins*), where they not only rent canoes and kayaks, but also lead guided trips from 8 miles to overnight. You'll also find several public put-ins where you can launch your own craft for free, including the hidden treasure of **Redwater Lake Scenic Site** (off FL 40, Lynne) and the **Upper Ocklawaha River** at the FL 19 bridge.

SCENIC DRIVES **FL 19** provides an excellent scenic drive through the Ocala National Forest, but if you really want to immerse in the Big Scrub, take **FR 88** (one of the few paved forest roads) from **FL 40** to **FL 314**. If you have four-wheel drive, there are hundreds of sand and clay forest roads to get yourself lost on.

SWIMMING Swimmers can enjoy a dip in several major springs, including **Alexander Springs**, **Juniper Springs**, **Salt Springs**, and **Silver Glen Springs** (see *Recreation Areas*). Bring your snorkeling gear, as the water at all of the springs is crystal clear and shimmering with fish; water temperatures hover around 72 degrees year-round. For a sandy beach on a large lake, stop at **Mill Dam Recreational Area** along FL 40; this day-use picnic and swimming facility is a CCC camp from the 1930s.

TRAIL RIDING **Rocking Horse Stables** (352-669-9982), 44200 FL 19, Altoona, offers trail riding into the southern portion of the Ocala National Forest, and accepts overnight campers with horses, as does **Fiddler's Green Ranch** (see *Working Ranch*), where you can take riding lessons ($35 hour; multilesson packages available), or enjoy a 2-hour ($40) or full-day ($75, includes lunch) trail ride.

Bringing your own horse? Try the trail systems at **Sunnyhill Restoration**

OAK SCRUB SHADES THE FOOTPATH THROUGH PAT'S ISLAND.

Sandra Friend

Area and the **Ocklawaha Prairie Restoration Area** (see *Restoration Areas*) along the southern edge of the Forest at Moss Bluff. For serious outings, the **Ocala One Hundred Mile Horse Trail** loops through the Big Scrub, with a trailhead at Swim Pond on FR 573. Stop by a visitors center (see *Guidance*) for a map of the route, which is still under construction. A 34-mile loop is now complete.

✷ Green Space

GREENWAYS **The Marjorie Harris Carr Cross Florida Greenway** is a 110-mile corridor from the St. Johns River to the Gulf of Mexico, encompassing Rodman Reservoir at the north end of the Forest. For maps and information, contact the Office of Greenways and Trails Ocala Field Office (352-236-7143), 8282 SE CR 314; there is a visitors center at the Buckman Lock off FL 19, open daily. Free.

RECREATION AREAS On CR 445A, **Alexander Springs Recreation Area** borders Alexander Spring and Alexander Run, where archeological evidence of Timucua culture dating to A.D. 1000 has been uncovered. Rent a canoe and float down the run, or take a swim in the chilly clear waters. A blue-blazed trail leads to the Florida Trail, while a short nature trail leads you through hammocks near the spring. Fee.

Off FL 42 in Paisley, **Clearwater Lake Recreation Area** is the gateway to the Paisley Woods Bicycle Trail (see *Bicycling*) and the Florida Trail (see *Hiking*), and offers fishing and canoeing.

Along CR 314, **Fore Lake Recreation Area** on Fore Lake offers swimming, fishing, and a pleasant picnic area. Fee.

One of the Forest's most popular destinations is **Juniper Springs Recreation Area** along FL 40 near FL 19. Developed in the 1930s, it centers on Juniper Springs (where you'll see eels shimmering in the depths) and Fern Hammock Spring, where sands dance in aquamarine shimmers beneath the glassy surface. The paddling trip down Juniper Run is one of the best in the state. Access the Florida Trail through the Juniper Prairie Wilderness from here. Fee.

If you're looking for a weekend's worth of outdoor activities to keep the whole family busy, head over to **Salt Springs Recreation Area** (1-877-444-6777; www.saltspringscampground.com), FL 19. Set up camp under the moss-draped oaks and take off in every direction: Explore the little-known Bear Swamp Trail with its giant cypresses, head out fishing on Salt Springs Run, rent a canoe or kayak to paddle the pristine waters, or snorkel across crystalline Salt Spring.

Silver Glen Springs Recreation Area, FL 19, provides a place for swimming and snorkeling as well as picnicking, paddling, and wandering along the hiking trails that parallel Lake George. Fee.

Wildcat Lake Recreation Area along FL 40 near Astor Park has fishing and canoeing; the alligators are pretty thick in here, so you won't want to take a dip in the lake. Fee.

RESTORATION AREAS Managed by the St. Johns Water Management District, both **Ocklawaha Prairie Restoration Area** (entrance on CR 314A, Moss Bluff) and **Sunnyhill Restoration Area** (entrance on CR 42, Moss Bluff) provide large open areas in which the Ocklawaha River is being restored to its natural meanders through wetlands. Birding is superb along the riverside levees, which serve as multiuse trails for hikers, bikers, and equestrians.

Sandra Friend

JUNIPER SPRINGS MILL

SPRINGS Numerous crystal-clear springs bubble up in the Ocala National Forest, forming some of the state's most pristine spring runs: The major springs lie within recreation areas. All are open to swimming and paddlesports, but paddling is best at **Juniper Springs** and **Alexander Springs**; swimming, at **Silver Glen Springs** and **Salt Springs**. Don't miss spectacular **Fern Hammock Springs** at the end of the nature trail at Juniper Springs Recreation Area; you can't swim in it, but you'll be mesmerized by the variety of unusual spring vents, from liquid pools like turquoise paint to swirling underwater dust storms.

WILD PLACES Designated wilderness areas are places of beauty: No roads mar the wilderness experience for hikers, and wildlife abounds. Along the **Florida Trail**, you'll pass through the wilds of the **Alexander Springs Wilderness**, south of Alexander Springs, which showcases wet flatwoods and bayheads; in **Juniper Prairie Wilderness**, prepare to immerse in the Big Scrub of the Ocala National Forest, where you'll be surprised to see crystal-clear streams and ponds in one of Florida's driest environments. Both wilderness areas can also be paddled; Juniper Run is one of the best canoe trips in the state.

Caravelle Ranch Wildlife Management Area (352-732-1225), FL 19 near the Ocklawaha River, is primarily managed for hunting but also has a network of forest roads marked for hiking.

✵ Lodging

Lodging in the Ocala National Forest tends toward the rustic, as it caters to folks interested in outdoor recreation. Camping is the norm, although there are a few small family-run motels near Salt Springs and Astor and fish camps along the lakes. In Paisley, the **Country Inn Guest House** (386-736-4244), 24970 CR 42, caters to independent travelers in a hostel-like setting. Private bedrooms with shared dining and living space, $39–89; reservations recommended.

MOTEL

Astor 32102

Astor Bridge Marina (866-BD-POTTS; www.astorbridgemarina.com), 1575 W FL 40. Zipping past on the Astor Bridge, you'd assume this is just another nondescript fish camp. But Hall's Lodge, built in the 1940s, has undergone serious renovation under the care of new owners Dale Potts and Betsy Dunn. Although the exterior still has that 1940s feel, these units impress. Four are tidy but small motel rooms, sharing a waterfront porch for sitting or fishing, but the six "cottages" (essentially efficiency apartments) facing the St. Johns River showcase classy furnishings in spacious suites, $65–79; guests arriving by water have their slip fee included; guests bringing their boats enjoy boat ramp use. Encompassing 8 acres, the marina also includes a waterfront café (see *Dining Out*) and docks, a ship's store, gas pumps, and 68 wet slips with electric power and pump-out service.

WORKING RANCH

Altoona 32702

Bring your horse or borrow one of theirs at **Fiddler's Green** (1-800-94-RANCH; www.fiddlersgreenranch.com), 42725 W Altoona Rd, a working ranch focused on training mounted police. Owner Glenn Barnard oversees 2-week clinics for riding instruction, but daily guests are welcome to enjoy the spacious facilities, which include several multibedroom villas ($110–215), an efficiency ($80–115), and RV sites ($20); bring your horse or use of one theirs. Guests share a swimming pool, private lake, and tennis court, and can arrange for guided trail rides into the nearby Ocala National Forest. It's an enchanting place, deeply shaded by ancient live oaks, providing respite for equestrians and their steeds.

CABINS **Ocklawaha Canoe Outpost & Resort** (1-866-236-4606; www.outpostresort.com), 15260 NE 152nd Place, Fort McCoy 32134, is just off CR 314 along the wild and scenic Ocklawaha River, a perfect place to arrange a paddling trip (see *Paddling*). Their luxurious new log cabins ($79–119) sleep up to nine guests and boast kitchenette, cable TV, and a screened porch; guests enjoy a complimentary continental breakfast. Tent camping (with bathhouse) available; bring your gear or rent theirs.

♿ **Lake in the Forest Estates & RV Resort** (see *Campgrounds*). You can't imagine a more tranquil retreat, tucked under live oaks with a view of Half Moon Lake. The rental cabin (more planned for the future) feels like it dropped right out of the Appalachian Mountains—a roomy log retreat with screened porch, cozy sleeping loft, and full kitchen, fully wheelchair accessible; $59, sleeps seven.

Colby Woods RV Resort (see *Campgrounds*). These are full-blown log homes ($65–75), with a large living room set off by the cathedral ceiling and fireplace, full kitchen, and two bedrooms sleeping three to six people. Grill burgers outside on the patio, stroll to the pool and hot tub for a swim, or wander down to the Ocklawaha River and cast from the riverbank.

CAMPGROUNDS

Altoona

Ocala Forest Campground (352-669-3888), 26301 SE CR 42, Umatilla

32784, sits on the south border of the Forest, with a nice mix of wooded and sunny sites, concrete pads and pull-throughs, and tent spaces. A small marsh with a boardwalk gives the kids somewhere to drop in a line and wait for a catfish to nibble. Recreation room, swimming pool, and camp store; sites start at $16.

Astor 32102

Camp along the St. Johns River at **Parramores Campground** (1-800-516-2386; www.parramores.com), 1675 S Moon Rd. Offering one- to four-bedroom cabins, some on the water; tent sites and full hookups.

Lynne

Ben's Hitching Post (352-625-4213), 2440 NE 115th Avenue, Silver Springs 34488. Located up a short stretch of dirt road, this is a pleasant, partially wooded campground with 56 full-hookup sites (some pull-through), a sparkling pool, heated spa, and clubhouse. RV $16, tents $14.

Whispering Pines RV Park (352-625-1295), 1700 NE 115th Avenue, Silver Springs 34488. At the south end of the same sometimes-bumpy dirt road, another pleasant choice set under the semishade of tall pines; ring the giant cowbell at the office for service! Fifty-six full hookups (some pull-through), large campsites, recreation hall, two bathhouses, on-site coin laundry, picnic tables at each site. $15.

Lake Waldena Resort (1-800-748-7898; www.lakewaldena.com), 13582 East FL 40, Silver Springs 34488. One of the larger campgrounds in the area: 104 sites, virtually all in the shade of beautiful old hardwood trees. Full hookups $16–18, includes use of swimming area, fishing and boat dock, and playground on Lake Waldena. The office also houses a camp store and recreation room.

Mill Dam

Lake in the Forest Estates & RV Resort (1-877-LIFES-OK; www.lakeintheforest.com), 19115 SE 44th St, Ocklawaha 32179. Set well off the beaten path off 183rd Ave Rd, this expansive campground shaded by grand live oaks slopes down to the edge of Half Moon Lake, with roomy spaces and full hookups. Pull-through spaces are in a sunny field. Each site has its own picnic table and fire ring; wheelchair-accessible rest rooms and showers in clubhouse. Rental boats for fishing or paddling. RV $18, tent $12.

Mill Dam Lake Resort (352-625-4500; www.milldamlake.com), 18975 E FL 40, Silver Springs 34488. An angler's delight—large campsites right on the edge of one of the larger lakes in the Ocala National Forest. Swim in the lake, or kick back in the screened pavilion; play shuffleboard, horseshoes, and other games, or pop in at the grocery store with deli on site. Partial hookups; dump station/shower fee $5. RV $16, tent $14. Lakefront park models ($49) sleep four.

Nuby's Corner

Colby Woods RV Resort (352-625-1122), 10313 E FL 40, Silver Springs 34488. Right on the Ocklawaha River, with canoe and kayak rentals available—your best private launch point for a trip up the Silver River. Full hookups, most spaces nicely shaded by pines, although the newer section is open and sunny. RV sites $19 May–Oct 1; $24 remainder of year; tents $15. Well-kept pool area with hot tub. The campground is undergoing some renovation; expect to see a second pool area and upgraded bathhouses. Great location, with easy access to Silver Springs and Ocala.

Salt Springs

Elite Resorts at Salt Springs (1-800-356-2460), US 19, Salt Springs 32134. Top-rated 70-acre camping resort with 465 paved full-hookup spaces, 40 furnished cottages, clubhouse, heated pool and spa, 18-hole mini golf, and many other amenities, including gated access and organized activities. Caters to snowbirds but accepts overnight guests; RV sites $29-plus, cottages $60–75.

USFS CAMPING Camping in the Ocala National Forest falls into three categories: developed (run by concessionaires), limited facility, and primitive. Individual sites at developed and limited-facility campgrounds are on a first-come, first-served basis. Fees vary. Primitive camping is allowed anywhere in the Forest (limit 2 weeks in one spot) for free, but campers must stay at designated campsites or established hunt camps during hunting season. These are a handful of the 26 campgrounds available; obtain *The Sunshine Connection* newsletter from a visitors center for the complete list with a map.

Developed campgrounds

Juniper Springs (352-625-3147), FL 40 west of FL 19, Silver Springs 34488. More than 70 shady trailer and tent sites, $15–17; hot showers, dump station, swimming area and canoe rental, camp store, access to Florida Trail and nature trails.

Salt Springs (352-685-2048; www.saltspringscampground.com), FL 19, Salt Springs 32134. Full-hookup sites in full shade ($20 paved, back-in) under beautiful moss-draped oaks and pines, separate primitive camping area ($14), recreation barn and hiking trail (see *Hiking*). Includes access to one of the best swimming holes (see *Swimming*) in the region. Reservations accepted (www.reserveusa.com).

Limited-facility campgrounds

Clearwater Lake, CR 42, Paisley. Forty-two campsites ($8) in two loops, flush toilets and warm showers, access to Florida Trail and Paisley Woods Bicycle Trail.

Fore Lake, CR 314A. Thirty-one lushly shaded sites ($8) with spaces up to 35 feet, no hookups. Access to lake with canoe put-in and fishing pier; pit toilets, no showers.

Grassy Pond, off FL 19 north of Salt Springs. Six sites, $5. Canoe launch.

Hopkins Prairie, FR 86, off FL 19 north of Silver Glen Springs. Twenty-one sites ($5) with a spectacular view across the prairie. Pitcher pump, pit toilets not always open. Boat ramp accesses some of the best bass fishing in the Forest.

Lake Delancy, N FR 75, off FL 19 north of Salt Springs. Fifty-nine sites in two campgrounds around the lake, $5. Pit toilets, no showers.

Lake Dorr, FL 19 north of Pittman. Thirty-four secluded sites hidden in the palmettos, $5. Warm showers, rest rooms. Boating and fishing on the lake.

Lake Eaton, CR 314. Fourteen sites, $6–8. Fishing pier and boat ramp on Lake Eaton. No showers or dump station.

Designated primitive campsites

During hunting season, primitive

campers can pitch a tent only at the 23 designated primitive campsites in the Forest, including **Little Lake Bryant**, **Clay Lake**, **Echo Pond**, and **Trout Lake**; pick up a locator map at a visitors center (see *Guidance*).

FISH CAMP

Umatilla 32784
Nelson's Fish Camp and Riverfront RV Park (352-821-FISH), 19400 FL 42. Right on the Ocklawaha River at FL 42, this old-fashioned fish camp dates back to the 1950s and has fabulous access to Lake Griffin and the wild marshes along the river heading north. Nelson's Store serves up its famous pork BBQ sandwiches, sells fishing tackle and bait, and even has venison and alligator in-season. Rustic cabins come with fully equipped kitchens and fresh linens, $45–72; many have river views. Full-hookup RV sites and campsites with electric and water are $19; tent sites, $15. Boat rentals and boat slips available.

✷ Where to Eat

DINING OUT

Astor
Stop in the **Galley Café** at the Astor Bridge Marina (see *Motels*) for mouthwatering pastries, or settle down for a gourmet breakfast ($2–4) with a view of the St. Johns River. Lunches and dinners include Key West–inspired fare like Tortuga kebabs and Jack Daniels steak, $5–13; menu changes weekly. Closed Mon.

Blackwater Inn Restaurant & Lounge (1-888-533-3422), 55716 Front St. Fine dining on the St. Johns River; tie up at the dock and enjoy fresh seafood entrées including rainbow trout, crab legs, frog legs, deviled crabs, and Canadian sea scallops as well as massive fried and broiled seafood platters. Opens 4:30 Tue–Fri, noon Sat–Sun; closed Mon. **William's Landing**, atop the Blackwater Inn, opens at 11:30, serving lunch and dinner in a more casual setting with the same riverfront view.

EATING OUT

Astor
Astor Mule (352-759-2854), E FL 40. This family restaurant serves up a speedy breakfast ($1 and up) "til we run out," with goodies like cream chip beef, corned beef hash, three-egg omelets with all the trimmings, and cinnamon toast. Pancakes come out so light and airy, you hardly need a dash of syrup to enjoy them. Lunch includes 12 types of burgers (starting at $3), sandwiches ($1–5), and "Salty Dawg" seafood plates ($6–10). Open for dinner Fri and Sat. Don't forget the dessert—either from the walk-up ice cream window or at your table with a slice of Mama's homemade pie ($2).

Forest Corners
The Chatterbox Café (352-625-4288), 16460 E FL 40. "We've got the best cook in the Forest," said my waitress, and I'll believe her. I've never had French toast this good: melt-in-your-mouth, with a touch of cream and cinnamon in the mix. Don't miss this tiny family-run café: It may have only eight tables, but it's a gem! Breakfast $1–5; lunch $1–5, includes such goodies as grouper sandwiches; daily dinners run $6–8, with southern-fried chicken always available; desserts, $1–3, run the gamut from ice cream cones to banana fudge sundae and hot fudge cake. Check the board for today's

specials. Open daily 6 AM–10 PM; take-out window for ice cream, or eat in.

Jake's Place (352-625-3133), 16725 E FL 40. Barbecue is the claim to fame at Jake's, where they serve up chicken, baby back ribs, and tender sliced beef available to go for a picnic or right here at your seat. Chef's seafood specials on Fri nights include rainbow trout, sautéed scallops, red snapper, and flounder, to $13. Open daily 7 AM–8 PM.

Lake Kerr

The 88 Store BBQ and Smokehouse (352-685-9015; www.the88store.com), FR 88, south of FL 316. Small take-out featuring shrimp po'boys ($3.50), big burgers ($3.25), sweet Vidalia onion rings ($1.50), and heaping mounds of moist and tender barbecue (dinners with baked beans, coleslaw, and roll, $4–5; ribs $9 and up). Try the pulled pork sandwich ($2.50 or $3.50), and pull up a seat either inside or outside adjoining Store 88, a popular bar and package store with live music most Fri and Sat nights. Offers hot showers ($3) and tent space to hungry hikers pulling in off the nearby Florida National Scenic Trail. Open Wed–Sun 11 AM–8 PM. Cash only.

Moss Bluff

Duck's Dam Diner (352-288-8332), 9748 SE CR 464-C. One of my favorites, the Dam Diner is a hot spot for home cooking, pure and simple, and lots of it. I love the real 1950s diner atmosphere—no replica here—from the black-and-white-tiled floor to the lunch counter. Breakfast includes cheesesteak omelets, their famous biscuits and gravy, and French toast ($2–9); lunch runs the gamut from barbecue to salad, and dinner (served Fri 3–8) might be an all-you-can-eat fish fry one week, spaghetti the next. Open 6–2 daily.

Nuby's Corner

Chuck Wagon Diner (352-625-0100), on the grounds of Colby Woods RV Resort (see *Campgrounds*). Open to the public Sun–Thu 7–2, serving country home-cooked breakfast and lunch, $2–6.

Roger's Barbecue (352-625-2020), FL 40 and FL 314. Enjoy tasty barbecue in hefty servings at budget prices: sandwiches $2–3, basic dinner platters $3–6, combination barbecue dinners $5–8. Take-out available. Daily specials. Open weekdays 10:30–8:30, weekends 10:30–9. Cash only.

Paisley

Big Oak Italian Restaurant and Pizza (352-669-4296; www.bigoakitalianrestaurant.com), 24929 CR 42. Eat in and enjoy a pizza or lasagna in the spacious dining room, or take out a sandwich and head to nearby Clearwater Lake for a picnic in the Forest. Lunch and dinner $6–15; closed Sun.

Salt Springs

Lenore's Restaurant (352-685-0527), US 19, is a great lunch stop after a morning's hike or paddle. Salads $6; entrées include down-home favorites like meat loaf, ham steak, fried chicken, and country-fried steak, $5–8. Pizza, burgers, and subs, too! Open lunch and dinner, Tue–Sun.

✷ Entertainment

Live music can be found in many of the bars on weekends, at places like **Cactus Jack's** (352-685-2244), 23740 NE CR 314 in Salt Springs, where you might catch a rock band or live acoustic country. At **The 88 Store** (see *Eating Out*), catch live performers most Fri and Sat nights, strumming bluegrass or singing country tunes to an appreciative local audience.

✷ Selective Shopping

Lynne

Forest Trading Post Antiques & Collectibles (352-625-3831), 14399 E FL 40. It's a place you must browse to believe: Step across the threshold and enter another world, where soft classical music drifts through the room as you ponder chain saw art, a one-of-a-kind bear bench, and intricate wooden puzzles as well as art glass, brass decor items, and pottery. Featuring not just neatly displayed antiques but also an excellent selection of original art and crafts from local artisans, the Forest Trading Post is a must-stop shop along FL 40. Open Tue–Sat 10–5.

Paisley

Miss Grace's Emporium (352-669-6989), 24959 CR 42. Housed in Paisley's original post office, this little gift shop features country crafts and collectibles and the local historical museum (see *Museums*); in the back you'll find **Paisley's Bait and Tackle**.

Salt Springs

Linda's House of Dolls (352-685-8600), 24330 CR 314. After miles of greenery, the bright pink house along CR 314 catches your eye well before the sign. Inside, proprietor Linda handcrafts dolls of all sizes from porcelain and fabric. During business hours, she offers free instruction in her workshop on making your own porcelain dolls; pick out the materials you want to use to paint and fire your own creations, or choose one of Linda's darlings off the shelf. Open Tue–Sat 9–5.

✷ Special Events

May: **Native American Spring Gathering** (352-625-2764), Orange Springs. Each spring, Native Americans from around the nation come together in celebration at a site near the Ocala National Forest; 2003 marked their 20th year. Open to outsiders, the powwow features tribal dancing, food, and crafts. Usually held at the Chambers Farm.

October: **Salt Springs Festival** (352-685-2954), in its 15th year, features music, arts, and crafts in the middle of the Ocala National Forest . . . and don't forget the barbecue! First Sat.

Atlantic Coast

THE SPACE COAST

DAYTONA & THE BEACHES

THE FIRST COAST

JACKSONVILLE

ST. JOHNS RIVER

Kennedy Space Center

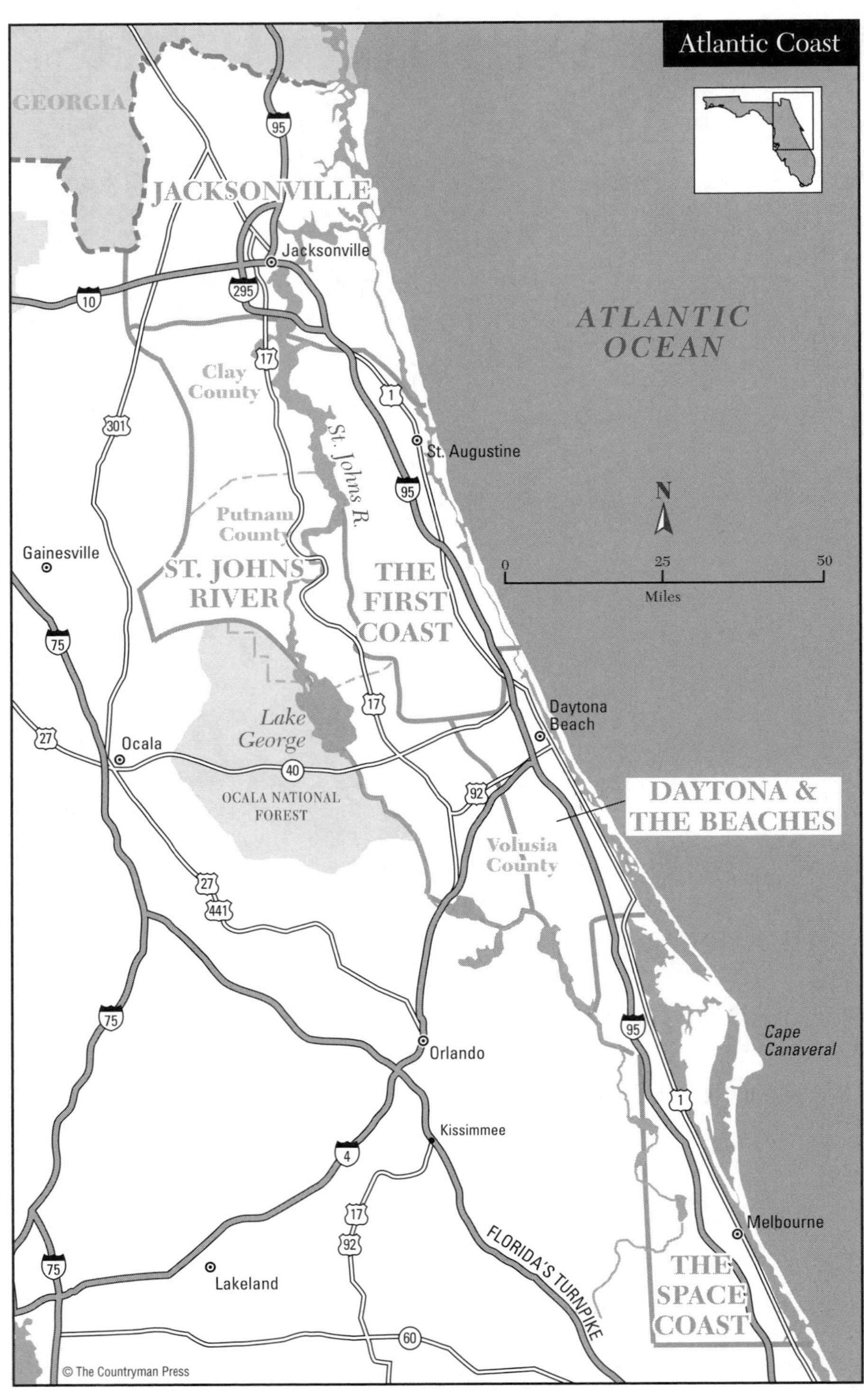
Atlantic Coast
GEORGIA
JACKSONVILLE
Jacksonville
ATLANTIC
OCEAN
Clay
County
St. Johns R.
St. Augustine
N
0
25
50
Miles
Putnam
County
Gainesville
ST. JOHNS
RIVER
THE
FIRST
COAST
Daytona
Beach
Lake
George
Ocala
OCALA NATIONAL
FOREST
DAYTONA &
THE BEACHES
Volusia
County
Cape
Canaveral
Orlando
Kissimmee
Melbourne
FLORIDA'S TURNPIKE
Lakeland
THE
SPACE
COAST
© The Countryman Press

THE SPACE COAST

CAPE CANAVERAL, COCOA, COCOA BEACH, INDIALANTIC, INDIAN HARBOR BEACH, MALABAR, MELBOURNE, MELBOURNE BEACH, MIMS, PALM BAY, PORT CANAVERAL, SATELLITE BEACH, TITUSVILLE, AND VALKARIA

Brevard County once stretched several hundred miles—all the way to the Dade county border. Cut back to its current geography in 1905, it's still quite a long county, stretching 75 miles along the Atlantic Coast and Indian River. The history of the area dates back more than 8,000 years, with several ancient middens and one of the best-preserved aboriginal sites in Florida, discovered in 1982.

The Ais Indians were a distinct tribe from their northern Timucua neighbors, and primarily inhabited the Indian River and Cape Canaveral areas. It is said that Ponce de León first encountered the Ais between 1513 and 1565 at a small village just south of Cape Canaveral. For nearly 200 years, the area was under Spanish rule, but because the land did not contain precious metals and lacked fertile soil for agriculture, the Ais remained largely unaffected. By the time the Spanish left in 1763, however, the Ais population was decimated beyond recovery by disease and warfare brought by the European settlers. It wasn't until the land boom of the 1920s that progress and development were brought to the seaside area, and in 1949 Brevard County launched into the space program at Cape Canaveral, one of the world's few quadruple-mode ports—sea, land, air, and space.

GUIDANCE **Cocoa Beach Area Chamber of Commerce** (321-459-2200; www.cocoabeachchamber.com), 400 Fortenberry Rd, Merritt Island 32952.

Cocoa Beach Tourist Information Center (321-784-3223), 3670 N Atlantic Ave, Cocoa Beach 32931.

Cocoa Village Tourism Association (321-433-0362), 216 Florida Ave, Cocoa Village 32922.

Melbourne–Palm Bay Area Chamber of Commerce (321-724-5400; www.melpb-chamber.org), 1005 E Strawbridge Ave, Melbourne 32901.

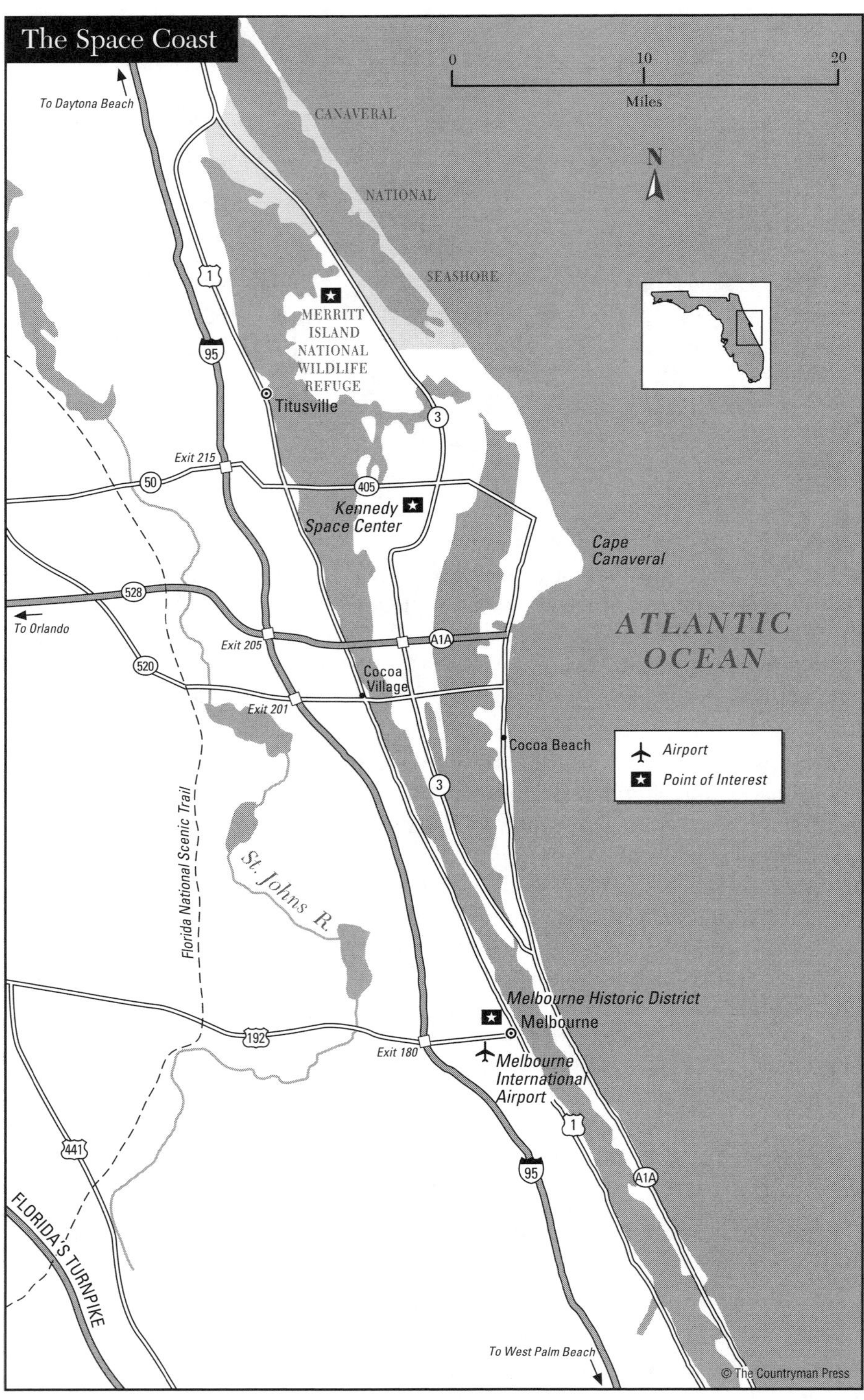
The Space Coast
0
10
20
Miles
N
To Daytona Beach
CANAVERAL
NATIONAL
SEASHORE
MERRITT ISLAND NATIONAL WILDLIFE REFUGE
Titusville
Exit 215
Kennedy Space Center
Cape Canaveral
To Orlando
Exit 205
Cocoa Village
Exit 201
ATLANTIC OCEAN
Cocoa Beach
Airport
Point of Interest
Florida National Scenic Trail
St. Johns R.
Melbourne Historic District
Melbourne
Exit 180
Melbourne International Airport
FLORIDA'S TURNPIKE
To West Palm Beach
© The Countryman Press

Space Coast Office of Tourism (321-868-1126 or 1-877-57-BEACH; www.space-coast.com), 8810 Astronaut Blvd, Suite 102, Cape Canaveral 32920.

Voyager Channel-Info Station (321-255-9670; www.voyagerchannel.com), 3270 Suntree Blvd, Suite 119, Melbourne 32940.

GETTING THERE *By air*: Only an hour from **Orlando International Airport** via FL 528 ("The Beeline"), Melbourne is also served by **Melbourne International Airport** (321-723-6227; www.mlbair.com).

By bus: **Greyhound** rumbles down US 1 with stops in Titusville (321-267-8760), Cocoa Beach (321-636-6531), and Melbourne (321-723-4323), as well as a terminal conveniently located at the Melbourne International Airport.

By car: From I-95, head east on **FL 520** or **FL 528**.

GETTING AROUND *By bus and beach trolley*: **Space Coast Area Transit** (SCAT; 321-633-1878; www.ridescat.com). Buses run Mon–Fri 6 AM–6:45 PM from Mims to Micco. Weekend service is available in some areas. The beach trolley runs Mon–Sat 7 AM–9 PM, Sun 8–5, from Port Canaveral to 13th St in Cocoa Beach. $1 full fare, 50¢ half fare (seniors, handicapped, and students). The I-4–FL 520 Connector takes you from the beach (FL A1A) along FL 520 over to Cocoa Village. There's no extra charge for transfers or for bikes and surfboards. Unlimited monthly passes $28.

By taxi: Melbourne (321-676-3100); Titusville (321-267-7061); Cocoa Beach (321-720-4342).

PUBLIC REST ROOMS All major parks have public rest rooms, but there are no rest rooms at crossovers.

LIFEGUARD STATIONS Stations are staffed at public parks Memorial Day–Labor Day only. Jetty Park (see *Parks*) has a lifeguard on watch year-round.

LAUNCH REPORTS NASA launches are listed on a recorded phone message (321-867-4636). For more information, go to www.kennedyspacecenter.com or www.ksc.nasa.gov.

SURF REPORTS Call ahead to check surf conditions and tides. For a live voice, call Cocoa Beach Surf Company (321-783-1530) or any of these recorded surf lines:

Cocoa Beach: **Natural Art Surf Report** (321-784-2400); **Ron Jon Surf Report** (321-799-8888, ext 3, then press 7).

Indialantic: **Groove Tube Surf's Up Line** (321-723-3879); **Spectrum Surf Shop** (321-725-5905).

MEDICAL EMERGENCIES **Cape Canaveral Hospital** (321-799-7111); **Health First, Inc.** (321-868-8313), Cocoa Beach; **Health First, Inc., Holmes Regional Center** (321-434-7000) and **Wuesthoff Medical Center** (321-752-1200),

Melbourne; **Health First, Inc., Palm Bay Community Hospital** (321-434-8000), Palm Bay; **Parrish Medical Center** (321-268-6111), Titusville.

✷ To See

ART GALLERIES

Melbourne

Walk through seven galleries at the **Brevard Museum of Art & Science** (321-242-0737), 1463 Highland Ave, which features ever-changing exhibits of internationally and nationally recognized artists. The **Children's Science Center** allows kids to touch, feel, and discover through hands-on exhibits. Fee.

Creative art exhibits and premier productions are found at the **Henegar Center for the Arts** (321-723-8698), 625 E New Haven Ave. Located in the heart of Historic Downtown Melbourne, it is also listed on the National Register of Historic Places.

Kennedy Space Center

Can you believe scientists have been mixing it up with artists? Left brain–right brain? Well, believe it! For more than 35 years, NASA has documented major events through its commissioned arts program. The gallery at **Kennedy Space Center Space Shuttle Collection** showcases an outstanding collection of traditional and modern art. Paintings by renowned artists, such as James Wyeth and Robert Rauschenberg, capture the emotion felt during a shuttle launch or while piloting a lunar module, and are immortalized in various styles and media from very realistic to abstract images and impressions.

CRUISE-SHIP-WATCHING Head out to Port Canaveral to watch cruise ships and pleasure boats set sail from the second largest cruise port in the world. See *Cruising*.

DINOSAURS **The Dinosaur Store** (407-783-7300; www.dinosaurstore.com), 299 W Cocoa Beach Causeway (FL 520), Cocoa Beach. I couldn't decide whether this was a store or a museum! What you'll find here is a fabulous collection of rare museum-quality fossils and minerals, amber, meteorites, dinosaur eggs, nests, and skeletons (many from right here in Florida). Several items are often on loan to museums. Knowledgeable owners Steve and Donna are real dino hunters and would be happy to discuss their various archeological expeditions. From serious to novice collectors, everyone has the opportunity to take home a historical treasure, priced from a few dollars to several thousand. Open daily except Sun.

HISTORIC SITES The 1848 **Cape Canaveral Lighthouse** stands 160 feet tall and has been automated since 1967. The U.S. Air Force is the current keeper and on rare occasions will open it for special groups like the Florida Lighthouse Association (www.floridalighthouses.org). It can be viewed from Canaveral Harbor Rd or looking southward from the beach at Cocoa Beach.

Originally built in 1962, the **Cocoa Beach Pier,** which stretches out 800 feet over the Atlantic Ocean, is where cars used to drive along its boardwalk planks and park at the end. Now a gathering spot of restaurants and shops, the pier is the social hub of the college crowd during spring break.

The small **Grant Historical House** (321-723-8543), 5795 US 1, Grant (circa 1916), shows the spirit of Florida's pioneers.

Several **middens** (ancient Indian garbage dumps) are located in the vicinity of Rockledge. **Persimmons Mound** is on the east bank of a former channel of the St. Johns about 10 miles from Rockledge. Standing a little over 4 feet, the 165-by-100-foot mound is said to date back to 4000 B.C.

The 1905 **Nannie Lee House**, 1218 E New Haven Ave, Melbourne, was often the center for social events and still is, as the fine-dining restaurant called Strawberry Mansion (see *Dining Out*).

Old Haulover Canal, on the north side of Merritt Island, is so named because Indians and traders actually had to portage (or haul) their canoes over a narrow strip of land at the current location of the 725-foot canal, dug in 1843. Great spot for kayaking and manatee viewing.

Porcher House (321-639-3500), 434 Delannoy Ave in the heart of Cocoa Village Historic District, was built by E. P. Porcher, a pioneer citrus grower and founder of Deerfield Citrus Groves. The beautifully restored, elegant 1916 mansion is an excellent example of Classical Revival adapted for the Florida environment. The semicircular portico with four fluted Ionic columns is absolutely breathtaking.

Step back in time to 1885 at **Travis Hardware** in Cocoa Village. The oldest business from Jacksonville to Key West, this shop has been operated by the Travis family since 1897. As a kid, I remember going to the hardware store with my dad. This place retains much of the same charm with its bins of nails and nuts, now placed next to modern electrical tools.

MUSEUMS

Cocoa

Brevard Museum of History & Natural Science (321-632-1830; www.brevardmuseum.com), 2201 Michigan Ave. Learn about the early inhabitants of Brevard County through hands-on activities and exhibits. Step into the archeological field and uncover fossils and artifacts. Then take a stroll in the 22-acre nature preserve. Open Tue–Sat 10–4, Sun 1–4. Fee.

Melbourne

The **Liberty Bell Memorial Museum** (321-727-1776), 601 Oak St, displays a full-sized replica of the famed bell along with 300 years of historical artifacts. Open Mon–Fri 10–4, Sat 10–2. Free.

Titusville

The **Policeman Hall of Fame** (321-264-0911; www.aphf.org), 6350 Horizon Dr, is the nation's first museum honoring all police—federal, state, county, and local departments. The solid marble wall memorializes over 60,000 officers who fell in the line of duty. See an electric chair, gas chamber, and the original police vehicle from the movie *Blade Runner*, along with more than 10,000 pieces of historical memorabilia. Have your photo taken in a real jail cell. The interactive and hands-on exhibits allow you to enter the world of forensics and test your detective skills, and the new indoor pistol range is now open to the public. Open daily. $12 adults; $8 ages 4–12, military, and senior citizens. Admission is free to law enforcement officers and survivors' families.

Vallant Air Command (321-268-1941), 6600 Tico Rd. World War II memorabilia and vintage warplanes are on display. See a T-28, Mig-17D, F-14A Tomcat, VAC Flagship Douglas C-47A, and more. Part of the Pastport Flight of Four. Open daily 10–6; $9 adults, $8 seniors and military, $5 children.

SAILING **Schooner Sails** (321-783-5274; www.schoonersails.com), Miss Cape Canaveral Dock, 670 Glenn Cheek Dr, Port Canaveral. Slipping silently among the monstrous cruise ships is the elegant tall ship the *Wanderer*. This 1903 replica of a Grand Banks fishing vessel has eight sails and impressive 60-foot double masts. Fitted in the finest hardwoods, the deck is solid mahogany with oak railings resting on hand-turned oak posts. Skilled seaman Captain Ken takes the elegant lady out to sea for gentle breezy Sunset Cruises: $30.

SPACE EXPLORATION Dedicated to the first 44 American astronauts, the **Astronaut Hall of Fame** (321-269-6101), 6225 Vectorspace Blvd, Titusville, lets you experience hands-on astronaut training. Suit up and get ready to blast off; you'll also enjoy exploring actual space capsules and viewing astronaut artifacts in this interactive exhibit, home of **U.S. Space Camp** Florida. Open daily. $14 adults, $10 children. Several money-saving combo packages with the Kennedy Space Center are available.

Kennedy Space Center Visitor Complex (321-449-4444; www.kennedyspacecenter.com), off FL 405. Walk through a full-sized replica of the Explorer shuttle, touch a real Mars rock, see *The Dream Is Alive* and the new *Space Station 3D* at the IMAX theater, take a stroll among giants in the Rocket Garden, then meet and talk with a real astronaut at the Astronaut Encounter. You'll also want to purchase the NASA Up Close guided tour, which will take you out past the Vehicle Assembly Building (VAB) to the launch pads for a breathtaking view of the island, and also includes admission to the **Astronaut Hall of Fame**. The VAB is one of the world's largest buildings in cubic volume, having as much interior space as nearly four Empire State Buildings and cov-

LAUNCH PAD AT THE KENNEDY SPACE CENTER
Kathy Wolf

ering more ground area than six football fields. It's so large, in fact, that the micro atmosphere inside is closely watched—it has actually *rained* inside the building. The KSC is also a successful National Wildlife Preserve managed by the Department of the Interior. It has over 220 miles of waterways, marshes, and beaches with more than 500 species, many of which will be pointed out to you on the guided tour. If you don't take the add-on tour, then check out the informative Nature Exhibit showcasing various Florida wildlife species. Art enthusiasts will also want to check out the Space Shuttle Collection (see *Art Galleries*). The best time to visit KSC is on the weekends when the 70,000-plus employees are off and the roads are not as congested. Maximum Access admission (includes Astronaut Hall of Fame and interactive space flight simulators) $35 adults, $25 ages 3–11. Standard admission $29/19. Combo pass (includes Maximum Access and NASA Up Close guided tour) $53/37. Add-ons: Lunch with an astronaut $20/13; the new Astronaut Training Experience costs $225 for those 14 and older.

MEMORIALS Honoring the men and women of the space program, **Space View Park**, 219 Indian River Ave, Titusville, is a popular launch-viewing area. The Mercury Monument is the centerpiece, with Gemini and Apollo Monuments as recent additions.

The **U.S. Space Walk of Fame Museum** (321-264-0434; www.spacewalkof fame.com), US 1, Titusville in the Miracle City Mall, offers a unique collection of space artifacts.

✷ To Do

AIRBOATS **Grasshopper Airboat Ecotours** (321-631-2990; www.airboat ecotours.com), FL 520 at the St. Johns River (4.5 miles west of I-95 on FL 520), Cocoa. USCG captain Rick Thrift takes you on a journey through the grassy marshes of the St. Johns River in his 60 -to-90-minute ecotour. Small groups (less than 12 people) learn about the history of the river and its wildlife inhabitants through the eyes and mind of Rick, who comes with a botany and zoology background. You'll not only see alligators and eagles, but also learn about them and their habitats. Elevated seats and complimentary binoculars make sure you don't miss a thing. This is the "limo" airboat ride, not the "taxi" version. Rick provides for your comfort with beverages and blankets when it's chilly. But for those who want a little thrill, you'll still get the adventure of an airboat without hanging on to your heart. Seasons dictate what time the boat goes out for best wildlife viewing and guest comfort, so call ahead for times. $28 adults, $18 children. For a more thrilling ride, take a tour on Rick's six-passenger boat where he'll make the airboat do 360-degree turns. Six passengers; $250.

Twister Airboats at Lone Cabbage Fish Camp (321-632-4199; www .twisterairboatrides.com), FL 520 at St. Johns River, Cocoa. This twisting, turning thrill ride will have you hanging on to your hat in these large watercraft. Round a turn to surprise an alligator, pass cattle in the field, and watch the grassy marshes carefully, as you just might see the bleached white skeleton of an

ZOOLOGICAL PARK The **Brevard Zoo** (321-254-9453; www.brevardzoo.org), 8225 N Wickham Rd, Melbourne, is unlike any zoo I have ever been to. Recently celebrating its 10th anniversary, this small community zoo has grown under the support of local residents and currently hosts more than 460 animals from Latin America, Australia, native Florida, and the newest addition, Expedition Africa, where you can pet and feed the giraffes Raffiki, Doc, and Duncan and watch rhinos Howard and Max from the observation deck. Among my favorite animals in the zoo are the rare and endangered breeding pair of native red wolves. Over the past decade several attempts have been made to reintroduce the red wolf into the wild, with one key location on a secluded island in Florida. From only 14 animals in 1977 to nearly 300 in 2004 (of which 220 are still in captivity), the red wolf is just beginning to see a comeback. Brevard Zoo is one of a handful of zoos working with the American Zoological Association and Species Survival Plan to increase their numbers and reintroduce them into their natural habitat.

The zoo also hosts a unique educational project. Each semester local fifth-grade students attend the Zoo School, where they spend their day on site learning about science and nature. I wish I had gone to school in classrooms like the Tree House (which sits high in the sky), or the Cave (which features stalactites and stalagmites and walls embedded with fossils), or the Swamp House (which sits atop a pond where students learn about wetland ecosystems). These classrooms are only the beginning, as this exciting zoo has just started to plan a new Education Complex, which will eventually open access to other residents and tourists.

The innovative Brevard Zoo is also the only zoo that kayaks! Paddle through the Florida Wetlands Outpost and learn about the "breakfast nook," where your guide tells you how to make pancakes and hash browns from native plants. Go on a journey through Expedition Africa, where you paddle past rhinos, giraffes, cotton-top tamarins, and gazelles on the African plains. Then pull your kayaks up on a sandy beach and climb the lookout tower to pet and feed the friendly giraffes as these gentle giants bat their long eye-

alligator that lost the battle for his territory. A 90-minute tour runs $50 adults, $25 ages 12 and under; 60 minutes costs $35/18; 30 minutes is $17/9.

ART CLASSES Carolyn Seiler's **Boatyard Studio** (321-637-0444), 118 Harrison St, Cocoa Village, offers drop-in drawing and painting classes for kids and adults. Get rid of some stress and open your creative spirit. Call for drop-in times and projects. A 1-hour class is $10.

Take a few hours for creativity and learn how to make beautiful beaded jewelry and accessories at **Tatanka Beads** (321-636-4104; www.tatankabeads.com), 121

KAYAKING THROUGH THE BREVARD ZOO

Kathy Wolf

lashes, begging for your affection. Go beyond the park and take a 4-hour kayak ecotour into the natural areas of Merritt Island with an expert naturalist. The Wild Side tour gets you up close and personal with Sinda the panther, anteaters, gray foxes, aviary birds, flying fox fruit bats, and more. The history of the zoo and its animals is also explained in this once-a-day limited tour. The zoo is open daily 10–5, with last entrance at 4:15. Regular admission $9 adults, $8 seniors over 60, $6 ages 2–12. Add-ons: the Wetlands Outpost ($3) or Expedition African ($3) 20-minute kayak tours, and the 1-hour Wild Side tour ($10). Call for prices on the Merritt Island excursion.

Harrison St, Cocoa Village. From a simple beaded pin to a Fairy Garden Bracelet, you'll learn how to master beautiful pieces using real glass beads in this quality art class.

AVIATION **Flying Boat** (321-689-0066; www.flyingboatadventures.com). When I found out that there was yet another craft that would take me in the air, I had to try it. Not your typical "air" boat, this ultralight aircraft really leaves the water. The two-seat trainer actually lifts off and flies several feet above the lagoon for an exhilarating one-of-a-kind adventure! The Introductory Flight ($40) gets you up for 20 minutes. Or take the First Class Flight ($100), where you'll learn how and then fly the boat for a full hour, get it all captured on a video, and receive a certificate of flight plus a really neat T-shirt.

BIRDING With over 330 species of birds in the Space Coast region, you'll want to take along a knowledgeable guide. **Birding & Photography Guide Services** (321-383-3088; www.cfbw.com), CFBW Enterprises, Inc., Titusville, offers half- and full-day guided tours through several diverse ecosystems such as wetlands, highlands, pinelands, grass plains, and scrubs. You'll see species from songbirds to raptors while exploring in small groups.

CRUISING Port Canaveral, the second largest port in the world, docks some amazing cruise ships, like **Carnival Cruise Line** (1-800-839-6955; www.carnival.com) and **Disney Cruise Line** (1-800-511-1333; www.disneycruise.com). Board partial-day gaming cruises with **Port Canaveral** (321-783-7831; www.portcanaveral.org) and **Sterling Casino Lines** (1-800-765-5711; www.sterlingcasino.com), which provides you free passage with a complimentary buffet and live Vegas entertainment. Watch these glamorous vessels set sail from Jetty Park (see *Parks*) or several restaurants along Port Canaveral.

ECOTOURS **Grasshopper Airboat Ecotours** (321-631-2990; www.airboatecotours.com). See *Airboats*.

Island Boat Lines Water Taxi and EcoTours (321-794-7717 or 1-800-484-7804; www.islandboatlines.com), 725 Acorn St, Merritt Island, Indian River Lagoon. Former Miss Florida Penny Flaherty is now known as Penny-the-Boat-Lady. Her 28- and 55-passenger pontoon boats (brightly decorated with Miss Florida colors of cherry red, lemon yellow, apple green, and orchid purple) have been sailing the Indian River Lagoon since 2002. Captain John Tweety, a retired school principal, skillfully guides a pontoon boat through an endangered manatee sanctuary while Brad Martin, an eco major, tells you about the Thousand Islands as manatees graze on the Serengeti of the sea. You'll graze, too, on free chips and salsa, nuts, and fresh fruit as you pass stately homes, Indian shell mounds, and hundreds of islands in the tidal delta. Beer and soft drinks are also available for purchase. This boat tour will satisfy everyone in your party with wildlife off the port and "wild life" off the stern. $19 for a 2-hour ecotour. Penny's new addition is the ***Indian River Queen*** paddleboat. Debuting in the 2003 movie *Out of Time* with Denzel Washington, it features a historical photo gallery and crew dressed in period costumes.

Space Coast Nature Tours (321-267-4551; www.spacecoastnaturetours.com). All tours depart from Titusville Municipal Marina (North End) at the Indian River Lagoon. This true ecotour operates from a solar-powered pontoon boat with propeller guards, uses recycled paper and soy-based ink in their marketing materials, and recycles all trash. Captain Ron takes you on a narrated journey. A variety of turtles, stingrays, and the smaller Indian River Lagoon dolphins will play off the side of the boat, while manatees approach with curiosity. Listen to fish, dolphins, and snapping shrimp with the underwater hydrophone as you sail around this sensitive and rare environment. The islands around the Mosquito Lagoon Sanctuary are a major breeding rookery where you'll see the neon plumage of double-crested cormorants, great blue herons, royal terns, roseate spoonbills, and more while eagles and ospreys soar overhead. You won't miss anything—they provide excellent binoculars for all, along with light beverages. And they'll even tuck you in with warm blankets when it gets breezy. Oh, and you'll find the "human viewing observation area" for manatees across from the pontoon landing and bridge. A 90-minute tour costs $14 adults, $13 ages 65 and older, $10 ages to 12. Day and night tours to all launches will take you as close to the launch site as the government will allow.

FAMILY ACTIVITIES ✐ Ride bumper boats, play miniature golf, or race go-carts at **Andretti Thrill Park** (321-956-6706; www.andrettithrillpark.com), 3960 S Babcock St, Melbourne.

✐ **TRAXX at Jungle Village** (407-783-0595), 8801 Astronaut Blvd, Cape Canaveral. Go-carts, batting cages, laser tag, miniature golf, and arcade games. Ninety-nine-cent mini golf for seniors on Wed. Open daily 10 AM–midnight.

FISHING

Off the jetty
Jetty Park Bait Shop (321-783-2771), 400 E Jetty Dr, Cape Canaveral. Fishing pole rentals and all the bait necessary to fish off the pier or from shore.

Charters
USCG-licensed **Captain Kelly Wiggins L/T Flats Fishing Charters** (321-269-4568 or 1-877-269-4568; www.ltflatsredfish.com), 1280 Old Dixie Hwy, Titusville, will take you fishing on the Indian River Estuary and Mosquito Lagoon for redfish, tarpon, sea trout, and snook. A full 8-hour day starts at $300, including lunch and drinks. Half-day and night rates available.

Go fly-fishing or use light tackle with **Strictly Business** (407-721-7889) as Captain Joey Aloe takes you around the Mosquito River Lagoon and Indian River Lagoon.

Sail out 20 to 40 miles offshore in a 28-foot Bertram with **Gettin' There II Sportfishing Charters** (321-784-2279; www.gettinthere.com), 201 International Dr #734, Cape Canaveral. The USCG-licensed captain and crew are great with both professionals and beginners.

Party boats
Miss Cape Canaveral (321-783-5274; www.misscape.com). This 85-foot boat takes up to 100 people for a lively day of great fishing for everyone. The daily special includes a hot breakfast, lunch, soda, coffee, beer, rod and reel, bait and tackle, and fishing license. $65 adults, $55 ages 11–17, $45 ages 6–10.

GOLF The **Habitat**, 3591 Fairgreen St, Valkaria, is an 18-hole, par-72 course in a completely natural environment. You won't even hear cars pass by.

KAYAKING **A Day Away Kayaking** (321-268-2655; www.nbbd.com/kayaktours), on the Mosquito Lagoon and Banana River. I can't say enough about my day with Rick Shafer and Laurilee Thompson. Call it a kayaking tour or an ecotour, I learned so much about the natural inhabitants of the Mosquito Lagoon while paddling around the bird rookery and in and out of inlets where manatees nosed right up to my the kayak with interest. The 3- to 4-foot lagoon makes a perfect kayak adventure for novices. And the view in the crystal-clear water is full of exciting creatures like fish, tiny crabs, rays, and jellyfish. I exclaimed that they had everything here but sea horses and Laurilee said, "Keep looking—they're there, too!" I loved this area so much, I've brought my own kayaks back for several trips. Prices start at $25.

Paddle the Thousand Islands tidal delta in either canoes or kayaks with **Adventure Kayak of Cocoa Beach** (341-480-8632 or 321-453-6952; www.advkayak.com), 4755 Orchid Lane, Merritt Island, exploring mangrove islands. Paddle next to manatees and dolphins while white and brown pelicans sail by on the 2- to 3-hour trip. Adults $25, $15 ages 8–16.

Go kayaking at the **Brevard Zoo** (321-254-9453; www.brevardzoo.org), 8225 N Wickham Rd, Melbourne (see *Zoological Park*). Discover a natural nursery for fish in the 20-minute Florida Wetlands tour where resident otters may come out to play early in the day, or go on an expedition through Africa past rhinos and giraffes. These add-ons to the regular park admission are a bargain at only $3. Go beyond the park and take a 4-hour kayak ecotour into the natural areas of Merritt Island with an expert naturalist. Call the zoo for details.

The skilled staff at **Village Outfitters** (321-633-7245; www.villageoutfitters.com), 113 Brevard Ave, Cocoa Village, offer tours locally or to faraway destinations like the Bahamas, Costa Rica, or even Alaska. Local half-day tours through the Thousand Islands, Canaveral National Seashore, Merritt Island Wildlife Refuge, and more start at $30 for one or $45 for two in a tandem kayak. Call for full-day tours.

SUNSET IN THE THOUSAND ISLANDS

Kathy Wolf

KITEBOARDING Not something you'll learn in a day, this exciting new sport is best viewed off the FL 520 Causeway. If you want to take lessons, contact the folks down at **Kite World** (321-725-8336), 109 S Miramar Ave, Indialantic. They'll help you with everything from your first "body drag" to logging some serious airtime.

SPAS **Studio 1 Salon & Spa** (321-636-5511; www.studiooneandtwo.com), 206 Brevard Ave, offers the best pricing around for facials ($15–40), pedicures and manicures ($15–35), full-body wraps ($45–60), and body waxing. Create your own package and stay for the day; they'll order you a healthy lunch from either Café Margaux or the Black Tulip (see *Dining Out*).

Essential Massage Therapy (321-631-5678), 311 Brevard Ave, Cocoa Village, offers therapeutic massages in a cocoon-like environment. The 40-minute Decadent Foot Massage ($40) is a must after a day of shopping. Or go all out with the Supreme Aromatherapy Massage for a full 85 minutes of head-to-toe indulgence with lavender, chamomile, or frankincense essential oils and lotions. Several other treatments are available.

WINDSURFING **Calema Windsurfing & Kayak Lessons, Rentals, and Pro Shop** (321-453-3223; www.calema.com), 2550 N Banana River Dr, Merritt Island. Tinho and Susie Dornellas have been teaching windsurfing for over 20 years. You'll set out from Kelly Park to sail next to dolphins in the Banana River Lagoon. This sport is easy to master and great for all ages, but you'll need a few days to really get it right. The Beginner's Clinic ($299) is 4 days and will guide you through all the basics with on-land simulators, lightweight equipment, and step-by-step technique. Private 3-hour lesson ($150) includes board rental. Board rentals are also available to experienced sailors for partial or full days.

SAILING Learn how to sail at **Performance Sail & Sport** (321-253-3737), 6055 N US 1, Melbourne, or **Boater's Exchange** (321-638-0090), 2101 S US 1, Rockledge, and then rent a Hobie Cat, Sunfish, or sailboat and glide alongside dolphins in the lagoon.

SKYDIVING **Skydive Space Center** (321-267-0016 or 1-800-823-0016; www.skydivespacecenter.com), 476 N Williams Dr, Titusville. At this drop zone Patty and Greg Nardi will take you way up to new heights. How high can you go? All jumps are 15,000 feet, or you can request the 18,000-foot jump—the highest tandem skydive offered anywhere in the world! Count me in, Patty! During the minute-and-a-half flight you'll see the Atlantic Coast, Indian River Lagoon, and an awe-inspiring view of the Kennedy Space Center. You'll fly as close to the Space Center runway and launch pads as NASA will allow. Not everyone in your group ready for a jump? A scenic ride is offered to those nonjumpers who want to see you leave a perfectly good airplane. Open daily. A 15,000-foot tandem jump runs $159; video and photos $90.

SURFING Who says you can't surf? I was up catching waves in less than 30 minutes! They love beginners. Under the guidance of professional surfer Craig Carroll and his staff at the **Cocoa Beach Surfing School** (321-868-1980; www.cocoabeachsurfingschool.com), 150 E Columbia Lane, Cocoa Beach, you too will be riding in on long or short boards. First you'll learn the necessary marine safety awareness, from shark and stingrays to riptides. Then you'll practice your "snap" and positioning while in the air-conditioned comfort of the training school. In just a short time you'll hit the water, where your instructor will stay by your side the entire time while offering positive support and guidance. Surf lessons are scheduled with the incoming tides, so call in advance of your trip for times. Private 1-hour lessons $45; semiprivate (two students/one instructor) 1-hour $40, 2-hour $55, 3-hour $75 per person. Not ready for the wide-open ocean? Craig also teaches over at Disney's Typhoon Lagoon Wave Pool (see "Theme Parks").

TRAIL RIDING Ride horses on the beach or a wilderness trail at **Ace of Hearts Ranch** (321-638-0104; www.aceofheartsranch.com), 7400 Bridal Path Lane, Cocoa. As you drive up to the barn you'll be greeted by an attractive Asian turkey that seemingly stands guard over his stable. Sandra Vann offers rides by the hour, day, or even overnight on well-groomed horses. Weight limit 220 pounds. Beach riders must be able to control a horse and at least 12 years old. Due to turtle nesting, beach rides are limited Nov–Apr 15.

WALKING TOURS *Historic Titusville* outlines a walking tour of more than a dozen sites in this circa-1880 outpost on the Indian River; pick up a brochure at the local Titusville Chamber of Commerce.

✷ Green Space

BEACHES **Alan Shepard Park** is at the east end of FL 520 on the ocean. The 2-acre park was named for astronaut Alan Shepard and provides an excellent view of space launches. Picnic, barbecues, and rest rooms with showers. Parking $3 for cars, $5 for RVs.

Canaveral National Seashore (321-267-1110; www.nps.gov/cana), 308 Julia St, Titusville. It's one of the rare places in America where you can backpack along the Atlantic Ocean, where surf and sand meet along a narrow strip of Barrier Island along the Mosquito Lagoon. Climb the midden at Turtle Mound for a sweeping view of the lagoon, or walk the shifting sands to quiet campsites along the beach. In the shadow of Kennedy Space Center, this protected seashore provides a place for solitude and beach fishing, sunning and camping. Access the Turtle Mound area via FL A1A, New Smyrna Beach, where you'll find the official visitors center; reach Playalinda Beach, a popular swimming beach, from Merritt Island National Wildlife Refuge. Playalinda has a local reputation for nudity, which is *not* sanctioned by park management. The park may close during space shuttle launches for security reasons.

Straddling this human-made cut through the barrier island that runs from Melbourne Beach to Vero Beach, **Sebastian Inlet State Park** (321-984-4852), 9700 S FL A1A, Melbourne Beach, offers beach access on the Atlantic side and nature trails and fishing along the Intracoastal Waterway, where a campground overlooks the Indian River Lagoon. It's a popular launch point for fishing and diving trips. The McLarty Treasure Museum, featuring Spanish doubloons and other treasures brought up from offshore wrecks, is open daily 10–4:30; fee except for nature trails.

BOTANICAL GARDENS **Florida Tech Botanical Gardens** (321-674-8000; www.fit.edu), 150 W University Blvd, Melbourne. The 30-acre botanical garden has one of the largest collections of palms in the state. The lush hammock contains oaks, maples, and hickories. A plant guide and nature trail map is available at the adjacent Evans Library.

DOG PARKS 🐾 Who let the dogs out? Not **Satellite Beach Recreation Department** (321-773-6458; www.satellitebeach.org), 731 Jamaica Way off Desoto Blvd. They are safely contained in a free-roaming pet-friendly landscaped environment. Canines love the unrestricted social interaction. The new dog park has some specific rules and requires your current shot documentation. Free dog clinics and events are scheduled throughout the year. $2 admits up to three vaccinated dogs and two of their human companions (who don't need shots).

PARKS Search out seashells at **Coconut Point Park** (321-952-4650), FL A1A south of Melbourne Beach. The popular surfing spot is also home to several sea turtle nests, so observe marked-off sections. Picnic area and showers. Open dawn–dusk.

Crane Creek Promenade and Environmental Education Center, Melbourne. The freshwater tributary of Crane Creek leads to the Indian River Lagoon. Walk along the boardwalk at this prime manatee-viewing area. Display cases under the pavilion show a variety of rotating exhibits.

Enchanted Forest Nature Sanctuary (321-255-4466), FL 405, is at once a forest preserve and a history lesson on Florida's settlement. The entrance road follows the Hernandez-Capron Trail, a military trail built by General Joseph Hernandez and his men in 1837 to link U.S. Army fortresses at St. Augustine and Fort Pierce. The Coquina Quarry at the south edge of the preserve slices into the Anastasia Formation of the Atlantic Coastal Ridge, and the creek that the trail system follows is the Addison Canal, created in 1912 to drain the extensive wetlands between the St. Johns River and the Indian River Lagoon for development. Ancient oaks and magnolias form a dense forest on one corner of the preserve. Before you walk the hiking trails, stop in at the educational pavilion to browse the interpretive displays; the building also houses a gift shop. Mon–Sat 9–5, Sun 1–5. Free.

Jetty Park (321-783-7111), 400 E Jetty Rd, Cape Canaveral. Off the FL 528 Causeway. The newly renovated boardwalk along the jetty makes a great place to view cruise ships or shuttle launches. Campsites, fishing, pavilions, beach, barbecue grills. Open 7 AM–9 PM. Parking $1 for cars, $5 for RVs.

Kelly Park, Banana River Dr off FL 528. Grab a picnic lunch and watch the many sailboarders (see *Windsurfing*).

Holmes Park, at the corner of Melbourne Ave and Melbourne Court. Kids will want to climb on the colorful manatee statues at this tiny, unassuming park near Historic Downtown Melbourne.

Lori Wilson Park (321-455-1380), 1500 N Atlantic Ave, Cocoa. The 32.5-acre park is bordered by I Dream of Jeannie Blvd and is also home to the **Johnnie Johnson Nature Center**. Beach access, seasonal lifeguards, picnic tables, showers, pavilions, playground, volleyball court, and maritime hammock. Open dawn–dusk. Parking is $1 for cars.

Sidney Fischer Park (321-868-3274), in the 2100 block of FL A1A, was named for Sidney Fischer, who served as the mayor of Cocoa Beach from 1956 to 1960. The 10-acre oceanfront park was recently renovated to include shower and rest room facilities. Parking fee $3 for cars, $5 for RVs.

Turkey Creek Sanctuary (321-952-3433), 1502 Port Malabar Blvd, treats visitors to a boardwalk through sand pine scrub and along Turkey Creek, a popular kayaking route. Tall cliffs above the creek provide scenic views; look up in the canopy overhead for bromeliads and orchids. At the entrance you'll find a butterfly garden and the Margaret Hames Nature Center, with interpretive displays, research materials, and rest rooms. Open 7–sunset; free.

WILD PLACES Thanks to the **Brevard County's Environmentally Endangered Lands** (EEL) program (321-255-4466; www.eelbrevard.com), the Space Coast has a patchwork of wilderness areas breaking up the urban mass. In addition to its flagship project, the Enchanted Forest Nature Sanctuary (see *Parks*), Brevard's EEL lands (primarily accessible only for hiking and biking) include **Buck Lake Conservation Area** off FL 46, with a network of forest roads for hiking, biking, and horseback riding along the prairies edging the St. Johns River; **Malabar Scrub Sanctuary**, off Malabar Rd, a quiet 400-acre tract just south of Palm Bay, where early-bird visitors enjoy bird sightings amid flatwoods and scrub; **Micco Scrub Sanctuary**, off Micco Rd, a 1,300-acre scrub preserve; and **Pine Island Conservation Area**, on Pine Island Rd just south of Kennedy Space Center, a great place to watch for manatees in summer along Sam's Creek. On the barrier island south of Melbourne Beach, enjoy exploring the coastal scrub on hiking trails through **Coconut Point Sanctuary** (just south of the Melbourne Beach Publix), where the trail leads through a variety of habitats along the Indian River Lagoon, and **Maritime Hammock Sanctuary**, South Beach, where orchids abound in the oak hammocks and you can watch wading birds from a mangrove-rimmed platform on the lagoon.

Adjoining Kennedy Space Center along the Indian River Lagoon, the **Merritt Island National Wildlife Refuge** (321-861-0667; www.merrittisland.fws.gov), east of Titusville on FL 402, offers some of the best bird-watching opportunities in Florida. Stop by the visitors center before you explore the refuge for information and maps. Renowned for its diversity of species, the park offers several hiking trails on which you'll want to bring your binoculars and camera for an opportunity to see some of the 310 different types of birds, including Florida scrub-jays, bald eagles, black-necked stilts, and roseate spoonbills. **Black Point Wildlife Drive** is a must-see one-way scenic drive out into the marshes of the Indian River Lagoon. Open Mon–Fri 8–4:30, Sat and Sun 9–5; fee. The visitors center is closed on Sun Apr–Oct; the park may be entirely closed during space shuttle launches.

The **St. Johns Water Management District** (321-329-4500; sjr.state.fl.us) is responsible for a string of conservation areas that serve as buffers to the St. Johns River and its tributaries. Most are open for fishing and paddling; some are open to hiking, equestrian use, and hunting. Check their web site for the *Recreation Guide to District Lands*, which will lead you to preserves like **Blue**

Cypress, **Three Forks**, and **River Lakes**. With nearly 23,000 acres, **St. Sebastian River State Buffer Preserve** (321-953-5004), 1000 Buffer Preserve Dr, Fellsmere, is the largest public land the district administers, where you can backpack or ride horses on nearly 40 miles of trails through pine flatwoods and scrub, or walk the nature trail along the river to watch manatees; up to 100 have been seen in the river at one time.

✷ Lodging

BED & BREAKFASTS

Cocoa Beach 32922
A sunny breakfast room awaits you at **Indian River House Bed & Breakfast** (321-631-5660; www.indianriverhouse.com), 3113 Indian River Dr. Later, kayak or canoe right from the inn's dock. The early-1900s home was built for Judge Samuel C. Graham as a winter hunting and fishing retreat and retains much of its Old Florida charm. Relax on the porch overlooking the Indian River. With only four bedrooms, innkeeper Suzanne is able to offer personal touches, like chocolates, sherry, or hot tea just before bedtime. $90–95.

Indialantic 32903
The beachfront **Windemere Inn by the Sea** (321-728-9334 or 1-800-224-6853; www.windemereinn.com), 815 S Miramar Ave, was built only in 1998, but was made to look like a house from the turn of the 20th century. Romance and relaxation abound as Thomas and Vivien Hay bring southern hospitality to the coral-colored mansion. Three buildings compose the inn. You might choose to stay in the Main House in the Enchantment Room with pearl and mocha coloring, a mahogany poster bed, and a Jacuzzi bath; or in the Windward Cottage, where the sun greets you each morning in the natural decor of the Honeysuckle Room with a wicker-and-twig queen-sized bed, twin daybed, Jacuzzi bath, and separate outside entrance. Each evening sherry is served with freshly baked dessert treats of the day. Then fall off to sleep to the sounds of the surf just outside your window. $110–225.

Melbourne Historic Downtown 32901
🐾 The beautiful 1925 **Crane Creek Inn B&B** (321-768-6416; www.cranecreekinn.com), 907 E Melbourne Ave, is decorated in the casual style of Old Key West and situated on the Indian River tributary Crane Creek, right at the edge of Historic Downtown Melbourne. Innkeepers Gillian and Bob Shearer know how to make you feel right at home and will chat with you about local wildlife and the downtown historic area or just let you relax in your own space. Take a moment to unwind at the gorgeous waterfront pool or hot tub, and then canoe along the creek to discover the varied wildlife, like waterfowl, blue-shell crabs, and even manatees. In the evening you might see or smell the blooming queen of the night, a cactus growing off the many palms on the property. Park your car or come by boat and moor at the dock. This is one of the few B&Bs that allow pets; both Gillian and Bob welcome and adore well-behaved canine companions. $100–175.

Mims 32754
The 1860 **Dickens Inn Bed & Breakfast** (321-269-4595; www.dickens-inn.com), 2398 N Singleton

Ave, was built as a grand manor house for a thriving citrus plantation. Several orange and grapefruit trees still stand on the property, assuring fresh seasonal juices. Innkeepers Ursula and Bill Dickens want you to feel right at home and combine southern and Old World hospitality with the vibrancy of this millennium. The natural decor is comfy, not stuffy, with touches of Old Florida and Ursula's homeland, Germany. After staying with this active couple, you'll leave feeling relaxed and rejuvenated. That's if you really want to leave. $85–114.

HOTELS AND MOTELS

Cape Canaveral 32920

Nicely appointed suites and penthouses are available at the oceanfront **Royal Mansions Resort** (321-784-8484; www.royalmansions.com), 8600 Ridgewood Ave, by the week or month.

Cocoa Beach 32931

A variety of Superior Small Lodgings are recommended on and off the beach.

A short drive to the beach: The funky **Fawlty Towers Motel** (321-784-3870), 100 E Cocoa Beach Causeway, is owned by a couple of Brits and, yes, named for the British TV show. Just a few steps from the beach, the motel also has a heated pool surrounded by lush tropical gardens and an authentic tiki bar featuring European beers and ciders. **Sea Esta Villas** (321-783-1739 or 1-800-872-9444; www.seaestavillas.homestead.com), NW Corner 7th St, is across from the beach with fully equipped kitchens and one- or two-bedroom suites.

On the beach: The **Cocoa Beach Club** (321-784-2457; www.cocoabeachclub.com), 5200 Ocean Beach Blvd, rents their fully equipped rooms only by the week or month; **Luna Sea Bed & Breakfast Motel** (321-783-0500; www.lunaseacocoabeach.com), 3185 N Atlantic Ave, serves continental breakfast with European coffees and teas; all rooms at **Cocoa Beach Oceanside Inn Cocoa Beach** (321-784-3126; www.cocoabeachoceansideinn.com), 1 Hendry Ave, have an ocean view. The tropical paradise also caters to golfers and will put together a golf package for you at several of the local golf courses. At **Surf Studio Beach Resort** (321-783-7100; www.surf-studio.com), 1801 S Atlantic Ave, slip into the oceanfront pool, lie in a hammock, or take your board to the beach; 🐾 **South Beach Inn-on-the-Sea** (321-784-3333 or 1-800-546-6835; www.southbeachinn.com), 1701 S Atlantic Ave, offers fully equipped kitchens with one or two bedrooms and welcomes your pet. **Beach Island Resort** (321-784-0459; www.beachislandresort.com), 1125 S Atlantic Ave, and **SeaGull Beach Club** (321-783-4441; www.seagullbeachclub.com), 4440 Ocean Beach Blvd, are time-share condominiums with comfortable suites.

Titusville 32780

The **Best Western Space Shuttle Inn** (321-269-9100; www.spaceshuttleinn.com), 3455 Cheney Hwy, may not be near the beach, but it's a great place to stay not only due to its proximity to I-95 (exit 215) and all local attractions, but also because it's one of just a handful of "Green Hotels" in the country. For $5 more a night, you can request an Evergreen Room with allergy-free soaps, linens, and separate air and water filtration systems, great for those suffering from allergies. Family rooms offer one or two bedrooms with separate TVs and baths. Starstruck lovers will want to land in one of the romantic suites, like the spacious Galaxy with in-room Jacuzzi. The Royal Honeymoon Suite has a king-sized canopy bed with heart-shaped Jacuzzi. And if you want to be an astronaut, reach for the stars in the Space Shuttle Fantasy Room, where your bed is converted into the cargo bay of a space shuttle. You can sip champagne with your special someone while a shuttle lands over the Jacuzzi tub. The Space Fantasy package also includes a 2-day Maximum Access admission to Kennedy Space Center. All guests will enjoy the more-than-you-can-eat continental breakfast, served every morning in the clubhouse.

RESORTS

Cocoa Beach 32931

The Inn at Cocoa Beach (1-800-343-5307; www.theinnatcocoabeach.com), 4300 Ocean Beach Blvd, could also be called a B&B if not for the 50 rooms. This wonderful European-style hotel offers fresh fruit, warm moist muffins, and rich coffee and teas each morning. Eat indoors or out on the beautiful patio, where you can visit with Tangee, the sociable tropical macaw. The inn is located across from Ron Jon Surf Shop, so you may want to rent a kayak and get innkeeper/seasoned kayaker Karen Simpler to go for a paddle with you! $125–295; some with Jacuzzis.

RV CAMPING

Cocoa Beach 32931

Oceanus Mobile Village & RV (321-783-3871; www.floridacamping.com), 152 Crescent Beach Dr, 23rd St.

Rockledge 32955

Space Coast RV Resort (321-636-2873 or 1-800-982-4233; www.spacecoastrv.net), 820 Barnes Blvd.

Elsewhere

These other RV parks cater to the fishing crowd with bait and tackle and boat rentals: **Loughman Lake Lodge** (321-268-2277), 1955 Hatbill Rd, Mims 32754; **Lone Cabbage Fish Camp** (321-632-4199), 8199 FL 520, Cocoa 32922; **Honest John's Fish Camp** (321-727-2923), 750 Mullet Creek Rd, Melbourne 32951.

✷ Where to Eat

DINING OUT

Cocoa Beach

You can't beat the view at the **Atlantic Ocean Grille** (321-783-7549) on the Cocoa Beach Pier. Since 1962, this historical landmark has served up great dishes in a comfortable setting with a nautical theme, surrounded by warm wood-paneled walls. Start with grilled alligator ($6) or oysters Rockefeller ($7), then order from a variety of fresh Florida seafood ($15–20)—but save room for their famous desserts, like key lime pie ($4) and Kahlúa cake ($5). Watch the sun rise over the ocean during Sunday champagne brunch. Early birds will enjoy specials ($7–11) only 5–6 PM, so get there early.

Pompano Grille (321-784-9005), 110 N Brevard Ave. Mark Siljestrom and Vicki Cooper whip up some tasty dishes in this unlikely location. You've got to explore to find them, tucked in a bland strip mall off on a side street, but this is one perfect gem. The former South Florida chef moved up the coast, and Cocoa Beach should be thrilled to have him. Mark's sister, Pam, greets everyone at the door, and with less than a dozen tables, you are assured prompt attention as you settle into intimate surroundings. The French Continental/northern Italian cuisine is accented with cozy recessed arches displaying natural pieces and fine art. The strategically placed track lighting helps transport you to the Old Country. With selections like blackened shrimp with creamy dill sauce, sea scallops in brandy cream, boneless breast of chicken layered with sautéed apples, and *pasta capellini el pesto*—made with fresh basil, pine nuts, and garlic in virgin olive oil, partnered with pesto vegetable curry with fresh vegetables, raisins, and apples over rice pilaf—I didn't know where to start. But I knew where to end and saved enough room for their homemade Oreo ice cream and moist chocolate cake. They also offer a very nice selection of fine wines. Entrées $12–20. Dinner Tue–Sat. in season; Thu–Sun in summer. 5:30–9:30.

The German **Heidelberg Restaurant** (321-783-6806), 7 N Orlando Ave (FL A1A), offers traditional German fare like bratwust ($6) and *gulasch* ($11), as well as more complete entrées like Wiener schnitzel ($19), Hausmacher Wurstplatte ($16), and beef fillet stroganoff ($20) in elegant surroundings. Open Tue–Sun lunch and dinner.

Cocoa Village

Both **Café Margaux Restaurant** (321-639-8343; www.margaux.com), 222 Brevard Ave, and the **Black Tulip** (321-631-1133), 207 Brevard Ave, offer elegant fine dining before a show at the Phoenix Theatre or Historic Cocoa Village Playhouse (see *Entertainment*).

Kathy Wolf

KEY LIME PIE AT CAFÉ MARGAUX

Malabar

The beautiful **Yellow Dog Café** (321-956-3334; www.yellowdogcafe.net), 905 US 1, is the same place that Stuart Woods writes about in his books. The elegant building overlooking the Indian River serves light lunches like grilled portobello Caesar salad ($8) and the California Dreamer sandwich ($8), along with sumptuous dinners like onion-crusted chicken with caramel citrus glaze ($17) and blackened tilapia with crab tower ($24).

Melbourne

Head to Nannie Lee's **Strawberry Mansion** and **Mister BeauJeans** restaurants (321-723-1900) for sunny breakfasts, graceful luncheons, and elegant dinners.

Sit outside on the porch or step into bright yellow rooms with tables dressed in crisp white linens for a relaxing midday treat at **Le Jardin Francais** (321-837-0028), 1900 Municipal Lane.

Titusville

Starting out as a small roadside smokehouse, **Paul's Smokehouse**

(321-267-3663), 3665 S Washington Ave, has grown into a fabulous dining establishment. But don't let the gorgeous architecture scare you away: The prices are reasonable ($8–17), the view of the Indian River is breathtaking, and you can't beat the location for a prime viewing spot for launches.

EATING OUT

Cape Canaveral

The Crooked Cajun Café (321-783-3456), 523 Glen Creek Dr, cooks up muffulettas and gumbo for lunch and dinner.

A fun place to go to watch the cruise ships or the eclectic crowd is **Grill's Seafood Deck & Tiki Bar** (321-868-2226; www.sunrisemarina.com), 505 Glen Cheek Dr, Cape Canaveral. Famous for their fantastic grilled fish of the day ($14), they get my vote! Also offering entrées like grilled tropical chicken kebabs ($10) and grilled seafood Alfredo ($12). You'll want to try the spicy brown Bahamian chowder or creamy traditional clam chowder ($2–4). For not-so-light meals there's a variety of juicy sandwiches ($6) and the famous Hurricane Burger ($5).

Cocoa

An eclectic mix of bikers, fishermen, and tourists converges at the rustic **Lone Cabbage Fish Camp** (321-632-4199), 8199 FL 520. The 100-year-old fish camp boasts a great selection of swamp food like 'gator ($10), frog legs ($10), catfish ($8), and sampler combos ($12). You'll want to come out for the Sunday Fish Fry with live band. Save room for key lime pie. Open daily.

Cocoa Beach

The Fischer family created a triple hit with **Bernard's Surf** (www.bernardssurf.com), **Fischer's Seafood Bar and Grill**, and **Rusty's Seafood and Oyster Bar** (www.rustysseafood.com), all located at the same address (321-783-2401): 2 S Atlantic Ave. Go casual at Bernard's and a little more upscale at Fischer's. And come right off the boat at Rusty's, where they still have 94¢ draft at happy hour. You'll also find Rusty's located at Port Canaveral (321-783-2033).

You'll find several hot spots on the **Cocoa Beach Pier** (321-784-4409; www.cocoabeachpier.com), 401 Meade Ave, Cocoa Beach. The **Marlins Good Times Bar and Grill** is a favorite of the college crowd with Buffalo wings, fish sandwiches, and burgers ($6–8). Grab a cool treat at **Ricky's Ice Cream Parlor** (321-868-2990), then play some video games in the arcade. Ricky's sundaes, malts, and shakes ($3–5) are made with Edy's Ice Cream. **Oh Shucks Seafood Bar** (321-783-7549) is world famous for their finger foods and has live reggae bands every Wed night. Out at the end of the pier, the **Atlantic Ocean Grille** (321-783-7549; also see *Dining Out*) offers finer dining with a breathtaking ocean view. Nightly entertainment can be anything from soft guitar at the open bar to lively reggae depending on the season. The college crowd dominates during the spring break with UCS functions and the annual Easter spring surfing festival.

Awesome appetizers, and oak-fired grilled rib chops and chicken, can be found at **Durango Oak Fire Steakhouse** (321-783-9988; www.durangosteakhouse.com), 5602 N Atlantic Ave. Serving lunch and dinner daily.

Great fitness shakes, smoothies, and coffees are at the **Juice 'N' Java Café** (321-784-4044), 20 N Brevard Ave, which also serves healthy soups and sandwiches.

The attractive muraled walls, by local artist Vern Matiolli, soften the sports-bar image in the comfortable **Rum Runners Grill** (321-868-2020), 695 N Atlantic Ave. This restaurant didn't waste any time putting their clam "chowdah" to the test with this native New Englander. Their version of the traditional New England chowder, made with real butter and heavy cream, not only won them a caseful of medals but also garnered my award. For a new twist, they offer cocktail sherry on the side, which gives it an unexpected kick. They also dish up some of the best crabcakes anywhere—delicate and full of crab, held together with just a few Ritz cracker crumbs. Don't miss their annual event, on the first Sat of May, where they fly in official glasses of the Kentucky Derby to fill with mint juleps.

Stop by **Simply Delicious Café & Bakery** (321-783-2012), 125 North Orlando Ave, Cocoa Beach on FL A1A southbound, for a fabulous breakfast with such items as malted waffles ($4) and eggs Benedict ($5), or lunches like the grilled mahi sandwich ($6) and crispy Oriental salad ($7). Get there early, as the best muffins, like pistachio and fresh peach, go fast. You'll enjoy sitting in the colorful rooms of this historic beach house while sipping cappuccinos and lattes.

Thai Dixie (321-868-0066), 24 N Orlando Ave (FL A1A), is open for lunch and dinner with specials priced at $6.

Cocoa Village

Take a stroll down Brevard Ave for afternoon tea at the **Haven Tea Room and Gift Shoppe** (321-631-0633), 602 Brevard Ave. The Queen Mum Tea ($13) includes a pot of tea, a scone with Yorkshire cream and preserves, finger sandwiches, fruit, tarts, and desserts. Nana's Tea ($6) includes a pot of tea and two scones with Yorkshire cream and preserves. Reservations required.

Gardener's Cottage Inc. Health Food Store and Restaurant (321-631-2030), 902 Florida Ave, is the place to go for home-style vegetarian dishes, fresh vegetable juice, and smoothies.

The Main Event Wrestler's Grill (321-638-0415), 3 Forrest Ave, has hearty meals like Body Slam Burgers ($5) and Head Lock Chicken ($10).

Mama D's (321-638-1338), 109 Brevard Ave, serves a great Greek salad ($5–7) and several Italian-style subs ($6–7).

For a light breakfast before shopping or deli-style sandwiches and subs for lunch, try the **Village Cappuccino** (321-632-5695), Brevard Ave; it's reminiscent of a Victorian parlor with rose wallpaper, hand-crocheted tablecloths, and needlepoint chair seats. And while you might expect tea, they serve rich coffee in a unique variety of mugs at this great resting spot in historic Cocoa Village.

Indian Harbor Beach

Great sandwiches and gourmet foods are found at the **Green Turtle Market** (321-773-2001), 855 E Eau Gallie Blvd.

Indialantic

Ocean View Diner (321-723-2270), 1 5th Ave. Perfect for watching the sunrise on the Atlantic, this 24-hour family diner has a Greek emphasis on the menu—not just the traditional *moussaka*, *souvlaki*, gyros, and *pastitsio*, but even Greek omelets made with feta, spinach, onion, and tomatoes. Breakfast ($2–7) served all day; sandwiches and salads, and entrées (lots of seafood choices!) for $9–14; children's menu, too!

Melbourne
Bellas (321-723-5001), 1904 Municipal Lane, serves up great pasta dishes like Amica Loretta—a meat tortellini sautéed with creamy Alfredo sauce and prosciutto ham ($12)—and Mama Anna's Traditional Lasagna with three imported cheeses, Bella's marinara sauce, and lots of beef ($10). Beer and wine also served. Lunch and dinner Mon–Sat.

Yes, it's true, **Sonic Drive In** (321-242-6041), 4011 N Wickham Rd, is a fast-food establishment, but one of my favorites. The "happy days" drive-in has great American food made the way it was back in the 1950s and '60s. And I love that a carhop on roller skates delivers a burger and root beer float right to my car.

Melbourne Beach
D&D's Shake Shop (321-733-9455), 2990 S FL A1A. Ice cream treats at the beach: How can you resist? D&D's serves up parfaits, splits, hand-dipped hard ice cream, and a soft serve flavor of the week, $1–4. Open noon–9 daily.

Melbourne Historic Downtown
The **905 Café** (321-952-1672), 905 E New Haven Ave, serves light salads ($6) and sandwiches ($5–7) on croissants, bagels, wraps, or wheat, white, or rye breads. They also have espresso drinks, beer and wine, and a great assortment of interesting desserts.

Not only does the **Greenhouse Gallery Café** (321-676-1243), 705 E New Haven Ave, offer great salads ($2–6), deli sandwiches ($4–7), and suitable lunches for kids ($2–3), but it also hosts a variety of local artists' works. The front garden patio makes for a great spot for relaxing while secluded behind the garden trellis.

'Tis a grand Irish pub, **Meg O'Malleys** (321-952-5510), 812 E New Haven Ave, which offers traditional dishes such as rosemary-scented Irish stew ($7), corned beef and cabbage ($9), and fish-and-chips ($8). A cup of the Irish Parliament Bean Soup is still served for 18¢. For dessert, Bushmill's bread pudding ($4) is made with the traditional recipe, served on a pool of sweet Irish whiskey cream with raspberry sauce or doused with their "drunken" raisin sauce. Stick around and have them pour your pint while you listen to the live entertainment.

Don't call this a tearoom. The folks over at **Melwood Creek Tea Company** (321-722-0107), 2013 Melbourne Court, prefer tea *bar*. After spending some time with them, you'll understand why. They take their steeping seriously at this brilliant tea bar. Those who really appreciate tea will love it. Come in and sample teas while sitting in the intimate garden room. They also offer children's parties and tea seminars, including boy-themed parties for the guys, because real men drink tea!

Vegetarian chili and fresh fruit smoothies are served at **Nature's Table, Inc**. (321-254-7075), 7640 N Wickham Rd.

A local favorite, **Pop's Casbah** (321-723-9811), 2005 S Waverly Place, has the best homemade pies ($3) and an award-winning home-style breakfast ($2–5).

You'll want to stop by **Zappala's Italian Restaurant Pizzeria** (321-255-3123), 2330 N Wickham Rd, for great Italian food, but especially for their tiramisu. Leah Lo Galbo and Mary Manuele have been operating this local favorite for over 30 years.

Titusville

Café Chocolat (321-267-1713), 304 S Washington Ave, specializes in everything chocolate, from Turtle Mocha coffee ($4) to their famous Chocolate Fondue Tray ($20) with melted Belgian chocolate, angel food cake, marshmallows, pretzels, chips, and seasonal fruit. Oh, and if you must behave, they have veggie burgers ($5), hot panini sandwiches ($6), and salads ($4–6). Open daily for breakfast, lunch, and dinner. Call ahead for the Fondue Tray.

Stop by the "almost famous" **Dogs R' Us Grill and Bar** (321-269-9050), 4200 S Washington Ave, for gourmet hamburgers ($6) and hot dogs ($3). This fun and funky place also serves dinners ($8–13) and a great selection of desserts ($3).

You know you're in for an adventure as you park your car next to the nature garden bordered by a 150-foot mural. **Dixie Crossroads Seafood Restaurant** (321-268-5000; www.dixiecrossroads.com), 1475 Garden St, knows shrimp! As you walk up from the parking lot, stop and take a picture next to the cute statues of Mr. and Mrs. Rock Shrimp, the adorable mascots of this local establishment. Cross the walkway where imported Egyptian fish swim in the pond below, keeping the pond's aquatic growth in control. This place packs them in, so you may have to wait for a table, but you won't mind—the friendly staff offer hot corn fritters while you wait. Once inside, you'll notice the lively, rustic rooms flanked with colorful murals as well as original wildlife paintings from local artists. As you sit down, you are immediately greeted with more corn fritters! Don't fill up, because dinner portions are generous, and this is where you'll find the largest selection of shrimp anywhere. Dixie Crossroads shrimp come straight off their own fleet of commercial shrimpers and are then processed only a few blocks away at their own Cape Canaveral Shrimp Company, Inc., where you can also buy raw shrimp to cook at home (see *Selective Shopping*). The vast assortment of shrimp is outstanding; you'll wonder why you haven't seen these varieties before now. Choose from pinks, "hoppers," brownies, whites, Royal reds, Cape Canaveral browns, and the shrimp that made them famous—the rock shrimp. This crustacean looks a bit prehistoric, but tastes deliciously like a mini lobster. And they'll cook them any way you like—blackened, fried, sautéed, broiled, and even crunchy with coconut. Dip them in homemade sauces like spicy orange mango, which is great with the rock shrimp, or mandarin orange sesame, which goes well with blue crab claws. Shrimp is their forte, of course, but the restaurant also serves a huge selection of freshly caught fish; steaks and chicken can also be ordered for the landlubbers in your party. Owner Laurilee Thompson and her family go way back and are among Titusville's original natives. An active voice in her community and environment,

Laurilee is an energetic woman. If you can manage to catch up with her, she'll be glad to tell you all about the historical and natural areas, along with the Great Birding Festival (see *Special Events*). Open daily, with most dinners $7–20.

Find your way into **Kloiber's Cobbler Eatery** (321-383-0689), 337 Washington Ave, for Joe's soup of the day ($3–4), quiche ($4), and a variety of salads and sandwiches ($3–6). Joe also makes his fresh fruit cobbler ($3) from scratch every day. Serving breakfast, lunch, and dinner.

For over 30 years **Steve's Family Diner** (321-268-3011), 2900 Washington Ave, has served the Titusville area with all-American favorites and good home cooking from hamburgers to prime rib. Open daily for breakfast, lunch, and dinner.

The Coffee Shoppe (321-267-9902), Baldwin Plaza, 125 Broad St. A down-home family restaurant with tasty, inexpensive breakfasts ($1–4) served 6–2, lunch sandwiches, and entrées (veal cutlet, grilled Salisbury steak) that run $2–8.

Hope's Tea Room & Treasures (321-259-9158), 814B S Washington Ave. Imagine my delight at stumbling across this family restaurant jam-packed with antiques and country crafts, many for sale! No matter what you order for breakfast—and the selection is huge; I recommend the crêpes—Hope greets you with a bucket of fresh-baked mini muffins. The creative morning menu includes orange cream cheese bagels, chocolate Belgian waffles, and fruit ambrosia ($3–8); in addition to wraps, sandwiches, and salads ($5–8) for lunch, try the dainty tea sandwiches with a hot pot of herbal tea. Closed Sat.

✷ Entertainment

The 500-seat **Historic Cocoa Village Playhouse** (321-636-5050; www.cocoavillage.com), 300 Brevard Ave, Cocoa, recently reopened after extensive renovations. Built in 1924, this quaint theater in the heart of the village shopping district is listed on the National Register of Historic Places.

The **Maxwell C. King Center for Performing Arts** (321-242-2219; www.kingcenter.com), 3865 Wickham Rd, Melbourne, offers Broadway shows, dance, opera, and children's theater in a spacious 2,000-seat facility.

Take in a play or musical at the intimate **Phoenix Theatre** (321-777-8936), 817 E Strawbridge Ave, Cocoa Village.

The fabulous 289-seat **Surfside Playhouse** (321-783-3127), 5th St S and Brevard Ave, Cocoa Beach, has been around since 1959 and is the only live theater on the Barrier Islands.

✷ Selective Shopping

Cocoa

There's something for everyone at **Frontenac Flea Market** (321-631-0241), 5605 N US 1, the largest flea market on the East Coast.

Cocoa Beach

The Dinosaur Store (407-783-7300; www.dinosaurstore.com), 299 W Cocoa Beach Causeway (FL 520), has a large selection of museum-quality dinosaur fossils, along with minerals, amber, and meteorites (see *To See*).

Ron Jon Surf Shop (321-799-8888; www.ronjons.com), 4151 N Atlantic Ave, Cocoa Beach, is Surf Central for all your beach and surfing needs.

Cocoa Village

Historic Cocoa Village (321-631-

9075; www.cocoavillage.com) is a true Main Street USA. Stroll throughout the tree-lined streets, stopping in on the charming mix of shops and boutiques—antiques, jewelry, arts, crafts—and fabulous gourmet restaurants. Saunter down the brick walkways to the waterfront park. Take a tour through 20th-century Classic Revival architecture at the Porcher House (circa 1916) on the walking tour.

Bushveld (321-427-3085; 321-363-4334; or 1-800-386-7407), 26 Oleander St, displays an artful collection of African crafts, including furniture and fabrics. Have your pet's portrait done by Lori in a unique style at **Pet Story Boards**, 4040 Brevard Ave, at the **Black Dog Gallery** inside the Thread Needle Street Mall. Shop for glass beaded jewelry and accessories at **Tatanka Beads & Artist's Jewelry** (321-636-4104; www.tatanka beads.com), 121 Harrison St, or take one of their classes and design your own. Take a walk down a tiny garden path to discover the dynamic duo of **Greg Wooten Pottery** and **Harry Guthrie Phillips** (321-636-4160), 116-B Harrison St. Greg turns fine porcelain clay in exquisite pieces for use in your home or on your table, while Harry, an avid scuba diver, sculpts unique saltwater fish. **Buy arthere.com** (www.buyarthere .com), 409 Brevard Ave, showcases the talents of 35 local artists. Nice home decor is at **The Pear Tree** (321-632-5432), 310-A Brevard Ave; **Carol's Unique Antiques & Collectibles** (321-632-5533), 643 S Brevard Ave, is a great place to find that signature piece.

Essential Massage Therapy (321-631-5678), 311 Brevard Ave. Put a roof on an alley and what do you get? Essential Massage makes use of the 6-foot-wide, 70-foot-long floor space, and the soothing aroma will draw you in from across the street. Display cases reaching the ceiling are filled with oil scents, aromatherapy candles made with pure palm and beeswax, painted glass bottles by Linda Elian, beaded necklaces, and beaded chain pulls for ceiling fans or lamps. Liquid castile soaps are scented with essential oils, and custom bar soaps come with a tiny vial of essential oil for your complete aromatherapy experience. Massage therapist on site offering a decadent foot massage for $40.

Indialantic

Eclectic shops and surfer stores are found in Indialantic, like **Kite World** (321-725-8336), 109 S Miramar Ave, which has a large selection of unique kites and can also teach you kite-boarding; and the **Longboard House** (321-951-0730), 101 5th Ave, which has a great selection of surfboards and beachwear.

Melbourne

Super Flea & Farmers Market (321-242-9124; www.superflea market.com), 4835 W Eau Gallie Blvd, Melbourne.

Melbourne Historic Downtown

A great selection of specialty shops, antiques stores, restaurants, and art studios is found all along New Haven and Strawbridge Aves. **Apple Barrel Gifts** (321-956-0026), 901 E New Haven Ave, has gourmet foods and gift baskets. **Antiques by Heidi** (321-722-2112), 821 E New Haven Ave, and **Seldom Scene** (321-768-8442), 724 E New Haven, have your grandmother's antiques and collectibles. Interesting creations by local artists are at **Heart Strings** (321-724-0111), 802 E New Haven Ave. Fine ladies' apparel, evening wear, and Brighton shoes and purses are at **Isabella's Ladies Apparel** (321-952-4489), 845 E New Haven Ave. You'll enjoy stopping in for some Turkish tea at **Shading International** (321-951-7560), 812 E Strawbridge, which has a fabulous collection of Turkish and Oriental rugs and Bursa silk scarves. The **Indian River Soap Co.** (321-723-6464), 804 E New Haven Ave, makes their own natural soaps on the premises, and the **Baby Patch** (321-676-7590; www.e-babypatch.com), 800 E New Haven Ave, is the place to go for complete layette and nursery furniture; individual themed vignettes are displayed. The real find at Baby Patch is **Tropical Rockers**, which has handcrafted wooden rocking helicopters, motorcycles, giraffes, alligators, dragons, and, of course, horses.

Satellite Beach

Karen & Charles L. Smith (321-773-0506), 309 Gemini Dr, often show their landscape and portrait oils at galleries along the Space Coast, but you can also see their works by appointment.

FRESH SHRIMP Cape Canaveral Shrimp Company, Inc. (321-383-8885), 688 Park Ave, Titusville. President Rodney Thompson watches over this immaculately kept processing plant where Dixie Crossroads gets their shrimp. Now you can take some home to cook, too!

✷ Special Events

The **Space Coast Arts Line** (321-690-6819) lists all the unique local festivals and events going on throughout the year.

Year-round, first Fri of the month: Listen to some music at **Jazz Friday** at the Brevard Museum of Art & Science (see *Art Galleries*).

Year-round, second Fri of the month: The shops stay open late, so saunter down to Historic Cocoa Village for **Friday Fest**, an evening of shopping, browsing, music, and art.

April: The annual **Cocoa Village Spring Gallery Walk** fills the historic district with fine arts and crafts. Contact the Cocoa Village Tourism Association (321-433-0362).

The harbinger of spring, the annual **Easter Surfing Festival** (321-453-5352) is held at Shepard Park at the foot of FL 520 and the Cocoa Beach Pier. The event features the best of professional surfing along with amateur competitions and various vendors.

For nearly 30 years the **Indian River Festival** (321-267-3036) has been just good old-fashioned family fun. Arts and crafts show, live national and local entertainment, duck race, river raft race, antique and custom car shows.

Out of 3,000 artists, only 250 are selected to display their crafts and artistry at the annual **Melbourne Art Festival** (321-722-1964; www.melbournearts.org).

May: The **Art of Harley's** annual motorcycle festival (321-690-6817) benefits Brevard's youth arts programs.

June–July: Turtle hatchlings race from their sandy nest to the ocean in a ritual that has been performed for millions of years. A 12-mile strip from Melbourne Beach to Sebastian Inlet is heavily monitored, as this is the largest nesting site in the United States. To see this natural phenomenon, go on a

Turtle Walk. The reservations-only 2-mile walk lasts from 9 PM until about midnight. Contact the Sea Turtle Preservation Society (321-676-1701) or the Sebastian Inlet Recreation Area (321-589-2147) for more information.

November: The annual **Space Coast Birding and Wildlife Festival** (321-268-5224) is one of the largest events of the year, with over 30 field trips, seminars, and workshops. The nature-based trade show draws a large crowd of outdoorspeople from miles around. Boat and kayak trips take you into significant natural areas of Florida's Space Coast, home of the largest collection of endangered wildlife and plants in the continental United States.

DAYTONA & THE BEACHES

DAYTONA, DAYTONA BEACH, NEW SMYRNA BEACH, ORMOND BEACH, PONCE INLET, AND PORT ORANGE

For more than 100 years tourists have been flocking to the white sand beaches of the Daytona area. From the late 1800s, wealthy northern tycoons have made this their winter home. In 1903 Ormond Beach became the Birthplace of Speed, with several land speed records broken right on the beach. In 1947 the National Association of Stock Car Auto Racing was founded in Daytona Beach; Daytona International Speedway was opened in 1959.

GUIDANCE

Ormond Beach to Port Orange
Daytona Beach Area Convention & Visitors Bureau (1-800-854-1234; www.daytonabeachcvb.org), 126 E Orange Ave, Daytona Beach 32114. **Daytona Beach Visitors Information Center** is located in the lobby of Daytona USA. The **Ormond Beach Welcome Center** (386-677-7005) and museum is in the MacDonald House at 39 E Granada Blvd.

New Smyrna Beach
Southeast Volusia Chamber of Commerce (386-428-2449 or 1-877-460-8410; www.sevchamber.com), 115 Canal St, New Smyrna Beach 32168.

GETTING THERE *By air*: **Daytona Beach International Airport** (386-248-8069; www.flydaytonafirst.com) is the closest airport. **Orlando International Airport** (407-825-2001; www.orlandoairports.net) is only an hour away.

By bus: **Greyhound** (1-800-231-2222).

By car: Take exit I-95 at **International Speedway Blvd** (US 92), then head east until you reach the beach.

GETTING AROUND **Votran and Trolley** (386-761-7700), $1; monthly passes available. Connects to West Volusia County. **Daytona-Orlando Transit Service** (DOTS; 1-800-231-1965).

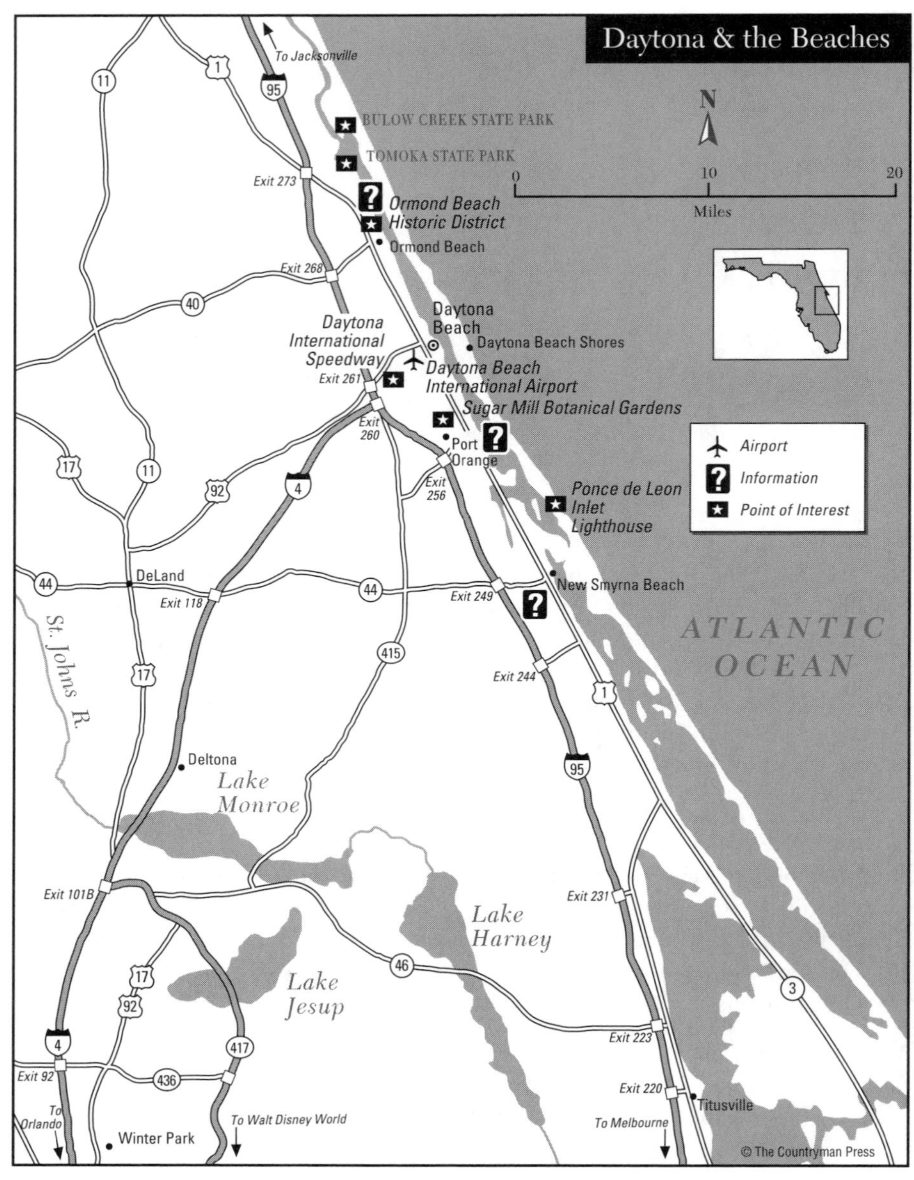

MEDICAL EMERGENCIES **Florida Hospital—Ormond Memorial** (386-676-6000), 875 Sterthaus Ave, and **Florida Hospital—Oceanside** (386-676-6444), 264 S Atlantic Ave, Ormond Beach.

✷ To See

AVIATION Take to the sky with **Air Florida Helicopters** (386-257-6993; www.airfloridahelicpoters.com) and see the racetrack and famous beach from the air.

For the best value, you'll want to lift off from the location nearest your scenic pleasure—the Daytona Flea & Farmers Market, the Daytona Beach Main Street Pier, or the Daytona Beach Kennel Club.

BOAT TOURS

Daytona
Select a narrated tour of the Halifax River watching dolphins, the exquisite riverfront estates, historic treasures, or a sunset cruise with Captain Jim on **A Tiny Cruise Line** (386-226-2343; www.visitdaytona.com/tinycruise), Halifax Harbor Marina, Show Dock, 425 S Beach St, Daytona Beach. Cruises last 1–2 hours ($11–18, with reduced rates for kids). Mon–Sat; call for times.

New Smyrna Beach
Join the **Florida Coastal Cruises, FCC the Manatee** (386-428-0201 or 1-800-881-BOAT; www.manateecruise.com) for a scenic tour of the Intracoastal Waterway. Boarding is at the Sea Harvest Restaurant between the North and South Bridges, New Smyrna Beach. $16 adults, $13 ages 3–12.

Port Orange
You have smooth sailing on pontoon boat river tours with the **Sunny Daze and Starry Nights River Cruises** (386-253-1796; www.sunnydazerivercruises.com), docked at Aunt Catfish's Restaurant. Fifth-generation captain Mark Sheets takes you on an ecoadventure around the Halifax River in search of pelicans, manatee, and bottle-nosed dolphins. Open daily, but reservations required. One hour $10; 2 hours $15; half-day inlet $30.

CHOCOLATE TOUR Satisfy your sweet tooth at **Angell & Phelps Chocolate Factory** (386-252-6531 or 1-800-969-2634; www.angellandphelps.com), 154 S Beach St, Daytona Beach. The confectioner offers free tours of a handmade chocolate factory, with sample! The half-hour tours run about every hour Mon–Fri, with the last tour at 4. Grab lunch and dinner next door with live jazz Thu–Sat.

DRIVE-IN CHURCH In an area dedicated to cars, it comes as no surprise that there's a drive-in Christian church. You'll park in an old drive-in theater while listening to sermons from the comfort of your car. Toot your horn during choir sing-alongs. Located at 3140 S Atlantic Blvd (FL A1A) in Port Orange.

GHOST TOURS **Haunts of Daytona** (386-253-6034; www.hauntsofdaytona.com) is one of the rare ghost tours owned and operated by a certified paranormal, blending science and folklore. You'll meet at sunset at the Quick Stop near the Boot Hill Saloon, then take a walking tour through the area while your ghost hunter, Dusty, weaves comical, sad, romantic, and sometimes macabre tales of local "inhabitants." You can't help but come away with a new appreciation of the paranormal in this articulately presented historical overview of past residents. $8.

Daytona

Howard Thurman Home, 614 Whitehall St. The 1899 two-story Frame Vernacular childhood home of Dr. Howard Thurman, a mentor of Dr. Martin Luther King, is also listed on the Florida Black Heritage Trail.

Baseball legend Jackie Robinson broke the color barrier in pro sports right here at **Jackie Robinson Ballpark** (386-257-3172), 105 E Orange Ave, and is honored with a bronze statue, on permanent display at the entrance.

An important educator in African American history, Mary McLeod Bethune established a school for young girls with only $1.50 and a few packing crates. Her persistent efforts led to the 1923 Bethune-Cookman College. The **Mary McLeod Bethune Home & Gravesite** (386-481-2122; www.bethune.cookman.edu), 640 Mary McLeod Bethune Blvd, is open Mon–Fri 9–4, weekends by appointment. Free.

Housed in the Bethune-Cookman College Carl S. Swisher Library, the **"New Deal" Permanent Exhibit** (386-481-2180), 640 Mary McLeod Bethune Blvd, showcases President Franklin D Roosevelt's "Black Cabinet" and depicts the life in the community of Rosewood from 1845 to the infamous massacre of 1923. Tue and Thu 11–1. Free.

Port Orange

The long-awaited reopening of the **Gamble Place Florida History Education Center at Spruce Creek Environmental Preserve** (386-255-0285), 1819 Taylor Rd, is slated for late 2004. The 150-acre preserve features historic buildings, including a 1907 "Cracker" house built by James Gamble (of Proctor and Gamble fame) as his hunting and fishing retreat. Also on the grounds is a 1907 citrus-packing house. But what I've been waiting for are the Snow White Cottage and the Witch's Hut, which were modeled after Disney's animated film. Originally built in 1938, both structures remained dormant and fell into disrepair. Now they will be available again for all to enjoy.

Ormond Beach

The former winter retreat of John D. Rockefeller, **The Casements** (386-676-3216), 25 Riverside Dr, is named for its charming casement windows. On the National Register of Historic Places, it now serves the community as a cultural center. The Boy Scout Historical Exhibit has been a permanent display since 1980. The home is open for tours Mon–Fri 10–3, Sat 10–noon.

Measuring 24 feet in circumference, the **Fairchild Oak** is the 15th largest tree in Florida. It can be seen in all its majesty on the east side of Old Dixie Hwy across from the James Ormond Tomb.

At Fortunato Park on the northeast end of Granada Bridge sits the **Hotel Ormond Cupola**. The red-roofed cupola sat atop the Hotel Ormond for 204 years. Thousands of visitors stop by to sign the guest book. A mural and memorabilia of the era are shown on Wed, Sat, and Sun 2–4.

LIGHTHOUSES Get a workout climbing Florida's tallest lighthouse. Even the fittest athletes were huffing and puffing as they worked their way up all 203 steps in the **Ponce de Leon Inlet Lighthouse** (386-761-1821; www.ponceinlet.org), 4931 S Peninsula Dr, Ponce Inlet. Completed in 1887, the beacon soars 175 feet high, tapering to just 12 feet at the top. Take it slow; once you get there the view is unsurpassed, and you'll want to enjoy it. The remainder of the grounds also warrants equal attention, from the original lighthouse keeper's dwelling to the museum featuring pirates' treasures and teacups from many of the ships passing through the area. The lens exhibit houses a magnificent, fully restored Fresnel lens that was used at Cape Canaveral until 1993. Open daily 10–5, until 9 in summer. Fee.

Kathy Wolf

THE FRESNEL LENS AT THE PONCE DE LEON INLET LIGHTHOUSE

MOTOR SPORTS Known throughout the world as a top-line racetrack, the **Daytona International Speedway** (386-253-7223; www.daytonainter nationalspeedway.com), 1801 W International Speedway Blvd, Daytona Beach, is where professional AMA Superbikes and NASCAR stock cars race up to 190 mph at such events as the annual Daytona 500. The track is also a venue for concerts, athletic events, and testing and development of race cars. Take a tour of the track and get a better view of the 31-degree banked turns.

Race fans will want to spend some time at **Daytona USA** (386-947-6800; www.daytonausa.com), 1801 W International Speedway Blvd, Daytona Beach, where you can test your skill changing tires at the timed pit stop, or buckle up in Acceleration Alley for a simulated ride of pure speed. Other interactive games, simulators, and historical exhibits are found at this official attraction of NASCAR. Open daily 9–7. Track tours available every half hour until 5, except on race days. $20 adults, $14 ages 6–12. Track tours extra.

MUSEUMS

Daytona Beach

The **Halifax Historical Museum** (386-255-6976; www.halifaxhistorical.org), 252 S Beach St, exhibits the history of racing and Daytona Beach. Open Tue–Fri 10–4, Sat 10–noon.

Located on the beautiful Tuscawilla Nature Preserve, **the Museum of Arts and Sciences** (904-255-0285; www.moas.org), 1040 Museum Blvd, offers an outstanding and varied collection of fine art, scientific, and historical items. It's hard to believe that the 130,000-year-old, 13-foot giant ground sloth came from right here in Florida. The Root family's collection showcases Americana, containing two fully restored railroad cars, a 19th-century apothecary, and hundreds of teddy bears. Coca-Cola fans will love the Coca-Cola exhibit with bottles, memorabilia, and machinery used to bottle the popular soda. The Cuban Museum collection spans 500 years of Cuban history with over 200 objects of Cuban fine and folk art, allowing all cultures a rare glimpse of material not usually seen outside Havana. A fine collection of African art features ceremonial masks and sculpted figures and is also part of the Black Heritage Trail. $7 adults, $2 students and children over 6.

SCENIC TOURS Don't miss the scenic drive the locals have come to know as **The Loop**. There have been concerted efforts to save this 22-mile country drive from encroaching developers, and I hope they succeed; even after driving a couple of hundred miles to get there I was revitalized by cruising this section. Begin on John Anderson Dr at the Granada Bridge in Ormond Beach and head north alongside the Halifax River. You'll pass through a historic residential area, and then the view turns to countryside, with several places to stop and take in the natural beauty. Continue on the winding road and then take a left (west) at Highbridge Rd over the Intracoastal Waterway. Make another turn on Walter Boardman Rd to go farther west to Old Dixie Hwy, where you'll take another left and go south back toward Ormond Beach. The canopy of oaks is enchanted as you reach Tomoka State Park (see *Parks*). Here you'll find one of the oldest oak trees in Florida, the Fairchild Oak.

THE APOTHECARY AT DAYTONA'S MUSEUM OF ARTS AND SCIENCES

Kathy Wolf

The **Ormond Beach Historic Trust, Inc.**, 38 East Granada Blvd, offers self-guided historic scenic tours (386-677-7005) of the Ormond Beach area. Ask for the publication *Historic Scenic Tours for Walking—Driving—Biking Beautiful Ormond Beach* to learn more about the homes, ruins, and Indian mounds along Granada Blvd, John Anderson Dr, US 1, Beach St, and Orchard Lane.

ZOOLOGICAL AND MARINE PARKS Not too far from the Ponce de Leon Inlet Lighthouse is the **Marine Science Center** (386-304-5545; www.marinesciencecenter.com), 100 Lighthouse Dr, Ponce Inlet. At this true working science center, you'll get to see rehabilitation in action from the turtle terrace; if you're lucky, you may be around for a beach release of various sea turtles, such as a loggerhead. A tour guide takes you through turtle rehabilitation, where you'll learn about the different endangered marine species, and then on to the exhibit gallery, where you'll see dioramas of Florida ecosystems, a 5,000-gallon artificial reef, marine mammal bones, and the largest mosquito you'll never want to meet. The small marine park is just right for a quiet day of exploration. Outside, you can take a walk on the nature trail or relax on the scrub oak observation deck admiring the view of the lighthouse. Tue–Sat 10–4, Sun noon–4. Modest fee.

RELEASED SEA TURTLE

Kathy Wolf

✷ To Do

BEACH CRUISING Drive your own car from dawn until dusk on 16 miles of the famous **Daytona Beach**—but there'll be no racing, as the speed limit is strictly enforced. $5.

For a better view, and more importantly to save your car from sand damage, rent an ATV from **JT's ATV's & Carts** (386-383-4063), across from the Bellair Plaza.

DIVING Swim alongside dolphins; see tropical fish, sharks, and barracudas as you scuba and snorkel with ecofriendly **Discover Diving Center** (386-860-3483), 92 Dunlawton Ave, Port Orange.

FAMILY ACTIVITIES

Daytona

🖍 Play miniature golf at **Congo River Golf & Explorations Co**. (386-258-6808), 2100 S Atlantic Ave, or **Pirate's Island Adventure Golf** (386-767-9397), 3420 S Atlantic Ave.

🖍 Chill out with some ice skating at **Sunshine Park Ice Arena** (386-304-8400), 2400 S Ridgewood Ave.

🖍 Go from 0 to 75 mph in under 3 seconds on drag-racing go-carts at **Speed Park Motorsports** (386-253-3278; www.speedparkdaytona.com), 201 Fentress Blvd. Cars run on a track. Riders must be 58 inches tall. $21 for two runs.

FISHING

Daytona Beach

Fish from the piers at **Main Street Pier** (386-253-1212); or **Sunglow Pier** (386-788-3364; www.sunglowpier.com). Fee.

Go charter fishing with **All Star Sport Fishing** (386-304-0105; www.fishallstar.com); **Adventure Yacht Harbor, Inc.** (386-756-2180); or **Halifax Harbor Marine** (1-800-343-2899).

Ponce Inlet

Critter Fleet (386-767-7676 or 1-800-338-0850; www.critterfleet.com) takes you on their 57-foot *Critter Gitter* bottom fishing or trolling; Captain Tad takes you out to sea on his 50-foot custom sportfisherman with **Heavy Hitter Sportfishing Charters** (386-767-2883; www.heavyhittersportfishing.com); **Inlet Harbor Marina** (386-767-5590; www.inletharbor.com) will hook you up with a guide on 35- to 65-foot deep-sea charters; **Sea Spirit Deep Sea Fishing** (386-763-4388; www.seaspiritfishing.com) is an offshore party boat—half day $40 adults, $25 ages 6–12, or full day $60 adults, $40 ages 6–12.

MOTORCYCLE RIDING Rent an Electric Glide or Road King by the day or week at **Daytona Harley-Davidson** (386-253-2453 or 1-800-307-4464; www.hdrental.com and www.daytonaharleydavidson.com), 290 N Beach St, Daytona Beach. Must have a valid motorcycle license. One day from $130, 2 days from $260, 7 days from $595. Rates are higher, with a 3-day minimum, during Bike Week and Biketoberfest.

PARASAILING **Action Water Sports** (386-257-4001), **Daytona Beach Parasail, Inc.** (386-547-6067; www.daytonaparasailing.com), and **Blue Sky Parasail** (386-334-2191), 2025 S Atlantic Ave, will all take you high overhead for spectacular views of the Atlantic coastline ($45–65).

RACE-CAR DRIVING **Richard Petty Driving Experience** (386-947-6530 or 1-800-BE-PETTY; www.daytonausa.com and www.1800bepetty.com), 1801 W International Blvd, Daytona Beach. Do you feel the need for speed? Ride as a passenger going 150 mph while banking 31-degree turns as you travel three times around the famed Daytona racetrack. $134 ages over 16. Want to drive the legendary high banks yourself? You'll need to call to see if you qualify.

* Green Space

BEACHES **Bethune Beach Park**, 6656 S Atlantic Ave, New Smyrna Beach, offers beach access with a playground and bathhouse on site.

Canaveral National Seashore (386-428-3384; www.nps.gov/cana), 7611 S Atlantic Ave, New Smyrna Beach. It's one of the rare places in America where you can backpack along the Atlantic Ocean, where surf and sand meet along a narrow strip of barrier island along the Mosquito Lagoon. Climb the midden at Turtle Mound for a sweeping view of the lagoon, or walk the shifting sands to quiet campsites along the beach. In the shadow of Kennedy Space Center, this protected seashore provides a place for solitude and beach fishing, sunning, and camping. Access the Turtle Mound area via FL A1A, New Smyrna Beach, where you'll find the official visitors center.

Smyrna Dunes Park (386-424-2935; www.volusia.org/park), Peninsula Blvd,

New Smyrna Beach. Tucked away at the northern tip of New Smyrna Beach, the 250-acre preserve of Smyrna Dunes Park protects several fragile coastal environments from the ongoing encroachment of development that has marred most of Central Florida's beaches. No signs lead you to this park, and the parking area holds less than 50 cars, but Smyrna Dunes provides several significant types of recreation—hiking, fishing, and the enjoyment of an unspoiled beach. Fee.

BOTANICAL GARDENS At **Sugar Mill Botanical Gardens** (386-767-1735; www.dunlawtonsugarmillgardens.org), 950 Old Sugar Mill Rd, Port Orange, enjoy a tranquil stroll with the family through this 40-year-old park past a reconstructed 19th century English sugar mill, statues of dinosaurs, and butterfly gardens. Walking under canopies of live oaks, past bromeliads and towering birds of paradise, you'll suddenly notice one of the four dinosaur statues made by Dr. Manny Lawrence in the early 1950s when the gardens were known as Bongoland and feel like you're back in prehistoric times. The 10-acre gardens are listed on the National Register of Historic Places. Please note that this is not a picnic area and food is not allowed in the park. Free; donations appreciated. Gift shop open Wed and Sat.

PARKS

Ormond Beach

The first beach racing began on this beach in 1903. The historic **Birthplace of Speed Park** commemorates this racing event at the corner of Ocean Shore Blvd (FL A1A) and Granada Blvd.

Bulow Creek State Park (386-676-4050), off Old Dixie Hwy, protects one of the South's oldest and largest live oak trees, the Fairchild Oak, thought to be more than 2,000 years old. A 7-mile hiking trail connects this preserve with its springs, ancient forests, and pine plantations to adjacent Bulow Plantation Ruins Historic State Park. Free.

At **Bulow Plantation Ruins Historic State Park** (386-517-2084), CR 2001/Old Kings Highway, the rough road beneath ancient oaks leads you back in time to an 1821 sugar plantation along Bulow Creek, where the ruins of the sugar-processing equipment, slave cabins, and spring will have you marveling at the ingenuity of Florida's pioneer settlers at making a living from the land. The Bulow Creek Trail parallels the creek and its tributaries, leading through one of the oldest forests remaining on Florida's east coast. Canoe rentals available for paddling Bulow Creek, $4 per hour or $20 per day; the park is open for day use only. Fee.

THE FAIRCHILD OAK, THOUGHT TO BE TWO MILLENNIA OLD

Sandra Friend

Ormond Tomb Park (386-257-6000, ext. 5953). Nine miles north of Granada Blvd on Old Dixie Hwy is the tomb of James Ormond, for whom the town is named. It's directly across from the Fairchild Oak and Tomoka State Park.

At **Tomoka State Park** (386-676-4050), 2099 N Beach St, walk in the footsteps of the Timucua as you explore the ancient village site of Nocoroco, once a thriving community on the shores of the Tomoka River. The park offers canoe rentals, a boat ramp, picnicking, fishing, and an extensive shady campground with 100 sites (all hookups except sewer; dump station available).

Port Orange

Spruce Creek Park (386-322-5133; www.volusia.org/parks), 6250 S Ridgewood Ave, Port Orange.

WILD PLACES **Tiger Bay State Forest** (904-226-0250), US 92, Daytona. It's called Tiger Bay because it's a wet place—more than 11,000 acres of boggy pine flatwoods and cypress swamps draining into the Tomoka River. The forest roads are open to hunting, biking, equestrian use, and hiking; the 2-mile Buncombe Hill interpretive trail introduces you to the forest and its history from a trailhead at Indian Lake, off Rima Ridge Rd. Pop a kayak in the lake and tour the wetlands, too!

✷ Lodging

BED & BREAKFASTS

Daytona

Built in 1871, the **Live Oak Bed & Breakfast Inn** (386-252-4667 or 1-800-881-4667; www.halifaxharbor.net/rosarios.htm), 444–448 S Beach St, Daytona 32114, is the oldest standing house in Daytona Beach. The homey inn overlooks the scenic Halifax River. All rooms have private bath, some with Jacuzzi. Continental breakfast. Off-season $90–115, high season $125–150.

The Villa (386-248-2020; www.thevillabb.com), 801 N Peninsula Dr, Daytona 32118, on the National Register of Historic Places, is set in a Spanish mansion in the heart of Daytona Beach. The luxurious home is only three or four blocks from the beach in a quiet neighborhood. You'll feel like royalty and won't want to leave the comfortable ambience of this private residence. Continental breakfast. Rooms $125–250.

New Smyrna Beach 32168

The historic 1883 **Little River Inn Bed & Breakfast** (386-424-0100; www.little-river-inn.com), 532 N Riverside Dr, is set on a 2-acre Floridian estate. The Library Room was the previous owner's law library and houses a complete wall of books as a headboard to the king-sized brass poster bed. The Lighthouse Room reminds you of a ship's captain quarters and faces the Ponce de Leon Inlet Lighthouse. Gourmet breakfast. $89–159.

Step back to 1906 at the **Night Swan Bed & Breakfast** (386-423-4940; www.nightswan.com), 512 S Riverside Dr, overlooking the Intracoastal Waterway. The home features 15 comfortable guest rooms, some with private Jacuzzi bath. $90–170.

HOTELS AND MOTELS

Daytona 32118

Tropical Manor (386-252-4920 or 1-800-253-4920), 2237 S Atlantic Ave, is a fun place to stay with the kids. One of the nicest beachfront motels, this place really shines. The tropical feel is everywhere from the brightly colored picturesque murals to the grassy lawn overlooking the heated king-sized swimming pool and beach. There's also a kiddie pool for the little tykes. One- to three-bedroom apartments, efficiencies, and rooms. For extended stays, ask about renting the house next door.

Other nonparty beachfront motels with rooms, suites, and efficiencies include **Aruba Inn** (386-253-5643 or 1-800-214-1406), $40–165; **Beach House Oceanfront Motel** (386-788-7107 or 1-800-647-3448), $38–99; and the **Cove Motel** (386-252-3678 or 386-828-3251; www.motelcove.com), $35–85.

Ormond Beach 32176

Simple and safe beachfront lodging is found at the **Symphony Beach Club** (386-672-7373; www.visitdaytona.com/symphony), 453 S Atlantic Ave. The clean efficiencies have everything you need, and the Murphy bed allows you extra room during the waking hours. The heated pool is small but inviting. You'll find solitude and comfort, as this place doesn't allow wild parties.

CAMPING AND RV PARKS

Daytona

Daytona Beach Campground (386-761-2663; www.rvdaytona.com), 4601 S Clyde Morris Blvd, Daytona 32129, and **International RV Park** (386-239-0249 or 1-866-261-3698; www.internationalrvdaytona.com), 3175 W International Speedway Blvd, Daytona 32124.

Ormond Beach 32174

Harris Village and RV Park (386-673-0494; www.harrisvillage.com), 1080 N US 1.

Port Orange 32129

Orange Isles Campground (386-767-9170; www.orangeislescampground.com), 3520 S Nova Rd.

✷ Where to Eat

DINING OUT

Daytona

You can't eat chocolate for dinner, so head next door after touring the chocolate factory (see *Chocolate Tour*) to **Angell & Phelps Restaurant and Wine Bar** (386-257-2677), 156 S Beach St, where they'll serve up fine dishes like Tuscan chicken with fettuccine ($14) and grilled filet mignon with port wine and wild mushroom sauce ($19). If your sweet tooth is still aching, try an Angell & Phelps chocolate ruffle cup filled with raspberry mousse and fresh berries ($5). Creative soups, salads, and sandwiches are served for lunch. Open Mon–Sat, lunch and dinner.

Ormond Beach

Stonewood Tavern and Grill (386-671-1200; www.stonewoodgrill.com), 100 S Atlantic Ave. Baked Brie, Emerald Bay crabcakes, oakwood-grilled chicken and steaks, herb-encrusted lamb, and fresh seafood. Open nightly for dinner.

EATING OUT

Daytona

The lively tropics greet you at the door at **Caribbean Jacks** (386-253-5557 or 1-877-525-2257; www.caribbeanjacks.com), 721 Ballough Rd, with a gorgeous view and reasonable prices, like surf and turf for $8 or

Jack's Jamaican jerk chicken for $13. Open for lunch and dinner.

Healthy breakfasts and lunches are served at the **Dancing Avocado Kitchen** (386-947-2022), 110 S Beach St, with crazy bread pizzas, sandwiches, wraps, and veggie burgers all around $6. They have a juice bar, too! Open Mon–Sat.

Get off your hog and settle into a half-pound burger at **Daytona Diner** (386-258-8488), 290½ N Beach St (located in the rear of the Daytona Harley-Davidson dealership). Open Mon–Sat for breakfast and lunch.

Enjoy a relaxing pace at **Rosario's Ristorante** (386-258-6066), 448 S Beach St, attached to the Live Oak Bed & Breakfast Inn (see *Lodging*). Reservations are recommended. Open Tue–Sat for dinner only.

Song Mongolian Grill (386-253-1133; www.songmongoliangrill.com), 132 N Beach St, will stir-fry fresh ingredients on flat-topped grills. Unlimited trips to the grill cost $19 adults, $5 ages to 10. Desserts are extra ($6). Open Tue–Sun for dinner and for Sun brunch noon–3 ($15).

As you walk into the **Starlite Diner** (386-255-9555), 401 North Atlantic Ave, a jukebox might belt out an old Elvis song. Old Americana graces the walls with aged *Time*, *Life*, and *Post* magazine covers of the 1950s. You'll want to get there early on Fri for the all-you-can-eat fish fry ($7).

Ormond Beach

Ormond's oldest restaurant, **Billy's Tap Room** (386-672-1910; www.billys-tap.com), 58 E Granada Blvd, displays photographic memorabilia in an English pub atmosphere. Open Mon–Sat for lunch and dinner (no lunch served on Sat).

Ponce Inlet

You'll think you're in the Caribbean at **Inlet Harbor Marina and Restaurant** (386-767-5590; www.inletharbor.com), 133 Inlet Harbor Rd. This lively tropical paradise has something for everyone. Hot baked bread with key lime butter comes first, followed by such delights as shrimp and pasta dishes ($9–11), fresh island sea scallops ($10), Jamaican-mon chicken breast ($8), juicy prime rib ($10), tropical drinks, and live entertainment. Take a walk on the large deck and 1,000-foot boardwalk overlooking the saltwater marshes and Ponce Inlet Lighthouse. Stop at the gift shop and check out their selection of hot sauces.

Port Orange

Drive away from the beach and head to **Booth's Bowery** (386-761-9464; www.boothsbowery.com), 3657 S Nova Rd at Herbert St. In 1984 Tim and Linda Booth started a small pub-style restaurant with only six employees. Two decades later they have 120 employees and a hoppin' family place. The food is what keeps everyone coming back. Keeping with fresh ingredients and making everything from scratch, they offer just about anything you can think of—shrimp Parmesan, broiled or blackened grouper, "hunger-buster" sandwiches—but they are famous for their Buffalo wings. The kids will enjoy the game room while waiting.

✷ Selective Shopping

Daytona

Daytona Flea and Farmers Market (386-253-3330; www.daytonafleamarket.com), 2987 Bellevue Ave, has new and used bargains galore and fresh produce.

Ocean Walk Village (www.oceanwalkvillage.com), 250 N Atlantic Ave. Upscale collection of shops, restaurants, and a cinema theater overlooking the Atlantic Ocean near the Adam's Mark Resort.

Spend the afternoon in the quaint downtown area at boutiques, antiques and collectibles shops, and intimate restaurants at the **Riverfront Marketplace** (386-671-3272; www.riverfrontmarketplace.com), 262 S–190 N Beach St.

Ormond Beach

"Main Street" shopping (386-676-3329) is in the heart of the historic district, running the length of Granada Blvd. Boutiques, antiques, gifts, and eateries.

✷ Special Events

February: **Speedweeks** (386-253-7223; www.daytonainternationalspeedway.com) features qualifying events culminating in the **Daytona 500**.

Harleys and Hondas cruise into **Bike Week** (1-800-854-1234; www.officialbikeweek.com), the world's largest motorcycle event. Racing at Daytona Speedway, concerts, exhibits, and street festivals dominate the scene for nearly 2 weeks.

March: **Semiannual Birthplace of Speed Celebration** (386-677-3454; www.ormondchamber.com). The first sanctioned time trials of auto racing actually took place on Ormond Beach. This event celebrates that memorable event, featuring reenactments of the historic beach race. Also in Nov.

Students from colleges all over the United States still come to Daytona Beach **Spring Break** (1-800-854-1234; www.daytonabreak.com) for sun and fun and an escape from serious studies.

Hot rods ride in with chrome and style at the **Spring Break Car Show and Swap Meet** (386-255-7355).

July: The biennial 2-week **Florida International Festival** (386-257-7790; www.fif-lso.org) is highlighted by the London Symphony Orchestra. Outside London, the LSO calls Daytona their official summer home.

One of the few races that run at night, the **NASCAR Pepsi 400** (386-253-7223; www.daytonainternationalspeedway.com) is one of the summer's best, with concerts, festivals, and fireworks surrounding the annual event.

October: An international event, with bikers riding coming down from Canada and over from Europe, **Biketoberfest** (1-800-854-1234; www.biketoberfest.org) gives riders one last time to ride before putting the bike up for the winter. This family event takes place throughout Daytona with street festivals, charity events, and wholesome fun.

November: **Semiannual Birthplace of Speed Celebration** (see *March*).

ANTIQUING IN DAYTONA

Daytona Beach CVB

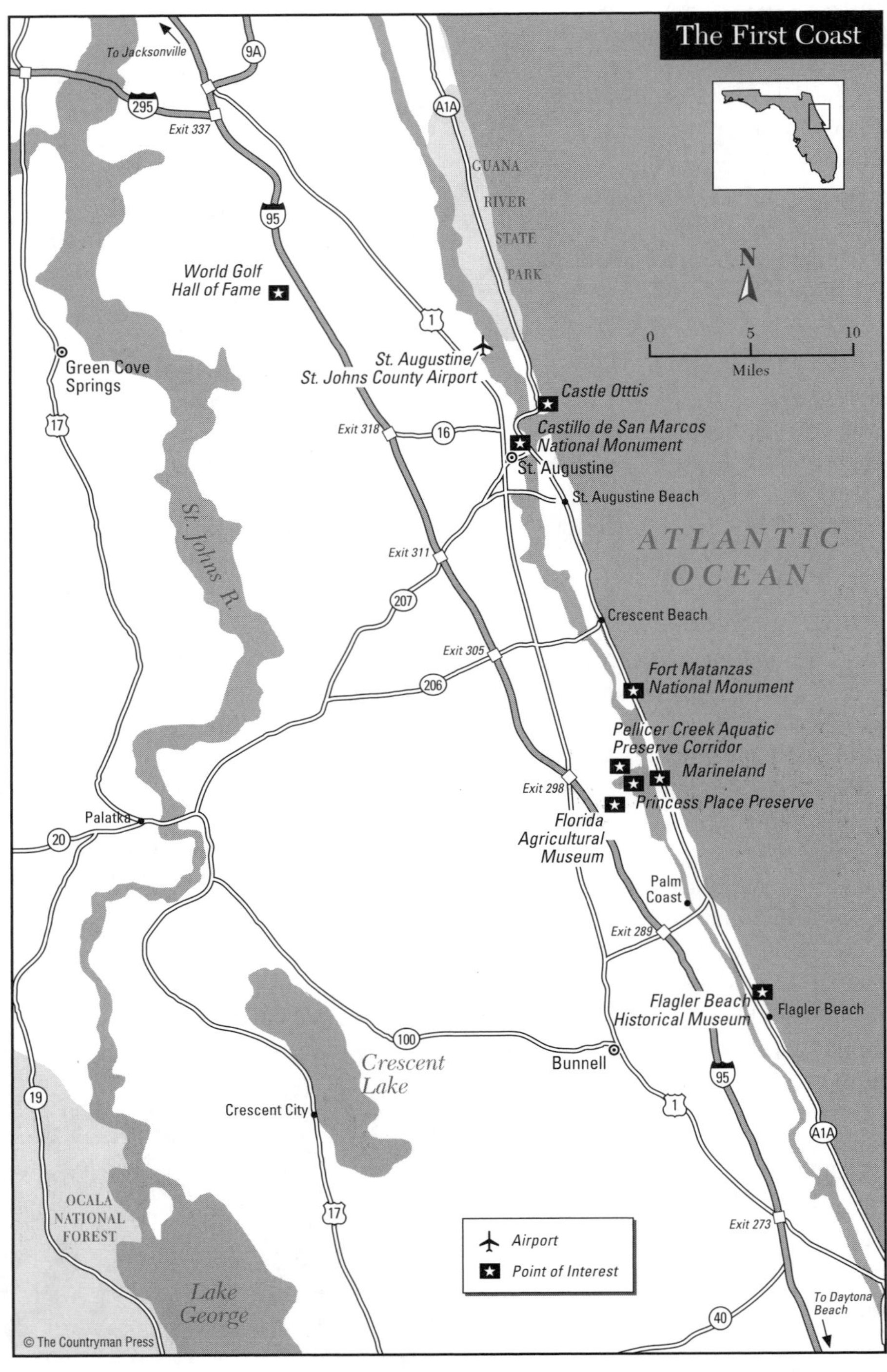
The First Coast
To Jacksonville
9A
295
Exit 337
A1A
GUANA
RIVER
STATE
PARK
95
World Golf
Hall of Fame
N
0
5
10
Miles
1
St. Augustine/
St. Johns County Airport
Green Cove
Springs
Castle Otttis
17
Exit 318
16
Castillo de San Marcos
National Monument
St. Augustine
St. Augustine Beach
St. Johns R.
ATLANTIC
OCEAN
Exit 311
207
Crescent Beach
Exit 305
206
Fort Matanzas
National Monument
Pellicer Creek Aquatic
Preserve Corridor
Marineland
Exit 298
Princess Place Preserve
Florida
Agricultural
Museum
Palatka
20
Palm
Coast
Exit 289
Flagler Beach
Historical Museum
Flagler Beach
100
Bunnell
Crescent
Lake
95
19
Crescent City
1
A1A
OCALA
NATIONAL
FOREST
17
Exit 273
Airport
Point of Interest
Lake
George
40
To Daytona
Beach
© The Countryman Press

THE FIRST COAST

ANASTASIA ISLAND, BEVERLY BEACH, BUNNELL, CRESCENT BEACH, FLAGLER BEACH, ST. AUGUSTINE, VILANO

Founded in 1565 by Spanish explorer Pedro Menéndez de Avilés, **St. Augustine** is the oldest continually occupied European settlement in the United States, a little slice of the Old Country on Florida's shores. Tall coquina and tabby walls hem in narrow alleyways between centuries-old buildings; each home, built defensively on orders of the king of Spain, has its main entrance off a courtyard brimming with greenery. It is a melting pot of cultures, a concentration of history in layers thicker than any other city in the United States, and the birthplace of Florida tourism in the 1890s thanks to Henry Flagler's grand hotels and railroad. It is a city infused with history and art, timeless and yet chic; it's also my favorite city, in my humble opinion the most vibrant and charming destination Florida has to offer.

GUIDANCE For the entire First Coast area, contact the **St. Augustine Visitor's Center** on San Marcos Ave, St. Augustine, and the **Beaches Visitors & Convention Bureau** (www.visitoldcity.com), which offers brochures, on-the-spot reservations, and an introduction to the area via exhibits and a video presentation; visit their web site for great pretrip research.

For additional information on Beverly Beach, contact the **City of Beverly Beach Town Office** (386-439-6888), 2770 N Oceanshore Blvd, Beverly Beach 32136; for Flager Beach, contact the **City of Flagler Beach** (386-517-2000; www.flaglerbeach.org, P.O. Box 70, Flagler Beach 31236, or **Flagler Beach Chamber of Commerce** (904-439-0995 or 1-800-298-0995).

GETTING AROUND St. Augustine is a place to park and get out on foot: The streets are narrow, with loads of pedestrian traffic. If you're planning to spend a day or more and aren't staying in the city (free parking is a great perk that comes with your room), ditch the car in one of the many flat-fee lots such as the one behind the visitors center or along Cordova Street. There is free 2-hour street parking along the waterfront and in residential neighborhoods, if you can find it; there are some short-term metered spaces downtown along King Street. And even to get to Anastasia Island, you truly don't need a car—the **Harbor Shuttle**

(904-460-0237; www.harborshuttletours.com) provides water taxi service across the Matanzas River from the City Marina to Lighthouse Park, Vilano Pier, and other stops: $3 one-way, $5 round-trip, $8 daily pass. Numerous tour operators run trams through the city; see *Sightseeing Tours* for details.

PUBLIC REST ROOMS There are several sets of public rest rooms along St. George St, at the visitors center on San Marcos Ave, and at the marina.

MEDICAL EMERGENCIES **Florida Hospital—Flagler** (386-586-2000), 60 Memorial Medical Pkwy, Palm Coast.

✱ To See

ARCHEOLOGICAL SITES The entire city of St. Augustine is one big archeological site, so much so that any new construction requires a team of archeologists to assess the site before building, since pottery shards, pieces of clay pipes, and the remains of 1800s yellow fever victims have routinely been discovered around town. The Tolomato Cemetery on Cordova Street, circa 1777, was formerly a Tolomato Indian village.

At the **Fountain of Youth** (1-800-356-8222), 11 Magnolia Ave, amble around the pleasant natural grounds at the site of the Timucuan village of Seloy, where Ponce de León stepped ashore on April 3, 1513, to claim the land of *La Florida* for Spain. In 1952 archeologists discovered the Christian burials of Timucua here circa 1565, proving the site was the first Catholic mission in the New World. A dripping rock spring is reverentially referred to as Ponce's Fountain of Youth, and you're invited to take a sip—I did so back in the 1960s, and everyone tells me I look 20 years younger than I am, so who knows? Judge for yourself; of course, you can take home bottled water from the spring for a small fee.

A little-known chapter in Florida history is that of **Fort Mose**, the first free black settlement in the southern United States. Founded in 1738 under the direction of the Spanish, this segregated community of emancipated slaves constructed a log fortress around their village along the salt marsh. In 1740 British invaders from Georgia overran the fortress; its inhabitants escaped to the Castillo de San Marcos in St. Augustine, where they joined a Spanish force to retake the strategic point. Visit the site at **Fort Mose Historic State Park** (904-461-2000; www.fortmose.org), at the end of Saratoga Blvd off US 1 north of St. Augustine.

ART GALLERIES St. Augustine is North Florida's cultural center, with more than 20 galleries showcasing local art. For ongoing arts events in St. Augustine, check in with the **St. Augustine Arts Association** (904-824-2310; www.staugustinearts.org), 22 Marine St, and the **Art Galleries of St. Augustine** (904-829-0065; www.staugustinegalleries.com), which holds Artwalks the first Fri of each month, 5–9, showcasing the galleries in a moving festival. For those who aren't up for walking, the St. Augustine Sightseeing Trains (see *Sightseeing Tours*) offer free rides along the art route. Pick up the *Art Galleries of Saint Augustine Guide* for the full scoop, and see *Selective Shopping* for additional galleries more strongly focused on retail sales.

The neon sign outside the **Butterfield Garage Art Gallery** (904-825-4577; www.butterfieldgarage.com), 137 King St, will catch your attention—stop inside for a blast of "high-octane art" from this 12-artist co-op. With large open spaces accommodating huge canvases, you'll find many different media on display, like Estella J. Fransbergen's raku elephant ear leaves and Wendy Tatter's batik.

Energy Lab Art & Restoration Gallery (904-808-8455; www.energylab gallery.com), 137 King St, has an urban feel, a vibrant co-op where member artists display works in oil, clay, papier-mâché, and more; I felt drawn to the bold acrylics of Becki Hoffman and the haunting, muted scenes of St. Augustine by photographer Taylor Fansset.

The **P.A.S.T.A. Fine Art Gallery, Inc**. (904-824-0251), 214 Charlotte St, has more than 200 original pieces of art on display and changing monthly exhibits.

The large, inviting spaces of the **Rachel Thompson Gallery** (904-825-0205; www.rachelthompsongallery.com), 139 King St, provide the perfect backdrop for Rachel's massive impressionist pastel still lifes, florals, and city scenes.

The oldest gallery in town is the **St. Augustine Art Association** (904-824-2310), 22 Marine St, dating back to 1924, with competitive shows and permanent exhibits.

Tripp Harrison Signature Gallery (904-829-2120; www.lovesemporium.com), 9 King St. In addition to glowing historical paintings by this local artist with a distinctive and popular style, the gallery includes works by two sculptors and seven two-dimensional artists; I fell in love with the vivid blue hues of *Manatee Sunrise*, a giclee by Victor Kowal.

HISTORIC SITES

Beverly Beach

As you drive along FL A1A from Beverly Beach to Vilano Beach, you'll notice an Irish castle off to the side. **Castle Otttis** (904-824-3274) was built in 1988 by Rusty Ickes as a landscape sculpture in "remembrance of Jesus Christ." The castle is an impression of one built over 1,000 years ago and was created under the guidance of the Catholic diocese to replicate the atmosphere of an Irish abbey. Amazingly, just two people, without outside aid, did all the masonry work. True to the castles of the period, the building is open to the environment. A privately owned structure, it is occasionally open for various church services.

Flagler

Princess Place Preserve (386-437-7474), Princess Place Rd, off Kings Rd in north Flagler County. It will take a few turns and a long drive down a dirt road to reach this unique historical treasure. It's magical! The oldest homestead in Flagler County, the beautiful 1886 home looks out over Pellicer Creek and the Matanzas River. Or go by kayak (see *Paddling*) and pull up on shore to have lunch on the veranda or by Florida's first in-ground artesian pool (no swimming in the pool is allowed, however).

St. Augustine

No other U.S. city can boast the number of centuries spanned by historic sites found in downtown St. Augustine. Along Matanzas Bay, the imposing **Castillo de San Marcos**, completed in 1695 of coquina rock quarried from Anastasia Island, provided the city's coastal defense. Although the wooden town was burned several times by invaders, residents survived by taking refuge behind the fortress walls; the sedimentary rock absorbed cannonballs. Now a national park, the Castillo offers interpretive tours, a fabulous bookstore, and excellent views of the bay, 10–5 daily; fee. From the outer walls of the Castillo, a wood-and-stone rampart enclosed the city; visitors entered through the **City Gates**, which still stand at the entrance to **St. George St**.

Dating back to 1874, the **St. Augustine Lighthouse & Museum** (see *Museums*) encompasses the entire light station complex. The light keeper's house is now a fun interactive museum with period items (including the original fourth-order Fresnel lens from the original tower, 1855–1871) and exhibits showcasing the history of light tending along the coast. From the top of the tower, you can see 35 miles on a clear day, fabulous for bird-watching from above. From before 1763, the **Oldest Wooden Schoolhouse**, 14 St. George St, is indeed the oldest school structure remaining in the United States, fun to take the kids through; fee.

Along US 1, you'll see the **Old Jail** (see *Family Activities*), which looks like an 1890s hotel—Henry Flagler had it built in 1891 to move the undesirables away from his hotels to the edge of town, and it served its purpose until 1953. Flagler's Gilded Age also brought the stately **Bridge of Lions** on FL A1A connecting St. Augustine with Anastasia Island. Residents have successfully fended off efforts to replace the bridge with a more modern structure, despite the traffic delays caused when the bridge opens to let ships through. If you're stuck on the bridge, grin and bear it—it's a small price for historic preservation of such a grand structure!

FIRING A VOLLEY AT CASTILLO DE SAN MARCOS

Sandra Friend

Take a free guided boat ride out to **Fort Matanzas National Monument** (904-471-0116) on Rattlesnake Island, where you may be joined by dolphins or manatees. The military outpost has been here since 1565. The small but impressive fortress, built in 1740, protected Spanish St. Augustine from British encroachment. Nature walks and torchlight tours. Call for schedule.

HISTORIC HOMES With the discovery of coquina came solid buildings of stone. The **Gonzales-Alvarez House** (904-824-2872; www.oldcity.com/oldhouse), 271 Charlotte St, is the city's oldest house, its tabby floors laid in the early 1700s; during the British period in 1776, the house served as a tavern. **Oldest House** tours hosted by the St. Augustine Historical Society interpret the lives and times of its visitors and residents; fee. The nearby **Sequi-Kirby Smith House** (904-825-2333), 6 Artillery Lane, houses the historical society research library and was the family home of Confederate general Edmund Kirby-Smith; the house dates back to the Second Spanish Period.

St. George and its cross streets are notable for homes dating back to the late 1700s—look for historical plaques with names and dates on each home. The **Peña-Peck House**, circa 1750, was the residence of the royal treasurer from Spain; it's managed as a house museum by a nonprofit, the Woman's Exchange (see *Selective Shopping*); fee. **Old St. Augustine Village** (904-823-9722), corner of Cordova and Bridge, provides an entire block's worth of historic homes to browse ($7 adults, $6 seniors, $5 students), nine houses from 1790 to 1910. The **Colonial Spanish Quarter** (904-825-6830), 53 St. George St, is a living history museum set in 1740, showcasing a dozen historic homes and structures in a complex with traditional craftsmen—coopers, smiths, shoemakers, and more—in period dress tending to everyday life in the Presidio de San Agustin, a fascinating look into Florida's past. Open for self-guided tours 9–5:30 except Christmas; adults $6.50, children $4.

HISTORIC HOTELS When railroad magnate Henry Flagler built his destination hotels in the 1880s, he kicked off Florida tourism as we know it today. Only one, the Cordova, remains a hotel, renovated in the 1990s into the elegant **Casa Monica** (see *Lodging*). The others are open to the public but serve different uses. **The Alcazar** is now city hall and the Lightner Museum (see *Museums*), where a café is tucked into the giant indoor swimming pool (the largest of its time in the 1880s), and visitors can wander through the original ballroom and baths. Flagler bequeathed his grand **Ponce de Leon** to become Flagler College (www.flagler.edu), a liberal arts college that started out as a women's school. Public access is limited, but you can join a walking tour (see *Walking Tours*) to immerse in the grandeur of Flagler's vision, as executed by interior decorator Louis Comfort Tiffany. The **Villa Zorayda**, built in 1883 by Franklin Smith as a one-tenth-scale replica of the Alhambra in Spain, became a casino in 1922 and then an attraction, Zorayda Castle, in 1936. It recently closed its doors, but stop by and take a look at the exterior—it's stunning.

HISTORIC CHURCHES When Father Francisco López de Mendoza Grajales offered the first Mass in St. Augustine, he did so at the **Mission Nombre de Dios** (904-824-2809), 27 Ocean Ave, more than four centuries ago. On the grounds of the ancient mission, a modern 208-foot stainless-steel cross marks the founding of St. Augustine in 1565; the statuette within the ivy-covered shrine of **Our Lady of La Leche** dates back to 1598. At St. George and Cathedral Sts, the **Cathedral Basilica**, the first Catholic parish in the New World, was built in 1797 with stones from the ruins of the original mission. The **St. Photios Greek Orthodox National Shrine** (904-829-8205), 41 St. George St, is the only Greek

Orthodox shrine in the United States. Henry Flagler and his wife are buried in a tomb within the **Memorial Presbyterian Church**, 32 Sevilla St, built in 1889 by Flagler.

MUSEUMS

Bunnell

Holden House Museum (386-437-0600), 204 East Moody Blvd, was built in 1918 by Mr. and Mrs. Tom Holden, who lived there until 1970. The rooms are decked with authentic furniture of the times, and the gables are inset with pieces of apothecary bottles, antique colored glass, and old pieces of dishes. Open Wed 10–1.

Flagler

Trace the history of the city to the early 1900s at the **Flagler Beach Historical Museum** (386-517-2025), 207 S Central Ave. Fossils, Indian tools, newpaper clippings, and old photographs are on display Tue–Fri 10–2 and the second Sat of the month noon–3.

Florida Agricultural Museum (386-446-7630), 1850 Princess Place Rd, Palm Coast, brings the First Coast's heritage alive in a 300-acre living history educational park. Learn about the first farmers—the Native Timucua—in a Native American village, the European influence and Spanish colonial agriculture through rare breeds of Cracker cattle and horses, and an 1890s rural town with a sawmill and turpentine operation.

St. Augustine

The **Governor's House Museum** (904-825-5033), corner of King and Cathedral Sts, exhibits St. Augustine's finest collection of historical artifacts, with more than 300 colorful displays recounting life from Timucuan times through the founding of St. Augustine, the Seminole Wars, and the Flagler era. Open Tue–Sat 10–4; fee.

Otto C. Lightner, founding editor of *Hobbies* magazine, was a collector of collections. I remember the **Lightner Museum** (904-824-2874; www.lightnermuseum.org), 75 King St, which opened in 1948, when it showcased its treasures in a way a kid could understand—open a hotel room door, and you'd find a room full of postcards. Or a room full of buttons. Or a room full of teacups. Then city hall moved into the Hotel Alcazar in 1971, saving the financially struggling museum but squeezing it into one segment of the hotel. Befitting its opulent setting, the museum shifted its emphasis to its upscale objets d'art—oil paintings, carvings, fine glasswork, and antique furnishings—although you can still find the button and matchbook collections tucked away in nooks, and one portion of the museum is devoted to the sciences, with minerals, archeological specimens, and an Egyptian mummy. As you stroll past the hotel's grand indoor swimming pool (the world's largest in 1888) and spa, you'll feel a part of the Gilded Age. Open 9–5 daily except Christmas; admission $8 adults, $2 ages 12–18, under 12 free with adult.

The **Museum of Weapons & Early American History** (904-829-3727; www.museumofweapons.com), 81-C King St, is a small space packed with authentic historical ephemera, including Florida's finest exhibit of Civil War armaments; check out their shop for period books and collectible papers. Open 9 AM daily; fee.

Old Florida Museum (904-824-8874; www.oldfloridamuseum.com), Old Jail Complex (see *Family Activities*), presents an excellent introduction to the region's long and storied past, from exhibits of Florida's First Peoples to the tale of Fort Mose (see *Archeological Sites*), the Spanish and British settlements, and the tale of Henry Flagler and his Model Land Company, the first snowbird real estate scheme in Florida history. 10–5 daily; fee.

The **Spanish Military Hospital** (904-827-0807), 3 Aviles St, provides a glimpse into 18th-century medical treatments at the Royal Hospital of Our Lady of Guadalupe on a narrated tour through this haunted building, with dioramas and artifacts like porcelain bedpans and scary-looking period medical instruments. Fee.

St. Augustine Lighthouse & Museum (904-829-0745; www.staugustine lighthouse.com), 81 Lighthouse Ave, isn't just a working historic lighthouse but an entire light station complex. Built in 1871 and outfitted with a first-order Fresnel lens (still functional, but repaired in 1986 after damage from a vandal's bullets), the 165-foot lighthouse is the second permanent tower to stand along this coastline. Climb the steep spiral staircase (219 steps with landings) for a 30-mile view of the coast; look down and you can catch flocks of ibises in flight between their roosts at the St. Augustine Alligator Farm and their feeding grounds on the mudflats of Anastasia Island. The museum in the light keeper's house provides excellent interactive interpretive exhibits. Admission $6.50 adults, $5.50 seniors, $4 for ages 7–11.

World Golf Hall of Fame (904-940-4000; www.wgv.com), 1 World Golf Place. I'll be the first to tell you that I don't play golf. But that doesn't mean that I'm not intimately aware of the game. After having learned the game from none other than Humphrey Bogart, my dad spent 70 years on fairways and greens from Maine to Florida. And my mom, at 81, continues to play 9 to 18 holes a day. They would love the World Golf Village, so it was with their eyes that I approached this monument to legends and deeply rooted history. The museum will take you from the birth of the game in St. Andrews, Scotland, all the way through to today's champions. I was surprised to find that as a nongolfer I was very interested in the historical artifacts and in particular the Shell Hall, where a stunning crescent of acrylic pedestals honors Hall of Fame members. The second floor is set up much like 18 holes, with the front 9 covering the historical game, where you can walk across a replica of the famed St. Andrews Swilcan Burn

THE WORLD GOLF HALL OF FAME

Kathy Wolf

Bridge, and the back 9 covering the modern game, where at one of the exhibits you'll see President Eisenhower's golf cart and at another discover the elements of golf course design. Test your swing at the virtual-reality exhibit. Open Mon–Sat 10–6, Sun noon–6. $12 adults, $7 ages 5–12.

WINERY At **San Sebastian Winery** (1-888-352-9463; www.sansebastianwinery.com), 157 King St, enjoy a tour of the processing plant in the arts district (the vineyards are off site at a sister winery) with a complimentary wine tasting thereafter. A wine and jazz bar offers a laid-back place to chat with friends, or browse the Wine Shop for gourmet foods, kitchen items, and the signature wines of San Sebastian. Open daily.

ZOOLOGICAL AND MARINE PARKS **Marineland** (904-460-1275 or 1-888-279-9194; www.marineland.net), 9600 Ocean Shore Blvd, just south of Summer Haven on FL A1A, is the world's oldest marine park, opened in 1938. Marineland's unique location on the Atlantic Ocean permits the constant flow of fresh salt water into its tanks, which reduces visibility but results in a healthy population of dolphins, sea turtles, sharks, and other marine life. One of the first things you notice is that they have safety for their animals in mind. The state-of-the-art filtration system cleans any unwanted bacteria and organisms from the ocean, making it safe for you, too. Marineland also prides itself on its generativity; one of its dolphins, Nellie, just celebrated her 50th birthday! Stop and talk to the volunteer docents and you'll discover their love for the park and its inhabitants, which range from horseshoe crabs and sea urchins in a tidal pool to dolphins and their young. Although small in size, the park has a heavy focus on interactive programs, from feeding to scuba and snorkeling with the dolphins. In addition, the park sponsors a unique public outreach program. "It's important that marine parks work to make a difference in the endangered marine populations," says manager Joy Hamph, and toward that end, Marineland actively manages Florida's only whale-watch program (see *Whale-Watching*). Open 9:30–4:30 daily, general admission $14 adults, $9 children; additional fees for interactive programs. Dolphin Encounter $120; Dive Marineland scuba $65 or snorkel $35; paint with a dolphin $45; and touch and feed a dolphin $20. Learn to scuba in the tank among real marine creatures with **Spruce Creek Scuba** (386-767-1727) or **Scuba Cove Adventures** (904-223-1300). Look for the new hard-hat diving in a real 1940s Miller Dunn helmet.

A MARINELAND DOLPHIN GREETS GUESTS.
Kathy Wolf

At the adjacent **Whitney Laboratories** (904-461-4000; www.whitney.ufl.edu), managed by the University of Florida, scientists and students delve into the secrets of the deep to apply to biomedical and biotechnical research. "Marine invertebrates are great models for human beings," said Maureen Welch as she showed me recent studies using sea slugs to model the neurological problems of Alzheimer's patients. In addition to its permanent exhibits at Marineland, the lab holds an open house each spring. Groups can arrange private tours. A free lecture series provides informative background on marine topics, Jan–May, on the second Thu of each month.

♿ I knew it as a kitschy place when I was a kid, with alligator wrestling and snake stunts, but the **St. Augustine Alligator Farm** (904-824-3337; www.alligatorfarm.com), FL A1A, is now a fully accredited zoological park. It hasn't lost its funky charm. Dating back to 1893, it's one of Florida's oldest tourist draws, with pits filled with alligators. Marvel at the many reptilian species represented here, including albino alligators from Louisiana, endangered Nile crocodiles, caimans, and gharials that share their space with tiny muntjac deer. My favorite part of the park has always been the Alligator Swamp Nature Trail and Native Bird Rookery, where more than a dozen species of birds (including wood storks, green-backed herons, and least bitterns) build their nests in early March and raise their young in the trees, protected from predators like egg-stealing raccoons by the alligators cruising below. It's one of the few places I know where you can get close enough to photograph fledgling herons without disturbing them. There are other themed sections to the park, including the Great Down Under with Australian creatures and a section with animals of the rain forest; daily shows now focus on interpretation of species behavior. Open daily 9–5, with admission $14.95 ages 12 and over, $8.95 ages 5–11, $7.48 wheelchair.

✷ To Do

BEACHES Heading north on FL A1A from Ormond Beach, **Gamble Rogers Memorial State Recreation Area** (see *Green Space*) provides a relaxed setting for sunbathing and swimming on soft orange sands. There isn't much beach left at Flagler Beach below the seawall promenade, so continue north past Beverly Beach for **Varn Park** on FL A1A, a county park with beach access, changing rooms, and outdoor showers. The **Coquina Beach at Washington Oaks State Park** (see *Green Space*) is a don't-miss geological treasure, but you can't swim there. Sunbathers enjoy the strand just south of **Marineland**, where a large county parking lot and boardwalk provide access, as well as the strips of shell-dotted sand along **Matanzas Inlet**. Parking areas and dune boardwalks flank the highway after you cross the inlet. In **St. Augustine Beach**, use Ocean Trace Road for drive-on access to the strand, or head up to my favorite hangout, **Anastasia State Park** (see *Green Space*), for 4 miles of unsullied sand with no cars allowed to intrude into your oceanfront experience. The 19 miles of **Flagler Beach** are unique, as the crushed coquina rock colors the beach a soft red.

BICYCLING A paved bicycle path stretches more than 12 miles south from Marineland toward Flagler Beach, paralleling scenic FL A1A.

BIRDING One of the best spots in the region for bird-watching is around the lagoons at **St. Augustine Alligator Farm** (see *Zoological and Marine Parks*), where the long-term presence of so many alligators assures the nesting colonies of egrets, herons, and wood storks that raccoons won't steal precious bird eggs. Along FL A1A in **Crescent Beach**, watch for nande conures, a variety of chartreuse parrot that has naturalized along the Intracoastal Waterway.

BOATING

St. Augustine

Rent or charter your own boat at the marina from **Bay Ray** (904-826-0010; www.bayrayrentals.com), 1 Dolphin Dr, which has miniature speedboats, pontoon boats, ocean kayaks, fishing charters, and a 33-foot sailing sloop. On **Sail Boat Adventures** (904-347-7183; www.villavoyager.com), Captain Paul Kulik provides an intimate sailing adventure for up to four people, $38 per person, tailored to your interests. The **Schooner *Freedom*** (904-810-1010), St. Augustine's one and only tall ship, takes guests out on relaxing 3- and 4-hour cruises on Matanzas Bay daily. This replica of a blockade-runner is a 34-ton clipper, a family operation that lets guests take the wheel after passing through the Bridge of Lions—ride this, and you can be the one who holds up bridge traffic instead of waiting in it.

THE SCHOONER *FREEDOM*

Sandra Friend

Sailing in to St. Augustine? You'll find plenty of slips at the **St. Augustine Municipal Marina** (904-825-1026); hail the harbormaster on VHF channel 16. Dockage (including use of showers and water) runs $4–5 per hour, $150 (minimum) weekly, $250 (minimum) monthly, electricity extra.

CHOCOLATE TOUR Whetstone Chocolates (904-825-1700; www.whetstonechocolates.com), 2 Coke Rd, St. Augustine. Now that you know there's a chocolate factory tour and outlet store, how can you miss it? In 1967 the Whetstone family started their handmade chocolate business in the historic district; as the public appetite for their goodies increased, so did their production. It's now a sleek factory along FL 312, where 25,000 pounds of chocolate pass through every 8 hours, and their signature chocolate oranges shouldn't be missed. Stop by for a free self-guided tour (10–5:30 Mon–Sat) and samples of chocolate!

DINNER THEATER At the **Garden Eatery** (904-471-2691), 4320 FL A1A S, St. Augustine, prepare to play sleuth as part of **MurderWatch Mystery Dinner Theatre** on Sun at 2 PM (see "Orlando Metro"). Or for those who've always wanted to hop up and down in front of a game-show host, join the hysterics of **Game Show Mania** Tue 6–9. Reservations are recommended for both shows.

ECOTOURS Go dolphin watching on the ***Victory III* Scenic Cruise** (1-800-542-8316; www.scenic-cruise.com), 4125 Coastal Hwy, St. Augustine, a narrated trip that departs from the St. Augustine Marina up to four times daily, or cruise with the *Lucky Ducky,* **Blue Water Marina's** (904-819-6741) dolphin trip twice daily from the marina.

FAMILY ACTIVITIES A fixture in St. Augustine, the **antique carousel** at Davenport Park on San Marcos Ave still costs only a dollar for a spin. The **Old Jail** (904-829-3800; www.historictours.com), 167 San Marcos, with huge kid appeal, is just across the street. It's a historic building tour with a kitschy spin, where a loony prisoner leads you, the new guy, into lockup. Open daily, 8:30–4:30; fee.

Looking like an escapee from a Charles Addams cartoon, the original **Ripley's Believe It or Not Museum** (904-824-1606; www.ripleys.com), 19 San Marco Ave, displays cartoonist Robert Ripley's weird stuff in a funhouse atmosphere; $10.95 adults, $6.95 ages 5–12, locals $5. At **Potter's Wax Museum** (1-800-584-4781; www.potterswax.com), 17 King St, the 160 wax stiffs don't move (mostly); in addition to the usual suspects (politicians and movie stars), there are lesser-known faces from history and art, including Voltaire, Sir Francis Drake, St. Augustine founder Menéndez, Rembrandt van Rijn, and Gainesborough. And what wax museum would be complete without a horror chamber, in this case direct from Vincent Price's *House of Wax*? Open 9–9; $7.95 adults, $6.95 seniors, $4.75 ages 6–12.

Play **miniature golf** at Anastasia Mini Golf, 701 Anastasia Blvd, or try your hand at the mini golf course between the marina and Bridge of Lions in the city limits.

FISHING **Coastal Outdoor Kayaks** (904-471-4144), 291 Cubbedge Rd, Crescent Beach, will rent you a boat, kayak (see *Paddling*), or canoe and all the gear and bait you'll need. Guides available.

A popular spot with saltwater anglers, the **Flagler Beach Pier** is a great place to try some saltwater fishing or just to get a great view of the beach. Anglers can check in at the **Bait and Tackle Shrimp Box**, FL 100, Flagler.

A public pier along FL A1A provides access for saltwater anglers to try their stuff at St. Augustine Beach. For outfitting and access to the Intracoastal Waterway, visit **Devil's Elbow Fishing Resort** (904-471-0398; www.devilselbowfishingresort.com), 7507 FL A1A S. A local landmark, Devil's Elbow provides everything from bait to guide service and boat rentals, and has a handful of fish-camp-style vacation rentals on site.

GOLF St. Augustine's newest offering is the **Royal St. Augustine Golf & Country Club** (904-824-GOLF; www.royalstaugustine.com), 301 Royal St. Augustine Pkwy, with 18 holes carved out from pine forests and wetlands.

HIKING All regional and state parks offer nature and hiking trails, but you can't go wrong with a visit to any of the conservation areas (see *Wild Places*) managed by the St. Johns Water Management District. Backpackers will appreciate the primitive campsite overlooking the Matanzas River at **Moses Creek Conservation Area**, while day hikers who like to stretch their legs can revel in half a dozen different habitats (and benches with scenic views) on a 9-mile loop on the undeveloped southern portion of **Guana River State Park**. One don't-miss short and free spot for families is the boardwalk at **Haw Creek Conservation Area** outside Bunnell, where alligator sightings are assured. For specifics on regional hiking trails, read *50 Hikes in North Florida*.

PADDLING With its dozens of uninhabited islands on which to stop and lunch or camp, the Matanzas River is a popular paddlers' getaway. You'll see manatees

GHOST TOURS The Ancient City has equally ancient ghosts—and a bevy of tour operators vying to introduce them to you. Standing atop the seawall, her scarf and 1790s attire fluttering in gusts of wind spawned by a distant hurricane, Amanda spun the tale of Jean Ribault's failed attack on St. Augustine, and his armada's untimely demise. "For three days, the bay ran red with blood . . . the fishermen say to beware, when looking into the water after dark, of the faces of the slaughtered Huguenots . . ." Around her, the audience stood rapt with attention. Wrapping legend around history and serving it up as entertainment, St. Augustine's ghost tours do a bang-up job of spinning spooky stories that'll have your hair standing on end. Amanda's outfit, the granddaddy of ghost tours, is **A Ghostly Experience** (1-888-461-1009; www.ghosttoursofstaugustine.com), which was founded to provide visiting school groups with something to do after dark. Each walk is different, touching on a handful of the thousands of stories that permeate this city. Reservations are generally recommended for any of the ghost tours, like **Spirits of St. Augustine** (904-829-2396), 18 St. George; the **Haunted Pub Tour** (1-866-PUB-TOUR; www.ghostaugustine.com), 123 St. George; **Ancient City Tours** (1-800-597-7177; www.ancientcitytours.net), 3 Aviles St; **Pirate Ghost Tours** (904-501-7508), 27 San Marco Ave; and **Ghosts & Gravestones** (904-826-3663; www.ghostsandgravestones.com), 2 St. George St, which also offers rides on the "Trolley of the Doomed." Or go "ghostbusters" with **Haunted St. Augustine** (904-823-9500; www.hauntedstaug.com), where you'll take electromagnetic and thermal readings as well as photos to reveal ghostly presences. Never has history been so much fun! Trips cost $6–10 and run 1–2 hours.

and dolphins cruising along this saline inland waterway, which runs between St. Augustine and Summer Haven. Although there is no official "blueway" route, a navigational chart will help you chart your course among the many public lands that border the waterway. Most visitors put in at Faver-Dykes State Park or at the county park in Summer Haven. Canoe and kayak rentals and put-in are available at Devil's Elbow Fishing Resort (see *Fishing*).

Brad and Joyce Miller at **Coastal Outdoor Kayaks** (904-471-4144), 291 Cubbedge Rd, Crescent Beach, have a great selection of kayaks, canoes, and ecotours available for everyone from the novice to the experienced paddler. And Joyce can tell you all about Princess Place Preserve (see *Historic Sites*) and how to get there—she used to be the caretaker! Take a 2-hour Kayak Birding Tour ($35) of local salt marshes to get close to migrating wading birds as they feed on exposed oyster bars and sandbars. A naturalist will take you on a 2-hour Naturalist Guided Walking Tour ($10) of Princess Place Preserve, Moses Creek Conservation Area, or Matanzas Inlet, pointing out local plant and wildlife. Or go on a 4-hour combo Naturalist Walking/Kayak Tour ($65), where you'll paddle to a small, remote island and lunch at Cresent Beach Café, followed by a walk around coastal marshes and upland pine while searching for wading birds and oysters. For about an hour and a half you can paddle at sunset ($25) on stable double kayaks through the saltwater marshes. If you have your Florida state fishing license, you'll want to try kayak fishing ($30 per hour). All instruction, bait, and gear are included. Or rent kayaks or canoes and explore on your own. And hey, on Mother's Day, moms paddle free!

Tropical Kayaks (386-445-0506; www.tropicalkayaks.com), at the Palm Coast Golf Resort Marina, Palm Coast. Take a 2-hour guided ecotour ($35) past historical treasures or rent a surfing kayak and explore the local beach and inlets for manatees, dolphins, and jumping mullet. Rentals: 2 hours, $15; 4 hours, $25; double kayaks for 24 hours, $35. Bicycle rentals also available.

PARASAILING **Smile High Parasail Inc.** (904-819-0980; www.smilehighparasail.com), 111 Avenida Menendez #C, St. Augustine, offers crew-supported soars above the Matanzas River; up to three can fly together.

WINDSURFING At Salt Run Inlet in Anastasia State Park (see *Beaches*), **Windsurfing St. Augustine** (904-460-9111; www.windsurfingstaugustine.com) rents windsurfers, sea kayaks, canoes, and catamarans, 10–6 daily. Sailing and windsurfing lessons offered by qualified instructors.

SCENIC DRIVES Few highways in the northern Florida peninsula match the beauty of FL A1A, the **Buccaneer Trail**, particularly in sections where the dunes remain preserved and free of development: between Ormond Beach and Flagler Beach, and north of St. Augustine through Guana River State Park. Designated a National Historic Scenic Byway, two-lane A1A provides a breezy seaside driving experience. Along the St. Johns River, FL 13 and CR 13 are designated the **William Bartram Scenic Highway**, passing through farmland and river bottom between Hastings and Jacksonville.

SIGHTSEEING TOURS Besides ghost tours and walking tours, St. Augustine offers some of the state's oldest narrated tours, including the **St. Augustine Sightseeing Trains** (1-800-226-6545; www.redtrains.com), 170 San Marco Ave, in operation since 1953 and offering complimentary pickup and drop-off at city motels as well as a truly educational tour of the city, with on/off privileges at all stops. Three-day ticket, $14 adults, $5 ages 6–12; package tours with historic and attraction admissions included run $20–70.

Old Town Trolley Tours (904-829-3800; www.trolleytours.com), running out of a depot at the Old Jail (see *Family Activities*), covers more than 100 points of interest with 20 stop-offs and reboarding privileges for 3 days on your ticket.

For a truly romantic tour, hop on board one of the sightseeing carriages along the bayfront near the Castillo de San Marcos, from **St. Augustine Transfer Company** (904-829-2391), $15 adults, $7 children 5–11. Or ride in style in a 1929 Model A or 1955 Chrysler Imperial on an **Antique Car Tour**; check with the Casa Monica Hotel (see *Lodging*) for details.

WALKING TOURS In addition to leading ghost tours, costumed guides from **Tour St. Augustine** (904-825-0087), 6 Granada St, lead walking tours touching on many different themes, from architectural history to the Victorian era, as do the folks at **Old City Walks, Etc.** (904-797-9733). Tours at **Flagler College** (904-823-3378; www.flagler.edu), May–Aug, offer a look at the grandeur of Henry Flagler's flagship, the **Hotel Ponce de Leon** (now the college campus); fee. For an immersion into the Gilded Age, join **Dr. Bronson and Friends** (904-377-2451) for a walking tour of the city's five 1880s hotels. **Walk About St. Augustine** (904-824-2872; www.walkaboutstaugustine.com), 14 St. Francis St, offers a portable guide for $15—an MP3 player providing layers of audio detail about the city's layers of history.

THE FORMER HOTEL PONCE DE LEON IS NOW FLAGLER COLLEGE.

Sandra Friend

WHALE-WATCHING Each winter, right whales migrate from sites near Newfoundland to the shores of St. Johns County and their ancestral calving ground, where they give birth and raise their young. The right whale is the most endangered whale on earth, with only about 350 members of the species remaining. Working through a program coordinated by Marineland and the Whitney Laboratory (see *Zoological and Marine Parks*), volunteer whale-watchers take up positions along beaches in Crescent Beach, Summer Haven, and Marineland to record whale sightings. Each whale has a unique pattern of spots, making it easier to positively identify specific individuals.

✷ Green Space

BEACHES **Anastasia State Park** (904-461-2033), 1340A FL A1A S, St. Augustine. It's my favorite place to take a walk on the beach—an 8-mile unsullied round trip to the tip of the island, right along Matanzas Pass, where you can sit and watch the sailboats come into the harbor at St. Augustine. Bird-watching is superb along the shoreline and the lagoons, and the campground in the coastal hammock can't be beat. Swimmers and surfers flock to these shores every summer, so it gets pretty busy on weekends. The park also includes the historic coquina quarries used by the Spanish to quarry blocks for the Castillo de San Marcos and other structures in the Ancient City, and windsurfing lessons and rentals are available at the lagoon. Fee.

The **Coquina Beach** at Washington Oaks Gardens State Park (see *Botanical Gardens*) is one of Florida's true geological treasures, a natural sculpture created by the sea digging into an outcropping of the shell-laden Anastasia limestone of the Atlantic Coastal Ridge. You can't swim here, but it's worth a visit to take a walk on the beach and marvel at the incredible rock formations and tidal pools sculpted from coquina. Fee.

Gamble Rogers Memorial State Recreation Area at Flagler Beach (386-517-2086), 3100 S FL A1A, Flagler Beach. With soft sands tinted orange by coquina shells and an expansive 144-acre beachfront, this is a park for relaxing and catching some rays. Thirty-four campsites (no shade) directly overlook the Atlantic Ocean, with 30-amp hookups, electric and water, hot showers, and a dump station. The park is also home to the annual Gamble Rogers Folk Festival. Fee.

BOTANICAL GARDENS **Washington Oaks Gardens State Park** (386-446-6780), 6400 N Oceanshore Blvd, Palm Coast. On the site of the first Spanish land grant in the region, these formal gardens were lovingly cultivated between 1936 and 1964 by Owen D. Young, chairman of the board of General Electric, and his wife. Meandering pathways lined with azaleas and camellias make a maze through a hammock of ancient live oaks, past benches set in scenic spots for quiet contemplation. On the wilder side of the park, walk the short Mala Compra Trail to explore mangroves and needlerush along the Matanzas River en route to a popular picnic area; hike the 1.7-mile Bella Vista Trail to see coastal scrub, maritime hammock, and dense hardwood forests. Fee.

PARKS **Lighthouse Park** on Anastasia Island has a playground tucked under the windswept oaks, a boat ramp with access to the inlet, a restaurant on the water, and a bait shop.

Faver-Dykes State Park (904-794-0997), 1000 Faver Dykes Rd, St. Augustine. Nestled in oak hammocks along Pellicer Creek, this peaceful park offers camping, nature trails, and some of the best paddling along the coast. Bring your kayak or rent a canoe (reservations required) to enjoy the Pellicer Creek Trail, gliding through mazes of needlerush as you paddle out to the Matanzas River. A new addition to the park, **Mellon Island**, is accessible only by boat and open to primitive camping. Fee.

A Flagler County park, the **Princess Place Preserve** (386-437-7490; www.flaglerparks.com/princess_place1.htm) off US 1 includes the historic Cherokee Lodge and Florida's first in-ground swimming pool (see *Historic Sites*); camp in the deeply shaded campground and walk the network of short hiking trails that take you to freshwater and saltwater marsh views and around a sulfur spring, or launch your kayak into Pellicer Creek or the Matanzas River (the preserve is at their confluence) and paddle away! Open Wed–Sun 7–6; free.

WILD PLACES The **St. Johns Water Management District** (386-329-4883; sjr.state.fl.us) is responsible for conservation areas that serve as buffers to the St. Johns River and its tributaries, and works with local land managers to administer the following preserves that offer hiking, biking, paddling, and trail riding. **Graham Swamp Conservation Area**, along Old Kings Rd south of Palm Coast, protects a freshwater floodplain that creates a barrier against saltwater intrusion from the Atlantic Ocean; a mile-long hiking trail lets you explore the swamp. **Haw Creek Conservation Area**, CR 2007, near Bunnell, has a fabulous boardwalk along a pristine creek; you will see alligators here. At **Moses Creek Conservation Area**, FL 206, Dupont Center, backpack or ride your horse to a distant campsite with a sweeping view of the Matanzas River salt marshes. **Pellicer Creek Conservation Area**, off US 1 near I-95, protects almost 4,000 acres of wetlands between Faver-Dykes State Park and Princess Place Preserve. **Stokes Landing Conservation Area**, Lakeshore Dr, St. Augustine, provides an outdoor classroom for local schools and beautiful panoramic views of the salt marshes along the Tolomato River for hikers.

✷ Lodging

BED & BREAKFASTS

St. Augustine 32080

With 28 historic B&Bs at last count, St. Augustine provides a wide range of choices for the history-minded traveler. Check **St. Augustine Historic Inns** at www.staugustineinns.com (immediate room availability at www.sahirooms.com) to find the best B&B to suit your needs. Here's a handful I personally explored:

Casa de La Paz (1-800-929-6269; www.casadelapaz.com), 22 Avenida Menendez. A prime bayfront location, this Mediterranean Revival home has operated as an inn since the 1920s. Innkeepers Sherri and Marshall Crews now present seven romantic rooms ($130–275), several with sweeping views of the bay. It's the perfect place to cozy up with a loved one, and you'll love their gourmet two-course breakfasts with treats like banana-almond pancakes, raspberry-stuffed French toast, and eggs Benedict.

♿ **Casa de Sueños** (1-800-824-0804; www.casadesuenos.com), 20 Cordova St. A chandelier sparkles over the whirlpool tub, funky black-and-white furnishings dress up the common areas, and each room uplifts the soul. That's the "House of Dreams," a 1920s Mediterranean Revival home along Cordova Street, where guests can watch the world drift by from the vibrant sunporch or settle down for a read in the parlor. Each of the five rooms is a relaxing retreat, with comfy robes, fine literature, and a decanter of sherry on the dresser; two rooms boast whirlpool. When owner Kathleen Hurley is away, Carol Ann whips up a tasty gourmet breakfast. $125–175.

The Kenwood Inn (1-800-824-8151; www.thekenwoodinn.com), 38 Marine St, dates back to the 1860s, when it served as a boardinghouse. It has that wonderful feel of an old-time hotel, with narrow corridors, low ceilings, and mismatched floors. Each of the 14 spacious rooms ($95–175) has its own particular character; many are two-room suites. I enjoyed my stay in the Porcelain Room, with walls the color of Wedgwood china, where I could sway in a hammock on the balcony and listen to the carriages go by. The Bridal Suite ($150–225), which occupies the whole third floor, has a view of Matanzas Bay. All guests enjoy use of a private pool and secluded garden courtyard, where you can borrow a bicycle for a ride around town.

The Old Powder House Inn (1-800-447-4149; www.oldpowderhouse.com), 38 Cordova St. An 1899 Victorian with classic charm entices with its second-floor veranda, ideal for people-watching from the porch swing. From the frilly Queen Ann's Lace to the Garden, a three-bed girls' getaway, each of the nine elegant rooms offers a perfect 1900s ambience. $95–225.

Our House (904-824-9204; www.ourhousestaugustine.com), 7 Cincinnati St. Tucked in a residential neighborhood behind the San Marcos Ave antiques district, Dave Brezing's intimate two-story Victorian has a snazzy urban feel befitting its owner, a former *USA Today* editor. Bold monochrome walls set off the restored heart pine floor, art and literature

Sandra Friend

AN ELEGANT BREAKFAST AT THE CASA DE SUEÑOS B&B

accent each room, and a piano stands at the ready in the parlor. The two guest rooms, Greenhaven and Morningview ($90–200), occupy the second floor. Greenhaven features a romantic clawfoot tub, while wraparound windows suffuse Morningview with soft morning light. Each room has a large bath and private balcony; guests also enjoy a common sitting room and a secluded garden with fountain. Dave brings newspapers and coffee up to you in the morning, and cooks a great gourmet breakfast.

🐾 🖉 **The Painted Lady** (1-888-753-3290; www.staugustinepaintedlady.com), 47 San Marco Ave. You can't miss this Victorian decked out in purples and greens—it looks like a funky dollhouse. And indeed, it's one of the few B&Bs in town that welcomes children and pets. Will and Carri Donnan welcome the curious into three rooms ($79-plus) of their haunted home, where Miss Martha trysts with her lover and a ghost orange tabby leaves impressions on the daybed. It's all part of the ambience, since Carri is a fourth-generation spiritualist running a metaphysical shop downstairs where you can have your tarot read and aura photographed, or just browse through the crystals, dream catchers, incense, and racks of Eastern clothing.

St. Francis Inn (1-800-824-6062; www.stfrancisinn.com), 279 St. George St. With not a straight angle in the place, this is a three-story home with charm—how many B&Bs in the USA date back to 1791? Every room has its own unique shape, size, and furnishings befitting the character of Señor Gaspar Garcia; I'm drawn to the romantic Balcony Room, with its park view, sitting room, fireplace, and in-room whirlpool. A small swimming pool sits off the lush garden courtyard, and guests can enjoy the peace of St. Francis Park next door. Two chefs share the honor of creating gourmet breakfasts and delicious complimentary desserts each evening. Rates run $89–269; at the high end, that's the rental of a family cottage across the street.

Southern Wind (1-800-781-3338; www.southernwindinn.com), 18 Cordova St. My sister raved about her stay here, so I had to check it out. Although the inn is in transition to new owners, it's a beautiful 1916 Victorian home with one key feature—a wraparound veranda that's the perfect place to hang out and relax. Period furnishings and antiques add to the Gilded Age ambience of the inn's 10 rooms ($99–239, ranging from cozy nooks to spacious suites), and little touches like bottled water, bathrobes, and hair dryers make you feel pampered. Breakfast is served buffet style but always features one hot entrée, like crabmeat omelets.

HOTELS AND MOTELS

Anastasia Island 32080

Anastasia Inn (1-888-226-6181; www.anastasiainn.com), 218 Anastasia Blvd. One of the newest motels in town, this pleasant, compact offering has a small heated swimming pool and Jacuzzi rooms, and a mini fridge, microwave, and coffeepot in every room; free continental breakfast.

Flagler Beach 32136

♿ Romance is in the air at **Island Cottage Villas by the Sea** (386-439-0092 or 1-866-845-5275; www.islandcottagevillas.com), 2316 S Oceanshore Blvd. Toni and Mark Treworgy radiate warmth and simplicity in this quaint "island" hideaway. The immaculate rooms and suites are just across from their own private beach, while the heated pool is the centerpiece, surrounded by lush gardens and enchanted surprises. Toni, an accomplished writer herself, is also a very talented watercolorist and has many of her lithographs and prints on display and for sale. One-bedroom villas start at $139 nightly, $693 weekly. Two-bedroom villas start at $175 nightly, $1,148 weekly.

St. Augustine 32080

On Anastasia Island, just across the Bridge of Lions, you'll find numerous small nonchain motels with rates in the $30s. Poke around the northern fringe of St. Augustine for similar bargains. You'll find excellent national chains along San Marco Ave and on St. Augustine Beach; a local fellow is in the process of breaking ground for his life's dream, a new beachfront hotel that should open by 2005.

♿ **Casa Monica** (1-800-648-1888; www.casamonica.com), 95 Cordova St. Stride into the Turkish-inspired lobby and take a step back into Henry Flagler's Gilded Age in this grand hotel, with its beaded Victorian lamps and painted beams, where the white-gloved staff usher you to your private abode. This is what Florida tourism meant in 1888, when the Casa Monica (built by Flagler's partner Franklin Smith) first opened its doors. After 4 months, Flagler bought the hotel and renamed it the Cordova. Restored to its original lavish glory several years ago by Richard Kessler, it now offers guests spacious rooms and opulent suites, $129–289, with modern appointments; it's a member of the Historic Hotels of America.

The Cozy Inn (1-888-288-2204; www.thecozyinn.com), 202 San Marco Ave. Staying at this Superior Small Lodging during my last big hiking expedition, I appreciated being able to spread things out across a like-new two-story town house with a full kitchen, great for multiday stays ($130–200). Sparkling standard rooms with a Florida coastal atmosphere sport queen beds, $69–89.

St. George Inn (904-827-5740; www.stgeorge-inn.com), 2 St. George St. This new entry to the local scene offers something no other motel can—it's in the heart of the historic district, blending in seamlessly with the shops and restaurants of St. George St at the City Gates. Large, well-appointed rooms boast killer views of the downtown area; 22 units, with some very roomy suites ideal for families, $79–159. My favorite is Room 25, with a balcony that looks out on the Castillo and Matanzas Bay.

St. Augustine Beach 32080

The Mediterranean-themed **La Fiesta Ocean Inn & Suites** (1-800-852-6390; www.lafiestainn.com), 810 FL A1A (Beach Blvd), has spacious rooms decorated in local artwork, tile entries, and great landscaping with a palm-lined pool. Oh, and the beach is just a stroll down the boardwalk over the dunes: Rooms 216–219 have a killer sunrise view. $80–290, depending on season, size, and location; continental breakfast included.

Vilano Beach 32084

I love a dog-friendly motel. **Vilano Beach Motel** (904-829-2651), 50 Vilano Rd, is light kitsch with pink flamingos and tropical decor. The clean 1950s motel is just off the beach and has cool tile floors in every room for your favorite pooch.

RESORTS

St. Augustine 32092

Adjacent to the World Golf Hall of Fame is the **World Golf Village Renaissance Resort** (904-940-8000 or 1-800-WGV-GOLF; www.worldgolfrenaissance.com), 500 S Legacy Trail. The resort borders the village's first championship course, at which hotel guests have full privileges, and offers hotel guests preferred tee times to the Slammer and the Squire. European accents, outdoor pool, professional golf simulators, 24-hour health club and sauna, billiards room, cigar room, and gift shop. *Complimentary parking at a resort!* Now, where do you see that anymore?

HOUSE RENTALS

Summer Haven

Beach Cottage Rent (1-888-963-8272; www.beachcottagerent.com). Large families and friends traveling together often find house rentals an economical way to visit the beach. For a taste of the charm of 1890s Summer Haven, stay at the Lodge, a restored five-bedroom dogtrot cottage sandwiched between the Summer Haven River and the Atlantic Ocean, with breezy wraparound porches and gorgeous beadwork walls and ceilings. Specializing in family reunions, agent Win Kelly-Joss also represents six modern but aesthetically pleasing homes in Summer Haven. Daily and weekly rentals range from $191 a night (3-night minimum) to $2,800 a week, depending on season.

CAMPGROUNDS

Beverly Beach 32136
You can't get any closer to the beach than at **Beverly Beach Campground and RV Resort** (386-439-3111 or 1-800-255-2706; www.beverlybeachcamptown.com). With your RV parked facing the Atlantic Ocean, you'll greet each day with a stunning sunrise.

North Beach 32084
North Beach Camp Resort (904-824-1806), 4125 Coastal FL A1A. Nestled on a barrier island between a remote stretch of A1A and the North River. Beautifully landscaped sites shaded by mature trees. Convenience store, playground, pool, Jacuzzi, fishing pier.

St. Augustine 32080
Indian Creek Campground (1-800-233-4324), 1505 FL 207. Tuck your camper into the shady forest, or choose a sunny pull-through space. RV spaces ($25) with gravel pads, each with picnic table; bathhouses scattered throughout the campground. Tent campers welcome but must check in before 6 PM.

St. Augustine Beach 32080
Bryn Mawr Ocean Resort (904-471-3353), 4850 FL A1A S. Just over the dunes from the Atlantic (with direct beach access), this campground has a mix of park models ($80–85), permanent residents, and RV spaces ($40 oceanfront, $47 beachfront), many with adjoining decks with picnic tables. Some sites are tucked in the maritime hammock, but most are out in the open along the ocean; the swimming pool is next to a nicely shaded playground area.

Ocean Grove Camp Resort (1-800-342-4007; www.oceangroveresort.com), 4225 FL A1A S. Set in a remnant maritime hammock with a grove of tall pines on Matanzas Bay, this campground with natural appeal has shady spaces (gravel and grass pads, $41), rustic one-room log cabins ($50, sleeps four), and tent spaces ($35) with beautiful views across the salt marsh. Dock with boat launch, fish-cleaning station; a camp store has marine items.

✷ Where to Eat

DINING OUT

Flagler Beach
Pier Restaurant. (904-439-3891), 215 FL A1A, if watching the pounding surf is high on your to-do list, stop in at the Pier Restaurant for a late lunch or early dinner with a spectacular view. Enjoy the delightful shrimp salad or a slice of their homemade key lime pie. Average entrée under $8. Take-out also available.

St. Augustine
95 Cordova. (904-810-6810; www.95cordova.com), 95 Cordova St. Settle back into that comfortable chair and savor St. Augustine's most upscale dining experience, presented by chef René Nyfeler and the staff of the Casa Monica (see *Hotels and Motels*). Take a trip back in time to the 1880s,

when Henry Flagler's railroad brought the crème de la crème of New England society to this very place—although evening attire isn't required, you'll want to be dressy for this occasion. The menu is a changing palette of entrées of the caliber of sesame-seared sea scallops ($26) and fusion herb-crusted redfish and polenta ($25); entrées $18–29. Winner of the *Wine Spectator* "Award of Excellence"; reservations recommended. One insider tip: **The Market at 95 Cordova**, the café along King St, serves gourmet food in a more casual atmosphere, with a bakery and fudge shop to tempt passersby.

❀ **Cortesses Bistro and Flamingo Bar** (904-825-6775), 172 San Marco Ave. Classy presentation and delightful textures in a perfect bistro setting—dining at this newcomer to the northern end of town is a delight. Step into the traditional courtyard with its booths and tables shaded by garden finery, and you won't want to leave. Indoors and out, intimate dining spaces set the tone for fine creations from executive chef Roger Millecan, including herb-crusted New Zealand lamb, Chicken Cortesse (chicken breast stuffed with prosciutto and provolone, sautéed in white wine), and Atlantic salmon grilled with a peppercorn mélange. An extensive wine list complements your meal. Don't pass up the appetizers, either: I savored the blue crab and corn cakes ($7) presented with a drizzle of lemon garlic aioli, and the daily special (grouper) was tender with a spicy edge. Entrées $15–24; Sunday live jazz brunch 1–5, $9–14, or catch live music most nights in the popular Flamingo Bar.

"I'm all right" at the **Murray Bros Caddyshack** in World Golf Village. Tee up with nachos with chili ($10) or chicken wings ($7), tour the greens with the Wedge Salad ($8), and check out the back nine with the Caddyshack Classic—a 12-ounce USDA strip steak ($21). The 19th Hole has domestic and imported beers.

Le Pavillion (904-824-6202), 45 San Marco Ave. In a grand old home in the antiques district, this elegant French restaurant is one of St. Augustine's top dining experiences. For lunch, enjoy the special oyster platter and salad ($9), or crêpes stuffed with seafood, beef, spinach, or chicken ($8–9); dinner entrées include filet mignon, half roast duckling, fresh trout sauté amandine, and their famous rack of lamb for one ($15–21).

Tucked into an 1879 Victorian home under the trees along the avenue, it's as inconspicuous as it is delicious. For more than 20 years, the **Raintree Restaurant and Steakhouse** (904-824-7211; www.raintreerestaurant.com), 102 San Marco Ave, has delighted diners with its award-winning entrées and extensive wine list. Choose from lamb shank osso buco, grilled portobello napoleon, beef Wellington, and more: $14–26. Don't miss the dessert bar, where the chef creates bananas Foster and crêpes tableside. Open for dinner; reservations suggested.

St. Augustine Beach

Kelley's (904-461-8446), 550 FL A1A (Beach Blvd). Chef Blake Kelley showcases his culinary talents in the classiest dining room on the beach, offering a southern seafood boil (Tue–Wed) and seasonal fish prepared with tasty trimmings. Dinner entrées $16–23; reservations preferred.

Vilano
Fiddler's Green Oceanside Bar & Grill (904-824-8897), 2750 Anahma Dr (FL A1A). The view says it all—right on the beach nestled into the dunes. Full bar.

EATING OUT

Anastasia Island
Gypsy Cab Company (904-461-8843; www.gypsycab.com), 828 Anastasia Blvd. Decked out in Caribbean pastels on the outside and with a jazzy New York bistro feel on the inside, the award-winning Gypsy Cab Company dishes out "urban Italian" treats like vegetable formaggia (one of the $4.99 weekday lunch specials served 11–3) with just-crunchy vegetables in a strong garlic and cheese sauce ladled over ziti and topped with fresh bread crumbs. Of the soup selections ($2.50 cup/$3.50 bowl), the wild mushroom bisque delivers with a velvety texture and just the right amount of mushrooms; sandwiches $7–8, salads $8, entrées $8–10. Top off your meal with tiramisu, or go for the chocoholics' favorite, their rich and creamy chocolate mousse.

They say fried shrimp was invented in St. Augustine, and **O'Steen's Restaurant** (904-829-6974), 205 Anastasia Blvd, is *the* local hot spot for fried shrimp and pileau (pronounced *per-loo*)—a classic regional dish of seasoned rice, shrimp, and Minorcan sausage. The lines get long here, so sign up at the window and browse next door in the antiques shop while you listen for your name on the loudspeaker. Dates back to 1965. Open Tue–Sat for lunch and dinner ($6–20), cash only.

Beverly Beach
Next to Beverly Beach Campground and RV Resort (see *Campgrounds*), bright lemon yellow and turquoise beckon you to come into the beachfront **Shark House Seafood Restaurant,** where the seafood is fresh and Elvis is in the building. Get your teeth into "Jaws" with Shark Bites ($6), or try a hot cup of conch chowder ($3) or tasty platter of coconut shrimp ($13).

Bunnell
For the best BBQ around, head inland to **Woody's Bar-B-BQ** (386-439-5010), 99 Flagler Regional Plaza. The Family Value Meal is your best bet and comes with a portion of chicken thighs and legs, ribs and sliced pork, and beef or turkey with four large sides ($19 for two; $29 for four).

Crescent Beach
South Beach Grille (904-471-8700; www.southbeachgrill.net), 45 Cubbedge Rd. It's a surreal scene: 1940s music spills across the dunes as you sip a margarita and watch the waves crashing on the beach. With a complement of beach drinks, from the Goombay Smash to Blue Island Ice Tea, the South Beach Grill is the hot spot to hang out in Crescent Beach. Choose the open-air back porch for best effect. Seafood fusion entrées make this menu a standout: Try the jerk blackened flounder ($16) for a taste of Caribbean spice, or the coriander black sesame tuna ($18) sprinkled with fresh-ground masala and served up in a pool of pineapple hoisin. Dense with shrimp, fish, mussels, and sausage, the seafood étouffée ($17) is a winner. My top pick: Stop by for a drink and a bowl of their outstanding blue crab corn chowder ($4), a crunchy, buttery concoction that will have you ordering seconds.

Flagler Beach

Grab a cup of coffee, pastry, or ice cream and say hi to Carol and Tony at **Cafe CARA** (386-439-3131), 420 S Central Ave.

Sea shanties and windjammer ships decorate the walls of **Fisherman's Net** (386-439-1818), 500 S FL A1A, where you get fresh seafood and fabulous service at a great price; reduced dinners 4–6. Simple, but a nice wine list.

Gail always has great hamburgers and beer-battered shrimp at **High Tides at Snack Jacks** (386-439-3344), 2805 S FL A1A, where you can relax on the screened porch and look out over the ocean. Valet parking available.

Enormous salad platters ($8) are found at **King's Oceanshore Cafe** (386-439-0380), 208 S Oceanshore Blvd. Order the prime rib sandwich when it's on special. Also serves breakfast items like King's Benedict ($7) and homemade corned beef hash with eggs ($6).

Manny's Pizza House (386-439-6345), 1848 S FL A1A, also packs them in for breakfast! Manny's Waffle Favorite comes with two eggs, waffle, bacon, sausage, or ham ($6); Surfer's Special is two eggs with two pancakes or two slices of French toast ($5).

There's always a line at **Martin's Restaurant & Lounge** (386-439-5830), 2000 S Oceanshore Blvd, as Kevin serves generous portions.

St. Augustine

A1A Ale House (904-829-2977), 1 King St. With its upstairs dining area (overlooking Matanzas Bay) jazzed up with fish tanks and snazzy nautical decor, this is a place for funky fusion seafood like a delicious blue crab BLT, a snapper burger (made with fresh-ground snapper topped with mango ketchup), and shrimp and grits. Lunch $5–14, dinner $13–20; open daily.

Acapulco's (904-804-9933), 12 Avenida Menendez, offers Mexican dishes like *carne asada*, *pollo colorado*, and *mole poblano* in the shadow of the Castillo de San Marcos, with a stellar view of Matanzas Bay from their upper floor; serving lunch ($5–6) and dinner ($8–14) in a comfortable atmosphere.

Decorated with murals depicting the founding and settlement of St. Augustine, **Athena Restaurant** (904-823-9076; www.athenacafe.com), 14 Cathedral Place, provides a unique setting for classic Greek dishes like *pastitsio*, *moussaka*, and *saganaki* (entrées $8–19, mezzes $4–8), but the big deal here is the desserts—baklava, napoleons, and more—that beckon from the front bakery case. Open for breakfast, lunch, and dinner.

Barnacle Bill's (904-824-3663; www.barnaclebillsonline.com), 14 Castillo Dr. My favorite stop in town boasts hearty seafood selections, fabulous chowder, and the don't-miss Datil Do-It Shrimp, a spicy delight seasoned with local datil peppers. Lunch and dinner, $8–16, plus market-price fresh catches. Additional location on FL A1A at St. Augustine Beach.

Creekside Dinery (904-829-6113; www.creeksidedinery.com), 160 Nix Boatyard Rd. Set off the mainstream of US 1, this gabled replica Cracker house looks like someone's home—until you step inside. The vast open rooms and wraparound porches along Oyster Creek blur the line between indoors and outdoors. Imagine toasting marshmallows tableside as the crickets buzz at twilight under the magnolia trees: You can do that at Creekside on an open tabby grill pit. The focus of the menu is seafood ($9–20), with fresh grouper, plank-cooked salmon, and other specialties presented on fish platters. Ask for the piquant and spicy house dressing on your salad, and if the squash casserole is available as tonight's vegetable, don't miss it! The fried entrées are a little heavy on the breading, but the grilled fish will leave you with a smile—I recommend the Crock a' Shrimp for shrimp lovers.

The Kings Head British Pub (904-823-9787), 6460 US 1 N, looks like it dropped out of an Elizabethan painting: an ivy-covered cottage with bright red British phone booth (à la *Dr. Who*) outside; inside, real Brit food from bangers and mash to Scotch eggs, ploughman's platter, various meat pies, and fish-and-chips. Lunch and dinner, $2–13; closed Mon.

A delightful restaurant with many vegetarian choices, **The Manatee Café** (904-826-0210; www.manateecafe.com), 525 FL 16, Westgate Plaza, offers breakfast goodies like burritos, fruit-topped pancakes, and omelets, and main dishes ranging from tofu Reuben and chili to Cajun chicken. Herbal teas, carrot juice, and other "good for you" foods, too! Serving breakfast and lunch 8–8 (except Sun, 8–3); a portion of all sales go to manatee preservation funds.

O. C. White's (904-824-0808), 118 Avenida Menendez. Jazz floats across the walled courtyard on a stiff breeze from Matanzas Bay. Classy but casual, this unique dining venue—the General Worth House, circa 1791—overlooks the bay at the marina, offering a large outdoor patio with live music nightly. Lunch and dinner offerings focus on seafood, like shrimp and scallop scampi and seafood gumbo over rice, $6–18.

St. Augustine Beach

Café Eleven (904-460-9311), 501 FL A1A (Beach Blvd), is a snazzy combination of bistro and performance space, with live music on weekends. Breakfasts include funky treats like a feta, spinach, and cheese croissant and praline French toast, but I gravitate to the enormous fresh salads—pear 'n' berry, bruschetta, tomato mozzarella—and big sandwiches; $4–6. The pastry case will tempt you, too. Open 6:30 AM–midnight.

Saltwater Cowboys (904-471-2332; www.saltwatercowboys.com), 299 Dondanville Rd. Good luck finding a parking space at this wildly popular fish camp on the Matanzas River; your best bet is arriving for lunch or a very early dinner. It's all about fish, of course—fried, broiled, baked, blackened, and steamed. Try a Florida Cracker specialty like frog legs or cooter, or the hot and spicy jambalaya. Entrées $9–18, plus market-price fresh catches.

Sea Market (904-461-9991), 4255 FL A1A (Beach Blvd). It's a restaurant, an oyster bar, and a seafood market rolled into one, and it's always busy. No wonder: The food at the Sea Market is authentic St. Augustine, made with the fresh fruits of the sea: steamed, boiled, seared, fried, and raw. Order oysters by the bucket ($4 and up) or crawfish by the pound ($6), or nab one of more than a dozen nightly specials ($9–15), like the tasty Minorcan shrimp boil over rice ($13). Expect carrots, celery, and captain's wafers to nibble on while you wait for dinner to simmer. Lunch and dinner daily.

Sunset Grille (904-471-5555; www.sunsetgrilleA1A.com), 421 FL A1A (Beach Blvd). Enjoy huge seafood pasta platters (shrimp and scallops Rockefeller, $15), the "world's best" coconut-crusted shrimp ($15), and the smoothest margaritas along the beach in this casual, award-winning local favorite. Lunch and dinner, $7–20, with nightly specials—AYCE crab legs on Mon!

✷ Entertainment

St. Augustine

Between Memorial Day and Labor Day, families gather at Plaza de la Constitucion for free weekly **Concerts in the Plaza**, Thu evening 7–9, with jazz, blues, folk, and country artists keeping the crowd swinging. Catch live music 5–8 and 9–close nightly at the **Tropical Trade Winds Lounge** (904-829-9336; www.tradewindslounge.com), 124 Charlotte St, where the house band Matanzas plays Jimmy Buffett and a jammin' collection of their own home-grown St. Augustine–style tunes, or settle back with a beer on the rooftop of the **Old Mill House** on St. George St for breezy acoustic music. For a real immersion into history, stop in at the **Taberna del Gallo**, one of St. Augustine's original watering holes, at the Colonial Spanish Quarter (see *Historic Homes*) to raise a toast to the Bilge Rats as they draw you back to 1734 with their repertoire of seafaring tunes. Open Thu–Sat 2–9:30, Sun noon–7.

The play's the thing at the **Limelight Theatre** (1-866-682-6400; www.limelight-theatre.org), 11 Old Mission Ave, with year-round performances ($10–24) that include professional productions like *I Hate Hamlet* and *The Diary of Anne Frank*. Florida's official state play, the *The Cross and Sword*, depicts the settlement of St. Augustine, with performances Thu–Sat at 8:30 PM at the St. Augustine Amphitheater on Anastasia Island (904-471-1965). Special plays are offered during Lent and Christmas.

Catch the **Comedy Club** at the Gypsy Bar & Grill (adjacent to the Gypsy Cab Company; see *Eating Out*) for live national acts Thu–Sat, tickets $10.50.

✷ Selective Shopping

Anastasia Island

Anastasia Books (904-824-0648), 13 Anastasia Blvd. Nice selection of Floridiana (new and used) as well as plenty of children's books and textbooks for homeschoolers. Large used-book section, including the area's largest selection of science fiction and fantasy.

St. Augustine

With more than 100 stores to choose from, you could spend most of a week browsing the shops of historic St. Augustine. There are three major shopping districts: **Old St. Augustine** tends toward touristy with a touch of art, especially along St. George St, which is lined with shops from end to end and has everything a tourist could want and more, from T-shirts and tchotchkes to postcards and paintings. **San Marco Ave** is the antiques district to the north of the City Gates, and **San Sebastian** is the up-and-coming arts district along King St near the San Sebastian Winery. Here are highlights for each area.

Old St. Augustine

Around the World Marketplace (904-824-6223), 21 Orange St. The burble of fountains makes browsing a pleasant experience as you poke through colorful imports—Tavalera porcelain, onyx chess sets, masks, statues, mirrors, and wall art.

Bouvier Maps & Prints (904-825-0920), 11-D Aviles St. If you're looking for a map to go with St. Augustine's history, this is the place to visit. Dealing in original antique maps and prints, this shop is as rare a find as its incredible inventory. Closed Tue and Wed.

The Camera Stop (904-819-0336; www.thecamerastop.com), 58 Spanish St. Bruce Andrews has an interesting meld of interests: As a photographer, he displays creative photographic art and original watercolors in a shop that's also a storefront for folks who'd like to shoot St. Augustine themselves. Rent an Olympus Stylus 300 (5 megapixel) with a 16MB card for $35 a day, and Bruce will download your images and burn CDs for as many shots as you care to take daily.

Dreamstreet Too (904-829-5220; www.dreamstreettoo.com), 64 Hypolita St, a place for the soul to soar, is a New Age shop replete with angels and fairies, music, and books; I love the uplifting sayings on the walls.

Flying Dutchman Colonial Art (904-824-0789), 59 Cuna St. Step back in time as you marvel at colonial crafts and working replica artifacts from St. Augustine's past, the handiwork of potters, weavers, coppersmiths, scribes, and minstrels, all historic reenactors who have come together to sell their unique wares.

Frantiques (904-823-1818), 6 Cordova St. Tourist trains stop here for a look at the "love tree," an intertwined growth of cabbage palm and live oak. Step inside for vintage clothing, furniture, glassware, and books, or grab a fresh fruit smoothie at the **Love Tree Juice Bar** in the back of the building.

Gallery 39 (904-825-0539), 63 Hypolita St. For more than a decade, this funky gallery has tempted me with silly sculptures, furnishings turned into pieces of art, and pottery with style; closed Mon.

Grover's Gallery (904-824-5738), 14B St. George St. Big pieces, low prices: That's the philosophy of artist Grover Rice, who has spent more than 30 years carving wood into art such as life-sized sea turtles and pelicans, tikis made from palm trunks, and model nautical villages.

Think *gifts with attitude* at **Materialistic** (904-824-1611), 125 St. George St, where even the T-shirts are smarmy. Pick up a punching rabbi, a dashboard hula dancer, or a Brahman lunch box.

At **Metalartz** (904-824-6322; www.metalartz.net), 58 Hypolita St, mobiles and glass balls dangle from the ceiling, and lizards and dragonflies cling to a tree that rises from the floor. With art glass, paintings, metal sculptures, and much more, this kaleidoscope of artistry represents 15 local artists and their very creative expressions.

The **Mullet Beach Gallery** (904-829-6831; www.mulletbeach.com), 51 Cordova St #B, features local artists in watercolors, acrylics, pottery, and more. Patrick Madden's bright acrylics jump off the walls, and Brenda Phillips creates oils on canvas with colors that'll jazz up any space. Don't miss Evie Auerbach's functional and fun fish platters!

Reflections of a Lifetime (904-819-0020), 6 Aviles St, reflects Doe Minteer's avenues of art—painted glass and family story paintings. Meet Doe in her working studio, and browse the creations of other artists who work in glass, pottery, mosaic, and more. Closed Mon.

Second Read Books (904-829-0334), 51 Cordova St, keeps a brisk business going with used books for sale or trade just a block from Flagler College. Look for a good local section, fine literature, and a broad young-adult selection.

The Secret Cove (1-800-821-1946; www.secretcove.com), 76 St. George, represents 40 artists, with glass, metal, and polished wood the canvas for wildlife sculptures.

St. Augustine Art Glass (904-824-4916), 54 St. George, isn't just about glass—check out the raku art sculptures and playful metal sculptures in the tranquil garden behind the building.

St. Augustine Toy Company (904-829-3266; www.saturdaytoy.com), 33 King St, is a don't-miss shop of funky fun stuff in a former Woolworth, where the lunch counter is in use as the **Jesterville Grill** (a soda fountain with great prices). Painted floors lead you through themed toy areas like the "Jesterpolitan Museum of Art." You'll find the eclectic here—how about a Sigmund Freud action figure for Christmas?

The **Woman's Exchange** (904-829-5064), 143 St. George St, is a volunteer organization dating back to 1892 that manages tours through the historic Peck Piña House (circa 1700) in order to run a consignment outlet for top-quality home crafters. Their motto is, "Creative need is as important as the financial need," and their creativity runs the gamut from watercolor notecards and cookbooks to clothespin dolls, hand-smocked dresses, handcrafted soaps, and hand-painted glass.

San Marco Ave

Bonaparte's European Antique Shop (904-824-3344), 60 San Marco. Poke around through two stories' worth of antiques, with an emphasis on 1800s–1920s English and French country furniture.

Creative Studios, Inc. (904-826-0004; www.createglass.com), 61 San Marco. Watch the sparks fly as Joan and Thomas Long spin glass in an open-air studio along the sidewalk; pop into the shop and browse their completed art glass creations.

St. Augustine Antique Emporium (904-829-0544), 62 San Marco Ave, features 22 dealer booths in a refreshingly open setting, making it easy to keep track of the rest of your group as you browse through the art glass, jewelry, postcards, saltcellars, stained glass, and other ephemera.

At **Uptown Antiques** (904-824-9156), 63 and 67 San Marco Ave, look through the mini mall of dealer booths and you'll unearth treasures like historic postcards of St. Augustine, movie memorabilia, posters, and books.

Wolf's Head Books (904-824-9357; www.wolfsheadbooks.com), 48 San Marco. I walked in here to look around and walked out with a rare book in my favorite field of study, Florida natural history. This is a true antiquarian bookseller—you will find books here you can't even find on the Internet, especially in the Florida section, with great prices and a superb selection.

San Sebastian
Avenue Books & Gallery (904-829-9744; www.avenuebooksandgallery.com), 142-A King St. A massive bookstore dealing in mostly used books, with a special focus on the fine arts, a good selection of new Florida books, and the impressionistic Florida scenes of artist-in-residence Kathleen Mulholland.

The heart of the arts district is **Rembrandtz** (904-829-0065), 131 King St, lovingly tended by Lynne Doten and Kimberly Hunt, the gallery that started it all back in 1995. Representing more than 75 artists, this funky shop carries art glass, fabric arts, paintings, photography, pottery, and more; my eyes were drawn to Ray Brilli's colorful scenes of St. Augustine.

St. Augustine Beach
Out at the beach, you'll find all the usual surf, swimming suit, and T-shirt shops you've come to expect from every beachfront town. Drive FL A1A to explore, and you'll find gems like **Sunburst Trading Company** (904-461-7255), 491 FL A1A (Beach Blvd), *the* shell shop for the region, with a selection of shell crafts, burbling Mexican fountains, Latin imports, and, of course, shells. Bring the kids: The incredible selection starts at 20¢, and there are fossils and coral to choose from, too.

With an atmosphere like a comfy school library, **Booktown** (904-471-5556), 4075 FL A1A S, offers a great selection of used books broken out by genre, stacks of puzzles and magazines, and a children's section; new books available via special order.

FARMER'S MARKETS, SEAFOOD STANDS, AND U-PICK

Flagler Beach
An old-fashioned market is set in the center of town with fresh-baked goods, fruits, vegetables, and nuts. Fri 7–2 at the corner of FL 100 and FL A1A.

St. Augustine
Indian River Fruit Market. Spanning a full block between San Marcos Ave and US 1 west of San Carlos, it's not just a fruit market—it's "Florida's largest fruit and gift shop," the largest collection of ticky-tacky in St. Augustine under one roof.

St. Augustine Beach
Farmer's and Art Market. Now here's a twist—a farmer's market that's evolved into a weekly art gathering, where you can peruse the works of local sculptors and painters while picking up the perfect peck of potatoes. Every Wed 7:30–noon at the pier.

✷ Special Events

February: **Menendez Festival**, St. Augustine. A weekend's worth of parades, music, and heritage celebrations commemorating the founder of St. Augustine, with events throughout the Old City.

April: Having been brought up on Maine potatoes—and an Irish lass—I had to inquire about Hastings's "Potato Capital of the World" **Annual Potato and Cabbage Festival**. So it was back to the basics with mouthwatering potato stew and cabbage soup, and some new treats like potato cupcakes and potato fudge (we call them needhams in Maine). The tiny town of Hastings really knows their spuds—ayuh!

May: **Gamble Rogers Folk Festival** (904-794-0222; www.gamblefest.com), St. Augustine Amphitheatre, first weekend. One of Florida's top folk music weekends, with dozens of performers honoring one of the strongest voices in Florida folk music, and vendors and craftspersons with Florida art. Weekend pass $45, ages 13 and up; daily performances $15–25, children free with paying adult (except Sat, $10).

June: **Drake's Raid**, St. Augustine, first weekend. I love the plug for this one: "Said to be the largest 16th-century reenactment in the United States." As if there could be many others? Only the most studious of history lovers know that swashbuckling pirate Sir Francis Drake came ashore and set fire to St. Augustine in 1586, sacking the city.

October: **Colonial Folk Arts and Crafts Festival**, St. Augustine, Spanish Quarter. Browse 17th-century arts and crafts—everything from weaving to blacksmithing—in one of the most interesting living history festivals in Florida.

JACKSONVILLE

AMELIA ISLAND, FERNANDINA BEACH, JACKSONVILLE, JACKSONVILLE BEACH, PONTE VEDRA, AND WEST NASSAU COUNTY (CALLAHAN AND HILLIARD)

The mouth of the St. Johns River is situated in the heart of downtown Jacksonville. Traveling more than 270 miles on its northern journey to the sea, the river has dominated this region since 1562, when Frenchman Jean Ribault established Fort Caroline. To the northeast of Jacksonville, on the Georgia border, is the only area in the United States to have been governed by eight different flags. The first inhabitants, the Timucua Indians, lived here more than 1,000 years before Amelia Island and the surrounding areas came under French rule. This lasted only a handful of years; then the region was occupied by the Spaniards in 1565. Because of its natural deep harbor, American patriots, British, Scots, French, Spaniards, and even pirates battled for the area. Spain held on to it the longest, with over 200 years of rule, before ceding the area to the United States in 1821. Jacksonville was named in honor of General Andrew Jackson in 1822.

GUIDANCE

Amelia Island and Fernandina Beach
Stop by the Old Railroad Depot building at the west end of Centre St in Fernandina Beach, where you'll find the **Amelia Island Chamber of Commerce** (904-261-3248; www.ameliaisland.com), P.O. Box 472, Fernandina Beach 32035. Another great resource is **Amelia Island Tourist Development Council** (904-277-0717; www.ameliaisland.org), 102 Centre St, Fernandina Beach 32034.

Jacksonville and Jacksonville Beaches
Jacksonville & The Beaches Convention and Visitors Bureau (904-798-9111 or 1-800-733-2668; www.visitjacksonville.com), 550 Water St, Suite 1000, Jacksonville 32202. **Jacksonville Chamber of Commerce** (904-366-6600), 3 Independence Dr, Jacksonville 32202. **Beaches of Jacksonville Chamber**

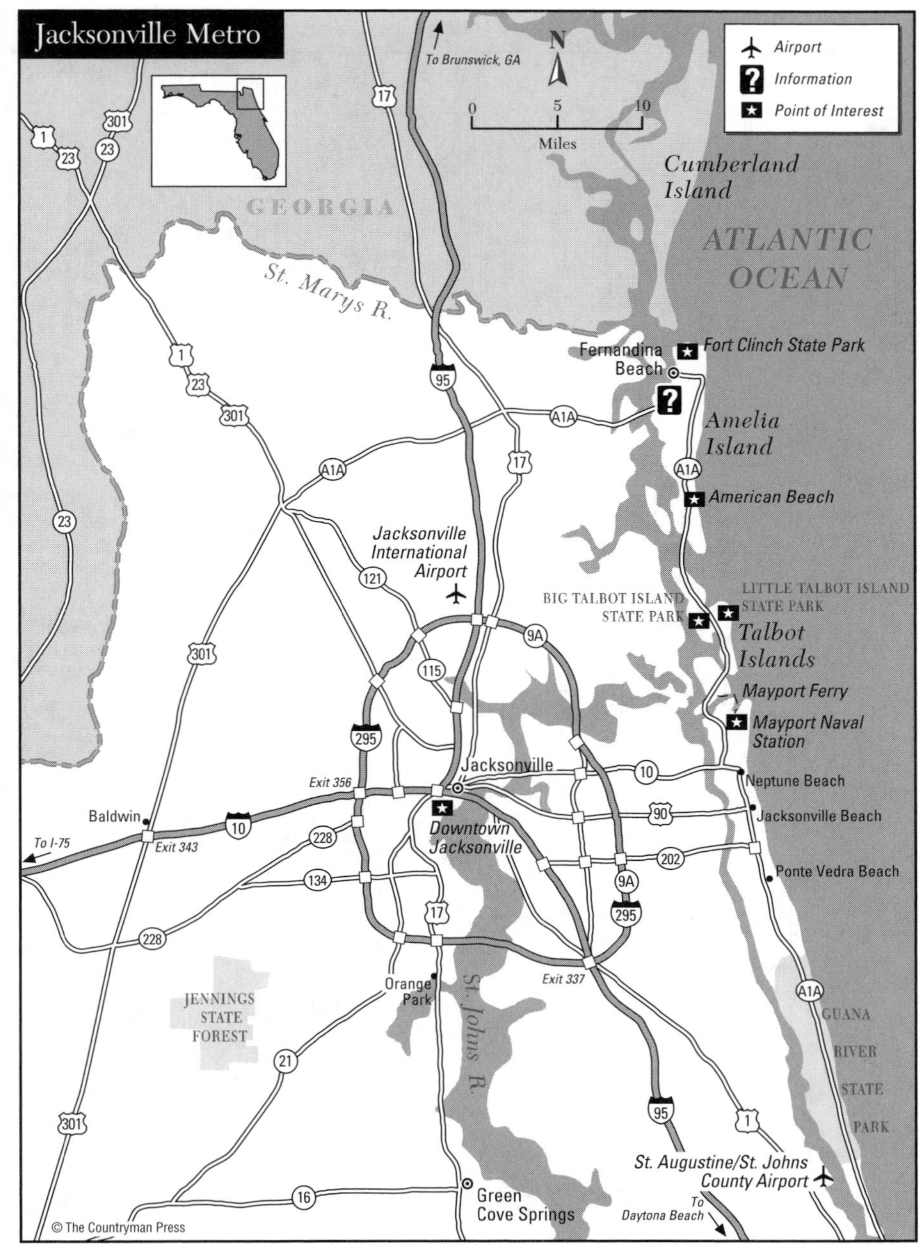

(904-249-3868), P.O. Box 50427, Jacksonville Beach 32240. **Beaches Visitor Center** (904-242-0024), 403 Beach Blvd, Jacksonville Beach 32250.

West Nassau County (Callahan and Hilliard)

West Nassau County Chamber of Commerce (904-879-1441), P.O. Box 98, Callahan 32011.

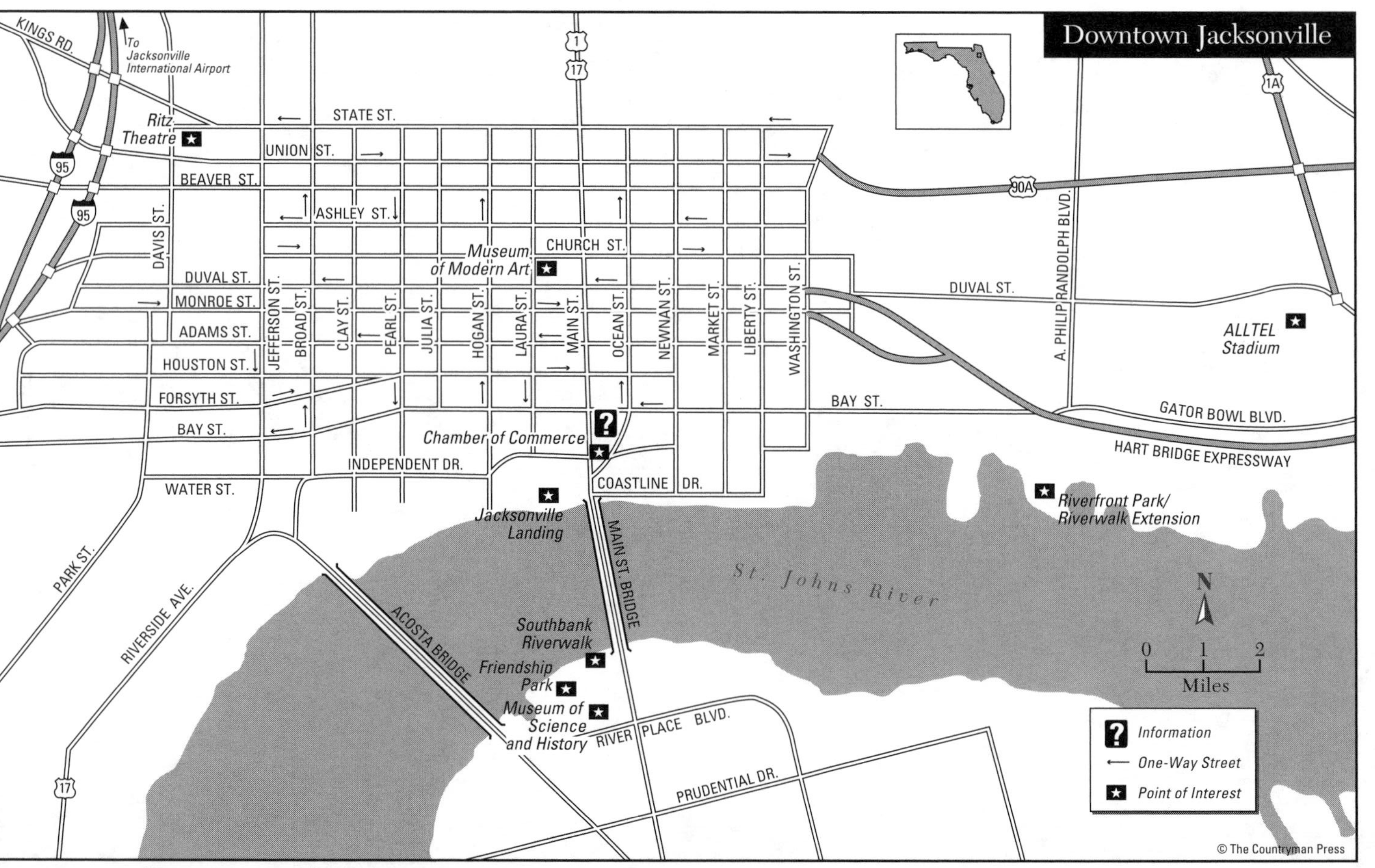
Downtown Jacksonville
KINGS RD.
To Jacksonville International Airport
95
95
1
17
1A
90A
17
Ritz Theatre
STATE ST.
UNION ST.
BEAVER ST.
ASHLEY ST.
CHURCH ST.
DAVIS ST.
DUVAL ST.
MONROE ST.
ADAMS ST.
HOUSTON ST.
FORSYTH ST.
BAY ST.
WATER ST.
JEFFERSON ST.
BROAD ST.
CLAY ST.
PEARL ST.
JULIA ST.
HOGAN ST.
LAURA ST.
MAIN ST.
OCEAN ST.
NEWNAN ST.
MARKET ST.
LIBERTY ST.
WASHINGTON ST.
Museum of Modern Art
Chamber of Commerce
INDEPENDENT DR.
COASTLINE DR.
Jacksonville Landing
DUVAL ST.
A. PHILIP RANDOLPH BLVD.
BAY ST.
ALLTEL Stadium
GATOR BOWL BLVD.
HART BRIDGE EXPRESSWAY
Riverfront Park/ Riverwalk Extension
St. Johns River
MAIN ST. BRIDGE
ACOSTA BRIDGE
PARK ST.
RIVERSIDE AVE.
Southbank Riverwalk
Friendship Park
Museum of Science and History
RIVER PLACE BLVD.
PRUDENTIAL DR.
N
0
1
2
Miles
Information
One-Way Street
Point of Interest
© The Countryman Press

GETTING THERE *By air*: **Jacksonville International Airport** (904-741-4902).

By bus: **Greyhound** (904-356-9976; www.greyhound.com) takes you into downtown Jacksonville, where transfers to city buses and Skyway are nearby.

By car: **Interstate 95** runs north–south through the heart of Jacksonville. Coming from farther west, take **I-10** to I-95. **FL 9** takes you to the Neptune and Atlantic beaches.

By train: **Amtrak** (904-766-5110; www.amtrak.com), 3570 Clifford Lane on the north side of Jacksonville, 7 miles from the downtown area.

GETTING AROUND

Amelia Island

From I-95, take FL A1A east to Amelia Island. A1A loops north through the Fernandina historic district, then turns east again to the beach. Head south on Fletcher Ave (FL A1A) through Fernandina Beach; the road turns west at Amelia City and connects with FL 105. The Buccaneer Trail (FL 105) continues past the roads leading to American Beach and then on to the end of the island, where you can take the car ferry to the mainland (see *Ferry Crossing*).

Jacksonville and Jacksonville Beach

There are three main streets that take you from Jacksonville to Jacksonville Beach. To go from downtown to the beaches, take **Atlantic Blvd** or **Beach Blvd**, or from I-95 take **J. Turner Butler (JTB) Blvd**.

Skyway Express Monorail, Trolley, and City Bus (904-743-3582 or 904-RIDE-JTA). The monorail weaves through the downtown area from Kings Ave Garage to the FCCJ campus and the Convention Center on Bay St for only 35¢. Buses take you to the beach or west to Orange Park for 75¢ to $1.50, depending on distance. The trolley runs only on weekdays and is free.

River Taxi (904-724-9068). North side at Jacksonville Landing; south side at Riverwalk. $2 one-way, $3 round-trip.

West Nassau County (Callahan and Hilliard)

FL 301 and **CR 15** from Jacksonville take you through the heart of Callahan and Hilliard, and then across the Georgia border.

MEDICAL EMERGENCIES **Memorial Hospital Jacksonville** (main number 904-399-6111; emergency 904-399-6156), 3625 University Blvd S, Jacksonville.

✱ To See

AVIATION TOURS The only way to see Fernandina Beach, Fort Clinch, and Cumberland Island is from the air with **Island Aerial Tours** (904-321-0904), 1600 Airport Rd, Amelia Island. Bob and Chong Murphy take you on a magical journey over kayakers paddling the emerald-green saltwater marshlands, wild horses running on the white sands, shrimp boats setting out to sea with dolphin escorts, and historic downtown Fernandina, including Fort Clinch. The small plane will hold two or three passengers. Call for customized tours and rates.

BIRD SANCTUARY More than 2,000 birds, like eagles and owls, are rescued and rehabilitated each year at **BEAKS—**Bird Emergency And Kare Sanctuary (904-251-2473), 12084 Houston Ave on Big Talbot Island. Guided tours at the visitors sanctuary help maintain the nonprofit facility. The annual Baby Bird Shower is in May (see *Special Events*). Open noon–4; free.

BOAT TOURS **Amelia River Cruises & Charters** (904-261-9972). Board the *Ryan-K* for fully narrated scenic tours exploring the backwaters of Amelia Island, discovering the area's rich history, or around Cumberland Island to see horses galloping across the pristine white sands. North Amelia River or North and South Amelia Sunset $14 adults, $10 children. Two-hour Cumberland Island $20 adults, $16 children. The Amelia Island Lighthouse tour is only on Mon.

A private ferry departs from the docks in Fernandina for day or dinner trips to **Greyfield Inn Cumberland Island** (904-261-6408; www.greyfieldinn.com), Cumberland Island, Georgia (see *Lodging*).

Not your typical boat tour, the one at **St. Marys River Fish Camp & Campground** (904-845-4440 or 966-845-4443), 28506 Scotts Landing Rd, Hilliard, is along a quiet stretch of the river where you'll simply enjoy the ride, in a small bass boat, looking for alligators, deer, eagles, owls, and fish jumping in the rivers. Ahhhh!

BREWERY TOUR **Anheuser-Busch Budweiser Brewery Tour** (904-751-8116; www.budweisertours.com) 111 Busch Dr, Jacksonville. This open-air tour overlooks the Brew Hall, where golden beers and amber ales are bottled and canned. Then sample the popular American beer. Great gift shop of logo items. Mon–Sat 9–4; free.

CARRIAGE TOURS **Old Towne Carriage Company** (904-277-1555), Amelia Island. Take a 30- to 40-minute ride in a horse-drawn carriage through the Fernandina historic district while your narrator points out the history and culture of the National Register of Historic Places in a 50-block area. $15 adults, $8 ages 3–12.

DINNER THEATER For nearly 40 years the **Alhambra Dinner Theatre** (904-641-1212), 12000 Beach Blvd, Jacksonville, has given Broadway-style performances like *Phantom of the Opera* coupled with a nice home-style dinner. Tue–Sun, $35–46.

FERRY CROSSING The only public ferry in the country, the **St. Johns River Mayport Ferry** (904-241-9969) operates from FL A1A through Mayport Village across to Heckscher Dr on Fort George Island, making the passage from northeast Florida along A1A a scenic journey. $3 toll.

FOOTBALL In 2005 the **Super Bowl** comes to Jacksonville, home of the **Jacksonville Jaguars** (904-633-2000; www.jaguars.com), 1 ALLTEL Stadium Place.

Amelia Island

This historic **American Beach** was established in 1933 as one of the few African American beaches. Sandwiched between two billion-dollar resorts, the community has managed to keep this important stretch of land open despite the encroaching development. It is important to note that Florida beaches were racially segregated until 1964; this was one of the few beaches where affluent African Americans could vacation. It is also the first of 141 sites on the Florida's Black Heritage Trail. If you're lucky enough to find her home, the "beach lady," MaVynee Betsch, will show you around.

Fort Clinch (904-277-7274), 2601 Atlantic Ave. Constructed in 1847, the restored pentagonal brick Civil War fort is surrounded by over 1,000 acres of sand dunes, maritime forest, and tidal marsh. Costumed reenactors walk around the fort providing period authenticity and will occasionally set off the cannons. The park also offers nature trails, picnicking, and camping. You'll want to see this one from the air (see *Aviation*). Fort open daily 9–5, park 8–sunset.

If you've seen the 1988 movie *Pippi Longstocking*, you'll find that most of the historic downtown area and Katie's Light (see *Vacation Homes*) were featured in the movie. It wasn't hard to create the magical "Rocksby Town," as Amelia Island has a magic all its own. No, Astrid Lindgrin didn't live at the famous redhead's "Villa Villa Kulla," but the young and young at heart will enjoy driving by the private residence in Old Town near the Posada San Carlos.

Jacksonville

Fort Caroline National Memorial (904-641-7155), 12713 Fort Caroline Rd, Arlington. A replica of Fort Caroline, the first colony in Florida, sits along the St. Johns River inside this deeply wooded preserve, its size and shape based on the paintings of Jacques Le Moyne. Clamber up the battlements and peer over the sides. In 1565 the founder of St. Augustine, Pedro Menéndez, marched here

A FORT CLINCH INTERIOR

Sandra Friend

with 500 of his troops to roust the French from Florida, after Jean Ribault attempted to attack the Spanish colony at St. Augustine. Taking the fort by surprise, they murdered 140 settlers, sparing only the women and children. Nearly 50 settlers, including Le Moyne, escaped by boat and returned to France. An interpretive center tells the story, and interpretive signs along the nature trails invoke the interaction between the French and Timucua. Open Mon–Sun 9–4:45; free.

Kingsley Plantation (904-251-3537), 11676 Palmetto Ave, Fort George Island. Established in 1791 by John McQueen, who sought his fortune under a policy of the Spanish government of Florida that invited Americans to homestead on land grants throughout eastern Florida, this Sea Island cotton plantation passed into the hands of Zephaniah Kingsley, a slave trader, in 1812. Zephaniah Kingsley lived here with his wife, Anna Madgigine Jai, a slave he had bought in Senegal and later freed, and their children. He strove to establish liberal policies for the freeing of slaves, and to ensure the rights and privileges of free blacks in Florida, but failed, and moved his family to Haiti in 1837. Tour the plantation home (a limited portion of it has been renovated) and the slave cabins; walk the waterfront along the St. George River. Open Mon–Sun 9–5; free.

Learn about the history of the railways and beaches at **Pablo Historical Park** (904-246-0093), 425 Beach Blvd. Take a free guided tour and discover the Mayport and Pablo Railways, which served the area's recreational beaches, along with the fishing and phosphate industries in the late 1800s. Mon–Sat 10–3. Donations appreciated.

Timucuan Ecological & Historic Preserve (904-221-5568), 13165 Mt. Pleasant Rd, Mayport. A preserve of archeological and historic importance due to its massive Timucuan middens and a trail on which the Spanish trod en route to Fort Caroline, this deeply wooded park encompasses coastal scrub, freshwater wetlands, shady oak hammocks, and saltwater marshes, with several miles of biking and hiking trails. Open Mon–Sun 9–5; free.

HOCKEY The fairly new **Jacksonville Barracuda Professional Hockey Team** (904-367-1423; www.jacksonvillebarracudas.com) checks the ice in the new Jacksonville Veterans Memorial Arena.

MUSEUMS

Amelia Island/Fernandina

Stop by the old Nassau County Jail on Centre St, home to the **Amelia Island Museum of History** (904-261-7378; www.ameliaislandmuseumofhistory.com). Learn about why Amelia Island is the only location in America to have been ruled under eight flags. Take a walking tour down Centre St, or a ghost tour beginning at St. Peters Cemetery. Open Mon–Fri 10–5, Sat 10–4.

Jacksonville

Alexander Brest Planetarium (904-396-7062). Take a cosmic family camping trip under the stars with Bear Tales or listen to music in the starry night with Cosmic Concerts. Part of the Museum of Science and History.

With 40-plus years of arts and gardens, the largest fine-arts museum in North Florida, the **Cummer Museum of Arts and Gardens** (904-356-6857; www.cummer.org), 829 Riverside Ave, displays its permanent collection from the Middle Ages to the present and is arguably one of the best fine-art museums in the state. As an art major I was in awe of the original works—from Glakens to Rubens—not often seen in Florida. One of the more important pieces is Thomas Moran's oil painting *Ponce de Leon in Florida* (1878), which depicts the Spanish conquistador in the company of Native Floridians deep in the natural and mystical forests around the St. Johns River. The quaint 2.5-acre English and Italian Gardens overlook the St. Johns River and are shaded by a 175-foot canopy from one of the oldest live oaks in the area. Other collections shown in the intimate galleries are 19th-century American landscapes, Renaissance, baroque, rococo, and impressionism. Open Tue and Thu 10–9; Wed, Fri, and Sat 10–5; Sun noon–5. $6 adults, $4 seniors, $1 children.

Museum of Modern Art (MOMA) (904-366-6911; www.jmoma.com), 333 N Laura St. Founded in 1924, the MOMA was the first institution in the city devoted to visual arts. It displays a fine selection of modern and contemporary works by locally and nationally acclaimed artists. A very special place is the **Art Exploration** loft, with lots of family interaction and education in the 16 interactive stations—and on Sunday it's free! All other days: $6 adults, $4 ages 12 and under.

Museum of Science and History (MOSH) (904-396-7062; www.themosh.com), 1025 Museum Circle. Permanent exhibits about the history and marine animals of northeast Florida along with special exhibits and programs, like railroadiana and prehistoric beasts. Open Mon–Fri 10–5, Sat 10–6, Sun 1–6; $6 adults, $4 ages 3–12.

Learn about the lifestyle and culture of the antebellum South at the **Museum of Southern History** (904-388-3574), 4304 Herschel St, covering prehistoric Florida, politics, fashion, home life, and military memorabilia. Adults $1, children free. Tue–Sat 10–5.

The history of African Americans in northeast Florida is depicted at the beautifully restored **Ritz Theatre and LaVilla Museum** (904-632-5555), 829 N Davis St, Jacksonville. The 400-seat theater is home to exciting musicals and theatrical performances. The museum is open Tue–Fri 10–6, Sat 10–2, Sun 2–5; $6 adults, $3 children and seniors. Call the Ritz Theatre for a current schedule of performances.

NAVAL TOUR Take a tour at one of the largest naval facilities in the nation at **Mayport Naval Station** (904-270-4111). You'll see frigates and destroyers along with a tour of the Mayport Lighthouse.

ZOOLOGICAL PARK You'll need to keep going back, because the **Jacksonville Zoological Gardens**

AT JACKSONVILLE'S MUSEUM OF MODERN ART

Kathy Wolf

(904-757-4463; www.jaxzoo.org), 8605 Zoo Pkwy, Jacksonville, continues to expand and bring in new exhibits each year. You'll enter the natural habitats of animals from around the world at the Main Safari Camp Lodge, with a hand-thatched roof created by 24 Zulu craftsmen from South Africa. You'll find a good showing of African wildlife from East Africa and the Rift Valley. In Wild Florida you'll discover the Florida panther, native bear, boar, eagles, and alligators in a wetlands environment. Kangaroos, wallabies, and koalas are in the Aussie exhibit, and the new 2004 Range of the Jaguar exhibit showcases the neotropical rain forest with four jaguars, along with golden lion tamarins, tapirs, capybaras, giant river otters, anteaters, and reptilians, including the anaconda. Daily 9–5; $10 adults, $5 ages 3–12.

Amy Stone

AUTHOR SANDRA FRIEND (& FRIENDS) AT THE JACKSONVILLE ZOO

✷ To Do

BICYCLING The **Jacksonville–Baldwin Rail Trail** (www.coj.net) comprises 14.5 miles of an old CSX railway line through a dense canopy of forests, wetlands, and fields between Imeson Rd and CR 121. There are three separate paths: one for walking, jogging, and in-line skating, one for mountain bikers, and one for horseback riding.

FAMILY ACTIVITIES ✐ **Adventure Landing** (904-246-4386), 1944 Beach Blvd, Jacksonville Beach. Get wet at **Shipwreck Island Water Park**, then compete with the kids on go-carts, miniature golf, and laser tag.

✐ **Dave & Buster's** (904-296-1525), 7025 Salisbury Rd, Jacksonville Beach. Interactive games, simulators, arcades, and food and drink. Daily. After 10 on Fri and Sat, the facility is reserved for the grown-ups.

FISHING At **St. Marys River Fish Camp & Campground** (904-845-4440 or 966-845-4443; www.stmarysriverfishcamp.com), 28506 Scotts Landing Rd, Hilliard (see *Fish Camps*), you're so close the Georgia border you can cast your line across it. Take a ride down the black waters of the St. Marys in a small bass boat as it curves past white sandbars, cypress trees, and alligators, then under a train trestle. Fish or just enjoy the view. The river winds along a 130-mile path from the Okefenokee Swamp to the Atlantic. Given the connection to the ocean, tides play a role even this far up. Watch for shallow and narrow areas during low tide when sandy banks are displayed, especially in the narrower sections. Half day 2–4 miles, full day 12–20 miles.

JET SKIING On Amelia Island, escape with a Jet Ski or parasail at **Adventure Amelia** (904-277-1161), located at Peter's Point, or **Island Water Sports** (904-261-1230).

PADDLING Rent a canoe or kayak from the folks at **St. Marys Canoe Country Outpost** (904-845-4440 or 966-845-4443; www.stmarysriverfishcamp.com), 28506 Scotts Landing Rd, Hilliard, and then explore the river on your own. Don't forget to pack a lunch: You'll want to stop for a relaxing break on the sandy banks.

Black Creek Outfitters (904-645-7003; www.blackcreekoutfitters.com), 10051 Skinner Lake Dr, Jacksonville, is one of the most complete outfitters in Florida, with a full line of kayaking, surf, hiking, mountaineering, and climbing equipment. Call Keith Keller, director of outdoor activities, for the extensive list of guided tours around North Florida and beyond.

Paddle on North Florida's scenic waterways with **Kayak Adventures** (1-888-333-2480), 413 2nd St, Jacksonville Beach, in search of ospreys and pelicans.

Learn the correct way to kayak at **Kayak Amelia** (904-251-0016; www.kayakamelia.com), 13030 Heckscher Dr, in the saltwater marshes between Big and Little Talbot Islands. Jody Hetchka shows you safety first, and then carefully fits you with top-of-the-line paddles and kayaks. Head out into the saltwater marshes while your guide explains the history of area and local wildlife. You'll take a break and pull up on a pristine sandbar, where you can go for a refreshing swim. Special treats are warm chocolate chip cookies in summer and hot cider in winter. A single kayak runs $25 for a half day, $40 for a full day. A tandem kayak or canoe costs $40 or $55; a 3-hour guided tour of the salt marsh ecosystem is $55.

SAILING Sail off the beaches of Fernandina with Charlie and Sandra Weaver on the ***Windward's Child*** (904-261-9125; www.windwardsailing.com), Fernandina Harbor Marina. Dolphins swim alongside the 34-foot Hunter sloop as you pass horses running on the beach on Cumberland Island. See Fort Clinch from the water, just as the Civil War blockade-runners saw it. Move under the power of the wind with the quiet sounds of a warm sea breeze. Half-day, full-day, and sunset cruises.

AUTHOR KATHY WOLF TAKES NOTES ON HER KAYAK AMELIA ECOTOUR.

Bonnie Barnes

SPA Ponte Vedra Inn & Club (904-285-1111; www.pvspa.com), 200 Ponte Vedra Blvd, Ponte Vedra Beach. Come to this perfect haven for relaxation after a long day on the golf course or exploring neighboring St. Augustine. Wrap yourself in an elegant spa robe and sit with a light beverage while awaiting your treatment in the relaxation room or in the 2,000-

square-foot Cascada Garden with oversized Jacuzzi and cascading waterfall. Then move on to your own private room for treatments like the Reflexology Massage ($80), a Deep Cleaning Facial or Men's Skin Care Treatment ($80), or a Honeysuckle Algae Scrub ($55).

TRAIL RIDING Jim Kelly holds the coveted Horseman of Distinction designation, so it's no wonder that his horses are in Class A shape and well trained to ride through the salt marshes, white sand, and frothy surf of Amelia Island. At **Kelly Ranch** (904-491-5166) you start out in a wooded area, and then ride along miles of open beach next to dolphins just offshore. One-hour rides $45, adults and ages 13 and up only. There's a 230-pound weight limit.

Country Day Stable (904-879-8383), Hilliard. Take a 1-hour trail ride ($25) through 40 acres of north woods past the owners' re-creation of a medieval castle. The Horse Discovery ($10) lets small kids groom their horse, followed by a hand-led ride.

✷ Green Space

BEACHES **Fort Clinch State Park** (904-277-7274), 2601 Atlantic Ave, one of the oldest parks in the Florida State Park system, was acquired in 1935 when developers who planned to build along the peninsula couldn't pay their taxes; the state paid $10,000 with the "fort thrown in." Workers from the Civilian Conservation Corps toiled from 1937 to 1942 to restore the fort. Opened to the public in 1938, Fort Clinch State Park offers an array of seaside activities. Besides hiking, biking, picnicking, and fishing, you can tour the historic fort, constructed in 1842, or enjoy the salt breezes through either of its two campgrounds on an overnight stay. Fee.

Kathryn Abbey Hanna Park (904-249-4700), 500 Wonderwood Dr, Mayport. Boardwalks lead through gnarled forests of sand live oak and over tall, windswept dunes topped with cabbage palms and sea oats to strands of white sand that attract sunbathers from all over the region. The park includes fishing ponds, separate hiking and biking trails, and two campgrounds—developed and primitive. Fee.

Talbot Island Geo-Park (904-251-2320), 12157 Heckscher Dr. Divided into two adjoining state parks, Big Talbot Island and Little Talbot Island, these barrier islands provide an immersion into an undeveloped Florida shoreline, a rare and glorious experience. Short hiking trails lead out to the beaches, none more interesting than Blackrock Beach, where the lava-like "rocks" are made of naturally eroded peat and sand. The popular

BLACKROCK BEACH

Sandra Friend

campground on Little Talbot Island sits in a bowl created by the dunes of the maritime forest; canoe rentals available. Fee.

PARKS

Jacksonville

On a hot summer day, catch the mist off the world's highest-spraying fountains at **Friendship Park & Fountain**, Southbank Riverwalk, on the St. Johns River.

One of the oldest and largest live oak trees in Florida is at **Treaty Oak Park**, Prudential Dr at Main St. The tree spreads 160 feet across the branches.

Ponte Vedra Beach

Guana River State Park (904-825-5071), 2690 S Ponte Vedra Blvd. Most visitors come here for the beaches—they go on forever, it seems, paralleling FL A1A for several miles, with two large parking areas at either end. But I like the hidden treasure on the Intracoastal side of the park at the dam, the hiking and biking trail system that loops for 9 miles through a variety of habitats and provides fresh salt breezes as you walk under the oaks lining the Tolomato River. Fishing is superb in the Guana and Tolomato Rivers, and a popular activity at the dam. Expect a beach parking fee during peak seasons and weekends.

WILD PLACES ♿ **Cary State Forest** (904-266-5021), US 301, Bryceville. Protecting pine flatwoods, cypress domes, and pitcher plant bogs, this state forest has an extensive network of trails open to equestrians. The 1.4-mile Cary Nature Trail is a great short jaunt for kids and people of limited mobility—well graded, good for a stroller, and wheelchair accessible with assistance. Families may wish to take advantage of the "primitive" campsite: tents only ($5 per night per tent), but with showers and rest rooms provided. Fee.

Over 4,000 acres in the **Ralph E. Simmons State Forest** (904-845-3597), off US 301, Hilliard, offer some of the most beautiful wildflowers in the state, and several nice campsites with a view of Georgia across the St. Marys River. The forest roads are used for hiking, biking, and trail riding; take a map along or you *will* get lost! Free.

✷ Lodging

BED & BREAKFASTS

Amelia Island 32034

The **Elizabeth Point Lodge** (904-277-4851; www.elizabethpointlodge.com), 98 S Fletcher Ave, just drew me in. Calling on my Maine roots, I suspect, the 1890s Nantucket shingle-style inn has a strong maritime theme. Just steps from the ocean, you can take in a breathtaking view from the porch or breakfast area. And even with 25 rooms, they are always booked. Rooms with breakfast $160–275.

Florida's oldest hotel, **Florida House Inn** (904-261-3300; www.floridahouseinn.com), dates back to 1857 and is located in the middle of the Fernandina historic district. With 25 rooms, it's more of a country inn than a B&B. Recently under new ownership, it has retained much of the original innkeeper's charm and staff and still offers breakfast, lunch, and dinner in boardinghouse style as well as an old English pub. Deluxe rooms feature vintage and decorator quilts, two-person Jacuzzi, and working fireplace. Economy $99, standard $149–169, deluxe $179–219.

Jacksonville 32204

The gorgeous 1912 Colonial-style **House on Cherry Street** (904-384-1999; www.houseoncherry.com), 1844 Cherry St, is set directly on the St. Johns River and is within easy walking distance of Avondale Village. You'll instantly relax surrounded by the elegant period antiques and Oriental rugs and in the nurturing hands of friendly innkeepers Victoria and Robert Freeman. There are many reasons why people stay at B&Bs—for the history, for the homemade food, for the camaraderie (all found here), or simply to know that someone cares if you get up in the morning. Nursing a bout of the flu while doing research, I got progressively worse and can't imagine what would have happened to me if I had been in a large chain hotel. Victoria not only nursed me back to health with motherly care, but also called to make sure I got home okay. The inn is one of grand elegance, but not stuffy or fussy. You won't want to miss evening conversations with these intelligent innkeepers and their worldly guests, sipping wine and sampling hors d'oeuvres on the spacious screened-in back porch while discussing everything from politics to the latest novel. Take a stroll on the large lawn overlooking the St. Johns, where you'll discover secret gardens and hidden treasures, then rest on the Crone's bench and watch the dolphins play in the river. Breakfast is equally elegant, with kayaker's quiche, fresh fruit, and baked goods. The small pecan grove and blueberry patch produce just enough to make fresh muffins for the four guest rooms. $75–130.

In historic Riverside, just a short trip from downtown, is the **Inn at Oak Street** (904-379-5525; www.innatoak street.com), 2114 Oak St. Expect the unexpected at this no-so-typical B&B. The 1902 Frame Vernacular has a warm, comfortable environment accented with a rich use of color, like the Cabernet Room with rich wine-colored walls and queen sleigh bed. The nature-inspired Hemingway with Audubon green walls has a king grand mahogany sleigh bed and whirlpool spa tub. The spacious 1854 Room with gold walls and rich bed linens has a French art deco queen bed, an 8-foot armoire with amber glass doors, and a wine refrigerator. $90–165.

Jacksonville Beach 32250

Reminiscent of a traditional southern beach home, the **Fig Tree Inn** (904-246-8855 or 1-877-217-9830; www .figtreeinn.com), 185 4th Ave S, was built in 1915 as a summer beach cottage and is serenely decorated in calm colors. The comfy themed rooms—like the Bird Room, with handmade willow bed—all have beautiful quilts and handiwork. Families will appreciate the adjoining Coral and Palm Rooms. $75–150.

The recently renovated **Pelican Path B & B** (904-249-1177; www.pelican path.com), 11 N 19th Ave, is great for couples and single travelers. This is the place where you can pamper yourself. The gorgeous dining room overlooks the ocean, and select rooms have bay window, king-sized bed, and spa tub. Senior getaway packages available.

HOTELS AND MOTELS

Jacksonville

From the classy **Adam's Mark Hotel** (904-633-9095 or 1-800-444-ADAM; www.adamsmark.com), 225 Coast Line Dr E, Jacksonville 32202, the largest new hotel downtown, you can stroll the Riverwalk to the Landing, downtown's hot gathering spot. Rooms come in two flavors: Riverview or Cityview ($79–279). Suites are available on the Concierge Level ($35 upgrade), where visitors enjoy private breakfast in the Concord Club. The 19th floor has a fitness center, hot tub, and pool overlooking the river, and there are two restaurants (see *Dining Out* and *Eating Out*) and two bars in the massive complex.

The **Sea Turtle Inn & Restaurant** (904-249-7402; www.seaturtle.com), 1 Ocean Blvd, Jacksonville 32233, is where John Grisham is said to have written *The Brethren*. Rooms and two-bedroom suites $105–599.

RESORTS

Amelia Island 32035

Most visitors to **Greyfield Inn Cumberland Island** (904-261-6408; www.greyfieldinn.com), Cumberland Island, Georgia, depart from the docks in Fernandina, where the private ferry takes you across to a great escape from the hectic pace of the mainland. The remote island is teeming with wildlife, making it a great place to go for a nature walk or bicycle ride, paddle around in a kayak, or take a 3-hour guided wilderness tour with a staff naturalist in the comfort of a Land Rover vehicle—all included in your overnight stay. Three fabulous gourmet meals are also included. If you can only stay for a brief visit, plan on a day trip with picnic lunch or dinner trip with candlelight gourmet dinner.

Ponte Vedra 32082

Step back in time to 1928 at the **Ponte Vedra Inn & Club** (904-285-1111; www.pvresorts.com), 200 Ponte Vedra Blvd, where you'll experience all the grandeur of a famed winter resort for the wealthy and famous. Generations of guests continue to come back, and generations of staff continue to cater to their every need. The main inn was opened in 1938 and has retained much of its original grandeur. Choose from lagoon or ocean views in any of the 18 luxury rooms. The ocean-side rooms are larger and feature two queen poster beds in a beautiful honey-blond finish. I wanted to have them ship one to my house. The European turndown service was new to me; the bed covers are removed, and two soft sheets surround your blanket for a much softer and more hygienic sleep. In the bathroom you'll find the television piped in so you won't miss the morning news; there's also a soft-lit magnifying mirror. This resort is all about the little details, from intimate corner nooks to friendly personal service. Rooms start at $200 in the historic inn and $240 oceanfront.

VACATION HOMES If you need more room, ask **Lodging Resources** (904-277-4851), 98 S Fletcher Ave, about **Katie's Light**, a three-bedroom, two-and-a-half-bath oceanfront home shaped like a lighthouse. This unique structure, with a 360-degree deck, also appeared in the movie *Pippi Longstocking*. Other beachfront properties are also available.

Hilliard 32046

Remember how life used to be? Down a dirt road in a quiet corner of the Ralph E. Simmons Memorial State Forest (see *Wild Places*), you come to **St. Marys River Fish Camp & Campground** (904-845-4440 or 966-845-4443), 28506 Scotts Landing Rd. Steve Beck's family-oriented environment provides a great getaway place for safe, clean fun. You'll often see the kids up late at night playing basketball with him at the basketball court, just off the porch of the community store. Everyone hangs out here, and the sense is of community, caring, and southern hospitality. Take to the water in fishing or pleasure boats to catch bream, catfish, or bass. Pull up on a sandy beach for a swim or picnic. Learn how to water ski. Search for the elusive goats on Goat Island. On weekends, watch a movie in the outdoor amphitheater, hike the many nature trails in the nearby state forest, or just relax and enjoy the beautiful solitude of the area—you'll run out of time before you run out of things to do. RV sites $25 daily, $120 weekly, $250 monthly. Primitive tent sites $10 daily.

SOLITUDE ON THE ST. MARYS RIVER

Kathy Wolf

✷ Where to Eat

DINING OUT

Amelia Island

Enjoy the charm of **Le Clos** (904-261-8100; www.leclos.com), 20 S 2nd St, while dining by candlelight in an intimate 1906 cottage. The creatively prepared French dishes by Cordon Bleu and Escoffier chef-owner Katherine Ewing are partnered with equally fine wines. Dinner nightly except Sun.

Jacksonville

Come for an earful at **Bravo!** in the Adam's Mark Hotel (see *Hotels and Motels*), where the singing wait staff entertains (some of them have gone on to Broadway, even!) while executive chef Charlie Sacher creates art in the kitchen—upscale Italian like portobello ravioli with sun-dried tomatoes, white truffle oil, and shaved Regianno, or dinner entrées that include maple-glazed crisp duck, saltimbocca, and cedar-planked salmon. Pasta, pizza, salads, and light dishes, $7–13; dinner entrées, $15–30.

Other great dining spots are **River City Brewing Co** (904-398-2299), 835 Museum Circle, for steaks and seafood; **Morton's of Chicago** (904-399-3933), 1510 Riverplace Blvd, world famous for steaks; the fun and hip **Bistro Aix** (904-398-1949), 1440 San Marco Blvd; the chic Manhattan-style café **bb's** (904-306-0100), 1019 Hendricks Ave, where "its groovy to b"; and **Biscotti's Expresso Café** (904-387-2060), 3556 St. Johns Ave, a trendy coffee bar with an extensive lunch and dinner menu and sinsational desserts.

EATING OUT

Amelia Island/Fernandina Beach

Your first stop should be the **Palace Saloon**, Florida's oldest continuously operating saloon, for some Pirate's Punch. Once your thirst is slaked, satisfy your appetite with fried or blackened shrimp ($14), crabcakes ($17), and Palace prime rib ($18).

Amelia Island Deli (904-261-9400), 5 S 2nd St. Light breakfast items, sandwiches, wraps, and platters ($4–6).

For a jolly time, you'll always find your way to an Irish pub, and **O'Kanes** (904-261-1000), Centre St, is extra friendly. The Davis Turner Band has been playing here for over a decade, every Wed–Sat night. Dine on great Irish fare like steak and Guinness pie ($11), Shannon seafood au gratin ($17), and fish-and-chips ($11) in the pub or the dining room.

For a funky Florida adventure, visit **Palms Fish Camp** (904-251-3004), south of Amelia Island at Clapboard Creek. Art Jennette prepares authentic Florida Cracker-style seafood at fish camp prices. Go early (before 6:30) to take advantage of the buffet on Fri and Sat nights.

The **Surf Restaurant** (904-556-1059; www.thesurfonline.com), 3199 S Fletcher Ave, serves up lunch, dinner, and late-night snacks with live music on the huge outdoor sundeck. Salads, fried oyster or butterfly shrimp baskets, crab burgers, and Hawaiian chicken wraps ($9). Catch the Fri- and Sat-night all-you-can-eat buffets ($19 adults, $9 ages to 12).

Catch a big T-burger or portobello mushroom burger at **T-Ray's Burger Station** (904-261-6310), 202 S 8th St, located inside the Exxon station at the corner of S 8th and Ash Sts.

Callahan

Traveling up US 1, my son and I began to get hungry about dark. The **Florida Room Restaurant** (904-879-2006), 1335 S Kings Rd, looked like it might have a selection to satisfy both of us. I don't know what such a talented chef is doing so far out in the country, but I was grateful to have found this talented soul. The family-owned restaurant has a wholesome, comfortable atmosphere, with simple but charming decor carefully selected to enhance but not "stuffy up" the place. The self-taught chef is passionate about his cooking, and so we followed his dinner suggestions. My Orange Blossom Chicken would rival that of any chef in South Beach, and my son's Bucky Burger had to be the most enormous burger I have ever seen. Even with his bottomless stomach, he just couldn't finish it! This road stop is worth taking a country drive out from Jacksonville.

Hilliard

Home-style southern cooking and barbecue is on the menu at **Patricia Ann's** (904-845-2113), 551705 US 1. BBQ beef or pork plate ($7), liver and onions ($5), country-fried steak ($5); you won't go hungry with the Family Feast ($30), which includes regular slab whole chicken and large portions of both beef and pork served with three sides and garlic bread.

Jacksonville

The elegance of the marble and glass lobby of the Adam's Mark Hotel (see *Hotels and Motels*) spills over to set the ambience of the **Riverfront**

Café, which looks out across the lobby to the St. Johns River. The creative dessert list caught my eye right off, with entries like sweet potato pecan pie, tangerine crème brûlée with tropical nut florentine, and the dainty banana coconut cream pie (best of both worlds!) that I simply had to try. The "famous grouper sandwich" stood up to its name, with fish so fresh it melts in your mouth; try it blackened for just a touch of spice. Breakfast, lunch, and dinner; sandwiches $7–8, entrées $12–20.

You'll want your fresh Cracker-style fish at **Clark's Fish Camp Seafood Restaurant** (904-268-3474), 12903 Hood Landing Rd, and good home-style cooking can be found at the historic **Starlite Cafe** (904-356-4444), 1044 Park St.

Jacksonville Beach
Lighthouse Grille (904-242-8899), 2600 Beach Blvd. Dine on steaks, ribs, and seafood surrounded by rich, dark wood in an open and inviting setting overlooking the Intracoastal Waterway. Oven-roasted salmon ($15), Danish baby back ribs ($14–16), and New York strip ($20) all come with honey-dribbled croissants. Salads, sandwiches, and burgers, $7–13.

✷ Selective Shopping

Amelia Island/Fernandina Beach
Centre St and many of its connecting streets are where you'll find great shopping like **Pineapple Patch** (904-321-2441), with Flap Happy and Fresh Produce kids' clothing. **Harbor Wear** (904-321-0061) has a great assortment of Life is Good women's quality sun and fun clothing. At the **Tilted Anchor** (904-261-7086) there's a nice selection of Brighton shoes and accessories along with interesting knickknacks like Cats Meow. The Irish-owned **Celtic Charm** (904-277-8009) takes me back to the motherland. **Amelia's Bloomin' Baskets** (904-277-2797) makes adorable gift baskets in a quaint island style. And the **Unusual Shop** (904-277-9664) really lives up to its name with artsy treasures. Expect the unexpected at Terri Rauleson's **Two Hearts** (904-321-1615), with whimsical gifts. Take the **Last Flight Out** (904-321-0510) and learn the history behind the name. The small shop offers a variety of gift and logo items and apparel.

Art galleries and studios showcase their works on Artrageous First Fridays (see *Special Events*). You'll enjoy such artists as **Sax/Designs on Gallery/Gifts** (904-277-4104), featuring American crafts, glass, wood, clay, and metal, and Susan's slightly off **Centre Gallery and Gifts** (904-277-1147), with unusual collections of ceramics, paintings, and glass, plus funky clothing.

Jacksonville
Jacksonville Landing (904-353-1188), 2 Independent Dr. A riverfront marketplace with dozens of shops and live entertainment.

Pier 17 Marine Inc (1-800-332-1072), 4619 Roosevelt Blvd. Gifts wrapped in nautical charts? That's part of the charm of this massive nautical store, where you'll find everything from floating key chains to kayaks, outboard engines, canvas sails, and sailboats. Billed as the "South's Largest Outdoor Store," there's no doubting it'll keep you busy browsing for hours.

Gourmet chocolates are prepared right before your eyes at **Peterbrooke Chocolatier** (904-398-2489), 1470 San Marco Blvd. The chocolate production center has antique chocolate molds on display and offers rich chocolaty samples with the tour. Mon–Fri 10–5; tours at 10 only. Fee.

Jacksonville Beach
Since 1973 **Aqua East Surf Shop** (904-246-9809; www.aquaeast.com), 696 Atlantic Blvd, has been Surf Central for northeast Florida. Surf, wave, and skate gear; pro events.

Just a peek in the window caught my curiosity at **Cats MEOW Boutique** (904-242-2560), 328 9th Ave N, where you'll find fine contemporary clothing that's just purr-fect.

Middleburg
Country Charm Mercantile (904-282-4512), 4544 Alligator Blvd. Handcrafted quilts bulge from the shelves; wind chimes dangle from the ceiling. This five-room home is jam-packed with gift items and home decor, from Heritage Village miniatures to Yankee candles, gourmet foods, and Beanie Babies. Closed Sun.

Ponte Vedra
Pineapple Post Gift Shop (1-877-757-7678; www.pineapplepostgifts.com), 2403 South 3rd St. Great gifts and home accessories with southern hospitality. Complimentary gift wrap.

You can't go wrong with the classics in **Talbots** (904-285-1011), 330 FL A1A N, at the Shoppe of Ponte Vedra.

FARMER'S MARKETS AND U-PICK

Callahan
Hildebrand Farms (904-845-4254). Strawberries, tomatoes, melons, and cucumbers.

Jacksonville
Dowless Blueberry Farms (904-772-1369). Blueberries.

✷ Special Events

Year-round, first Fri of the month: The **Artrageous First Fridays** is an art walk with over a dozen art studios and galleries open 6–9 PM in historic downtown Fernandina.

Year-round, first weekend of the month: See the blacksmith shop, jail, laundry, and kitchen come alive as park rangers reenact everyday life along with marching drills and artillery demonstrations at **Fort Clinch State Park** (see *Historic Sites*). Guided candlelight fort tours after sundown.

March: **Concours d'Elegance** (904-636-0027), Fernandina, is one of the nation's largest classic car shows, with over 230 rare cars from private collections on display.

May: **Isle of Eight Flags Fernandina Shrimp Festival** (904-277-7274), in downtown historic Fernandina, celebrates the shrimping industry with music, fine arts and crafts, antiques, pirates, and shrimp, shrimp, shrimp.

Annual **Baby Bird Shower** at BEAKS (see *Bird Sanctuary*), Big Talbot Island. The 2-day event benefits the wildlife sanctuary for injured birds and animals. Music and fun for all ages.

In Jacksonville, the **Jacksonville Beer & Food Festival** at the Morocco Shrine Temple Auditorium features over 130 exotic beers and food. The multicultural **World of Nations Celebration** in Metropolitan Park serves up exotic foods and fun. Take a self-guided **Historic Home Tour** through Riverside-Avondale. The

Kuumba Festival celebrates African American heritage at Clanzel Brown Park, while high-flying dogs catch Frisbees at the **Florida State Canine Frisbee Championships**, Bolles School.

June: Get your reservations well in advance for the **Amelia Island Chamber Music Festival** (www.islandchamber.org). World-renowned musicians perform chamber music at venues throughout the island in this fabulous annual event.

June–August: **Seawalk Pavillion Moonlight Movies and jazz concerts** take place in Jacksonville Beach throughout the summer.

September: The **Riverside Arts Festival** arts and crafts show takes place at Riverside Park in Jacksonville.

October: The **Amelia Book Festival** in Fernandina features book signings, readings, and workshops. Have "lunch with an author" or go on a "beachwalk with an author."

The **Jacksonville Agricultural Fair** features livestock, a petting zoo, arts and crafts, midway rides, and live entertainment.

November–December: The **Ritz-Carlton** (1-800-241-3333) does it up big for Christmas as Santa and Mrs. Claus arrive in a horse-drawn carriage, giving the reindeer a rest before the big night. Enjoy a bonfire on the beach with hot chocolate and s'mores, campfire music, and storytelling. For the kids, there's an afternoon tea and storybook performances, and Santa will even tuck your little one in at night.

December: **Amelia Island Historic Christmas Tour of B&B Inns**. Not sure which B&B to stay at next time? Or just want to see the beautiful architecture decked out in holiday splendor? You'll want to make this favorite trek. The self-guided driving tour features 10 B&Bs filled with holiday music and light refreshments.

The **Holiday by the Sea Festival** takes place at the Seawalk Pavilion in Jacksonville Beach.

ST. JOHNS RIVER

The St. Johns River is one of only 14 rivers designated an American Heritage River. The top fishing spot covers 70 square miles of rivers and lakes, with several towns settled along its banks. In 1513 Ponce de León is said to have discovered the Fountain of Youth at De Leon Springs, an area still open to the public. Around 1570 the resident Timucua Indians were beginning to lose their foothold on their land; by the 1700s the area was populated with early pioneers and traders. With the timber and turpentine industries well established, the steamboats of the late 1800s brought the wealthy down from the north to vacation near the mineral-rich springs. This section is divided by counties, with East Clay and Putnam Counties at the north end of the river and West Volusia County, the south. The river meets the Atlantic Ocean at Jacksonville.

CLAY COUNTY: GREEN COVE SPRINGS, ORANGE PARK, AND PENNEY FARMS

GUIDANCE **Clay County Tourism Division** (904-264-2651; www.claychamber.org), 1764 Kingsley Ave, Orange Park 32073.

GETTING THERE *By air*: **Jacksonville International Airport** (904-741-4902).

By bus: **Greyhound** (1-800-231-2222).

By car: From Jacksonville, take **US 17** about 50 miles south. From the St. Augustine area, take **CR 16** from I-95.

By sea: From Jacksonville, follow the St. Johns River south and dock in Orange Park or Green Cove Springs.

GETTING AROUND **US 17** runs from Orange Park south along the St. Johns River past Green Cove Springs to Putnam County. **CR 16** runs east–west through the county, from Green Cove Springs past Penney Farms and

ALONG THE ST. JOHNS RIVER

Sandra Friend

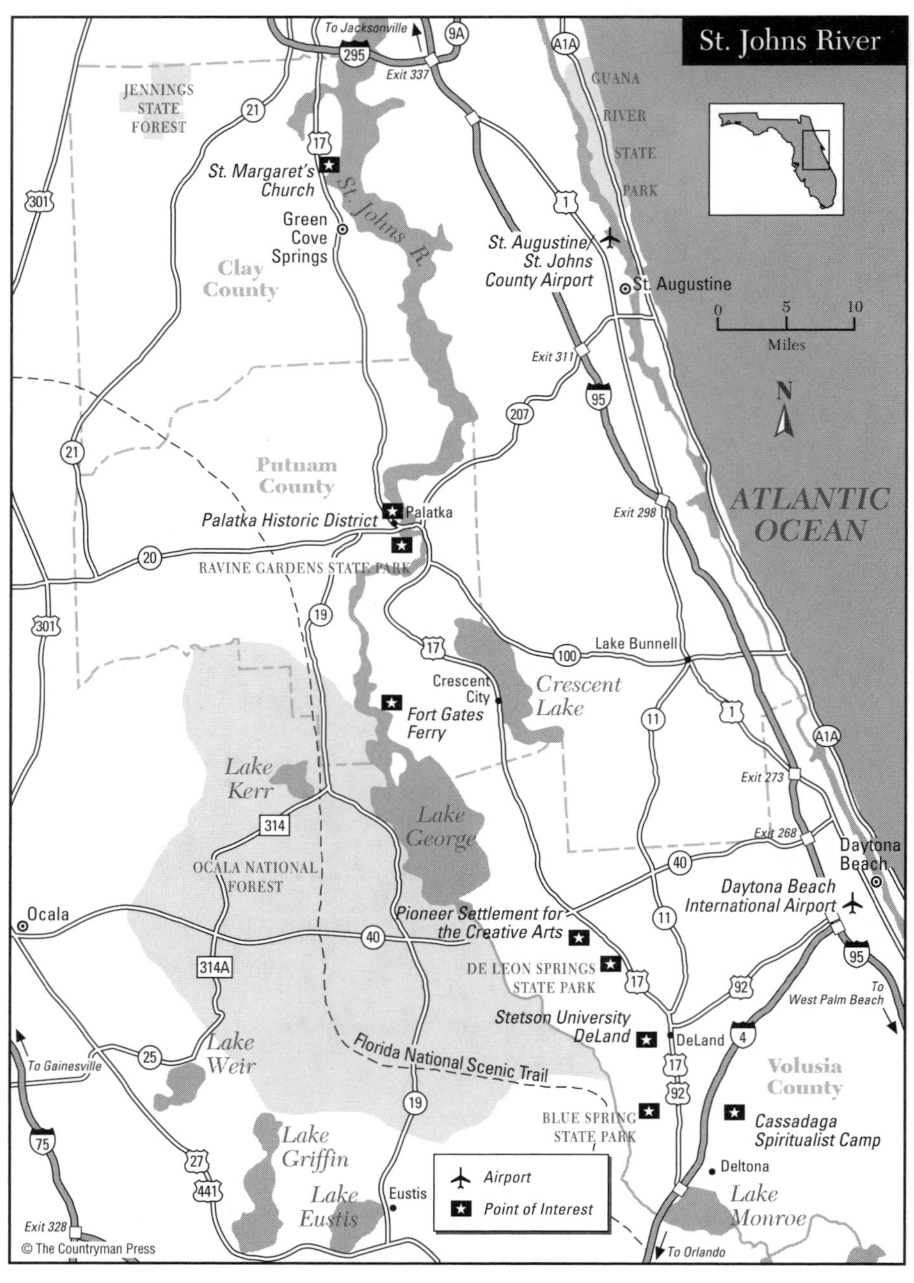

Camp Blanding in Starke to the Bradford county line. Take **CR 21** from Orange Park south to reach Middleburg and Keystone Heights.

MEDICAL EMERGENCIES Orange Park Medical Center (904-276-8500; www.opmedical.com), 2001 Kingsley Ave, Orange Park. **Memorial Hospital**

Jacksonville (main number 904-399-6111; emergency 904-399-6156), 3625 University Blvd S, Jacksonville.

✷ To See

MUSEUMS

Green Cove Springs
♿ Local history is well documented at the **Clay County Historical Museum** (904-284-9644 or 904-284-5243), 915 Walnut St. And with the addition of the **Railroad Museum** you'll enjoy the collection of photographs, fine china and silverware, timetables, bells and whistles, step boxes, and baggage tags once part of the Clay Street Hill Railroad. Look for Phantom Train ACL 76. Sun 2–5.

Middleburg
Black Heritage Museum (call Maude Jackson at 904-282-4168, Mamie Oliver at 904-282-5223, or Sarah Weeks at 904-282-5205 for tours), Longmire Ave at Hunter-Douglas Park. A sensitive and thought-provoking view of black culture during the late 1800s displayed in a one-room schoolhouse.

Photographs and displays of the early turpentine, timber, and phosphate industries depict one of the oldest continuous communities in Florida at the **Middleburg Historical Museum** (904-282-5924), 3912 Section St. Sun 2–4.

HISTORIC SITES **Bubba Midden** is located on the east bank of Black Creek, 2 miles north of its confluence with the St. Johns River in the vicinity of Hibernia.

Green Cove Spring and Swimming Pool, a popular tourist spot in the late 1800s, is thought to be Florida's first therapeutic mineral springs. A decorative railing surrounds the clean and clear spring, about 20 feet in diameter, set amid tall oaks and palm trees. You can look down about 31 feet, where it tapers to a narrow entrance into the cavern. This section is out of sight, but opens to 25 feet wide and descends another 150 feet before flowing toward the St. Johns River. The spring keeps the neighboring 50-by-100-foot swimming pool at a constant 72 degrees year-round, then overflows down a stream about 300 feet to the St. Johns. You'll note the sulfurous odor, but the water is safe for swimming and at one time was bottled as drinking water. The spring is open year-round; swimming in the pool is allowed only during summer months.

A long drive down a narrow dirt road is richly rewarded when you reach the quaint **St. Margaret's Episcopal Church** (904-284-3030; www.stmargarets.org), Old Church Rd, Hibernia. George Fleming emigrated from Ireland and established Hibernia (Latin for "Ireland") Plantation on the 1,000 acres now known as Fleming Island. The church, a gift for his wife, Margaret Seton Fleming, was completed in 1878. With only 50 seats, the Gothic-style sanctuary requires three services on Sun. The annual Tour and Tea (see *Special Events*) re-creates the Civil War era with guided tours of the plantation grounds; high tea is served.

Middleburg Methodist Church Cemetery and the 1847 **Middleburg United Methodist Church** are next to the Middleburg Historical Museum (see *Museums*).

Since 1921 the Loyal Order of Moose at **Moosehaven** (904-278-1210) has been a part of the Orange Park community. The fraternal organization dedicated to bettering the lives of children and the elderly, along with helping their communities, donated many sites and buildings, which are now the town hall, fire station, and library, to the town of Orange Park. The retirement community resides on 63 acres along the St. Johns River and has its own chapel, library, and a state-of-the-art assisted-living health care center.

See the register from the Parkview Resort Hotel (circa 1890) and rare photographs from the late 20th century at the **Orange Park Town Hall** (904-264-9565), 2042 Park Ave, Mon–Fri 8–5. The **J. C. Penney Memorial Church** (904-529-9078) and surrounding area was built in 1927 as a community for retired ministers.

✷ To Do

BICYCLING Whether you ride city streets or rough and rural, several great off-road touring and mountain bike paths can be found throughout the county. The Northeast Regional Planning Council (904-363-6350) produces *Bikeways of Northeast Florida, Clay & Putnam Counties*, which can be picked up at the Clay County Tourism Division (904-264-2651; www.claychamber.org), 1764 Kingsley Ave, Orange Park. There is a nice paved bicycle path along US 17 from Doctors Lake south about 7 miles; or you can veer off onto Pine Ave for views of the St. Johns River. For off-roaders, head to the rolling sandhills of Gold Head Branch State Park, then down FL 21 to CR 352 for a leisurely lakeside ride.

BOATING **Dock Holiday Boat Rentals** (904-215-5363; www.dockholidayboatrentals.com), 3108 US 17 S, Orange Park. Fishing boats $150–250; pontoon boats $175–275; houseboats $600 and up.

Venture Up (904-291-5991), 2216 S Mimosa, Middleburg. Canoes or paddle boats $25 a day; kayaks $20 a day.

DRIVING TOURS Fans of Lynyrd Skynyrd will search for **Brickyard Road**. Look for the sign.

GOLF In Green Cove Springs, try **Cattail Creek Golf Club** (904-284-3502). Orange Park has **Eagle Harbor Golf Club** (904-269-9300) and **Golf Club at Fleming Island** (904-269-1440); in Middleburg you'll find **Ravines Golf Resort** (904-282-1111).

GREYHOUND RACING **Jacksonville Kennel Club** (904-680-3647), 20455 Park Ave, Orange Park. **Orange Park Greyhound Track** (904-646-0001), Orange Park.

SWIMMING Revive yourself in the chemical-free community pool. The constant 72-degree water of the **Green Cove Spring** (see *Historic Sites*) feeds directly into the pool and then out to the St. Johns River, ensuring clean, mineral-rich water at all times. The pool is open only during summer months.

WALKING TOURS The Clay County Historical Society (904-284-3615) provides guided tours through two historic districts on the National Register of Historic Places. You'll find 85 structures in the **Green Cove Springs Historic District**, mostly around Walnut St and bounded by Bay St, the CSX railroad tracks, Center St, Orange Ave, St. Elcom St, and the St. Johns River. There are a dozen buildings in the **Middleburg Historical District** along Main and Wharf Sts.

✻ Green Space

SPRINGS The spring and pool are the focal point of the pretty little park on the edge of the St. Johns River. But the view from the **Spring at Spring Park** (904-529-2200), Green Cove Springs, looks out over the St. Johns River, making this a great place for picnics. Gentle breezes blow through the shady canopy of tall and graceful live oaks covering the children's play area.

WILD PLACES **Bayard Point Conservation Area** (904-529-2380), FL 16, Green Cove Springs. Access this 10,000-acre preserve from the John P. Hall Sr. Nature Preserve entrance off FL 16 near the St. Johns River Bridge to follow the trails through pine flatwoods and scrub out to a beautiful campsite on the banks of the St. Johns River. It's a popular place for trail riding and fishing, and is used for environmental education classes for the local school district. Free.

GREEN COVE SPRINGS PARK

Kathy Wolf

Black Creek Ravines Conservation Area (904-269-6378), Green Rd north of CR 218, Middleburg. If you've always wanted to see pitcher plants in bloom, stop here and walk the trails out to the vast pitcher plant bogs beneath the high-tension lines. The reason for this preserve, however, is the rugged terrain—bluffs up to 90 feet above sea level, deeply cut with ravines that channel rainwater down to Black Creek. Primitive camping, biking, and horseback riding are permitted—but bring your camera for the showy parade of spring wildflowers! Free.

Jennings State Forest (904-291-5530), 1337 Long Horn Rd, Middleburg. Popular with equestrians for its dozens of miles of riding trails, this high-and-dry forest amid the sandhills outside Jacksonville also offers several hiking trails; try out the Fire & Water Nature Trail for an interpretive introduction to the habitats found here, including seepage slopes with pitcher plants. The North Fork Black Creek Trail offers primitive camping within a stone's throw of the waterway. Free.

✱ Lodging

BED & BREAKFAST Take in the cool river breeze of the St. Johns while sitting on the veranda of an 1887 inn on the National Register of Historic Places. Just across from the Green Cove Mineral Spring (see *Historic Sites*) is the **River Park Inn Bed & Breakfast** (904-284-2994; www.riverparkinn.com), 103 S Magnolia Ave, Green Cove Springs 32043. During its heyday in the late 1800s and early 1900s, the spring was a mecca for wealthy tourists. This three-story Frame Vernacular home is just one of the "cottages" built to accommodate the well-heeled crowd. Five guest rooms, all with private bath, feature vintage decor. The Master Suite has a two-person Jacuzzi and sitting room. As part of the historic district, the inn is within easy walking of the fishing pier, antiques shopping, dining, and movies. Rooms with breakfast $75–200.

RESORT While it bills itself as a bed & breakfast, the **Club Continental and River Suites** (904-264-6070 or 1-800-877-6070; www.clubcontinental.com), 2143 Astor St, Orange Park 32073, is so much more. Still owned by heirs of the Palmolive Soap Company, the 27-acre estate retains the privacy of a private club. Walk amid the splendor of the carefully manicured gardens and fountains set in intimate courtyards. Towering 200-year-old live oaks bend to frame the three swimming pools. The seven rooms in the main Mediterranean-style mansion reflect Old World elegance, while 15 river suites, some with Jacuzzi and four-poster king-sized bed, all have a private riverfront balcony. Rooms with continental breakfast $80–175.

CAMPGROUNDS **Whitey's Fish Camp** (904-269-4198), 2032 CR 220, Orange Park 32003, has 44 sites with full hookups, a restaurant (see *Eating Out*), boat and canoe rentals, and, of course, fishing.

✱ Where to Eat

DINING OUT Looking for a romantic evening? You'll find it at the restaurant at **Club Continental** (904-264-6070 or 1-800-877-6070; www.clubcontinental.com), 2143 Astor St, Orange Park. Tall ceilings, white tablecloths, candles, and an incredible view of the St. Johns River are just part of the Old World elegance in the main house, where an extensive gourmet menu is complemented by fine wines and rare cognacs. This members-only restaurant allows you exclusive entrance only if you stay over in the main house or river suites (see *Resort*). Open Tue–Fri for dinner, Sun brunch.

EATING OUT Watch for seaplanes as they land and take off by **Outback Crabshack** (904-522-0500), 8155 CR 13 N, just south of Green Cove Springs at Six Mile Marina. You'll get your money's worth, as they dish out enormous platters of fried scallops ($14), alligator ($12), and catfish ($15). Lobster, crawfish, blue crab, and clams are steamed to perfection. They'll even blacken or stir-fry your meal. Get your daily requirement of veggies with the steamed Low Country tender potatoes, onions, corn, broccoli, mushrooms, and sausage for $5. Open daily for lunch and dinner.

Whitey's Fish Camp (904-269-4198), 2032 CR 220, Orange Park. Catfish is the specialty at this recently renovated restaurant with Florida flair. All-you-can-eat catfish ($13) is only for those with a big appetite. Petite eaters can order a basket with slaw, fries, and hushpuppies ($6). If you're not into catfish, then there's just about any other type of fish available—grilled, blackened, broiled, fried, or pecan crusted. Seafood platters ($14) include shrimp, oysters, scallops, and grouper. A really healthy appetite commands the Deluxe Dinner ($19), which seems to cover just about everything on the menu, including frog legs and 'gator tail. Fear not, landlubbers: You can get a 16-ounce rib eye ($19) or marinated chicken breast ($10). The outdoor terrace has live music on the weekends.

Ronnie's Wings Oysters & More (904-284-4728), 232 Walnut St, Green Cove Springs.

✷ Entertainment

Be one of the first to see a performance at the **Thrasher Horne Center for Performing Arts** (904-276-6815; www.thcenter.org), 283 College Dr, Orange. This state-of-the-art 84,666-square-foot theater is fully equipped with a multiuse theater and two art galleries. Its first event is scheduled for fall 2004. Expect performances of professional theater, dance, and music, along with visual arts exhibits.

✷ Selective Shopping

Fleming Island ("the Island," as the locals refer to it) is located on US 17 in Hibernia and is the community's center for restaurants and modern shops. The **historic district** in Green Cove Springs is an excellent place for antiquing.

✷ Special Events

♿ *May*: Not to be missed is the annual **St. Margaret's Tour and Tea** (904-284-3030; www.st.margarets.org), Old Church Rd, Hibernia. The 1-hour tour of Margaret's chapel (see *Historic Sites*) and the Fleming family plantation is followed by high tea. Civil War

EVENTS AT CLAY COUNTY FAIRGROUNDS Throughout the year there are several events at the Clay County Fairgrounds (904-529-3617), 2497 County Road 16 W, Green Cove Springs. In Jan equestrians gather for the $25,000 **Hunter Jumper Grand Prix**. In Feb, celebrate Celtic heritage with the **NFL Scottish Highlands Games** (904-264-2635). The **Clay County Agricultural Fair** (904-281-1615; www.claycountyfair.org) is in Apr. By Nov, get ready for 234 hours of bluegrass and gospel music at **Sheila's Bluegrass Festival** (904-923-5222), while later in the month canines jump for joy at the **Paws and Pals Agility Dog Show**.

reenactments, Virginia reel dancing, period costumes, and southern hospitality are just some of what's on offer. Limited number of golf carts available for handicapped or those unable to walk the area. $9 for ages 12 and up, $6 seniors.

August: **Soul Food Festival and Parade of Pride**, Vera F. Hall Park, Green Cove Springs.

December: **Clay County Historical Society Holiday Tour of Homes & Sites**, Green Cove Springs. Walk through authentic Victorian homes decorated for the holidays. $10.

PUTNAM COUNTY: CRESCENT CITY, PALATKA, INTERLACHEN, AND WELAKA

GUIDANCE **Putnam County Chamber of Commerce** (386-328-1503; (www.putnamcountychamber.org), 1100 Reid St, Palatka, or in Crescent City (386-698-1657) at city hall.

GETTING THERE *By air*: **Jacksonville International Airport** and **Daytona International Airport**.

By bus: **Greyhound** (1-800-231-2222).

By car: From Jacksonville, take **US 17** about 50 miles south. From the St. Augustine area, take **FL 207** off I-95. Go west about 22 miles to US 17. From Daytona, take **FL 100** approximately 45 miles. You can reach the western part of the county from I-75 by traveling 10 miles east on **FL 26**, then taking **FL 20** to Interlachen.

By sea: From Jacksonville, follow the St. Johns River south approximately 55 miles into downtown Palatka.

By train: **Amtrak** (1-800-872-7245; www.amtrak.com) provides regularly scheduled service to Palatka.

MEDICAL EMERGENCIES **Putnam Community Medical Center** (386-328-5711), FL 20 W, Palatka. **Memorial Hospital Jacksonville** (main number 904-399-6111; emergency 904-399-6156), 3625 University Blvd, Jacksonville.

✷ To See

AGRICULTURAL TOURS Visit fern fields, potato and cabbage farms, and an agricultural museum on the **Putnam County Agricultural Extension** (386-329-0318) agritours.

AQUACULTURAL TOURS Learn about warm-water fish production and native Florida fish conservation at **Welaka National Fish Hatchery and Aquarium** (386-467-2374), CR 309, Welaka. Open daily 7–4; guided group tours. Free.

ART GALLERIES **Florida School of the Arts Galleries** (386-328-1571), 5001 St. Johns Ave, Palatka.

Serving as a public library until the 1980s, the **Larimer Arts Center** (386-328-

8998), 216 Reid St, Palatka, is now the home of the Arts Council of Greater Palatka and the council's monthly exhibits. The gallery is open Thu and Fri 1–5, Sat 10–2.

BIRDING Hundreds of osprey nests top the trees and beacon markers along the St. Johns River. Great blue herons and snowy egrets are a common sight along the banks, especially around the fish camps.

The roadside observation tower at the Beecher Unit of the **Welaka National Fish Hatchery and Aquarium** (see *Aquacultural Tours*) provides excellent viewing, in winter and spring, of sandhill cranes, southern bald eagles, and a variety of egrets and herons.

Just south of the fish hatchery, the **Welaka State Forest** (see *Wild Places*) Mud Trail is a good place to see woodpeckers, Osceola turkeys, and owls.

Thousands of azaleas bloom in spring, making **Ravine Gardens State Park** (see *Parks*) a great place to view cedar waxwings, cardinals, hummingbirds, and a variety of butterflies.

View limpkins, gallinules, anhingas, and white ibises at **Kenwood** and **Rodman** recreation areas off US 19 (see Ocala National Forest).

HISTORIC SITES

Crescent City

Charles & Emily Cheatham House, 102 Main St. Emphasizing horizontal planes and wide eaves, this Prairie-style home showcases the American architectural style of Frank Lloyd Wright.

Henry G. Hubbard, who was the first to bring the camphor tree and Japanese persimmon to Florida, built the **Hubbard House**, 600 N Park St. Now a private residence, the circa-1879 dwelling is surrounded by elaborate botanical gardens.

Interlachen

The quaint 1892 **Interlachen Town Hall** (386-684-3811), 311 Atlantic Ave, on

FOLKLORE While traveling through the small community of Bardin off FL 100, peer into the piney woods and look closely; you might just catch a glimpse of the **Bardin Booger**. Local legend has it that a giant shaggy-haired creature, much like the elusive Sasquatch, was first sighted in the mid-1980s. Said to smell much like rotting cabbage and stand 13 feet tall, the ape-like creature has been touted as northeast Florida's Bigfoot. The Bardin Booger was immortalized in the late Billy Crain's "Bardin Booger" song, which is still played at many festivals and events along with the occasional appearance of the Booger itself. The curious and disbelievers can view a scrapbook filled with news clippings and illustrations at Bud's Store, the Bardin community gathering spot. You'll also find Jody Delzell's 1995 book *The Enigmatic Bardin Booger* at Andrea's Book Store in Palatka.

Kathy Wolf

THE BRONSON-MULHOLLAND HOUSE

the National Register of Historic Places, was the social center in the early 1900s, holding such town hall activities as dances, ladies' society meetings, and voting—events it hosts to this day.

Palatka

The 1854 **Bronson-Mulholland House** (386-329-0140), 100 Madison St, has seen its share of history. The former residence of Judge Isaac Bronson, the home also served as a school for freed slave children and a Red Cross center in both world wars. The beautifully restored antebellum plantation home is open Tue, Thu, and Sun 2–5.

Built by the Atlantic Coast Line in 1908, the **Historic Union Depot** (see *Railroadiana*) showcases the architectural style of H. H. Richardson with its random window openings and hexagonal dormered bays.

The Georgian-style **Tilghman House** (386-325-8750), 324 River St, built around 1887, now operates as an active arts center. Note the half-gabled veranda supported by Greek Doric columns and the Palladian window in the gable dormer. Open Mon–Fri 9–5.

Welaka

Mount Royal Indian Temple Mound, CR 309, is believed to be the largest shell mound in the state. The 100-foot-high site of the Timucua Indian ceremonial ground dates back to A.D. 1200–1600.

MURALS Pick up a map at the Chamber Visitor Center at 1100 Reid St and stroll through the "Mural City of Northeast Florida" seeking out the 25 **Palatka Murals** (386-328-6500) scattered throughout the downtown historic district. These building-sized, breathtaking murals beautifully depict the history, landscape, and culture of Palatka. You'll find a cattle drive, Ravine Gardens (see *Parks*), and the sailboats of the annual Mug Race (see *Special Events*). Look for the tiny gray church mouse in the Billy Graham mural (it's on the church porch).

PALATKA MURAL

Kathy Wolf

MUSEUMS

Crescent City

The Crescent City Women's Club takes on a labor of love filling the **Little Blue House Heritage Museum and Art Center** (386-698-4711 or

386-698-1991), 602 N Summit St, with pieces of the past. The former home, dating back to 1871, showcases the history and art of South Putnam. Open Tue–Sat 2:30–5.

Palatka

Originally part of Fort Shannon during the Indian Wars (1832–1845), the **Putnam Historic Museum** (386-325-9825), 100 Madison St, is the oldest dwelling in the Palatka area. Open Tue, Thu, and Sun 2–5.

RAILROADIANA All aboard at the **Historic Union Depot** (386-329-5538) and **David Browning Railroad Museum** (386-328-1539) at the corner of 11th and Reid Sts, Palatka. The Union Depot is open daily with railroad memorabilia, historical documents, and photographs of the Palatka area. But you'll want to plan your trip when all the members run their trains at the Browning Museum—only on the first Sun and third Sat of the month. Look for the 31-foot HO-scale model train, one of the longest in the world, chugging along the tracks for the enjoyment of young and old. The museum is open daily.

✷ To Do

BICYCLING The publication *Bikeways of Northeast Florida, Clay & Putnam Counties* can be picked up at the Clay County Tourism Division (904-264-2651; www.claychamber.org), 1764 Kingsley Ave, Orange Park. For a challenge, start at the Maintenance Building on Putnam County Blvd in East Palatka and head west on FL 207A, traveling 17.8 miles through riverfront farmlands and neighborhoods reflecting rural Florida. The trail ends at Federal Point Rd.

BOATING River Adventures (1-866-OUR-BOAT; www.riveradventuresinc.com), Crystal Cove Marina, Palatka. Motor down the St. Johns River while living on board a 60-foot luxury houseboat. Stretch out on the sundeck, then slip down the water slide for quick refreshment. These large houseboats accommodate up to 20 people and can be rented daily starting at $575, which includes a captain. Or they'll show you how to pilot the boat yourself, then let you take it for a week ($2,400–3,000). Groups of five or less can take advantage of the well-equipped fishing boats ($65 a day).

DRIVING TOURS For the shortest route from US 17 to US 19, take the **Fort Gates Ferry** (386-467-2411), CR 309, Welaka. The oldest operating ferry in Florida, this tiny two-car barge has transported auto passengers back and forth across the St. Johns River continuously since 1856. Access to the ferry dock is a mile off CR 309 on the east at Gateway Fishing Camp (see *Fish Camps*) and 17 miles through the Ocala National Forest from the west. Caution should be observed in the wet season, as both are dirt roads. If arriving from the west, honk your horn to alert the ferry captain. Autos $9, motorcycles $5. Open 7–5:30. Closed Tue.

ECOTOURS Learn more about the environment and local waterways with **Whole Earth Outfitters of Florida** (904-471-8782; www.wholeearthoutfitters.com).

Canoe, kayak, and camping tours take small groups through lakes, rivers, and coastline inlets to discover natural and historic Florida. Launch from the family homestead in Georgetown and paddle the St. Johns River, Lake George, and Salt Springs Run in search of bald eagles and alligators. Push off from a sandy beach in St. Augustine (see "First Coast") into a sheltered waterway for a different view of the St. Augustine Lighthouse, Castillo de San Marcos, and Bridge of Lions. Half- and full-day trips $45–85. Overnight trips available.

FISHING The well-known places to fish here are Lake George, the Rodman Pool, and of course the St. Johns River, but don't pass up the deep waters of **Crescent Lake**. Often neglected by anglers, this 12-mile body of water quickly drops from the 3-foot shoreline flats to depths reaching 14 feet. You may want a depth finder to locate the 12- and 13-pound bass lurking under the tea-stained water, or catch them as they move to the shallows to feed in such places as Shell Bluff and Sling Shot Creek.

When fishing Crescent Lake, stop by **Landing Lake Crescent Resort** (386-698-2485; www.lakecrescent.com), 100 Grove Ave, Crescent City (see *Fish Camps*), for all your bait, tackle, and marine needs. Fifteen-foot fiberglass fishing boats are available for half-day ($35) or full-day ($65) rentals. Pontoon boats run $75 for a half day, $130 for a full day.

Off CR 309 several marinas and fish camps (see *Fish Camps*) lead down to the St. Johns River, where bait and tackle is plentiful and you can rent boats, guides, or lodging.

WALKING TOURS The "Golden Age" is beautifully represented in **Crescent City**, whose streets are lined with ornately decorated Victorian architecture under a generous canopy of live oaks. A brochure, detailing the location of 20 of these historical homes (see *Historic Sites*), churches, and commercial buildings, is available from City of Crescent City (904-698-2525), 115 N Summit St.

Seek out the many murals (see *Murals*) and extensive Victorian architecture in historic downtown **Palatka**. A map is available at the Putnam County Chamber of Commerce (see *Guidance*).

✷ Green Space

PARKS You'll want to take in the burst of color Jan–Apr at **Ravine Gardens State Park** (386-329-3721), 1600 Twigg St, Palatka, when thousands of azaleas burst into full bloom. Drive 1.8 miles through canopies of live oaks surrounded by thick blankets of tropical and subtropical flora. Stroll through the 182-acre park, stopping at the observation terraces 100 feet above the ravine, or just sit and watch hummingbirds and butterflies in the formal gardens. There's a great place to picnic near the amphitheater. Open daily 8 AM–sunset; fee.

WILD PLACES **Etoniah Creek State Forest** (386-329-2552), FL 100 N, Florahome, protects one of Florida's most beautiful ravines at Etoniah Creek, where hikers can look down a 40-foot bluff to see tapegrass waving in the current of the stream at the bottom; visit in springtime, when the azaleas and dogwoods put on a show. The **Florida Trail** runs through the state forest, with designated campsites and a screened-room camping shelter at Iron Bridge. Free.

Owned by Georgia Pacific, the **Rice Creek Sanctuary** is a very special preserve off FL 100 N, west of Palatka. From the new trailhead, follow the main road back to the T intersection and turn right to find the **Florida Trail**. A 2-mile blue-blazed loop follows impoundments built in the 1700s by British settlers, who scraped an indigo and rice plantation from the floodplain forest; dozens of bridges carry you across blackwater waterways between ancient cypresses. Free.

The **St. Johns Water Management District** (904-529-2380; sjr.state.fl.us) is responsible for conservation areas that serve as buffers to the St. Johns River and its tributaries. While most provide access to waterways for paddling and fishing, some are also opening to hunting, equestrian use, and hiking. In Putnam County, **Dunns Creek Conservation Area** (386-529-2380), off FL 100 S of San Mateo, has a splendid array of bog wildflowers along its trails in spring; there's one primitive campsite. **Murphy Creek Conservation Area** (386-329-4883), CR 309-B, is a two-part preserve with a loop trail through floodplain forest off Buffalo Bluff Rd, near Welaka, and a loop trail on Murphy Island, leading to rare high bluffs above the St. Johns River, accessible only by boat; camping permitted. Free.

Welaka State Forest (386-467-2388), CR 309 south of Welaka, is one of the best places in the area for an overnight campout. Grab your backpack and walk 4 miles along the Johns Landing Trail out to one of two spectacular primitive campsites right on the St. Johns River. Or take the kids on an easy stroll through the floodplain forest on the nature trail at the fire tower, or along the short Mud Spring Trail to see Mud Spring, a crystal-clear garden of aquatic plants. Fee.

✷ Lodging

BED & BREAKFAST Talking with Doug de Leeuw about the love and enthusiasm he and his wife, Jill, have for the 1878 **Azalea House Bed & Breakfast** (386-325-4547; www.theazaleahouse.com), 220 Madison St, Palatka 32177, I couldn't help but feel that I'd come home. Surrounded by over 100 pieces of needlework, you'll want to create some of your own. And you can! Jill not only stocks needlework supplies, but also offers a Stitcher's Retreat complete with culinary delights and a special commemorative sampler kit. Jill, an accomplished pastry chef, also prepares a delicious full breakfast served in the formal dining room. Wander throughout the Victorian home and relax in the formal parlor and library-style living room or step outside to the open verandas that stretch around the home overlooking the tropical swimming pool, gardens, and fishpond. When you're ready to retire, curl up in an iron sleigh bed overlooking a magnolia tree in the Magnolia Room or (my favorite) the large Garden Room, with mission-style furnishings and "Button Bunny" needlework, reminiscent of the rabbits in Richard Adams's *Watership Down*. This former home of Benjamin Alexander Putnam's grandson Benjamin Alexander Calhoun, and former vice president John C. Calhoun, has six rooms with 14-foot ceilings, four of which have private bath. Open all year, $70–135.

FISH CAMPS

Lake Crescent

Landing Lake Crescent Resort (386-698-2485; www.lakecrescent.com), 100 Grove Ave, Crescent City 32112, sits on the west side of the largely undeveloped Crescent Lake (see *Fishing*). It's here you'll find black crappie, bream, black and striped bass, and catfish. Fish from the pier or rent a boat and explore the hidden depths of the lake. The camp features efficiency rooms (one has a fireplace), suites, RV sites and covered marina slips, cable TV, full kitchens, swimming pool, recreation room, pub/deli, and bait-and-tackle store. Rooms $58–120, RV sites $19–23, marina slips $5–10.

St. Johns River

Quiet and rustic, the **Gateway Fishing Camp** (386-467-2411), 229 Fort Gate Ferry Rd, Crescent City 32139, is located in the heart of bass fishing country, between Little Lake George and Big Lake George. Stay in the air-conditioned cottages, complete with stove, where you can fry up your catch of the day. Fish off the private boat ramp or take to the river in a rental boat. Cottages $35–50 daily, $210–300 weekly. Rental boats $35 a day. You can also pitch your tent for $10.

The vintage **Stegbone's** (386-467-2464; www.stegbones.com) will take you back to the way life used to be: RVs, Jet Skis, and cell phones are not allowed.

At the other end of comfort is the **Floridian Sports Club** (386-467-2181; www.floridiansportsclub.com), with in-room Jacuzzi, wet bar, and screened porches overlooking the river.

✳ Where to Eat

EATING OUT What a treat to find **3 Bananas** (386-698-2861), 11 South Lake St, Crescent City. This tropical paradise, just off the lake, offers up a large chicken Caesar salad ($7), Caribbean jerk chicken ($6), lightly fried Crescent catfish $9), and a half-pound paradise burger ($5). Sit on the outside deck and look for the sunken pirate ship while drinking rumrunners and piña coladas for only $3. Live island music on weekends. Open every day except Tue.

Inside the cozy **Country Cabin Bar-B-Que** (904-282-6700), 2216 S Mimosa, Middleburg, Gail and Smokey Boston prepare some of the best barbecued delights around in their own oakwood smoker. The "Feast for Two" ($19) includes a hefty portion of barbecued ribs, pork, beef, or turkey, along with coleslaw and garlic toast.

The fresh and friendly **Musselwhite's Seafood & Grill** (386-326-9111), 125 US 17 S, East Palatka, serves up such dishes as Florida alligator tail ($4) with a tangy twist, tangerine tuna marinated with citrus, soy, ginger, and honey ($16), and New York strip ($11–15) cut and grilled to your liking. Save room for dessert: Key lime pie and chocolate peanut butter pie are only $3.

Other great spots are **Corky Bell's Seafood of Palatka** (386-325-1094), 211 Comfort Rd, and **San Mateo Seafood** (386-325-1871), 480 S US 17.

✳ Selective Shopping

Andrea's Book Store (386-325-2141; www.andreasbookstore.com), 308 S

US 19, Palatka, has a great selection of local folklore (See *Folklore*) along with national best-sellers. The web site provides excellent reviews of selected favorites.

FARM STANDS Stop by **County Line Produce**, near the Putnam–St. Johns line, as you travel along FL 207.

Get buzzing and head to the self-serve 1947 **Honey Stand** (386-749-3562), 303 E FL 100, San Mateo, where you'll find pure, raw Florida honey. Choose from orange blossom, gallberry, or wildflower in 1-, 2-, and 5-pound jars.

✷ Special Events

January: The **Putnam County African-American Cultural Arts Festival** (386-325-9901), downtown Palatka, always on Martin Luther King Day, is a celebration of African American history, arts, and culture.

March: Downtown Palatka hosts the annual **Florida Azalea Festival** (386-326-4001), always the second weekend.

You'll find traditional agricultural exhibits, entertainment, and midway rides at the **Putnam County Fair** (386-329-0318), Putnam County Fairgrounds, East Palatka.

April: Best place to skin a catfish is at the **Catfish Festival** (386-698-1666), Crescent City. The championship catfish-skinning contest is one of many events, including the catfish run, a parade led by King Catfish, a bluegrass concert, an antiques show, and an arts and crafts fair.

On the St. Johns River you can watch the rowing regatta of the **Gainesville Crew Classic and Masters** (352-378-6837).

May: One of this area's main events, the 42-nautical-mile **Mug Race** (904-264-4094) sails from the Palatka riverfront and races to Jacksonville on the St. Johns River.

You'll find not only hot steaming blue crabs at the annual **Blue Crab Festival** (386-325-4406; www.bluecrabfestival.com), downtown Palatka, but also such delights as soft-shell crabs, shrimp, and alligator. Four days of entertainment, rides, and arts and crafts. Always on Memorial Day weekend.

June: Wake up early and head to the **Bostwick Blueberry Festival** (386-329-2658) for the blueberry pancake breakfast, where you can pick up blueberry-related foods, arts, and crafts.

October: Get your caboose to the **Palatka Railfest** (386-649-6137), Palatka Railroad Depot, corner of 11th and Reid, where you can learn about model and full-scale trains or enhance your HO, S, and N collection at the many railroad exhibits.

November: The Bronson-Mulholland House (see *Historic Sites*) is centerpiece to the **Fall Antique Fair** (386-329-0140), where local and out-of-town vendors display and sell several fine antique and estate pieces.

Relive the **Battle of Horse Landing** (386-328-1281), Rodeheaver Boys Ranch on the St. Johns River, with living history demonstrations including a Civil War reenactment and military ball.

December: Take a **tour through Crescent City**, where many of the grand and glorious homes are decorated in holiday splendor (386-649-4534).

VOLUSIA COUNTY: ASTOR, BARBERVILLE, CASSADAGA, DEBARY, DELAND, DE LEON SPRINGS, DELTONA, LAKE HELEN, ORANGE CITY, AND PIERSON

GUIDANCE **St. Johns River Country Visitors Bureau** (386-775-2006 or 1-800-749-4350; www.stjohnsrivercountry.com and www.volusia.org), 101 N Woodland Blvd, Suite A-308, DeLand 32720.

GETTING THERE West Volusia County is centrally located just 23 miles east of Daytona Beach and 36 miles northeast of Orlando.

By air: **Daytona Beach International Airport, Sanford Orlando International Airport**, and **Orlando International Airport**.

By bus: **Greyhound** (1-800-231-2222).

The Votran (386-756-7496)—West Volusia County Transit—runs throughout DeLand, Deltona, Orange City, Pierson, and Seville. On weekdays only, routes connect with the Orlando Express bus at the Saxon Park & Ride on weekdays. $1; monthly passes available.

By car: From I-95 S, take I-4 westbound to exits 118 through 108. From I-75 S, take I-4 eastbound to exits 108 though 118.

By train: **Amtrak** (1-800-872-7245; www.amtrak.com) provides regularly scheduled service to DeLand's historic train station in the heart of St. Johns River country. Built in 1918, this old train station was restored in 1988.

MEDICAL EMERGENCIES **Florida Hospital Deland** (386-943-4522), 701 W Plymouth Ave, DeLand, and **Florida Hospital Fish Memorial** (386-917-5000), 1055 Saxon Blvd, Orange City.

✷ To See

ART GALLERIES **The Duncan Gallery of Art** (386-822-7266), 421 N Woodland Blvd, DeLand, at Stetson University.

HISTORIC SITES

Cassadaga

New Yorker George Colby founded the **Cassadaga Spiritualist Camp** (386-228-3171), 355 Cassadaga Rd, in 1895 after being told in a séance that it was his destiny. The community, established as a winter retreat for spiritualists, encompasses over 60 historic buildings circa 1895–1938. At the Colby Memorial Temple you can experience a Candlelight Healing (see *Psychic Readings*) and attend a Sunday service that recognizes all religions.

DeBary

The **DeBary Hall Mansion Historic Site** (386-668-3840), 210 Sunrise Blvd, includes the beautifully restored two-story Italianate mansion, an icehouse, a stable with kennels for hunting dogs, and several small working houses. Built in 1871 by wine importer Samuel Frederick deBary as a winter retreat, the two-story southern plantation home has a stunning two-pier veranda around three of its sides. Open Thu–Sat 10–4, Sun noon–4.

DeLand

Thinking it would be a nice place for his kids to go to college, Henry A. DeLand opened DeLand Academy in 1884. By 1889 Mr. DeLand's friend, the Philadelphia hat manufacturer John B. Stetson, was forced to rescue the financially strained academy and renamed it **Stetson University** (www.stetson.edu), now one of the top-ranked universities in the Southeast. **DeLand Hall** is the oldest structure in Florida in continuous use for higher education. You'll find the 1886 **John B. Stetson House** on 1031 Camphor Lane.

Lake Helen

Take a drive or stroll through the quaint neighborhood of the **Lake Helen Historic District**. The town, named for Henry DeLand's daughter, was intended to be the "prettiest and pleasantest" town in Florida. And I have to agree. Start your tour on Euclid Ave under canopies of live oak decorated with Spanish moss, then cross back and forth along the side streets of this residential community. You'll find more than 70 formal homes built for wealthy businessmen of the era in the designs of Queen Anne, Classic and Gothic Revival, and Italianate. Pick up *A Walking Tour of Euclid Ave* at the Lake Helen public library, which details 13 of these homes.

Orange City

A postage stamp of a philatelic museum, the **U.S. Postal Service Museum** (386-774-8849), 1876 Heritage Inn, 300 S Volusia Ave, Orange City, offers a unique perspective on Florida by displaying Postal Service artifacts and postal history from around the state. Young stamp collectors will appreciate the freebie canceled stamps at the front desk. Open daily 9 AM–4 PM, Sat 9 AM–noon. Free.

HORSE RACING The largest standardbred training facility in the world is in Paris, France. The second largest is tucked back off the road in De Leon Springs, but you'll think you're in Kentucky. The **Spring Garden Ranch Training Center** (386-985-5654), 900 Spring Garden Ranch Rd, started life as a turn-of-the-20th-century dairy farm. Housing fewer than 100 horses in 1949, it now holds over 600 standardbred horses in state-of-the-art barns. Watch from the observation deck as up-and-coming horses, as well as legends, train on the 1-mile clay track. The restaurant offers a front-seat view (see *Eating Out*).

MURALS The **DeLand Mural Walk** (see *Guidance*) is a fine compliment to the Historic Main Street community. The first in a planned series depicts the early life of settlers in the up-and-coming town, complete with a steam locomotive. If this is any indication of the artistic talents to come, I can't wait to see the rest.

MUSEUMS

Barberville

At the **Pioneer Settlement for the Creative Arts** (386-749-2959), 1776 Lightfoot Lane, you'll discover what life was like around the turn of the 20th century.

Dedicated to preserving the past, this pioneer community not only has historic buildings and artifacts, but also demonstrates and offers classes on candle dipping, batiking, basket weaving, blacksmithing, quilting, and even dancing. Walk through the settlement and discover the past through historic farm equipment and buildings, such as an 1885 post office and 1920s pottery shed. The exposed turpentine quarters where slaves were forced to live will alarm you. The modest admission includes an informative tour with a guide. Fee.

DeLand

Since its opening in 1995, the **African American Museum of the Arts** (386-736-4004), 325 S Clara Ave, has been slowly building their collection of over 150 artifacts, including sculptures and masks from several African countries. The only museum in the area devoted to African American and Caribbean American cultures, it also houses a revolving gallery of established and emerging artists. Open 10–4 Wed–Sat. Donation.

Black Heritage Exhibit (386-734-5333), 230 North Stone St, portrays life when the first freed slaves settled in the West Volusia community. The exhibit, housed in a small building behind the DeLand Memorial Hospital, portrays life in the black community through photographs, personal artifacts, and memorabilia. Elephant Fantasyland (see below) is in the same building.

Interestingly enough, the **Henry A. DeLand House Museum** (386-740-6813), 137 W Michigan Ave, was owned by several leaders of the community, but never by Mr. DeLand. He sold the piece of land where the house sits to the city's first attorney, George Hamlin, who then passed it on to John Stetson for university faculty housing. The home changed ownership several times, and during the Civil War was divided into apartments. Nearly 100 years later, the Conrads (see Elephant Fantasyland, below) rescued the house and donated it to the city. The home is filled with period furniture and accessories, along with the history of western Volusia County depicted in period photographs. Behind the house is a gazebo in the center of a small garden. This monument commemorates **Lou Gim Gong the Citrus Wizard**, who is credited with developing a new citrus orange resistant to cold. An immigrant from China, his dedication to the groves also produced a new grapefruit. Some of the original trees are still there on the grounds. The **Robert M. Conrad Educational and Research Center** (386-740-6813) is also found on the grounds.

FORMER SLAVE QUARTERS AT THE PIONEER SETTLEMENT FOR THE CREATIVE ARTS

Kathy Wolf

Look into a real 1920s surgical room at the **DeLand Memorial Hospital Museum** (386-734-5333), 230 N Stone St. You'll also find historical medical equipment (some a bit barbaric), and a hospital dispensary. Another section of the hospital hosts one of the few electrical collections in

the country: The **Gallery of Ice and Electricity** is filled with rare artifacts from the late 1800s, like the colorful rainbow of insulators. DeLand became the first city in Florida to enjoy an electrical system in 1887.

Elephant Fantasyland (386-734-5333), 230 N Stone St. It took over 40 years for Hawtense (Fuzzy) Conrad to amass this collection of pachyderms, some dating back to the 1940s. More than 1,000 pieces are on display, from cloth to blown glass.

With works from national exhibitions, like Ansel Adams, Audubon Treasure, and celebrated local artists, the **DeLand Museum of Art** (386-734-4371), 600 N Woodland Blvd, provides cultural enrichment to the surrounding community. The museum shop is a great place to find beautiful handcrafted works and unique gifts. Open Tue–Sat 10–4.

World War I dive-bomber pilots trained right here in DeLand, flying the Douglas Dauntless SBD. Located out at the DeLand Airport, the **DeLand Naval Air Station Museum** (386-738-4149), 910 Biscayne Ave, displays naval uniforms, photos, and other memorabilia. Down the street the **Historic Hangar**, 1380 Flightline Blvd, features a MASH helicopter and 1914–1918 Curtis JN4 "Jenny" World War I trainer.

On the campus of Stetson University, the **Gillespie Museum of Minerals** (386-822-7330; www.gillespiemuseum.stetson.edu) is Florida's only museum entirely devoted to minerals—and yes, there's more to Florida than limestone. In addition to native microminerals and crystals, check out the gemstone and fluorescent mineral displays. This is the largest mineral museum collection outside the Smithsonian. Open Tue–Fri 10–4 during school sessions; free.

Deltona

Deltona Arts & Historical Center (386-575-2601; www.deltonaarts.com), 682 Deltona Blvd. The area's rich historical heritage comes alive here with paintings by local artists. Art classes available.

NASCAR RACING You can find great NASCAR-sanctioned auto racing, at reasonable prices, just 15 miles west of Ormond Beach at **Volusia Speedway Park** (386-985-4402; www.volusiaspeedwaypark.com), 1500 E FL 40, De Leon Springs (5 miles east of Barberville). Watch as late-model and street stock cars speed around the 0.5-mile clay oval dirt track taking turns on the on the 9-degree semibanked corners. And as if one track wasn't enough, the speedway also has a 0.4-mile semibanked asphalt oval for special events. Pits and grandstands open every Sat night at 5; racing starts at 7:30. Free parking at both tracks.

WILDLIFE VIEWING Many endangered species roam freely in their natural environment throughout the entire county. **Lake Woodruff National Wildlife Refuge** (386-985-4673), 2045 Mudlake Rd, De Leon Springs, and **Gemini Springs Park** (386-668-3810), 37 Dirksen Dr, DeBary, are two of the best places to view endangered species, such as the bald eagle, manatee, eastern indigo snake, American alligator, wood stork, and snail kite. **Lyonia Preserve**

(407-736-5927), 2150 Eustace Ave, Deltona, provides a perfect habitat to view the threatened Florida scrub-jay and gopher tortoise. During the winter months, over 100 manatees swim in the crystal-clear waters of **Blue Spring State Park** (386-775-3663), 2100 W French Ave, Orange City. Stop by **De Leon Springs State Park** (386-985-4212), 601 Ponce de Leon and Burt Parks Rd, De Leon Springs, to take a swim in the mineral springs, learn about the area on a pontoon boat ecotour, or grab some pancakes at the Old Spanish Sugar Mill & Griddle House (see *Eating Out*).

✷ To Do

BOAT TOURS Located inside De Leon Springs State Park, **Safari River Tours** (386-740-0333), De Leon Springs State Park (see *Springs*), 601 Ponce de Leon Rd, brings you into the heart of the wilderness. You'll see river otters, manatees, alligators, and a wide variety of birds, all in their natural habitat in and around Lake Woodruff Wildlife Refuge (see *Wild Places*). Daily tours at 11 and 1:30. $16 adults, $14 seniors, $10 children 6–10; under 5 free with parent.

Experience the romance of an authentic side-wheel paddleboat: the **Beresford Lady Tour Boat** (386-740-4100), 1905 Hontoon Rd, DeLand. For 3 hours you can enjoy the sights on the river in air-conditioned comfort or go topside on the open-air deck. Cruises daily at 11 and 4. Adults $27, children $14.

St. John's River Cruises (407-330-1612), 2100 W French Ave, Orange City, really show you the river as they take you on a journey to its shallow backwaters. Take your camera—you're sure to see lots of local wildlife on this quiet pontoon boat. Two-hour tours daily at 10 and 1. Adults $16, children $10.

CONTRA DANCING While I chatted with two local ladies at dinner one night, they asked if I was going to the **Cassadaga Contra Dance** (386-255-6286 or 386-943-9142), and I thought: *Why not get into the spirit of things!* So I followed them to the Andrew Jackson Davis Building opposite the Cassadaga Hotel to find out what this was all about. Nothing at all like country line or square dancing, this fun-for-all activity is comparable to the Victorian dances of the great English balls—though you'll want to wear casual clothes and sneakers, and it's a *lot* faster. You don't need a partner for this, either, so it's a great opportunity to meet and talk with the townspeople. Most of the dance patterns are very simple; the caller walks you through a few times before the live band, playing tunes with Scottish and Irish roots, picks up the pace. A great way to work off your vacation pounds, the nonsmoking, nondrinking activity is perfect for families and a hometown treat. Second Saturday of the month 8–11; $6 adults, $1 children.

DRIVING TOURS Itineraries for self-guided driving tours are available from the Tourist Information Center at the DeLand Area Chamber of Commerce.

FISHING From the novice fisherman to the serious bass angler, St. Johns River country offers a variety of fishing adventures. Many top names in fishing have cast off in these waters, landing trophy bass, stripers, and speckled perch. Dotting the banks of the river are many fish camps (see *Campgrounds*) and marinas

HOUSEBOATING Holly Bluff Marina (1-800-237-5105; www.hollybluff.com), 2280 Hontoon Rd, DeLand. For 20 frustrating minutes, I cast into the shallows on the edge of the Hontoon Dead River, where the bass have been surfacing, nibbling at flies, since we anchored. It's my first attempt at using a rod and reel; nothing bites. Around us, the river awakens as the sun slips behind Hontoon Island. A kingfisher chatters as it swoops low across the placid water. Two anhingas find a perch in the high branches of a cypress. Deer crash through the woods. White ibises honk as they settle down on a tall Carolina willow. With the generator cut off, all is still. It could be 2000 B.C., when the Timucua slipped down this channel in canoes made from hollowed-out cypress logs. It could be 1765, when botanist and explorer William Bartram paddled along the St. Johns. Then the roar of a jet taking off from the Sanford Airport breaks the stillness of twilight. We open the sliding glass door to step back into the mosquito-free comfort of our houseboat.

To immerse yourself in the primeval environment that is the St. Johns River between DeLand and Palatka, consider a houseboat rental. No special boating license is required to pilot a houseboat, but if your boating skills are limited, you may want to hire a captain. These massive craft putter along like a box on water, but it only took me and my crew a day to get the hang of steering and navigation. Houseboats range in size from 38 feet for one-bedroom models to 53 feet for four bedrooms, and have air-conditioning, heat, and hot water for your shower. All linens, utensils, and cookware are supplied, and each boat comes with a fully equipped kitchen and a gas grill on the front deck. Other amenities include a television and VCR, and deck chairs. Prices vary by season, time of week, and size of boat, but generally run $675–2,550 for a 3- to 4-day outing, plus the cost of fuel. A $500 security deposit is required.

that will rent you everything you need, from bait to gear to boat. If you want the inside scoop on where to find the best fish, consider hiring a local fishing guide, who will gladly help you weave your own special fish tale.

Before you cast your line you'll need a Florida freshwater license. Resident fees are $13.50 for 12 months; nonresident fees run $16.50 for 7 days or $31.50 for 12 months. Children under 16 do not need a license. Contact the Florida Fish and Wildlife Conservation Commission for license information at www.florida fisheries.com or www.myfwc.com; you can also obtain an Instant Fishing License at 1-888-FISH FLORIDA (1-888-347-4356). A $3.25 plus 2.5 percent surcharge of the total sale per person will be added to your purchase.

Many fishing guides are available and can be found at almost any marina. Here are some recommended by locals: **Captain Larry Blakeslee** (386-736-9151),

Captain Roger Dillon (352-759-2446), **Captain Jeff Duval** (386-789-3914), **Captain Bill Flowers** (386-734-5211), **Captain Red Flowers** (386-734-6656), **Captain Robert Hees** (386-649-4185), **Captain James Hillman** (386-734-2334), **Captain Curtis E. Lucas** (386-749-2707 or 386-749-2505), **Captains Rick and Ron Rawlins** (386-734-2334 or 1-800-525-3477), **Captain Mark Smith** (386-738-1836), and **Captain Bob Stonewater** (386-736-7120).

PSYCHIC READINGS You won't find witchcraft or black magic at **Cassadaga Spiritualist Camp** (www.cassadaga.org), or anywhere else in Cassadaga; that's not what this spiritualist community of psychic mediums and healers is all about. What it *is* about has more to do with your own instincts. Based on the philosophy that we are more than our physical body, mediums "channel" information from outside the physical realm, bringing in bits of information that relate to your individuality. I experienced this with a thud. Sitting in the Candlelight Healing in the Colby Memorial Temple, I was in a state of total relaxation. The meditation and calm music enveloped me like a warm, soft blanket. Toward the end of the ceremony, participants are invited to come forward while those of the spiritualist community channel healing energy. I was a bit hesitant but finally went forward. Sitting on a stool, my healer touched my head and shoulder; I could feel the warmth radiate from her hands. It was very comforting and put me at ease. After a few moments she leaned over and told me that a woman wrapped in a quilt wanted me to know that this will be a very exciting year for me. Hmmm? Sitting back in the pew I pondered who the woman might be—my grandmother maybe? Then I felt an invisible *thud* and voice proclaiming, *"No you idiot, it's me!"* I immediately knew it was my recently deceased friend Sunny, who no doubt would have whacked me in the head to get my attention. And indeed it has been a very exciting year.

The Candlelight Healing service is at 7:30 on the second Friday of each month. For an individual reading, first walk through the town and feel the energy permeate from the historic homes. One of these will stand out and feel comfortable to you. Those with mediums typically have a name and phone number posted outside. Depending on their availability, you may have to schedule your reading for another day. For those who can't wait, there's a list of certified mediums on call at the Camp Bookstore (see *Selective Shopping*); one is sure to stand out. You may not experience the eye opening I got, but you will most definitely receive insightful information and leave relaxed and rejuvenated. Readings $40–60 for about half an hour; or check out the monthly mini readings for only $20.

Purple Rose (386-228-3315; www.cassadega-purplerose.com), 1079 Stevens St. Cassadega's reputation as a psychic center brings in the curious from around the globe. Some visitors steer toward the warmth of the spiritualist camp, but many take their chances with readings offered at various shops around the village. What's the allure of these modern-day fortune-tellers? Curious, I signed up for a reading with the Reverend Galen at Purple Rose (see *Selective Shopping*). Entering through a beaded curtain, I sat down in a darkened room where New Age music and incense set the mood.

After shaking my hand, Galen "channels the spirit," telling me what she sees. I ask about romance and finances, and the things she says fit like pieces of a jigsaw puzzle. I marvel: *How could she know these details about the men in my life, or the projects I am pursuing, when I haven't said a word about myself?* I realize, of course, that the mind grasps to make order from chaos, and her words can be fit into my frame of reference, but I still find the experience intriguing—especially when I return a few months later and discover continuity in predictions made during the last visit. Whether you call it entertainment or New Age guidance, it's an experience you won't forget.

SIGHTSEEING Take a walk down at least one street in each of the three National Historic Districts in DeLand, Lake Helen, and Cassadaga. Walking tour maps providing historic descriptions of architecture, from the turn of the 20th century, can be picked up at the DeLand Chamber of Commerce (386-734-4331), 336 N Woodland Blvd; the Cassadaga Spiritualist Camp Bookstore and Information Center (386-228-2880), 1112 Stevens St; or the Lake Helen City Hall (386-228-2121).

SKYDIVING Whether your rush is free fall or tandem, **Skydive DeLand** (386-738-3539; www.skydivedeland), 1600 Flightline Blvd, will take you to new heights. The adrenaline soars at a high altitude at this world-class diving center where the best of the best practice and compete. Bring your binoculars—all the action is well over 5,000 feet in the air. Fretting family members and nonfliers can watch the drop zone from the spacious observation deck. And yes, this is the place where Cruise and Kidman learned to dive.

✷ Green Space

GREENWAYS The new **Spring to Spring Trail** (386-736-5953), a 1.3-mile multiuse trail, links DeBary with Gemini Springs via a shady paved path; park at the trailhead at US 17-92 at Dirksen Dr in DeBary.

PARKS **Bill Dreggors Park**, 230 N Stone St, DeLand. Local celebrity, town storyteller, and historian Bill Dreggors was honored in 1991 with his own park. The kids will love Freedom Playground, while the adults will enjoy the DeLand Memorial Hospital (see *Museums*), containing eight galleries and exhibits.

Just east of the center of Cassadaga off Colby Lane you'll find **Colby Alderman Park and Lake Colby** (386-736-5953), 1099 Massachusetts St. The casual footpath travels from the Cassadaga Spiritualist Camp past a small citrus grove with tangerine, grapefruit, and orange trees, then a healing spring next to Lake Colby where George Colby is said to have drunk and recovered from a fateful illness. Moving north through a beautiful cluster of live oaks, you may spot two resident gopher tortoises, Mabel and Gertrude, then pass Clauser's B&B (see *Lodging*) and head up to Lake Macy. The path is self-guided, but a map with more details can be picked up at the bookstore (see *Selective Shopping*).

Lyonia Preserve (407-736-5927), 2150 Eustace Ave, Deltona. Covering 400 acres of relict sand dunes, this preserve hosts Florida's least common bird: the endemic Florida scrub-jay. Walk the trails in the early-morning hours, and you're guaranteed to see not just one or two of these colorful blue-and-white birds but dozens of them, flitting through the oak scrub in search of breakfast. Free.

Hontoon Island State Park (386-736-5309), 2309 River Ridge Rd, DeLand. Florida's state park system includes several island preserves, but Hontoon Island State Park is the only one surrounded by fresh water, and the only one to which the state provides a free ferry. Once on the island, walk out to an ancient Timucua shell midden at the end of the Indian Mound Trail, or carry your gear back to the campground for a quiet night's sleep. The two Timucua totem poles represent originals dredged out of the mud offshore, the only totem poles found in the United States outside the Pacific Northwest. The park also offers picnicking, a marina, a nature center, and miles of forest roads to walk or bike. Fee.

SPRINGS **Blue Spring State Park** (386-775-3663), 2100 W French Ave, Orange City, is one of Florida's don't-miss state parks. In addition to its abundant wildlife, camping and swimming facilities, picnic grounds, and historic treasures, it hosts two trails that provide two very different looks at habitats along the St. Johns River. Ideal for families, the riverside boardwalk parallels beautiful Blue Spring Run as it flows from Blue Spring, where swimmers and divers can play in the deep spring. The rugged Pine Island Hiking Trail attracts backpackers with its pristine primitive campsites along the St. Johns River at the end of a 3.6-mile trek. Rent a canoe and paddle the run, or take a tour of the Thursby House, one of the original plantation homes on the St. Johns River circa 1872. In winter months this is the top site in Florida to see manatees—more than 150 cluster in the warmth of the spring run. Fee.

A FLORIDA SCRUB-JAY AT LYONIA PRESERVE

Sandra Friend

De Leon Springs State Park (386-985-4212), 601 Ponce de Leon and Burt Parks Rds, De Leon Springs. It was the wintering ground for the Clyde Beatty Circus, and it was the plantation owned by Colonial Orlando Rees before he died by the shores of Lake Eola. But more important, it might have been Ponce de León's famed Fountain of Youth. Exploring the St. Johns River, De León discovered this spring in 1513, a place "which the Indians call 'Healing Waters.'" In springtime the azaleas are in bloom; all year long, the hiking trails treat you to the deep shade of the floodplain forests of Spring Creek

Run. Swim in the spring, take a quiet hike, paddle down the run (rentals available), or pile up the pancakes at the Old Spanish Mill (see *Eating Out*).

WILD PLACES The **St. Johns Water Management District** (386-329-4883; sjr.state.fl.us) is responsible for conservation areas that serve as buffers to the St. Johns River and its tributaries. In western Volusia, their lands include **Crescent Lake Conservation Area**, off US 17 at Crescent Lake, with several miles of trails through pine flatwoods open to hiking, biking, and equestrians; and **Heart Island Conservation Area**, between FL 40 in Barberville, US 17, and FL 10 in DeLand, a massive preserve of wetlands and wet flatwoods where you're welcome to walk the forest roads.

Lake Woodruff National Wildlife Refuge (386-985-4673), 2045 Mudlake Rd, De Leon Springs. Looking for sandhill cranes? You'll find them here—and more. One of the region's top birding sites, the refuge was established in 1964 and encompasses more than 20,000 acres of water and marshes along the St. Johns River. Walk the dikes slowly to watch for alligators, gallinules, and deer; this is an excellent place for wildlife-watching, with more than 6 miles of hiking trails. The visitors center and bookstore is open 8–4:30 Mon–Fri.

✷ Lodging

Imagine piloting a houseboat on the St. Johns River or spending a romantic weekend at a cozy bed & breakfast. Get back to nature and pitch a tent or park your RV in one of the many campgrounds in the area. Kick back at a local fish camp or go au naturel at a clothing-optional resort. A wide variety of accommodations are available throughout the county.

BED & BREAKFASTS

Lake Helen 32744

Cabin on the Lake B&B (386-228-2878; www.cabinonthelake.com), 222 Tangerine Ave. This cozy cabin has it all! Take in the beauty of the butterfly garden, grape arbor, azaleas, and grand oaks. Explore the area with a leisurely bicycle ride down the street to the historic districts of Lake Helen or over to Cassadaga for a spiritual reading. Then return to relax on the porch overlooking the lake. Slip a canoe into the water for a sunset paddle. This B&B is all about relaxation. The Captain's Room on the first floor has French doors that open to your own private porch, along with its own hot tub. The Island and Antique Rooms are on the second floor and have their own private baths. In the morning you'll wake up to a full country breakfast served in the front room on the plank farm table or outside on the deck. Ask about the ladies' "Ya Ya" parties. $85–125.

Red rocking chairs greet you from the porch at **Clauser's Bed & Breakfast** (386-228-0310), 201 E Kicklighter Rd. Marge and Tom Clauser host this two-story National Register of Historic Places (circa 1895) home with warmth and camaraderie. You don't visit this place—you come home. And you won't want to leave. Hot coffee and friendly conversation are served early in the country kitchen of the 19th-century farmhouse; then guests move to the main dining room, where delectable delights such as poached pears and baked Italian omelets are dished up on warmed plates. The carriage house, although built 100 years later, stays true to the period. All rooms have king or queen beds; some also have daybeds. Every carriage house room has its own private screened porch. There are eight rooms to choose from—some with their own Jacuzzi—including the English garden Windsor with rich floral fabrics, hardwood floor, and English antiques; the homey Cross Creek, with handmade quilts and wicker in the Old Florida style; and the Laredo, a log cabin room complete with cowboy and western antiques (most of which are Tom's), a ranch house bathtub, and a unique king-sized log bed with all the romance of the Old West. In the gazebo you'll find a hot tub to sooth your aching muscles after bicycling down to Cassadaga for spiritual renewal or walking along the Cross Volusia Trail past Lake Colby and beyond. $100–140. No children under 16. No pets.

HOTEL

DeLand 32720

DeLand Artisan Inn (386-736-3484; www.delandartisaninn.com), 215 S Woodland Blvd. This small three-story hotel, located in the heart of downtown DeLand, has only eight suites, so you are assured individual attention. Each suite of the 1924 Mediterranean Revival building is located on the third floor, providing a great view of the historic district. Decorated in a different theme and named for local pioneers of the community, suites like the literary Stetson reflect their namesakes' personalities and accomplishments. On the first floor, live entertainment and good conversation can be found in the full-service lounge, where happy-hour drinks are under $2. The richly appointed on-site restaurant has an extensive menu and also offers room service (see *Dining Out*). Suites $90–120; $150–180 during special events.

RESORT

Pierson 32180

Sunny Sands Naturist Resort (386-749-2233), 502 Central Blvd. Where else but in the "Fern Capital of the World" would you find a nudist resort? This secluded not-for-everyone resort offers 35 acres of natural beauty. Private mobile home trailers can be rented for $95 a night or $76 with ANA membership. Sun lovers will enjoy the privacy of the heated swimming pool and hot tub. Take in some golf on the nine-hole chipping course or go on a leisurely hike on the nature trail. Restaurant open weekends. Gated security.

CAMPGROUNDS AND MARINAS

Astor 32102

There are no RVs at **Front Street Bait & Tackle** (352-759-2795; www.frontstreetbait.com), 55522 Front St (previously Big Bass Bait & Tackle). Just seven comfy cabins set along the St. Johns River—all with refrigerator, stove, and everything you need to fry up your big bass or catfish. If you just can't eat fish every day, the **Beans BBQ** is open 11–6 weekends, serving platters ($5–14) of pork ribs, beef, chicken, and good ol' country beans. Come by the river: One covered boat slip comes with each cabin. Well-stocked bait shop on site. $50–80 night; $250–400 per week.

Whether you're looking for a cedar log cabin or modern mobile home, or just want to pitch your tent,

♐ ♿ **Parramore's Fantastic Fish Camp & Family Resort** (386-749-2721; www.parramores.com), 1675 S Moon Rd, has the lodging for you. Kids will love petting the donkeys and goats. Take out a canoe or pontoon boat out for a little sightseeing, then cast your line and catch your own dinner. This is a great place for families with a large pool and playground.

DeBary 32713

♿ **Highbanks Marina & Camp Resort** (386-668-4491; www.campresort.com), 488 W Highbanks Rd. Bring your RV or tent to this 25-acre RV campground nestled along 2,300 feet of the St. Johns River. Then relax on a guided tour of the river on their *River Queen*. Don't have an RV or tent? Rent an air-conditioned RV "Cabin." Cable TV, playground, and swimming pool are just some of the many amenities.

DeLand 32720

Cast off for the backwaters at **Highland Park Fish Camp** (386-734-2334; www.hpfishcamp.com), 2640 W Highland Park Rd, where it seems everything is biting. On the boundaries of Lake Woodruff National Wildlife Refuge (see *Wild Places*), you'll be fishing some of the best spawning sites around. Tents $16, RVs $20 nightly. Cabins available in-season. Boat rentals $15 and up.

You'll see the wonders of natural Florida on your own houseboat from **Holly Bluff Marina** (386-822-9992), 2280 Hontoon Rd (see *Houseboating*). Alligators line the banks, while eagles and ospreys soar above. You may even see a Florida sea cow (manatee) in the crystal-clear waters.

There's more than fish stories at **Hontoon Landing Resort & Marina** (386-734-2474), 2317 River Ridge Rd. Resident celebrity Stumpy, a true Florida "snow bird," returns each year to this resort after being rescued one year from a fishing accident. I guess he knows where his fish is fried! Standing on his only leg, this great white egret has been the resident mascot for over a decade. And he's selected a fine place. The immaculate motel is right on the water, with rooms from $75 a day to the $195 executive suite. Or rent a houseboat and change your view each day. The resort also has a charming hummingbird garden and gorgeous pool.

You'll want to roll right into the RV sites in the family-owned **Tropical Resort & Marina** (386-734-3080), 1485 Lakeview Dr on Lake Beresford. The lush natural landscape has full hookups; those without motor coaches can stay in one of the 14 spacious suites. Pool, marina, boat rentals, and bait shop. Suites $48–69 a day, $270–390 a week.

✳ Where to Eat

DINING OUT

DeLand

The all-day bistro menu at the **DeLand Artisan Inn and Restaurant** (386-736-3484), 215 S Woodland Blvd, will satisfy those with creative taste buds. Crunchy salads might be enhanced with Gorgonzola, candied walnuts, and cider honey vinaigrette ($6). The grilled chicken breast sandwich is complemented with rosemary, bacon, Swiss cheese, red leaf lettuce, and beefsteak tomato ($7). Chef Ian C. G. Huddleston continues his culinary expertise with cavatelli pasta ($12) and curry-seared Atlantic salmon ($16). The lounge is one of the few places in town that are open late.

Emmy's Time Out Tavern (386-734-0756), 2069 Old New York Ave. An institution in DeLand, Emmy offers food from her Germanic roots—rouladen, goulash, pork chops, and schnitzels—in a convivial atmosphere that'll have you singing *zige zake zige zake ho ho ho!* Sides include red cabbage, potato dumplings, German potato salad, applesauce, and spaetzle. If you're not into the authentic Old Country food, locals swear the prime rib here is the best in town, and there are seafood and chicken entrées to choose from, too. Four special German dinners served Wed, \$8–13; dinner entrées \$7–17. Enjoy live country and 1960s bands in the lounge at 9 PM Fri and Sat.

Step down the stairs to **MainStreet Grill** (386-740-9535), 100 E New York Ave, just to view the waterfall cascading over the tiled manatee mural. This upscale grill serves mouthwatering steaks (\$10–16) and a long list of seafood (\$8–14). Open lunch and dinner daily. The Sunday brunch buffet is only \$9.

Mr. Phad Thai's Restaurant (386-740-0123), 217 N Woodland Blvd, cooks with four types of curry (red, green, yellow, and panang), mixing them with vegetables, coconut milk, and chicken, beef, or pork (\$10–13). Start your meal with crispy tofu (\$3) or chicken satay (\$4). And save room for dessert—sweet sticky rice with fresh mango (\$4).

EATING OUT

DeLand

Next door to Mr. Phad Thai's (see *Dining Out*) is a great selection of snacks and exotic groceries at the **Asian Food Market** (386-734-4968), 217 N Woodland Blvd.

Calamari, cavatelli, cannoli, and everything in between. Eat in or take it out at **Bellini's Delicatessen** (386-736-1747), 111 E Rich Ave. This place has been making subs, salads, pizza, and Italian dinners for local patrons for over 30 years (\$3–8). A small salad is under \$2.

Bellybusters (386-734-1611), 930 Woodland Blvd. A favorite with the college crowd, Bellybusters dishes up enormous sandwiches at reasonable prices, \$2–5. Ask for your sandwich "all the way," with mayonnaise, slaw, onions, sweet pickles, and their special sauce.

Take a break from shopping and grab a cappuccino, bowl of soup, or glass of wine at **Celery City Coffee Co.** (386-740-8555), 139 N Woodland Blvd. Then settle into the overstuffed chairs or couch and listen to classical performances of cello or violin while browsing the selection of natural soaps, candles, and fine gifts.

Countryside Café (386-775-8881), 2200 N Volusia Ave. Also known as The Cow Place (check out the Holstein lawn chairs), this tiny country diner serves up great fluffy pancakes to a country beat. Breakfast \$2–9; lunch and dinner choices include liver and onions, fried oysters, catfish strips, and veggie plates, \$4–10.

Looking for healthy supplements and organic foods? The staff at **Debbie's Health Foods** (386-734-6502), 140 N Woodland Blvd, will help you find everything from herbs to wheat germ. A second shop is farther south in Orange City at 816-2 Saxon Blvd (386-775-2931).

What's a town without an Irish pub? The **Dublin Station** (386-740 7720), 105 W Indiana Ave, has excellent food and spirits. And that's no blarney!

Established in 1849, **Hunter's Restaurant** (386-736-7957), 202 N Woodland Blvd, is DeLand's oldest family-owned restaurant and a local hot spot, serving country breakfast and soups and sandwiches for less than $5. Open daily, except Sun.

Ahoy mates, stow your appetite and get ye to **J. C.'s Lobster Pot** (386-734-7459), 2888 W FL 44, where platters ($14–19) come with chowder, hushpuppies, and lots and lots of seafood. From the butcher block, there's chicken, ribs, and steaks ($10–16). Beer by the mug or jug. Lunch and dinner.

You'll smell warm bread, fresh from the oven, long before you get near **Mac's Bread Barn** (386-734-5019), 142 S Woodland Blvd. Named for the owners' young daughter, Mackenzie, the town got lucky when not one but two graduates from the Culinary Institute of America decided to settle here. Russ and Heather Cunningham knead and bake danish, pastries, savory croissants, and such specialty breads as chocolate espresso cranberry and rosemary shallot. After stopping here twice, I even made a special trip from Daytona to get several loaves. Breads are made from scratch in a way not often found in Florida bakeries. Get there early, as they sell out fast.

Step back to the good ol' days at **Nookler's Homemade Ice Cream** (386-736-6262), 208 N Woodland Blvd. This old-fashioned soda fountain with red retro chairs and a colorful wall of penny candy is set inside a building (circa 1921) on the National Register of Historic Places. Owner Jerry Risting and son Michael Lawson are behind the counter serving up all-natural fountain treats like egg creams, sundaes, and thick malts and shakes ($3). Whether you're pregnant or not, ask Jerry for some pickles. These crunchy slices are made with 19 ingredients. Sloppy Joes for $2 can't be beat. Open Mon–Sat 11–9.

Vera Smaldone shares her passion for cooking at **They Call It Macaroni** (386-740-0618), 124 N Woodland Blvd. Using family recipes from the Old Country, she cooks up fine Italian dishes like stuffed peppers with fresh herbs and homemade pasta, Aunt Rose's Ravioli stuffed with lots of ricotta, and spicy arrabiatta pasta with jalapeños. Open daily except Sun. Lunch and dinner $7–14.

De Leon Springs

The Old Spanish Sugar Mill & Griddle House (386-985-5644), De Leon Springs State Park. It's one of Florida's most unusual and fun family dining experiences: Cook your own pancakes made from stone-ground flour on the griddle built into your table. All you can eat, $4 per person; additional for sides. Open Mon–Fri 9–4; Sat, Sun, and holidays 8–4. Closed Thanksgiving and Christmas.

Trot up to the breakfast buffet at **Spring Garden Ranch Restaurant** (386-985-0526), 900 Spring Garden Ranch Rd, while watching standardbred racing at the second largest training facility in the world. The hot roast beef Breeder's Crown served open faced with mashed potatoes and the Shady Daisy Reuben are just two of the winners lined up on the menu. Open daily. Breakfast buffet on weekends and for special events.

Orange City

Pier 16's Fish House (386-775-2664), 1081 N Volusia Ave. With its wagon-wheel lamps, wood bench seats, and enormous fireplace, you'd assume Pier 16 was a steak house. And indeed, steaks are on the menu. But seafood is their strong suit—this is the home of the best lunch value in Orange City, where for $3 you can pick up a heaping plateful of breaded fish or popcorn shrimp, Texas toast or hushpuppies, and coleslaw. Lunch and dinner entrées $7–13.

River City Landing (386-775-2626; www.rccatering.com/landing), 1501 S Volusia Ave. You'll find the parking lot crowded every morning at River City Landing, where big portions of home-cooked omelets, pancakes, and French toast come cheap. Daily lunch and dinner specials provide excellent value at $6–12. Breakfast served 6 AM–4 PM. Don't miss the manatee paintings in the back room!

Orange Park

Larry's Giant Subs (904-278-2276; www.larryssubs.com), 562 Kingsley Ave, Orange Park, does everything in a very big way, with over 50 subs and sandwiches ($3–7). Get your mouth around such hot and cold subs as the Destroyer, Big Boss Man, and Turkey Reuben. They even have peanut butter and jelly! You'll also spot this local chain in towns along the St. Johns River, the northeast coastline, and dotted throughout Jacksonville—their home base.

✷ Entertainment

Take in a show at **the Sands Theater Center at the Cultural Arts Center** (box office 386-738-7456; www.sandstheatercenter.com), 600 N Woodland Blvd, DeLand. This venue offers professionally directed theatrical productions for all ages and tastes. Enjoy classic or contemporary on either the Main Stage or the more intimate Stage II. Children's Storybook Theater keeps the kids entertained with classics and interactive performances. DeLand's own community orchestra—the DeLand Little Symphony—is also on site.

Shoestring Theater (386-228-3777), 380 S Goodwin St, Lake Helen. Check out the local talent in a 150-seat theater housed in an old schoolhouse. Geared towards families. Sept–May.

✷ Selective Shopping

Pick some fresh produce at the farmer's market, find peace and serenity in Cassadaga, or spend the day strolling down the beautiful tree-lined streets in DeLand. West Volusia has many unique shops and boutiques worth discovering.

Barberville

Two Sisters Antiques & Gifts (386-749-0795), 180 W FL 40. Chat a while with Bobbie Jefferson and Margaret Grimes in this treasure box full of quality antiquities. Then browse each room of the 1936 home, decorated as if you lived there.

Cassadaga

Cassadaga Spiritualist Camp Bookstore and Information Center (386-228-2880; www.cassadaga.org), 1112 Stevens St, in the Andrew Jackson Davis Building. Not only will you find a large collection of books from spiritualism to metaphysics, and gifts from crystals to meditation tapes, but this building is also your first stop for all the activities in town (see *Special Events*). Open daily till 5, later on Mediums Nights.

Purple Rose (386-228-3315; www.cassadaga-purplerose.com), 1079

Stevens St. In addition to featuring a wide selection of minerals at reasonable prices, the warm and relaxing Purple Rose offers "down to earth" items such as dream catchers, bubbling fountains, stone jewelry, and New Age books. Several psychics offer readings of the past, present, and future for you to get in touch with your inner self; or you can ask for a demonstration of the aura-cleansing crystal bowls.

DeLand

You could spend all day shopping throughout the historic downtown area. From Woodland Blvd to just a few steps down a side street, you'll find a variety of antiquities, bric-a-brac, galleries, eateries, and boutiques.

Antiques and collectibles: Over 50 dealer displays cover three floors at the **Rivertown Antique Mall** (386-738-5111) 114 S Woodland Blvd. You'll find your grandmother's bits and pieces at **Back Home Antiques** (386-738-9967), 110 S; **Silver Rose Antiques** (386-740-1911), 120-A N; and **Furniture By Design** (386-734-4965), 136 N. Look for the giraffe outside **Junque Exchange** (386-738-3735), 212 N. Off Woodland there's **Just Olde Stuff** (386-740-4842) at 115 W Rich Ave, and **DeLand Coins & Collectibles** (386-738-5472), 109 W Indiana Ave.

Concerned with the demolition of architecturally significant properties, Mark Shuttleworth (also mayor of Lake Helen) started to salvage the building materials from these houses and opened **Florida Victorian Architectural Antiques** (386-734-9300; www.floridavictorian.com), 112 W Georgia Ave. If you've been remodeling your vintage home and you just can't seem to find the right trim molding or hardwood flooring—or you just want a unique doorknob or stained-glass window—you'll most likely find it here. Leave the kids at home, as a lot of materials are lying around. Open Mon–Sat 9–5 or by appointment.

Looking for that heirloom Barbie? The **Doll & Hobby Shop** (386-734-3200; www.doll-hobby.com), 138 S Woodland Blvd, has one of the largest collections of Barbie and her friends, clothes, and accessories. You'll find vintage Sun Loving Malibu Barbie and Dream Date Ken along with lots of other collector and artist dolls. Three Barbie experts are always on staff. Boys and tomboys won't be disappointed, either: The side room is devoted to Hot Wheels, Johnny Lightning, Matchbox, and other collectible toys.

Galleries and bookstores: Several fine galleries are almost within the same block on Woodland Blvd. You can stop by and see Mike at **Gold Leaf Gallery and Framing** (386-943-4001), 110 N, for fine art limited-edition prints and custom framing. Discover the secret art of Dr. Seuss and Disney fine art and animation at **Florida Art Gallery** (386-740-1209), 139 N. Ceramic works are showcased at **Clay Pigeons** (386-734-1100), 120 S, and the artist-owned co-op **Gallery 142** (386-740-9744), 142 S Woodland Blvd, has a diverse collection of different media. For fine art there's **Fithian's Studio** (386-734-2929), 116½ N Woodland Blvd, and bibliophiles will enjoy **The Muse Book Shop** (386-734-0278), 112 S Woodland Blvd.

Boutiques and shops: I stepped inside the **Quilt Shop of DeLand, Inc.**

(386-734-8782), 116 E Rich Ave, and looked at all the walls of beautiful fabric, and immediately wanted to start a quilt, but didn't know how. And that was okay, because they'll teach you everything you need to so you can make your own family heirloom. From fabric selection to rotary cutting and finishing, the talented women of this quilt shop will guide you every stitch of the way.

Shop for fine natural clothing at **Goosefeathers** (386-943-9955), 102 S Woodland Blvd, or upscale garments and designer labels at **Laura's Upscale Consignaree** (386-822-4010), 212 N Woodland Blvd. **Anitas Lingerie** (386-736-2549), 101 N Woodland Blvd, has sensuous and delicate attire, along with mood-enhancing incense and potpourri. Stop by **Danny's Shoe Service** (386-734-1645), 206 N Woodland Blvd, just to view the vintage cobbler tools. Danny loves to chat and can tell you just about anything about his hometown.

Wild and wonderful, **Primitive Expressions** (386-740-0022), 118 N Woodland Blvd, has some great pieces from all over the globe. African masks, imported furniture, textiles.

Inside Nooklers (see *Eating Out*), just about any type of rubber stamp can be found at **Stampworks of Florida** (386-736-6262), 208 N Woodland Blvd. Peruse the walls filled with a great assortment of business or craft stamp and inks. Custom work can be done to your design.

Can't wait to get those vacation pics developed? Shutterbugs will want to stop into the **Camera Store & Studio** (386-734-2440), 122 E Rich Ave, for 1-hour developing—and you can frame it here, too!

FARMER'S MARKETS Stock your cupboards Dec–July with fresh local produce picked at the **West Volusia Farmers Market** (386-734-9514 or 386-734-1613; www.volusiacountyfair.com), Volusia County Fairgrounds, FL 44, where you will also find a large variety of garage sale items.

✷ Special Events

Year-round, last Thu of the month: The downtown galleries open their doors 6–9 with great art, wine, and snacks on the **Gallery Stroll**, DeLand.

Year-round, second Fri of the month: **Candlelight Healing Service**, Colby Memorial Temple, Cassadaga, is at 7:30 PM (see *Psychic Readings*).

January: For everything you always wanted to know about the Florida sea cow, the **Blue Spring Manatee Festival** (386-804-6171; www.themanateefestival.com), Valentine Park, French Ave, Orange City, is the place to go. A complimentary bus takes you to the park so you can view manatees in their natural habitat. Lots of environmental exhibits, food, and music. Fee.

Over 200 dealers ride in to the **11th Annual Railroad Show** (407-656-5056), Volusia County Fairgrounds, to display and sell model trains and collectibles.

February: 🐾 Forget New Orleans: DeLand has great tail-wagging fun at the **Canine Cabaret Parade** and **Mardi Gras on Mainstreet** (386-734-4243), Woodland Blvd. Dogs and owners dress up and march down the center of town in the largest parade of the year. Dog-gone activities galore, and awards for both dogs and their human companions.

Buckler Craft Show (407-860-0092; www.volusiacountyfair.com), Volusia County Fairgrounds. Two hundred award-winning Volusia County craftspeople exhibit and sell.

Speed Week Dirt Racing, Volusia Speedway Park (386-985-4402; www.volusiaspeedwaypark.com), 1500 E FL 40, De Leon Springs (5 miles east of Barberville).

The Pioneer Settlement for the Creative Arts (see *Museums*) offers mini workshops in many of the folk art fields at **Pass It On Folk Art Days** (386-749-2959). You'll learn all about such long-ago skills as basket weaving and blacksmithing at this 2-day event.

March: Hear from Florida authors from all over the state as they read and discuss their writings at the **Annual Florida Author's Book Fair** (386-228-0174), Hopkins Hall, Lake Helen. The free event also has a silent auction and café.

For over 25 years the annual **Motorcyle Swapmeet & Special Bike Show** (301-336-2100; www.volusiacountyfair.com), Volusia County Fairgrounds, has put on a blast of a show full of stunts, thrills, and bikes, bikes, bikes. $8.

Fall: **Volusia County Fair**, Volusia County Fairgrounds, FL 44, DeLand. This large county fair shows breeding and market livestock: goats, ewes, swine, poultry, rabbits, lamb, and beef. Entertainment includes nationally recognized talent, live bands, a petting zoo, puppet shows, a pie-eating contest, and the Little Miss, Mr., and Senior Fair Queen contests. Admission $7 adults, $3 children 6–12. All-you-can-ride bracelets for midway amusements can be purchased for $12–15 with special sponsor coupons.

One of the largest events around, the annual juried **DeLand Fall Festival of the Arts** attracts over 200 talented artisans, who exhibit their talents all along Woodland Blvd.

November: **Annual Fall Country Jamboree** (386-749-2959) celebrates a weekend of Florida pioneer life at the Pioneer Settlement for the Creative Arts (see *Museums*). Continuous folk music, lively storytellers, and creative activities like indigo dyeing and cane grinding are just some of the activities. Juried arts show, crafts, and antique autos. Call for admission prices.

December: The whole community of DeLand comes out for one of the largest, and longest (2½ hours), holiday parades—half the town is in it, the other half watches. Woodland Blvd.

The Original Florida

4

ALACHUA AND THE HISTORIC LAKE DISTRICT

THE LOWER SUWANNEE

THE BIG BEND

THE UPPER SUWANNEE

Sandra Friend

ALACHUA AND THE LAKES

ALACHUA, BRADFORD, AND UNION COUNTIES

In 1765 botanist William Bartram described a visit to the village of Cuscowilla, on the edge of a vast prairie, where he met with the great chief Cowkeeper. Cowkeeper's descendants, the Seminoles, were pushed south off their ancestral lands by settlers eager to claim the rich prairies, oak hammocks, and pine flatwoods as their own. After Florida became a U.S. territory in 1821, Congress authorized the construction of the Bellamy Road, a wagon route from St. Augustine to Tallahassee, leading settlers to this region. But it was not until the establishment of the University of Florida in 1853 that **Gainesville**, now the largest and most vibrant city in the region, became a major population center. All three counties maintain their rural roots, where farming and ranching surround small historic communities.

Gainesville started out as Hogtown, an 1824 settlement of 14 inhabitants on a creek that snaked its way into the vast prairie south of town. Named for General Edmund Gaines, commander of U.S. Army troops in Florida during the Second Seminole War, Gainesville won out over Lake City for the location of the newly formed University of Florida, becoming the county seat in 1854. Civil War skirmishes in downtown streets added a touch of excitement in the 1860s, but it wasn't enough to dissuade a steady stream of settlers. Gainesville incorporated as a city in 1869.

Historic but hip describes the towns north along US 441, mingling old and new, with historic structures reinvented into cafés, art galleries, and theaters. Settlers coming down the Bellamy Road moved into **High Springs** on the Santa Fe River as early as the 1830s; Florida's phosphate boom accelerated the town's growth in the 1870s, and it retains that turn-of-the-century feel. The Bellamy Road also brought settlers to the pastoral town of **Alachua** (see map on p. 449), founded in 1905. Blink, and you'll miss the turnoff from US 441 to Alachua's Main St, just a mile south of I-75. But it's worth the stop. Although only a few blocks long, downtown Alachua is crammed with unique shops and restaurants.

In Bradford County, the county seat of Starke lives in infamy as the home of

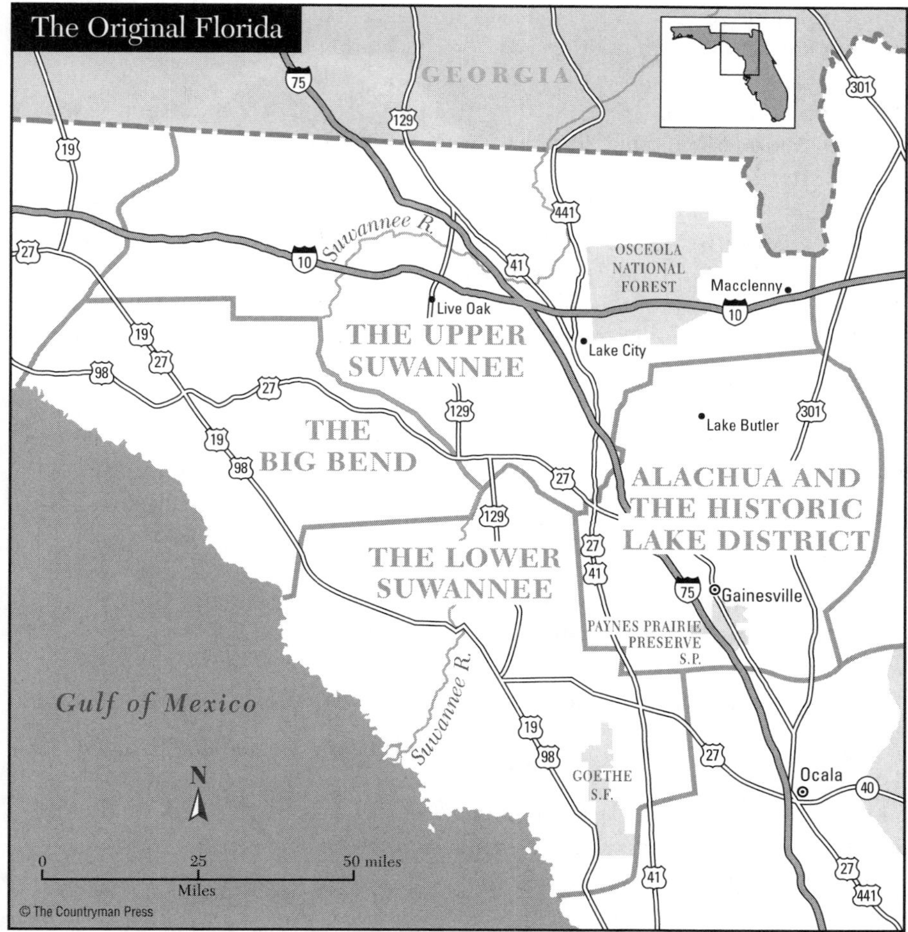

the Florida State Prison and its electric chair, but downtown Call St shows the genteel side of this historic city. South of Starke on US 301 is **Waldo**, founded in 1858 as a railroad town. In the 1960s Waldo became infamous for its speed traps along US 301, so much so that a former officer wrote a book about it. *Waldo* remains a synonym for *speed trap* in Florida, so watch that gas pedal when you drive through!

The railroads also ran through **Hawthorne**, established in 1880 as a junction for trains from Gainesville to Ocala and Waldo. On nearby Lake Santa Fe, **Melrose** was established along the Bellamy Road in 1887, and you won't find a better place to study early Florida architecture: There are nearly 80 buildings in town on the National Register of Historic Places. At the north end of Lake Santa Fe, **Keystone Heights** shows off its 1920s charm. The Lake District continues in a sweep southward past Newnans Lake and the historic village of **Rochelle** down to Lake Lochloosa and Orange Lake, where Pulitzer Prize–winning author

Marjorie Kinnan Rawlings put the fishing village of **Cross Creek** on the map. Nearby **Evinston**, established in 1882 on the Marion County border, was a major citrus center until the deep freezes of the 1890s killed the groves. And **Micanopy**, founded in 1821 near Paynes Prairie, is one of Florida's top destinations for antiques shopping, its downtown a snapshot of the late 1800s.

In western Alachua County, history buffs will appreciate tiny **Archer** for its railroad museum and Civil War history. Florida's phosphate boom built the town of **Newberry** in 1870, where workers dug deep pits to extract the black nuggets used for fertilizer. In more recent times, paleontologists have had a field day in Newberry's phosphate pits, pulling out fossilized crocodiles, turtles, and other creatures whose bones are on display at the Florida Natural History Museum in Gainesville.

GUIDANCE **Gainesville/Alachua County Visitors & Convention Bureau** (352-374-5231; www.visitgainesville.net), 30 E University Ave, Gainesville 32801.

North Florida Regional Chamber of Commerce (904-964-5278; www.northfloridachamber.com), 202 S Walnut St, Starke 32091.

GETTING THERE *By air*: Both Delta (ComAir) and USAir provide daily commuter service to the **Gainesville Regional Airport** (352-373-0249), located east of town off FL 20.

By bus: **Greyhound** (352-376-5252), 516 SW 4th Ave.

By car: **I-75** runs through the heart of Alachua County, paralleled by **US 441**; **US 301** passes by the lakes of Bradford and Union Counties. **FL 20**, **24**, and **26** radiate out of Gainesville to reach points east and west in Alachua County, and **US 41** provides an often canopied scenic rural route between High Springs, Williston, and Archer.

By train: **Amtrak** (352-468-1408) stops in Waldo, west of Gainesville.

GETTING AROUND *By bicycle*: Gainesville is one of Florida's most bicycle-friendly cities, with rail-trails, dedicated urban bike paths, and bike lanes connecting the city core and the University of Florida with the suburbs.

By bus: Given the University of Florida's large student population, local bus service via **Regional Transit System** (352-334-2600) is frequent and comprehensive; call 352-334-2614 for a schedule.

By taxi: **A1 Yellow Cab** (352-374-9696).

PARKING Although there are some free parking spaces in downtown **Gainesville** (2-hour limit), it's mostly metered parking (50¢ hour, 2-hour limit in most places). One parking garage serves the downtown district. At the University of Florida, if you can't find metered parking along the edge of campus, it's essential to pick up a visitors pass (free) at one of the staffed parking permit kiosks off University Blvd or SW 13th St. Park only in permit areas that match the color of your pass—even in metered areas—or you'll face a parking ticket, payable immediately at the main parking office on North-South Rd. In **Alachua**, **High**

Springs, and **Starke**, you'll have no problem finding free street parking within easy walking distance of shops and restaurants.

PUBLIC REST ROOMS You'll find public rest rooms in **High Springs** in a replica train depot housing the chamber of commerce at the south end of the antiques district.

MEDICAL EMERGENCIES In Gainesville, **Shands Medical Center** (352-265-0111), 1600 SW Archer Rd, is one of the nation's top medical facilities; you also have the option of **North Florida Regional Medical Center** (352-333-4000), 6500 W Newberry Rd.

✷ To See

ARCHEOLOGICAL SITES

Gainesville

Thanks to the archeologists of the University of Florida, many significant sites have been identified throughout Alachua County. Some, like the **Law School Burial Mound**, are open to public inspection. Located on the University of Florida campus near Lake Alice, this burial mound dates back to A.D. 1000. It contains the remains of the ancestors of the Potano culture, also known as the Alachua Tradition peoples. The **Moon Lake Villages** were a series of Alachua Tradition villages on the site now occupied by Buchholz High School in Gainesville. Accessed by the trails in **Gum Root Swamp Conservation Area** (see *Wild Places*), villages along Newnans Lake were occupied as early as 3000 B.C., and more recently by the Seminoles, who called the lake Pithlachocco: "the place where boats are made." More than 100 aboriginal canoes were unearthed from the lake in 2000, the largest such find in Florida. Most remain buried in the mud. Another Paleo-Indian site has been identified near the boardwalk along US 441 in the middle of **Paynes Prairie**. At **San Felasco Hammock Preserve State Park** (see *Wild Places*), one of the first Spanish missions in North America was established in 1608 and occupied until 1706. Its exact location is not marked, but you can walk through the woods around the mission along the Old Spanish Way trail, where Alachua County's original seat, **Spring Grove**, has also vanished under the thick cover of hardwood forest.

ART GALLERIES

Gainesville

✐ ♿ **Samuel P. Harn Museum of Art** (352-392-9826; www.harn.ufl.edu), SW 34th St and Hull Rd. Now more than a decade old, the Harn Museum of Art showcases thematic exhibits of fine arts from their extensive collections as well as rotating traveling exhibits. The tall, open rotunda provides access to the main galleries. In the Richardson Gallery, you might encounter an exhibit of fine turn-of-the-20th-century American oils, but you'll always find the museum's masterpiece on display—Monet's *Champ d'Avoine*. Take a seat and enjoy some quiet time studying this impressionistic masterpiece. Looking for more to aid your art appreciation? Stop in the **Bishop Study Center** to peruse their library of fine art books, or examine the computers for exhibits from virtual galleries. In addition to books, jewelry, and fine art reproductions, the **Museum Shop** carries artsy games and toys for kids, and the artistic works of several local artisans. Tue–Fri 11–5, Sat 10–5, Sun 1–5. Closed on state holidays. Donation.

Santa Fe Gallery (352-395-5621; www.inst.santafe.cc.fl.us/~cah), 3000 NW 83rd St, Building P, Room 201. As the first community college approved for loans of high-security exhibits from the National Gallery of Art and the Smithsonian Institution, Santa Fe Community College displays rotating exhibits of contemporary art. Mon–Fri 10–3, Tue 6–8. Free.

Thomas Center Galleries (352-334-5064), 302 NE 6th Ave. Serving the community as the Hotel Thomas from 1928 to 1968, this is now a cultural center housing a small history museum, an art gallery with rotating exhibits, and the city's Department of Cultural Affairs. Roam the galleries and enjoy the beautiful surrounding gardens. Free.

University of Florida Galleries (352-392-0201; www.arts.ufl.edu/galleries) include the University Gallery in Fine Arts Building B, with contemporary national and regional art displays (Tue–Sat); the Focus Gallery in Fine Arts Building C (Mon–Fri), featuring student art and emerging artists; and the Grinter Gallery in Grinter Hall, with its international art displays (Mon–Fri). Free.

HISTORIC SITES

Archer

In 1865 David Levy Yulee, U.S. senator and head of the Florida Railroad, stashed the personal effects of Confederate president Jefferson Davis at his **Cottonwood Plantation** while Davis attempted to flee to Florida after the surrender of the Confederacy. Yulee's servants led Union soldiers to the prize, and Yulee was jailed for treason. A plaque near the old **Archer Depot** (see *Museums*) tells the story; the plantation house burned in 1939.

Cross Creek

At the **Marjorie Kinnan Rawlings Homestead Historic State Park** (352-466-9273), CR 325, house tours take you through the living and working space of this Pulitzer-winning novelist beloved by regional historians for her accurate depictions of rural North Florida. Set in what remains of her original orange grove from the 1940s, this dogtrot Cracker home offers some quirks specific to its northern resident, including the "liquor cabinet" with firewater on top and firewood on the bottom, as well as her use of inverted mixing bowls as decorative fixtures for lights. Cary Grant, Spencer Tracy, and many other legends stayed in Marjorie's guest room. Costumed guides explain what life was like in Cross Creek when Marjorie sat on the front porch and typed the drafts of her novels, including *The Yearling*. Fee.

Gainesville

Several historic districts surround the city core of downtown Gainesville, where the original **Courthouse Clock** (circa 1885) resides in a new housing at the corner of University and 1st St in front of the new courthouse. B&Bs (see *Lodging*) stake a claim in the historic **Southeast Residential District**, Gainesville's earliest suburb, settled in the 1880s. Wander through these streets for some fine examples of Victorian and Cracker architecture. In the lushly canopied **Northeast Historic District**, covering a few blocks around the Thomas Center, 12 historic homes show off their Victorian charm beneath the live oaks and magnolias. Start your tour at the **Thomas Center** (see *Art Galleries*). Built in 1906, this restored Mediterranean Revival hotel began as the home of Major William Reuben Thomas, the man instrumental in attracting the University of Florida to Gainesville. Founded in 1853, the **University of Florida** boasts its own historic center. In 1989 the **Pleasant Street District** was placed on the National Register of Historic Places, the first predominantly African American community in Florida to gain that designation. Comprising a 20-block area to the northwest of downtown, it contains 35 points of historic interest, including the **St. Augustine Day School**, 405 NW 4th Ave, an 1892 mission for African Americans, and the **Dunbar Hotel**, 732 NW 4th St, a favorite of jazz musicians and the only Gainesville lodgings available to African American travelers from the 1930s through the 1950s.

High Springs

High Springs itself is a historic downtown; many of its buildings date back to the late 1800s. A remnant of the original wagon road that brought settlers to this region, the **Old Bellamy Road** can be accessed from US 41 north of High Springs: Follow the Bellamy Road east to the interpretive trailhead. Just south on US 41 is the De Soto Trail monument, commemorating the route of explorer Hernando de Soto and his men as they traversed the Florida peninsula in 1539.

Kanapaha

Established in 1855, the **Historic Haile Homestead** (352-372-2633), 8500 SW Archer Rd, provides a glimpse into the life of Florida's territorial settlers on a 40-acre remnant of the original 1,500-acre Sea Island cotton plantation. Open Sun for tours noon–4; adults $7, under 12 free.

Keystone Heights

Keystone Beach (see *Swimming*) dates back to 1928, with its historic bathhouse and dance hall perched on Lake Keystone.

Melrose

Boasting one of the highest concentrations of historic sites in Florida, with 79 classic homes and businesses, **Melrose** is a town where history is part of everyday life. Many buildings are more than a century old, but remain well kept and occupied as residences; see *Walking Tours* for how to explore local history.

Micanopy

More than 35 historic sites crowd Micanopy's small downtown, best enjoyed as a self-guided walking tour (see *Walking Tours*). Some don't-miss stops along the tour include the **Old Presbyterian Church**, built 1870; the 1890 **Thrasher Warehouse**, housing the Micanopy Historical Society Museum (see *Museums*); the 1880 **Calvin Merry House**, the oldest home on the east side of the street; the Victorian Gothic Revival **Powell House**, from 1866; the 1895 **Brick School House**; the 1875 **Simonton-Herlong House** (see *Lodging*); and the **Stewart-**

Merry House, built around the 1855 log cabin where Dr. James Stewart practiced medicine. None of the homes is open for public inspection, although many of the historic business buildings now house the town's shops.

Newberry

For a ramble through a preserved homestead, visit **Dudley Farm Historic Site State Park** (see *Farms*), where rangers in period costume take you through a day in the life of a turn-of-the-20th-century Florida farmer. The museum at the visitors center interprets the several generations of family who lived here, and how farming changed over the years; the tour will open your eyes to how difficult life was for Florida's early settlers.

Starke

The historic **Bradford County Courthouse** anchors the west end of Call St to US 301; the **Gene Matthews Museum** marks the east end of the historic district, with several antiques shops (see *Selective Shopping*) and **Bobkat's Café** (see *Eating Out*) in the old Rexall Drug Store in between. A restored theater shows first-run movies. As renovation of the historic district continues, expect to see more of the storefronts fill in.

MUSEUMS

Archer

Housed in the former railroad depot, the **Archer Historical Society Museum** (352-495-9422), Magnolia and Main Sts, displays local history and railroad memorabilia, including a lab-model Edison phonograph, an original telephone and telegraph from the depot, and the curator's antique camera collection. Open Sat 3–6, Sep–June. Donation.

Gainesville

Alachua County Historic Trust and Matheson Museum (352-378-2280), 513 E University Ave. In addition to its interpretation of Alachua County's history, the museum houses a historical library and archives, with an extensive collection of Florida history books and documents. Closed Mon. Free. The trust also administers the historic **Matheson House**, the second-oldest residence in Gainesville, and the **Tison Tool Museum**, both open by appointment only. Fee.

✐ ♿ **Florida Museum of Natural History** (352-846-2000; www.flmnh.ufl.edu), SW 34th St and Hull Rd. Interactive and engaging, the Florida Museum of Natural History continues to evolve with new picture-perfect 3-D dioramas and hands-on activities. Kids and adults love the walk-through Florida cave, which now funnels you into the permanent exhibit called Northwest Florida's Waterways and Wildlife—showcasing everything from karst topography and carnivorous plants to indigenous peoples and the creatures of the salt marsh. In the South Florida People and Environments gallery, shrink down to the size of a killifish to explore the world beneath the mangroves, and walk into the home of a Calusa chieftain. Dinosaurs never walked Florida's soil, but we've had saber-toothed tigers, mastodons, and shoveltuskers; learn more about them in the newly refurbished Florida Fossils exhibit. Rotating exhibits fill the remainder of the museum. Don't miss the **Collectors Shop**, a must for picking up educational toys and books for the kids. Mon–Sat 10–4:30, Sun 1–4:30. Donation.

The **Institute of Black Culture** (352-392-0895), 1510 W University Ave, exhibits African, African American, and Caribbean art on the University of Florida campus. Mon–Fri 8–9; free.

Hawthorne

Hawthorne Historical Museum (352-481-4491), 7225 SE 221st St, is housed in a restored 1907 church; artifacts, exhibits, and primitive arts illustrate the long history of this rural village.

Keystone Heights

On 170,000 acres of sand pine and scrub oak in the heart of the Florida wilderness, Camp Blanding was home to 800,000 World War II soldiers from 1940 to 1945. Nine infantry divisions trained in ankle-deep sand on arguably one of the toughest training grounds anywhere while preparing for conflict. The **Camp Blanding Museum and Memorial Park** (904-682-3196), Starke, is dedicated to these soldiers, but also honors all who served in Korea, Vietnam, and Desert Storm. The newest addition is the Black Soldiers Memorial Park, dedicated in 1998. Life at Camp Blanding during the 1940s is depicted in the museum through colorful displays of weaponry, photos, memorabilia, and even a life-sized bunkhouse. In the Memorial Park, monuments honor the original nine army infantry divisions and the 508th Parachute Infantry Regiment; several World War II aircraft and vehicles are on display. Actors Demi Moore and Viggo Mortensen worked out long hours in the harsh environment during the filming of *GI Jane*, and real military drill instructors put 16 civilians through basic training for TV's *Boot Camp*. The current site, now reduced to about 73,000 acres, continues to train members of the U.S. National Guard, Active Army, and Army Reserves from all over the United States. The museum gift shop has a fine selection of books, pins, and patches. Open noon–4 daily.

AT THE FLORIDA MUSEUM OF NATURAL HISTORY, GAINESVILLE

Alachua County VCB

Micanopy

Micanopy Historical Society Museum (352-466-3200; www.afn.org/~micanopy), corner of Cholokka and Bay Sts. Housed in the Thrasher Warehouse (circa 1890)—the "Home Depot of its day," says volunteer Paul

Oliver, built along the railroad tracks—this small but comprehensive museum gives an overview of life in and around Micanopy, from the ancient Timucua and William Bartram's visit to Cuscowilla in 1774, through the town's settlement as a trading post in 1821, and on into this century, with special exhibits of historical railroad items, relics from the Thrasher Store (now Tyson Trading Company), and period pieces from the Simon H. Benjamin Collection. There's also a small gift shop and bookstore with historical tomes on the region. Open 1–4 daily. Donation.

Starke

Boat Drain School Museum, 581 N Temple Ave. In 1893 this one-room pine board schoolhouse served the needs of Bradford County's small population; today it's a small museum dedicated to the history of Bradford High School. The **Gene Matthews Bradford County Historical Museum** (904-964-4606), 201 E Call St, showcases Bradford County's history, with a special emphasis on turpentine, logging, and railroads. Open 1–5 Tue–Sun; free.

RAILROADIANA At Magnolia and Main in Archer, the **Archer Historical Society Museum** (see *Museums*) occupies the old railroad depot; across the street at the Maddox Machine Works, a gleaming **Seaboard Air Line steam engine** circa 1910 is on display. Visit the **Micanopy Historical Society Museum** (see *Museums*) for historical information and relics from the Gainesville, Rocky Point & Micanopy Railroad, circa 1895. After it became the Tampa & Jackson Railroad, locals called the T&J the "Tug & Jerk." It stopped at Thrasher's Warehouse, which now houses the museum.

High Springs grew up around Henry Plant's Seaboard Air Line. The man credited with putting Tampa on the map selected High Springs as his distribution center. On Railroad St (south of Main), look for the original **passenger depot**, a historic site now housing the Station Bakery & Café (see *Eating Out*). To the west of the station, vast rail yards, roundhouses, and engine shops kept busy with mighty steam engines; the only reminder of their passing is a bright red **Seaboard Coast Line caboose** tucked behind city hall.

Railroads shaped the towns of Starke, Waldo, and Hawthorne as well. You'll find a **working railroad depot** at East Brownlee Street (FL 16) in Starke at the railroad crossing just west of US 301, and a retired **caboose** sitting on a siding southwest of the junction of US 301 and FL 20 in Waldo.

ZOOLOGICAL PARK ✐ **Santa Fe Community College Teaching Zoo** (352-395-5604; www.inst.sfcc.edu/~zoo), 3000 NW 43rd St, Gainesville. For more than 20 years, this unique hands-on zoo has taught generations of animal technicians (once known as zookeepers) how to create exhibits and handle animals. Guests travel with a guide through the deeply forested complex, learning about bald eagles, muntjac, otters, and more while seeing students at work learning how to care for their charges. Open weekends 9–2, with tours held every 10 to 15 minutes. Weekday tours by reservation only; closed holidays and semester breaks. Free.

✱ To Do

ALLIGATOR SPOTTING In 2002 artists created alligator sculptures that were placed throughout Gainesville, then auctioned off as a fund-raiser for the arts. To track down the remaining whimsical pieces, ask around for the *Gator Trails* brochure, or look it up online on the *Gainesville Sun* web site (www.gainesville sun.com). To spot hundreds of live alligators, visit **Alachua Sink** in Paynes Prairie Preserve State Park (see *Wild Places*) or visit the University of Florida campus, where a network of nature trails surrounds **Lake Alice**. Visitors get up close and personal with the university's real-life namesakes—but don't ramble down the pathways after dark! The daytime sightings of 10-foot alligators sunning themselves along the trail are thrill enough. Parking areas on Museum Rd are restricted to student use until 3:30 PM.

BAT-WATCHING On the University of Florida campus at Lake Alice, the **Bat House** in the Student Agricultural Gardens on Museum Rd contains a colony of more than 20,000 brown bats. Visit at dusk to see the incredible display of bats pouring out of the house and into the skies. At the **Lubee Center** (352-485-1250) north of Gainesville, researchers care for endangered fruit bats under the auspices of the Lubee Foundation, formed by Bacardi Rum magnate Louis Bacardi. Group tours are offered by reservation only.

BICYCLING Gainesville is a city for serious bicycling; many residents use bikes as their sole means of transportation. For a map of the urban bikeway network, contact the **Gainesville Bicycle/Pedestrian Program** (352-334-5074), 306 NE 6th Ave, Gainesville 32602. The **Gainesville-Hawthorne State Trail** (see *Greenways*) runs from Bouleware Springs Park in southeast Gainesville to downtown Hawthorne, providing riders with a 34-mile round trip. **San Felasco Hammock Preserve State Park** (see *Wild Places*) has more than 12 miles of shady rugged mountain biking routes. Check on bike rentals at **Spin Cycle** (352-373-3355), 424 W University Ave in Gainesville, and **Santa Fe Bicycle Outfitters** (352-454-BIKE), 10 N Main St, in High Springs.

BIRDING At **Paynes Prairie Preserve State Park** birders head for open ground—the observation platforms at Bolen's Bluff and at the end of the La Chua Trail both provide just enough altitude to let you see far across the open prairie. You'll encounter dozens of trilling species around the water gardens at **Kanapaha Botanical Gardens**. Any spot with a marsh is a major haven for birds; check the *Green Space* section for ideas.

DIVING Northwestern Alachua County lies along the spring belt, offering open water and cave diving at **Poe Springs** (see *Springs*) as well as underwater adventures in adjacent Gilchrist County at **Ginnie Springs** and **Blue Spring** (see "The Lower Suwannee"). At High Springs check in at **Extreme Exposure Adventure Center** (1-800-574-6341; www.extreme-exposure.com), 15 S Main, for rental equipment, instruction, and pointers on the area's best dives. **Water World** (352-37-SCUBA), 720 NW 13th St, a full-service dive shop, rents snorkeling and scuba gear, holds dive training, and offers information on more than 50 dive sites within an easy drive of Gainesville.

ECOTOURS Author and river rat Lars Anderson runs regular guided kayaking trips out of his **Adventure Outpost** in High Springs (see *Paddling*).

GOLF **Ironwood Golf Course** (352-334-3120), 2100 NE 39th Ave, is a city-owned public course with PGA pro Bill Iwinski on staff; 18 holes, par 72, on an Audubon-approved natural course established in 1962. West of I-75 on FL 26, the **West End Golf Course** (352-332-2721) features the world's largest and longest night-lighted course (18 holes, par 60), along with a driving range.

HIKING Home to the state office of the **Florida Trail Association** (1-877-HIKE-FLA; www.florida-trail.org), 5415 SW 13th St—where you can stop in and pick up hiking information and hiking-related gifts—Gainesville is ringed with dozens of excellent opportunities for hikers, including more than 20 miles of trails at **Paynes Prairie Preserve State Park** and another 12 miles of trails at **San Felasco Hammock Preserve State Park** (see *Wild Places*). Or opt for an easier stroll at one of the nature centers or wilderness areas. The nearest completed segment of the **Florida Trail** runs through **Gold Head Branch State Park**, just outside Camp Blanding. Check out *50 Hikes in North Florida* (Backcountry Guides) for details on the best hiking in the region.

PADDLING Two outfitters in High Springs can get you in the water and down the Santa Fe or the nearby Ichetucknee in Columbia County. At **Santa Fe Canoe Outpost** (386-454-2050; www.santaferiver.com), US 441 at the Santa Fe Bridge, rent a canoe (shuttle included) or take a guided trip (including overnight trips!) on the Santa Fe or Ichetucknee Rivers. In addition to their "Menu" of guided trips and a selection of canoes and kayaks for sale or rent, the **Adventure Outpost** (386-454-0611), 815 NW US 441, has technical clothing, camping equipment, and a nice selection of regional guidebooks. Owners Lars and Patsy keep the shop well stocked: You'll even find pottery and other gift items from local artists. Kick back in the "parlor" and thumb through a book, or relax at the picnic tables outside under the trees.

PRAIRIE OVERLOOK **Paynes Prairie Overlook**, I-75 rest area southbound. Notice the DANGEROUS SNAKES warning signs around the rest area, intimidating visitors from getting too close to the edge of Paynes Prairie, North Florida's largest prairie. Reflecting this theme, the Florida Department of Transportation built a snake-shaped walkway out to an observation deck overlooking the prairie. To northbound travelers, the walkway and deck look like an enormous snake, complete with a ribbon of concrete creating a forked tongue.

SCENIC DRIVES The **Old Florida Heritage Highway** (www.scenicus441.com), a newly designated Florida Scenic Highway, circles the Gainesville area, using US 441, CR 346, CR 325, and CR 2082 to create a beautiful drive around Paynes Prairie and along canopied roads. Along **CR 234**, from FL 26 south through Rochelle to Micanopy along the east side of Newnans Lake, you'll cruise past historic homes under a canopy of ancient live oaks.

SWIMMING Step back in time at **Keystone Beach** (352-473-7847), 565 S Lawrence Blvd, Keystone Heights. Established in 1924, it's a place where you can splash around on a sandy beach outside the historic bathhouse on Lake Geneva. Visit the region's springs (see *Springs*) for more swimming options.

WALKING TOURS

Gainesville

Check with the Thomas Center (see *Historic Sites*), the Gainesville CVB (see *Guidance*), or the Matheson Center (see *Museums*) for brochures outlining walking tours of historic Gainesville, such as the *Pleasant Street Historic Walking Tour* and *Historic Gainesville: A Walking Tour*, which covers the Northeast Historic District around the Matheson Center.

Micanopy

Stop in at the **Micanopy Historical Society Museum** (see *Museums*) to purchase an inexpensive walking tour booklet giving the history and location of 38 significant sites in the historic district.

Melrose

The *Historic Melrose 125 Years: A Celebration Tour* brochure outlines a walking tour of the 79 historic sites in town, from businesses to private homes, churches, and cemeteries. I found a copy of the brochure while visiting the Micanopy Historical Society Museum, but you may want to write to Historic Melrose, P.O. Box 704, Melrose 32666, for a copy. Or just explore on your own: Amble down the narrow back streets (many unpaved) along the Lake Santa Fe chain of lakes on foot or by car to see genteel homes set in lush landscaping under ancient live oaks.

✷ Green Space

BEACHES The sandy beach and crystal-clear water at **Keystone Beach** (352-473-4807), Keystone Heights, make this a great place for swimming, snorkeling, and catching some rays.

FARMS ✐ Bring a bag of carrots for admission to the **Mill Creek Farm Retirement Home for Horses** (386-462-1001; www.millcreekfarm.org), CR 235A in Alachua, open Sat 11–3. In the 1840s farmstead at **Morningside Nature Center** (see *Nature Centers*) kids learn what life in Old Florida was really like during living history demonstrations on weekends. Let them visit with the barnyard animals and join in on a cane-grinding session. At **Dudley Farm Historic Site State Park** (352-472-1142), 18730 W Newberry Rd, visitors amble through a working 19th-century Florida farm, where park rangers in period costume present ongoing living history demonstrations of sugarcane harvesting and daily farm chores. Farm open Wed–Sun 9–4, grounds 8–5. Guided tours available. Fee.

BOTANICAL GARDENS 🐾 ♿ **Kanapaha Botanical Gardens** (352-372-4981; www.hammock.ifas.ufl.edu/kanapaha), 4700 SW 58th Dr. With more than 14 distinct garden areas spread across 62 acres bordering Lake Kanapaha, Kanapaha Botanical Gardens provides a peaceful retreat on the western edge of Gainesville. Come in spring to revel in the aromas of azalea and camellia in bloom; come anytime to walk more than a mile of pathways between the burbling water gardens, the palm hammock, and the woodland gardens, where you can pause and sit on a bench next to a reflective pool, or watch an artist at work painting one of the many lovely garden scenes. Plant identifications add to your understanding of native plants and popular botanicals. Children will appreciate the new children's garden, as well as the many places to duck beneath bowers of plants. Art glass aficionados should note the collection assembled in the gift shop; you'll always find fine art on display in the Summer House, and plants available from the on-site nursery. Managed by the North Florida Botanical Society, this is one of Florida's little-known beauty spots. Small admission fee; dogs on leash permitted. Closed Thu.

SAGO PALM ALONG A WALKWAY AT KANAPAHA

Sandra Friend

GREENWAYS The paved **Gainesville-Hawthorne State Trail** (352-336-2135) runs along a 17-mile section of the old railroad line between the two towns, with termini at Bouleware Springs Park in southwest Gainesville and in downtown Hawthorne, and additional parking areas at all major road crossings. Enjoy biking, hiking, or horseback riding along the adjoining grassy strip. Passing through Hampton on US 301, the new Palatka–Lake Butler State Trail, when completed, will connect these towns on a ride through rural Putnam and Bradford Counties.

NATURE CENTERS **Bivens Arm** (352-334-2056), 3650 S Main St, Gainesville. Stroll the interpretive paths under shady live oaks along the edge of this marshy extension of Paynes Prairie, a great spot for bird-watching. Daily 9–5; free.

Morningside Nature Center (352-334-2170; www.natureoperations.org), 3540 East University Ave. Preserving 278 acres of forest on the eastern edge of Gainesville, the Morningside Nature Center provides a living history farm, interpretive exhibits, and a network of hiking trails through longleaf pine flatwoods and sandhills. Free except during special events.

PARKS As befits a large town with a lot of greenery, Gainesville has an extraordinary number of small parks with picnicking, playgrounds, and other fun family activities. One of the more unusual parks in the area is the **Devil's Millhopper Geologic State Park** (352-955-2008), 4732 Millhopper Rd, where you can walk down 232 steps to the bottom of a 120-foot sinkhole lush with vegetation. At **Bivens Arm Nature Park** (352-334-2056), 3650 S Main St, nature trails and boardwalks circle a willow marsh.

Dogs are welcome to roam off-leash at **Squirrel Ridge Park**, 1603 SW Williston Rd, a city park with an open fenced area for dogs to play. For a theme park for your dog, visit **Dog Wood Park** (352-335-1919; www.dogwoodpark.com), 5505 SW Archer Rd, where Fido can romp and play across a 15-acre preserve, a true doggy delight with swimming ponds, a walking trail, and doggy playground equipment. Open to nonmembers Sun only; $8.25 for first dog, $2.50 for additional pooches (accompanying human free).

Mike Roess Gold Head Branch State Park (352-473-4701), 6239 FL 21, Keystone Heights, centers on an incredible ravine dripping with ferns, from which the sand-bottomed Gold Head Branch is born. Nature trails let you climb down into the deep ravine and follow the stream's course to Little Lake Johnson, where you can grab a canoe and paddle across the expanse. Three miles of the **Florida Trail** pass through the park, with a primitive campsite along the way; developed camping and cabins from the Civilian Conservation Corps era are also available.

SPRINGS On CR 340 outside High Springs, there are three major parks centered on the region's largest springs. **Blue Springs** (386-454-1369) forms the centerpiece of a county park with picnicking, nature trails, and camping, but most visitors dive and snorkel in the springs. Open 9–7 daily. $10 adults, $3 children 5–12; no pets. In neighboring Gilchrist County, **Poe Springs Park** (386-454-1992) is a 197-acre county park with rolling hills and steep bluffs along the

Santa Fe River. At nearby **Ginnie Springs** (386-454-7188; www.giniesprings outdoors.com), overnight campers can swim in the springs until midnight; it's a mecca for cave divers. Tube and canoe rentals available, open 8–sunset.

WATERFALLS Visit **Devil's Millhopper** (see *Parks*) during the rainy season, and you'll see cascades dropping more than 100 feet down the walls of this steep sinkhole, creating an atmosphere much like a tropical rain forest for Florida's southernmost natural waterfall.

WILD PLACES Nowhere else in North Florida can compare to **Paynes Prairie Preserve State Park** (352-466-3397), 100 Savannah Blvd, a 22,000-acre wet prairie defining the southern edge of Gainesville. Herds of bison and wild horses roam the vast open spaces, while alligators collect en masse in La Chua Sink at the north end of the prairie. With more than 20 miles of hiking, biking, and equestrian trails and a beautifully shaded campground, it's one of the best places in the region for wildlife-watching. Open 8–sunset daily; fee.

Enjoy 12 miles of rugged trails through the hills of **San Felasco Hammock Preserve State Park** (386-462-7905) on Millhopper Rd, a lush preserve with Appalachian-like landscapes formed by Florida's limestone karst. Open 9–5 daily; fee.

Conservation areas are some of the wilder spots around the region's lakes, where hikers, bikers, and equestrians can roam miles of old forest roads and developed trails through floodplain forests. Visit **Gum Root Swamp Conservation Area** on FL 26 for a glimpse of Newnans Lake; the **Newnans Lake Conservation Area** (with three tracts: Hatchet Creek, North, and South) off CR 234 and FL 26; and the **Lochloosa Conservation Area**, where you can hike out to an observation platform on Lake Lochloosa from a trailhead adjoining the fire station in Cross Creek. All are managed by the **St. Johns Water Management District** (386-329-4483; sjr.state.fl.us).

✷ Lodging

BED & BREAKFASTS

Gainesville 32601

♣ ♿ **The Laurel Oak Inn** (352-373-4535; www.laureloakinn.com), 221 SE 7th St. After 2 years of renovating this roomy Queen Anne in Gainesville's historic residential district, Monta and Peggy Burt can be proud of the results—they won the city's top beautification award in 2003. The Laurel Oak Inn is a place to unwind. Sit on the spacious porches and watch the owls from the comfort of your rocking chair, or enjoy the pampering afforded by the soft robes, fragrant lotions, and candles that accompany your in-room hydro-jet massage tub. It's a hit with honeymoon couples, and business travelers appreciate the DSL Internet access in every room ($75–135). You won't go away hungry, as a steady parade of artfully presented gourmet treats appears on your breakfast plate. A ground-floor room accommodates wheelchairs with an appropriately sized wheel-in shower.

The Magnolia Plantation Inn (1-800-201-2379; www.magnoliabnb .com), 309 SE 7th St. In 1991 Joe and Cindy Montalto opened the Baird

House, an 1885 Victorian, as the first B&B in Gainesville. In addition to the five lavish rooms in the main house, each with private bath ($90–125), their plantation now encompasses six lovingly restored cottages ($175–300) connected by lush, shaded gardens developed by Joe, a landscape architect. Full breakfast served in the Baird House.

♿ **Sweetwater Branch Inn** (1-800-595-7760; www.sweetwaterinn.com), 625 E University Ave. Cornelia Holbrook's complex of four historic buildings just outside downtown provides a selection of tastefully themed rooms and the private Honeymoon Cottage, popular with newlyweds who take their vows at McKenzie Hall, the Victorian-style banquet room on site. Sit on the broad, breezy veranda to enjoy complimentary wine and hors d'oeuvres each evening, or stroll the lush gardens and listen to the burble of the fountains. $80–155.

GAINESVILLE'S LAUREL OAK INN

Sandra Friend

Hampton 32091

Hampton Lake B&B (1-800-480-4522; www.hamptonlakebb.com), US 301. On Lake Hampton, this massive winged A-frame with a native stone fireplace and pecky cypress walls is the dream home of Freeman and Paula Register; the antique gas pumps were handed down from Grandpa, who was the local Gulf Oil distributor in the 1930s. This is a retreat for those who love the outdoors, with fishing tackle and a pedal boat waiting at the pier, walking trails winding through 18 acres of pines, a porch swing and rockers overlooking the lake, and a hot tub for relaxing after play. Outdoorsy decor accentuates the spacious Wade Room, big enough for an entire family. Four rooms of varying sizes, $70–120. Fisherman's packages available; dinner prepared for an additional fee with notice.

High Springs 32643

Enjoy spacious accommodations in a romantic setting at the **Grady House** (386-454-2206; www.gradyhouse.com), 420 NW 1st Ave, a charming two-story mansion from 1917 with intimate formal gardens in the backyard. The aroma of home-cooked muffins wafts through the dining room; settle down by the fireplace and read a book. Five rooms, $85–115.

At the **Rustic Inn** (386-454-1223; www.rusticinn.net), 3105 S Main St, Tom and Wendy Solomon offer relaxation in six modern rooms ($79–109) with nature themes, from the Everglades to sea mammals; settle into a rocking chair on the porch or take a lap around the pool on this 7-acre mini ranch. A continental breakfast basket is left at your room each evening so you can set your own pace in the morning.

Micanopy 32667

The Herlong Mansion (1-800-HERLONG; www.herlong.com), 402 NE Cholokka Blvd. When guests come to this neoclassical 1875 mansion, they take to the verandas, where comfortable chairs overlook the expansive lawns. Of the four suites, five rooms, and two private outbuildings, sisters and girlfriends traveling together will especially appreciate Pink's Room with its two antique cast-iron beds and a daybed; brothers will like the masculine Brothers' Room, with a double bed and a daybed. The mansion features private baths, classy antiques, and original push-button electric switches throughout. For a touch of history, settle back in the Music Room and watch *The Yearling* or any of several other movies filmed in the region. Full breakfasts on weekends; continental breakfasts weekdays; no special orders. No children, no pets, no smoking on premises. $99–179.

HOTELS AND MOTELS

Gainesville 32601

Cabot Lodge (352-375-2400), 3726 SW 40th Blvd. It's always happy hour at the Cabot Lodge, where guests get cozy in the massive great room, sharing cocktails, snacks, and stories as the sun sets. The large, comfortable rooms ($80–105) ensure a good night's rest, with all the usual amenities.

♿ **Howard Johnson Express Inn** (352-371-2500; www.howardjohnsongainesville.com), 3820 SW 13th St. Pleasant, newly renovated property with a swimming pool, all-new furnishings, and small but well-appointed rooms ($42–66), some with whirlpools. Four home office suites with DSL; bring your own router. Full continental breakfast served.

♿ **University of Florida Hilton** (352-371-3600), 1714 SW 34th Place. Top-notch chain hotel with T-1 lines to every room, fitness center, heated pool and spa; visit **Albert's Restaurant** for fine dining, American-style, including a Sun brunch with complimentary mimosas. Shuttle provided to airport.

High Springs 32643

Cadillac Motel (386-454-1701), 405 NW Santa Fe Blvd. Built by Dynamite Jones in 1950, this modest family motel has clean, spacious rooms, each with cable TV and coffeemaker; $38–45.

High Springs Country Inn (386-454-1565), 520 NW Santa Fe Blvd. This 1960s family-run offering has cute landscaping outside its period rooms ($38 for one bed, $55–68 for two), which vary in size from small to suite; each is sparkling clean, with small tiled bathroom, fridge, microwave, and cable TV.

CABINS

Cross Creek 32640

Secret River Lodge (352-466-3999), 14531 S CR 325. Tucked behind the Yearling Restaurant (see *Dining Out*), this eclectic collection of restored fish camp cabins on Cross Creek provide a quiet venue for relaxing in a sleepy little town. Each cabin is named for one of Marjorie Kinnan Rawlings's books.

CAMPGROUNDS

High Springs 32643
High Springs Campground (386-454-1688), 24004 NW Old Bellamy Rd, provides camping in a family-oriented atmosphere, with playground, swimming pool, and full hookups.

River Rise Resort (386-454-7562; www.riverriseresort.com), 252 SE Riverview Circle. With horseback riding, camping, canoeing, swimming, and nearby hiking trails, it's a centrally located mecca for outdoor recreation along the Santa Fe River.

Keystone Heights
On the sandy shores of spring-fed Lake Kingsley at **Camp Blanding** (see *Museums*) you can lay your tent under shaded trees. The primitive site has latrines, showers, and a designated swimming area. The RV-only site is separate from the primitive site and has full-hookup facilities with a children's playground. Contact the Morale, Welfare, and Recreation office (904-682-3104) for sites. The MWR also rents canoes, inner tubes, camping gear, and bicycles.

Starke 32091
Fish, swim, or just lounge around at **Kingsley Beach RV Park Campground and Resort** (904-533-2006; www.kingsleybeach.com). There's a lot to do at this family-oriented 30-acre park. Scuba lessons, banana boat rides, paddle boats, and Jet Skis are just some of the water amenities on this clear blue lake. If you don't want to cook, the restaurant serves all three meals. Bait-and-tackle shop, game room, and live outdoor entertainment. RV sites $25–40 a day, $125–300 a week. Don't own an RV? The resort also rents one- to three-bedroom furnished cabins for $50–145 a day and $175–650 a week.

KOA (904-964-8484; www.starkekoa.com), 1475 US 301. Large campground, partially shaded, with exceptional amenities like free modem hookup and wide 70-foot pull-through spaces. Heated swimming pool, playground, cabins, tent camping area.

✸ Where to Eat

DINING OUT

Cross Creek
The Yearling Restaurant (352-466-3999), CR 325. A regional favorite since 1952, the Yearling reopened in 2002 under new ownership with the same devotion to quality Cracker fare. Although the outside looks like an old shack along Cross Creek, the main dining area features dark, rich wood and windows on the creek. If you're lucky enough to end up in the overflow section, it's an antiques shop replete with a fishing skiff, booths from the original restaurant, and shelves lined with classic books like the sci-fi thriller *Thuvia, Maid of Mars* by Edgar Rice Burroughs. This is a funky place celebrating the legacy of their neighbor Marjorie Kinnan Rawlings, where you're as likely to rub elbows with the poet laureate of Tennessee as you are with local fishermen. Cheese and crackers kick off each meal, which you can supplement with an appetizer ($4–8) like the large portion of freshly battered fried mushrooms. Outstanding "Cross Creek Traditions" ($12–28) include crawdads, alligator, frog legs, venison, soft-shell crab, catfish, and pan-fried quail, as well as a variety of steaks and combination platters. Coated in a light breading, the fresh venison medallions are surprisingly tender

and juicy; the stuffed flounder contains a mass of succulent buttery crabmeat. Lighter fare ($8–10) is available between noon and 5 PM on weekends, including a unique "Creek Boy" sandwich served up with your choice of fried shrimp, oyster, or alligator with coleslaw and Jack cheese. For dessert, try the sour orange pie, a tiger-striped creation with the taste of a chocolate orange truffle ($4.50). Live music Fri and Sat.

Gainesville

Amelia's (352-373-1919), 235 S Main St, Suite 107. Gainesville's top pick for fine Italian cuisine, Amelia's Italian bistro entices you off the street with the aromas of fresh sauces bubbling in the kitchen. Pasta dishes $10–13, meat dishes $15–33. Open for lunch Thu and Fri, dinner Tue–Sun. Closed Mon.

dinner (352-378-7850), 11 SE 1st Ave. A newcomer to downtown, this boutique bistro serves dinner and nothing but, with a heavy emphasis on fusion foods. Starters $5–8, entrées $18–21, desserts $6–7. Adventuresome dining companions can partake in the "tasting menu" ($35 per person), where everyone at the table gets samplings from several entrées, a starter, and dessert. Opens at 6; closed Mon.

Dragonfly Sushi & Sake Company (352-371-3359), 201 SE 2nd Ave, Union Street Station. Purple walls and velvety black and red chairs accentuate the op art feel of sushi served up by Gainesville's only certified sushi chef. Lunch and dinner served à la carte ($1 per piece, $8 per roll) or as platters ($7–15).

Emiliano's Café (352-375-7381), 7 SE 1st Ave. With a daily selection of Spanish tapas, Cuban and Caribbean sandwiches, and Cuban entrées in a setting with a special Spanish-Caribbean flair, Emiliano's provides Gainesville's best choice for fine Latin cuisine. Lunch ($7–9) served Tue–Sat; dinner ($12–20) every day but Mon; Sun brunch.

Mildred's Big City Food Café and Wine Bar (352-371-1711; www.mildredsbigcityfood.com), 3445 W University Ave. Winner of numerous awards, Mildred's is a hot spot for those who love wine, good food, and desserts to die for. Setting a mood with gleaming chrome, dark wood, and snappy 1940s jazz, the **Next Door** (open 11–5, Mon–Sat) provides quick-stop diners with creative quiches, pasta du jour, salads, and sandwiches such as grilled ham and Brie, fried eggplant and prosciutto, and the delicious hummus, which comes loaded with layers of roasted peppers and a black olive tapenade on fresh focaccia (lunch $6–9). Don't walk out without a slice of cake ($5, huge portion). I couldn't resist the chocolate mocha ganache, but it was a tough choice stacked up against a raspberry whipped cream torte, a French silk torte, and the decadent Chocolate Fudge Corruption.

Panache (352-372-8446), 113 N Main St. Part of the Wine & Cheese Gallery (see *Selective Shopping*), this upscale lunch (11–2:15) spot serves up unusual daily specials, such as the sweet potato quesadilla ($7.15), a hot blue cheese and green apple sandwich ($6.50), or the cheeseboard ($9) with three cheeses, French loaf, and fruit du jour. Sandwiches $6 on your choice of bread; tasty salads, $5–6, come with homemade dressings. Daily quiche, soup du jour, dessert specials, and featured cheeses. For atmosphere, sit out in the shaded patio garden to sip your choice (4 to 10 options daily) from the wine bar ($5–6 glass). My lunch companions gave the Florida Sunshine Cake "delightful" and "scrumptious" ratings for the orange-rich flavor, delicate frosting, and white chocolate garnishes.

Paramount Grill (352-378-3398), 12 SW 1st Ave. In this sophisticated downtown European-style bistro, chef-owner Clif Nelson draws on nearly 20 years of local experience to create provocative fusion food. I enjoyed my chilled cucumber, yogurt, and almond soup du jour ($4) and artfully presented salad ($4–8), with four types of farm-fresh berries and baby asparagus over baby greens. Entrées include such creative gems as spicy Thai-style prawns with Asian vegetables, linguine, fresh basil, and coriander ($20); seared garam masala spiced tuna steak served over green onion hummus with tomato cucumber chutney, grilled papadam, and vindaloo vinaigrette ($24); and pan-roasted prime Angus fillet served over garlic mashed potatoes with shiitake mushroom sherry wine sauce, poached asparagus, puff pastry, and white truffle oil ($28.75). Lunch weekdays 11–2, dinner daily; Sun brunch 10–4. Reservations suggested.

High Springs

The Great Outdoors Trading Company and Café (386-454-2900; www.greatoutdoorscafe.com), 65 N Main St. Housed in the 1895 opera house, it's like a Cracker Barrel for hikers and paddlers; you'll be so distracted by the gear and outdoor guidebooks that your waiter will need to track you down when your table is ready. Superb entrées, fabulous service; entrées $11 and up. Open for lunch and dinner daily. Live entertainment (see *Entertainment*) Fri and Sat evenings in the Theatre of Memory, upstairs.

Melrose

Blue Water Bay (352-475-1928), 319 FL 26. With a formal dining room in shades of oceanic blue, this classy restaurant pulls in patrons all the way from Gainesville with entrées ($13–40) like lemon-steamed snow crab legs, Cajun étouffée, and their famous seafood platters. French night, Tue; buffets on Fri and Sat at 5.

BROWSE AND DINE AT THE GREAT OUTDOORS TRADING COMPANY.

Sandra Friend

Alachua

Conestogas Restaurant (386-462-1294; www.alachua.com/conestogas), 14920 Main St. Loyal customers just keep filling up the dining room at Conestogas, where they're celebrating more than 15 years in the business. In this unpretentious western-themed restaurant, you'll nibble on peanuts while waiting for one of the tender house sirloin steaks ($10–17), marinated in the family's secret marinade recipe. Burgers are the other big thing—fresh handmade burgers ($5–7) cooked the way *you* want them. The Main Street Monster Burger ($18) challenges *Guinness Book of World Records* appetites with 48 ounces of beef on an extremely oversized bun. Open for lunch and dinner; closed Sun.

Harvest Thyme Café (386-462-4633; www.harvestthymecafe.com), 14816 Main St. It's the gathering place of Alachua, somewhere to kick back and read the morning paper while sipping coffee, tea, or chai. Enjoy shakes and smoothies, fresh fruit, sandwiches, soups, salads, and wraps, $5–7; my fave is 32 South Main, stuffed full of homemade hummus. Open 8–4; menu posted on colorful chalkboard over the kitchen. Additional location at 2 W University Ave in Gainesville.

Gainesville

Bistro 1245 (352-378-2001), 706 W University Ave. This tiny speck of a café near the busiest corner in Gainesville serves fabulous lunches in a classy atmosphere: I was impressed by my choice of portobello mushroom with apple jam, smoked Gouda, and red pepper aioli on fresh bread. Sounds odd, but it works! Sandwiches run $5–10, dinner entrées $11–15; wine tastings and live jazz on Fri 5–8, Sun brunch 11–4.

Book Lovers Café (1-888-374-0090), 505 NW 13th St. Tucked inside busy Books Inc. (see *Selective Shopping*), the Book Lovers Café serves creative vegetarian and vegan salads and entrées ($3–7), going well beyond tofu burgers and sprouts. Check the artsy menu board for today's offerings, which include gourmet salads such as Thai cucumber, with crunchy fresh cucumbers in rice vinegar, and red beans in walnut sauce, a tasty combination of textures in olive oil. If you can't make up your mind, try the 3 Salad Sampler. Savor a cup of authentic Indian chai, or enjoy freshly squeezed lemonade. Seating is scattered throughout the bookstore, but if you sit near the kitchen, you'll smile at the young chefs singing along to mellow music behind the counter as they prepare your meal. Themed dinners showcase macrobiotic and ethnic foods.

Burrito Brothers Taco Company (352-378-5948; www.burritobros.com), 16 NW 13th St. Here's a Swedish chef serving up Mexican take-out—and it works. Popular student stop just off campus with vegetarian and vegan choices; don't miss the excellent fresh guacamole! $3–6; order from the web site—they ship!

Cabana Café (352-373-7003), 2445 SW 13th St. Surrounded by soft music and colorful murals, you're served up Latin delights, kicked off by a helping of fresh chips and salsa. Try one of the many unique tapas ($2–5), sandwiches served up with plantain chips ($6–7), soups, salads, or real Mexican favorites from chimichangas and *carne asada* to *mole poblano* ($6–9). Vegetarian options let you choose tacos or burritos stuffed with tofu and vegetables; I'm partial to the beef enchiladas, some of the best I've ever had. Daily lunch specials and, of course, margaritas! Open daily for lunch and dinner.

Cameo Tea Room (352-379-5889; www.cameotearoom.com), 230 NW 2nd Ave, is a classy Victorian tearoom where you don hats, gloves, and feather boas to become part of the past. Enjoy traditional tea ($8–13) served with scones, baked desserts, tea sandwiches, and soup. A gift shop is on the premises, too.

Chop Stix Café (352-367-0003), 3500 SW 13th St. Vietnamese noodle bowls, Thai and Chinese entrées, a sushi bar, and a wide variety of vegetarian choices, all presented in a soothing Asian atmosphere with giant carp and a sweeping view of the alligators cruising Bivens Arm. Fabulous food, fabulous prices—$5–8 covers everything from giant noodle bowls to combination platters. It's packed at dinner, so try them out for lunch. Closed Sun.

Copper Monkey Restaurant & Pub (352-374-4984), 1700 W University Ave. It's a popular local hangout with fabulous burgers; entrées $5–8.

David's Real Pit BBQ (352-373-2002; www.davidsbbq.com), 5121 NW 39th Ave. Cheap, fast, *and* good: It's not supposed to be possible, but this award-winning barbecue place pulls it off. Plates of barbecued ribs, chicken, beef, turkey, and pork run $7–9, hearty sandwiches $3–4, and you can choose your sauce from the "wall of fire." They even do omelets and pancakes for breakfast, $2–6. The surroundings are nothing fancy, but the food is sublime.

The Top (352-337-1188), 40 N Main St. Think *pop art* and *paint by number*: This place is a step back into the 1970s, with chairs like my 1976 high school cafeteria. But it's a hip young crowd that hangs here, with food to match: I loved the spinach salad with roasted peppers, onions, pecans, goat cheese, and a mango vinaigrette, and the speedy service made it possible to get back to my conference in record time. Lunch $5–7; dinner entrées ($8–13) like pecan-crusted tofu and ginger orange stir-fry show off the chef's creativity.

Wise's Drug Store (352-372-4371), 239 W University Ave. Since 1938, Wise's has had an old-fashioned soda fountain in their drugstore—and they charge less than $1 for a scoop of ice cream! They'll make sundaes, shakes, banana splits, and flavored sodas, too. Lunch sandwiches, burgers, and dogs for under $5. Open 8:30–4.

High Springs

Floyd's Diner (386-454-5775; www.floydsdiner.com), 615 Santa Fe Blvd. Gleaming chrome, glass block, classic hot rods, and a neon pink flamingo welcome you to a great diner experience along US 41, where you'll step back into the 1950s and sink your teeth into huge burgers, overflowing salads, and pan-sautéed pastas. There's a dizzying array of menu choices, from a BLT ($4.49 with sides) to filet mignon ($14.99), so I can only say: Explore! And save room for an old-fashioned shake or malted milk. Lunch and dinner 11:30–9 daily.

In the old railroad depot, the **Station Bakery & Cafe** (386-454-4943), 20 NW Railroad Ave, offers great sandwiches on fresh-baked bread ($2–4), including the classic "fluffernutter," as well as salads, ice cream, and fresh-baked goods. Open for lunch daily.

Keystone Heights

Johnny's Bar-B-Q Restaurant (352-473-4445), 7411 FL 21. Eat in, walk up, or drive through at this busy local icon, where families gather for great barbecue and burgers. The waitresses know everyone by name, and service is in a snap, even during the lunch rush. Historic photos and memorabilia from Keystone Heights line the walls. Daily lunch specials ($5) and dinner plates ($6–8) pack in the crowds; salads (with your choice of barbecue meat) appeal to the lighter palate.

Keystone Inn Family Restaurant (352-473-3331), FL 100 W. Just good ol'-fashioned country food, hot and cold bar, seafood and steaks. Open daily for breakfast, lunch, and dinner.

Sabo's Italian-American Restaurant (352-473-2233), 7448 FL 21. The portions are huge, the blue cheese dressing homemade, and the prices can't be beat: $7–10 for baked-to-order entrées with salad and tasty garlic rolls. My friends raved about their traditional Italian favorites at Sabo's; you won't be disappointed. Lunch and dinner; closed Mon.

Micanopy

Old Florida Café (352-466-3663), 203 NE Cholokka Blvd. A funky antiques-shop-*cum*-lunch-spot under the shade of giant live oaks, the Old Florida Café provides tasty homemade soup ($3), black beans and rice ($3), and chili ($3) as well as a gamut of "generous sandwiches," hot Cubans and Reubens ($5), and fabulous thick BLTs ($5). Browse the shelves while waiting for your order, or stake out a place on the front porch and watch the world wander past. Don't miss out on their desserts ($4), especially the piquant McIntosh wild orange pie. Open 11–4 daily.

Pearl Country Store (352-466-4025), US 441 and CR 234. On the outside, it looks like your basic convenience store. Step inside, and you'll be treated to down-home breakfast sandwiches, hotcakes, French toast, and omelets served 6–11 AM ($2–5), followed by a parade of barbecue: sandwiches ($4–5), dinner platters ($5–10), and barbecue-by-the-pound, as well as daily $2.50 dinner specials. It's all tucked away in David Carr's eclectic country store, where local baked goods, organic veggies, and books on natural Florida share the floor with more traditional convenience store fare. Barbecue served Sun–Thu 11–7, Fri and Sat 11–8.

Starke

Bobkat's Café (904-964-7997), 127 E Call St, is the only eatery in Starke that does its own baking; your sandwich is served up on thick slabs of homemade bread. Grab a cherry Coke at the old soda fountain, or sit down in a booth for a daily blue plate special like shepherd's pie, meat loaf, or a Reuben sandwich. Country music accents the country crafts (all for sale) decorating the place, and the place gets hopping at lunchtime. Serving breakfast 6:30–10 ($1–7) and lunch 11:30–2:30 ($3–6). Take a slice of homemade pie ($2) with you on the way out! Open daily; Sun lunch buffet 11–2.

✷ Entertainment

Gainesville

Check with the **Gainesville Cultural Affairs Office** (352-333-ARTS; www.gvlculturalaffairs.com) for their latest slate of **free public concerts** downtown on Fri night, presented year-round. Since this is a university town, the place to see and be seen is downtown, of course, on the patio bars and cafés surrounding Sun Center and the **Hippodrome State Theater** (352-373-5968), 25 SE 2nd Place, where vibrant live theaters take the stage. For those into student-driven nightlife, nightclubs line Main and University.

Dance aficionados enjoy the **Gainesville Ballet Theatre** (352-372-9898; www.gainesvilleballettheatre.org), 1501 NW 16th Avenue, a 30-year-old nonprofit regional ballet company; **Dance Alive!** (352-371-2986; www.dancealive.org), 1325 NW 2nd St, presents modern works and classic ballet as the State Touring Company of Florida. After 20 years, the **Gainesville Chamber Orchestra** (352-336-5448), performing at a variety of venues around the city, continues to delight its fans. One of those venues, the **Philips Center for the Performing Arts** (352-392-2787), can be counted on for a wide variety of shows.

High Springs

Above the Great Outdoors Café (see *Eating Out*), the **Theatre of Memory** coffeehouse (386-454-2900) presents live folk, bluegrass, and other down-home performances; shows run Fri and Sat at 8 PM amid a historical display of local artifacts; $7 donation. The **Priest Theater** (386-454-SHOW), 15 NW 1st Ave, is Florida's oldest movie theater, showing films on Mon, Fri, and Sat evenings for $3.50. Watch for live theater at the **High Springs Community Theatre** (386-454-2900); tickets and a playbill available at the Great Outdoors Café.

✷ Selective Shopping

Alachua

Angel Gardens (386-462-7722; www.angelgardens.com), US 441. Set in a restored Victorian farmhouse along US 441, this peaceful retreat displays fountains, statuary, antiques, plants, and garden supplies in a beautifully landscaped setting.

Exotic Boutique (386-418-8211), 14844 Main St. Take a trip back to the 1960s with incense, Asian art, embroidered Indian dresses, wall hangings, and comic books.

Little Hearts Desire (386-462-7706), 14925 Main St. A sweet little shop with local country crafts and ceramics accenting an array of consignment antiques. Closed Sun.

Evinston

Wood & Swink (352-591-1334) 18320 SE CR 225. Built in 1884 of heart pine, this general store and local post office is one of the few remaining historic post offices in the United States, complete with original decorative (and still functional!) postboxes. Postmaster Wilma, a descendant of original postmaster Fred Wood (who served for 44 years), waits on her customers amid a jumble of antiques, crafts, groceries, fresh produce, books on local culture and history, and gift items. Stop by and say hello!

Gainesville

Artisans' Guild Gallery at Greenery Square (352-378-1383; www.gainesvilleartisansguild.com), 5402

NW 8th Ave. It's *the* place in Gainesville for local art, from colorful textiles to turned wood, art glass, and pottery, in an artists' co-op representing more than local 50 artisans. Open 9–6, Sun noon–5.

Artworks Boutique and Gallery (386-454-1808), 702 W University Ave. More than 900 artists are represented in this downtown shop, an eclectic collection of pottery, jewelry, clothing, and linens mixed up with painted mirrors, scenes of Florida in acrylic and watercolor, and witch balls hanging from the gnarled limbs of a potted tree, as well as April Cornell linens and clothing, Pre de Provence soaps, and Burt's Bees products.

Books Inc. (352-384-0090), 505 NW 13th St. Roam through this house of new and used titles, surveying the book-lined walls of every room. You're sure to find something offbeat, like a well-worn tome on hiking the Caribbean or one of those fabulous Penguin travelogues published in Great Britain. Rotating exhibits by local artists grace the walls. The aromas emanating from the Book Lovers Café (see *Eating Out*) will draw you toward the kitchen before you leave. As the owners say, "Come for the books . . . stay for the food."

Brasington's Adventure Outfitters (1-888-438-4502; www.brasingtons.com), 2331 NW 13th St. If you're headed out to the trail or to one of the pristine nearby rivers, stop in and get outfitted at Brasington's, one of only a handful of outdoor adventure outfitters in Florida where you can pick up backpacking gear. With paddling equipment, camping supplies, technical clothing, and a wide variety of travel and outdoor adventure guides, you'll find everything you need for outdoor recreation in North Florida.

Goerings Book Store (352-378-0363; www.goerings.com), 3433 W University Ave. Truly a bookstore in touch with its town, this well-established independent bookseller offers an interesting intellectual mix of books, from modern fiction and nonfiction to poetry, with an emphasis on Florida authors. Gainesville best-sellers are placed prominently in the front of the store. Grab a coffee and browse Gainesville's most comprehensive newsstand, especially deep in political and spiritual enlightenment magazines. The children's section provides breadth and depth, and features little nonbook goodies like science toys and stuffed animals. Several bookcases are devoted to books on Florida, including an antiquarian section. If you're looking for an offbeat literary or artistic gift, perhaps a calendar by Edward Gorey or a set of magnetic poetry, you'll find it here. A smaller location is on the UF campus at Bageland, 1717 NW 1st Ave.

Gypsy Palace (352-379-1116), 4000 Newberry Rd. Its gaily-painted front will catch your eye as you drive down Newberry Rd, with only a hint of the exotic experience to come. Step into the shop for a true sensory experience, where a cloud of incense accents the Asian music as you browse through Rajasthani pillow covers, carvings of gods and goddesses, and clothing imported from India, Turkey, Morocco, China, and Japan.

Harold's Frames & Gallery (352-375-0260; www.haroldsframes.com), 101 SE 2nd Place. Showcases stunning images of natural Florida by local photographers.

Hyde & Zekes (352-376-1687), 1620

W University Ave. A fixture since my college days, Hyde & Zekes helps university students gain a little pocket cash while spreading a wealth of out-of-print music across Gainesville and beyond. If you're looking for small bands and independent labels, this is the place—and yes, they still sell vinyl!

Still Life in G (352-372-5155), 201 SE 2nd Ave. Step into this classy art gallery on the Hippodrome Square, featuring both local and national artists, for an eyeful of fine art. Frequent special events including weekly wine-and-cheese do's.

Thornebrook Village (352-378-4949), 2441-6D NW 43rd St. A trendy and popular collection of galleries and boutiques at the north end of Gainesville.

Wild Iris Books (352-375-7477), 802 W University Ave. It's loud, it's proud, and it's feminist. The merchandise at Wild Iris runs the gamut from raunchy greeting cards and comics to tomes on Zen Buddhism, Wicca, and artistic inspiration. The back room houses used books, while culturally sensitive children's books rate their own special corner, and the main section contains a special emphasis on strong female voices in fiction and nonfiction.

The Wine & Cheese Gallery (352-372-8446), 133 N Main St. More than 4,000 types of wine line the floor-to-ceiling shelves at this 30-year fixture in downtown Gainesville, a necessary stop for the discriminating gourmand. In addition to the perfect wine, you'll find imported chocolates, microbrew beers, and a wide array of gourmet food items. Lunch served at adjoining Panache (see *Dining Out*).

High Springs

Fitzpatrick's Irish America (386-454-0242), 30 NW 1st Ave. Irish books and music, imported foods including scone mixes and a range of teas, fine china, jewelry, mohair scarves—a little bit of all things Gaelic.

Housed in an 1895 opera house, the **Great Outdoors Trading Company and Café** (see *Dining Out*) is my kind of store—filled with gear to make hikers and paddlers very, very happy. Check out the Lexan canoes!

In a 1905 home, **Heartstrings** (386-454-4081), 215 N Main St, has a country feel, with room after room of primitives, painted windows, glass and china, and a smattering of gift items.

High Springs Emporium (386-454-8657), 625 S Main St. South of downtown, detached from the rest of the retail district, this shop has a heavy focus on beautiful Asian- and African-import home decor items: sculptures and carvings, jewelry, wall hangings, and trinkets. But the real reason to stop here is to check out their collection of rocks and minerals, with everything from New Age quartz points to assemblages of crystals that will impress the most serious mineral collector—as will the owner, who knows her stuff about geology.

High Springs Gallery (386-454-1808; www.highspringsgallery.com), 115 N Main St. Representing works from more than 700 artists (with 30 percent local content), this gallery soars with art with a natural feel, from the playful painted metal flowers and creatures of Sarasota artist Brian Meys to the large amount of art glass on display.

Take the kids to **His & Her Hobby**

Shop (386-454-5365), 65 NW 1st Ave, for a real treat—a huge eight-car slot car track where they can race each other. Their stock also includes model aircraft and model trains, including HO and N track and cars.

Joann's Antiques, Gifts, and Collectibles (386-454-7505), 70 N Main St, intersperses McCoy pottery, classic glass, and Barbie dolls with large items like 1890s cash registers and huge measuring scales.

Main Street Antique Mall (386-454-2700), 10 S Main St, is chock-full of small items like saltcellars, antique glassware, and kitchen items.

Main Street Stained Glass Studio (386-454-1611), 206 Main St. An open, airy presentation of art glass by local artists, with mosaics, wall hangings, lamps, and sun catchers; stained-glass supplies and classes found in the back.

Paddywhack (386-454-3751; www.paddiwhack.com), 25 NE 1st Ave. "Art for Life" is the theme of this most eclectic of art shops, where creativity molds colorful, playful, vibrant pieces ranging from mirrors and wall hangings to large pieces of furniture, each signed by one of the many artists represented.

Wisteria Cottage (386-454-8447), 225 N Main St. A true period piece, this tin-roofed Cracker home with bead board walls and ceilings has numerous spacious rooms filled with country crafts and collectibles, a kitchen filled with gourmet foods, and an Americana room.

Keystone Heights

Nobody's Teddy (352-473-9996), 330-A S Lawrence Blvd. A sweet little shop featuring teddy bears, teddy bears, and more teddy bears; home decor items and Yankee candles. Open 10–6; closed Sun.

Melrose

Ann Lowry Antiques (352-475-2924), 1658 SE 5th Ave, housed in a historic church under a canopy of ancient live oaks, showcases classy home decor items and furnishings. Ann shares the building with **East Coast Antiques** (352-475-5771), which offers an eclectic selection of furniture, books, home ephemera, and a bargain basement with more books and board games.

Melrose Bay Gallery (352-375-3866), 103 FL 26, represents fine regional artists in a variety of media. Open Fri–Sun.

Micanopy

One of the top antiquing towns in Florida, downtown Micanopy dates back to the 1820s. Enough shops crowd Cholokka Blvd (Micanopy's "Main Street") to allow you to spend the entire day shopping. Some of my favorites include:

O'Brisky Books Inc. (352-466-3910), 112 NE Cholokka Blvd. Bursting with books, O'Brisky deals mostly in used nonfiction, and features an excellent Florida section in the front of the store. Bring your want list—I've been surprised at the gems I've discovered in the stacks, and manager Gary Nippes runs a free search service for those tough-to-find items.

Tyson Trading Company (352-466-3410), 505 Cholokka Blvd. With its focus on antique Florida art, Tyson's started the statewide craze for painting by the "Highwaymen," a group of African American artists trained by A. E. Backus. In the 1950s these artists sold their impressionistic Florida landscapes by the side of the road.

Now one of their paintings—all of which capture the spirit of Old Florida—will set you back $2,000 or more. Isaac (a Highwaymen painter) and Lily Knight oversee the adjacent Highwaymen Gallery, and it's a pleasure to talk with them. Tyson's also deals in folk art, miniature buildings, and Seminole quilting and dolls. Open Thu–Sun.

The Twisted Sister (352-466-4040), 108 Cholokka Blvd. Dealing in vintage clothing from the 1890s to the 1970s, milliner Sharon Sutley can set you up in the perfect period attire.

The Micanopy Country Store (352-466-05100), 202 Cholokka Blvd. Open daily. Focus on antique glassware, dishes, and bottles, including those elusive milk bottles.

House of Hirsch Too (352-466-3744), 209 Cholokka Blvd. High-end antique furnishings, modern quilts, and home decor items.

The Garage at Micanopy, Inc. (352-288-8485), 212 Cholokka Blvd. Fun ephemera fills the booths in this 1920s garage, from figurines and postcards to toys and glassware at reasonable prices.

The Shop (352-466-4031), 210 Cholokka Blvd. Every nook and cranny brims with botanical gifts in this garden-themed shop, where you'll also find crafts, antique glassware and furnishings, and quilts. Closed Tue.

Treasured Collection by Macy (352-466-8000), 190 Cholokka Blvd. Macy's salute to Victoriana includes flower-topped women's hats, original art and prints, and a secret garden behind the store.

Smiley's Antique Mall (352-466-0707), CR 234 and I-75 (Micanopy exit). With more than 200 booths, this mini mall of antiques will keep you browsing for hours. Open daily 9–6.

Starke

When I was a kid, US 301 was Main Street for tourists headed down to Central Florida, and the shops and attractions along the way were geared to wide-eyed northerners. Signs proclaimed RARE 16 FOOT ALBINO ALLIGATOR!, SEE THE WALKING CATFISH!, and FREE ORANGE JUICE! Most of those old-time tourist traps (and I say that with affection) are now gone, but the stretch of US 301 north from Starke to Lawtey hosts a few hangers-on. At **Textile Town** (904-964-4250), housed in an old Stuckey's, you can

TYSON'S SELLS PAINTINGS BY FLORIDA'S FAMED "HIGHWAYMEN."

Sandra Friend

nab chenille bedspreads, towels by the pound, and T-shirts at three for $10. With its giant tepee out front, the **Silver Lining American Indian Trading Post** (904-964-5448) has Native crafts, moccasins, antiques, and turquoise jewelry. And a former Horne's restaurant hosts **Florida Souvenir Land**, with pecans and candies, T-shirts and towels, and all sorts of ticky-tacky ephemera that the kids will love.

Scarlett's Custom Framing and Gallery (904-964-9353), 139 East Call St, deals in antique advertising and sheet music, as well as a fine selection of quilts. Thu–Sat.

Forget-Me-Not Antiques and Gifts (904-964-2004), 320 Call St, the largest shop in town, has primitives and home decor items; full place settings of dishes are shown off on antique dining room tables.

Waldo

Waldo Antique Village (352-468-3111), US 301. Adjoining the flea market, this big barn full of antiques has been around for more than 20 years—the large farm implements outside are just a sample of the primitives and country items you'll find here. Open daily.

Waldo Farmer's and Flea Market (352-468-2255), US 301. *The* reason to stop in Waldo: a sprawling complex of more than 800 vendors across 40 acres on both sides of the highway, showcasing the best produce that North Florida has to offer. Sat and Sun 7–4.

FARMER'S MARKETS, PRODUCE STANDS, AND U-PICK

Gainesville

Alachua County Farmer's Market (352-371-8236), 5920 NW 13th St, corner of US 441 and FL 121. Fresh produce from local farmers, Sat 8:30–1.

Downtown Farmer's Market (352-334-7175). Fruits and plants, vegetables and fruits—bountiful local produce stacked up at the corner of SE 1st St and University Ave. Wed 4–6:30 PM.

Union Street Farmer's Market (352-462-3192), downtown at the Hippodrome. Local produce, baked goods, candles, plants, and live acoustic music. Wed 4–7:30 PM.

Hawthorne

Brown's Produce (352-475-2015), FL 26 east of US 301. A permanent roadside stand selling straight from the farm; stop in for fresh honey, veggies, and fruits.

High Springs

High Springs Farmer's Market, next to the railroad tracks, downtown, has local vendors with seasonal fresh produce. Thu 4–7 PM.

Starke

In addition to the **Starke State Farmer's Market**, US 301, and **Wainwright's Pecans, Produce, and Seafood** (904-964-5811), 302 N Temple Ave, the bountiful produce of Bradford County (well known for its excellent strawberries) fills fruit and vegetable stands all along US 301 from Starke north to Lawtey. Some are permanent locations, like **Kings Kountry Produce** (904-964-2552), N US 301, open daily, and **Norman's Roadside Market** (904-964-9152), US 301; others are transient stands that show up during the growing season.

✷ Special Events

March: **Spring Garden Festival**, Kanapaha Botanical Gardens (see *Botanical Gardens*), Gainesville. A weekend's worth of gardening tips, landscaping tricks, and environmental awareness set in the beauty of this region's largest garden.

April: **Farm & Forest Festival**, Morningside Nature Center (see *Nature Centers*), Gainesville, features cane grinding and other pioneer crafts, displays of fire engines, and hands-on activities for the kids.

May: **High Springs Pioneer Days** (386-454-3120; www.highsprings.com). Annual celebration of local history, arts and crafts, held the first weekend of the month.

June: **Yulee Day**, Archer, second Sat. Celebrating the birthday of David Levy Yulee, Florida's first U.S. senator and founder of the Florida Railroad, the town that was his home hosts exhibits, crafts, and vendors at the historic railroad depot.

November: **Alachua County Fair** (352-372-1537; www.alachuacountyfair.org), first week, at the fairgrounds on 39th Ave, Gainesville. A traditional county fair attracting farmers from around the region, showing off their cattle, chickens, vegetables, and more in friendly competition. Top country music acts and exhibitions from vendors; fee.

Micanopy Fall Harvest Festival, Micanopy (352-466-7026; www.afn.org/~micafest). Since 1973, this celebration of harvesttime brings together artisans, craftspeople, and musicians with more than 200 display booths throughout town.

FEBRUARY **Hoggtown Medieval Faire** (352-334-ARTS), at the Alachua County Fairgrounds, 39th Ave, Gainesville. The largest and longest-running (18 years in 2004) Renaissance Faire in Florida, the Hoggtown Medieval Faire spans two weekends each February with active participation by the Society for Creative Anachronism, a playful bunch that usually keep their events off-limits to the public. At Hoggtown more than a third of the crowd dresses in medieval drag; it's a place to get in touch with your inner knight (or princess), where wandering minstrels strum on mandolins; fairies, dwarves, and witches roam the streets; and the vendors take "Lady Visa and Master Card." Kids will have a blast with street theater, magic shows, medieval carnival games, and manually powered amusement rides you won't see anywhere else, like the Barrel of Bedlam and the Hippogriff. Vendors include an alchemist with real charms, tarot readers and other mediums, and artisans crafting in fiber, wood, and wax. Even the food court is a little different: You'll see knights fresh off the battlefield toasting each other with cobalt bottles of frothing cherry ale. Daily events include jousting, live chess battles, and the court processional through the streets of Hoggtown. Fee.

THE LOWER SUWANNEE

PURE WATER WILDERNESS: DIXIE, GILCHRIST, AND LEVY COUNTIES

If you've come to Florida for peace and quiet, you'll find it "way down upon the Suwannee River" in the Pure Water Wilderness, a region known best for its rivers, springs, and estuaries. Settlers trickled into the region in the 1850s when state senator David Yulee (son of Moses Levy, founder of Levy County) ran his Florida Railroad from Fernandina Beach to **Cedar Key**, providing the first shipping link across Florida. In 1867 naturalist John Muir followed the path of the Florida Railroad on his 1,000-mile walk to the Gulf of Mexico. Arriving at the Cedar Keys, he fell ill with malaria and spent several months living in the village, which had a booming pencil industry. The fine southern red cedars and white cedars growing on scattered islands throughout the Gulf made the perfect housing for pencil leads. The original settlement on Atsena Otie Key included several houses and the Eberhard Faber Pencil Mill. After the island was devastated by a tidal surge in 1896, business shifted to Depot Key, today's downtown Cedar Key.

Cedar Key sits between the mouth of the Withlacoochee River, on which the towns of **Yankeetown** and **Inglis** sprang up, and the mouth of the Suwannee River, home to the fishing village of **Suwannee**. The railroad line (now the Nature Coast State Trail, a rail-trail) connected Fanning Springs, where Fort Fannin was built along the river in 1838 as part of a chain of forts during the Seminole Wars, with the turpentine and lumber towns of **Old Town** and **Cross City**. On the southern shore of the Steinhatchee River, the fishing village of **Jena** grew up around the abundant mullet and crab, with packing houses shipping out seafood to distant ports. Dixie County boasts the lowest per-capita population in the state, and Gilchrist County has only a single traffic light, at the crossroads in the county seat of **Trenton**. Sleepy riverside hamlets and end-of-the-road fishing villages provide a natural charm found only in rural Florida.

GUIDANCE **Pure Water Wilderness** (352-486-5470; www.purewaterwilderness.com), P.O. Box 779, Cedar Key 32625, is the primary contact for the region, which comprises six distinct chambers of commerce.

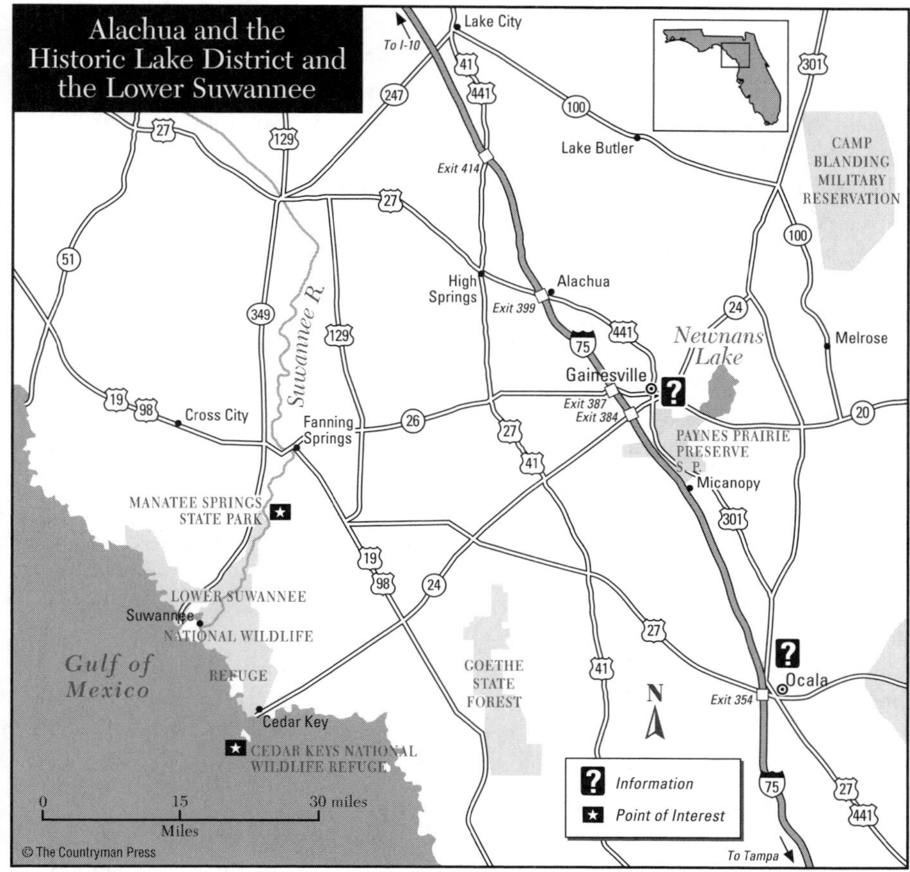

GETTING THERE *By air*: Gainesville (see "Alachua and the Historic Lake District") provides the only "nearby" commuter access, an hour or more from most points on the Nature Coast.

By bus: **Greyhound** stops along US 19 in Cross City and Chiefland.

By car: **Alt US 27**, **US 129**, **US 27**, and **US 19** are the major north–south routes through this trio of rural counties. To reach them from **I-75**, use **US 27** from Ocala or High Springs, or **FL 24** or **FL 26** west out of Gainesville.

MEDICAL EMERGENCIES Serious emergencies should be deferred to Crystal River (see "Nature Coast") or Gainesville (see "Alachua and the Historic Lake District"); call 911. For lesser problems, contact the **Cedar Key Health Clinic** (352-543-5132) or the **Nature Coast Regional Hospital** (352-528-2801), US 41, Williston.

Important: In these rural counties, cell phone coverage is sporadic to nonexistent, depending on your carrier.

✷ To See

ARCHEOLOGICAL SITES At the end of CR 347 in the **Shell Mound Unit** of Lower Suwannee NWR (see *Wild Places*), a short trail takes you to the most significant archeological feature in this region, a 28-foot-tall shell midden created between 2500 B.C. and A.D. 1000 by the ancestors of the Timucua who once inhabited this coastline. Just off CR 351 at Old Railroad Grade in Dixie County, the **Garden Patch Archeological Site** at Horseshoe Beach has several burial and ceremonial mounds and two large middens.

HISTORIC SITES **Atsena Otie Key**, abandoned by most of its settlers after an 1896 hurricane-driven storm surge, is now part of the **Cedar Key NWR** (see *Wild Places*), only accessible by boat (see *Ecotours* and *Paddling*). Buried under cover of maritime hammock along the short hiking trail from the dock are reminders that this was the original town of Cedar Key. Bricks scattered around a deep hole are all that's left of the Eberhard Faber Pencil Mill. The deep hole contained the machinery of the mill, driven by water flowing through a sluice. Workers sawed cedars into the small slats required for making pencils. In an ironic twist of nature, a grand cedar now crowns the spot. The trail ends at the town's cemetery, set on a bluff overlooking the salt marshes. The marble tombstones date back to 1882, some fallen, some as clean as the day they were erected. A wrought-iron fence cordons off one tiny corner, a private family plot under the windswept oaks. Seahorse Key, part of the island chain, has a small cemetery with Union soldiers who died while occupying the **Seahorse Key Lighthouse**, which can be visited twice a year on open-house days: during the fall seafood festival and on the first Sat of July.

In Fanning Springs work is under way to reconstruct **Fort Fanning** on its original site just north of US 19. Back in 1838, U.S. Army troops built and manned a small wooden fortress at the river crossing, Palmetto, as part of a string of defenses during the Second Seminole War. Renamed Fort Fannin in honor of Colonel Alexander Fannin, the name became corrupted over time to Fanning. As the war raged on and Fannin attempted to round up Seminoles for deportation to the West, the garrison grew from a dozen men to nearly 200 in 1843. Yellow fever ravaged the troops. Abandoned in 1849, the remains of the fort vanished back into the forest.

RAILROADIANA Although the railroad no longer carries cypress logs through Bell, the **historic train depot** (circa 1905) along US 129 now houses the town hall. On US 19 in Cross City, the old **railway freight station** sits along the rail-trail near Barber Avenue; you'll find the Chiefland **railway depot** undergoing restoration at the southern terminus of the Nature Coast State Trail (see *Greenways*). At Cedar Key the **depot** marking the historic **western terminus of the Florida Railroad** is still on Railroad St, but the trestle leading to the coast has been obliterated by condos. South on US 19, watch for "3 Spot," a **steam engine** circa 1915 in a small wayside park just north of the blinker at Gulf Hammock. One of the few pieces of original rolling stock displayed in Florida, it pulled logging cars to the Patterson-McInnes sawmill.

MUSEUMS

Cedar Key

Cedar Key Historical Society Museum (352-543-5549), 609 2nd St. Exhibits and artifacts trace the history of this coastal town from its founding through Civil War occupation, the rise and fall of the pencil industry, and current advances in aquaculture; an excellent resource for researchers and amateur historians in understanding Florida's Gulf Coast. Open Mon–Sat and holidays 11–4, Sun 1–4; donation.

Cedar Key Museum Historic State Park (352-543-5340). Follow the signs out through the residential area to this large compound established in 1962 as the first museum to capture Cedar Key's long history as presented by St. Clair Whitman, a colorful local man who started his own personal museum of artifacts and seashells. Whitman's house is under restoration on the property; a small trail leads along the edge of the estuary. Closed Mon and Tue; fee.

SEAHORSE KEY LIGHTHOUSE

Sandra Friend

Levyville

♿ Amid the farms and fields of Levy County, quilting is one of the favored pastimes. At the **Levy County Quilt Museum** (352-493-2801), 11050 NW 10th Ave, quilters come together to perfect their craft. The modern log structure contains plenty of space for active quilting while displaying prizewinning quilts (and other related handicrafts) around the rooms.

WINERY ♿ **Dakotah Winery & Vineyards** (352-493-9309; www.dakotahwinery.com), 14365 NW US 19, Chiefland. Established in 1985, this premier Florida winery features wines and other products produced from cultivated muscadine grapes. It's a unique place with a touch of the romantic: Antique windmills stand tall over the vineyard, and visitors relax under an arbor overlooking the vines and a duck pond. Inside the tasting room, owner Rob Rittgers buzzes around, answering questions and pouring wine for each new group of guests. Art fills the spacious room, from hand-painted wine bottles with Florida scenes to woodcraft, paintings, quilts, and sketches by local artists. Mon–Sat 10–5, Sun noon–5.

* To Do

BICYCLING On the **Nature Coast Trail** (see *Greenways*), enjoy a 32-mile paved bike path connecting the communities of the Lower Suwannee. Mountain bikers frequent the trail system at **Manatee Springs State Park** (see *Springs*).

BIRDING You'll always see pelicans at the **Cedar Key dock**, but don't miss the Pelican Man, who tosses fish to a crowd of pelicans every evening. At **Cedar Key NWR** (see *Wild Places*), each island has colonial bird rookeries and beautiful beaches; beware of the high snake population in forested areas. **Seahorse Key** is off-limits to all visitors Mar–June due to its fragile pelican rookery. **Lower Suwannee NWR** (see *Wild Places*) offers great birding opportunities along the trails at the **Shell Island Unit**, where you'll see Louisiana herons, willets, and other wading birds in shallow saline ponds near Dennis Creek, and belted kingfishers along the hammocks. In spring follow the **Road to Nowhere** (see *Scenic Drives*) through the **Jena Unit of Big Bend WMA**, and take the side roads (if wet, only navigable by four-wheel drive or on foot) west to the Gulf hammocks to see seaside sparrows, clouds of migratory birds (from robins to vireos and warblers), and nesting pairs of black rails. At any time, you'll see wading birds roadside in the salt marshes.

BOATING For a map of boat ramps along the **Suwannee River**, contact the Suwannee River Water Management District (386-362-1001); one of the easiest to access is off US 19-98 at the Gilchrist-Dixie county line. Recreational boaters enjoy playing on a segment of the **Cross Florida Barge Canal** accessed at Inglis, off US 19. In **Cedar Key** parking gets tight around the public marina (downtown) on weekend mornings. **Island Hopper Tours** (352-543-5904; www.cedarkeyislandhopper.com), City Marina, rents boats and provides guided tours and drop-offs (see *Ecotours*) on the **Gulf of Mexico**. At **Suwannee** several marinas provide access to the Suwannee River and the Gulf of Mexico.

DIVING Scuba divers have several unique venues to try out their skills. At **Devil's Den** near Williston (see *Lodging*), a shimmering pool of 72-degree ice-blue water fills an ancient cave. As you descend stone steps to access the open water underground, a chandelier of ivy dangles down through the sinkhole, with rays of sunlight filtering through the opening. It's a surreal and beautiful scene. Divers delight in discovering prehistoric fossils on the limestone bottom. Dive fee $27, additional $10 for night dives, gear rental $62 (includes dive fee). Cave certification not required. Full dive shop and instruction on site. At nearby **Blue Grotto** (352-528-5770; www.divebluegrotto.com), 3852 NE 172nd Court, cave-certified divers can descend up to 100 feet into the Floridan Aquifer, dropping down into a cave system from the bottom of a sinkhole; dive shop with rentals on site. The many springs of the **Suwannee River** are open to open-water diving, but only cave-certified divers should venture *into* the crevices from which the waters pour. **Wreck diving** is a popular pastime, as divers can visit sunken steamboats such as the *City of Hawkinsville*, the very last of the Suwannee River steamboats, sunk just south of Fanning Springs in 1922. It's a designated underwater archeological preserve. For support, check with **Suwannee River Scuba** (352-463-7111), 17950 NW 90th Court, for guided trips, cold air, rentals, and instruction.

ECOTOURS **Island Hopper Tours** (see *Boating*). Catch a ride out to the outer islands of the Cedar Keys with the Island Hopper, offering island drop-offs (perfect for exploring Atsena Otie or Seahorse Key), 1-hour scenic cruises, and sunset cruises. $12 adults, $6 children under 12.

🐾 **Lady Pirate Boat Tours** (352-543-5141), Slip 16, City Marina. Take the 22-foot pontoon on any of several tour options—bird-watching, sand dollar collecting, sunset trips, or island drop-offs. $12 adults, $6 children.

Nature Coast Expeditions (352-543-6463) runs photographers' field trips along the Suwannee River and the Cedar Keys; enjoy an afternoon with a professional guide for $75 for up to three people.

Paddle with Brack Barker at **Wild Florida Adventures** (1-877-WILD-WAV; www.wild-florida.com), where you'll explore the estuaries at a leisurely pace; destinations include Cedar Key, Steinhatchee, Waccassa, and Suwannee, and half-day tours ($50) include a gourmet picnic.

FISHING For recommended fishing guides and charters in **Cedar Key**, check with the Cedar Key Chamber of Commerce (see *Guidance*). Bait and tackle are available at **Fishbonz** (352-543-9222) in Cedar Key. In Suwannee the full-service **Suwannee Marina** (352-542-9159), 219 Canal St, has a boat ramp, charters, dry dock, gasoline, bait and tackle, and mechanics on site. At Inglis, **Lake Rousseau** is a hot spot for bass anglers; check in at the fish camps (see *Fish Camps*) along CR 40 for guides.

A LAZY DAY FISHING THE ESTUARY NEAR SHELL MOUND

Sandra Friend

HIKING Hiking in the region is limited to short day hikes leading out to scenic points along the Suwannee River and the Gulf estuaries, mainly in the **Lower Suwannee National Wildlife Refuge** and state parks; I especially enjoy the nature trails at **Manatee Springs State Park**. At **Andrews Wildlife Management Area**, trails lead past state and national grand champion trees.

HOUSEBOATING **Miller's Suwannee Houseboats** (see *Fish Camps*) rents houseboats for cruises up the 70-mile meander of the Suwannee River from Suwannee to Fanning Springs—head out for an overnight, a few days, or a week. You have all the amenities of home, minus the yard, as you drift past shorelines crowded with red maple and sweetgum, and sight a manatee or two. Rates vary by season and number of days, starting at $400 for 2 days and going up to $1,300 for a week; special deals for active military personnel on leave.

HUNTING Off US 19 in Fanning Springs, **Andrews Wildlife Management Area** (386-758-0531) is a popular fall hunting ground for deer and wild hogs.

PADDLING Freshwater paddlers have numerous launch points into the **Suwannee River**; contact the Suwannee River Water Management District (386-362-1001) for a map. There are canoe liveries at Manatee Springs State Park, Fanning Springs State Park, and Hart Springs Park, and rentals are available at some of the riverside campgrounds such as Big Oaks River Resort (see *Campgrounds*).

Outfitters with rentals for exploration of the Cedar Keys include **Fishbonz** (352-543-9922) and **Nature Coast Expeditions** (352-543-6463). From Cedar Key, you can launch into numerous wilderness waterways; see *Wild Places* for details. With or without a guide, there are hundreds of miles of saltwater passageways to explore. The southern terminus of Florida's longest and most rugged sea kayaking route, the 91-mile **Historic Big Bend Saltwater Paddling Trail**, is the town of Suwannee. From there, you follow the coastline north along the Big Bend Aquatic Preserve, with stops at Shired Island, Horseshoe Beach, and Sink Creek before reaching Steinhatchee to begin rounding the Big Bend (see "The Big Bend"). This is a vast wilderness area, so don't set out unless you have appropriate maps and navigational aids, camping gear, and an adequate supply of fresh water and food. Obtain information about the trail from the Office of Greenways and Trails (850-488-3701), 325 John Knox Rd, Bldg 500, Tallahassee 32303. For a gentler immersion in this part of the Gulf estuary, head down the Road to Nowhere (see *Scenic Drives*) and put your kayak in at the **Cow Creek** Bridge, where a maze of estuarine waterways cut through the plain of black needlerush out to the Gulf. Similarly, you can launch into the creeks off the Dixie Mainline Trail (see *Scenic Drives*), but be sure you find somewhere to park that isn't blocking the road. On a day trip into the estuary, consider carrying a GPS, and make sure you mark a waypoint at your car so you can find it again.

SCALLOPING Charters run from **Gulfstream Marina** (352-498-8088; www.gulfstreammotelmarina.com), CR 358 in Jena, where they'll be happy to set you up with a captain who knows the prime scalloping grounds. See "The Big Bend" for more details on this unique take on fishing along the Gulf of Mexico.

SCENIC DRIVES Imagine, if you will, a lengthy paved road in the wildest and most inaccessible portion of a generally wild and inaccessible part of Florida, ending abruptly in the salt marshes of the Big Bend Aquatic Preserve: the **Road to Nowhere**. This highway didn't access a single home or a fishing pier: It was a clandestine airstrip. During the 1970s and 1980s, smugglers landed planes as big as a DC-9 on this highway to drop off loads of marijuana destined for points north. After the operation was shut down by law enforcement, a legacy remains—a ribbon of pavement with unparalleled views of the salt marshes, now used by anglers and paddlers, bikers and birders. One warning: If you drive down the Road to Nowhere, there are two short unpaved sections. Don't go too fast on the second one, or you'll miss the end of the road—and end up in the salt marsh! The Road to Nowhere runs through the Jena WMA (see *Wild Places*), and is most easily accessed from CR 358 from the Steinhatchee Bridge (see "The Big Bend").

Showcasing the remote southern fringe of Dixie County in Lower Suwannee Wildlife Refuge, the **Dixie Mainline Trail** is a one-of-a-kind scenic drive, a 9-mile one-lane hard-packed limestone road through the wilds of the cypress-and-gum floodplain of the California Swamp, with one short stop at Salt Creek for a walk out on a boardwalk. Don't expect to drive more than 20 mph, and keep alert for oncoming traffic. There are pull-offs every mile to allow vehicles to pass. Check with the refuge before utilizing the drive to ensure it's not flooded.

ALONG THE ROAD TO NOWHERE

Sandra Friend

SKYDIVING At **Skydive Williston** (352-528-2994; www.skydivewilliston.com), US 41 just south of Williston, you can tandem jump with professional instructors certified with USPA as you learn to skydive.

SWIMMING For refreshing plunges into cool, fresh water, try the swimming area at **Fanning Springs State Park** and the open springs at **Hart Springs** and **Blue Spring** (see *Springs*). At **Cedar Key City Park**, a small waterfront park adjacent to the City Marina provides the village's only public beach on the Gulf of Mexico; several motels have their own private beaches, but the best ones are found on the outer islands, accessed only by boat. Shallow Gulf waters invite at **Shired Island** and **Horseshoe Beach**.

TRAIL RIDING **Goethe State Forest** (see *Wild Places*) is a favorite for trail riding, with more than 100 miles of equestrian trails. Look for trailheads at Black Prong, Apex, and Tidewater along CR 336. Equestrians can also parallel the paved Nature Coast Trail (see *Greenways*).

WALKING TOURS Stop in at the Cedar Key Historical Society Museum (see *Museums*) for the official walking tour of **Cedar Key**, which leads you past sites in the old town and explains the history of the outlying islands.

✷ Green Space

GREENWAYS From its start in Dixie County at Cross City, the 32-mile **Nature Coast Trail** (352-493-6072) forks in Fanning Springs. One prong heads east to Trenton, ending at the historic train depot; the other heads south to end at the Chiefland railroad depot. Equestrians may use the grassy strip parallel to the paved biking trail.

SPRINGS There's a big reason they call this the Pure Water Wilderness—fresh water abounds! Large public springs accessible by road include **Poe Springs Park** (386-454-1992), a 197-acre county park with rolling hills and steep bluffs along the Santa Fe River, and **Ginnie Springs** (386-454-7188; www.ginniespringsoutdoors.com), a 200-acre park that's a mecca for cave divers. Open 8 AM–sunset; canoe and tube rentals available. **Hart Springs** at Hart Springs Park (352-463-3444), 4240 SW 86th Ave, is a Gilchrist County park with swimming, hiking, and camping; the crystalline spring pours out 62 million gallons each day. **Fanning Springs** at Fanning Springs State Park (352-463-3420), US 19-27, has a well-developed swimming area and canoe rentals. **Manatee Springs** at Manatee Springs State Park (352-493-6072), NW 115th St, outside Chiefland, has swimming, boating, fishing, hiking and biking trails, and a large campground. At the end of CR 339A off Alt US 27 between Bronson and Chiefland, **Blue Spring** creates a natural 72-degree pool as it feeds the Waccasassa River. Spend an afternoon picnicking under the shady oaks at this Levy County park. Fee for all but Blue Spring; contact the Suwannee River Water Management District for a map of additional spring locations in the Suwannee River for diving and swimming.

WILD PLACES Encompassing more than 40,000 acres, the **Lower Suwannee National Wildlife Refuge** (352-493-0238), 16450 NW 31st Place, protects the floodplain of the Suwannee River as it reaches the Gulf of Mexico. Most of it is inaccessible except by boat, although there are short hiking trails at Shell Mound and the park headquarters. In Fanning Springs, **Andrews Wildlife Management Area** (386-758-0531) off US 27 is notable for the number of national and state champion trees in its dark riverside forests, reached by dirt roads and short hiking trails. Near Blue Spring, **Devil's Hammock WMA** off Alt US 27 is crisscrossed with old logging roads usable for hiking, biking, and horseback riding; be mindful of hunting season for your own safety. Extending through most of southern Levy County, **Goethe State Forest** (352-447-2202), 8250 SE CR 336, has three large tracts for recreation. At **Cedar Key Scrub State Reserve** (386-758-0531) off FL 24, hikers meander through a coastal scrub, rare in this wetland region. Hunters make more use of **Jena WMA**, a massive preserve along the Road to Nowhere (see *Scenic Drives*), where rugged side roads reach pristine beaches along the grassy shores of the Gulf estuary.

Sandra Friend

NESTING PELICANS, CEDAR KEY NATIONAL WILDLIFE RESERVE

Boaters and paddlers have an extensive watery wilderness to explore. In addition to the backwaters of the Lower Suwannee NWR and the 90-mile **Big Bend Aquatic Preserve** to the north of Suwannee (see *Paddling*), they can visit the islands making up **Cedar Key National Wildlife Refuge** (352-493-0238), off Cedar Key. And at **Waccasassa Bay State Preserve** (352-493-0238), 31,000 acres between Cedar Key and Yankeetown, boaters have the place all to themselves—it's a wet wilderness suitable for paddling and fishing, with primitive campsites available to paddlers.

✱ Lodging

BED & BREAKFASTS

Cedar Key 32625

Cedar Key Bed & Breakfast (352-543-9000 or 1-877-543-5051; www.cedarkeyBandB.com), corner of 3rd and F Sts, P.O. Box 701. Innkeepers Bill and Alice Philips take you back in time to Cedar Key's heyday as an exporter of fine cedar for buildings and pencils. Built in 1880, this home was used as a boardinghouse by the daughter of one of Florida's first senators, David Levy Yulee. Within an easy walk of shopping and the docks, it's an ideal place to unwind under the paddle fans with a good book. Five romantic rooms and a Honeymoon Cottage, each decked out with period antiques, $95–135.

Island Hotel (352-543-5111 or 1-800-432-4640; www.islandhotel-cedarkey.com), 2nd and B Sts. Don't look for right angles in this historic tabby-and-oak hotel, built just before the Civil War—it's the place in town to sleep with history. Each room ($80–125) has a private bath; full breakfast in the restaurant downstairs is included with your stay.

Inglis 34449

Pine Lodge Country Lodge (352-447-7463; www.pinelodgefla.com), 649 CR 40 W. Enjoy lazy days and quiet nights amid romantic Victorian decor (rooms and cabins, $99–149) in this charming inn, where a beautiful sunset is just steps away on the antique porch rockers. Elvis fans will appreciate being immersed in part of the set of *Follow That Dream*, which was filmed along this highway out to the Gulf.

Old Town 32680

Suwannee River Inn (352-542-0613), HC 3, Box 206, US 19. A Victorian-style home with a river view: the only one along the Lower Suwannee. Five beautifully appointed rooms and landscaped grounds leading down to the river, $69–119; pontoon boat rentals available.

Suwannee 32692

The Pelican's Roost (352-542-9712 or 1-888-91-ROOST), 23566 CR 349, at the end of the road, overlooks a vast sweep of estuary where Salt Creek meets the many mouths of the Suwannee River. Outside their spacious rooms ($75–125), guests share a massive great room with a wraparound view; hosts Frank and Margie Narki provide complimentary bicycles and canoes.

Williston 32696

The Ivy House (352-528-5130), 106 NW Main St. Built by the founder of Williston, the Ivy House once served as a hospital. You wouldn't guess that today by the broad parlor filled with Victorian furnishings, nor by the three bedrooms (Blue Willow, Rose, and Wisteria), each bed piled with pillows, each room with its own private bath. With breakfasts prepared by the kitchen staff of the adjoining fine-dining Ivy House restaurant (see *Dining Out*), you'll be in the lap of luxury.

Yankeetown 34498

Izaak Walton Lodge (1-800-611-5758; www.izaakwaltonlodge.com), One 63rd St. Two riverside efficiency units ($69) at a fishing lodge with a long history: It's the site of the founding of the Izaak Walton League, a conservationist organization more than a century old, and the Compleat Angler Restaurant (see *Dining Out*).

Circa 1924, the first schoolhouse in Yankeetown is now the **Whippoorwill House** (352-447-3510; www.whippoorwillhouse.net), 6202 Riverside Dr, where Matt and Gail Fleming invite you to join them in their celebration of Yankeetown's history—you'll find artifacts and historic photos throughout the building. In the Schoolhouse Room, a historic real estate pamphlet selling the town to northerners is a great read, and you'll appreciate the full tub with dual showers; the Tarpon Room opens onto a pleasant screened porch. Upstairs, the Loft has enough room to house a family—two full beds and a twin. Rooms run $99; special fishing trip packages available.

HOTELS AND MOTELS

Cedar Key 32625

Although it's one of the older lodges on Dock Street, **Dockside Motel** (1-800-541-5432; www.dockside-cedarkey.com), 491 Dock St, delivers with large well-kept suites overlooking either the marina or the Gulf ($55–77; Captains Quarters with full kitchen $85). Open up those massive picture windows and let the sea breeze pour through. Ten units; small pets accepted.

Faraway Inn Motel & Cottages (352-543-5330; www.farawayinn.com), 3rd and G Sts. Harking back to vacation memories, the rooms and cottages ($90) at the Faraway Inn sweep you back into the great age of Florida tourism—the funky beach cottage of the 1940s. Small pets accepted.

The Gulf Side Motel (1-888-543-5308), P.O. Box 3. Located at the very end of FL 24, the 1950s Gulf Side Motel sits right on the Gulf, enabling visitors to kick back and relax on the fishing pier, porch swing, or Adirondack chairs overlooking the Gulf of Mexico. Neat and nautically decorated, all rooms have been renovated and are nonsmoking. Choose from efficiencies ($65–75) or standard rooms ($55–60), and be sure to check out Room 8, with its great Gulf view. Nine units; small pets accepted.

Harbour Master Suites (1-800-559-6327; www.cedarkeyharbourmaster.com), 390 Dock St. Settling in for an extended stay? Here's luxury for you—a choice of six suites with apartment-style amenities, available by the night, week, or month. Rates start at $70. Each suite features tastefully furnished rooms with large windows; two provide full kitchen.

Sawgrass Motel (352-543-5007), P.O. Box 658. Perched above the classy Sawgrass Gallery (see *Selective Shopping*) on Dock St, this duo of immaculate rooms ($70) overlooking the marina presents a quandary—to choose the darker nautical theme, or the bright and airy space? Both include a microwave, coffeemaker, refrigerator, and TV; no phone.

Seahorse Landing (1-877-514-5096; www.seahorselanding.com), 4050 G St, provides a fabulous view of sunset over the Gulf from newer large condo units (1,024 square feet, sleeping four or six) equipped with washer and dryer, dishwasher, microwave, full dishes and linens, television and VCR; DSL available in some units. $125–150.

Sunset Isle Motel & RV Park (1-800-810-1103; www.cedarkeyrv.com), FL 24. Along the estuary, this pleasant family motel has rooms with refrigerator, microwave, and coffeemaker ($45) as well as cottages ($85) and RV spaces ($16); tent campers welcome.

Chiefland 32626

Best Western Suwannee Valley Inn (352-493-0663), 1125 N Young Blvd, has the feel of a small family motel, with a coin laundry and soda machines in the breezeway and a pleasant pool out front. Central to everything, they have 60 large rooms, many with desk and dataport, some with microwave and refrigerator; $60–95.

Cross City 32628

Carriage Inn (352-498-3910), US 19-27-98. At this family motel, the wrought-iron railings remind me of the French Quarter. Enjoy well-kept reasonably sized 1960s-style rooms, $37–45, with a swimming pool, shuffleboard court, and adjacent restaurant; across the road from the Nature Coast Trail.

Fanning Springs 32693

Cadillac Motel Inn & Suites (352-463-2188), 7490 N US 19, has real curb appeal: a tropical oasis, from the sparkling swimming pool to the flowering bushes in front of the rooms. This well-kept family-run motel dates back to the 1950s, with large rooms and original small tiled baths in retro colors. Furnishings are bright and tropical, and each room has a microwave and mini fridge. Twenty-nine units, including family-sized multibed suites, $40–48; walk to Fanning Springs State Park and the Nature Coast State Trail.

Suwannee 32692
Suwannee Shores Motor Lodge (352-542-7560), 525 Canal St. At this pleasant family-owned motel, enjoy being able to walk down the boardwalk to the river's edge and cast in a line, or put in your boat at the ramp. Older, spacious rooms (some kitchenettes) with a nautical atmosphere, $55–65.

COTTAGES

Cedar Key 32625
My friends love to stay at **Mermaid's Landing** (1-877-543-5949), FL 24, an easy stroll from town and a great place to launch a kayak. Set in a funky beach atmosphere, each cottage ($42–64) comes with an equipped kitchen. Kayak rental on site.

At **Pirates Cove** (352-543-5141; www.piratescovecottages.com), FL 24, each cottage ($54–69) comes fully equipped with dishes and linens; free use of bicycles for exploring Cedar Key, or fishing equipment to settle back on the shore and cast a line.

CAMPGROUNDS

Bell 32619
Hart Springs Park (see *Green Space*) on SW CR 344 west of Trenton offers both primitive tent and hookup sites, dump station, grills, picnic tables, and hot showers. $11–13; weekly and monthly rates available. No pets.

Branford 32008
Ellie Ray's River Landing Campground (386-935-9518; www.ellieraysriverlanding.com), 3349 NW 110th St. A high canopy of oaks shades this expansive campground along the Santa Fe River, a great place for river rats to hang out. You've got swimming in a horseshoe-shaped spring on the river, canoeing and kayaking down to the Suwannee River, boating, fishing, plenty of springs nearby for divers, canoe and paddle boat rentals, and an on-site lounge. $19–25; weekly and monthly rates available. Leashed pets only.

Cedar Key 32625
Shell Mound County Park (352-543-6153), CR 326, on the edge of Lower Suwannee NWR, provides basic tent and camper sites cooled by breezes off the salt marsh. Ideal for hikers, paddlers, and anglers who like to get an early start; boat ramp, picnic tables, and privies.

Inglis 34449
Big Oaks River Resort and Campground (352-447-5333; www.bigoaksriverresort.com), 14035 W River Rd. An extremely appealing spot on the Withlacoochee River, with full-hookup ($18) and tent ($10–12) sites, cabins with cable TV ($40–50), swimming pool, and campground store. Renting canoes and kayaks, johnboats and pontoon boats, and tubes (rentals include shuttle service).

Old Town 32680
Suwannee River Campground (1-888-884-CAMP), FL 349. With campsites tucked in the deep shade of the river forest, this is one beautiful hideaway set above the river. Choose from tent sites ($18), pull-through sites with full hookups ($22), or camping cabins (no bathrooms, $30). Swimming pool, boat ramp, and fishing dock.

Suwannee River Hideaway Campground (352-542-7800; www.riverhideaway.com), CR 346-A. You're greeted by a cute replica of an old general store at check-in at this new campground along the Suwannee, with pretty full-hookup spaces ($22–24) under the pines and oaks. Tenters ($12) get the primo access to the river; a boardwalk leads from the bathhouse area down to the river.

The only area campground with a significant amount of river frontage, the **Yellow Jacket Campground** (352-542-8365; www.yellowjacketcampground.com), FL 349, blends well into its natural surroundings. Over more than 2 years, the new owners renovated this former fish camp into a place of beauty. A rope swing with a grand view of the Suwannee River hangs off an ancient live oak tree next to shady riverside campsites; guests enjoy a beautiful swimming pool and spa area. $20 tents, $30 riverbank RV sites, $85 for their extremely pleasant cottages.

Shired Island

It's the epitome of rustic—a flush toilet (not in the best of shape) your only amenity. But if you *really* want to get away from it all, pitch your tent or bring your trailer to **Shired Island County Park**, the most remote campground on the Nature Coast, at the end of CR 357 right on the Gulf. Launch your sea kayak from the beach, and enjoy a sunset that's all yours. Self-serve $9; nearby boat ramp.

Yankeetown 34498

B's Marina and Campground (352-447-5888; www.bmarinacampground.com), 6621 Riverside Dr. Campsites ($20) along the pine-and-palm-lined Withlacoochee River, with paved pads and picnic tables. Bring your boat and take advantage of the dock, or come by boat and arrange overnight dockage. It's a great place to launch a kayak and head out to the Gulf, with rentals available.

DIVE RESORT

Williston 32696

Devil's Den (352-528-3344; www.devilsden.com), 5390 NE 180th Ave. Surrounding its world-renowned dive venue (see *Diving*), Devil's Den provides a full-service dive resort with 30 RV sites ($22), 20 tent sites ($7–11), and three kitchenette cabins ($75–80, sleeping four) perched on the rim of a large sinkhole. Campers enjoy use of bathhouses and a heated pool on site. In addition to the must-dive grotto, enjoy swimming, snorkeling, and scuba in spring-fed Ray's Fish Pond, ranging up to 22 feet deep, and picnicking in the covered pavilions or open tables under the forest canopy. No pets permitted.

FISH CAMPS

Inglis 34449

Big Bass Village Campground (1-877-GO-FISH2; www.bigbassvillage.com), 10530 SE 201st St, on Lake Rousseau, is the place to go if you're after trophy-sized largemouth bass on this snag-filled lake. In addition to primitive ($12) and full-hookup sites ($15), they have rustic cabin rentals (cable TV, fully equipped kitchens), $35–50, a bait-and-tackle shop, and boat rentals.

Suwannee 32692

In a pretty cedar forest along the Suwannee's side channels, **Miller's Marina and Campground** (352-542-7349 or 1-800-458-2628), P.O. Box 280, has RV sites ($24) with concrete pads or grassy sites, both with full hookup, as well as rustic park models. Check here for houseboats, too.

HOUSEBOAT ON THE SUWANNEE Original Florida CVB

✷ Where to Eat

DINING OUT

Cedar Key

The Island Room Restaurant at Cedar Cove (352-543-6520), Cedar Key. The island's dressiest restaurant serves up proprietor-chef Peter Stefani's specialties, like grouper Savannah (pecan crusted, served with a sherry beurre blanc) and New Zealand rack of lamb; entrées $13–25. Reservations suggested.

Williston

The Ivy House (352-528-5410), 106 NW Main St. Featuring recipes handed down for more than 50 years through the Hale family, the Ivy House presents gourmet southern cooking in a 1912 Victorian home; five differently themed rooms provide unique backdrops to the main attraction, the food. From southern-fried grouper ($10) to a Big South sampler of a Delmonico steak, grouper, and shrimp ($19), you'll find something to fit every appetite, served up with roasted vegetables, corn bread, yeast rolls, and their trademark baked potato with cheese. Leave some room for a homemade dessert, like their classic milk cake. Open for lunch and dinner; closed Sun. A gift shop occupies one room near the entrance, with an array of feminine gift items.

Yankeetown

The Compleat Angler Restaurant at Izaak Walton Lodge (1-800-611-5758; www.izaakwaltonlodge.com), One 63rd St, is the classy place on the coast for a big meal, serving seafood and Black Angus beef with a Withlacoochee River view enjoyed by patrons for more than a century. The original hunting and fishing lodge burned down some years ago, replaced by this replica that captures the spirit of Old Florida. Serving lunch and dinner, with a special three-course prix fixe menu for $16 served Tue–Thu and Sun.

EATING OUT

Bell

Captain Hugh's (352-463-7670), US 129. If you're in the mood for mounds of food, stop by Captain Hugh's, where buffets will keep you sated. Breakfasts under $4, lunches $3 and up, and dinners $9–14, including local favorites like catfish, clams, grouper, quail, shrimp, and snow crab.

Cedar Key

The Captain's Table (352-543-5441), 222 Dock St. Savor the sunset while partaking in the fabulous mullet dip at the Captain's Table, a great choice for seafood on the Gulf. Save some room for the excellent key lime pie. Closed Tue.

🏵 **Pat's Red Luck** (352-543-6840), 490 Dock St. Consistently excellent for both lunch ($5.50–10.75) and dinner ($6–17), Pat's now serves up unique breakfasts ($3.25–7), including their tasty fruit pancake, a thin crêpe smothered in sautéed bananas and strawberries, topped with cinnamon sugar and your choice of creamy topping. The oysters here are always fresh and lightly breaded, making my top lunch pick the New Orleans Peacemaker ($7.25), a rendition of the po'boy sandwich.

♿ **Seabreeze on the Dock** (352-543-5738), 520 Dock St. One of the few eateries in Cedar Key that a wheelchair can reach, the Sea Breeze offers good fresh Gulf seafood with a great view. Try their creamy oyster stew ($3.75 or $4.95) as a starter, and move on to entrées ($10.25–23.95) showcasing local favorites—grouper strips, mullet, roast clams, blue crab claws, and stone crab. For something completely different, try the hearts of palm salad as a side—served with peaches, dates, and pineapples, and topped with peanut butter ice cream dressing. Yum!

Chiefland

Bar-B-Q Bill's (352-493-4444), US 19 and FL 320. This place is always packed, and it took but one meal to understand why: fine barbecue that even impressed my friends from Texas. Served with traditional fixings, barbecue comes as sandwiches ($2 and up) and plates ($6 and up), with optional salad bar. Daily lunch specials 11–3.

Bells Family Restaurant (352-493-4492), 116 N Main St. The buffet is the centerpiece of this longtime hometown favorite, where even at lunch you can grab piles of fresh peel-'n'-eat shrimp and stacks of fried fish. Every day means a slightly different feature on the buffet, from frog legs and 'gator tail to quail and catfish; $7.99–13.95, with daily specials. There's an extensive menu, too, with items like country-fried steak and grouper Reubens. Country breakfasts served 7–11, $1.49–6.99. Breakfast buffets Sat and Sun, $4.99.

Cross City

Cypress Inn Restaurant (352-498-7211), US 27 and CR 351-A. Since 1928, they've been serving up heaping helpings of southern cooking in this beautiful pecky cypress building; sit down and make yourself at home. Prime rib special ($10), seafood dinners ($7–9, including fresh mullet and grouper), and everything comes with your choice of home-style sides like fresh acre peas, baby limas, fried okra, and corn nuggets. Open 5–9:30; cash or ATM debit cards only.

Fanning Springs

Always packed for dinner, the **Lighthouse Restaurant** (352-463-2644), US 19, serves fresh Gulf seafood and thick steaks that folks come for from miles around. Try the Swamp Thing ($17), with 'gator tail bites, catfish strips, and golden-fried deviled crab, or the Dinghy ($9) for small appetites, with flounder, shrimp, crab, and oysters. Entrées $8–28; open 11–11 daily.

Suwannee

Salt Creek Restaurant (352-542-7072), CR 349, is a spacious restaurant, with seating overlooking the Gulf estuary. It's worth the drive to the end of the road for their succulent seafood, including fresh oysters, mullet, bay scallops, and their steamer pots (six choices of seafood, $9 and up) cooked with veggies and red potatoes. Entrées run $11–19, including a Fisherman's Platter with blue crab. Open 11–10, Wed–Sun.

Trenton

Inside the spacious Suwannee Valley Quilt Shop (see *Selective Shopping*), the **Cypress Swamp Café** offers delightful daily specials like crab salad on croissant: $5 including tea or coffee. You'll be tempted by slices of pie like cashew, sawdust, and tin roof, displayed prominently in a bakery case on the edge of this garden-like space inside the historic Coca-Cola bottling plant. Open 10–5, Tue–Sat.

Williston

Driftwood Grill (352-528-5074), 515 E Noble Ave. Enjoy a heaping helping of comfort food in this comfy downhome café, where a plateful of pancakes with your choice of toppings (blueberry, chocolate chip, or peaches and cream) will run you less than $3; lunches $2–7, southern-style dinners $6–13.

Hale's General Store (352-528-5219), 8 NW Main. It's a gift shop (check out the quilts) *and* an old-fashioned ice cream parlor open 10–3, serving deli sandwiches and salads as well as steamed seafood. Closed Sun.

✷ Entertainment

Catch live music at **Frog's Landing** (352-543-9243), 490 Dock St, Cedar Key, on weekends.

✷ Selective Shopping

Cedar Key

From gift and home decor items to one-of-a-kind pieces of art, you'll find a great selection in artsy Cedar Key. The shopping district encompasses 2nd St, its cross streets, and Dock St along the Gulf. A handful of places you shouldn't miss:

The Cedar Keyhole (352-543-5801), 457 2nd St. Representing more than 20 local artists and a handful of consignments, this gallery tempts with art in virtually every medium. Fused art glass captures the motion of ocean waves, and Cindy's gourd handbags add a touch of humor. Despite ceramic slugs and hand-painted dresses, the art reflects island themes. Ongoing gallery events, including nationally juried exhibits, occupy the second floor.

Dilly Dally Galley (352-543-9146), 390 Dock St. Dark woods accent the nautical theme in this seaside shop, with wooden signs, wood carvings, and antique ephemera tucked away in the back rooms. The front desk also serves as the check-in for the Harbour Master Suites (see *Lodging*).

Haven Isle (352-543-6806), 582 2nd St. Dating back to 1884, this little white gingerbread cottage houses the usual gift items found in small tourist towns, but with a twist—the owner is a well-respected stained-glass artist, and the back of the shop serves as his studio. Look high up on the walls for original art in glass, wood, and metal by local artists.

Island Arts (352-543-6677), C St. Just around the corner from 2nd St, this vibrant artists' co-op features playful art with a maritime theme. Follow the purple fish inside for a parade of pop art, clever cards, and other island treasures.

The Natural Experience (352-543-9933), 334 2nd St. A working wood and clay studio occupies one corner of this classy gallery, where Don Duden works the lathe, creating hand-turned wood vessels. In addition to Don's fine work, several other artists are represented, including noted author and photographer Jeff Ripple and his stunning "One With Nature" collection of original outdoor photography. Pottery and art glass, enameling and impressionistic Florida landscapes round out the collection.

Curmudgeonalia (352-543-6789), corner of 2nd and D Sts. Every little town needs an independent bookstore, and none so much as Cedar Key, being an enclave of artists and writers. Pen Names fills the niche, with an excellent selection of tomes on Florida and by Florida authors, and a children's section that caters to inquisitive outdoorsy kids.

Sawgrass Gallery (352-543-5007), 451 Dock St. Featuring artists from around America, the Sawgrass Gallery displays an eclectic mix of glass, metal, ceramic, and fabric art. My eyes immediately locked on the "sublimely weird sculptures" of Julie Borodin, a parade of one-of-a-kind pillows, and the free-form pottery of Connie Mickle, flowing shapes expressed in earth tones. From fused glass to foam-core 3-D collages, the artistry sings.

The Suwannee Triangle Gallery (352-543-5744; www.suwanneetriangle.com), 491 Dock St. Take a pinch of Connie Nelson, with her island watercolors of houses, waterbirds, and Florida's colorful flora, and add a dash of Kevin Hipe, with his offbeat mosaics and photography that captures the spirit of the Cedar Keys, and you've been drawn into the Suwannee Triangle. In addition to the prolific output of these two excellent local artists, the gallery features fine jewelry, prints of collages, and Brian Andrews's distinctive "story people."

Chiefland

Every weekend Chiefland has flea markets as bookends—**Shaw's**, a small enterprise, at the south end of town near SW 4th Ave, and the **Chiefland Farmers Flea Market** (352-493-3022), Sat and Sun 8–4. Comb through the stalls for country bargains!

Magnolia Mist Unique Gifts & Antiques (352-493-7877), 711 N Main, stands out along US 19 in downtown Chiefland with a good selection of antiques and gift items.

Fanning Springs

October Rose Antiques (352-463-7367), US 19 at the bridge, is housed in an 1960s "Textile Town" building, permitting plenty of broad open space for classic furniture to be neatly arranged much like a furniture showroom, with dining room tables set with dishes, living room suites, and the like. The antiques are top-notch, and prices are fantastic, especially on Carnival glass and other glassware.

Inglis

Big Tepee Trading Post (352-447-2442), 16 US 19 S, carries Native American art, clothing, and artifacts; closed Sun.

From the road, it looks like fun: **World Shells & Sea Forest Gifts** (352-447-1455), 14440 US 19, has funky coral gifts and a shell shop that shell collectors will love, plus art from local artists.

Old Town

Intrigued by the stacks of driftwood outside **Catch the Drift** (352-542-7770), 410 US 19 S, I stopped to take a look and was glad I did. C. Emery Mills's decade-old gallery is all about nature as art, with 10 local artists creating sculptures from wood, shells, and coral.

Suwannee

You'll find **Souvenirs & Things,** CR 349, with original stained-glass art, carved wooden fish sculptures, and other nautical gifts along Salt Creek adjoining the Salt Creek Restaurant (see *Eating Out*).

Trenton

Suwannee Valley Quilt Shop (352-463-3842), 517 N Main St. It's not just a quilt shop; it's a piece of history. Grab lunch at the Cypress Swamp Café (see *Eating Out*) or browse the selection of stained-glass supplies. But if fabric's your thing, you'll find plenty of options here!

Williston

Cedar Chest Antiques (352-528-0039), 48 E Noble Ave. Modern home decor items like carved hope chests share space with beaded Victorian lamps, Vaseline glass, and collectible dolls in a virtual showroom of antique furniture. Open Wed–Sat.

Dixies Antiques (352-528-2338), 131 E Noble Ave. It's a mini mall overflowing with antiques and collectibles, with a heavy emphasis on kitchenware and dishes—look for your missing Fenton glass, Fiestaware, and enamelware here. But you'll also find country crafts, western home decor, rustic wooden furniture, and ironworking by a local blacksmith in among the stacks of paperbacks, Hardy Boys mysteries, and soda pop bottles—a little something for everyone. Closed Sun. Produce stand in the parking lot carries seasonal fresh fruit and vegetables.

Williston Peanut Factory Outlet (352-528-2388), 1309 US 41. Small outlet with offerings of peanut goodies made on site, from roasted peanuts to peanut butter and peanut brittle; open during production hours.

Yankeetown

Riverside Antiques & Gallery (352-447-2717), 3B 63rd St. An antiques mall and art gallery featuring local artists, with primitive art, nautical-themed items, and garden art in the historic Yankeetown Garage.

U-PICK **R&S Produce** (352-528-0100). Fresh fruit and vegetables out of a permanent canopied fruit stand just west of US 41 on FL 121, south of Williston.

✷ Special Events

February: **Suwannee Valley Bluegrass Festival** (1-800-576-2398), Trenton. Enjoy live bluegrass from Florida performers.

March: **Suwannee River Fair** (352-486-5131) is the combined county fair for the three-county region, with livestock and vegetable judging, rides and crafts, and more. Suwannee River fairgrounds.

April: **Cedar Key Sidewalk Arts and Crafts Festival** (352-543-5600; www.cedarkey.org). Enjoy the works of local artists, with a taste of seafood for good measure.

May: **Red Belly Day** (352-463-3310; www.dixiecounty.org), Fanning Springs State Park. One of the most amusing Memorial Day weekend celebrations in Florida, centered on the town's favorite member of the bream family (which makes for a great fish fry), with families participating in sack races, melon chunking, and the ever-popular belly-flop contest.

September: **Down Home Days** (352-463-3467), Trenton. More than 180 artists, craftspeople, and food vendors, with music for a "down-home" time.

October: **Cedar Key Seafood Festival** (352-543-5600; www.cedarkey.org), third weekend. Thousands converge on this tiny village for samplings of local seafood and a large arts and crafts show, as well as special tours of the Cedar Key lighthouse.

THE BIG BEND

TAYLOR AND LAFAYETTE COUNTIES

Encompassing the sweep of Florida's coastline where the peninsula meets the Panhandle, the Big Bend is a wild and wondrous place. Once the domain of the Timucua Indians, the region saw Spanish explorers in 1529, when Pánfilo de Narváez came looking for gold and marked Deadman's Bay on the map; he was soon followed by Hernando de Soto and his men. Building two small missions near the Fenholloway River, the Spanish attempted to convert the Timucua, but diseases ran rampant, decimating the tribes. By the 1700s, the Seminoles, descendants of Maskókî peoples, moved south to take their place. In 1818 General Andrew Jackson brought U.S. forces against the Seminoles at the Econfina River, and marched his troops south across the Steinhatchee River at the falls. During the Seminole Wars of the 1800s, the area was a hotbed of military activity, with Fort Frank Brook erected near the mouth of the Steinhatchee River, and four more forts built along the Econfina and Fenholloway Rivers. General Zachary Taylor led more troops into the region in 1838, attempting to force the Seminoles to reservations in the West. Taylor County bears his name.

Along the Gulf Coast, you'll find **Steinhatchee** near the mouth of the Steinhatchee River, founded by pioneers looking for cedar to feed the pencil factories in the Cedar Keys (see "The Lower Suwannee"). In the 1940s Greek sponge divers moved into the area to work the vast sponge beds in the Gulf of Mexico, and the fishermen followed. Although the sponge divers are long gone, you can see reminders of Greek culture in the offerings on local menus. Up the coast, **Adams Beach** and **Keaton Beach** are quaint fishing villages along the vast estuary of the Big Bend. **Perry**, the seat of Taylor County, grew up around farming in the 1860s, but the economy shifted to lumber and turpentine after Reconstruction, when timber companies removed vast tracts of virgin pines and cypress, processed in two enormous timber mills. The Forest Capital State Museum (see *Museums*) tells the story of Florida's timber industry, centered at Perry.

Lightly populated and agrarian, both Taylor and Lafayette Counties provide quiet getaways for folks looking to get well off the beaten path.

GUIDANCE Contact the **Lafayette County Chamber of Commerce** (386-294-2510), P.O. Box 416, Mayo 32066, and the **Perry/Taylor Chamber of Commerce** (1-800-257-8881; www.taylorflorida.com), P.O. Box 892, Perry 32348.

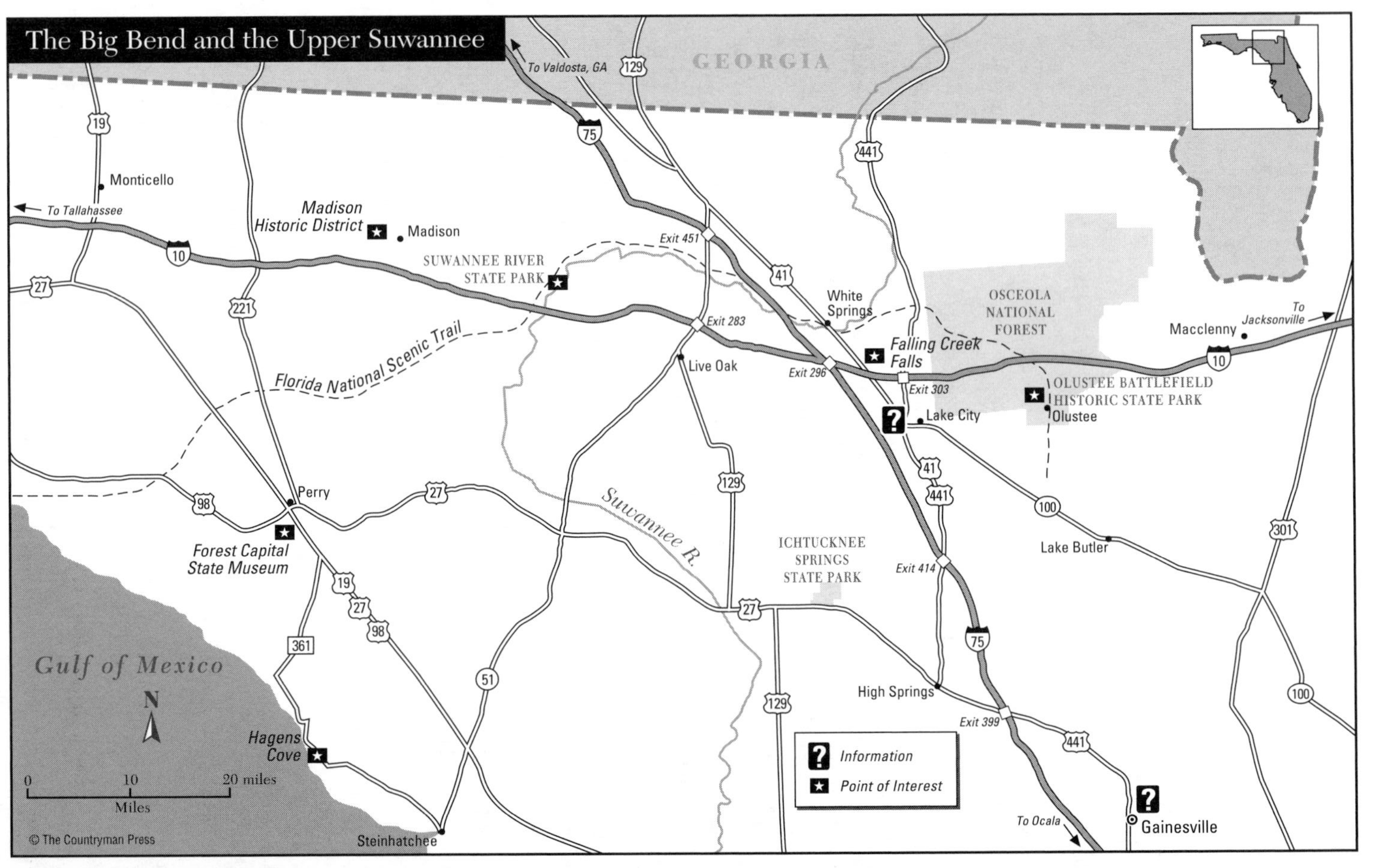

The Big Bend and the Upper Suwannee
GEORGIA
To Valdosta, GA
To Tallahassee
Monticello
Madison Historic District
Madison
SUWANNEE RIVER STATE PARK
Florida National Scenic Trail
Exit 451
Exit 283
Exit 296
Exit 303
Exit 414
Exit 399
White Springs
Falling Creek Falls
OSCEOLA NATIONAL FOREST
Macclenny
To Jacksonville
OLUSTEE BATTLEFIELD HISTORIC STATE PARK
Olustee
Lake City
Live Oak
Perry
Forest Capital State Museum
Suwannee R.
ICHTUCKNEE SPRINGS STATE PARK
Lake Butler
High Springs
Gainesville
To Ocala
Gulf of Mexico
Hagens Cove
Steinhatchee
Information
Point of Interest
0 10 20 miles
Miles
© The Countryman Press

GETTING THERE *By car*: **US 19-27** runs through the heart of Taylor County, but you'll want to take **CR 361** and **FL 51** to explore its Gulf Coast communities. FL 51 and US 27 meet at Mayo, the center of Lafayette County, passing through all of its major towns. Steinhatchee is a 3-hour drive north from Orlando.

MEDICAL EMERGENCIES The nearest medical center is in adjoining Suwannee County at Live Oak (see "The Upper Suwannee"). Call 911 for emergencies.

✷ To See

GHOST TOWNS In 1870 **New Troy**, near Troy Springs, boasted busy steamboat docks and steady commerce. It was the seat of Lafayette County, but after an arsonist torched the courthouse in 1892, county residents voted to move the courthouse to Mayo; New Troy was abandoned soon after.

HISTORIC SITES **Steinhatchee Spring**, a historic spa and the birthplace of the Steinhatchee River, is off FL 51 north of US 27. Visit downtown Perry for a look at the historic district, centered on the **Taylor County Courthouse**; the **Lafayette County Courthouse** in Mayo dates back to 1908. At **Steinhatchee Falls** (see *Waterfalls*), examine the rock above the falls closely; when the water is low, you can see ruts left behind by heavy wagon wheels from territorial settlers crossing in the 1820s.

MUSEUMS **Forest Capital State Museum** (850-584-3227), 204 Forest Park Dr, Perry. In Florida's heart of forestry, this lively museum focuses on the importance of Florida's timber, particularly its pine forests. In addition to a diorama on the historic turpentine and naval stores industries, there are life-sized replica habitats and a talking tree to teach the kids about the life cycle of Florida's trees. A wooden map of Florida showcases the variety of native trees in the state (314 types), with each county made out of a different type of wood. Outside the museum, walk beneath the stately longleaf pines through a reconstructed Cracker homestead. Open 9–5; closed Tue and Wed.

THE FOREST CAPITAL STATE MUSEUM FOCUSES ON FLORIDA'S TIMBER.

Original Florida CVB

✷ To Do

BICYCLING Perfect for beginners, the **Allen Mill Pond** bike trail runs 4.2 miles between Allen Mill Pond and Lafayette Blue Springs along the Suwannee River. For information, contact the Suwannee River Bicycle Association (386-397-2347), White Springs.

BIRDING **Cooks Hammock**, hidden in a maze of forest roads off FL 51 at the Lafayette Hunt Club, has a colony of white and glossy ibises; hang out at **Hagens Cove** (see *Beaches*) to watch flocks of shorebirds, including black skimmers.

BOATING In Steinhatchee you can rent boats and pontoons at many marinas, including **Gulfstream Motel** (see *Lodging*), **Sea Hag** (352-498-3008; www.seahag.com), **Ideal Marina and Motel** (see *Lodging*), **River Haven Marina & Motel** (1-877-907-0709; www.steinhatchee.com/riverhaven), **Paces Cabins** (352-498-0061), and **Woods Marina and Campground** (352-498-3948). Marinas provide dockage and storage (including dry dock) at varying rates. A public boat ramp is located at the end of CR 358 on the north side of the river; turn right at the end of the bridge.

DIVING From diving and snorkeling offshore on the reefs of the Big Bend and around its submarine springs to diving in the crystalline waters of the Suwannee River, this area offers many options for divers. Check in at the dive shop at **Ideal Marina and Motel** for offshore opportunities and outfitting, and at **Jim Hollis' River Rendezvous** for freshwater diving (see *Lodging* for both). *Important note*: Many open-water divers have died in this region while attempting cave diving. Do not enter an underwater cave or spring unless you are a certified cave diver. Most springs must be accessed by boat, and a DIVER DOWN flag is necessary while diving.

FISHING With more than 60 miles of wilderness coastline, the Big Bend has always attracted a steady clientele of saltwater anglers in search of grouper, cobia, and trout. Toward that end, you'll find plenty of fishing guides, especially around **Steinhatchee**. Ask around at the marinas (see *Boating*) regarding specific captains' specialties, and expect a day's worth of guided fishing (which includes your license) to cost $350–700, depending on what you're after. At **Keaton Beach**, a fishing pier provides access to the Gulf.

Inland, anglers head for **Koon Lake**, a 110-acre fish management area west of Mayo on US 27, where largemouth bass and bluegill provide spring sport. If you're fishing along the banks of the **Suwannee River**, target sunfish around the snags and channel catfish in the deep holes.

HIKING The **Florida Trail** traverses two particularly scenic areas in this region—**Goose Pasture** and the **Aucilla River Sinks** (see *Wild Places*). Don't miss **Steinhatchee Falls** (see *Waterfalls*) with its 6-mile round-trip trail along the Steinhatchee River. Two short hiking trails in the Tide Swamp Unit of Big Bend WMA lead through coastal pine flatwoods along the tidal marshes near Hagens Cove.

HUNTING Deer hunting is big sport between Thanksgiving and Christmas in the thousands of acres of natural lands making up the Big Bend Wildlife Management Area, which stretches south into Dixie County. Check the Florida Fish and

Wildlife Conservation Commission web site, www.floridaconservation.org, for hunt locations and dates.

MUD BOGGIN' Ever wonder what folks do with those monster pickup trucks? Stop by **North Florida Mud Boggin'**, US 27 between Branford and Mayo, on the second and fourth Sat each month at 6 PM to watch the gears grind and the mud fly.

PADDLING For a tiny taste of white-water thrills, head to **Steinhatchee** with your kayak to leap the **Steinhatchee Falls** (see *Waterfalls*). The 8-mile trip from the falls to Steinhatchee along this obsidian-colored waterway winds through dark river hammocks and forested residential areas before meeting the tidal basin, offering several Class I rapids. Rent kayaks from Steinhatchee Outpost (see *Campgrounds*); take-out is at Fiddler's Restaurant. Of course, the **Suwannee River** is the region's prime canoeing venue, outlining the eastern border of Lafayette County. Put in at **Troy Springs State Park** (see *Springs*) or the CR 51 bridge crossing north of Mayo to follow the central section of the **Suwannee River Canoe Trail**.

Estuary dominates the central and most remote portion of a rough but scenic 91-mile saltwater paddle attempted by a handful of people every year: the **Historic Big Bend Saltwater Paddling Trail** (see "The Lower Suwannee"). Paddlers on this segment can find services at Steinhatchee, Keaton Beach, and Econfina, where sea kayakers put in at **Econfina River State Park** (see *Wild Places*) for direct access to the Gulf of Mexico. On US 98 you'll find picnic tables and a boat ramp on the **Econfina River**, a jungle-like paddling route that heads south 6 miles to the state park. A little farther west, paddlers can also put in at the **Aucilla River** and head upstream along the **Wacissa River Canoe Trail** into Jefferson County; the Aucilla quickly peters out as it disappears through its famed sinks.

SCENIC DRIVES Contact the Perry/Taylor County Chamber of Commerce (see *Guidance*) for a brochure on **The Loop** in Taylor County, a nearly 100-mile circuit taking you through the scenic fishing villages along the Gulf Coast and through the heart of the "Forest Capital of Florida." A truly wild and scenic drive, the **Road to Nowhere** (see "The Lower Suwannee") in Jena is best accessed from Steinhatchee.

✷ Green Space

BEACHES The Big Bend isn't noted for its beaches—it's an estuary. But you will find a soft white strand at **Hodges Park** in **Keaton Beach** at the end of CR 361, along a grassy strip with rest rooms and a covered picnic pavilion. Between Steinhatchee and Keaton Beach on CR 361 in the Tide Swamp Unit of Big Bend WMA, **Hagens Cove** is a prime destination for scalloping, especially for families with small children. Don't expect a beautiful white sand beach here. It's an accessible piece of shoreline along an infinite stretch of mudflats, a beautiful place to sit and watch the sunset.

SCALLOPING Dropping off the back of a 32-foot Ocean Cat, I plunge into the warm waters of the Gulf of Mexico, mesh bag in hand. It's my first time snorkeling in many years, and the fins on my feet feel unfamiliar, the scene surreal, dreamlike. I glide noiselessly through hues of green above a waving pasture of turtle grass, where silvery pinfish glimmer against the shifting textures and a jellyfish pumps briskly against the seafloor. I spot my goal ahead, a patch of rocks and bright white sand with tall strands of Christmas tree grass rising to the surface. There, at the base of the waving grass—bay scallops! It takes a few swift kicks of the flippers to make the dive and then surface with the clacking shellfish in hand, the beginning of a seafood dinner gathered under my own power.

THE QUARRY Sandra Friend

For many years the estuaries of the Big Bend have been the only place where enough scallops naturally breed to be harvested; their estuarine nurseries in other parts of the state had been overcollected and poisoned by runoff. Although more counties along the Gulf Coast have had their waters reopened for an annual scalloping season, **Steinhatchee** remains the destination of choice for serious scallopers. Your success is in direct proportion to the weather: Too much rain, and the scallop population suffers. The season runs Jul 1–Sep 10, and you must abide by state-mandated limits of 2 gallons of whole scallops per person per day. If you snorkel from your own boat, you must have a saltwater fishing license and display a DIVER DOWN flag. Many local marinas arrange charters; **Captain Brian Smith** with **Big Bend Charters** (352-498-3703; www.bigbendcharters.com) specializes in scalloping trips. No fishing license is required when you scallop with a charter, nor if you head for Hagens Cove (see *Beaches*), where you can wade into the Gulf and collect to your heart's content.

SNORKELING IN THE GULF OF MEXICO Sandra Friend

PARKS In downtown Mayo, ancient live oaks shade **Mayo Town Park**, which has a playground, picnic area, and historic Cracker home. Just off US 27 near Cindy's Motel (see *Lodging*).

SPRINGS Contact the Suwannee River Water Management District (386-362-1001) for a map of spring locations in the Suwannee River for diving and swimming. In this region you can visit tiny **Conviction Springs** at Jim Hollis' River Rendezvous (see *Lodging*), but you shouldn't miss **Troy Springs State Park** off US 27 near Midway, where the water is nearly 75 feet deep and contains the remains of the *Madison*, a steamboat scuttled in 1861 when her owner left to fight for the Confederacy in Virginia. Adjoining **Ruth Springs** is a third-magnitude spring open for swimming and diving; **Lafayette Blue Springs** (386-294-1617) along CR 350A has primitive camping, nature trails, picnic pavilions, and a boat ramp.

WATERFALLS **Steinhatchee Falls** rates as Florida's broadest and most interesting waterfall—this limestone shelf along the Steinhatchee River served as a crossing point for wagons as settlers pushed their way south along the Gulf Coast, and the wagon ruts are still visible in the limestone on both sides of the river. A riverside park has interpretive information, picnic tables, and a boat launch; a hiking trail starts just outside the gate. The trailhead and falls are off CR 51, 2 miles west of US 19-27.

WILD PLACES During hunting season, you'll see plenty of pickups pulling into **Hickory Mound WMA** near Perry, and the **Big Bend WMA** surrounding Steinhatchee. Off-season, Hickory Mound's extensive dike trails are great for birding and alligator watching; the **Jena Unit** of Big Bend WMA provides fabulous birding (accessed best from Steinhatchee, it's actually in adjoining Dixie County). The **Tide Swamp Unit** of Big Bend WMA is the home of Hagens Cove, the region's swimming and scalloping beach. Off CR 355, the **Mallory Swamp WMA** provides access to nearly 30,000 acres of remote wilderness south of Mayo. Off US 98 east of the Aucilla River bridge, the **Aucilla River Sinks** and **Goose Pasture** provide access to one of the strangest rivers in Florida—after rushing across rapids, it vanishes beneath the limestone bedrock and pops up time and again in "windows" in the aquifer, deep sinkholes with water in motion. Use the Florida Trail to explore this unique area. At the end of CR 14, **Econfina River State Park** (850-922-6007) gives paddlers a put-in to the vast Gulf estuary.

THE AUCILLA RIVER, ONE OF FLORIDA'S STRANGEST

Sandra Friend

✷ Lodging

BED & BREAKFASTS

Hatchbend 32008

Seeking a truly rural escape? Settle into your comfortable cabin at **The Smoakhouse Ranch** (386-935-2662 or 1-877-258-9686; www.smoakhouseranch.com), 4321 SE CR 500 (Rt 1, Box 518), a working ranch where the kids can feed the cows or walk past the fishpond to the swimming pool. It's a place to relax and rejuvenate yourself, yet convenient to hiking, biking, and paddling trails in parks along the Suwannee River. Wake up and find your refrigerator stocked with fresh fruits, pastries, and bread; have breakfast at your own pace. Along with a re-creation of the Earl farmhouse from the original family farm in Marion County (as described in *The Last Cracker*, by Joyce Hart Smith), the "country modern" cabins ($65–125, double occupancy) sleep entire families ($14 per extra person); camping available on request.

Mayo 32066

The Chateau (386-294-2332; www.southernchateau.com), Bloxham and Fletcher Sts. Step back in time in these tastefully appointed romantic suites in the former county courthouse (1883–1907), restored to its historic splendor and lovingly cared for by Leenette McMillan and Dewey Hatcher. Three rooms, $65–85, include continental breakfast; full breakfast available. Fine dining Fri and Sat evenings in the Savannah Room (see *Dining Out*).

HOTELS AND MOTELS

Keaton Beach 32348

Keaton Beach Marina Motel & Cottages (850-578-2897), 20650 Keaton Beach Dr. Sandy Beach (honest!) runs this family motel with spacious rooms; the unit I checked out had a glassed-in porch overlooking the channel. It's an older building, with uneven floors, but that just adds to its charm. $59 for motel rooms, $89 for cottages (which require a 2-night stay).

Mayo 32066

Cindy's Motel (386-294-1242), US 27. A blast from my past: a spotless 1950s motel (period furnishings, even!) harking back to family road trips in the days before interstate highways, where every room has ample space for Mom, Dad, and the kids. The property is shaded by grand live oaks and sits just across from the city park and behind the Mayo Café. A/C, cable TV. $40–55.

Perry 32348

Chaparral Inn (850-584-2441), 2519 S Byron Butler Pkwy. From the pre-interstate days when Perry was a bustling junction of major U.S. highways, the Chaparral has aged gracefully. Each modest room ($38–45) includes cable TV, phone, and air-conditioning; enjoy the pool or sit in a porch swing on the well-manicured grounds.

♿ **Hampton Inn** (850-223-3000), 2399 S Byron Butler Pkwy. The newest motel in Perry comes with a guarantee of top-notch customer service: It's ranked fifth in the nation for its chain. In addition to an expanded continental breakfast, look for cookies and chocolate-dipped strawberries in the dining area every afternoon; families crowd the swimming pool on weekends. $75–85; reservations recommended, especially during football season, when they catch the spillover of fans from Tallahassee.

Steinhatchee 32359
Gulfstream Motel and Marina (352-498-8088; www.gulfstreammotelmarina.com), CR 358, is actually in Jena (Dixie County) but part of the Steinhatchee community. With 20 newly refurbished units in the middle of the action, it's perfect for folks headed out on fishing or scalloping trips. Large, well-maintained units ($69–99) feature kitchenettes, television, and plenty of beds for the kids; there's even a unit with bunk beds, and family-friendly cabins ($109). Connecting rooms make it possible to bring the extended family. You'll find **Andrew Dowd's Smokehouse** (open Thu–Sun, with AYCE breakfast buffets) and a tiki bar on the premises, as well as charters, boat rentals, live-aboard marina slips, marina store, and fish-cleaning stations. Guests receive docking and launching privileges with their room.

Ideal Marina and Motel (352-498-3877; www.steinhatchee.com/ideal), 114 Riverside Dr. Jody and Scott Peters run this pretty little place right on the river, with walk-out-the-door access to your boat at the marina. Each sparkling room has pine board walls and tile floors, cable TV, and nice-sized bathroom; most have a small refrigerator, and guests share a patio and grill area. Boat slips are included in the room price, $59–89, and a full two-bedroom, two-bath rental house is available for $139. A full-service marina, they offer boat rentals, guide service, fishing licenses, bait and tackle, marine supplies, and a dive shop. The Peterses also own the small **Fisherman's Rest Motel** across the street, $50–69.

Pelican Pointe Inn (352-498-7427), 1306 SE Riverside Drive. With condos converted to motel rooms in 2002, Pelican Pointe offers a riverfront view and dockage in front of your room, adjacent to Fiddler's Restaurant (see *Dining Out*). Amenities vary, but all of the spacious rooms have cable TV and screened balconies; $65 and up.

Steinhatchee River Inn (352-498-4049), Riverside Dr, has 17 large and tidy units on a hillside above the river, offering a variety of room configurations (most are two-room suites) at $55–65. The swimming pool overlooks the river.

Sunset Place Resort Motel (352-498-0860), 115 1st St SW. Every condo has a full kitchen and sweeping view of the Gulf estuary along the Steinhatchee River, where you can watch the sunset from your balcony or at the pool; $75–105.

RESORT

Steinhatchee 32359
Steinhatchee Landing Resort (352-498-3513; www.steinhatcheelanding.com), FL 51. It's a magical place, with the feel of a turn-of-the-20th-century village on the shores of the Steinhatchee River, where ancient live oaks shade Old Florida and Victorian gingerbread homes that melt into the landscape. When owner Dean Fowler came to Steinhatchee from Georgia in the 1970s to fish, he saw a need for a place where the whole family could come and relax while the family angler was out on a fishing trip. At Steinhatchee Landing, the 31 tasteful old-fashioned homes come with modern interiors: a step from Florida Cracker into a page out of *House*

Sandra Friend

THE STEINHATCHEE RIVER AT STEINHATCHEE LANDING

Beautiful, with hardwood and tiled floors, high ceilings, gleaming modern kitchens, and inviting overstuffed beds. Most of the homes are owned privately and leased for rental through the 35-acre resort, where guests are free to roam and enjoy the riverside pool, health center, petting farm, children's playground, and miles of walking trails; canoes and kayaks, guided pontoon tours, and bicycles are available for a nominal fee. In addition to a conference center accommodating 60 guests, the newly christened Dancing Waters Chapel provides a lovely natural nondenominational setting for weddings and other special events. This family-friendly venue hosts many reunions, including get-togethers of the Carter clan of Plains, Georgia, and caters to newlyweds with romantic Honeymoon Cottages, each with fireplace and hot tub. Rates start at $120 off-season for a one-bedroom, 1-night stay in one of the Spice Cottages, modeled after old Florida seaside village homes; discounts apply to stays of weekends and longer.

CAMPGROUNDS

Keaton Beach 32348

Old Pavilion RV Park & Camping (850-838-1776), Keaton Beach Rd, offers scenic, sunny full-hookup spaces surrounded by a salt marsh with sweeping view of the Gulf; $25–30 with full hookups, including cable TV, or $8 for tent camping. This is a family-friendly place, and the bathhouse is wheelchair accessible.

Perry 32348

Southern Oaks Campground (850-838-3221), US 19 S, provides a mix of shady and sunny pull-through sites with full hookups; swimming pool.

Steinhatchee 32359

Fisherman's Rest (352-498-3877), 115 Riverside Dr. Across from and owned by the Ideal Marina and Motel (see *Hotels and Motels*), this relaxing campground offers high, dry campsites shaded by live oaks, with full-hookup (including cable) pull-through sites ($20) and a tent camping area with bathhouse ($8). Easy walk to restaurants and the marina.

Steinhatchee Outpost (1-800-589-1541; www.steinhatcheeoutpost.com), US 19 and FL 51, offers open and shaded sites ($8–22) for tents and RVs, adjacent to the Steinhatchee River, as well as a private pond for paddling, canoe and kayak rentals for trips on the river, and quiet rental cabins ($50–175).

Wood's Gulf Breeze Campground & Marina (352-498-3948; www.woodsgulfbreeze.com), 2nd Ave N, has shady sites ($23) overlooking the estuary, including some prime tent spots along the marshes of Deadman's Bay. Forty RV sites, eight tent sites with electric, and a dump station.

DIVE RESORT

Mayo 32066

Tucked under a canopy of live oaks on the river bluffs, **Jim Hollis' River Rendezvous** (1-800-533-5276; www.jimhollis.com), Rt 2, Box 635, has more than 90 spaces on the Suwannee River ranging from primitive tenting ($5) to full hookup ($12); rental cabins and rooms available, including a riverside A-frame. This expansive riverfront resort features a large playground, swimming area, canoe and kayak rentals, pontoon boat rides, game room, pistol and rifle range, and restaurant on site. Perfect for your diving expedition: An on-site dive shop has rental gear and instruction.

✷ Where to Eat

DINING OUT

Mayo
The Savannah Room (386-294-2332; www.southernchateau.com), Bloxham and Fletcher Sts. Serving up steak, chicken, and local seafood favorites ($9–20) such as lobster tail, blue crab claws, grouper, and frog legs, the classy dining room of the Chateau B&B (see *Bed & Breakfasts*) opens to the public on Fri and Sat evenings for fine dining. Reservations recommended.

Steinhatchee
Fiddler's Restaurant (352-498-7427), 1306 Riverside Dr, is set in a giant fishpond (complete with koi) overlooking the river. Kick back and enjoy the view out the picture windows as you feast on specialties like grilled grouper with caper sauce, caprice chicken, and Greek shrimp with feta over linguine. Entrées run $11–18 for fresh local seafood, from mullet and shrimp to crab claws, and the steaks are fantastic: Delmonico, prime rib, and filet mignon, $16–22. The lunch menu offers salads and sandwiches, $5–8, including grouper, shrimp salad, and pecan chicken salad on a croissant. Stop in the lobby on your way out and look over the great selection of Guy Harvey T-shirts. Open daily.

EATING OUT

Keaton Beach
At the end of Keaton Beach Rd, the **Keaton Beach Hot Dog Stand** (850-578-2675; www.keatonbeach-florida.com) is *the* place to eat in this seaside town, and they serve seafood and breakfast (Sat and Sun) as well as milk shakes and sundaes—good eats for cheap, with sandwiches $2–4, seafood dinners $6–12.

Mayo
At 3 PM on a Monday, the parking lot at the **Mayo Café** (386-294-2127), US 27, is packed. That's because everyone in the tricounty area knows Belinda Travis and Shirley Watson, and knows that these ladies dish up great home cooking, buffet style. Try the tempting salads at the salad bar, and southern comfort foods like fried chicken, fried okra, and collard greens. Breakfast served 5–10:30 ($1.95–5.95); lunch and dinner ($1.25–16.95) until 9 (10 on weekends). Buffet $5.80, or $11.95 on Fri evenings, when it includes delicious fresh Gulf seafood—from shrimp to crab claws.

Perry
Sisters' Tea Room & Gallery (850-838-2021; www.sisterstearoom.com), 121 E Green St, pours on the charm with your choice of three formal teas ($5.95–11.95): a cream tea with scones and fresh fruit; a light afternoon tea including sandwiches, tea breads, and pastries; or a full afternoon tea adding on quiche and desserts. Offering themed teas and

unique varieties of tea, they're an unexpected find in downtown Perry.

Steinhatchee

Bridge End Café Restaurant (352-498-2002), 310 10th St. In a cozy little Cracker cottage at the south end of the bridge over the Steinhatchee River, Jude McDaris and Robin Marable present local seafood favorites and comfort food served with a smile. The baked goods will catch your eye on the way in—leave some room for favorites like cherry pie, coconut cake, and the Steinhatchee Mudslide, a concoction involving brownies, ice cream, and chocolate syrup. Breakfasts (buffet $5 on weekends) include omelets made with fresh shrimp; a selection of salads and sandwiches ($2–7) dominates the lunch menu, and dinner entrées with heaping helpings of sides and a salad bar run $7–12, including the unique Steinhatchee Steamer Pot of fresh steamed clams, potatoes, corn-on-the-cob, onions, broccoli, and celery for $9. If you need a box lunch for a scalloping trip, stop in the night before!

Everyone raves about **Roy's** (352-498-5000), Riverside Dr, a fixture since 1969 with a killer view of a Steinhatchee sunset. Their mashed potato salad goes down smooth as silk, and the barbecue attracts folks from several counties. Offering a wide variety of steaks and seafood, Roy's is a place for fresh locally caught specialties including bay scallops, shrimp, oysters, and tender mullet. Entrées $9–15.50; open for lunch and dinner. When you can tear your eyes away from the entrancing view of the estuary, enjoy the many scenes of the region painted by local artist Linda K. Della Poali. They're for sale, as are the goodies in **Gold N' Gifts** (352-498-0202), with jewelry and local art inside a niche in the restaurant.

✷ Selective Shopping

Perry

You'll find both old and new books at the **Book Mart** (850-584-4969), 2115 S Byron Butler Pkwy, where I was enthralled with the collection of Florida books out front, and was pointed toward an essential book for learning about this region, *Along the Edge of America*, by Peter Jenkins.

Michelle's Bull Pen (850-584-3098), 3180 US 19 S, is a great westernwear shop with moccasins, boots, hats, and jewelry as well as tack for your steeds.

In addition to jewelry, **Rebecca's Gold & Gifts** (850-584-2505), 117 E Green St, has a nice selection of home decor items and gifts, including candles and potpourri.

Perry Flea Market (850-838-1422), US 27 S, held Fri–Sun, is a good old-fashioned flea market featuring antiques, collectibles, and tools.

Shady Oaks Antiques (850-584-7971), 5451 US 27. Open daily 9–5. Not only is this shop stuffed to the brim with antiques, but the ephemera spills outside as well: Look for claw-foot tubs, gaily-painted bed frames, and pink flamingos under the live oaks. **Em's Emporium**, a separate but affiliated shop, sits out back.

Sisters' Tea Room & Gallery (see *Eating Out*) has an adjoining shop with arts and crafts from regional artists and general gift items.

Steinhatchee

Deadman's Bay Trading Company is a fun and funky collection of tiki huts with local artists showing off flint knapping, photography, primitives, flea market under tarps, fresh produce, seashells.

The Goldfish Gift Shop & Café (352-498-0277), 800 1st Ave. This sweet little shop showcases nautical gifts and local art on consignment, as well as light breakfasts and tea. Open Thu–Sun 9–6.

The Sea Witch, 12th St and Riverside, carries nautical items, local arts and crafts, and T-shirts.

PRODUCE AND FRESH SEAFOOD **Old Hickory** (352-498-5333), Steinhatchee, has fresh seafood you can't do without, including smoked mullet dip, fresh crabmeat, jumbo crab, and, of course, scallops.

Produce Place Farm Market, US 19, Perry. Fresh local produce and good Georgia peaches in-season.

✷ Special Events

October: **Pioneer Day Festival**, Mayo, second Sat. This pioneer-themed event mixes up history and fun: Southern belles drift through town as staged gunfights rage; the crowd whoops and hollers at the rodeo while more sedate visitors amble through hundreds of craft booths and an arts show.

THE UPPER SUWANNEE

BAKER, COLUMBIA, HAMILTON, MADISON, AND SUWANNEE COUNTIES

As settlers trickled into the new territory of Florida in 1820, they found the red clayhills and deep ravines of North Florida reminiscent of the terrain they'd left behind in Georgia and the Carolinas. Building farms and plantations along the Suwannee River and its tributaries, they founded villages and cities with a Deep South feel. **Fort White** grew up around a frontier fortress from the Second Seminole War, while **Branford** was once an important steamboat-building town. Antebellum homes grace **Madison**, **Lake City**, **Greenville**, and **White Springs**. A post-1900s building boom associated with railroad commerce sets the tone for **Jasper** and **Live Oak**. Covering only 1 square mile, **Lee** is one of the state's smallest incorporated towns. Established in 1913 by the Advent Christian Church, **Dowling Park** remains a religiously oriented retirement village with a beautiful slice of waterfront on the Suwannee River. **Macclenny**, the seat of rural Baker County, dates back to 1886, and was once known as the horticultural capital of Florida; the Glen St. Mary Nursery, established 1907, was responsible for the citrus industry's standardization of orange varieties. **Lake City**, the heart of the region and the seat of Columbia County, was first known as Alligator Town, a Seminole village ruled by the powerful chief Alligator in the 1830s, and was to have been the home of the University of Florida, but political supporters in Gainesville wooed the college down their way.

Imbued with the grace of the Old South, the towns of the Upper Suwannee offer a reflection on Florida's start as a state during a period of national upheaval. This is a part of Florida that's remained almost untouched since Reconstruction. The economy is based on agriculture, not tourism. Amber waves of grain wave along the highways, and barefoot youngsters walk the clay roads down to the springs. You'll encounter many postage-stamp-sized towns as you pass through vast swaths of beautiful rural Florida: Stop and sit a spell.

GUIDANCE When you arrive in the region, stop at the **State of Florida's Nature & Heritage Tourism Center** (386-397-4461), FL 136 and US 41, White Springs 32096. As Florida's official outdoor recreation tourism center, it provides a bounty of information on activities throughout the state. Browse their library of guidebooks, or pick up a handful of brochures and a state parks guide. Open daily 9–5. If you're headed out on the rivers, you'll want a map showing boating access and springs: Contact the **Suwannee River Water Management District** (386-362-1001; www.srwmd.state.fl.us), 9225 CR 49, Live Oak 32060; you can also download their recreational guide from the web site. For an overview of the region, contact **Original Florida** (1-877-746-4778; www.original florida.org or www.springs-r-us.org), which has a welcome center at 601 Hall of Fame Dr in Lake City and can put you in touch with county tourism boards.

GETTING THERE *By air*: The nearest commuter service comes into **Tallahassee** (see "Capital Region") and **Gainesville** (see "Alachua and the Historic Lake District"); however, **Jacksonville International Airport** (see "Jacksonville") provides a broader choice of carriers and is a 1½-hour drive by I-10.

By bus: **Greyhound** (1-800-229-9424; www.greyhound.com) makes stops in Lake City, Live Oak, and Madison.

By car: **I-75** and **I-10** provide quick access to most of the region, but you'll want to wander the back roads to see the sights. Heading north from High Springs, **US 41** passes through downtown Lake City before becoming Hamilton County's "Main Street," running through its three major towns—White Springs, Jasper, and Jennings. **US 129** also runs north–south, linking Branford, Live Oak, and Jasper. For the scenic east–west route, take **US 90** from Olustee west to Lake City, Live Oak, Lee, Madison, and Greenville; **US 27** takes a more southerly route, tying together High Springs, Fort White, and Branford on its way to Tallahassee.

By train: **Amtrak** (1-800-USA-RAIL) has regular service along the main line running through Olustee, Lake City, Live Oak, Lee, Madison, and Greenville.

MEDICAL EMERGENCIES Regional hospitals include **Shands at Lake Shore Hospital** (386-755-3200), 560 E Franklin St, Lake City; **Shands at Live Oak** (386-362-1413), 1100 11th St SW, Live Oak; and **Madison County Memorial Hospital** (850-973-2271), 201 E Marion St, Madison.

✷ To See

DE SOTO TRAIL In 1539 Spanish explorer Hernando de Soto and his troops crossed Florida in pursuit of gold. Roadside markers along US 90 interpret his route.

EQUESTRIAN EVENTS **Suwannee River Riding Club, Inc**. (386-935-0447), US 129 north of Branford. Stop by their arena to watch team roping (first and third Fri) and speed events (first and third Sat) each month.

GHOST TOWNS The towns of **Columbus** and **Ellaville** vanished not long after steamboats stopped chugging up the Suwannee, supplanted by railroads. You'll find the Columbus Cemetery within Suwannee River State Park (see *Green Space*). Directly across the Suwannee, the remains of Ellaville (primarily foundations and loose bricks) lie along the Florida Trail through Twin Rivers State

Forest just north of the former site of the **Drew Mansion** off old US 90, on the west side of the Suwannee River bridge.

HISTORIC SITES

Falling Creek

First established as a Baptist congregation in a log cabin prior to 1866, the current **Falling Creek Methodist Church and Cemetery**, Falling Creek Rd, dates back to the 1880s, the land donated to the church after 1855 by heirs of one of the original settlers of the area, Thomas D. Dicks from South Carolina. Wood frame weathered by age, original water glass, shaded by ancient live oaks and southern magnolias; the deep gorge of Falling Creek rings the property (see *Waterfalls*).

Jasper

Built in 1893, the **Old Jail** (386-792-1300), 501 NE 1st Ave, functioned as a prison until 1984, but now serves as the Hamilton County Historical Society Museum (see *Museums*) and gives a glimpse into what it was like on both sides of the bars—the sheriff and his family occupied living quarters connected to the jail. Visit the living quarters and walk through the creepy jail cells. Saved from the wrecking ball by a determined group of women, the structure is still undergoing restoration, as is the adjoining **Heritage Village** complex, where Jasper holds its annual cane-grinding festival (see *Special Events*), and a cotton gin, a small church, and two shotgun houses await restoration.

Lake City

In downtown Lake City, check out the old **Columbia County Courthouse**, circa 1902. The **Columbia County Historical Society** (see *Museums*) sits in a neighborhood dominated by beautiful 1890s Victorian houses, including the **Chalker-Turner House**, 104 E St. Johns. Stop at the historical society for information on walking tours in the city's antebellum neighborhoods.

Live Oak

Take a look at that **Wrigley's ad** painted on the side of a building on W Howard St: It's been there since 1909. Glance at Sperring's Muffler and Lube, and you'll realize it's a **1960s Sinclair gas station**. That's the way history is in Live Oak: all around you, but transformed into something utilitarian, from the **1890s downtown block** filled with businesses to the pillared **Thomas Dowling** house on FL 136, renovated into a community center. There's plenty of interest for the history buff who's willing to poke around. Stop first at the Suwannee County Historical Museum (see *Museums*) to get your bearings for a walking tour of downtown.

AN OLD COTTON GIN AT JASPER'S HERITAGE VILLAGE

Sandra Friend

Macclenny

Now serving as the town's library, the original **Baker County Courthouse** is an architectural landmark at the corner of 5th and McIver Sts. The old **Baker County Jail**, built 1911–1913 (see *Genealogical Research*), is next door. The sheriff's family lived on site and prepared food for inmates. Stop in at the Macclenny Chamber of Commerce, 20 E Macclenny Ave, to browse through their book of historic sites and get directions to see the town's historic homes from the late 1800s, all privately owned.

Madison

With more than 30 buildings from the 1800s and nearly 50 historic sites dating to 1936, downtown Madison has the highest concentration of historical architecture in the region. Start your walk by picking up the *Walking/Driving Tour of Madison County* brochure from the chamber of commerce; it contains a map and detailed information on each historic site. The **Wardlaw-Smith-Goza Mansion** (850-973-9432), 103 N Washington St, is a Classical Revival mansion built in 1860, once known as Whitehall. North Florida Community College uses the mansion as a conference center, and tours are offered Tue–Thu 10–2 (closed mid-Dec to mid-Jan). Other historic homes of note include the **W. H. Dial House**, 105 E Marion St, a Victorian mansion circa 1880; the **J. E. Hardee House**, 107 E Marion St, a two-story Mediterranean villa from 1918 designed by Lloyd Barton Greer (who also designed the classy **Madison County Courthouse**); and the **Livingston House**, 501 N Range St, Madison's oldest home, from 1836. In continuous use for worship services since 1881, the small wood frame **St. Mary's Episcopal Church** (850-973-8338), 108 N Horry St, permits tours by appointment.

Dedicated in memory to Captain Colin P. Kelly Jr., a Madison resident and the first American casualty of World War II on December 9, 1941, at Clark Field in the Philippines, the **Four Freedoms Monument**, downtown, reflects on the "Four Freedoms" speech made by President Franklin Delano Roosevelt prior to the outbreak of the war.

Near the old Madison Depot, a **giant steam engine** sits along Range Road at 109 W Rutledge. It's a relic of what was once the largest cotton gin in the world, combing through Sea Island cotton at the Florida Manufacturing Company in the 1880s.

Olustee

Olustee Battlefield Historic State Park (386-758-0400), US 90, is the site of Florida's largest and bloodiest Civil War battle, a patch of hallowed ground beneath the pines, preserved as a memorial by the 1899 Florida legislature to the men who fell during the 4-hour conflict. Sparked by a push by Union general Truman A. Seymour, whose success at capturing Baldwin tempted him to send his troops toward the railroad bridge at Columbus without orders from his superiors, the Union forces were met by the largest Confederate buildup to defend Florida—thanks to Florida's crucial role as a beef supplier to the Confederate army. On February 20, 1864, more than 10,000 met in combat in these pine woods; casualties topped 2,000. An annual reenactment (third weekend of February)

Sandra Friend

YOUNG SOLDIERS PLAYING CHESS AT THE ANNUAL OLUSTEE BATTLE REENACTMENT

re-creates the battle and encampments; with nearly 10,000 participants, it's one of the South's largest encampments. It's an excellent educational experience, especially for those unschooled in Florida's Civil War history. Interpretive center open daily 9–5; an interpretive walk takes you through the battlefield stations. Free.

White Springs
White Sulfur Springs Spa. Behind the Nature & Tourism Center, follow the wooden staircase down to the original White Sulfur Springs Spa, built in the late 1800s. Standing on the balcony, you can look down into the spa, and down along the rapid flow of the Suwannee River. During World War II the spa and its grounds served as an internment camp for German prisoners of war.

MUSEUMS After you learn about Florida's most significant Civil War battle at the visitors center at **Olustee Battlefield** (see *Historic Sites*), stop in the **Olustee Visitor's Center and Museum** at the old railroad depot (off US 90) for an interactive walk through life in this logging and railroad community. In downtown Lake City, the **Columbia County Historical Museum** (386-755-9096) offers exhibit rooms with furnishings that capture the period of this southern Italianate manor circa 1870, including artifacts from the Civil War.

Housed in the former Atlantic Coast Line freight depot from 1903, the **Suwannee County Historical Museum and Telephone Museum** (386-362-1776), 208 Ohio Ave N, Live Oak, presents dioramas and an extensive collection of historic objects—including a working telephone switching station—to bring history alive. At the Old Jail in Jasper (see *Historic Sites*), the **Hamilton County Historical Society Museum** shows off historical documents, display cases with exhibits, and photos of historical structures throughout the county, along with a small gift shop with local art.

A repository of Madison County history, with information on long-lost historic sites like the San Pedro Mission and the Drew Mansion, the 1883 **Old Jail Museum** (850-973-3661), 405 W Pickney St, Madison, is open Mon–Sat 10–2. The funky **Beggs Museum & Art Exhibit** at T. J. Beggs & Company (see *Selective Shopping*) is literally a walk through an old attic, with an eclectic collection of local ephemera including World War II memorabilia and an extensive section on funerary equipment, another of the Beggs family's historical enterprises.

RAILROADIANA Many settlements of the Upper Suwannee started as railroad towns, so their railroad history remains. You'll find turn-of-the-20th-century railroad depots still standing in **Fort White**, **Live Oak**, **Madison**, and restored depots at **Olustee** (housing a beautiful visitors center with regional railroad history), and Macclenny (with a red caboose outside the depot). A historic iron boxwork bridge crosses the Suwannee River at **Dowling Park**. The east–west main line paralleling US 90 through the region remains a busy thoroughfare (great train spotting for rail fans); its Suwannee River crossing (as seen from within **Suwannee River State Park**, or from the old US 90 bridge, now a walking trail) is fairly dramatic and has significant historic import—the military objective of the Union troops stopped at Olustee (see *Historic Sites*) was to blow up the original railroad bridge here, severing commerce between North Florida and the Panhandle. Stop in the **Suwannee County Historical Museum** (see *Museums*) for information on Live Oak's railroading history. Live Oak grew up around the Seaboard Air Line railroad, which came through in 1903, and the locally owned Live Oak, Perry & Gulf Railroad, affectionately known as the "Lopin' Gopher." Railroad shops in Live Oak once turned out steam locomotives and parts for the Plant System.

✷ To Do

BEACHES While none of the counties in this region touches either the Atlantic or the Gulf, you'll find beautiful white sand beaches suitable for sunning, swimming, and camping along the **Suwannee River** at Suwannee Springs and Big Shoals (see *Green Space*), at Spirit of the Suwannee Music Park (see *Lodging*), and along the Florida National Scenic Trail (see *Hiking*).

BICYCLING Mountain bikers have a blast on rugged riverside trails built and maintained by the **Suwannee Bicycle Association** (386-397-2347), P.O. Box 247, White Springs 32096. Stop by their office to pick up maps of local biking routes, including the popular Swift Creek, Gar Pond, Disappearing Creek, and Big Shoals routes. Each provides challenges to bikers with the undulating terrain along the Suwannee River and its tributaries; trails are posted for three levels of difficulty, from beginner to gung-ho. **American Canoe Adventures** (see *Paddling*) rents mountain bikes in White Springs. For a tamer outing, a paved rail-trail runs along the **Suwannee River Greenway** (see *Green Space*) from Little River Springs County Park in Suwannee County to Ichetucknee Run in Columbia County, passing through the town of Branford. Madison County boasts **The Loop**, a 100-mile marked bike route running down paved rural byways; pick up a map from the chamber of commerce (see *Guidance*).

BIRDING Top sites in the region include **Alligator Lake** (see *Green Space*), where colonies of nesting egrets occupy the islands, and the **Nice Wander Trail** in the **Osceola National Forest**, where an early-morning visit lets you watch rare red-cockaded woodpeckers, marked with white bands, emerging from their holes in longleaf pines. Part of the **Florida National Scenic Trail**, which also affords access to red-cockaded woodpecker colonies much deeper in the forest, the 2-mile accessible-with-assistance Nice Wander Trail starts at a trailhead at the **Olustee Battlefield Historic State Park** entrance. At the **Ladell Brothers Environmental Center** in Madison you can borrow a pair of binoculars from the Hamilton Library and go birding in this lush oasis of hardwoods in the middle of the North Florida Community College campus.

BOATING Most of the rivers in this region have shallows, sandbars, and rapids. Unless your craft has a very shallow draft, don't take it any farther up the Suwannee River than its confluence with the Withlacoochee—snags and sandbars are very real hazards, and have flipped many a Skidoo. See *Paddling* for details on the best river routes in the region.

DIVING Where the Santa Fe meets the Suwannee, the town of Branford calls itself the "Spring Diving Capital of the World." Stop in at the **Steamboat Dive Inn** (see *Lodging*) for information about open-water dive sites. Cave divers also flock here for both spring diving in the **Suwannee River** and the extensive underwater cave system at **Peacock Springs** (see *Green Space*). For cold air, gear rentals, instruction, and a friendly chat with Cathy about cave diving, stop at the **Dive Outpost** (386-776-1449; www.diveoutpost.com), 20148 180th St, en route to the park. *Important note*: Many open-water divers have died in this region while attempting cave diving. Do not enter an underwater cave or spring unless you are a certified cave diver. Most springs must be accessed by boat, and a DIVER DOWN flag is necessary while diving the river.

FAMILY ACTIVITIES One of the favorite pastimes of local families is to get the kids in the van and head on down to **Suwannee Springs** (see *Springs*) for some freebie swimming and sunning on the natural white sand beaches of the Suwannee River, or to the water park at **Jellystone Campground** (see *Lodging*) in Madison, where a 60-foot-tall, 300-foot-long spiral water slide splashes down into a small lake lined with kids' activities, from playground equipment, boats, and water sprinklers to the nearby mini golf, tractor-train rides to a ghost town in the woods, and cartoons in the Yogi Theatre. $9 person for day use; water park and other kids' activities open weekends and for special events only.

FISHING From **Ocean Pond** at Olustee to **Lang Lake Public Fishing Area**, north of White Springs on US 41, you'll find plenty of stillwater opportunities as well as more than 100 miles of the Suwannee River to explore. Don't miss **Cherry Lake**, a WPA reservoir north of Madison popular for bass fishing. Looking for bream? Head for the **Aucilla River** west of Greenville.

GENEALOGICAL RESEARCH In Madison, **Elmer's Genealogical Library** (386-929-2970), 115 W Base St, caters to researchers digging into their family roots, with more than 1,700 rolls of microfilm, 3,000 books, and 4,000 genealogical newsletters to review. Open weekdays 10–4, or by appointment. Housed in the old Baker County Jail in Macclenny, the **Baker County Historical Society Family History Library** (904-259-0587), 42 W McIver, opens Tue 1–8, Sat 1–4 for folks doing historical and genealogical research; you can also make an appointment to visit. Both sites provide fabulous resources for people researching their local connections to the Civil War.

GOLF **Pineview Golf and Country Club** (904-259-3447), 1751 Golf Club Rd, Macclenny, offers golfing in an open, uncluttered environment with pleasing landscaping under the Florida pines. Eighteen holes $16–22, nine holes $7–13.

HIKING Starting at Olustee Battlefield, you can backpack more than 100 miles of the **Florida National Scenic Trail**, following the Suwannee River for nearly 70 miles from the southern shore of Big Shoals through White Springs to Mill Creek. To pass through sections of private land along the river, you must be a member of the **Florida Trail Association** (1-877-HIKE-FLA; www.florida-trail.org). You can also find excellent hiking at **Alligator Lake**, **O'Leno State Park**, and numerous other locations detailed in *50 Hikes in North Florida* (Backcountry Guides). Don't miss the easy 2-mile round trip to Big Shoals from **Big Shoals Public Lands** north of White Springs, where you can watch the rapids froth like cola, and the easy 0.25-mile walk down to **Falling Creek Falls** (see *Waterfalls*). Pursue your Florida State Forests Trailwalker patch with several qualifying trails in **Twin Rivers State Forest**, or take an easy amble along the Suwannee River waterfront on the **Milford Clark Nature Trail** at Dowling Park, a 4-mile round trip starting behind the Village Lodge (see *Lodging*). Area hikers also vouch for the beauty of the new **Four Freedoms Trail**, a 6-mile round trip to the Withlacoochee River (see *Greenways*).

PADDLING The **Suwannee River** is one of the top paddling destinations in Florida, thanks to its length and lack of commercial boat traffic—it has enough shoals and sandbars to discourage most motorboats from heading any farther north than Ellaville. It takes 2 weeks to paddle the river from its headwaters in the Okeefenokee Swamp in Georgia to the town of Suwannee on the Gulf of Mexico. With its broad sand beaches and beautiful springs, the Suwannee is a perfect choice for a long-distance canoe outing. To read about one man's adventure on the river, check out *From the Swamp to the Keys: A Paddle Through Florida History* by Johnny Molloy (University Press of Florida, 2003); a dated but useful guidebook is *Canoeing and Camping the Beautiful Suwannee River* by William A. Logan.

Several outfitters provide rentals and shuttles along the Upper Suwannee. In White Springs stop in at **American Canoe Adventures** (1-800-624-8081; www.aca1.com), 10610 Bridge St, where they can set you up with a canoe or kayak and shuttle service, or arrange a multiday outing. They also handle Florida's only white-water rafting excursions (see *White-Water Rafting*). Where US 129 crosses the Suwannee north of Live Oak, the **Suwannee Canoe Outpost** (1-800-428-4147; www.canoeoutpost.com) provides canoe and kayak rentals and shuttles out of **Spirit of the Suwannee Music Park** (see *Lodging*). In Pinetta, **Twin Rivers Outfitters** (850-929-2200; www.twinriversoutfitters.com), 4718 NE Belleville Rd, gets you out on the lesser-known (but just as fun) Withlacoochee and Alapaha Rivers, which flow into the Suwannee, and the Upper Aucilla, which makes its way down toward the Gulf of Mexico. Canoeists putting in on the Ichetucknee and Santa Fe Rivers near Bradford can contact the **Santa Fe Canoe Outpost** (386-454-2050), US 441, for rentals.

SWIMMING Swimmers have plenty of choices in the region: from the water park at Jellystone Campground in Madison (see *Family Activities*) to the many springs open for swimming along the Suwannee River and its tributaries (see *Springs*).

TRAIL RIDING Rent horses and tack at **Spirit of the Suwannee Stables** (386-364-1683) inside the Spirit of the Suwannee Music Park (see *Lodging*) to ride the many miles of equestrian trails along the south side of the Suwannee River in Holton Creek Wildlife Management Area. Trail rides run $20 per hour or $90 per day; stall rentals and riding lessons are available. Equestrian trails also wind through **Twin Rivers State Forest** in Madison County and crisscross the **Osceola National Forest** (see *Wild Places*), with opportunities for overnight camping.

TUBING The most popular tubing route in the state, the **Ichetucknee River** flows forth from Ichetucknee Springs to create a crystalline stream that winds through deep, dark hardwood forests. Pick up a rental tube ($2 a day) at any of the many small shops along US 27; **Joanne's Tubes** is the closest to the park's south entrance, off US 27. A shuttle takes you up to the north end of the park for launch; leave your rental tube in the tube corral at the end of the day for the outfitters to reclaim.

WALKING TOURS In Lake City the Lake Isabella Residential District covers 30 blocks, and the downtown historic district encompasses another 15 blocks. Pick up a walking tour brochure at the Columbia County Historical Museum (see *Museums*). At White Springs grab a walking tour brochure at the State of Florida's Nature & Heritage Tourism Center (see *Guidance*); interpretive signs add to your understanding of the town's history as you walk. The Madison Chamber of Commerce can also provide you with a walking tour brochure for their extensive historic downtown.

WHITE-WATER RAFTING Believe it or not, you *can* go white-water rafting in Florida! When conditions are right, the **Big Shoals of the Suwannee River** provide more than a mile of Class III white-water fun. Contact **American Canoe Adventures** (see *Paddling*) in White Springs to find out if the river level is up to par. They'll set you up with a raft and all the necessary gear, leaving you the option of running the rapids multiple times (possible thanks to a canoe portage path on the south shore) or shooting them once, then paddling downstream to White Springs.

✳ Green Space

GREENWAYS Running between Little River Springs County Park and Ichetucknee Run, the **Suwannee River Greenway** provides a paved bicycle path with limited shade along an old railroad route; parking area in downtown Branford. Ten miles north of Madison, the 3-mile **Four Freedoms Trail** starts at Pinetta and heads to the state border at the Withlacoochee River. Now unpaved but providing a pleasant hike, this new greenway project will eventually link the Georgia border to Madison with biking, hiking, and equestrian trails.

NATURE CENTERS Tucked away in the middle of the North Florida Community College campus west of Madison, the **Ladell Brothers Outdoor Environmental Center** (850-973-1645), 1000 Turner Davis Dr, is a little hard to find: Park on campus near the Hamilton Library and walk between Building 5 (Biology) and the Student Success Center to reach the green space beyond. Follow the lakeshore to the trees, where you'll find the trailhead to this shaded network of hiking trails perfect for wildlife-watching.

PARKS

Branford
On the east shore of the Suwannee River at US 27, **Ivey Memorial Park** has a bait-and-tackle shop, a boat ramp, picnic tables with an expansive view of the Suwannee River, and a swimming hole at **Branford Spring** accessed via a boardwalk near the park entrance. It also provides parking for people using the Suwannee River Greenway.

High Springs
One of the oldest state parks in the system, **O'Leno State Park** (386-454-1853), US 41, has two campgrounds with 64 spaces, and 17 stone-and-log cabins nestled along the Santa Fe River, which vanishes into a riversink and flows underground for several miles. A network of hiking trails winds through shady hardwood forests, leading to the river rise.

Lake City
Alligator Lake Recreation Area (386-755-4100), SE Country Club Rd. More than 6 miles of hiking trails surround Alligator Lake and its adjacent impoundments, where colonies of herons nest in the willows. Paddle a kayak across the placid water, or walk the gentle trails with your family.

Lee
Behind city hall the historic **McMullen Farm House** forms the centerpiece of a small city park with a fishpond, picnic tables, and walking trail. Drive 10 miles east of Lee on US 90 to reach **Suwannee River State Park** (386-362-2746), 20185 CR 132. Although this beautiful riverfront park boasts a pleasant campground, gentle and rugged nature trails, historic Civil War earthworks, and some of the best views you'll get of the Suwannee River, you're missing out if you don't visit its wild side along the north shore of the Suwannee, accessible only via the **Florida Trail** (see *Hiking*).

Macclenny
♿ Along US 90 west of town, **Glen St. Mary River Park** affords access for boaters and canoeists to the Little St. Mary River, with several fishing decks on a dredged channel out to the river.

White Springs
The mission of **Stephen Foster Folk Culture Center State Park** (386-397-2733), US 41, is to preserve Florida's folk culture heritage, with the state's

folklorist on staff, a permanent craft village, and the **Florida Folk Festival** (see *Special Events*), the state's premier venue for cultural preservation. In addition to the cultural exhibits, there is a pleasant campground, and the **Florida Trail** passes through the park, following the Suwannee River.

SPRINGS Imagine a mirror-smooth surface of clear water reflecting hues of robin's-egg blue. That's **Ichetucknee Springs**, found at the north end of **Ichetucknee Springs State Park** (386-497-2511), 8294 SW Elim Church Rd. In addition to swimming and diving at the spring, visitors grab tubes and float down the placid spring run (see *Tubing*), or take to the stream with canoes and kayaks for a serene trip down one of Florida's purest rivers.

Contact the Suwannee River Water Management District for a map of spring locations in the Suwannee River for diving and swimming; most can only be accessed by boat. In Suwannee County, small county parks provide access to **Charles Spring** (south of Dowling Park), **Little River Springs**, **Royal Springs** (north of Branford), and **Branford Spring** (at Ivey Park in Branford), all of which invite swimmers and divers to plunge into their chilly depths.

🐾 ♿ At **Peacock Springs State Park** (386-497-2511), 180th St (follow signs east from FL 51), a one-lane dirt road winds through deep woods past pulloffs leading to sinkholes that interconnect underground, forming a karst playground for cave divers. $5 dive fee. You *must* be cave certified to dive in these springs. No solo diving. Swimming is permitted in Orange Grove and Peacock Springs. Limited facilities, including composting toilet, picnic tables, ramp to Orange Grove Springs. Leashed dogs only.

Open Sat 10–6, **Madison Blue Spring State Park** (386-362-2746) provides visitors a cool natural pool along the Withlacoochee River at FL 6. Along US 90 near Suwannee River State Park, **Falmouth Springs** creates a popular swimming area. At **Suwannee Springs** (north of Live Oak off US 129 before the river bridge), a warm sulfur spring pours into a turn-of-the-20th-century spa building before flowing out into the river. Expansive beaches make this a cool weekend hangout (see *Family Activities*).

WATERFALLS Although Florida isn't known for its waterfalls, the Upper Suwannee boasts a high concentration of scenic spots with waterfalls along streams feeding the Suwannee River basin. Start your tour with a peek at **Falling Creek Falls**, located north of Lake City off US 41 just north of I-10. Turn right on Falling Creek Road (CR 131) and follow it 0.8 mile to the trailhead parking area. It's a 0.2-mile walk to the spectacular root-beer-colored cascade, which plummets more than 10 feet over a deep lip of limestone and flows away over limestone boulders at the bottom of a ravine. Continue your drive along US 41 through White Springs and turn off on CR 25A. Look for the small sign on the left, and park at the trailhead. Follow the broad bike trail down to **Disappearing Creek**, which drops through a churning set of hydraulics before plunging down into a deep sinkhole. Feeling adventuresome? A blue-blazed trail of less than a mile leads up and around the creek to give you optimum views and a total hike of about 2 miles.

The Florida National Scenic Trail crosses US 129 north of Live Oak, presenting two more waterfall-viewing opportunities. Park on the northbound shoulder of the road and follow the orange blazes east for less than 0.25 mile to the log bridge crossing over **Sugar Creek**, which cascades a couple of feet between the cypress knees as it flows down to the Suwannee River. Members of the Florida Trail Association (www.florida-trail.org) can also take the trail west through private lands on a round-trip hike of 7 miles to visit scenic **Mill Creek Falls**, which plunges in a double cascade of more than 15 feet over a limestone escarpment into the river.

WILD PLACES **Osceola National Forest** (386-752-2577) is the smallest of Florida's three national forests. For an orientation to recreation in the forest, stop at the ranger station on US 90 at Olustee (open Mon–Fri 7:30–4) or at the Olustee Depot Visitors Center (open 9–4:30, closed Tue) at CR 231; the railroad depot dates back to 1888. Walk the short nature trail at **Mount Carrie Wayside** for an introduction to the longleaf pine and wiregrass habitat, then head to **Olustee Battlefield Historic State Park** to walk the **Nice Wander Trail**, a 2-mile accessible loop along the Florida Trail through red-cockaded woodpecker habitat. **Ocean Pond** is one of the most beautiful camping areas in North Florida, especially as the sun sets over the cypresses. To see the wildest side of the forest, visit the **Big Gum Swamp Wilderness**, where the Florida black bear roams.

Along CR 135 north of White Springs, **Big Shoals Public Lands** (386-397-2733) encompasses river bluffs and uplands overlooking the roughest whitewater on the Suwannee River.

Spanning both sides of the Suwannee at its confluence with the Withlacoochee, **Twin Rivers State Forest** (386-208-1462) covers nearly 15,000 acres of thick hardwood forest and timberlands. In addition to seasonal hunting, it provides access to the Suwannee River for anglers and boaters, and hosts an extensive network of biking, equestrian, and hiking trails, including the **Florida Trail**.

* Lodging

BED & BREAKFASTS

Greenville 32331

At **Grace Manor** (1-888-294-8839), 117 SW US 221, you'll fall in love all over again. In this 1898 Victorian with a genteel Old South feel, it's the mission of David and Tammy Nusbickel to provide a peaceful retreat for their guests to restore their relationships and mend their souls. Each of the four guest rooms has a private bath and lavish furnishings, $75–115; pets are permitted in a two-bedroom cottage ($125) near the

AT GRACE MANOR B&B

Sandra Friend

swimming pool and gardens. Full gourmet breakfast, dietary restrictions honored; can arrange dinners by request.

Madison 32340

Walk into the **Manor House** (850-973-6508), 111 N Range St, and you're swept up somewhere in time—it's been serving guests since 1883. So it's a surprise to open a door on the narrow upstairs hallway and discover a full-blown 900-square-foot apartment suite behind it, featuring all the amenities you'd need to move in for a month. Most of the five suites can accommodate a family of four. $98–125, including breakfast delivered to your door; weekly and monthly rates available.

White Springs 32096

Sophia Jane Adams House (386-397-1915), 16513 River St. Perched above the Suwannee River on a street lined with historic landmarks, the Sophia Jane Adams House offers massive rooms, comfortable porches, and a delightful back patio with a river view. Built in 1893, this home was commissioned by innkeeper Watkins Saunders's great-uncle, and has been passed down through the family to his care today; his extensive renovations in the 1990s permitted him to open it to the public. Four lavish rooms/suites, $85–115, with full breakfast, in what I consider one of the most beautiful B&Bs in Florida.

White Springs (386-397-1665 or 1-888-412-1665; www.whitesprings.org), 15117 SE 100th Way. In the heart of White Springs, a white picket fence surrounds this former 1905 boardinghouse; my friends rave about their Dogwood Suite, great for families. Complimentary hot drinks; does not include breakfast, which can be arranged in advance for an additional fee. Rates begin at $65 a night.

HOTELS AND MOTELS

Branford 32008

Cave divers visiting Branford stay at the **Steamboat Dive Inn** (386-935-2283), corner of US 129 and US 27, providing basic motel accommodations with dive instructors and "ice cold air" on site.

Dowling Park 32060

In the Advent Christian Village, the **Village Lodge** (1-800-371-8381) at Village Landing, CR 136 and CR 250, provides something I haven't found anywhere else on the Suwannee River—large, immaculate riverfront motel rooms in a tranquil setting. Rocking chairs outside each room await your arrival; sit and enjoy the view. Follow the walkways (where you can lounge in a porch swing and watch the river) to the Milford Clark Nature Trail, a gem of a hike along the river bluffs. Two rooms enhanced for wheelchair use. No pets. Rooms $53–70; Copeland Suite $85–93.

Lake City

For the traveler on a tight budget, Lake City offers a wide variety of older motels just east of the US 90/I-75 interchange, with rates below $30 a night. Quality and cleanliness vary, so ask to see a room before checking in. Rates in major chains at the same interchange tend to stay below $50 per night.

Madison 32340

Deerwood Inn (850-973-2504), St. Augustine Rd, is just off I-75 at exit 258, with spacious rooms ($42–45) featuring a large work space for working travelers, although modem connections must be arranged through the front office. Located in Madison Campground (see *Campgrounds*), it shares amenities such as the pool, game room (classic Pac-Man and pinball lurk here!), tennis, and shuffleboard.

White Springs 32096

The friendly **Suwannee River Motel** (386-397-2822), P.O. Box 412, on US 41, provides basic and clean 1950s-style accommodations for $23–27 except during the annual Florida Folk Festival (see *Special Events*). Each room contains a small microwave and refrigerator, and some have full kitchenette. Small dogs permitted.

CAMPGROUNDS

Fort White 32038

Ichetucknee Family Canoe & Cabins (386-497-2150 or 1-866-224-2064; www.ichetuckneecanoeandcabins.com), CR 238, just west of the state park. Primitive cabins and tent camping just upstream from one of the region's most beautiful springs; full-hookup sites, too. Offers float trips ($14–16) with pickup at take-out.

Live Oak 32060

Spirit of the Suwannee Music Park and Campground (386-364-1683; www.musicliveshere.com), 3076 95th Dr, off US 129 at the Suwannee River. It's a campground. It's a concert venue. And it's so much more. Spread out across 700 thickly wooded acres along the Suwannee River, the Spirit of the Suwannee holds events that draw up to 20,000 people—and they still don't run out of space. You can pitch your tent ($15–17) anywhere, including the soft white sand banks of the Suwannee River. RVs and campers have their choice of spaces along four separate loops ($18–25), and a wide range of rentals (from the cozy but popular "Possum" trailer to the virtual skybox "Treehouse" overlooking the concert grounds) suit everyone's needs (to $99). There's even a special horse camping area with stables ($17–22). Some visitors come for a weekend; others stay for 6 months. Canoe rentals, horseback riding, mini golf, swimming, pontoon boat rides, and a classy private floating dining room are just a few of the on-site offerings, along with the camp store, Heritage Village shops (weekends), and SOS Café (see *Eating Out*). Rates increase during special events.

Madison 32340

Jellystone Park Campground (1-800-347-0174; www.jellystoneflorida.com), Old St. Augustine Rd. This family-oriented camping resort (see *Family Activities*) has a little something for everyone, with campsites and cabins to accommodate all needs and special events held almost every weekend. $25–30 sites; $65–225 cabins, which range from a playful chuck wagon with bunk beds to comfortably refurbished portable classrooms with enough rooms for the entire family. No bathrooms provided in low-end cabins; nearby bathhouses are shared with campers. Pets permitted, but not in cabins.

Madison Campground (850-973-2504), St. Augustine Rd. Eighty sites set under the trees, suitable for tents or campers, providing picnic tables, grills, and shared amenities such as shuffleboard, tennis, horseshoes, a spacious adult-oriented game room, and an inviting pool. Thirty- and

50-amp service. All major club discounts. Leashed pets permitted. $12–18.

White Springs 32096

Kelly's RV Park (386-397-2616; www.kellysrvpark.com), 142 NW Kelly Lane, off US 41 south of town, has sites for tents ($10–19) and roomy rental cabins ($49–59) with screened porch, A/C, and heat set in a deeply shaded park with nature trails that lead to the adjoining Gar Pond Tract.

Lee's Country Campground (386-397-4132), I-75 and FL 136, has more than 30 sites in an open field, suitable for RVs, vans, and tents. $17 for six people per site, includes use of dump station; hot showers and laundry facility. Overnight stays only. Pets permitted.

Stephen Foster Folk Culture Center State Park (1-800-326-3521), P.O. Drawer G, US 41. Set up your tent at one of 45 sites under the ancient live oaks. Leashed pets welcome.

Suwannee Valley Campground (386-397-1667; www.suwanneevalleycampground.com), Rt 1, Box 1860, off FL 136. Perched well above the Suwannee River, this peaceful campground provides a special primitive tenting area ($12) as well as full-hookup pull-through sites ($19) and cabins with private bath ($39). Amenities include a large clubhouse with general store, canoe and kayak rentals, swimming pool, hiking trails, and a special dog activity area.

✷ Where to Eat

DINING OUT

Lake City

Do Mo Japanese Steakhouse (386-758-7931), US 90 at I-75. Granted, North Florida isn't where you'd seek out sashimi or tempura. But Do Mo delivers with sushi offerings comparable to any big-city restaurant. Choose from 16 individual types ($2–3), 21 varieties of maki sushi rolls ($3–9), or 10 different combination dinners ranging from $17 for regular sushi to $40 for sashimi for two. Not a sushi fan? Enjoy traditional Japanese chicken, steak, and seafood dishes prepared tableside. Opens Mon–Sat at 5, Sun at noon.

Tucker's (386-755-5150), N Marion St, offers fine dining inside the century-old Hotel Blanche (now an office complex). Enjoy Italian entrées like sausage pomodoro, or seafood specialties like shrimp supreme (large crab-stuffed shrimp wrapped in bacon) or shrimp fra diavolo. Subs, salads, and pasta at lunch, $6–11; dinner entrées $10–23.

Madison

At **Miss Virginia's Café** (850-973-6508), 111 N Range St, a classy restaurant showcasing the inner courtyard of the Manor House, you'll find ever-changing delights like shrimp Creole and veggie wraps on the chalkboard menu ($6–7). Open 11–2; closed Mon. Don't miss the homemade desserts, including Mom's Chocolate Cake, made from an old family recipe.

EATING OUT

Branford

Gathering Café (386-935-2768), 100 Suwannee Ave. Western-themed restaurant open daily at 7 AM, serving breakfast (under $4), lunch (sandwiches and salads, $4–6), and dinner favorites like rainbow trout and lemon-pepper chicken.

Nell's Steak and Bar-B-Q House (386-935-1415), 403 Suwannee Ave. Serving up good southern cooking for more than 30 years, Nell's is a regional favorite with breakfasts under $4 and big buffet spreads. Buffet daily 10–2:30, breakfast buffet on weekends 6–10:30; $5.50 or $6.50. Lunches $2–4.

Dowling Park

The Village Café (386-658-5777) at Village Landing serves breakfast 7–11 ($3–5). Lunch and dinner options range from hot dogs to crabcakes ($4–7). Open until 8 most evenings.

Fort White

Good food en masse draws the masses to the **Goose Nest Restaurant** (386-497-4725), US 27, with daily lunch buffets ($7) Tue–Sun 11–2; dinner buffets ($9) Fri and Sat 5–8. Stop in for breakfast, too, with cinnamon French toast, grits and eggs, and other favorites for under $6. Closed Mon.

Jasper

Covered in barnyard murals, **Roosters Diner** (386-792-2800), 108 NE 1st St, is a popular local hangout for good southern cooking. Breakfast under $4, served anytime; sandwiches and subs $2–5; daily blue plate special $4 or $6 (all you can eat). Open 6–3; closed Sun.

Lake City

Chasteen's (386-752-7504), 204 N Marion Ave. Sandwiches, salads, and daily lunch specials ($5–9); don't miss the homemade pimiento and cheese spread! Serving lunch Mon–Fri.

Desoto Drug (386-752-9958), 405 N Marion Ave. Creative salads and tasty sandwiches bring this old-fashioned soda fountain into the 21st century—but you can still order a real vanilla Coke or an egg cream with lunch. Creative daily specials such as sherry wild rice mushroom soup and date bacon walnut chicken salad ($3–6), and a full range of desserts ($1–3).

Ken's Barbecue (386-752-6725), US 90. Mmmm . . . barbecue. This regional chain offers simply the best. Additional locations at South Oak Square on US 129, Live Oak; FL 100 in east Lake City; S 1st St in Lake City; and US 90 (near the college) in Madison. Closed Sun.

Ruppert's Bakery and Café (386-758-3088), 134 N Marion Ave. For breakfast, enjoy a fresh orange muffin at Ruppert's, served up in a former drugstore soda fountain on the square downtown. Tempting bakery items include coconut macaroons, fruit turnovers, and a chocoholic's selection of brownies. Lunches $3–5; frozen cappuccino slush and old-fashioned fountain drinks, too!

Lee

Everyone eats at **Archie's** (850-971-5567), US 90 and FL 255, where they serve up huge burgers and country favorites between 11 and 2. On Thu, dinner (5–8) features premium Black Angus prime rib; Fri (noon–9) brings out the popular seafood buffet ($14). Sun buffet.

Live Oak

Dixie Grill & Steer Room (386-364-2810), 101 Dowling Ave. With mouthwatering pies on display when you walk in, you know you'll save room for dessert. This is the *in* place in Live Oak, where the politics of Suwannee County get resolved over coffee. Daily specials ($5 and up) offer heaping helpings of home-cooked favorites like fried chicken and meat loaf.

Live Oak Sub Shop (386-362-6503), 603 S Ohio Ave. Boasting "World Famous Subs," this Live Oak landmark piles it on with massive sandwiches good for a picnic on the Suwannee River. Open 10–6 daily.

SOS Café (386-364-1703), 3076 95th Dr, at Spirit of the Suwannee Music Park (see *Campgrounds*), has family favorites; stop by for a bowlful of homemade cream of mushroom soup ($2) or a meat loaf dinner ($7). Open 11–10; closed Mon.

Macclenny

Pier 6 Seafood & Steak House (904-259-6123), 853 S 6th St. When I asked friends where I could get great seafood near Jacksonville, I was surprised when they didn't point me to the coast—they sent me to Baker County. Pier 6 has a loyal clientele devoted to their heaping seafood platters for two: Order fried, which comes with a lot of 'gator tail, or steamed, my preference, with shrimp, crabs, and clams. Lunch ($5–7) and dinner ($9–14) daily, 11–9.

THE SUWANNEE RIVER DINER IS A WORK OF ART INSIDE AND OUT.

Sandra Friend

Madison

Food for Thought (850-973-4248), 108 E Pinckney St, serves up entrées so huge you can easily split one into dinner for two. Their "world famous burgers" ($5–7) run from 5 to 16 ounces, and dinner selections ($9–16) include southern favorites like grilled pork chops, country-fried steak, butterfly shrimp, and a 16-ounce rib-eye steak. Open Mon–Fri 11–8.

For an old-fashioned soda fountain with quick counter service, try the **Ladybug Café** (850-973-2222) inside the Norris Pharmacy, 110 S Range St, where you can pick up a grilled panini sandwich ($3) or egg salad ($2) to go with your vanilla Coke and hot fudge sundae ($2). Serving breakfast and lunch.

White Springs

Country Café (386-397-2040), 16750 Spring St. It's a down-home place with great country cooking—enjoy eggs and grits in the morning, chicken gizzards for lunch, and all-you-can-eat mullet for dinner. Call ahead, and you can pick up your order at the drive-through window! Breakfast options start at $2 for a short stack of pancakes; fish dinners run $5–10, steak entrées $9–18, and all-you-can-eat snow crab legs are $21 on Fri and Sat nights.

Suwannee River Diner (386-397-1181), 16538 Spring St. It's a work of art outside and in, with a vivid wraparound mural depicting the journey of the Suwannee River from the Okeefenokee Swamp to the Gulf of Mexico. Owners Rose and Wayne Stormant handcrafted the booths as well. Try one of their cooked-to-order breakfasts or omelets ($4), or stop in for the all-you-can-eat lunch and dinner bar with daily specials served up with salad bar, hot biscuits, corn bread, dessert, and a beverage ($6). For something offbeat, go for the quail platter ($9). Dinner entrées include vegetables (often collard greens or black-eyed peas), corn bread, beverage, and dessert ($6–10). Open at 5 AM for breakfast.

✻ Entertainment

Spirit of the Suwannee Music Park (see *Campgrounds*), Live Oak. Hosting everything from the Suwannee River Gospel Jubilee to the Further Festival, this massive music venue has concerts on an ongoing basis in both indoor and outdoor locations. Check their web site (www.musicliveshere.com) for the current schedule of events, which also ranges to antique car shows, national trail riding meetings, and other large gatherings.

At **Thayer's Grove** enjoy free bluegrass and folk music Sat at 6 PM, off FL 18 just west of I-75.

✻ Selective Shopping

Dowling Park

In the shops of **Village Landing** on CR 136, **The Rustic Shop** (386-658-5273) stands out with its mix of antiques, import items, and crafts, including fine quilts, pillows, and crocheted baby sets made by local residents. Open 10–5; closed Sun.

Glen St. Mary

Franklin Mercantile (904-259-6040), CR 125 S, is an old-time general store and post office in this once thriving citrus town. Step back a century as you browse through antiques, local crafts, and gifts. Open Wed–Sat 10–5.

Jasper

The Lemon Tree (386-792-1527), 202 NW Central Ave. A distinctly

Sandra Friend

THE FRANKLIN MERCANTILE IN GLEN ST. MARY

feminine shop hidden inside the Jasper Ace Hardware, it's a real counterpoint to the rest of the merchandise in the store, with country gift and home decor items.

Stephanie's (386-792-2233), SW Central Ave, next to the chamber of commerce. In a century-old building with an original stamped-tin ceiling and bricks made locally with a brick-making machine picked up in trade for a tank of gas, this 30-year landmark offers brassware, figurines, a smattering of antiques, and other home decor items, as well as a wide selection of ladies' attire in the back room.

Lake City

12 Baskets (386-758-7995), 2277 SE Baya. Inside a replica Cracker home wrapped in the welcoming scents of aromatic soaps and candles, this relaxing, down-home floral shop feels like the outdoors inside. Browse the handmade soaps, quilts, sculptures, and unique turned wood bowls by local artisan Everett Smith, or order a natural floral arrangement from the in-house florist.

Antiques North-South Connection (386-758-9280), I-75 and US 441, exit 414. Five thousand square feet. One owner. Loads of antiques. Literally: A new truckload comes in every week. Look for beaded Victorian lamps, quilts, milk bottles and country kitchen implements, Christmas decor, and, my favorite, row upon row of funky saltcellars.

Creative Stitches Quilting and Embroidery (386-754-3741), 318 E Duval St. Looking for a new frock to wear to the Confederate ball at Olustee? This popular local quilting shop carries a broad stock of Civil War reproduction fabrics and a nice complement of fat quarters, as well as supplies for embroidery and appliqué and specialty sewing machines.

Webb's Antique Mall (386-758-5564; www.webbsantiquemalls.com), US 441-41 and I-10. With 300 dealer booths to roam, you can get lost in here for days, checking out items from vintage tools and golf clubs to fine china, collectible Barbies, and church pews. Plan a day—you'll need it to absorb everything!

N Marion Ave: With small antiques and artsy venues lining the avenue, downtown Lake City offers a good afternoon's worth of shopping, complete with several pleasant eateries:

A Company of Angels (386-752-5200), 313 N Marion Ave. Uplifting gifts, from spiritual books, candles, and New Age music to wind chimes, custom-recipe aromatherapy, and, of course, angel-themed items.

The General Store (386-752-2001), 308 N Marion Ave. A Chippendale escritoire stands next to statues of King Tut: That's the nature of this unique shop, with its mix of country and exotic items.

Linda's Antiques & Collectibles (386-755-6674), 318 N Marion Ave. Dealer booths with a little bit of everything: glassware, dishes, furniture, primitives, and local arts and crafts.

Nana's Antiques & Collectibles (386-752-0272), 327 N Marion Ave. Lovely antique oak china cabinets, country gifts and antiques, collectible Heritage Lace and Boyd Bears—a little bit of collectibles, a lot of home decor.

Rowand's Mall (386-752-3350 or 1-888-904-9045), 261 N Marion Ave. A bit of everything in this multidealer mall, from collectible coins, stamps, baseball cards, and postcards to minerals, Depression glass, and a smattering of books.

Simply Southern by JoAnna (386-754-6999), 148 N Marion Ave. Catch JoAnna McManus at work, and you'll find her painting wildflowers and country scenes on antique tables, dressers, and saws—her dream business. Browse through her original art, candles, antiques, and home decor, and you'll find something delightful and country.

Live Oak

Antique Gallery (386-362-3737), 227 W Howard St. Fine antiques and collectibles; look for classic glassware.

Early Bird Collectibles (386-364-4120), 215 W Howard St. Browse for books (if you don't, I will) and paintings amid the antiques and collectibles; you'll find antique pottery here!

Macclenny

Glass Menagerie, College St. Depression glass, fine china, and collectibles adorn the shelves of this little shop just off US 90.

Rachel's Farmhouse, 238 Macclenny Rd. Step inside this old-time mercantile set in a historic home to browse primitives, local crafts, and old-time farm implements. Antique furniture in various stages of restoration is scattered throughout the house and the porches. Open Wed–Sat.

Madison
Madison Antiques, Etc. (850-973-4344), corner of US 90 and Range St. Offering classic furniture and furniture refinishing, as well as a nice selection of glassware, kitchenware, and books.

The Old Bookstore (850-973-6833), 115 W Pinckney. Bring your life list! Heavily stocked with out-of-print fiction, especially vintage paperbacks, the Old Bookstore is a bibliophile's dream, a place to spend hours browsing the narrow aisles. Their Florida section includes both used and new books. Record collectors—ask about 78s and other vinyl.

T. J. Beggs & Company (850-973-6163), 106 S Range St. Since 1886, the Beggs family has managed a mercantile store out of this location, now focusing on masculine gift items, menswear, home decor, and Madison-themed gifts. A grand chandelier from the Old Capitol Building (Tallahassee) hangs over the staircase leading up to the eclectic Beggs Museum & Art Exhibit (see *Museums*); ask to see the museum when you shop.

White Springs
Spring Street Antiques (386-397-4385), Spring St. Housed in a restored 1890s cottage and focusing primarily on glassware and dishes, Spring Street Antiques displays its wares on fine period furniture. Look for a good complement of Fiestaware and saltshakers worth poring over. Specializing in matching antique silverplate patterns. Open Wed–Sat 10:30–4:30.

FARMER'S MARKETS

Lake City
K. C.'s Produce (386-752-1449), 2275 SE Baya. The most popular spot in Lake City to pick up a bunch of bananas or a pound of peppers—a great selection of fresh fruits and vegetables sold wholesale and retail. Closed Sun.

Live Oak
Suwannee County Farmer's Market (386-776-2362), 1302 SW 11th St. Fresh produce from local farms every Saturday 9:30–1 at the Suwannee County Agricultural Colosseum, year-round.

Madison
O'Toole's Herb Farm (850-973-3269), Rocky Ford Rd (CR 591). Culinary herbs and flowers grown organically—that's the mainstay of Jim and Betty O'Toole's lovely gardens, and their greens garnish platters in fine restaurants around the region. Their 150-year-old family farm also has a gift shop and tearoom. Mon–Fri 9–6, Sat 9–4; closed Jan, Jul, and Aug.

Pinetta
At **Emmolyn Gardens** (850-929-4580), 3344 NE Oak Hill Rd, you can pick your own seasonal vegetables and have peas and butter beans shelled on the spot. Open all year.

Wellborn
Scott's Blueberry Farm (386-963-4952), US 90. Watch for the sign that says FOLLOW THE YELLOW DIRT ROAD and do just that to one of the region's most popular U-picks.

MEMORIAL DAY WEEKEND Florida Folk Festival (1-877-6FL-FOLK; www.floridastateparks.org/folkfest), Stephen Foster State Folk Culture Center, White Springs. If you truly want to know Florida and its people, plan your vacation around this incredible Memorial Day weekend extravaganza of folk music and Florida culture, now more than half a century old. The Folklife Area brings together Florida's melting pot of cultures, and 14 concert stages scattered throughout the park host more than 250 concerts daily. Each evening the spotlight shifts to the main stage, where Florida troubadours continue the tradition of Will McLean and Gamble Rogers with their haunting ballads of our state, its history, its beauty, and its troubles. Nationally acclaimed folk acts perform on Sat evening, and the Florida State Fiddle Contest brings on a hoedown atmosphere Sun night. As the weekend unfolds, follow the orange blazes in search of the Seminole Camp and homemade churned-on-site ice cream, or join in one of the 75 music, dance, and storytelling workshops. And don't forget the ethnic food vendors! It's your annual opportunity to touch the soul of Florida. Daily admission costs $20 adults, $5 children; weekend pass $40 adults, $50 families. For optimum comfort, bring your own folding chair.

TRADITIONAL WEAVING AT THE FLORIDA FOLK FESTIVAL

Sandra Friend

✷ Special Events

February: **The Battle of Olustee**, Olustee, third weekend. It's the largest Civil War reenactment in the Southeast, featuring living history encampments, a large sutler's (period shopping) area, and battle reenactments on Sat and Sun.

March: **Wild Azalea Festival** (386-397-2310), third Sat, White Springs. Celebrate the fragrant blossoms that usher in spring on the Suwannee with arts, crafts, music, and food.

Suwannee County Fair (386-362-7366; www.suwanneecountyfair.com), 1302 11th St, at the Suwannee County Fairgrounds, held the last week of March. A traditional old-time county fair with judged livestock and vegetables, quilting, fine arts, and other crafts; commercial and educational exhibits, a popular midway, talent show, and the "politician bake off" (this, I've gotta see!).

April: **Lee Days**, Lee, first Sat. A celebration of the heritage of this tiny Florida town, with arts and crafts and food vendors at the park.

May: **Hamilton County Rodeo** (386-792-1415) first weekend, Hamilton County Arena, Jasper.

Down Home Days, Madison, third weekend. Step back to pioneer days in downtown Madison with traditional crafts and foods.

November: **Cane Grinding Festival** (386-792-1300), second weekend, at Jasper's Heritage Village. Learn how sugarcane becomes molasses at this annual celebration of agricultural history.

December: **Christmas on the Square**, featuring arts and crafts and entertainment in Live Oak's historic downtown.

Festival of Lights, Live Oak. A drive-through wonderland of light in Spirit of the Suwannee Music Park (see *Campgrounds*), including a miniature Victorian Christmas Village and Santa's workshop. $5 per car.

The Florida Panhandle

CAPITAL REGION

APALACHICOLA REGION

WESTERN PANHANDLE

Sandra Friend

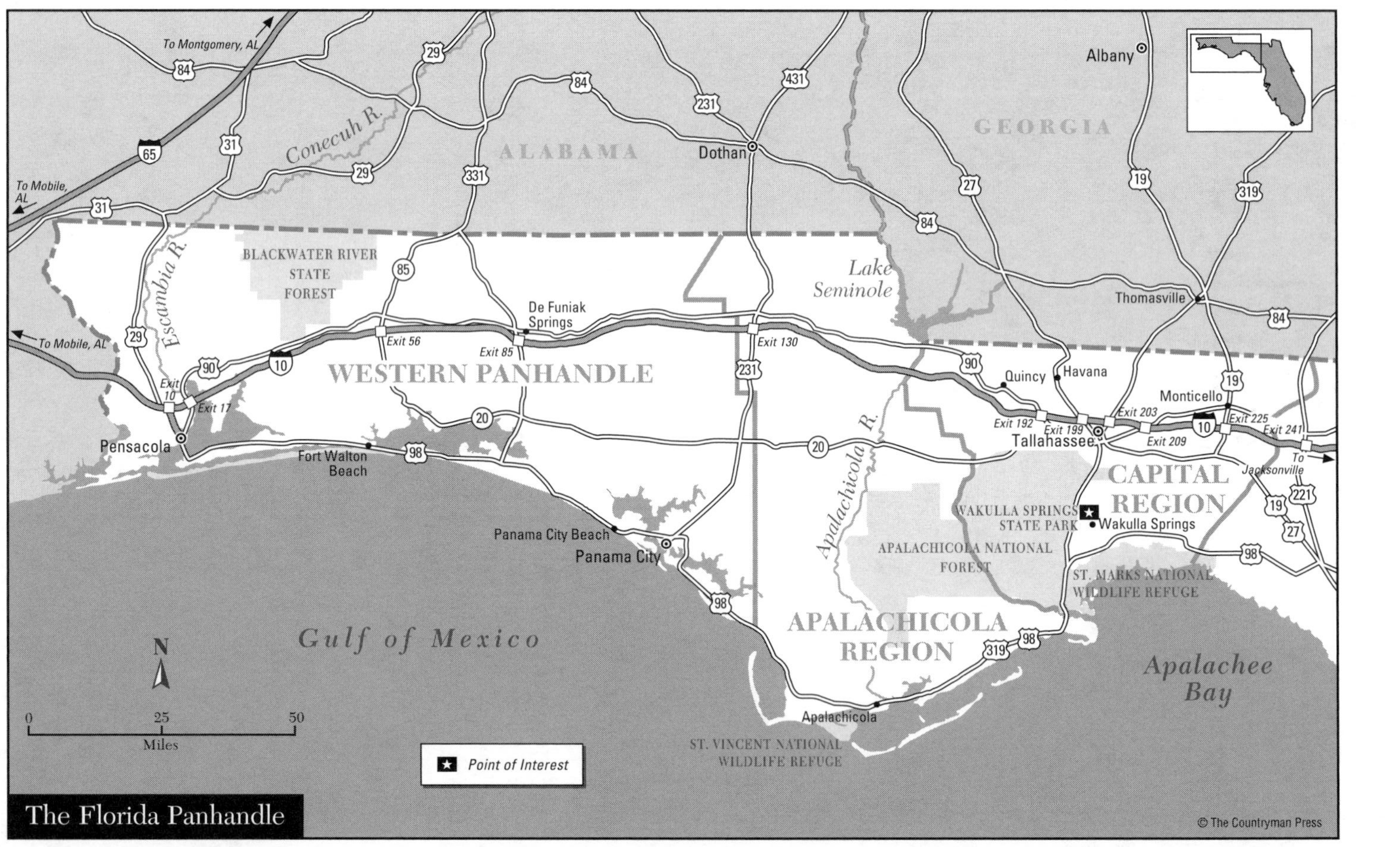

The Florida Panhandle

THE FLORIDA PANHANDLE

Disconnected by geography from the bulk of the Sunshine State, the Florida Panhandle is a world onto itself. It's a place where Florida's history runs deepest, where Spanish missionaries traced trails west from St. Augustine to found missions among the Apalachee in the 1600s, where the French, British, and Spanish fought for control of the deep-water port at Pensacola, where Florida's capital, Tallahassee, was founded in 1824 as a halfway meeting point between the state's only truly populous cities, St. Augustine and Pensacola.

The Panhandle is a place where the genteel Old South remains intact: In the early-morning sun, Spanish moss casts shadows on centuries-old antebellum mansions, and a light mist rises from the cotton fields. Along the Gulf of Mexico, the shrimpers come in at dawn after a hard night's work of harvesting the sea. Time moves slowly here; the farther you stray from the interstate, the more relaxed you'll find the pace of life.

The Panhandle is a place where agriculture and fishing are a way of life, where you can settle back on a sandy beach and listen to the wind blow without fighting your way through crowds—excepting those that now flock to Panama City Beach, Fort Walton, Destin, and Pensacola Beach during the annual spring break. Alas, the coming of crowds means the rising of condos along the shoreline in these popular beach areas. Stray farther east along the coast, and you'll find the wind rustling through the pines along the shore.

The Panhandle is a place of natural wonder, where rugged clay cliffs rise high above clear sand-bottomed rivers, where rhododendron, azalea,

APALACHICOLA SHRIMPERS

Sandra Friend

and mountain laurel bloom in profusion along streams that seem straight out of the Appalachians, where columbine and trillium add splashes of color to rugged limestone slopes, where vast savannas of endangered pitcher plants shake their draping lemon-yellow blooms in a March breeze.

The natural divide of the Apalachicola River forms the division between Eastern and Central Time Zones in Florida—it's a big region, however narrow, and you'll spend a lot of time between towns taking in the rolling Piedmont-like sandhills and clayhills topped with pine forests. Slow down and savor the views.

CAPITAL REGION

LEON, JEFFERSON, GADSDEN, AND WAKULLA COUNTIES

On Mar 4, 1824, Florida's politicos decided on a meeting place halfway between the thriving cities of Pensacola and St. Augustine, and dubbed it **Tallahassee**—a corruption of the Creek word for "abandoned village." A log cabin served as the first capitol building, replaced by a more grandiose structure completed just in time for Florida's induction into the Union in 1845. Tallahassee's classy downtown, a mix of old brick buildings and modern architecture with side alleys just wide enough for a horse and carriage, has incredible hills for a Florida city—you'll think you're in New England.

Atop the tallest hill in **Monticello**, the Jefferson County Courthouse evokes déjà vu: It's a replica of Thomas Jefferson's famous home. The namesake of **Havana** is indeed Cuba, as the Red Hills region supplied the Cuban cigar industry with tobacco until Fidel Castro came to power. The old tobacco drying barns and downtown infrastructure now make up the region's top antiquing town. Two generations ago folks in the nearby tobacco community of **Quincy** invested in a young company called Coca-Cola, and their dividends show in the Victorian homes that dominate this artistic town.

As you head toward the Gulf of Mexico, red clayhills give way to the densely forested Woodville Karst Plain, a wonderland of sinkholes and springs defining **Wakulla County**. It's a green, wet place, with lushly canopied roads edged by floodplain forests and salt marshes. The medicinal qualities of the sulfur and magnesium springs near **Panacea** lead to its unusual name, but this coastal town is best known for its seafood. Buy it roadside direct from the fishermen, or have it fried or broiled at one of the local eateries. Also renowned for seafood, the fishing village of **St. Marks** sits along the St. Marks River and the vast estuaries where it meets the Gulf of Mexico. The U.S. Congress created this town in 1830 as a port of entry to the United States before Florida's first major railroad, the Tallahassee & St. Marks, joined the two cities in 1837.

GUIDANCE The **Tallahassee Area Visitor Information Center** (850-413-9200 or 1-800-628-2866; www.co.leon.fl.us/visitors/visitor.htm) has a delightful walk-in storefront at 106 E Jefferson St, downtown, with a wall of brochures and a gift shop serving free iced tea Mon–Fri 8–5, Sat 9–1. Parking may be tricky, so head

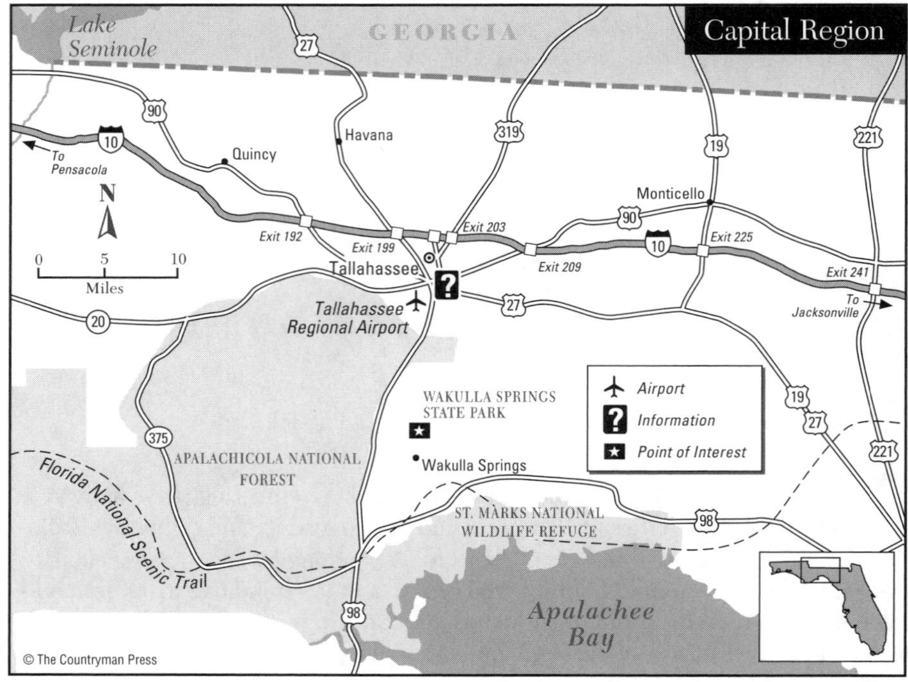

to nearby Kleman Plaza. You'll find the **Wakulla County Chamber of Commerce** in the county seat of Crawfordville along US 319, housed in the historic old County Courthouse (behind the new courthouse), open Mon–Fri 8–noon, 1–5.

GETTING THERE *By air*: **Tallahassee Regional Airport** (850-891-7800), 3300 Capital Circle SW, has commuter service on Atlantic Southeast, Continental, Delta, Northwest, and US Airways.

By bus: **Greyhound** (850-222-4240) pulls into 112 W Tennessee St, downtown Tallahassee.

By car: **I-10** is the major east–west corridor through Florida's Panhandle, with **US 98** providing the scenic route connecting coastal villages and **US 90** running through the northerly Red Hills region.

By train: **Amtrak** (850-224-2779 or 1-800-872-7243) connects Tallahassee via New Orleans with Los Angeles with the transcontinental Sunset.

GETTING AROUND *By car*: With its many one-way streets, downtown Tallahassee can be a bit confusing: Watch for signs that direct you to points of interest. Roads radiate out of Tallahassee like spokes on a wheel: **US 27** leads northwest to Havana, southeast to Perry; **US 319**, north to Thomasville, Georgia, and south to Crawfordville; **FL 363** south to St. Marks; **US 90** northeast to Monticello, northwest to Quincy. Capital Circle defines the wheel's rim.

By bus: Weekdays, catch a free ride between downtown Tallahassee points of interest on the **Old Town Trolley**, every 20 minutes, 7–6. **TalTran** (850-891-5200), the public bus service, runs routes to suburban neighborhoods, fares $1, or $2.50 for a 1-day pass.

By taxi: **Ace Taxi** (850-521-0100), **City Taxi** (850-562-422), **Red Cab** (850-425-4606), **Yellow Cab** (850-580-8080).

PARKING Havana, Monticello, and Quincy have free street parking for shopping. But in busy Tallahassee, metered on-street spaces have time limits from 30 minutes to 10 hours. If you're visiting a museum or restaurant, it's best to pop into a parking garage. **Kleman Plaza**, between Bronough and Duval, is roomier than the **Eastside Parking Garage** on Calhoun and offers easy access to museums and downtown historic sites; $1 an hour, $10 a day.

MEDICAL EMERGENCIES **Tallahassee Memorial Hospital** (850-681-1155), 1300 Miccosukee Rd, Tallahassee. In outlying areas, call 911; it may take up to an hour to reach the emergency room.

✷ To See

ANTEBELLUM PLANTATIONS Most of Florida's remaining antebellum plantations are found in the Capital Region—the visitors bureau lays claim to 100 plantations between Tallahassee and Thomasville, many still working farms, some owned by folks like Ted Turner. Although specifically noted for its formal gardens, the grounds of **Alfred B. Maclay Gardens State Park** (see *Botanical Gardens*) encompass an antebellum quail hunting plantation.

A corn-and-cotton plantation dating back to the 1830s, **Goodwood** (850-877-4202), 1600 Miccosukee Rd, is the most accessible of the region's grand antebellum plantations. With period furnishings (including many European antiques) dating back to the home's ownership by Senator Hodges circa 1925, the classy interior is beautiful to behold. Crystal chandeliers dangle from the ceilings, velvet drapes add a touch of Europe, and the ornate ceiling in the salon is considered the oldest existing fresco in Florida. Traditional dogtrot architecture is broken up by a half-curved stairway in the center of the building, leading up to the bedrooms, which are extremely roomy for their period. An ornate canopied alabaster bed frame sports an original lace bedspread; the medallion above the master bed is painted with delicate roses, as is the bath. It is a place of romance and history, where Granny slyly smiles like Mona Lisa from the picture frame. Step inside, and touch a Florida long gone. Sixteen buildings make up the complex, but the main house is truly the crown jewel. Fee.

In 1896 the **Hickory Hill Plantation** encompassed 2,800 acres along the Georgia border. Architect Henry Beadel designed a grand home overlooking Lake Iamonia, now known as the **Beadel House**. With four rooms upstairs, and four downstairs decked out in original furnishings, this unique plantation home reflects the sensibilities of its New York owners, who added an Adirondack-style hunting lodge in 1923. A skilled photographer and painter (whose watercolors are signed with the number of minutes it took to complete each piece), Henry

Beadel was an avid sportsman who felt that the lack of controlled burns of plantation fields limited quail populations. In 1958 Beadel founded the **Tall Timbers Research Station** (850-893-4153; www.ttrs.org), 13093 Henry Beadel Dr, which occupies much of the original plantation and serves as a facility for the study of fire to regenerate habitats. Tall Timbers, with walking paths above Lake Iamonia, is open daily; the plantation home opens for docent-led tours once monthly on the third Sun (except on holidays). Fee.

Evoking *Gone with the Wind*, the **Brokaw-McDougall House** (850-891-3900), 329 N Meridian Ave, shows off its 1850 Classical Revival charm with its balcony and verandas behind the Corinthian columns. Nearby, **The Grove**, home of Florida's first territorial governor, Richard Keith Call, isn't open for tours, but you can drive by (100 E 1st Ave) and admire this 1825 beauty dubbed the finest Greek Revival building in Florida. The current **Governor's Mansion** (850-488-4661) is not an antebellum plantation, but it looks like one—it's patterned after Andrew Jackson's Hermitage and is open for tours.

ARCHEOLOGICAL SITES Two extraordinary earthen temple sites in the region are the **Lake Jackson Mounds** (850-922-6007), 3600 Indian Mounds Rd, and **Leitchworth Mounds**, off US 90 west of Monticello. On the north shore of Lake Jackson, the temple complex of Lake Jackson Mounds consists of six earth-

GOODWOOD PLANTATION

Sandra Friend

en temple mounds and a burial mound, part of an A.D. 1200–1500 village. At **Leitchworth Mounds** you can walk around the base of the tallest and most complex ceremonial mound in Florida, 46 feet high, from the Woodland Period circa A.D. 500.

One of the more unique ways to tour the region's archeological treasures is to paddle the **Apalachee Archeological Boat Trail** along Ochlocknee Bay, with 11 points of interest including middens, ceremonial mounds, and fisheries. Pick up a tour brochure from the Wakulla County Chamber of Commerce (see *Guidance*).

ART GALLERIES

Havana

First Street Gallery (850-539-5220), 204 1st St NW, is a local fine-arts co-op with sculpture, paintings, and photography by area artists. Open Fri–Sun.

Florida Art Center and Gallery (850-539-1770), 208 1st St NW, handles consignments from area artists in a large, open gallery space, showcasing ceramic tiles, paintings, photography, and other fine art.

Quincy

Gadsden Art Center (850-875-4866; www.gadsdenarts.com), 13 N Madison St, showcases fine visual arts in a historic 1910 hardware store, with one of North Florida's top collections. Massive wood sculptures by Mark Lindquist dominate the lobby. Climb upstairs to see the **Bates Children's Gallery**, with the fine works of local schoolchildren, and don't miss the gift shop, with its one-of-a-kind works of art. Open Tue–Sat 10–5, Sun 1–5; closed holidays.

Tallahassee

The **Le Moyne Art Foundation** (850-222-8800), 125 N Gadsden St, encompasses a complex of three major buildings connected with a sculpture garden, where fine arts from local, regional, and national artists fill the galleries and gardens. Closed Mon and major holidays; fee. Near Florida State University, **Railroad Square** (850-224-1308), 567 Industrial Dr, contains a cluster of art galleries and gift shops surrounding a sculpture garden and a diner inside a railroad caboose. **The Museum of Fine Arts at Florida State University** (850-644-6836; www.mofa.fsu.edu), 250 Fine Arts Bldg, features changing exhibits from students and national artists, and the **Foster Tanner Art Center** (850-599-3161) at Florida A&M focuses on world art, with an emphasis on African American artists.

GHOST TOWNS There isn't much left of **Port Leon**, founded in 1838 as the terminus of Florida's first railroad, the Tallahassee Railroad. Located southeast of San Marcos de Apalache (see *Historic Sites*), scattered bricks and the outlines of streets are all that remains in the salt marsh. In 1843, soon after Port Leon became the seat of the newly formed Wakulla County, a hurricane obliterated the town; water covered the streets up to 10 feet deep. The survivors decided not to rebuild, and moved inland to establish the village of Newport.

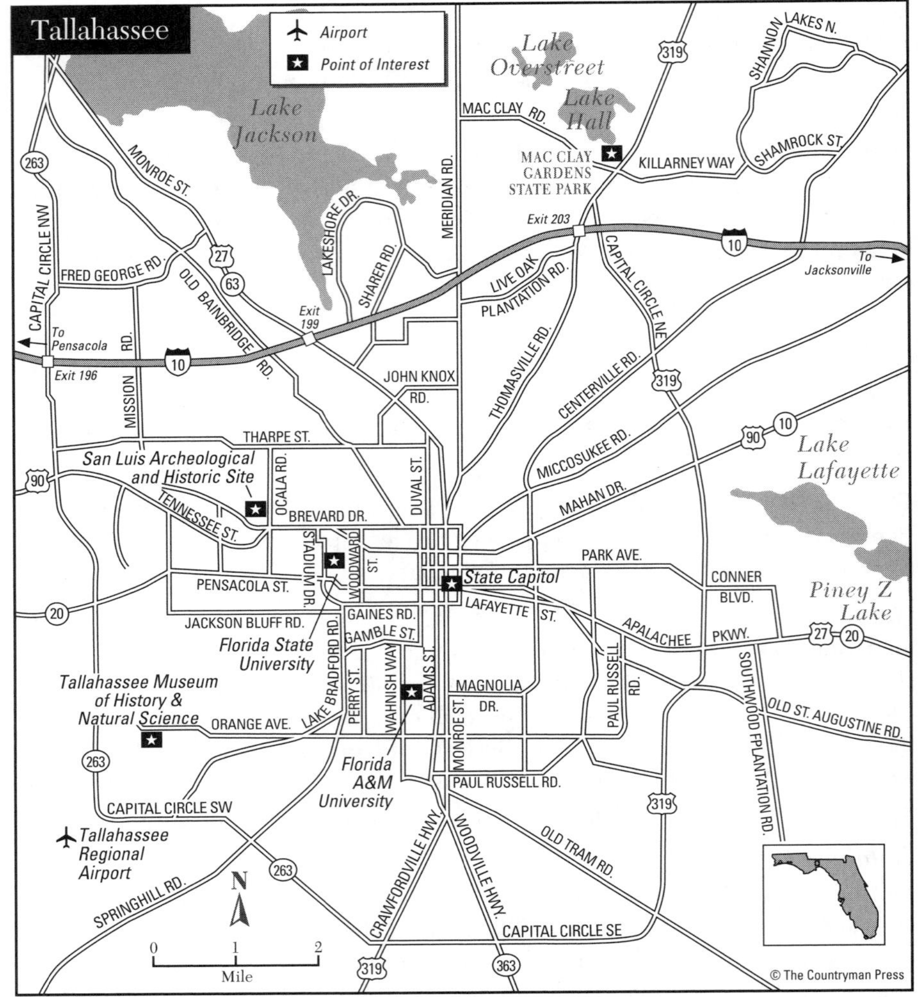

HISTORIC SITES

Chattahoochee

Since the early 1900s, the historic **Chattahoochee Arsenal**, site of Florida's first arsenal in 1839, has been part of the grounds of the Florida State Hospital, a sanitarium.

Crawfordville

The original **Wakulla County Courthouse** houses the chamber of commerce and has exhibits on regional history. Across the street, the **Old Jail** is undergoing renovation for use as a county history museum.

Greensboro

Dating back to 1875, the picturesque **Shepard's Mill** (850-875-2694), CR 12 on

Telogia Creek, is Florida's last working water-powered gristmill. Stop by on Fri or Sat, 10–5, to see how cornmeal and grits are ground from corn.

Monticello

A Florida Heritage downtown, Monticello has more than 40 historic buildings, including the 1908 **county courthouse** that mimics Thomas Jefferson's grand home. Since 1890, the **Monticello Opera House** has dominated the town square; peer in the windows of the office to see historical artifacts like a 1928 Greta Garbo poster found under the stage. Built in 1852, **Monticello High School**, west on US 90, is Florida's oldest brick school building. Walk around downtown to enjoy other residential and business structures with fine Classical and Greek Revival architecture.

Newport

One of the most photographed structures in the region is the **St. Marks Lighthouse** at the end of the road in St. Marks National Wildlife Refuge (see *Wild Places*), which dates back to 1842. During the Civil War, the Fresnel lens was removed and hidden in the salt marshes to make the lighthouse useless to the Union Blockading Squadron. Lighthouse keepers and their families lived in the structure until 1960, when the U.S. Coast Guard automated the beacon.

Quincy

Quincy has an extraordinary number of historic buildings in excellent condition; all are privately owned but can be viewed from the sidewalks. Stop by the **United Methodist Church** to see the handiwork of Louis Comfort Tiffany, who also installed windows in homes around town. Around the corner, the **White House**, constructed in the early 1840s, became the home of Pleasants Woodson White, chief commissary officer for the Confederate army in Florida. Both the **Alison House** and **McFarlin House** (see *Bed & Breakfasts*) offer glimpses into Quincy's storied past; many more structures are explained in the walking tour handbook available at the Gadsden Art Center.

St. Marks

San Marcos de Apalache (850-922-6007), 148 Old Fort Rd. Significant as the site of the first coastal fortress along Florida's Panhandle, this historic site protects several generations of battlements, from the faint tracings of the original wooden stockade fort completed by the Spanish in 1679 at the confluence of the St. Marks and Wakulla Rivers to the remains of the masonry structure occupied up through the Civil War. Visit the small museum before walking the interpretive trail along the rivers. Open 9–5; closed Tue and Wed. Fee.

Tallahassee

There are more than 100 historic sites in the Tallahassee area; pick up a copy of *Tallahassee Treasures* and *Touring Tallahassee* from the visitors center to start your exploration. Downtown contains many historic treasures, including some narrow old brick alleyways reminiscent of those in New England cities. **The First Presbyterian Church** (850-222-4504), 102 N Adams St, built in 1838, is Tallahassee's only church remaining from territorial days, complete with frontier accoutrements like rifle slits in the basement. The massive pipe organ was built to fit the building, and the North Gallery served as a segregated congregation for plantation owner's slaves. Across the street, the **Old U.S. Courthouse** (850-224-2500) has murals depicting great moments in government—honest! At **The Columns** (850-224-8116), 100 N Duval St, the Greek Revival columns say it all: It was built for the first president of the Bank of Florida. The **Old Capitol Building** dates back to 1845, and the 1843 **Knott House** is one of several houses in town built by George Proctor, a free black man (see *Museums* for both). Both the **Park Ave** and **Calhoun St** historic districts are lined with antebellum and early-1900s homes. Tallahassee's two universities, **Florida A&M** and **Florida State**, also merit their own historic districts.

To step farther back in time, head for **Mission San Luis de Apalachee** (850-487-3711), 2020 Mission Rd, the site of the first Spanish mission in this region, 1656–1704. The mission oversaw all Spanish missionary work in La Florida during that period. The complex re-creates the residences of 17th-century Apalachee as well as the old Spanish fort and Franciscan religious complex.

Outside Tallahassee, a drive up Centerville Rd will take you to **Bradley's Country Store** (850-893-1647; www.bradleyscountrystore.com), 10655 Centerville Rd, a general store in continuous operation since 1927. Stop in for their signature country smoked sausage and milled grits.

Woodville

Natural Bridge Historic State Park (850-922-6007), Natural Bridge Rd. An important site in Florida's Civil War history, Natural Bridge speaks to a time when the Confederacy was close to collapse. On March 6, 1865, Union troops marching north from their landing point at the St. Marks Lighthouse met the Florida 5th Cavalry and cadets from the West Florida Seminary (now Florida State University). The Confederate troops routed the Union attack, and are credited with keeping Tallahassee the only Confederate capital east of the Mississippi that did not fall into Union hands during the war—although some historians surmise that the Union objective was to capture the key port of St. Marks rather than invade the capital city, and they came to this spot to utilize the Natural Bridge, a place where the St. Marks River dives underground at a river sink and reemerges less than 0.25 mile south at a spring.

MARINE CENTER At **Gulf Specimen Marine Laboratory** (850-984-5297; www.gulfspecimen.org) along US 98, Panacea, you can interact with the native marine life of the Gulf estuary. You'll find no sharks or dolphins here: The center has a special focus on the small side of Florida sea life, scallops and crabs, snails and lobsters, sea fans and sea urchins, shrimp and oysters, and other tiny denizens of the coastline. Open daily; fee.

MUSEUMS

Tallahassee

In addition to commemorating the former senator's accomplishments, the **Claude Pepper Center** (850-644-9309), 636 W Call St, contains research materials dating back to the New Deal era and an art gallery with a focus on political activism. A true believer in liberalism, Senator Pepper received the Presidential Medal of Freedom while working to improve life for his fellow Americans. Open Mon–Fri 8:30–5; free.

At the **Knott House** (850-922-2459), 301 E Park Ave, step into 1928 and learn about the lives of William Knott, a former state treasurer, and his wife, Luella, a temperance advocate and whimsical published poet who wrote about and attached short poems to virtually every piece of the home's original furnishings, earning the home the nickname "The House that Rhymes." The home was designed by George Proctor, a free black man, in 1843, commissioned as a wedding gift for Catherine Gamble from her husband-to-be, attorney Thomas Hagner; on May 20, 1865, the Emancipation Proclamation was read from its front steps. Tours on the hour Wed–Fri 1–3, Sat 10–3; free.

At the **Museum of Florida History** (850-245-6400), 500 S Bronough St, prepare to have your eyes opened about Florida's rich and colorful past. In addition to rotating thematic exhibits, the state's official history museum includes a climb-aboard replica of an early steamboat, tales of buried treasure, a citrus-packing house from the 1930s, information on Florida's role in the Civil War, and much more—interactive exhibits that'll keep the kids hopping. The adjoining **History Shop** contains classy reproductions and a great selection of Florida books. Open Mon–Fri 9–4:30, Sat 10–4:30, Sun noon–4:30. Free.

Old Capitol Museum (850-487-1902), 400 S Monroe St. Construction began in 1839 to replace the old log cabin used as a meeting place for Florida's first legislators. Although the new Capitol Building opened in 1845, a hurricane damaged

TALLAHASSEE'S KNOTT HOUSE MUSEUM

Sandra Friend

it in 1851. Restoration and expansion followed; the building continued to sprawl until the 1970s, when the state replaced it with a tall modern structure next door. Saved from the wrecking ball by public support, the Old Capitol, restored to its 1902 Classical Revival glory, is now a museum devoted to Florida's legislative history.

Sandra Friend

THE OLD CAPITOL BUILDING

John G. Riley Center and Museum of African-American History & Culture (850-681-7881; www.tfn.net/Riley), 412 E Jefferson St. In this 1890 home designed by John G. Riley, a black architect, you'll find a museum of regional African American history from Reconstruction through the civil rights movement, with a special focus on historic cemeteries. Mon–Wed and Fri 10–4; fee.

Tallahassee Antique Car Museum (850-942-0137; www.tacm.com), 3550 US 90 E. From the first steam-powered car ever built (the 1894 Duryea) to prop vehicles from several Batman movies, Devoe Moore has a car collection to put Jay Leno to shame. But it's not just about the autos. Moore is a collector of collections, and his grand display (in addition to the top antique-car collection in the nation) includes more than 80 classic vehicles, sports memorabilia, children's pedal cars, brass fans, antique toys, and the finest collection of antique outboard motors in the world. $7.50 adults, $5 students, $4 children under 10.

Tallahassee Museum of History & Natural Science (850-575-8684), 3945 Museum Dr, isn't at all what you'd expect from a museum. Gentle footpaths blend into the natural surroundings, winding through Florida habitats alive with native wildlife like bald eagles, alligators, Florida panthers, and river otters; I looked up in a tree and saw a gray fox peering calmly down at me. In the Discovery Center, interactive natural science exhibits change every 4–6 months. Kids were busy in a fossil dig as I continued on to the Big Bend Farm, a living history area where workshops show off Florida how it used to be: shucking corn, pressing cane for sugar. On the opposite side of the main building (with a gift shop full of fun toys for the kids) are several historic structures, including the 1897 Concord School, the first post-Reconstruction school where blacks were taught, and Catherine Murat's 1850s manor home, moved here from the Bellevue cotton plantation. To truly enjoy the historic exhibits on display, rent the audio tour, which lets you plug codes into a cell-phone-like device to get audio clips from the Florida State Archives—oral histories, music, interviews, and narrations. What impressed me the most? Inside the 1924 Florida East Coast Railroad caboose, I pressed a button and heard a recording from the 1940s of Zora

Neale Hurston singing a railroad lining chant. Now, that's bringing history to life. $7 adults, $6.50 seniors, $5 ages 4–15.

The **Union Bank Museum** (850-487-3803), Apalachee Pkwy, is Florida's oldest surviving bank building, dating back to 1841. Mon–Fri 9–4, Sat and Sun by appointment; free.

RAILROADIANA In addition to **Tallahassee's Railroad Square** near FSU, be sure to see the railroad exhibit at the **Tallahassee Museum of History & Natural Science** (see *Museums*) and make a stop at the **Sopchoppy Railroad Depot**, currently under renovation. The **Tallahassee–St. Marks Historic Railroad Trail State Park** (see *Greenways*) traces the route of Florida's earliest lengthy railroad, circa 1837, and in downtown Chattahoochee, **Heritage Park** has a red caboose parked next to a beautiful mural of the *John W. Callahan* steamboat on the Apalachicola River.

WINERY **Monticello Vineyards & Winery** (850-294-WINE; www.fgga.org/monticello.htm), 1211 Waukeenah Hwy, is a small operation at Ladybird Organic Farm on CR 259 south of Monticello. All wines are certified organic, processed from muscadine grapes grown on site. Call to arrange a visit.

✷ To Do

BEACHES The vast salt marshes of the Gulf estuary yield to several small beaches, found off the side roads south of US 98; look for signs to **Shell Point** and **Wakulla Beach** near Wakulla, and **Mashes Sand Beach** at Panacea.

BICYCLING The **Tallahassee–St. Marks Historic Railroad Trail State Park** (see *Greenways*) is the region's longest bike trail, ideal for overnight trips. Or follow FL 12 through Gadsden County on the **North Florida Art Trail**; signs lead the way.

BIRDING **St. Marks National Wildlife Refuge** (see *Wild Places*) can't be beat for the number of species to spot during the winter migration. Stop by the **Henry M. Stevenson Memorial Bird Trail** at Tall Timbers Research Station (see *Historic Sites*), open Mon–Fri 8–4:30, for prime birding along Lake Iamonia.

DIVING The Woodville Karst Plain draws cave divers from all over the world for exploration of the interconnecting underground waterways at **Leon Sinks Geological Area** (see *Wild Places*); cave diving certification required.

FAMILY ACTIVITIES

Tallahassee

✐ At the **Challenger Learning Center and IMAX Theatre** (850-644-IMAX; www.eng.fsu.edu/challenger), 210 S Duval St, most folks are there for the big-screen IMAX with 20,000 watts of sound and the incredibly crisp digital planetarium in its 50-foot dome, where dazzling graphics immerse you into space like no other planetarium show I've ever seen. But with reservations, your kids can also spend 3 hours taking over Mission Control and become astronauts on a space station mission to collect data on a comet in two realistic training laboratories (minimum age 10). This collaborative effort between the FSU College of Engineering and NASA is a living memorial to the Challenger crew. Mon–Thu 10–8, Fri–Sat 10–1, Sun 1–7.

The **Mary Brogan Museum of Art and Science** (850-513-0700; www.thebrogan.org), 350 S Duval St, an associate of the Smithsonian Institution, offers an interesting mix—science for the kids, art for you. And it works! Rotating first-floor exhibits feature colorful hands-on play stations; the second floor showcases permanent science exhibits such as the Ecolab (check out the Florida watershed map), WCTV weather station, and the Early Childhood Area for the smallest of small fry. Third-floor exhibits celebrate the merging of art and science; I enjoyed a stroll through the History of Photography, which kicked off with Matthew Brady's classic photo of Abraham Lincoln. Special stations focused on the science behind photography. Stop in the **Museum Store** for a delightful selection of creative gifts to spark any budding artist. Open Mon–Sat 10–5, Sun 1–5; closed Thanksgiving and Christmas. $6 adults, $3.50 students and seniors.

At **Cross Creek Driving Range & Par 3 Golf** (850-656-GOLF), 6701 Mahan Dr, practice your putts on the driving range, or challenge the kids to a round of par 3. Open daily at 8 AM.

Tallahassee Rock Gym (850-224-ROCK), 629-F Industrial Dr, Railroad Square, offers a popular climbing wall in a historic railroad warehouse; take lessons, or practice your skills!

FISHING Saltwater anglers head for **St. Marks**, the region's launch point into the Gulf of Mexico; ask after guides at **Shell Island Fish Camp** (see *Fish Camps*). Inland, **Lake Talquin**, a hydroelectric reservoir on the Ochlocknee River, has plenty of speckled perch, sunfish, and the tantalizing trophy-sized largemouth bass for the patient angler. There are numerous fish camps off FL 267 and several off FL 20 on the **Upper Ochlocknee River**. Use Chattahoochee Landing off US 90 as your access point to the **Upper Apalachicola River**.

GAMING Greyhound racing is the focus of the **Jefferson County Kennel Club** (850-997-2561), US 19 north of Monticello, but I'm told their dining room offers good old-fashioned southern hospitality; dress for the occasion!

GENEALOGICAL RESEARCH You'll hit the jackpot for all sorts of historical research at the **Florida State Archives** (850-245-6700; dlis.dos.state.fl.us/barm/fsa.html), 500 S Bronough St, but most folks who quietly sit at the long tables inside are digging through their ancestors' roots. Tip: Use their online resources first, and then come to Tallahassee to look through manuscripts and letters you couldn't otherwise view.

GOLF In Tallahassee enjoy a round at **Hilaman** (850-891-3935), 2737 Blair Stone Rd, with 18 holes and driving range, $15–18; **Jake Gaither** (850-891-3942), 801 Tanner Dr, 9 holes, reservations on weekends, $8–22; **Seminole** (850-644-2582), 2550 Pottsdamer St, an 18-hole course with lighted driving range, reservations required, $18–32; and the semiprivate **Players Club** (850-894-4653), Meridian Rd, 18 holes, membership $100–195 a month, green fee $25–48. For nine-hole par-3 fun, head to **Cross Creek** (850-656-4653) on US 90 at I-10 to play on the rolling greens. Wakulla County boasts **Wildwood Country Club** (850-926-4653; www.golfatwildwood.com), a par-72 semiprivate club with lush landscaping along US 98 in Medart, $20–35.

HIKING The **Florida Trail** winds its way from St. Marks National Wildlife Refuge through the entire width of the Apalachicola National Forest: One of the trail's wildest and most remote sections is through the Bradwell Bay Wilderness, a watery swamp forest with ancient trees. For a close-up look at the wondrous world of the Woodville Karst Plain, a place where water vanishes underground to flow through caverns into springs, hike 6 miles of trails at **Leon Sinks Geological Area** (850-926-3561), US 319 in the Apalachicola National Forest. **Lake Talquin State Forest** (see *Wild Places*) has several excellent hiking trails, as do **Eleanor Klapp Phipps Park** (see *Parks*) and the **Lake Overstreet Trails** at Maclay Gardens (see *Botanical Gardens*) in Tallahassee.

PADDLING With the **Sopchoppy**, **Aucilla**, **Ochlocknee**, **St. Marks**, and **Wakulla Rivers** sluicing through this region (and goodness knows, I've forgotten others I haven't yet explored), paddlers will find plenty of challenges. The Aucilla offers rapids, while the Sopchoppy is a twisting, winding blackwater river. The Ochlocknee, St. Marks, and Wakulla Rivers pour out into the Gulf of Mexico through a mazy meander of salt marshes, much fun for kayakers. In Crawfordville, **Williams BP Home & Garden** (850-926-3335), 3215 Crawfordville Hwy, rents canoes for $25 per day, including paddles and PFDs. Take 'em with you to a nearby put-in, and return them at the end of the day. You can also set up float trips (including pickups) through **The Wilderness Way** (850-877-7200; www.thewildernessway.com), 4901 Woodville Hwy, an outfitting shop that offers paddling instruction and ecotours. Check in at Backwoods Pizza (see *Eating Out*) to connect with **Sopchoppy Outfitters** for Sopchoppy and Ochlocknee expeditions. Along US 98 you'll find **Hide Away Rental** at the Wakulla River Bridge and **Lighthouse Center Canoe and Bait** (850-925-9904) at the St. Marks River Bridge; the **Riverside Café** (see *Eating Out*) in St. Marks rents canoes, too. For a trip on the Wacissa River, the **Canoe Man** (850-997-6030) rents canoes and runs shuttles Mar–Nov.

SCENIC DRIVES In addition to cruising Tallahassee's many "official" **canopy roads**, such as Meridian Road—which is wonderful in late March when azaleas and wisteria are in bloom—you'll want to pick up the ***North Florida Art Trail*** brochure and follow rural CR 12 and FL 269 across Gadsden County from Havana through Quincy, Greensboro, and Chattahoochee to enjoy the rolling farmland and stops for art aficionados along the way.

SKYDIVING **Seminole Skydiving** (850-297-2127; www.seminoleskydiving.com), US 98 at the Wakulla County Airport, Medart, offers extraordinary scenery for skydive training and tandem dives, as well as helicopters and airplane rides over the Gulf estuaries.

SWIMMING At **Wakulla Springs State Park** (see *Springs*), dive into Florida's deepest spring and paddle back to the sandy shoreline; stay within the ropes, since the 'gators play just outside them!

WALKING TOURS In **Tallahassee** grab *Touring Tallahassee* at the visitors center and hit the bricks for a **self-guided walk** around more than 60 historic sites downtown. You can watch the Florida Legislature at work by hooking up with a walking tour at the **Capitol Building**; don't miss the view from the 22nd-floor observation deck! **Quincy** also offers *On the Trail in Historic Quincy*, a self-guided walking tour booklet of 55 historic homes and churches; drop by the Gadsen Arts Center for a copy.

✷ Green Space

BOTANICAL GARDENS **Alfred B. Maclay Gardens State Park** (850-487-4556), 3540 Thomasville Rd. Walk through the iron gate and up the brick path—the azaleas are in bloom, and the air is strong with their street fragrance; a thousand shades of green march down the hill to Lake Hall. It's spring, and it's just as New York financier Alfred Maclay envisioned his retirement home—surrounded by blooms. When Maclay purchased an antebellum quail hunting lodge in 1923, he turned his landscape design skills to the surrounding hills. Several years after Maclay died, his widow opened the formal gardens as a tourist attraction, and turned it over to the state a decade later. The flow of form is subtle: As you approach the house, the gardens yield from wild woodlands to formal Italianate walled gardens, with burbling fountains and stands of cypress. Prime blooming months run from Dec to early summer, but the gardens are a joy to explore any time of year; adjacent **Lake Overstreet** is a wild, wooded addition to the park with miles of hiking and biking trails. The antebellum home, furnished in antiques bought and used by the family, is open for tours 9–5 Jan–Apr. Fee.

MACLAY GARDENS

Sandra Friend

GREENWAY **Tallahassee–St. Marks Historic Railroad Trail State Park**

(850-922-6007), 1022 Desoto Park Dr. Although the trail runs up into the southern suburbs of Tallahassee, the trailhead along FL 363 provides ample parking, rest rooms, picnic tables, and a historic marker that explains it all: The Tallahassee–St. Marks Railroad began operation in 1837 with mule-drawn cars and switched to steam locomotives in 1839, connecting ships coming into Port Leon with Tallahassee. This paved bike trail runs through wilderness areas along its 23-mile route to its southern terminus in St. Marks, so take plenty of water and ride with a friend if possible. An equestrian trail runs parallel to the forested right-of-way.

PARKS **Lake Jackson**, the largest lake in Tallahassee, is one of those oddball geological mysteries: Every 25 years or so, the lake's waters vanish "down the drain" into a sinkhole, and it takes a few years for the lake to brim with water again. Bordering Lake Jackson's east shore on Meridian Road, **Eleanor Klapp Phipps Park** (850-891-3975) has an excellent hiking loop as well as biking and equestrian trails; on the west shore of Lake Jackson, **J. Lee Vause Park,** 6024 Old Bainbridge Rd, has a boardwalk along the lake and nature trails as well as picnic shelters. Off to the west along FL 20, **River Bluff State Picnic Area** gives you a scenic panorama of Lake Talquin with a fishing dock and nature trail. In downtown Tallahassee, folks like to stroll around **Lake Ella** in **Fred O. Drake Jr. Park**, Monroe St, where you can picnic under the pines, or at **Dorothy B. Oven Park**, 3205 Thomasville Rd, a 1824 land grant with a manor house and formal azalea and camellia gardens. For a longer stroll, visit **Lake Munson Preserve**, just south of Capital Circle on US 319.

In Panacea the **Otter Creek Unit** of St. Marks National Wildlife Refuge (see *Wild Places*) has a boat launch, fishing area, hiking trail, and shady picnicking along the shores of Otter Lake. **St. Marks River City Park**, with rest rooms, picnic tables, a fishing pier, and a boat ramp on the St. Marks River, marks the southernmost terminus of the Tallahassee–St. Marks Historic Railroad Trail (see *Greenways*). **Ochlocknee River State Park** (850-962-2771) sits just south of Sopchoppy on US 321 and has hiking trails, camping, and plenty of waterfront for fishing the estuary.

SPRINGS ✐ **Edward Ball Wakulla Springs State Park** (850-224-5950), 550 Wakulla Park Dr. Showcasing Florida's deepest spring, where the water is so clear you can see the bones of mastodons and giant sloth resting at the bottom of the 180-foot pool, Wakulla Springs State Park offers swimming facilities (69 degrees year-round) with a high diving platform, nearly 3 miles of shady nature trails, and daily boat tours (River Tour or glass-bottomed boat), where you're bound to see dozens of alligators and innumerable waterfowl. At the center of it all is the classic **Wakulla Lodge** (see *Lodging*); don't miss the marble-topped soda fountain in the gift shop!

WILD PLACES The **Apalachicola National Forest** (850-643-2282) is the wildest place in the Florida Panhandle. Sweeping around the southern edge of Tallahassee, it's also Florida's largest national forest. Some of its special spots include

Leon Sinks Geological Area, popular for hiking (see *Hiking*) and cave diving; **Bradwell Bay**, a wild and lonely wilderness area along the Florida National Scenic Trail; and the cypress-lined **Sopchoppy River**, a great paddling route.

Established in 1931 to protect the fragile Gulf estuaries, **St. Marks National Wildlife Refuge** (850-925-6121; saintmarks.fws.gov), 1255 Lighthouse Rd, spans three counties. Monarch butterflies rest here in October on their annual migration to Mexico, carpeting the saltbushes in shades of orange and black. Although the refuge is broken up into several units, most visitors arrive at the visitors center south of Newport off US 98. Browse the exhibits and learn about this mosaic of habitats before setting off down the road. The **Florida Trail** crosses the entire length of the refuge. Shorter nature trails give you a taste of the salt marshes, pine flatwoods, and swamps. Drive to the end of the road to visit the historic **St. Marks Lighthouse** (see *Historic Sites*).

Encompassing more than 16,000 acres, **Lake Talquin State Forest** (850-627-9674) is spread across 10 tracts on the shores of the Ochlocknee River and Lake Talquin. You can hike through forests of magnolia and beech along trails on the **Fort Braden Tract** and **Bear Creek Tract**, or ride horses on the equestrian trails. Bicycling is permitted on forest roads, numerous boat ramps allow access for anglers, and there is seasonal hunting on some of the tracts.

* Lodging

BED & BREAKFASTS

Monticello 32344

The **John Denham House** (850-997-4568; www.johndenhamhouse.com) is a classic piece of history, built by a Scots immigrant in 1872. Luxuriate in the silky sheets under a down comforter, or relax in a clawfoot tub. Each of the five large rooms has a fireplace accented with candles. $70 and up; children and pets are welcome in a safe, family-friendly environment.

Tallahassee 32312

At the **Little English Guest House** (850-907-9777; www.bbonline.com/fl/littleenglish), 737 Timberlane Rd, you'll step right into London in the company of Thom and Tracey Cochran, who re-created a slice of Tracey's homeland with two roomy guest rooms with four-poster beds topped with fluffy duvets from England, comfy whirlpool tubs, English towel warmers, and a pretty English garden. Share time with guests in the common dining and living areas, where the *Union Jack* newspaper is on prominent display. Oh yes, and there's tea. Two rooms, $99–120, in a quiet house in the suburbs.

Quincy 32351

Allison House Inn (1-888-904-2511), 215 N Madison St. The former home of General A. K. Allison, who stepped into office as governor of Florida at the end of the Civil War, this 1843 Georgian-style house is one of the oldest in North Florida. Extensive renovation in 1925 added a story to the house and gave it an English country look. Step into Florida's genteel past and enjoy one of the six spacious guest rooms ($85–130) and fine crumpets and orange marmalade offered by innkeepers Stuart and Eileen Johnson; many of the rooms have multiple beds in this family-friendly inn.

McFarlin House (1-877-370-4701; www.mcfarlinhouse.com), Love St. Decorated with Tiffany windows original to the home and 11,000 square feet of imported Italian tile, this century-old Queen Anne Victorian showcases the good life that Quincy's well-to-do gentry enjoyed. With renovations completed in 1996, this was a finalist for an award as one of the top homes in the USA. The three-story mansion has nine elegant rooms, each unique in size, shape, and decor, offering romantic amenities such as Jacuzzi and fireplace as well as cable TV, phone, and Internet access; $85–175.

Millstone Farms (850-627-9400; www.millstonefarms.com), 3895 Providence Rd. Off the beaten path in the rolling farmlands west of Quincy, this unique B&B offers a stay on a peaceful 78-acre working beef cattle ranch (tours available on request). Settle into a truly country atmosphere in this grand farmhouse with three large guest rooms ($85) and a hot tub and pool out back; enjoy the big-screen TV, walk the nature trails, or sit under the pines and read a book. A camping cottage plus multi-bed rooms makes this a good choice for families, especially when the kids meet pet goats Lucy and Ethel or find the Secret Garden.

St Marks 32355

The Sweet Magnolia (850-925-7670; www.sweetmagnolia.com), 803 Port Leon Dr, offers an interesting meld of old-fashioned charm and updated facilities; it's a former railroad boardinghouse from 1923, but the interiors are sparkling new. Of the seven roomy bedrooms ($85–135), five offer a Jacuzzi for two. I especially like the beautiful water gardens behind the home, a perfect place to settle in and read a book. Gourmet breakfasts served; dinner on request.

HOTELS AND MOTELS

Tallahassee

As the hub of regional activity, Tallahassee boasts a large number of hotels and motels, primarily major chains such as **Homewood Suites** (850-402-9400; www.tallahasseehomewoodsuites.com), 2987 Apalachee Pkwy, Tallahassee 32301; **Quality Inn and Suites** (850-877-4437), 2020 Apalachee Pkwy, Tallahassee 32301; and **Wingate Inn** (850-553-4400), 2516 Lakeshore Dr, Tallahassee 32303. Despite the many choices, it can still be hard to find a room in town—lobbyists and football fans often book the place full. Your best bet is to call the **Hotel Hotline** (850-488-BEDS), as they update availability hourly during peak occupancy periods.

♿ **Cabot Lodge** (1-800-223-1964; www.cabotlodge.com), 2735 N Monroe St (US 27), Tallahassee 32303. The lobby and room decor are reminiscent of a Maine lodge, including a spacious wraparound porch with rocking chairs overlooking the swimming pool. Each large, comfortable room ($72–84) has special touches for business travelers: a pinewood desk with lamp; a hair dryer, an iron, and an ironing board in the vanity area. Mingle with other guests over free cocktails every evening in the great room, or in the morning as you enjoy a continental breakfast with fresh fruit and pastries. An additional location on Thomasville Rd (1-800-255-6343) features interior hallways.

The Governors Inn (850-681-6855 or 1-800-342-7717; www.the

govinn.com), 209 S Adams St, Tallahassee 32301. This intimate boutique hotel (rooms, $129–159; suites, $159–229), created in the heart of a historic warehouse and stable in the shadow of the Capitol Building, showcases the finest that Tallahassee has to offer, with complimentary valet parking, breakfast, and cocktail hour. Learn a little history, too—each room is named for one of Florida's former governors. The refined atmosphere extends from the common spaces into the rooms, where you'll enjoy a large bath, writing desk, and terry robe for lounging.

Wakulla Springs 32305

Dating back to 1937, **Wakulla Lodge** (850-224-5950), 550 Wakulla Park Dr, overlooks fabulous Wakulla Springs at Wakulla Springs State Park (see *Springs*). This is Florida's only state park lodge, a true step back in time, with gleaming Tennessee marble floors and period furnishings in each of the 27 rooms ($79–99), and no television—except in the lobby, where guests mingle as they enjoy checkers, cards, and conversation at the marble tables in front of "Old Joe," an 11-foot alligator shot by a poacher in 1966. Look up and take in the artistic beauty of the hand-decorated wooden beams, completed by a Bavarian artist, or thumb through the album of clippings that spell out the history of the lodge and its builder, Edward Ball, once the wealthiest philanthropist in Florida, who donated up to $27,000 a day to charity at age 93! As night falls, a soft mist rises from the springs, and alligators crawl up onto the beach as you peer from the windows of the Ball Room (see *Dining Out*) during dinner. In the morning head out on a boat tour or a hike, or hit the 33-foot diving board for a jump into Florida's deepest spring.

Sandra Friend
HISTORIC WAKULLA LODGE

FISH CAMPS Six fish camps cluster around Lake Talquin off FL 267, offering anglers a place to retreat from busy Tallahassee. The busiest is **Whippoorwill Sportsman's Lodge** (850-875-2605), 3129 Cooks Landing Rd, Quincy 32351, which has cottages, two rooms in the lodge, a campground, and a marina. For saltwater fishing, visit **Shell Island Fish Camp** (850-925-6226), St. Marks 32355, on the Wakulla River. They offer basic, clean motel rooms with a small fridge, cable TV, no phones, $49; cottages and mobile homes also available. Boat ramp $3, overnight docking $5.

CAMPGROUNDS

Chattahoochee 32324

Perched on a high bluff above the Apalachicola River off US 90, the county-owned **Chattahoochee RV Resort** (850-663-8000) offers flat spaces ($12, full hookup), older cabins

($50), a playground, fishing pond, and nature trails, and easy access to the river for your boat. No credit cards. Near I-10, the **Chattahoochee KOA** (850-442-6657), 2309 Flat Creek Rd, is just what the family needs—camping cabins ($32) and shady spaces ($18–26) clustered around a playground and swimming pool.

Newport
Newport Recreation Area (850-925-6171), US 98, Wakulla, with picnicking, playground, and deeply shaded campsites in the forest along the St. Marks River, sits just outside St. Marks National Wildlife Refuge (where camping is not permitted).

Panacea 32346
Holiday Campground (850-984-5757; www.holidaycampground.com), US 98 at the Panacea Bridge, is a large family campground with a steady breeze off Ochlocknee Bay; great views from many of the sites. They can accommodate anything from a tent to a big rig ($22–31), and offer full 30- and 50-amp service, nice bathhouses, playground, 200-foot pier for fishing the bay, a swimming pool, and camp store. Dump station available.

Tallahassee
Big Oak RV Park (850-562-4660; www.bigoakrvpark.com), 4024 N Monroe St, Tallahassee 32303, offers shady spaces under grand old oaks just north of Tallahassee, perfect for antiquing excursions. A mix of back-in and pull-through full-hookup sites, $25—self-contained RVs only.

Tallahassee RV Park (850-878-7641; www.tallahasseervpark.com), 6504 Mahan Dr, Tallahassee 32301, has azalea-lined roads with shaded spaces, picnic tables and full hookups ($24–26) at each site, and a swimming pool. Travelers have use of the central modem hookup at the clubhouse; cable and phone lines available for long-term stays.

* Where to Eat

DINING OUT

Monticello
Three Sisters Restaurant (850-342-3474), 370 S Jefferson St, serves up Angus beef and fine cuisine in a comfortable home-style atmosphere. Lunch Wed–Sat 11–2, dinner Fri–Sat 5–8. Reservations suggested.

Panacea
Angelo's Seafood Restaurant (850-984-5168), US 98 at the bridge, stretches out over Ochlocknee Bay into the next county, providing gorgeous waterfront views while you dine on dishes with a Greek flair. It's a seafood lover's delight—choose from fresh Florida lobster stuffed with crab ($19–25), charbroiled mullet, grouper, amberjack, or snapper ($13–19), stuffed pompano ($23), and several dozen other seafood entrées. Dinner only; closed Tue.

Tallahassee
Andrew's 228 (850-224-2935), 228 S Adams St. The upscale big brother to Andrew's Capital Bar & Grill (see *Eating Out*) presents a very different face than its neighbor, featuring fine continental cuisine, with entrées $20 and up.

Bahn Thai Restaurant (850-224-4765), 1319 S Monroe St. Melding Chinese and Thai cuisine, Bahn Thai presents a wide array of fresh Asian food for discriminating palates in an unassuming locale. Nothing is precooked, save the items on the nightly all-you-can-eat buffet ($11), and there are more than 126 menu options, including 15 different soups and an extensive selection of vegetarian dishes; entrées $10–19. The convivial staff can be caught breaking into traditional song and dance in honor of their patrons' birthdays. Serving Tallahassee for more than 20 years, Chef Sue deserves her many top ratings from local reviewers. Open for lunch on weekdays, dinner daily.

Carlos Cuban Café (850-222-8581), 402 E Tennessee St, takes high marks from local reviewers for their excellent presentation of authentic Cuban cuisine.

Chez Pierre (850-222-0936; www.chezpierre.com), 1215 Thomasville Rd, is French, as the name indicates—but with a southern twist. Chalk paintings greet you along the walk, and flamboyant modern impressionism dresses up the tasteful maroon walls, setting a festive mood that spills over to Chef Eric's parade of fresh French cuisine—hors d'oeuvres ($3–11) like *gallettes au crabe de Chef Eric* and *saumon fumé*, sandwiches ($8–9) and quiche du jour, and entrées ($7–13) such as a traditional cassoulet of duck leg confit, ratatouille, or meat loaf deveau with whipped potatoes and porcini mushroom gravy. Save room for a selection from the elegant pastry tray! The wine selection, of course, is broad ($20–180 per bottle), and Le Piano Bar hosts jazz weekends. Stop in on Bastille Day, and find yourself surrounded by festivity—more than 1,000 people show up for dancing, arts and crafts booths, and wine tastings.

Always reserve ahead at the **Cypress Restaurant** (850-222-9451), 1350 W Tennessee St, as it's a favorite of the local politicos: and can I blame them? Chef-proprietor David Gwynn serves up creations like warm duck confit salad on chive potato cakes with cranberry vinaigrette; entrées start around $20. Open Tue–Sat for dinner, Tue–Fri for lunch 11–2.

The Silver Slipper (850-386-9366; www.thesilverslipper.com), 531 Silver Slipper Lane, a Tallahassee institution since 1938, is the classy place to bring a date for dinner. The entrées ($11–60) range from a vegetable platter to seafood Alfredo and châteaubriand for two, accompanied by an extensive wine list. Lunch Mon–Fri 11–2, dinner Mon–Sat at 4 PM.

Wakulla Springs

Large windows open out onto a view of the Wakulla Springs as you settle back into a fine-dining experience at **The Ball Room** at Wakulla Lodge (see *Hotels and Motels*). With backlit photos of the park, it feels a little like an interpretive center, although classical music drifts through the air and your food comes served on period dishes. And what food! Breakfast brings fluffy stacks of pancakes and eggs with grits ($3–5), and after you spend a day out on the water, it's tough to choose between the fresh-as-can-be Apalachicola fried oysters ($13) for lunch or and the traditional "Old South" fried chicken ($14) for dinner, a patrons' favorite since 1946; their world-famous navy bean soup ($3) is a must.

EATING OUT

Crawfordville

Myra Jean's Restaurant (850-926-7530), 2669 Crawfordville Hwy. For nearly 20 years this fun family restaurant and ice cream parlor has entertained kids young and old with the model railroad running around the restaurant; order some comfort food like a gravy dip sub and a chocolate shake ($2–8) and settle in to hear the whistles blowing. Don't miss the adjoining bakery, **Myra Jean's Cakes Etc.**, with its great selection of fresh-baked confections.

Havana

Nicholson's Farmhouse Restaurant (850-539-5931; www.nicholsonfarmhouse.com), 200 Coca-Cola Ave. It's not just a meal—it's a destination. Dr. Malcolm Nicholson's plantation lives on with a collection of four historic buildings centered on the old family home. High-raftered country-style dining halls inside the renovated buildings set the stage for tasty steaks, quail, lamb, and seafood entrées, $11–33. The meat is guaranteed fresh—they have their own butcher on the premises. Leave room for the homemade pies! Enjoy wagon rides on weekends, walk around the farm and visit the horses, chickens, and peacocks, or settle down to listen to a hoedown on the porch of the old filling station. Open Tue–Sat 4–10; reservations suggested.

Monticello

Jake's Subs & Grill (850-997-0388), 100 W Washington. Busy all times of the day, this local favorite opens at 6:30 AM and keeps dishing out until dinner; salads and sandwiches start at $3. Don't miss their great ice cream—I savored a banana pudding shake on my way to Tallahassee.

Panacea

Posey's Up the Creek (850-984-5243), 1506 Coastal Hwy. I stopped here for dinner late one day and ate a mess of shrimp and a slice of key lime pie . . . yum. Next time I came through, they were closed (Wed). But the nearby **Posey's Restaurant** (850-984-5799), 1168 Coastal Hwy (closed Mon), has a spectacular broiled seafood buffet the first Fri of each month; baskets and sandwiches run $6–11.

Quincy

Gucchidadi's (850-627-6660), 7 N Madison St, serves up tasty tomato, onion, and bacon pie (the family's variant on quiche) each morning, and a selection of pasta and garden salads for lunch, $3–6. Open Mon–Fri 8:30–2.

Sopchoppy

Backwoods Pizza (850-962-2220), 106 Municipal Ave. You won't miss the full-sized gorilla outside, nor the barnacle-encrusted bicycle in the front window of this classy pizza parlor, housed in the renovated 1912 drugstore that served this once bustling railroad town. Choose from specialty pizzas like the Extreme, Veggie Garden, or Carnivore, $7–17, or try a gourmet Greek or Mexican pizza; sandwiches, salads, and lasagna, too, with a side of music on Fri evening. Ask about canoe and kayak rentals via **Sopchoppy Outfitters**, which will be moving from this building to the old railroad station soon.

Spring Creek

Spring Creek Restaurant (850-926-3751), 33 Ben Willis Rd. Tended by the Lovel family since 1977, this off-the-beaten-path seafood restaurant draws folks from all over for fresh locally caught seafood, including grouper, mullet, and soft-shell crabs. Landlubbers can choose from fried chicken or rib eye. Lunch and dinner; sandwiches $5–7.50, entrées $9.95–27.50.

St. Marks

Posey's (850-925-6172; www.poseys.com), 55 Riverside Dr. In an unassuming two-story Cracker home along the St. Marks River, Posey's presents smoked mullet ($4) and fine local oysters and shrimp ($4–6) in its waterfront bar; patrons have papered the walls with dollar bills. Catch live music with your seafood Fri and Sat nights.

Riverside Café (850-925-5668), 69 Riverside Dr, is the epitome of Old Florida waterfront dining—open air, with the breeze coming right in off the river. Chow down on a variety of sandwiches from oyster to BLT ($4–7), or savor a dinner of bacon shrimp kebabs ($11), stone crab claws ($15) in-season, or any of several vegetarian specialties. They rent canoes as well ($20); ask at the front counter. Breakfast served daily 9–11, lunch and dinner thereafter.

Tallahassee

At **Andrew's Capital Grill & Bar** (850-224-2935), 228 S Adams St, the sandwiches come named for Florida politicos—try the "Jeb Burger" or the "Bob Gra-HAM burger" for lunch ($7–9). Looking for something more substantial? G.O.P. (Grand Old Pastas) start at $10, and the Executive Branch features entrées like cedar-planked salmon, lemon grouper, and wasabi tuna with wilted greens ($11–23). Open daily at 11:30.

Big-band music drifts into the **Black Dog Café** (850-224-2518), 229 Lake Ella Dr, from the adjoining American Legion, filling this hangout where friends chat and singles tap on their laptops, hoping to be noticed. Be the scene: Order up a latte and settle into a comfortable chair. Anywhere that hosts Scrabble Nights is all right by me!

Higher Taste (850-894-4296), 411 St. Francis St, offers vegetarian fare with flair inside a historic Tallahassee home. The lunch buffet (Mon–Fri) features organic salads, curried vegetables, Indian-style soups, and more. Dinner served Wed and Fri.

Metro Deli (850-224-6870), 104½ S Monroe St. Since 1942, this tiny downtown sub shop packs 'em in at lunchtime with its full slate of deli sandwiches, hot subs, melts, and grinders, $4–7. The aroma of cheddar bacon soup will draw you in!

Mon Pere et Moi (850-877-0343; pvchocolates.com), 3534 Maclay Blvd. Casual but classy, this premier chocolaterie and café presents freshly baked croissants and bagels each morning, followed by French favorites for lunch: from starters of escargots ($6) and *pâté au mousse de canard* ($8), a smooth duck pâté flavored with truffles, to salade Niçoise ($8) and entrées ($7–9) of crevettes, crêpes, and quiche. Don't forget a glass of wine ($5–8) to accompany these delights. The food, however, is just a sideline. A selection of sinful chocolate confections awaits: more than 20 varieties to explore. Served chilled, the dark chocolates are delicate, rich, bittersweet—a sensual experience when you bite into the liquid center of a framboise barrel with a raspberry inside, or gently chew on a mocha bean with its velvety ganache filling. At $32 a pound, these are the top of the line; choose carefully. Serving lunch 11–3.

Paradigm Restaurant & Lounge (850-224-9980), 115 W College Ave, draws in the lunch crowd with tasty wraps (including a wrap of the day, $7), a dressy BLT with baby spinach, Roma tomatoes, and provolone ($5), and fresh fruit salad ($6).

Po'Boys Creole Café (850-224-5400; www.poboys.com), 224 E College Ave, dishes up more than 20 types of po'boy sandwiches (from crawfish to tuna salad, $3–7) and authentic Creole favorites like crawfish roll and southern pork for dinner ($8–9). Stop in on Sun for the Bayou Brunch, 10–2, with omelets stuffed with crabmeat and shrimp, soufflés with andouille sausage, and more.

San Miguel (352-385-3346), 200 W Tharpe St. Authentic Mexican in a comfortable atmosphere, with à la carte items $1–3, and entrées $5–8, like the tasty *enchiladas verde*, smothered in spicy green tomatillo sauce. Murals brighten the intimate spaces; I couldn't help but notice the Aztec warrior carting off a maiden toward a raging volcano!

Shell Oyster Bar (850-224-9919), 114 Oakland Ave, is a hot spot for the Capitol crowd, where the raw and steamed oysters are the talk of the town. It's a small family-owned business focused on fresh seafood—I hear tell that the grouper, shrimp, and blue crab claws are superb. No credit cards.

The Soul Vegetarian Restaurant (850-893-8208; www.kingdoofyah.com) is a weekday lunchtime pushcart on Kleman Plaza that's served up vegan specialties for 9 years. Try a spicy jerk tofu platter, lentil soup, or a slice of sweet potato pie. Daily entrées $8, sandwiches $4, platters $7.

Uptown Café (850-222-3253), 111 E College Ave, is an old downtown standard serving breakfast and lunch goodies like made-from-scratch buttermilk biscuits ($1) and fresh banana bread; my hearty grilled Greek salad wrap kept me filled for hours ($5), but I was also tempted by the Eggzotic Express, made with curry and green onions ($5). Wash it all down with a cool glass of sweet mint iced tea.

Vintage Lace Tea Parlor (850-561-6944), 917 N Monroe St, is a haven of elegant Victoriana, a meld of a tearoom with a gift shop filled with antiques, where frilly hats decorate walls throughout the house and I found my childhood Mother Goose book on display. Open for lunch, afternoon tea, and dinner; call to reserve teatime, which ranges from a simple children's tea ($8) or cream tea ($7) to a full tea with finger sandwiches ($19).

Woodville

No matter the hour, **The Seineyard** (850-421-9191), 8159 Woodville Hwy, hidden in a strip mall along FL 363, is a busy dining spot serving up the best local seafood—I have friends who'll drive 2 hours to have dinner here. Fresh Gulf shrimp is featured prominently on the menu; have your seafood fried, broiled, or blackened to taste. Entrées run $9–14, including combination platters; this is one of the rare places where you can have a mullet sandwich ($6) for lunch.

✷ Entertainment

Watch your representatives at play: Legislators and lobbyists hang loose at **Clyde's and Costello's** (850-224-2173), 210 S Adams, a city pub with pool tables. But Tallahassee has a classy side, too: 25 years old, the annual **Tallahassee Bach Parley** (www.tfn.net/bach_parley) features classical music in venues like Goodwood; the **Tallahassee Symphony Orchestra** (850-224-0461; www.tsolive.org), 1345 Thomasville Rd, has a decade of concert series behind them, playing Sep–May. The **Big Bend Community Orchestra** (850-893-4567) offers Sun-afternoon classical and "pops" in area parks, and the **Artist Series** (850-224-9934) brings in philharmonic orchestras and soloists from around the globe. **Theatre A La Carte** (850-224-8474; www.theatrealacarte.org) bills itself as North Florida's premiere musical company, putting on two musicals each year, and the **Tallahassee Film Society** (850-386-4404; www.tallahasseefilms.com) shows indie, art, and retro films twice monthly at the EFC Miracle 5 Theatre.

More off the beaten path, you'll find live music (bluegrass, country, and classic rock) on the waterfront at both **Riverside** and **Posey's** in St. Marks on Fri and Sat nights (see *Eating Out*) and at the **Sopchoppy Opera**, a country music and bluegrass jam venue along US 319 where country legend Tom T. Hall hangs out. The Apalachee Blues Society meets at the **Bradfordville Blues Club** (850-906-0766), Moses Lane off Bradfordville Rd, where you can catch live blues concerts on Fri and Sat evenings.

✷ Selective Shopping

Crawfordville

Simple Things Antiques and Collectibles (850-926-9617), 3299 Crawfordville Hwy. Decked out with Coca-Cola signs, wind chimes, and other ephemera, this little Cracker home houses a nice mix of arts and crafts; the shelves and antique furnishings are crowded with baskets, pottery, old-time tins, and paintings with a regional flair. Open 10–5; closed Mon.

Tattered Pages Books & Espresso Bar (850-926-6055), 2807 Crawfordville Hwy. The hub of this shop, its small café, serves cappuccino, lattes, and smoothies, but the big attraction here is the books—all new. There's an excellent selection of new releases, literature, and fiction, books of regional interest, and an entire room devoted to titles just for kids. Open Mon–Fri 7–8, Sat 9–5, Sun 10–4.

Havana

Havana is the Panhandle's antiques hub, with more than 20 shops filling the downtown buildings, old railroad station, and tobacco barns to overflowing with a little bit of everything country. Prices are great, too. Here's a selection—but spend a day and see them all!

It feels like stepping into an old-time library at **Beare's Books 'n Things & Historical Bookshelf** (850-539-5040), 101 W 7th Ave, where stacks of historical books and antiquarian ephemera beckon—browse their large selection of Civil War and American history books.

Furniture shopping? **Custer's Last Stand** (850-539-1902), 208 1st St NW, had some of the nicest writing desks I've seen, as well as other fine furnishings in dark, rich woods.

Little River General Store (850-539-6900; www.littlerivergs.com), 308 N Main St, is a page from the past, where kids gaze at the penny candy while Mom picks up a bar of Fels-Naptha soap; mixed in are comfy throws, old-fashioned toys, and gourmet foods.

Mirror Image Antiques (850-539-7422), 303 1st St NW, is a sprawling complex with an eclectic selection of items—it's not just antiques. You'll find an art gallery, a gourmet food room stocked with British imports, rooms filled with books, and intriguing items from the Far East, like a Vietnamese Buddha.

At **Traditions on Main Street** (850-539-0622), 206 N Main St, you can spend hours wandering through this sprawling building if you take the time to look closely at everything—and it's worth your while to do so. While the primitives caught my eye, one vendor, **The Vintage Bookshelf** (850-875-4525), kept me busy for a long time as I paged through the vintage children's books.

With a female backpacker gracing their sign, how could I not visit **Wanderings** (850-539-7711), 312 1st St NW? This roomy shop, part of the 1906 Havana depot, deals in exotic home decor and primitives—arts, crafts, and furnishings.

Medart

Just Fruits & Exotics (1-888-926-7441), 30 St. Francis St. Along US 98 east of Medart, this sprawling native plant and exotic fruit emporium has everything from ferns and *Sarracenia* (carnivorous pitcher plants) to persimmon and guava trees. A must-stop for the serious gardener.

Monticello

Stroll downtown Monticello, and you'll find more than a dozen funky little shops, old-fashioned drugstores, and mercantile shops filled with collectibles and not-so-antiques, like the **Old Bank Antique Mall** (850-997-8163), 100 N Jefferson St.

I found perfect Christmas gifts at **Great Adventure Outfitters** (850-997-8675), 225 N Jefferson St, where you can buy mosquito head nets, Nalgene bottles, hiking boots, and technical clothing as well as fun Life is Good logo items, retro lunchboxes, and local crafts.

South of town, look for the **Southern Friends Antique Mall** (850-997-2550; www.southernfriends.net), I-10 and US 19. It's a large mall with many dealer booths, and lots of Coca-Cola memorabilia and china. The owner specializes in postcards and vintage paper collectibles.

Town Square Antiques (850-997-2127), 220 W Washington St, is an open, roomy shop with plenty of room for browsing their selection of saltcellars, glassware, and plates; look for larger items like fine furniture, primitives, and old washing machines in the back.

Sopchoppy

The Book and Art Tea Room (850-962-1900), 114 Municipal Ave. Featuring Florida titles and a nice concentration of books of regional interest, this small bookstore offers chai for $1 and monastery tea for 50¢—what a deal! Kick back and relax and browse while sipping a cup of tea.

George Griffin Pottery (850-962-9311), 1 SunCat Ridge Rd. It's a rough road back to George's place, a little cabin in the woods where he's practiced his craft for more than 30 years. But you'll be glad you made the detour to his tin-roofed gallery, as George's pottery is a wonderful, fluid thing; it's natural sculpture in a very natural setting, reflective of his inherent love of the craft. Stroll the shaded grounds and enjoy the outdoor art; sculptures rise along the fishpond, looking like the pitcher plants that grow in the surrounding forest. Little sheds contain earth-toned treasures, and inspirational quotes (along with

Polaroids of folks who've come to learn at the studio) are interspersed among pieces with form and function inside the main gallery. Open Tue–Sun.

St. Marks

Cabin Fever (850-925-6138), Riverside Dr, is the one and only quaint little shop down in St. Marks, featuring gifts that speak of Old Florida—nautical items, manatee figurines, and local crafts.

Tallahassee

Artworks (850-224-2500), 110 S Monroe St, offers the finest in local art on consignment from artists creating original oils, dichrotic glass and glass bowls, sculpture, and literature.

Stop by the shops of **Betton Place** at 1950 Thomasville Rd to browse through the **Museum Shop** (850-681-8565), filled with unique educational gifts for all ages; continue down a few doors to **My Favorite Things** (850-681-2824), where Tallahassee brides walk into the faux southern mansion to register for fine china, elegant home decor, and Swarovski crystal.

At Lake Ella (1650 N Monroe St), it's fun to browse the historic tourist cottages that now make up the **Cottages at Lake Ella**. My favorites include **Quarter Moon Imports** (850-222-2254) and their new Quarter Moon Annex, filled with exotica like lush tapestries from India, sensuous sushi platters, and Moroccan tea sets; **Barb's Southern Style Gourmet Brittles** (850-385-9839), for a sweet treat; **Glasswork by Susan** (850-222-5095), a stained-glass studio with supplies and original art; and **Lofty Pursuits** (850-521-0091; www.loftypursuits.com), where you can buy a kite, a yoyo, or a board game.

At the **Mary Brogan Museum of Art and Science** (see *Family Activities*), the **Museum Shop** offers creative and fun science toys, a great selection of children's books and art books, and beautiful works of art—art glass tables, bowls, limited-edition baskets, and more.

Native Nurseries (850-386-8882), 1661 Centerville Rd. It's a nursery for nature lovers, a shop where you'll learn about native plants and animals as you browse. Be sure to check out the Children's Nature Nook and the Wren's Nest Nature Shop, and if you're in town for a while, sign up for one of the many free workshops on native creatures and gardening.

Offering both new and used titles, the **Paperback Rack** (850-224-3455), 1005 N Monroe St, has been around for more than 20 years, and shines with an incredible diversity of titles (I found Alison Lurie, Gerald Durrell, and Jack Keroauc all in a few minutes' search), with an especially deep selection in fine literature but also a great variety in travel, black studies, and children's books. An extensive genre paperback section fills the front of the store.

Funky castoffs and mod art fill **Remember When** (850-425-4755), 115 W 6th Ave, an antiques and collectibles shop focusing on the 1930s through the 1960s, where lava lamps sit side by side with Parisian hats and lingerie.

Someone's in the Kitchen (850-668-1167; www.someoneskitchen.com), 1355 Market St. A fun stop for culinary items: gourmet foods and wines, plus kitchen accessories that would make a chef proud.

Something Nice (850-562-4167), 5019 Metzke Lane. The former Metzke Pewter Designs building is now a collection of gallery shops filled with antiques, collectibles, and handcrafted children's furniture; they also hold a flea market the first Sat monthly, 8–1.

The **Tallahassee Area Visitor Information Center** (see *Guidance*) has its own shop featuring art, books, and CDs from Tallahassee artists, including photo cards, primitives, bold acrylics, fiber arts, paintings on slate, and more.

Trail & Ski (850-531-9001), 2748 Capital Circle NE. With nearly 30 years serving Tallahassee, Trail & Ski is *the* shop where backpackers and campers head when they're gearing up for a trip. The store features a fine selection of outdoor guidebooks, travel items, and technical clothing; rental gear available.

FARMER'S MARKETS, FRESH SEAFOOD, AND U-PICK

Havana

Get your hands dirty at **Beare Blueberry Farm U-Pick**, 1.7 miles west of Havana on FL 12, where organic berries are the name of the game—it's $2.50 per pound, payable by the honor system. Open May 15–July 15.

Lamont

A 1960s-style roadside stand, **Robin Hood's Pecan House** on US 19 (south of I-10 at Monticello) sells fresh fruit, jumbo pecans, and country smoked sausage.

Medart

Captain Hook's, along US 98 in Medart near the junction with US 319, features "Hot Boiled Green Peanuts," watermelon, and other seasonal fruits. Pick up your fresh fish and smoked mullet at nearby **Fishbonz** on US 98.

Monticello

Turkey Hill Organic Farm (850-216-4024), 3546 Baum Rd. Organically grown veggies on an 89-acre family-run farm; holds an annual open house but otherwise sells produce every Sat at Market Square Shopping Center, Timberland Rd. Get your peaches and grapes in-season at **Windy Hill Farm**, 1 mile west of FL 59 on US 90.

Newport

Where FL 267 meets US 98, you'll find a longtime local vendor selling **tupelo honey**, **mayhaw jelly**, and **cane syrup** out of the back of his pickup truck on weekends.

Panacea

Known for its fresh fine seafood, the fishing village of Panacea boasts the largest number of roadside seafood stands in Wakulla County. In addition to folks selling shrimp and oysters out of the backs of their trucks, some of the old standbys with storefronts on US 98 include **Rock Landing Seafood**, featuring "live crabs when light is flashing," **D. L. Thomas Seafood**, the oldest outlet in town, and **My Way Seafood**.

Quincy

Davis Farm Fresh Fruits & Vegetables, a large farm stand on FL 65 S, sells direct from this family grower; you'll always find green boiled peanuts and vine-ripe tomatoes in-season.

St. Marks

Lighthouse Seafood Market (850-925-6221), Port Leon Dr, features fresh fish caught daily.

Tallahassee
Don't miss the **Downtown Marketplace** (850-980-8727; www.downtownmarket.com) in Ponce de Leon Park (Park Ave between Monroe and Adams), where vendors haul in the freshest of local produce while local musicians play on stage, poets and authors offer readings under the grand live oaks, and kids can join in fun activities like pumpkin carving, sidewalk chalk art, and other hands-on arts and crafts. Sat 8–2, Mar–Nov; free.

A community co-op, **New Leaf Market** (850-942-2557; www.newleafmarket.coop), 1235 Apalachee Pkwy, is more than 30 years old and invites the public in to shop for organic produce, ecofriendly household goods, alternative diet foods, and more.

✷ Special Events

March: **Natural Bridge Civil War Re-enactment** (850-922-6007), first weekend at National Bridge Historic State Park, Woodville. Reenactment of the Battle of Natural Bridge.

Red Hills Horse Trials (850-893-2497; www.rhht.org), Eleanor Klapp Phipps Park, Tallahassee. A nationally recognized equestrian competition with Olympic riders, educational exhibits, and special activities for the kids. Fee.

April: **Gold Cup Antique Car Race and Show** (850-653-9419), Tallahassee, first Sat. Nearly two decades old, this special event features classic automobiles winding through the city's streets.

Sopchoppy Worm Grunting Festival (850-962-5282), first Sat. If you didn't know how to grunt an earthworm out of the ground, you will by the end of this festival, featuring live bluegrass, arts and crafts, and the annual worm grunters' ball. No jokes, folks—this is an honest profession in the Apalachicola woods!

May: **Panacea Blue Crab Festival** (850-227-1223), first weekend. A parade and craft booths are an adjunct to seafood, seafood, and more seafood from the folks who know crabs!

October: Celebrated at St. Marks National Wildlife Refuge (see *Wild Places*), the **Monarch Festival** offers guided naturalist tours to view butterflies along hiking trails, environmental exhibits (including a great butterfly tent for the kids), arts and crafts, and the opportunity for you to volunteer to tag butterflies for research (I couldn't believe it was possible until I saw it done!). During the same weekend, the **St. Marks Crab Festival** draws visitors to the riverside restaurants with massive fixed price feeds, live bluegrass, and a small arts and crafts festival.

November: **North Florida Fair** (850-878-3247), Tallahassee, is the region's largest agricultural fair, featuring major country music acts, midway rides, agricultural competitions, and food vendors. Fee.

December: **Just One More Invitational Art Festival** (850-980-8727), second Sat, Park Ave, Tallahassee. Featuring live music, food, children's activities, and works from selected southeastern artists.

APALACHICOLA REGION

LIBERTY, FRANKLIN, GULF, CALHOUN, AND JACKSON COUNTIES

History runs deep along the Apalachicola River, the meandering 108-mile watercourse that defines the boundary between the Eastern and Central Time Zones in Florida. Spanish traders and British seafarers fought over commerce here in the 1700s, and merchants established the town that is now **Apalachicola**, the vibrant heart of the region, in 1829. Soon after, **Carrabelle** and **Port St. Joe** grew up around Florida's first railroad connections with the sea; along with **Eastpoint**, these coastal towns are defined by their working shrimpers and oystermen, who provide a bounty enjoyed in local restaurants and elsewhere—Apalachicola harvests 90 percent of Florida's oysters. White sand beaches and rolling dunes define the barrier islands of **St. George**, **St. Vincent**, **Dog Island**, and **Cape San Blas**, where spectacular public lands like St. Joseph State Park let you enjoy the beauty of the "Forgotten Coast."

In the northerly counties along the watershed, expect pine-topped ridges and high bluffs above the rivers, where Old Florida thrives in settlements like **Wewawitchka**, **Blountstown**, and **Bristol**. Working downtowns characterize these small towns—islands in a sea of cotton fields and cattle ranches. **Marianna** anchors the northern corner of the region, with genteel historic homes and outstanding outdoor recreation. The Apalachicola region is a friendly place, where you can share small talk with shopkeepers and innkeepers, or hoist a beer with the locals down at the waterfront. And don't be surprised to see the sheriff wave hello as he drives past on US 98!

GUIDANCE You'll easily find the **Apalachicola Bay Chamber of Commerce** (850-653-9419; www.apalachicolabay.org), downtown on Market St, but the **Carrabelle Chamber of Commerce** (850-697-2585; www.carrabelle.org) and the **Gulf County Tourist Development Council** (1-800-482-GULF; www.visitgulf.com) are best contacted in advance. Take time to visit the **Jackson County Chamber of Commerce** (850-482-9633; www.jctdc.org), 4318 Lafayette St, in the beautifully restored Russ House in Marianna (see *Historic Sites*).

GETTING THERE **US 98** is "Main Street" for the coast, running east–west through Franklin and Gulf Counties. Use scenic **FL 65**, **67**, and **71** to parallel

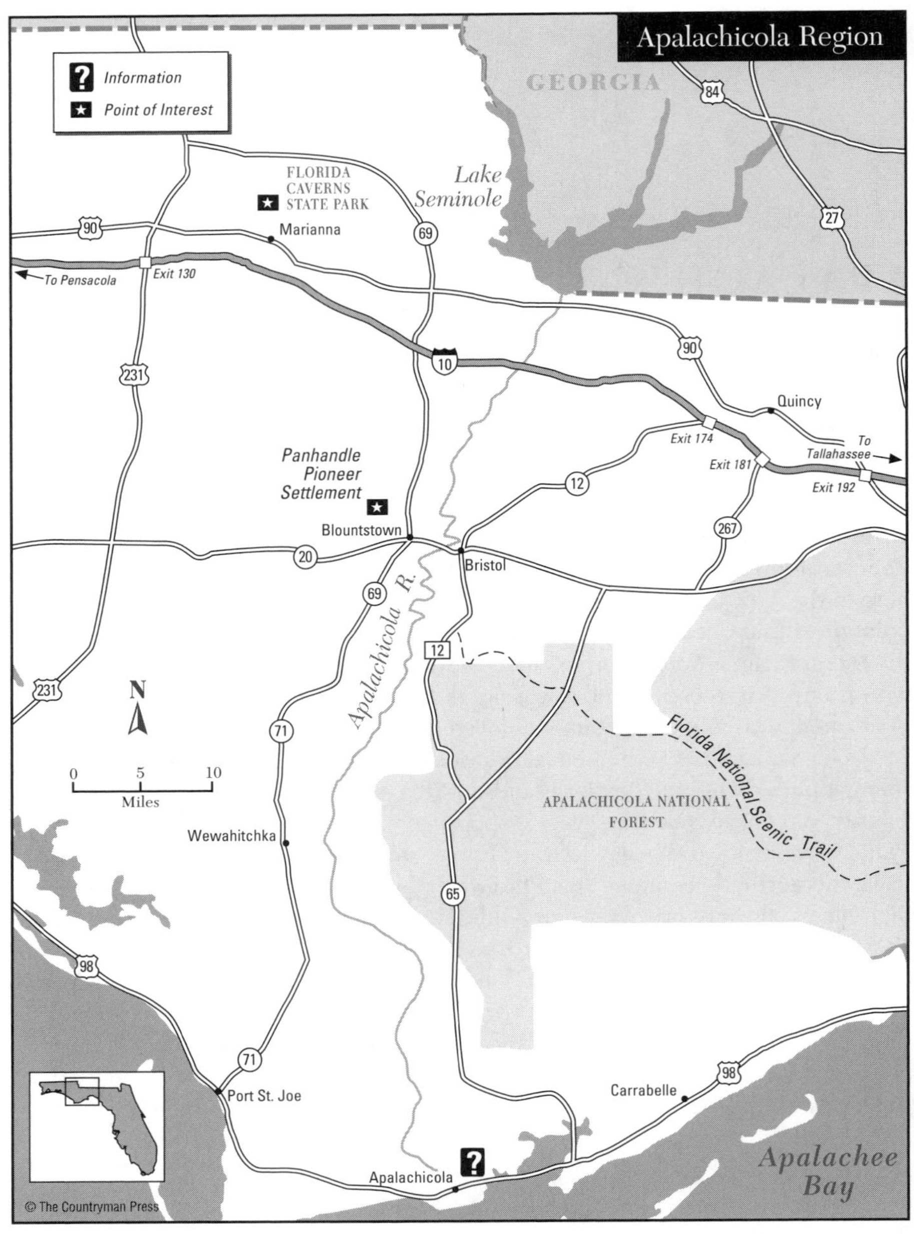

the Apalachicola River to reach the northern part of the region, where **I-10** and **US 90** provide access to towns near the Georgia-Alabama border.

MEDICAL EMERGENCIES Emergency treatment can be received at **George E Weems Memorial Hospital** (850-653-8853), 135 Ave G, Apalachicola, and at **Jackson Hospital** (850-526-2200), 4250 Hospital Dr, Marianna. *Important note*:

Most of this region is extraordinarily remote, and cell phone service isn't guaranteed in the vast wilderness areas between I-10 and US 98.

✷ To See

ART GALLERIES

Apalachicola

I am in love with Apalachicola's artists, and can't wait for the day when my checkbook says I will patronize them properly. At the Grady Market (see *Selective Shopping*), visit **Richard Bickel Photography** (850-653-4099; www.gradymarket.com/bickel.htm) for black-and-white images that capture the soul of this region. The **Alice Jean Art Gallery** (850-653-3166), 29 Ave E, showcases Alice Jean Gibbs's haunting coastal scenes, Jane Tallman's pastels, and the photography of **Alecia Ward**. See *Selective Shopping* for other outlets for local artists.

Carrabelle

Carrabella Cove (850-697-8984), 1859 US 98, across from the beach, showcases coastal art, pottery, and sculpture, all by local artists who love the estuaries they call home.

St. George

Sea Oats Gallery (850-927-2303; www.forgottencoastart.com), 128 E Pine St, has four rooms filled with scenes of Apalachicola and the Panhandle, featuring artists like Ellen Sloan and Roger Leonard, who deftly capture the coastal light. The sculptures of Cass Allen Pottery are joyful figures of angels in flight. Don't miss this place!

HISTORIC SITES Driving through this rural region, you'll uncover Florida's pre–Civil War plantation history, where cotton grows on lands handed down through the generations. Most of the small towns have an old-time county courthouse, and sometimes the entire downtown district is a Florida Heritage site. Here are a few of the most significant stops along the way.

Apalachicola

Downtown Apalachicola is a Florida treasure. Pick up a walking tour map at the chamber of commerce (see *Guidance*) and explore the many unique sites, such as the **1836 Greek sponge exchange**, the **1831 Chestnut Street Cemetery**, the Greek-built shrimp boat ***Venizelos***, and this port city's **Customs House** from 1923, now the post office. On a high bluff above the river, the **Orman House** (850-653-1209), 177 5th St, was built by early settler and shipping magnate Thomas Orman with wood shipped from Syracuse, New York, in 1838. It's now a state park with history-packed tours on the hour (9–11, 1–3) led by ranger John Winfield Thu–Mon. Fee.

Carrabelle

Although the police force has outgrown its old digs, the **World's Smallest Police Station**, a phone booth downtown, remains, with a squad car always parked next door. It dates back to 1963, and I was going to ask the officer on duty about it, but he was busy giving a ticket to a speeder. I crept past and headed on to the **Crooked River Lighthouse** along US 98, built in 1895 to replace a lighthouse destroyed in a hurricane on Dog Island. A citizens group is working on its restoration.

Greenwood

Established in 1869, **Pender's Store** on Bryan St is one of the oldest continuously operated stores in Florida, retaining its original shelving and heart pine floors. On the way there, you'll pass stately **Great Oaks**, known as Bryan Plantation during the Civil War. The **Erwin House** on Fort St is perhaps the oldest structure in Jackson County, circa 1830. All three structures are on the National Register of Historic Places.

Marianna

First settled in the 1820s, Marianna formed the commercial center for a hub of busy plantations, including **Sylvania**, the home of Civil War–era governor John Milton, now the grounds of Florida Caverns State Park (see *Parks*). During the war, Marianna became a target because it was the governor's hometown. On September 17, 1864, the Battle of Marianna pitted the Home Guard (a militia of old men and teenagers) against invading Union troops. They fought in and around **St. Luke's Episcopal Church**, which was burned during the conflict. A Union officer preserved and returned the Holy Bible to the church, where it remains on display. Faced with surrendering the state to the Union army, Governor Milton returned home on April 1, 1865, and shot himself, 8 days before Lee surrendered the Confederacy. Milton is buried at St. Luke's.

THE RUSS HOUSE IN MARIANNA

Sandra Friend

Down the street, the distinctively rounded **Russ House**, built 1895 by prominent merchant Joseph W. Russ, had its fancy neoclassical pillars added in 1910. It now houses the Jackson County Chamber of Commerce (see *Guidance*), where you can pick up a walking tour guide to Marianna's many other historic structures.

GHOST TOWNS Off FL 65 in the Apalachicola National Forest at New River, **Vilas** has little more to note its passing than some scattered building materials and a long-unused railroad

SUMATRA Fort Gadsden (850-643-2282). Constructed during the War of 1812 to defend British colonial interests, the original fortress encompassed a 7-acre tract along the Apalachicola River as a base to recruit runaway slaves and Indians to the British cause of wresting control of Florida from the Spanish. In 1815 the British abandoned the effort but left behind a force of 300 former slaves and Seminoles to watch over the river from what was then dubbed the "Negro Fort." When American colonel Duncan Clinch sailed upriver under the auspices of General Andrew Jackson in 1816, the inhabitants of the fort fired on his gunboats. Clinch returned fire. A single cannonball hit the ammunition pile inside the fort, causing a massive explosion that blew apart the fort and its defenders. Only 30 survived, and Clinch had several of them executed. Jackson ordered a new fortress erected on the spot as a base of operations for his missions during the First Seminole War. Lieutenant James Gadsden and his men held the fort until Florida became a U.S. territory in 1821. The fort fell into disrepair, although it was briefly occupied by Confederate troops guarding the gateway to the Apalachicola River. Reached by dirt roads from FL 65 south of Sumatra, a mile-long interpretive and nature trail showcases the key points. Fee.

siding; the Florida Trail meanders through the remains of this turn-of-the-20th-century turpentine town.

MUSEUMS

Apalachicola

Apalachicola Maritime Museum (850-653-8700), 71 Market St. Learn about the Gulf Coast's long and storied maritime history through the permanent and changing exhibits of this museum, including the fully restored 1877 schooner the *Governor Stone* moored along the waterfront. It's considered the oldest operating sailing vessel in the American South.

John Gorrie Museum State Park (850-653-9347), 46 6th St. Living in malaria-stricken Florida in the 1850s, Dr. John Gorrie had a problem: how to keep his recovering patients cool? With a great deal of engineering savvy, Gorrie found a way to use compressed air and condensation to make ice, then ran a fan across the ice to keep his infirmary cool. By doing so, he developed the world's first system for mechanical refrigeration, patented in May 1851: an icemaker. At the time, ice for refrigeration was cut from frozen northern lakes and packed in sawdust for transport. Gorrie died in obscurity, his achievement too "far out" for his time. It wasn't until the 1890s that ice merchants discovered the magic of Gorrie's system, which led to the design of air-conditioning. In 1911 Gorrie was honored with a statue as one of two representatives of Florida history in the U.S. Capitol Building in Washington, DC. The museum is open 9–5; closed Tue and Wed. Fee. Across the street, Gorrie is buried in **Gorrie Square**.

Blountstown

Hidden behind the Sam B. Atkins Recreation Complex off Silas Green Street, the **Panhandle Pioneer Settlement** (850-674-3050; www.panhandlepioneer settlement.com) brings together vintage buildings from towns along the Apalachicola. Outfitted with period furnishings, each tells a story of Florida's frontier days. Volunteer docents lead informative tours, Tue and Thu–Sat, noon–4 (summer 9–1). Fee.

Carrabelle

Bet you didn't know that the first amphibious landing craft didn't land at Utah Beach on D-Day: They tried them out in Carrabelle first! From 1942 to 1946, the Gulf Coast from Ochlocknee Bay to Eastport was Camp Gordon Johnson, a training facility for more than 250,000 amphibious soldiers as they practiced storming the beaches of Normandy. The **Camp Gordon Johnston Museum** (850-697-8575; www.campgordonjohnston.com), 302 Marine St, honors the World War II troops who trained here and preserves the history of that important effort that clinched the Allied liberation of France, with artifacts and archives of special interest to vets and history buffs. Mon–Tue, Thu–Fri 1–4; Wed 10–4; Sat 10–1. Donation.

Port St. Joe

At the **Constitutional Convention State Museum** (850-229-8029), 200 Allen Memorial Way, interpretive exhibits and artifacts put a face on Florida's frontier days, with a special focus on St. Joseph. Established by homesteaders who were kicked out of Apalachicola thanks to a sneaky land deal called the Forbes Purchase (1830), St. Joe was Florida's first real tourist destination, a deep-water port that was the Las Vegas of its day. Some said it was the hand of God that wiped out Sin City in 1841, with a triple whammy of yellow fever, hurricane, and wildfire. A stone marker, cemetery, and this museum are all that's left of the old city. In 1838 St. Joe hosted Florida's Constitutional Convention. A replica meeting room has bios of all of the delegates, and gives a nice glimpse into a time when Mosquito County took up most of the southern peninsula. Thu–Mon 9–noon, 1–5. Fee.

A 1915 ST. JOE STEAM ENGINE

Sandra Friend

RAILROADIANA Inside the **Constitutional Convention State Museum** you'll find a scale replica of **Florida's first steam engine**, which ran on an 8-mile route, the St. Joseph & Lake Wimico Canal & Railroad, between St. Joseph and Depot Creek in 1836. Outside the museum, look for a **1915 steam engine** belonging to the St. Joe Lumber Company. In Marianna, the **L&N Railroad Depot** dates back to 1881.

✷ To Do

BICYCLING A dedicated bicycle path runs down the middle of **St. George Island**; rent bikes at **Journeys of St. George Island** (see *Ecotours*). The region's scenic rural roads lend themselves to long-distance excursions as well.

BIRDING On nearly 100 miles of back roads in the **Apalachicola River Wildlife and Environmental Area** (see *Wild Places*) look for hundreds of bird species, including swallow-tailed and Mississippi kites roosting in tall cypresses. Shorebirds abound on the tidal flats of the barrier islands.

BOAT EXCURSIONS To get to the remote barrier islands, you'll need a shuttle, such as **St. Vincent Island Shuttle Services** (850-229-1065; www.stvincent island.com), **Dog Island Water Taxi** (850-697-3989), or **Journeys of St. George Island** (see *Ecotours*). Or kick back and enjoy a pleasurable sail on a 1950s sloop, the ***Wind Catcher*** (850-653-3881), which offers daily trips and can be chartered out to the islands.

BOATING Located at the Port St. Joe marina, **Seahorse Water Safaris** (850-227-1099; www.seahorsewatersafaris.com) rents everything from a kayak to a 23-foot pontoon boat. Bringing your own boat? Look for public ramps at Carrabelle, Eastpoint, Apalachicola, and Indian Pass.

DIVING Offshore wrecks make exploring this region exciting. **Carabelle Fish & Dive** (850-697-8765; www.cbellefishdive.com) runs deep-sea trips and has cold air on premises; **Burkett's Diving** (850-647-6099), 212 Gulf St, Port St. Joe, can set you up in style, as can **Seahorse Water Safaris** (see *Boating*) and **The Moorings Dive Shop** (see *Lodging*) in Carabelle.

ECOTOURS **Apalachicola Estuary Tours** (850-653-TOUR; www.apalachicola tours.com) runs informative 2-hour cruises on a 40-foot, 32-passenger boat out of Scipio Creek Marina; $20 adults, $10 children. **Journeys of St. George Island** (850-927-3259; www.sgislandjourneys.com) has a complete menu of tours ranging from guided paddling trips to ecotours to St. Vincent and Dog Islands, deep-sea fishing, and bay fishing. They also rent sailboats, motorboats, and kayaks, and run environmental summer camps and special kid-oriented trips; call for details.

FAMILY ACTIVITIES **Putt-N-Fuss Fun Park** (850-670-1211), 236 US 98. Mini golf, bumper boats, and an arcade clustered around a miniature mountain at the gateway to St. George Island. Open daily, hours vary by season; adults $8, children $7.

FISHING No matter whether you prefer deep-sea excursions or bank fishing, the entire **Apalachicola River** watershed is a huge destination for sport fishing, with tournaments held nearly every month. In Carabelle ask about fishing guides at the **Dockside Marina** and **C-Quarters Marina** (850-697-8400), US 98. **Top**

Knot Charters (1-800-446-1639; www.topknotcharters.com) is one of the long-established services in the area. Ask around Apalachicola and Port St. Joe for top guides like the **Robinson Brothers** (850-653-8896; www.FloridaRedfish.com), or **Boss Charters** (850-853-8055) for deep-sea fishing on *Miss Emily*. Depending on the guide, length of trip, and location, you'll pay $250–700 for a guided trip. To fish the Apalachicola River on your own, put your boat in the river at any of many ramps along FL 71 or FL 67. Stop in at **Forgotten Coast Outfitters** (850-653-9669), 94 Market St, Apalachicola, for fly-fishing tackle and homespun advice.

Trophy-sized lunkers lurk along the Dead Lakes at **Dead Lakes State Park** and in **Lake Seminole** at **Three Rivers State Park** (see *Parks*). You won't want to miss the serenity of cypress-lined **Merritts Mill Pond** along US 90, Marianna, and **Spring Creek** for fly-fishing.

GOLF Built by the CCC in the 1930s, the **Florida Caverns Golf Course** (850-482-4257), 3309 Caverns Rd, has nine holes under the tall pines adjoining the state park, $10–15. Off US 90 east of Marianna, **Indian Springs Golf Club** (1-800-587-6257), 5248 Club House Dr, offers 18 holes, par 72, $24–32.

HIKING The **Florida Trail** passes through true wilderness in the Apalachicola National Forest between Porter Lake and Camel Lake, with rare pitcher plant savannas (best seen during their blooming period in March) around Memery Island. See *Green Space* for other excellent backpacking and day-hiking locales in the region.

HORSEBACK RIDING Several outfitters offer horseback riding on the shifting sands of St. George Island and Cape San Blas, including **Hoofprints in the Sand** (850-227-5454; www.hoofprintsinthesand.com). Expect to pay $35–50 for a ride along the surf.

PADDLING Along FL 65 you'll find numerous put-ins for paddling adventures into **Tate's Hell** and on the **Apalachicola River**; watch for the yellow-and-black signs at places like Graham Creek. Eleven such routes are outlined in the free ***Apalachicola River Paddling Trail System*** map available from the Apalachicola River Wildlife and Environmental Area office (850-488-5520; www.wildflorida.org/nbr). The **Chipola River Canoe Trail** starts at Florida Caverns State Park (see *Parks*) and flows 50 miles south to Dead Lake at Wewahitchka, a 3-day trip with a stretch of whitewater (portage recommended) near the FL 274 bridge. For canoe rentals and shuttling, check with **Scott's Ferry Landing** (see *Lodging*) or **Bear Paw Adventures** (850-482-4948; www.bearpawadventures.net), Magnolia Rd off FL 71, which runs half-day, full-day, and overnight trips Mar 16–Sep 30 ($27–50). For day trips on the Upper Chipola, rent a canoe at **Florida Caverns State Park**, $10–25. On St. George Island, **Journeys of St. George Island** (see *Ecotours*) runs guided kayaking trips and rents and sells kayaks. Explore the needlerush marshes along St. Joseph Bay by launching in the state park or at the public launch. Rent kayaks at **Happy Ours** (850-229-1991),

775 Cape San Blas Rd, or at **The Entrance** (850-227-PLAY; www.escapetothe-cape.com) in front of St. Joseph State Park.

SCALLOPING **St. Joseph Bay** is scalloping central on the coast, July 1–Sep 10. You can wade in at the public beaches and sift through the shallows for free, or book a charter—check in at **Port St. Joe Marina** (850-227-9393; www.brandy marine.com/psjmarina), or drop in at **Scallop Cove** (850-227-7557; www .scallopcove.com), 4310 Cape San Blas Road, where they also rent canoes and run ecotours.

SCENIC DRIVES One of Florida's best scenic drives is a little-known treasure through Liberty and Franklin Counties. Start at **FL 20** in Bristol; head south on **CR 12** into the Apalachicola National Forest. This designated scenic route merges with **FL 65** and continues south through nearly 50 miles of unspoiled old-growth longleaf pine forest as the road parallels the Apalachicola River. When the road ends, turn left. Atop a high sand bluff, **US 98** offers sweeping views of St. George Sound for the next 22 miles. At Carabelle, head north on **FL 67** through the national forest to return to FL 20 at Hosford. Total drive time: 3 hours. Alternatively, **CR 379** south of Bristol is the **Apalachee Savannas National Forest Scenic Byway**, which dovetails into the above route onto FL 65 at Sumatra. Along this route, you'll see vast pitcher plant savannas blooming each spring.

SWIMMING In addition to the region's many beaches (see *Beaches*), swimmers flock to pristine **Blue Hole** at Florida Caverns State Park (see *Parks*) and to **Blue Spring** in Marianna (see *Springs*).

TUBING **Bear Paw Adventures** (see *Paddling*) sets up 4-mile tubing trips down crystal-clear, cypress-lined Spring Creek; Mar–Sep, $9.

WALKING TOURS Stop at the **Apalachicola Bay Chamber of Commerce** (see *Guidance*) for a copy of their historic walking tour booklet that highlights 34 sites, most within seven blocks of Market St. In Marianna, **Main Street Marianna** (850-482-6046), 2880 Green St, has a 44-page self-guided tour of historic sites in Jackson County.

WATER SPORTS Check on the beach in front of the **Blue Parrot** (see *Eating Out*) on **St. George Island** for summer season stands with Hobie Cat rentals and parasail rides.

✴ Green Space

BEACHES East to west, you can sample public beaches off US 98 at **Baldy Point State Park** (see *Parks*), **Carabelle Beach** (used for D-Day invasion practice in 1942), **St. George Island State Park**, **Cape Palms Park** and **Salinas Park** at Cape San Blas, and **Beacon Hill Park** at St. Joe Beach. Don't miss **St. Joseph Peninsula State Park** (see *Parks*) with its stunning tall dunes and

Florida Caverns State Park (850-482-9598), 3345 Caverns Rd. Built by the Civilian Conservation Corps "Gopher Gang" from 1938 to 1942, this park's gem is the state's only show cave tour. Active features glisten with calcite crystals: shimmering rimstone pools, translucent soda straws, and rippling cave bacon underscore the delicate world inside Florida's limestone karst as you walk, duck, and squeeze through places like the Wedding Room, the Cathedral, and the Catacombs. For the claustrophobic, a video tour plays constantly in a big theater at the visitors center, where informative exhibits explain the unique habitats found in this park. Hikers, bikers, and equestrians share the 6.7-mile Upper Chipola Trail System, and hikers enjoy rugged limestone bluffs along the 1.5-mile Caverns Trail System, where the Bluff Trail goes right through a cave used by ancient peoples for shelter! Campground $8–14, picnic pavilions, canoe rentals, and adjacent state-run golf course. Fee. Additional fee for cave tour; go directly to the visitors center to buy your ticket, as tours frequently sell out.

DUCKING UNDER THE FORMATIONS AT THE FLORIDA CAVERNS

Sandra Friend

beaches, voted best in the nation by *Condé Nast Traveler* magazine. If you have the time and inclination, kayak out or catch a charter to the unspoiled coasts of **Dog Island**, **Cape St. George State Reserve**, and **St. Vincent Island**, where you can sun without the crowds.

BOTANICAL GARDENS The small **Chapman Botanical Garden** on Martin Luther King Jr. Ave, Apalachicola, honors native son Dr. Alvin Wentworth Chapman (1809–1899), an internationally renowned botanist. Sidewalks wind through green space; boardwalks carry you over wetlands. The park seems somewhat neglected; it would be nice to see it with blooming beds again, especially since clouds of butterflies stop here on their fall migration. Free.

NATURE CENTER ✐ At the end of Market St, the **Apalachicola Nature Center** (850-653-8063) at Apalachicola National Estuarine Research Reserve gives a great introduction to the estuary, with interpretive and hands-on exhibits, microscopes to watch sea critters, a little-kid corner with games and puzzles, open tanks with turtles and fish, and a popular boardwalk to an overlook on the estuary. Mon–Fri, 8–5.

PARKS **Apalachicola Bluffs and Ravines Preserve** (850-643-2756; www.tnc.org), CR 12, Bristol, provides hikers with a look at unique natural areas along the bluffs of the Apalachicola River along the extremely rugged 3.5-mile **Garden of Eden Trail**, where the world's most endangered conifer, the torreya tree, grows along with rare varieties of magnolias and the showy Florida anise—look for bright red blooms in spring!

Baldy Point State Park (850-349-9146), 146 Box Cut Rd, provides Alligator Point with its only sandy beaches along a peninsula of scrub oaks and pines. Nature trails and bicycle paths following old roads wind through the hammocks.

Dead Lakes State Park (850-639-2702), FL 71. This strangely beautiful 6,700-acre lake with dark tannic waters is located on the Chipola River near the town of Wewahitchka. The lake is accessible off FL 71 just north of Wewahitchka on State Park Rd and south off Land Rd. There are fish camps located around the lake. Care should be taken when operating a motorboat in this lake—it's filled with cypress snags and stumps. This lake enjoys a wide reputation for its bluegill (bream) and redear (shellcracker) fishing in spring.

St. George Island State Park (850-927-2111), 1900 E Gulf Beach Dr, has a pleasant campground nestled in among the pines at the east end of the island, and primitive camping for folks who hike the Gap Point trail. But the big draw here is the miles and miles of unspoiled beach. Enjoy! Fee.

St. Joseph Peninsula State Park (850-227-1327), 8899 Cape San Blas Rd, has the distinction of having the top beach in the United States, according to Stephen Leathermann, "Dr. Beach." Is it the white sand beaches or the tall sand dunes? You decide. The campgrounds are spectacular, as are the hiking trails—this is one of the few places you can really get away from it all on a backpacking trip to the western tip of the cape. There are well-appointed cabins, too. It's an excellent state park experience.

SAND DUNES AT ST. JOSEPH PENINSULA STATE PARK

Sandra Friend

Three Rivers State Park (850-482-9006), 7908 Three Rivers Park Rd, Sneads. Defined by the confluence of the Chattahoochee and Flint Rivers creating the Apalachicola, this expansive recreation area includes Lake Seminole, a top-notch bass fishing destination, as well as a large lakeside campground ($8–10) with a new wheelchair-accessible rental cabin, picnic pavilions, two hiking trails, and canoe rentals.

Torreya State Park (850-643-2674), FL 271 between Bristol and Greensboro. From the 150-foot bluffs above the Apalachicola River, you can see for miles. An 1849 mansion, the Gregory House, dominates the skyline. The star attraction, however, is the 11.5-mile hiking trail system, offering one of the most rugged backpacking experiences in the state as you pass earthen battlements built during the Civil War and walk through ravines with the aroma of the rare torreya tree, also known as the stinking cedar. Enjoy the peaceful, scenic developed campground for $8–10, where you can try out a yurt!

♿ **Rish Park** (850-227-1876), Cape San Blas Rd, deserves special note as Florida's only state park designated specifically for and limited to wheelchair-bound residents and their families. Boardwalks and tunnels allow access to swimming, cabins, the beach, fishing piers, and nature trails on both sides of the highway. Only Florida residents with developmental disabilities may utilize the facilities; call in advance of your visit. In Marianna, tiny **Spring Creek Park** on US 98 provides a wheelchair ramp right down to the water for fishing.

SPRINGS Marianna's **Blue Spring Park** (850-482-9637; www.jacksoncountyfl.com), 5461 Blue Springs Hwy, offers a sandy beach, diving boards, and playground fringing a 70-degree first-magnitude spring bubbling more than 64 million gallons of water daily. Open Memorial Day–Labor Day. Fee.

WILD PLACES **Apalachicola National Forest** (850-643-2282) encompasses more than half of Liberty County, with some of the world's finest pitcher plant savannas on its western edge. Walk the Florida Trail west from **Camel Lake Recreation Area** for an immersion into this unique marshy environment; the brightest blooms occur in late March. Adjoining the forest, the **Apalachicola River Wildlife and Environmental Area** (850-488-5520; www.wildflorida.org/nbr) encompasses thousands of acres of floodplain forests and marshes along both sides of the river, with more than 10 boat ramps and an interpretive trail at Sand Beach Recreational Area. Primitive camping (no permits, no fees required) is permitted in the upland areas of the preserve.

Several of the region's wild places are barrier islands, accessible only by boat. **Cape St. George Island**, a 9-mile stretch of beach sheltering Apalachicola Bay, has a historic lighthouse and plays host to families of red wolves being acclimated to the wild, as does adjacent **St. Vincent National Wildlife Refuge** (850-653-8808). Off Carrabelle, **Dog Island Preserve** can only be reached by boat. Coastal scrub and coastal pine forests are the predominant ecosystems on these barrier islands, where day-use visitors are welcome to roam the beaches and watch for birds; no overnight visits are permitted.

♿ **Tate's Hell State Forest** (850-697-3734), 1621 US 98, Carrabelle. With nearly 150,000 acres of mostly wetlands, this is one helluva swamp. It's an important chunk of land, a giant natural filtration system for water flowing out of the swamps of the Apalachicola National Forest and into the bay and estuaries.

Hunting, fishing, and paddling are the main recreation here, but hikers have two spots to explore: the short wheelchair-accessible **Ralph G. Kendrick Dwarf Cypress Boardwalk** (look for signs on FL 67) leading out over a rare (for North Florida) dwarf cypress swamp, and the **High Bluff Coastal Nature Trail** along US 98.

✷ Lodging

BED & BREAKFASTS

Apalachicola 32320

Bryant House (1-888-554-4376; www.bryanthouse.com), 101 6th St. European elegance infuses this grand 1897 home, where Brigitte (enjoying her dream job) brings a touch of Germany to Florida, and Einstein, the resident blue-and-gold macaw, will call out a cheery greeting on your arrival. Period antiques (with price tags attached—buy one if the mood strikes!) embellish each of the three lavish rooms: Blue, Gold, and Red. Business travelers will appreciate DSL access, while the romantically inclined will fall in love with this very grand setting. Brigitte's traditional German breakfast of thinly sliced smoked meats, cheeses, fresh fruit, and a soft-boiled egg is simply superb. $117–140.

Coombs House Inn (850-653-9199; www.coombshouseinn.com), 80 6th St. One of the grandest restored mansions in the South (circa 1905) and one of the nation's top inns, the pride of lumber baron James Coombs will amaze you. Step inside the doorway into a grand hall lined with black cypress walls and a high-beamed ceiling. Each room offers spacious Victorian elegance with careful restorative touches, such as the gleaming colored tile on the coal-fired fireplaces (a relic of the days when ships from Liverpool swapped coal ballast for cotton) and built-in cabinets moved into the bathrooms. You'll feel like royalty amid the lush furnishings and art, and the aroma of home-baked breads will ensure you come to the breakfast table. Eight rooms, each with en suite bath, $79–225.

Cape San Blas 32456

Along a tiny finger of St. Joseph Bay, the **Cape San Blas Inn** (1-800-315-1965; www.capesanblasinn.com), 4950 Cape San Blas Rd, offers five spacious guest rooms ($80–150) with DVD and VCR, phones, small refrigerators, and extraordinarily comfortable beds. Stroll down to the dock and put in your kayak for a paddle, or head up the road to one of the top beaches in the United States.

Carrabelle 32322

The Old Carrabelle Hotel (850-697-9010; www.oldcarrabelle hotel.com), 201 Tallahassee St, circa 1890, is a former railroad hotel, lovingly restored by Skip and Kathy Frink in 2000. Like a sea captain's home (which it once was), it's filled with treasures from abroad, fine art from the tropics and from Florida's coasts, reflecting the owners' exotic and artistic tastes. Kick back and read the morning paper in the Monkey Bar, or curl up with a good book in the Hemingway Room, which certainly appealed to me with its literary theme and decor evoking dreams of Africa. Each room is a quiet private retreat, or you can mingle with your fellow guests in the parlor or on the veranda and watch the sunset shimmer on the Carrabelle River. $75–95, includes full breakfast Fri and Sat.

Marianna 32446
It's always Christmas at the **Hinson House** (1-800-531-4786; www.phonl.com/hinson_house), 4338 Lafayette St, a Victorian gem in Marianna's historic residential district. Choose from two regular rooms or three spacious suites (including the Home Guard Suite, which looks over the site of the Battle of Marianna), with your choice of multiple beds—great for friends and relatives traveling together. $59–89; Judy welcomes well-behaved children.

Port St. Joe 32456
Turtle Beach Inn (850-229-9366; www.turtlebeachinn.com), 140 Painted Pony Dr. Along a relaxing stretch of remote Gulf beachfront at Indian Pass, the inn features four comfy modern rooms ($95–175) and several cottages ($150–250); enjoy a full breakfast with an ocean view. The large wooden sea turtles set amid the pines and palms remind you that in the proper season, you can watch loggerheads nesting or hatching. Walk by moonlight—no lights, please!

GUEST HOUSES

Apalachicola 32320
As the historic hub of the region, Apalachicola is blessed with several guest houses, where you're left to your own devices after checking in. The settings are just as comfy as the B&Bs, with rates to match. Your selections include the 1835 **Raney Guest Cottage** (850-653-9749; www.apalachicola-vacation.com), 46 Ave F, at $125; the **House of Tartts** (850-653-4687; www.houseoftartts.com), Ave F and 4th St, $80–125, a restored 1886 home; the **Witherspoon Inn** (850-653-9186), 94 5th St; and the new kid on the block, the **Wind-de-Mer Guest House** (850-653-1675; www.floridaforgottencoast.com), 102 5th St, $75–95.

HOTELS AND MOTELS

Apalachicola 32320
At the **Apalachicola River Inn** (850-653-8139) all of the pleasant, large rooms come with a river view and boat slips (excepting Fri and Sat). Kick back on your riverfront balcony and watch the shrimpers come in. $95–140; two-bedroom apartment, $200–250.

The Gibson Inn (850-653-2191; www.gibsoninn.com), Market St, dominates downtown with the classic charm of 1907. This three-story restored beauty offers 31 moderate rooms and spacious suites (check out Room 209!), each different, decorated in period antiques (I love the shawl canopied beds) but with full bath and television, $75–145. Wraparound porches let you sit back and watch the world go by. Best of all—and rare for a historic property like this—they love kids and pets. Downstairs, **Nola's Grill** is open Wed–Sun for fine dining.

Carrabelle 32322
The Moorings (850-697-2800; www.mooringscarrabelle.com), 1000 US 98. This popular full-service marina overlooking the Carrabelle River offers large waterfront condo-like suites with docking slips just outside your door; $75–120, more for multi-bedroom units. Swimming pool, dive shop, and charter captains on site.

Marianna 32446
Chain motels such as **Holiday Inn Express** (850-526-2900), **Microtel** (850-526-5005), **Hampton Inn** (850-526-1006), and **Comfort Inn** (850-

526-5600) cluster around I-10, exit 142, at FL 71.

Port St. Joe 32456

Port Inn (850-229-PORT; www.portinnfl.com), 501 Monument Ave. This snazzy new motel resurrects the original, circa 1913, with 20 spacious rooms ($65–165) reflecting modern sensibilities such as cable TV, Internet access, and a sparking pool. But you can still sit on the front porch rocking chairs and dine on the complimentary breakfast while watching the fishing boats on St. Joseph Bay.

St. George 32328

The Inn at Resort Village (1-800-296-9518; www.resortvillage.com), 1488 Leisure Lane, has an unparalleled setting for a hotel: It's nestled into the coastal scrub, peering over the dunes to the sea. Resort Village (see *Beach Rentals*) surprised the heck out of me by showing good ecofriendly sense in the way its buildings share the natural environment, peering out from beneath centuries-old pines along rolling dunes covered in Florida rosemary. The 24-room inn shares these sensibilities, with a beautiful pool hidden in the natural habitat, boardwalks to carry you over the dunes to the beach, and a minimalist parking area. All rooms have a great view. Some come with Jacuzzi or kitchenette, and there are three large rooms outfitted for wheelchairs. Full of amenities like writing desks, dataports, and private balconies, this seaside hotel offers serenity for $95–255.

St. George Inn (1-800-332-5196; www.stgeorgeinn.com), 135 Franklin Blvd. Built to look like a turn-of-the-20th-century hotel, this pleasant modern inn is a short walk from beach and bay and features large well-appointed rooms, a wraparound porch with rockers, and a swimming pool; $79–159.

BEACH RENTALS **Anchor Vacation Properties** (1-800-624-3964; www.florida-beach.com) manages classy properties like Casablanca, a well-appointed two-story beach home that tips its hat to Bogey. Traveling solo, I felt a little lonely kicking around this four-bedroom rental at Resort Village on St. George Island, but borrowing someone's lifestyle is the fun of a beach rental. You'll find it cost-effective if you split the tab with enough people to fill the house. Anchor's properties run from Carabelle to Mexico Beach. Other rental agencies in the region include **Ochlocknee Bay Realty** (850-984-0001; www.obrealty.com), with a focus on Alligator Point; and **Collins Vacation Rentals** (1-800-423-7418; www.collinsvacationrentals.com) and **Prudential Resort Realty** (1-800-332-5196; www.stgeorgeisland.com), both covering St. George Island.

CABINS

Port St. Joe 32456

If you loved to play "fort" as a kid or are a history buff, don't miss the **Old Saltworks Cabins** (850-229-6097; www.oldsaltworks.com), CR 30A. Hidden in a pine forest at the historic St. Joseph Saltworks, the cabins share a big play fort and a nice slice of St. Joseph Bay. Look for artifacts and Civil War dioramas at the office—the Confederates produced salt here, after all. Eleven upscale cabins with various configurations of bedrooms, $59–130, perfect for families.

Wewahitchka 32465
Fish camps are clustered around Dead Lakes State Park (see *Parks*), catering to anglers looking for peace and quiet amid the cypresses. Your choices include **Gate's Fish Camp** (850-639-2768), FL 71; **Lakeside Lodge** (850-639-2681), just 1 mile north of Wewahitchka on FL 71; and **Dead Lakes Sportsman Lodge** (850-639-5051) at the old Dead Lakes Dam, 2001 Lake Grove Rd.

CAMPGROUNDS

Blountstown 32424
Scott's Ferry Landing and General Store (850-674-2900), 6648 FL 71, along the Chipola River, offers a back-to-nature campground under the pines along the Chipola River, with RV and tent sites ($16) and cabins ($49–55) built on stilts above flood level. A restaurant is under construction. They also rent canoes (see *Paddling*), and there's a fish-cleaning station and boat launch ($2).

Carrabelle 32322
Carrabelle Palms RV Park (850-697-2638), 1843 US 98, sits right across from the public beach, with nice views and sea breezes from the sunny spaces; full hookups, $23.

Eastpoint 32328
Apalachicola Bay Campground (850-670-8307), US 98, has nicely shaded sites with partial or full hookups, $20. Enjoy the swimming pool, or walk the kids over to Putt-N-Fuss (see *Family Activities*). Tents welcome.

Indian Pass 32456
At the end of CR 30A, **Indian Pass Campground** (850-227-7203; www.indianpasscamp.com), 2817 Indian Pass Rd, encompasses a small peninsula surrounded by estuary, with sites set under gnarled oaks. There's plenty to do, with the newly renovated pool, fishing charters (they'll set you up with a local guide), excursions to St. Vincent Island, canoe and kayak rentals, and bike rentals. Choose from RV sites with water and electric for $25–30, waterfront tent camping $17, or the new Stewart Lodge camping cabins (I love 'em!) for $70–120.

Marianna 32446
On beautiful cypress-lined Merritts Mill Pond, **Arrowhead Campground** (850-482-5583; www.arrowheadcamp.com), 4820 US 90, has several rental cabins ($35–45) in addition to its full-hookup spaces shaded by tall pines ($18). Swimming pool and general store; canoe rentals available. The sites at **Dove Rest RV Park & Campground** (850-482-5313), FL 71 S, are nicely tucked under the pine trees. $10 tents, $20 full hookups.

✷ Where to Eat

DINING OUT

Apalachicola
After I saw the VW "staff car" outside **Chef Eddie's Magnolia Grill** (850-653-8000; www.chefeddiesmagnoliagrill.com), 99 11th Ave, I was especially sorry I'd missed meeting the chef—he's bound to be a personality. Hailing from Boston, Eddie Cass takes Apalachicola's fruits of the sea and gives them an upscale twist in bisques and gumbo, or fried and broiled with select sauces. There's even a gourmet kids' menu. Honest! You can view his superbly presented entrées ($12–23) on the web site. Serving dinner daily.

Owl Café (850-653-9888), 15 Ave D, treats your taste buds with fun dishes like Apalachicola Bay oyster salad ($9.95), the blue crab Café Quesadilla ($7.95), and grilled chicken with grapes, berries, and red onion ($7.95). Lunch and dinner, to $20.95.

Tamara's Café Floridita (850-653-4111), 17 Ave E, serves up funky fusion foods orchestrated by its South American owner. Look for tapas on Wed evening, paella, pecan-crusted grouper, and grouper tacos with fresh cilantro sauce. Trust me, they're fabulous! Entrées $16–21. Lunch and dinner; closed Mon.

Marianna

Pesce's (850-482-8005), 2914 Optimist Dr. Off I-10, exit 136, this newcomer to the region has captured locals' palates with Maine lobster, Ipswich clams, and snow crab. Featuring Italian and seafood entrées. Lunch and dinner; closed Sun.

Red Canyon Grill (850-482-4256), 3297 Caverns Rd. One of Florida's "Top 200" restaurants, this innovative grill serves up intriguing entrées like fried pumpkin-crusted chicken salad ($9) and blue corn catfish ($10) inside a brick house next to Florida Caverns, with an unexpected atmosphere inspired by New Mexico. Dinner $6–15; closed Sun and Mon.

Port St. Joe

Sunset Coastal Grill (850-227-7900), US 98. Settle back and watch the sun set over the bay in this New Orleans–influenced restaurant, where fresh local seafood has a twist of Cajun spice and hand-cut steaks sate the hungry landlubbers. Dinner served nightly.

St. George Island

Finni's Grill & Bar (850-927-3340; www.finnisgrillandbar.com), 200 Gunn St, is the island's bayside hot spot, serving the only sushi in Franklin County. Enjoy the view of Apalachicola Bay while feasting on ahi tuna, fresh grouper, and crabcakes served up with their signature garlic mashed potatoes.

EATING OUT

Apalachicola

Apalachicola Seafood Grill (850-653-9510), 100 Market St. With the best people-watching view in town (big picture windows and an unobstructed view down to the shrimp boats) and fabulous fresh fish, this is a century-old (yes, *century*) landmark in a city best known for its seafood. I sampled the oysters and of course they were perfect, but you won't go wrong with shrimp, grouper, or "the world's largest fried fish sandwich." Lunch and dinner $6–14; closed Sun.

Kick back and enjoy the view of Cape St. George Island at **The Hut** (850-653-9410), US 98, where the fried mullet ($12) and stuffed grouper ($17) come with a heap of cheese grits and an AYCE salad bar. Daily seafood specials; closed Mon.

Blountstown

The Callahan (850-674-3336), 19900 FL 20 W, named for one of the grand steamboats of the Apalachicola River, serves up home-style cooking in a comfy café with pecky cypress walls and a country-dining atmosphere, 10–8; sandwiches $3–6, entrées $6–12. Live entertainment Fri and Sat, no alcohol served—bring the kids!

Carrabelle

Carrabelle Station (850-697-9550), 88 Tallahassee St, feels like an old-time eatery, thanks to Ron Gempel's eye for antique signs and ephemera adding to the original 1940s soda fountain decor. Grab a sundae or a sandwich ($2–5), or enjoy one of his nicely done salads or made-from-scratch soups ($3–5).

Julia Mae's (850-697-3791), US 98, is *the* place in town for succulent seafood. Order the "oyster burger" ($7), as I did, and you'll end up with a heaping pile of perfect seafood—who cares about the bun! Try the seafood plates, $9–16; sandwiches and seafood "burgers," $3–8; entrées, $13–22 (for lobster. Lobster!); grouper chowder, oyster stew, and fried squid, too. Open for lunch and dinner; closed Mon.

Eastpoint

That Place on 98 (850-670-9898; www.thatplaceon98.com), with a deck overlooking Apalachicola Bay, provides dinner fresh from the sea, with legendary mounds of fresh oysters and crabmeat. Closed Wed; lunch served weekends.

Indian Pass

Indian Pass Raw Bar (850-227-1670; www.indianpassrawbar.com), 8391 CR 30A, looks like an old general store, where folks hang out drinking cold beer while chowing down on some of the freshest seafood in these parts. Grab oysters and shrimp by the dozen ($6–14), steamed crab legs ($16), or get the kids a corn dog. Lunch and dinner Tue–Sat.

Marianna

Bobbie's Waffle Iron (850-526-5055), 4509 Lafayette St, is your best bet for a cheap, hearty breakfast, $2–6; don't miss the home-cooked hash browns! Open 6–3 daily.

Gazebo Coffee Shop & Deli (850-526-1276), 4412 Lafayette St, is a popular downtown coffee shop and lunch stop. Open 7–3 Mon–Fri.

Jim's Buffet & Grill (850-526-2366), 4473 Lafayette St, is all about buffet—a massive daily spread. You can order off the menu as well, but buffet is king here. Try the Fri seafood buffet ($14), or catch the Senior Special buffet ($5) on Mon. A nice touch is the suggestion board at the exit encouraging patrons to suggest additions to the buffet. Lunch and dinner, $7–18.

At the **Old Ice House** (850-482-7827), 4829 US 90, I dined on catfish while watching an egret spear his dinner along cypress-lined Spring Creek. Housed in the original icehouse circa 1900, it's a simple family restaurant with a herd of deer on the wall and an extensive Weight Watchers menu. Lunch and dinner $4–13; closed Sun.

Port St. Joe

Dockside Café (850-229-5200), at the marina, offers a nice selection of local seafood, including some creative entries like crab-stuffed grouper, mandarin spinach salad, and sea scallops Alfredo. Lunch and dinner $4–20; watch for AYCE mullet on Wed evening.

St. George Island

The **Blue Parrot Café** (850-927-2987), 68 W Gorrie St, offers the island's only oceanfront dining; feast on oyster and grouper while the sea breeze blows in your face. I loved the fact that I could have gumbo instead of fries with my sandwich, but watch out for the tropical drinks at the tiki bar—they're potent! Serving lunch and dinner, $7–22.

St. George Island Gourmet (850-927-4888), 235 W Gulf Beach Dr, feeds the famished with deli delights and salads ($6–8); don't miss the fancy desserts, like coconut gelato.

Gourmet foods and imported beers and wines, too. Daily 9–6:30.

✱ Entertainment

Apalachicola

The restored **Dixie Theatre** (850-653-3200; www.dixietheatre.com) on Ave E hosts musicals, plays, jazz and folk concerts, and ballroom dancing.

Carrabelle

Catch the spirit of the Gulf at **Harry's Bar** (850-697-3420), 306 Marine St, an old-time fisherman's hangout; shoot some pool and shoot the breeze 7 AM–10 PM daily. Up the street, **Carrabelle Station** (see *Eating Out*) hosts live jazz on Wed night, and the **Tiki Hut** on Carabelle Island is a favorite hangout at the marina.

Marianna

Chipola Junior College (850-718-2301), 3094 Indian Circle, sponsors an annual performing arts series that includes Broadway shows, musicians, choral groups, and opera; Sep–Jan, Fri and Sat evenings.

✱ Selective Shopping

Alford

Old School House Antique Mall (850-579-3915), Park Ave, off US 231. Browse this massive (17,000 square feet!) selection of dealer booths housed in the town's old school, and you're bound to come away with a bargain; adjoining flea market. Open daily 9–5.

Apalachicola

You can spend hours wandering the downtown shops and never see everything. It's tough to narrow down choices—there's not a bad apple in the bunch. Here's my short list, but don't miss the others!

Chez Funk (850-653-3885), 88 Market St, captured my eye straightaway with their gleeful sign, and the shop is filled with Florida funk, including way-cool lamp shades and light switch plates celebrating Florida's past through postcards, created by artist Nanci Kerr. And who couldn't love Nunzilla?

At **All That Jazz** (850-653-4800), 84 Market St, I love the local arts and crafts, especially the clever coin catchers—socks topped with open-mouthed ceramic faces. Crème brûlée coffee tempts, too.

Looking for nautical antiques? **The Tin Shed** (850-653-3635), 170 Water St, has everything from portholes and ship's bells to lobster traps, buoys, and even a ship's binnacle or two.

Gaily painted scenes decorate the floors of **Betsy's Sunflower** (850-653-9144), 14 Ave D, where you can pick up splashy enamelware, fine linens, and gourmet foods. Step through the back door into busy **Downtown Books** (850-653-1290), 67 Commerce St, which features an excellent range of literary fiction, Florida books, and a small newsstand; 10–5:30 Mon–Sat. I knew Apalachicola was my kind of town when I discovered there are *two* independent bookstores to browse. At 54 Market St, **Hooked on Books** (850-653-2420) focuses mainly on used books but has a good Florida selection.

The **Sponge Exchange Emporium** (850-653-1402), 16 Ave E, has antiques worthy of a sea captain's home. Paintings hung on the brick walls of this historic building depict Apalachicola's history. Across the street, **Avenue E** (850-653-1411; www.avenuee.biz), 15 Ave E, features home decor worthy of any coastal home, with a nice mix of antiques, contemporary items, and local art (paintings, photography, and pottery). You'll find unique toys for the kids, too.

On the waterfront, the renovated **J. E. Grady & Co. Market** (850-653-4099), 76 Water St, Apalachicola's ship's chandlery circa 1884, is now a department store with tin ceilings and its original wooden floor. Browse for everything from dressy apparel, classic reproduction toys, and "Wild Women" gear to the photographic art of Richard Bickel.

I'm an outdoorsy gal, but **Riverlily** (850-653-2600), 78 Commerce St, caught my feminine eye with the wedding gown of my dreams and other delightful items—dresses, scarves, purple satin slippers, aromatherapy, incense, and candles—to uplift a woman's spirit.

Blountstown
The Bargain Corner (850-674-1000), FL 20 and FL 71, is a large antiques shop dominating the downtown corner, furnishings and glassware their stock-in-trade.

Carrabelle
At the **Beach Trader** on US 98, ALL OUR DUCKS ARE IN A ROW says the yellow sign with concrete ducks beckoning you into this collection of driftwood art, lawn ornaments, seashells, and more. Open Thu–Sat.

Two Gulls (850-697-3787), corner of US 98 and Marine St. You'll find nautical gifts, inspirational items, toys, candles, and local art—a little bit of everything. Closed Sun.

Marianna
Our Secret Garden (850-482-6034; www.secretgardenrareplants.com), US 90 E, has been in business for 35 years selling both native and unusual plants, including bonsai, water gardens, ferns, and bog plants. Mon–Sat 8–5.

P. C. Oak & Brass (850-482-5150), S Green St, can take hours to explore—it fills a three-story Victorian hotel and overflows with garden items and antique signs out into the yard. Every room brims with goodies, from antique walking sticks and Oriental swords to primitives and kitchenware. Open daily.

Port St. Joe
Bay Artiques (850-229-7191), 301 Reid Ave, displays classy coastal art from local and Panhandle artists, interspersed with antiques. Thu–Sat 10–5.

Portside Trading Company (850-227-1950), 328 Reid Ave, has home decor and goodies with a nautical flair—painted stemware, glass sea horses, and gourmet foods from the Blue Crab Bay Company. Closed Sun.

St. George Island
At **Hooked on Books** (850-927-3929), Judy Shultz hangs out in an old Cracker beach house with cats draped everywhere and a great selection of books. Check out the Florida authors corner, or browse the used-book shelves. Closed Sun.

Sometimes It's Hotter (1-888-468-8372; www.sometimesitshotter.com), 37 E Pine St. Showcasing spicy, unusual foods, including boutique beers, private-label hot sauces, and their own award-winning seasonings. Open daily.

Wild Woman Mall (850-927-3259), 240 E 3rd St, at Journeys of St. George Island, is part outfitter, part beach shop, with kayaks for sale under one roof and sarongs, teeny dresses, and Hawaiian shirts in the next room. Closed Sun and in Feb.

PRODUCE AND SEAFOOD MARKETS

Apalachicola
At **Seafood-2-Go Retail Market** (850-653-8044), 123-A Water St, buy today's catch direct from the fishermen—it doesn't get any fresher than this! Overnight shipping available; closed Sun.

Marianna
Operating Apr–Aug, the **Jackson County Farmers Market** (850-592-5848) at the county administration building is an open-air fete starting every Tue, Thu, and Sat at 7 AM.

Port St. Joe
St. Patrick's Seafood Market (850-229-0070) along FL 71 packs your shrimp, oysters, and other seafood treats for travel.

Sneads
Along US 90, **Buddy's Picked Fresh Produce** stand offers farm-fresh fruits and vegetables all year long.

Two Egg
This tiny town amid the cotton and cane fields of northern Jackson County has a dozen explanations for its very odd name; take away a piece of its history from **Robert E. Long Cane Syrup**, a roadside stand along CR 69 selling fresh cane syrup by the quart and gallon. If you stop in at the crack of dawn on the first Saturday of December, you'll catch the crew grinding cane and cooking up a big breakfast for visitors.

✷ Special Events

April: **Panhandle Folk Life Days** (850-674-3050). Demonstration of traditional arts and crafts at the Panhandle Pioneer Settlement. First weekend, 9–3. Free.

Apalachicola Classic & Antique Boat Show (850-653-9419), last Sat. Free.

Carrabelle Riverfront Festival (850-697-2585), last weekend, features arts and crafts, lots of fresh seafood, and an open house at the FSU Turkey Point Marine Lab.

May: On the **Apalachicola Annual Spring Tour of Historic Homes** (850-653-9550), tour up to 20 historic private homes on a guided walking tour; $10 donation.

Tupelo Festival (850-227-1223), mid-May. They've been making tupelo honey in Wewahitchka for more than a century, and the town celebrates this heritage with food, crafts, and entertainment at Lake Alice Park. Free.

August: **St. Joseph Bay Scallop Festival** (850-227-1223), Port St. Joe, last weekend. It's educational and entertaining—learn all about scallops and scalloping along the bay. Free.

October: **Florida Panhandle Birding & Wildflower Festival** (850-229-9464; www.birdfestival.org), Port St. Joe. Tours and lectures held at various locations along the coast; varying fees, check web site for details.

November: **Florida Seafood Festival** (1-888-653-8011; www.floridaseafoodfestival.com), Apalachicola. The granddaddy of seafood festivals is now more than 40 years old and simply shouldn't be missed—from oyster shucking to the annual blessing of the fleet, it's a huge event.

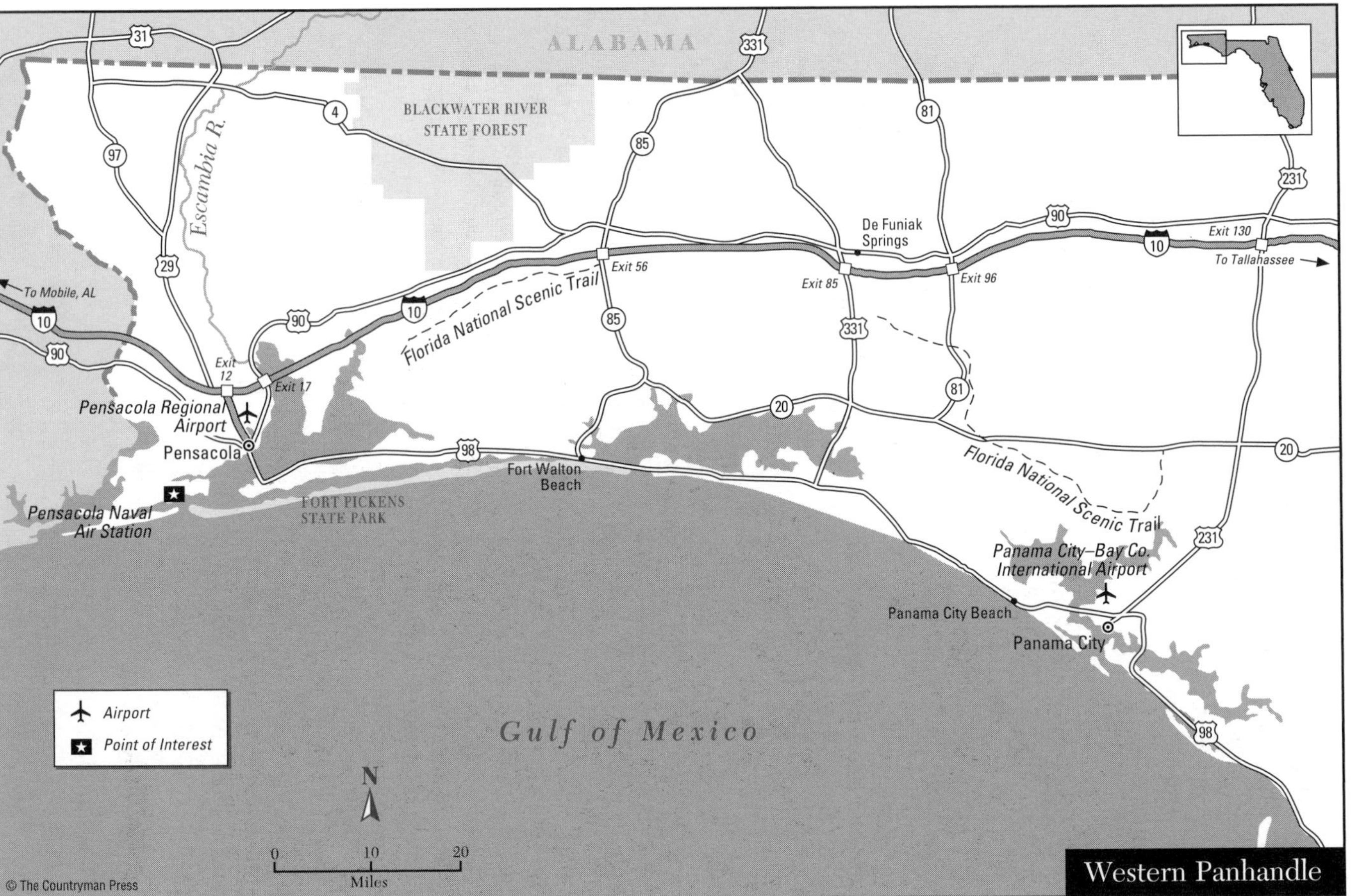

Western Panhandle
ALABAMA
BLACKWATER RIVER STATE FOREST
Escambia R.
To Mobile, AL
To Tallahassee
De Funiak Springs
Exit 12
Exit 17
Exit 56
Exit 85
Exit 96
Exit 130
Florida National Scenic Trail
Florida National Scenic Trail
Pensacola Regional Airport
Pensacola
Pensacola Naval Air Station
FORT PICKENS STATE PARK
Fort Walton Beach
Panama City–Bay Co. International Airport
Panama City Beach
Panama City
Gulf of Mexico
Airport
Point of Interest
N
0
10
20
Miles
© The Countryman Press

WESTERN PANHANDLE

Founded in 1698, **Pensacola** drew interest from Spanish explorers because of its large and easily defended natural deep-water harbor in Escambia Bay. Located in the extreme northwest section of Florida, the Western Panhandle is an area filled with miles of white sugar-sand beaches, fine museums, and outdoor adventure. Fort Walton, Pensacola Beach, Gulf Breeze, Navarre Beach, Destin, South Walton, and Panama City are all known as the **Emerald Coast**, due to the beautiful emerald-green waters and sugar-sand beaches.

GUIDANCE

De Funiak Springs
Walton County Chamber of Commerce (850-892-3191; www.waltoncounty chamber.com), 95 Circle Dr, De Funiak Springs 32435.

Destin and Fort Walton
Greater Fort Walton Beach Chamber of Commerce (850-244-8191; www.fwbchamber.org), 34 Miracle Strip Pkwy SE, Fort Walton 32549. **Destin Chamber of Commerce** (850-837-6241; www.destinchamber.com), 1021 US 98 E, Suite A, Destin 32541.

Panama City
Panama City Beach Convention and Visitors Bureau (850-233-5070; www.800pcbeach.com), P.O. Box 9473, Panama City Beach 32417.

Pensacola
Pensacola Visitors Bureau (850-434-1234 or 1-800-874-1234; www.visit pensacola.com), 1401 E Gregory St, Pensacola 32502.

GETTING THERE *By air*: **Okaloosa Regional Airport** (850-651-7160), **Panama City/Bay County International Airport** (850-763-6751), **Pensacola Regional Airport** (850-436-5005).

By bus: **Greyhound** (1-800-231-2222).

By car: **I-10** and **FL 90** run east–west along the Panhandle. **FL 29** and **FL 90** bring you through Pensacola, then south to Pensacola Beach. **FL 85** will take you from Crestview down past Eglin AFB and into Fort Walton; **CR 87** will take you from Milton to Fort Walton and Navarre Beach; and **FL 231** will take you into Panama City. **US 98** also runs east–west and will take you along the beaches from Panama City right up to Pensacola.

GETTING AROUND **The Okaloosa County Transit/The WAVE** (850-833-9168) is the local bus service for Destin and Fort Walton. Full fare is 50¢; senior and handicapped, 25¢.

A free shuttle service between Destin, Fort Walton, and Okaloosa Island is provided on the **Okaloosa Island and Destin Shuttles**. Contact the Emerald Coast Convention and Visitors Bureau in Fort Walton for routes (850-651-7122; www.rideoct.org).

MEDICAL EMERGENCIES In the Destin and Fort Walton area, **Fort Walton Beach Medical Center** (850-862-1111) and **Twin Cities Hospital** (850-678-4131). In Panama City, **Bay Medical Center** (850-769-1511) and **Gulf Coast Medical Center** (850-769-8341). In Pensacola, **Sacred Heart Hospital** (850-416-7000).

✷ To See

HISTORIC SITES

De Funiak Springs

The centerpiece of **De Funiak Springs** is one of only two naturally round spring-fed lakes in the world. The 1800s railroad town it full of quaint historic homes, many on the National Register of Historic Places.

Destin and Fort Walton Beach area

The 1912 **Camp Walton School House** (850-833-9596), 107 1st St, was in use until 1936 and is now restored and maintained by the Junior Service League. Open by appointment only.

The **Indian Temple Mound** (850-243-6521), 139 Miracle Strip Pkwy, is a monument to Native Americans. Over 4,000 artifacts describe the history of Native Americans dating back 10,000 years.

Tour the **Wesley House** and gardens at **Eden State Gardens** (850-231-4214), CR 395. The southern mansion was built in 1898 and is open for tours Thu–Mon 9–4.

Harold

Paralleling US 90 between the Harold Store and CR 87, the **Old Pensacola Highway** is a stretch of historic roadway now used as a footpath for the Florida Trail. Completed in 1921, this early brick highway known as Florida Highway 1 connected Pensacola with Jacksonville, enabling Model Ts to putter across the state.

Milton

Arcadia Mill Site (850-628-4438), 5709 Mill Pond Lane. Take a tour through one of the earliest industrial complexes in Florida. The site is home to a cotton textile mill, a sawmill, a mule-powered railroad, a rock quarry, a bucket factory, and workers' living quarters. Free tours by appointment.

Housed in the historic Milton Depot, the **West Florida Railroad Museum** (850-623-3645; www.wfrm.org), 206 Henry St, focuses on the railroad history of the historic logging districts of northwest Florida and southern Alabama, particularly the L&N Railroad. Open 10–3 Fri–Sat, or by appointment.

Pensacola

After Pensacola was selected to be a federal naval yard in the early 1800s, four forts were built (or shored up) to protect it. Originally built by the British Royal Navy as a log redoubt in 1763, **Fort Barrancas** sits on a hill above the western shore of Pensacola Bay. The Spanish added their touches in 1797, and the fort went through another update between 1839 and 1844, supervised by Major William H. Chase. The nearby **Advanced Redoubt of Fort Barrancas** was built between 1845 and 1859 to protect the Pensacola Naval Yard but was never used. **Fort McRee** on Perdido Key dated back to 1834, with 128 cannons trained on the entrance to Pensacola Bay. It succumbed to erosion by wind and waves over the decades; only a single battery built in 1942 remains. But of the four forts, **Fort Pickens** on Santa Rosa Island has the most storied history. Chase supervised construction between 1829 and 1834. Construction materials came from all over the world, including copper from Switzerland for the drains and granite from Sing-Sing; the fortress contains 21.5 million locally made bricks. The night before Florida seceded from the Union (Jan 10, 1860), Federal commander Lieutenant Adam J. Slemmer moved his men from the mainland to Fort Pickens to hold what President Lincoln considered a key position in coastal defenses. Confederate troops attempted to rout the entrenched Federals on Sep 2, 1861, during the Battle of Santa Rosa Island but failed, and subsequently turned the city over to the Union forces. In 1886 the Apache chief Geronimo was imprisoned at the fort as a tourist attraction. Fort Pickens came into play during World War I with new defensive batteries constructed to protect Pensacola, but no shots were fired. All of Pensacola's forts are part of Gulf Islands National Seashore (see *Beaches*); fee.

FORT PICKENS

Sandra Friend

The stucco on the circa 1932 **Crystal Ice Company Building**, 2024 N

Davis St, conveys the impression of a block of ice. The one-story building is one of the few remaining examples of vernacular roadside commercial architecture in Pensacola.

In the Seville Historic District, the **Old Christ Church** is one of the oldest in the state, circa 1830–1832. Several concerts are performed under the shady trees across from the church in Seville Square. Guided tours 11 and 1. Fee.

First lit in 1859, the **Pensacola Lighthouse** stands on a 40-foot hill above Fort Barrancas at the Pensacola Naval Station. Its first-order Fresnel lens was removed during the Civil War for safekeeping, since the lighthouse made an easy target for cannonades, and reinstated in 1869. Open for tours May–Oct, Sun noon–4; fee.

MEMORIALS The historic **St Michael's Cemetery** (www.stmichaelscemetery.org), at the corner of Alcaniz and Chase Sts in Pensacola, dates back to 1822, with 3,200 marked burials. Open daily.

The **Florida Vietnam Veterans Memorial** on Bayfront Pkwy near 9th Ave is the nation's only full-name, permanent replica of the Vietnam Veterans Memorial in Washington, DC.

MUSEUMS

Baker

The **Baker Block Museum** (850-537-5714; www.rootsweb.com/~flbbm/baker.htm), 1307 Georgia Ave (corner of FL 189 and CR 189), provides a pictorial history of rural Okaloosa County's cotton and lumber heritage with a dramatic mural; inside, browse through artifacts and archives, including extensive genealogical records. Historic farm buildings brought in from their original rural settings surround the museum. Open Tue–Fri 10–3:30 and third Sat. Free; donations appreciated.

Panama City

You'll have hands-on fun and learn about science, history, and culture at the **Junior Museum of Bay County** (850-769-6128; www.jrmuseum.org), 1731 Jenks Ave. See northwest Florida pioneer life portrayed through a gristmill, cabin, barn, smokehouse, and 1943 Bay Line Engine. The nature boardwalk winds through 12 acres of hardwood swamp. Open daily, except Sun. Fee. Florida residents are no charge.

Pensacola

Bearheart Gallery at Native Paths Cultural Heritage and Resource Center (850-497-8224; www.perdidobaytribe.org), 400 S Alcaniz St. Learn about the heritage and culture of the Lower Muskogee Creek Indians from the chief of Perdido Bay Tribe.

Civil War Soldiers Museum (850-469-1900), 108 S Palafox Place. A fascinating look into Florida's Civil War history, in which Pensacola played a pivotal role—Abraham Lincoln sent troops to take Fort Pickens before the first shots were fired at Fort Sumter, South Carolina. Don't miss the video *The Civil War in Pen-*

sacola for the details. Browse one of the country's largest displays of Civil War medical artifacts. Open Tue–Sat 10–4:30; fee.

Eglin Air Force Armament Museum (850-882-4062; www.florida.flyer.co.uk/airforce.htm), 100 Museum Dr, Eglin AFB, explores the history of military aviation with exhibits of U.S. Air Force armament and aircraft. Open daily 9:30–4:30. Free.

Cafés border the grassy **Historic Seville Square**, in the center of **Historic Pensacola Village** (850-595-5985; www.historicpensacola.org). Take a walk around the neighboring blocks to see furnished period homes spanning from the earliest Spanish settlements to the heyday of the 1920s. Guided tours are available through 18th- and 19th-century homes, featuring the Julee Cottage built in 1804, home to Julee Panton, a free woman of color during the era of slavery. Admission varies.

♿ Exhibits of the navy's role in the nation's defense are found at **National Museum of Naval Aviation** (850-452-2311), 750 Radford Blvd, with over 140 beautifully restored aircraft from U.S. Navy, Marine Corps, and Coast Guard aviation. You'll see wood-and-fabric biplanes, an NC-4 flying boat, and a Douglas "Dauntless" bomber in Hangar Bay. Then fly an FA-18 flight simulator on a mission in Desert Storm. See *The Magic of Flight* on the seven-story-high IMAX screen. If the Kennedy Space Center is the place to be on the east coast, then this is the place to be on the west. Open daily. Free.

Pensacola History Museum (850-438-1559), 405 S Adams St. Learn about the city of five flags through extensive exhibits on and artifacts from Pensacola's colorful history—from the clay deposits that provided the city's brick streets through the "Gallant capture of a lady's wardrobe" Civil War–era cartoon poking fun at Florida's troops. Open Mon–Sat 9–4:30; fee.

SCENIC DRIVES The city park on the **Pensacola Scenic Bluffs Highway** offers an outstanding view of Escambia Bay. Designated a Scenic Byway in Apr 1998, the Bluffs takes you amid moss-draped oaks and stately magnolias with scenic vistas along the way. At one point you'll reach the highest point along the entire coastline of Florida. Then continue through freshwater and tidal wetlands down to the Escambia River.

ART GALLERIES AND MUSEUMS

Destin and Fort Walton Beach

The Mimi Bash collection is housed at the **Fort Walton Beach Art Museum**, 38 Robinwood Dr SW, Fort Walton Beach, along with other American paintings, sculptures, and pottery. You'll also find Chinese, Thai, and Cambodian art objects and relics. Donations welcome.

Panama City

The **Visual Arts Center of Northwest Florida** (850-769-4451; www.vac.org.cn), 19 E 4th St. The building itself is a piece of art. Built in the 1920s, the Spanish Revival facility also reveals art deco influences, combining neoclassical, Gothic, and baroque features. Inside, it's the only museum of its kind for over

100 miles. Permanent and rotating exhibitions from local and nationally acclaimed artists in a variety of media are shown in the Main, Higby, and Permanent Galleries. The Impressions Gallery is a hands-on experience for children.

Pensacola

Pensacola Museum of Art (850-432-6247; www.pensacolamuseumofart.org), 407 S Jefferson St. The museum's permanent collection is of 19th-, 20th-, and 21st-century artists, including John Marin and Salvador Dalí, with rotating exhibits by world-renowned artists such as George Rodrigue. The museum also has a superb collection of European and American glass, and African tribal art. Open Tue–Fri 10–5, Sat and Sun noon–5. Fee.

ZOOLOGICAL AND MARINE PARKS The **Florida Gulfarium** (1-800-247-8575; www.gulfarium.com), 1010 Miracle Strip Pkwy SE, Fort Walton Beach, is the oldest continuously operated marine show aquarium in the world. In 1952, while doing research at the University of Miami, Brandy Siebenaler had a dream of creating a marine facility that would teach the general public about marine life. Only 3 short years later, in 1955, he realized his dream, opening the small research facility on Fort Walton Beach. While pioneering several research projects, the marine facility has undergone a great deal of growth and renovation. As Gulfarium was celebrating its 40th birthday, Hurricane Opal pummeled the coast, but that didn't stop the dedicated staff and supporters. Since 1996, the facility has undergone extensive rebuilding and now has a 400,000-gallon dolphin tank and 60,000-gallon living sea aquarium. Visit places like Dune Lagoon, which has a large variety of marine fowl, or Fort Gator, where you'll see a pair of American alligators; compare seals and sea lions at the Seal and Sea Lion Rookery; watch the unique eating habits of lemon and nurse sharks; and enjoy colorful tropical birds and unique tropical penguins, which are native near the equator in South America. Open daily 9–6, last admission at 4. $17 adults, $15 ages 55 and over, $10 ages 3–11. Free parking.

Ride the Safari Line train through 30 acres of free-ranging wild animals at **Gulf Breeze Zoo** (850-932-2299; www.the-zoo.com), 5701 Gulf Breeze Pkwy, Gulf Breeze, where you'll see wildebeests, pygmy hippos, capybaras, and more. Then walk along the perimeter enclosures to get an up-close look at lions, tigers, and bears. Oh my! Open daily 9–5. $11 adults, $10 ages 62 and up, $8 ages 3–11.

✳ To Do

BICYCLING Love the salt air in your lungs while pedaling? You've come to the right place. The coastal **Navarre Bicycle Path** links Navarre Beach with Gulf Islands National Seashore; the link is almost complete to the **Pensacola Bicycle Path**, which extends through the commercial district out to the entrance to Fort Pickens. Inside this segment of the national seashore, there are several more miles of hard-packed biking trail between Battery Langdon and Fort Pickens. The **Blackwater River Heritage Trail** (850-983-5363), 7720 Deaton Bridge Rd, is the region's premier forested cycling venue, a paved rail-trail on the old Whiting Naval Railway. It stretches 8.5 miles, following the Blackwater River north from Milton. The 9-mile **Crooked Creek Trail** in Pine Log State Forest (see *Wild Places*) was built with mountain bikers in mind; access the trailhead off FL 79, 1 mile south of the main entrance for the forest's recreation area. The **Eastern Lake Bike/Hike Trail** in Point Washington State Forest offers up to 10 miles of doubletrack riding through natural areas accessed via **Grayton Beach State Park**; the trailhead is on CR 395.

BOAT TOURS

Destin and Fort Walton

The glass-bottomed boat at **Boogies** (850-654-7787; www.boogiewatersports.com), at the foot of Destin Bridge, features dolphin encounters and bird feeding on a narrated cruise.

Take a sunset cruise aboard **Moody's *Emerald Magic*** (850-837-1293; www.moodysinc.com), 194 US 98, and see dolphins and birds in their natural habitat. $15 adults, half price ages 3–11.

Panama City

The **Glass-Bottom Boat Cruise** (850-234-8944), 3605 Thomas Dr, takes you to Shell Island, where you can swim or search for shells along the sugar-sand beach. This unique trip also explains shrimp nets and crab trap operations. Located at Treasure Island Marina.

Swashbucklers will want to step back in time aboard the 85-foot authentic pirate ship ***Sea Dragon*** (850-234-7400; www.piratecruise.com), 3601 Thomas Dr. You'll enjoy cruising the Gulf while pirates blast cannons, hang from the riggings, and then have a sword fight. You may even be asked to join in the sword fight. $15 adults, $15 seniors, $13 ages 3–14.

FAMILY ACTIVITIES

Destin and Fort Walton

Rent Jet Skis and Waverunners at **Bayside Watersports** (850-664-0051 or 850-302-0021) or **Boogies Watersports** (850-654-4497), which also offers parasailing.

Panama City

Play a game of mini golf at **Barnacle Bay Mini Golf** (850-234-7792; www.barnacle-bay-mini-golf.panamacitybeachfanatic.com), 11209 W US 98, which has two tropically landscaped 18-hole golf courses with rope bridges, waterfalls, and dark caves. Drive extreme go-carts at **Cobra Adventure Park** (850-235-0321), 9323 Front Beach Rd, where 9-horsepower go-carts race up and down three-story coils more than 30 feet high. Experience the Alien Arcade, bungee bounce, and bumper boats at **Emerald Falls Family Entertainment Center** (850-234-1049), Thomas Dr at Joan Ave. Play 1950s mini at the original 1959 **Goofy Golf** (850-234-6403), 12206 Front Rd. Race on the longest go-cart track in North Florida at **Hidden Lagoon Super Racetrack & Super Golf** (850-233-1825), 14414 Front Beach Rd, or on a winged Sprint Track at **Great Adventures Family Entertainment Center** (850-230-1223), 15236 Front Beach Rd.

Destin and Fort Walton

Captains Paul and Cathy Wagner of **Back Country Outfitters** (850-654-5566) will take you into the shallow flats to fish for speckled trout, redfish, and tarpon day or night on their 4-, 6-, or 8-hour charters.

Go bottom fishing for snapper, triggerfish, sea bass, flounder, and grouper aboard **Moody's *America Spirit*** (850-837-1293; www.moodysinc.com), 194 US 98. $35 for a half day, half price for ages 3–12 and riders.

Drop a line from the "ultimate fishing machine," the ***Swoop*** (850-337-8250; www.harborwalk-destin.com), 66 US 98. This 65-foot-long fishing boat, with air-conditioned cabin, takes up to 49 passengers, for half- or full-day charters, $40 and up.

HIKING The **Florida Trail** is the country's only National Scenic Trail to traverse a beach—and not just any beach, but the sparkling white sand strands of Santa Rosa Island, up to the trail's northern terminus at Fort Pickens. My pick for a coastal day hike, however, is where the trail scoots across CR 399 and travels for several miles through the undulating bayside dunes of the **University of West Florida Dunes Preserve**; access from the Pensacola Bicycle Path. Three sections of the Florida Trail provide excellent backpacking through this region: along **Econfina Creek** (trailheads on FL 20 and off Scott Rd in Fountain), through **Eglin Air Force Base** (nearly 50 miles of trail complete between US 331 and FL 85, with beautiful backcountry campsites set in old-growth forests), and through **Blackwater River State Forest** (more than 40 miles of trail, with trail shelters).

St. Andrews State Park (see *Parks*) offers two excellent short hikes through coastal scrub and pine flatwoods habitats.

PADDLING **Adventures Unlimited Outdoor Center** (850-623-6197 or 1-800-239-6864; www.adventuresunlimited.com), 12 miles north of Milton off CR 87, offers canoeing, tubing, and kayaking down Coldwater and Sweetwater Juniper Creeks. You'll also enjoy land activities such as the ropes course, hiking, biking, and hayrides. Stay right on site at their cabins, bed & breakfast, or campgrounds. Paddling excursions start at $20.

THE BLACKWATER RIVER

Sandra Friend

Whether you want a short or long canoe or kayak trip or just want to go tubing, **Blackwater Canoe Rental** (850-623-0235), Milton, has several rental packages on the pristine Blackwater River. The snow-white sandbars are graced on each side by magnolias and river cedar. Can't you just smell the fresh air?

At **Bob's Canoe Rental** (850-623-5457), FL 191, rent tubes, canoes, and kayaks for a paddle down Coldwater Creek, one of the most beautiful of the Blackwater River's tributaries; shuttles included in price.

SURFING Surf's often up at **St. Andrews State Park** (see *Parks*), where wave action is almost guaranteed along the zone between the jetty and fishing pier.

Navarre Beach Chamber of Commerce

FEEDING THE BIRDS ON NAVARRE BEACH

✷ Green Space

BEACHES Along CR 399, the public strands at **Navarre Beach State Park** abut the easternmost point of **Gulf Islands National Seashore**, which corners the market on public beachfront with several distinct tracts along Florida's Gulf Coast: Opal Beach and Fort Pickens on Santa Rosa Island, and across the bay on Perdido Key. Don't miss the beaches of **St. Andrews State Park** (see *Parks*), the high point of Panama City Beach—it's the only place where condos won't be staring you in the face.

BOTANICAL GARDENS **Eden Gardens State Park** (850-231-4214), CR 395, Point Washington. A century ago this grand plantation belonged to the William Henry Wesley family. Tour the manor by candlelight, picnic at the old mill, or come out and enjoy the fragrant camellia blooms each spring. Free; fee for tours given daily 10–3, on the hour.

GREENWAYS ♿ **Blackwater Heritage Trail State Park** (850-245-2052), 5533 Alabama St, Milton, is a paved linear 8.5-mile biking and hiking trail following the historical route of the Florida & Alabama Railroad, with nice views of the Blackwater River. Free.

PARKS **Big Lagoon State Park** (850-492-1595), 12301 Gulf Beach Hwy, Pensacola. Along the edge of Pensacola's Big Lagoon, this 712-acre park provides camping, picnicking, fishing, and a nature trail leading to a tall observation tower. Fee.

Blackwater River State Park (850-983-5363), 7720 Deaton Bridge Rd, Holt. Bask on a sandy freshwater beach, hike the Chain of Lakes Trail along ancient oxbows in the floodplain, or drop in your kayak for a scenic trip along one of the purest sand-bottomed rivers in the world. Offers a campground with electric and water hookups, plus primitive camping for backpackers along the Juniper Creek Trail, part of the Florida Trail System. Fee.

Camp Helen State Park (850-233-5059), 23937 Panama City Beach Pkwy, Panama City Beach. A peninsula that once served as a vacation getaway in the 1940s, the new Camp Helen State Park borders the Gulf of Mexico, Phillips Inlet, and Lake Powell, and is an excellent site for birding. Hike along the trails and beaches, or cast your line from the shore. The lodge and cottages date back to the 1940s. Fee.

Deer Lake State Park (850-231-0337), CR 30A, Santa Rosa Beach. This small state park offers beautiful views from its dune boardwalk/crossover, and access to a peaceful stretch of white sands along the Gulf of Mexico. Free.

Falling Waters State Park (850-638-6130), 1130 State Park Rd, Chipley. On my first visit to the park, I was disappointed that Florida's tallest waterfall wasn't falling—it drops 67 feet into a perfectly cylindrical sinkhole. But the Sinkhole Trail, on boardwalks over the rugged fern-lined karst, was a delight. Stop by in the rainy season to get the full feel of this unusual geological site. The park offers camping, hiking, and picnicking; fee.

Fred Gannon Rocky Bayou State Park (850-833-9144), 4281 FL 20, Niceville. Scenic nature trails and great fishing on the tidal bayou draw visitors to this beautiful park on an arm of Choctawhatchee Bay; enjoy camping in one of their 42 spacious, shaded sites.

Grayton Beach State Park (850-231-4210), 357 Main Park Rd, Santa Rosa Beach. With more than 2,000 acres of coastal dunes, coastal scrub, pine flatwoods, and beachfront, this is one of the Western Panhandle's most beautiful state parks. Laze on the beach, enjoy the nature trail, and camp with a sea breeze in the 37-site campground (or rent one of 30 fully furnished cabins). Fee.

Gulf Islands National Seashore (850-934-2600; www.nps.gov/guis/), 1801 Gulf Breeze Pkwy, Pensacola Beach. Broken into seven segments from Fort Walton Beach to Perdido Key, this expansive seaside park includes Pensacola's historic forts, great swimming beaches on Santa Rosa Island and Perdido Key (with backcountry oceanfront camping permitted!), and the Naval Live Oaks Preserve with its ancient live oak grove culled for shipbuilding over the centuries. Fee.

Hawkshaw Lagoon Memorial Park (850-434-1234), part of the Habitat Restoration, is a perfect location for spotting cormorants, pelicans, and great blue herons. The pedestrian bridge spanning the lagoon serves as a platform for the memorial sculpture *The Sanctuary*, the National Memorial for Missing Children.

A coastal oasis amid the sprawl of condos that has grown up along the Emerald Coast—that's **Henderson Beach State Park** (850-837-7550), 17000 Emerald Coast Pkwy, Destin, where you can get back to nature on more than a mile of scenic shoreline backed by coastal dunes topped with scrub vegetation. Fish for pompano, camp in the full-service campground, or walk the nature trails. Fee.

Navarre Beach State Park (850-936-6188), 8579 Gulf Blvd, Navarre. No fishing license is required to drop a line off the 900-foot Navarre Pier, the main feature of this small state park; fee.

At **Perdido Key State Park** (850-492-1595), 12301 Gulf Beach Hwy, Pensacola, you're as far west as you can get in the Florida State Parks system; the coastal scrub and beaches preserved here are home to the tiny, federally endangered Santa Rosa beach mouse.

St. Andrews State Park (850-233-5140), FL 392, Panama City Beach, is the one pristine getaway on the coast that you won't want to miss. Encompassing 1,200 acres of undisturbed forests and sand dunes, the park has miles of beaches; you can swim and snorkel in the protected pool behind the jetty, or cast a line off one of two fishing piers. Two beautiful natural campgrounds under the pines have sea breezes as a bonus, and two hiking trails introduce you to the splendor of one of Florida's most threatened habitats, the coastal scrub. I was entranced by my first visit, since it is truly an escape from the overpopulated mass that is Panama City Beach. The nature trail through the coastal pine flatwoods is a delight, and I was surprised to see an alligator in a freshwater pond less than 0.25 mile from the beach. This is Surfer Central, too—catch big waves near the jetty; camping, fishing, and picnicking round out the activities at this park at the end of CR 392. Fee.

Protecting more than 1,600 acres of vanishing coastal habitats like dune lakes, undisturbed beaches, sand pine scrub, and ancient longleaf pines, **Topsail Hill Preserve State Park** (1-877-232-2478), 7525 W CR 30A, Santa Rosa Beach, offers one of the top campgrounds in the nation, with 156 sites. Hike the 2.5-mile Morris Lake Nature Trail, or swim along more than 3 miles of beautiful beaches. Fee.

SPRINGS Surrounded by the town that bears its name, **De Funiak Springs** is a perfectly circular spring-fed lake. **Pitt Spring**, along FL 20 at Econfina Creek west of Fountain, offers a crystalline venue for swimming; my hiking buddies stopped there to fill their water bottles from the chalky-blue water.

Ponce de Leon Springs State Park (850-836-4281), 2860 Ponce de Leon Springs Rd. Chalky-blue 68-degree water tempts swimmers in for a chilly dip in this first-magnitude spring, gushing forth 14 million gallons of water daily. Fish, picnic, or walk the nature trails through the lush hardwood forest. Fee.

WILD PLACES At **Blackwater River State Forest** (850-957-6140), 11650 Munson Hwy, Milton, immerse yourself in the largest state forest in Florida—190,000 acres surrounding

PERDIDO KEY

Sandra Friend

the Blackwater River and its tributaries. Fingers of red clay seep down from Alabama, exposed in outcroppings like the tall cliffs above Juniper Creek. With high ground topped with longleaf pine and wiregrass, the undulating landscape seems to stretch on forever. Paddling, hiking, and hunting are the major draws to this vast wilderness: enjoy backpacking 38 miles of the Florida Trail, drop your kayak in at Red Rock, or utilize one of three reservoirs built especially as fish management areas—Karick Lake, Hurricane Lake, and Bear Lake. With six campgrounds and recreation areas to choose from, you won't run out of things to do!

Florida's oldest state forest is **Pine Log State Forest** (850-872-4175), FL 79, Ebro. Established in 1936, it covers 6,911 acres of sandhills, flatwoods, cypress-lined ponds, and titi swamps, with several extensive trail systems introducing you to this variety of habitats; the Florida Trail passes through here as well. A campground with electric and water hookups, showers, and rest rooms provides respite beneath the pines. Bring your canoe and paddle across East Lake, or fish in the natural streams and ponds. Trail riding is permitted on numbered forest roads.

Point Washington State Forest (850-231-5800), 5865 E US 98, Santa Rosa Beach. Sea breezes filter through the pines in this state forest protecting a vast swath of southern Walton County; access the forest for nature study, biking, and hiking via the Eastern Lake Bike/Hike Trail (see *Bicycling*). Fee.

✷ Lodging

BED & BREAKFASTS

Penascola 32501

Located in historic North Hill in Pensacola is the 1905 Tudor Revival **Noble Manor Bed & Breakfast** (850-434-9544; www.noblemanor.com), 110 W Strong St. Each room is nicely appointed with an eclectic mix of antique reproductions. The property also has a heated pool and outdoor hot tub. $79–119.

The Queen Anne Victorian **Pensacola Victorian Bed & Breakfast** (850-434-2818 or 1-800-370-8354; www.pensacolavictorian.com), 203 W Gregory St, was once a ship captain's home. Awaken each morning to fresh fruit, waffles, omelets, or quiche; you'll also be treated to complimentary fresh-baked treats and beverages throughout your stay. $75–110.

Just a short stroll from the historic downtown area is the **Springhill Guesthouse** (850-438-6887 or 1-800-475-1956; www.springhillguesthouse.com), 903 N Spring St. Your hosts will take you to Hopkins House (see *Eating Out*) each morning for breakfast, or you can request a continental basket outside your door. $89–99 per night, with longer stays encouraged.

Santa Rosa Beach 32459

The seven-bedroom **Highlands House Bed & Breakfast** (850-267-0110; www.ahighlandshousebbinn.com), 4193 W Scenic CR 30A, is a welcome retreat. Situated between Destin and Seaside directly off the sugar-sand beach, the re-created antebellum-style home is private and peaceful. Sit on the porch overlooking the beautifully landscaped lawn, sand dunes, and emerald-green water. Queen- and king-sized beds in most rooms; one room has two double beds. $110–195.

Seagrove Beach 32459
Just a short walk from the picturesque town of Seaside is the **Sugar Beach Inn Bed & Breakfast** (850-231-1577; www.sugarbeachinn.com), 3501 E Scenic CR 30A. Cheerfully decorated rooms have queen and king brass canopied and poster beds; some offer Jacuzzi and fireplace. $110–200.

MOTEL

Ebro 32437
Ebro Motel (850-535-2499), 5312 Captain Fritz Rd, offers nine clean, comfortable rooms ($34–40) in a family-owned motel with a swimming pool, just around the corner from acres of outdoor recreation at Pine Log State Forest.

RESORTS

Fort Walton 32548
With the completion of a $5 million renovation in 2003, the **Radisson Beach Resort** (850-243-9181; www.radisson.com/ftwaltonfl), 1110 Santa Rosa Blvd, is a new lady. The brand-new 500-foot beachfront Lay-Z River Ride with complimentary rafts and the Kids Pirate Ship Playground are just some of the fun things you'll find. Guest rooms have been updated with new furnishings and the addition of microwave and refrigerator, so you can take that doggie bag home for a late-night snack.

Sandestin 32550
Centrally located between Pensacola and Panama City, **Sandestin Golf and Beach Resort** (1-877-870-5915; www.sandestin.com), 9300 Emerald Coast Pkwy W, is only 8 miles from Destin. Choose from several types of accommodations: beachside condos, villas overlooking a picturesque lake, cottage-style homes just off the fairways, or penthouse suites overlooking the Gulf. Grouped in unique neighborhoods, one will surely suit your taste and budget. $69–637.

VACATION HOMES **Ocean Reef Resort Properties** (850-837-3935; www.oceanreefresorts.com) offers furnished cottages, beach homes, condos, town homes, luxury homes, and resorts by the day, week, or month.

One of the largest suppliers of fully furnished homes, the folks at **ResortQuest** (www.resortquest.com) can select which home will be right for you—from condos in resort-style settings to portfolio homes with private pools. By the day, week, or month.

Rosemary Beach (1-888-855-1551; www.rosemarybeach.com), established in 1995, will rent you upscale cottages and carriage houses by the night or week. Carriage Houses are 400–1,000 square feet with rates from $155 a night to $2,100 a week. Cottages run 1,000–5,000 square feet, with rates from $250 a night to $8,000 a week.

CAMPGROUND/MARINA

Milton 32570
Adventures Unlimited Outdoor Center (850-623-6197 or 1-800-239-6864; www.adventuresunlimited.com), 12 miles north of Milton off CR 87, offers a wide variety of accommodations, with cabins, bed & breakfast, or campgrounds. Stay in the School House Inn with Old Southern Charm ($79–119), housed in a renovated historic schoolhouse, the inn features

large rooms, each themed after an American author. The broad, shared porch has rocking chairs and porch swings. Or Granny Peadon's Cottage with period furnishing and a back porch overlooking Wolfe Creek ($109–119). The rustic one- and two-room camping-style cabins have air-conditioning and bunk beds ($39–59), while primitive campsites are $15 ($20 with hookup).

✷ Where to Eat

DINING OUT

Destin
The emerald waters glimmer past white sands as you gaze out the glass wall of the **Beach Walk Café** (850-650-7100; www.beachwalkcafe.com), 2996 Scenic US 98 E. Located on the first floor of the **Inn at Crystal Beach**, this fine-dining establishment offers fresh Gulf seafood and meats accented with French, Italian, and Asian flair, such as pepper-crusted tuna with sautéed spinach and a soy ginger sauce. Award-winning chef Tim Creehan dazzles your palate at this romantic getaway. Author of several cookbooks, Creehan also offers a cooking class once a month.

EATING OUT

Bruce
Bruce Café (850-835-2946), corner of FL 20 and FL 81. Generals and lumberjacks rub elbows at this great family café, where Lillie Mae serves up $5 specials like beef tips, fried chicken, and barbecued pork with three country-style veggies on the side. Seat yourself and look over the menu board, which includes burgers and a pork chop sandwich, $2–3. Save room for one of the 10 choices of cakes and pies! Open 6 AM–7 PM; closed Sun and Mon.

Crestview
Coco's Mexican Grill (850-689-1787), 2520 Ferdon Blvd. Tasty Mexican food, freshly made, with 21 options for lunch ($5) and dinner specials like Acapulco-style fried shrimp burritos and guacamole tacos: combos $6–7, entrées $6–13, $2 margarita specials; closed Sun.

Destin and Fort Walton Beach
The Candymaker (850-654-0833 or 1-888-654-6404; www.thecandymaker.com), 757 US 98 E, Destin. The "Grouchy Old Candymaker," Tom Ehlke, isn't so grumpy after all. Once he decided there had to be a better saltwater taffy, he set his sights and shop up in Destin and since 1992 has been satisfying locals and tourists alike with not only his saltwater taffy but other confections as well. You'll find sumptuous delights like crunchy, rich, South Georgia–style pralines, creamy, buttery fudge, and chewy caramels. Other locations in Sandestin (850-351-1986) and Mystic Port (850-534-0030).

✐ A 12-foot giraffe greets you at the door at **Harry T's** (850-654-4800; www.harryts.com), 320 US 98 E, Destin, a souvenir from his circus days. Harry loves to make kids laugh, so every Tue is Kids Night, with lots of clowns and balloons. Moms and dads will enjoy the 99¢ kids menu every day 11–7. But don't be misled: Harry also has grown-up food, like Grouper Beurre Blanc ($19)—a char-grilled grouper topped with shrimp, crabmeat, and creamy beurre blanc sauce—and filet mignon kebabs ($18). Open for lunch, dinner, and Sun brunch.

Just 1 mile east of the Destin Bridge is the world-famous **Hogs Breath Café** (850-837-5991; www.hogsbreath.com), 541 US 98, Destin. Established in 1976, this is the original café to its porcine cousin in Key West. The saloon features live music, restaurant and raw bar, great beer, and even fishing charters. Open daily for lunch and dinner.

Munson

Ruth's Country Store (850-957-4463), corner of FL 4 and CR 191. Established in the 1940s in a onetime timber industry boomtown, this quaint country store has deep local roots—Bobby (Ruth's son) grew up sleeping under the cash register, and his wife, Patty, offers a great little breakfast in the back room. Gather around the picnic table and order up fresh pancakes, omelets, and eggs and bacon, or stop in for burgers and dogs at lunch on your way to Blackwater River State Forest. Open 6–2, meals $1–5.

Panama City

Bayou Joe's (850-763-6442), 112A E 3rd Court, serves all three meals on the bayou.

Since 1978, the Old English–style **Boars Head Restaurant & Tavern** (850-234-6628; www.boarsheadrestaurant.com), 17290 Front Beach Rd, has been serving up great prime rib and fresh Gulf seafood at a casual eatery. Open daily at 4:30 with live music on the weekends.

The **Boatyard** (850-240-9273; www.boatyardclub.com), 5323 N Lagoon Dr. Executive chef Doug Shook of Key West's Louie's Backyard fame spent the better part of a year developing the menu here, which features fresh seafood treasures along with many of his renowned recipes. Sit back and relax in the Key West tradition with live entertainment and tropical dishes at the base of the beach's only lighthouse. Lunch $5–16, dinner $5–24.

Grab dessert and a hot cup of joe at the eclectic **Panama Java Coffee Bar** (850-747-1004), 233 Harrison Ave.

The top dog in town is at **Tom's Hot Dogs** (850-769-8890), 555 Harrison Ave, where they are consistently voted number one, for best hot dog, year after year.

Take a break from shopping at the charming English teashop **Willows** (850-747-1004), 207 E 4th St.

Pensacola Beach

All over Florida you can find places that serve 'gator, frog legs, turtle, crawfish, and other Florida fare, but I believe **Ard's Cricket Ranch** (850-433-3838), 827 Lynch St, is the only spot to serve crickets. Yes, you can get them fried with a glass of beer. This is where to pick up your bait and supplies, too—Ard's is also a bait shop and convenience store.

Flounder's Chowder House (850-932-2003; www.flounders

PANAMA CITY BEACH

Sandra Friend

chowderhouse.com), CR 399 at Fort Pickens Rd. Since 1979, this casual beach bar has been a Pensacola favorite, set in a playful tropical atmosphere befitting its setting on Santa Rosa Sound—right down to a lively pirate ship playground for the kids. From the oyster and corn chowder ($4) to Floyd Flounder's Flawless Full Flavored Florida Flash Fried Fresh Flounder ($20), you won't go wrong with the fresh seafood cramming the menu. Here for the band? Hoist a "dirty old Mason jar" full of "Diesel Fuel" while you toast your buddies over platters of baked oysters ($6–11) and seafood nachos ($13). Add speedy, friendly service for lunch and dinner daily, and this one's a winner.

You'll be greeted with southern hospitality at the **Hopkins House** (850-438-3979; www.hopkinsboardinghouse.com), 900 N Spring St. Since 1949, this restaurant has been serving southern-style cooking in a one-of-a-kind boardinghouse atmosphere. You'll need to get there early, and I mean before 5 on Tue and Fri, as everyone lines up to get the all-you-can-eat fried chicken. Expect a wait and you won't be disappointed. Once seated, you'll be served big bowls of southern-style food like turnip greens, black-eyed peas, steamed cabbage, fried okra, and more, along with a selection of chicken and dumplings, fried chicken, baked ham, or roast beef. The menu changes, so call ahead or be pleasantly surprised. With only seven boardinghouse tables, you'll be seated with strangers, but isn't that half the fun? Open for breakfast ($6) and lunch ($8) Mon–Sat. Dinner ($8) is only on Tue and Fri nights. Dessert and iced tea are included. Cash only.

Lively Irish folk music and traditional fare are found at **McGuire's Irish Pub** (850-433-6789; www.mcguiresirishpub.com), 600 E Gregory St. Sing-alongs are encouraged; if you don't learn the words, you'll have to kiss the moose, and that's no blarney. Senate Bean Soup is still only 18¢.

Perdido Key

Florabama Lounge (850-492-3048; www.florabama.com), 17401 Perdido Key Dr on the state line, prides itself on being the "last authentic American Roadhouse," where you can stop in for a brew and a stack of oysters and stumble upon Jimmy Buffett playing acoustic out on the porch, unannounced. It's a laid-back, rambling beachside bar and grill serving burgers, seafood baskets, and fresh seafood platters for lunch and dinner, $5–20; it also hosts the Annual Interstate Mullet Toss, first full weekend of Apr, with prizes for successful tosses across the river from Florida to Alabama (you have to see it to believe it!). Cover charge for bands and special events.

✱ Entertainment

The art-deco-style **Ritz-Martin Theatre** (850-763-8080; www.martintheatre.com), 409 Harrison Ave, Panama City, first opened in 1936 as part of a movie house chain. During the 1950s, the Martin family purchased the aging facility and operated it for over 20 years. It then sat dormant for more than a decade; only in the late 1980s were major renovations brought about by the Panama City Downtown Improvement Board. With the historic theater gracefully restored to life, the state-of-the-art facility now serves the community as an intimate venue for comedy, plays, and musical performances.

✷ Selective Shopping

Destin and Fort Walton Beach

The shoe fits everyone but Cinderella at **Allen Edmonds Shoes** (850-654-4790), 10406 Emerald Coast Hwy (US 98) E, Destin. The fine footwear establishment has sizes 5–18, widths AAA–EEE, but only for the men.

Great beachwear is found at **Beach Bums** (850-837-7111), 9539 US 98; **Beach Zone** (850-837-4500), 34871 Emerald Coast Pkwy; and **Wings** (850-650-9115), 1115 US 98 E, all in Destin, with brand names from Anne Klein to Tommy Bahama.

Fudpucker Trading Company (850-654-4200), 20001 Emerald Coast Pkwy, Destin, features "fudnominal" shopping and the world-famous Fudpucker merchandise. You'll also enjoy the eclectic mix of Clay Works pottery, Cow Parade cows, Maryhoonies, raku pottery, neon clocks, and kids' toys.

Over 100 designer-name stores at the **Silver Sands Factory Stores** (850-654-9771; www.silversandsoutlet.com), 10562 Emerald Coast Pkwy, Destin, offer something for everyone, from Black & Decker and Brooks Brothers to Jones New York and Maternity Works.

Wyland's Pardise Galleries (850-650-6240), 51 US 98 E in HarborWalk, Destin, features limited-edition prints, sculptures, jewelry, and collectibles from the famous marine artist.

Panama City

🐾 Don't forget Fluffy and Rover while you're on vacation. They'll want to go to the **Downtown Pet Salon** (850-769-9786), 547 Grace Ave, for conditioning and grooming after the dog days of summer.

The gallery and studio of internationally known watercolor artist **Paul Brent** (850-785-2684), 413 W 5th St, features originals and prints of coastal scenes and wildlife art, along with pottery, jewelry, and glassware from other talented artists.

The **Gallery of Art** (850-785-7110), 36 W Beach Dr, houses original art, sculpture, and pottery by local artists.

Vision Quest Gallery and Emporium (850-522-8552), 230 W 15th St, displays art, antiques, and jewelry and offers classes.

Along Harrison Ave, you'll find an extensive selection of antiques, jewelry, and collectibles at the **Antique Mall** (850-763-9993), along with a nice art collection. For more antiques, fine furniture, and collectibles, seek out **Second Edition Antique and Uniques** (850-215-1420). Grab a new or used book to read on the beach at **Books by the Sea** (850-784-8100). Fine women's clothing, including plus sizes, can be found at **DeHerberts** (850-769-0592), while **Elegante Heirs** (850-769-0245) has nice clothing and gifts for your little ones. Learn some new recipes and then pick up a fine wine to complement your new culinary skills at **Somethin's Cookin'** (850-785-8590).

Pensacola

For the absolute freshest seafood, head to **Joe Patti's** (850-432-3315; www.joepattis.com), South A St and Main. Since 1931, this world-renowned fish market has had locals and international clients picking out freshly cleaned fish and seafood. They even ship around the world. It's worth a visit just to see the frenetic fish market in operation.

Seaside

Follow CR 30A to the quaint village that served as the backdrop for *The Truman Show* starring Jim Carrey. More than 40 shops, quaint cafés, and eateries line the storybook streets, some of which are cobblestoned. At the heart of town is the Ruskin Place Artist Colony, where you'll find a nice collection of arts, crafts, and galleries.

✷ Special Events

January: Don't miss the popular **Polar Bear Dip** at the Florabama Lounge (see *Eating Out*). This annual splash in the Gulf of Mexico isn't as cold as its New England counterparts, but it's fun nonetheless. Afterward, join in the tradition eating black-eyed peas. Whoever finds a dime in their peas has good luck for the year.

Area Sandestin restaurants compete at the **Great Southern Gumbo Cook-off** (850-267-8092), with live Cajun music and door prizes.

Don your favorite costume or penguin suit at the **Annual Mardi Gras Ball** (850-244-8191; www.mardigras ontheisland.com), Fort Walton. The fun continues throughout the weekend with the Island Festival and Parade.

Let's hope they continue the tradition of the **Big Band Concert Series** at the National Museum of Naval Aviation (850-453-2389). The museum hosts 5 spectacular evenings of the best in big-band music for only $18.

January–February: **Mardis Gras** (1-800-874-1234) celebrations continue in Pensacola throughout January and February with numerous parades, where moonpies and beads are tossed from floats, just like in New Orleans. Many festival and entertainment events throughout the city.

February: **Penascola Bay International Film & Television Festival** (1-866-611-9299; www.pensacolafilm andtv.com) takes place over 4 days. Submissions come from the United States, Britain, France, and Spain and include feature films, series and documentary television, and student shorts.

March: The Arts Council of Northwest Florida sponsors **Gallery Night** (850-432-9906). Enjoy touring arts and culture in downtown Pensacola at this quarterly event. The free trolley makes a great way to see the area, while stopping off at various galleries along the way.

April: The **Annual Interstate Mullet Toss** (850-492-6838; www .florabama.com) at the Florabama Lounge (see *Eating Out*), first weekend, is not to be missed. This wacky tournament is a local tradition, with real mullet tossing, live music, food, and drinks throughout the weekend.

Historic Bartram Park is host to the **Annual Pensacola Crawfish Creole Fiesta** (850-433-6512; www.fiesta offiveflags.org), celebrating the Cajun influence in northwest Florida. The crawfish boil is one of the largest in the state, with other Cajun fare like spicy chicken, red beans and rice, jambalaya, and étoufée.

July: The biggest event of Penascola's summer is the **Red, White, and Blues Week**. The event starts with the Fourth of July fireworks display, packs in lots of music, food, and fun, then concludes with the world-famous **Blue Angels** performance.

Gallery Night (see *March*).

September: One of the top five beach volleyball events in the United States takes place in Destin at the **Fud-**

pucker's Fall Classic Beach Volleyball Tournament (1-800-447-7954).

🐾 How could you miss doggy square dancing at the **Annual Dog Daze** (850-664-6246), Fort Walton Beach Landing? Field events and other doggy delights take place throughout this 1-day event.

October: A monthlong fishing frenzy goes on at the **Annual Destin Fishing Rodeo** (850-837-2711), one of the most prestigious fishing events in the world.

There's fun for all at **the Boggy Bayou Mullet Festival** (850-678-1615), Niceville, with food, crafts, and national country music stars performing.

Visit 39 sites on the **Haunted House Walking and Trolley Tour** (850-433-1559), led by costumed guides, around the historic Seville and North Hill districts.

November: The **Okaloosa County Fair and Fine Arts Show** takes place at the Okaloosa County Fairgrounds (850-862-0211).

The **Annual Pow-wow** (850-822-1495) celebrates Native Americans with storytelling and intertribal dancing at the corner of FL 85 and College Blvd, Niceville.

The **Blue Angels** (850-452-BLUE; www.blueangels.navy.mil), the navy's precision flying team, perform a spectacular air show when they return to their home base.

Gallery Night (see *March*).

INDEX

B

C

D

F

J

M

N

O

S

T

U

V

W

Follow The Countryman Press to your favorite destinations!

Explorer's Guide & Great Destination Series

NORTHEAST

The Adirondack Book: A Complete Guide
The Berkshire Book: A Complete Guide
Berkshire Hills & Pioneer Valley of Western Massachusetts: An Explorer's Guide
Cape Cod, Martha's Vineyard & Nantucket: An Explorer's Guide
The Coast of Maine Book: A Complete Guide
Connecticut: An Explorer's Guide
The Hamptons Book: A Complete Guide
The Hudson Valley Book: A Complete Guide
Hudson Valley & Catskill Mountains: An Explorer's Guide
Maine: An Explorer's Guide
The Nantucket Book: A Complete Guide
New Hampshire: An Explorer's Guide
New York City: An Explorer's Guide
Rhode Island: An Explorer's Guide
Touring East Coast Wine Country

MID-ATLANTIC

The Chesapeake Bay Book: A Complete Guide
The Finger Lakes Book: A Complete Guide
Maryland: An Explorer's Guide

MIDWEST

The Shenandoah Valley Book: A Complete Guide

SOUTHEAST

Blue Ridge & Smoky Mountains: An Explorer's Guide
The Charleston, Savannah, & Coastal Islands Book: A Complete Guide
The Sarasota, Sanibel Island & Naples Book: A Complete Guide

WEST

The Monterey Bay, Big Sur & Gold Coast Wine Country Book: A Complete Guide
The Napa & Sonoma Book: A Complete Guide
Oregon: An Explorer's Guide
The Santa Fe & Taos Book: A Complete Guide
The Texas Hill Country Book: A Complete Guide

General Travel

NORTHEAST

Adirondack Odysseys
The Colors of Fall
Covered Bridges of Vermont
A Guide to Natural Places in the Berkshire Hills
Dog-Friendly New England
Dog-Friendly New York
Eating New England
In-Line Skate New England
Hudson River Journey
Hudson Valley Harvest
Maine Sporting Camps
New England Seacoast Adventures
New England Waterfalls
New Jersey's Great Gardens
New Jersey's Special Places
Off the Leash
The Other Islands of New York City
The Photographer's guide to the Maine Coast
Shawangunks Trail Companion
Weekending in New England

MID-ATLANTIC

Waterfalls of the Mid-Atlantic States

WEST

The California Coast
The Photographer's Guide to the Oregon Coast
Weekend Wilderness: California, Oregon, Washington

INTERNATIONAL

Bicycling Cuba
Switzerland's Mountain Inns

We offer many more books on hiking, fly-fishing, travel, nature, and other subjects. Our books are available at bookstores and outdoor stores everywhere. For more information or a free catalog, please call 1-800-245-4151 or write to us at The Countryman Press, P.O. Box 748, Woodstock, Vermont 05091. You can find us on the Internet at www.countrymanpress.com.